LOTTO
Wheel Five
To Win

Gail Howard

Library of Congress Cataloging-in-Publication Data
Howard, Gail
    Lotto Wheel Five to Win
        ISBN 0-0-945760-25-6
Library of Congress Catalogue Card Number: 98-60117

First Edition Printing 1992
Fifth Printing, Revised 1993
Eighth Printing 1994
Tenth Printing 1995
Twelfth Printing 1996
Fourteenth Printing 1997
Second Edition Printing 1998

Published by:
Smart Luck Publishers
P.O. Box 81770
Las Vegas, Nevada 89180-1770.

Web Address: www.smartluck.com

Printed and bound in the United States of America

TABLE OF CONTENTS

i

Balanced Wheels — Win 3 with 5 Right

ONE Power Number Wheels   Win 5 with 5 Right

ONE Power Number Wheels — Win 4 with 4 Right

vi

THREE Power Number Wheels — Win 4 with 4 Right

YOU MUST HAVE A WHEEL TO WIN

The phenomenal success of Florida's Fantasy Five game convinced lottery officials across America that players really did want Lotto games with lower odds and easier to win prizes—not just games with huge jackpots. Now almost every Lotto state has its own pick-5 game, or offers one of the multi-state games—The Big Game or Powerball.

Pick-5 Lotto games are those in which five numbers are marked on one game panel. Whether the game is called Cash-5, Easy-5, Fantasy-5, Take-5, Lucky-5, Match-5, Little Lotto, etc., they are all, generically speaking, pick-5 Lotto games.

The easier-to-win pick-5 games are becoming increasingly more popular as people are discovering that they can win small prizes more often than in the higher odds pick-6 games. Many players use pick-5 games to win "seed" money to invest in pick-6 Lotto tickets when the jackpots are big.

The pick-5 games have much lower odds than pick-6 games even with the same amount of numbers to choose from. The 5 out of 39 (5/39) Lotto game is an odds bargain compared to the 6 out of 39 (6/39) Lotto game.

The odds of winning a jackpot with all five winning numbers in a 5/39 game are one in only 575,757, while the odds of winning a jackpot with all six winning numbers in a 6/39 game are one in

3,262,623. The lower the jackpot odds, the better are your chances of winning *any* of the prize categories.

Pick-5 Lotto games not only offer better odds, but they are easier to handicap as well.

Number selection strategy is covered in depth in my book, *Lottery Master Guide*. (See page 53.) The key to winning more Lotto prizes is to use *both* wheeling systems and number selection strategies to lower the odds against you.

Scientific number selection and wheeling are equally important. Balanced Wheels™ are mathematical tools that give your money more leverage and dramatically improve your odds of winning. They should be used *every* time you play Lotto.

The wheeling systems in this book allow you to choose a large group of numbers in a pick-5 game, play scientific combinations of those numbers, and get a specific minimum win guarantee—if some or all of the winning numbers are in the group.

How often have you experienced the frustration of having chosen all the winning numbers, yet missed the prize because no ticket had more than one or two correct numbers? Balanced Wheels™ force all the winning numbers that are in your chosen group to *come together* to give you at least one specific prize.

Wheeling is merely a guide—but an absolutely essential guide—to show the order in which to place your chosen numbers when filling in your bet slips.

Wheeling does NOT choose the numbers for you. You choose your own numbers. Wheeling arranges your numbers into scientifically determined combinations that guarantee a specific minimum prize if you have the required number of winning numbers in your chosen group.

The object of using my Balanced Wheeling Systems™ is to create mathematically correct combinations that give you the most efficient coverage of the group of numbers you have chosen to play. Wheeling arranges your chosen Lotto numbers into a certain mathematical order on your bet slips as indicated by the patterns in the wheel.

When I use the word "combination," it means one set of five Lotto numbers, which is one game panel.

Each Balanced Wheel™ guarantees at least one specific prize if the five (four or three) winning numbers are in the group of numbers you have chosen. If you are lucky, you may win several prizes. Winning several prizes all at once makes these wheels exciting and fun to use.

If you are very lucky, you may even win the first prize jackpot—as dozens of my readers already have. In addition to the guaranteed minimum prize, my books and software also tell you the *maximum* number of multiple prizes that are possible to win with each Balanced Wheel.™

In *Lotto Wheel Five to Win*, the minimum and maximum prizes you could win appear in chart form above each wheel. **Read page 21 carefully, so you understand how to read the prize charts.** You will be amazed to see just how many prizes you could win all at once!

Full Wheels cover every possible combination of a group of numbers. Balanced Wheels™are shortened or abbreviated versions of Full Wheels. They cover just enough combinations to give the desired win guarantee of a four or three-number prize—which makes wheeling many numbers affordable. The more numbers wheeled, the greater the chances of trapping the winning numbers.

If you were to play every possible five-number combination (the Full System Wheel) of 24 numbers, you would have to play 42,504 games for just one drawing. But by using my abbreviated Balanced Wheeling System™, you can cover 24 numbers in just 54 games—with a minimum win guarantee.

The lower the win guarantee, the fewer combinations required—this means a lower ticket cost and more numbers that can be wheeled for the money.

If you were to take a group of Lotto numbers and create your own sets of five-numbers in the same amount of games, you would not be covering all possible combinations of the required prize category and you would not have a win guarantee. To cover the most Lotto numbers in the fewest combinations and have a win guarantee, you must use my mathematically correct Balanced Wheeling Systems™.

More important, I improved on the wheeling concept by creating totally different wheeling systems, not available anywhere else in the world. These wheeling systems were created to produce the most Balanced Games™ possible within each system itself.

Balanced Wheeling Systems™ are one of the two most important tools Lotto players can use to get the odds more in their favor. You will be amazed at your change in "luck" once you start wheeling your numbers. You can't expect to win every time, but you certainly will win more often if you wheel your numbers than if you don't—and you will win more prizes.

If you have access to a computer, you can wheel your numbers in an instant with one key stroke. All the wheeling systems in this book (and more—475!) are available in my Wheel Five Plus™ software. See page 67.

HOW TO WHEEL

It's really remarkable that such powerful systems can be so simple and easy to use. There is no faster, easier, yet effective way to get immediate odds improvement. And these wheels will work for any pick-5 Lotto game in the world. The size of the number field doesn't matter.

They could be used even in games in which five numbers were picked out of 100.

Once you understand how to use one system, you will know how to use all of them. They all work the same easy way. You won't believe how simple it is to wheel your numbers until you try it. Let's do one sample system before you go off on your own. This is the way it works. Assume, for this example, that you have decided to use Balanced Wheel 54108 for wheeling eight numbers.

Before using this system, choose eight *different* Lotto numbers. You can't use the same number more than once in any wheeling system. Look closely at the chart. You'll see room for your eight numbers in the eight boxes below the letters A through H. After you have chosen the eight Lotto numbers you want to play, write them in the boxes under the letters A through H, below "**Your 8**

Numbers to Wheel." Your numbers can be entered in any order, or from low to high.

Then in the five games below (under **The 5 Games to Play**), write the number you have placed under the **A** in all the boxes that have little A's in them. Next, write the number you have placed under the **B** in all the boxes that have little B's in them. Continue with the rest of the numbers you have written under the other letters until all 5 games in the system are filled in.

BALANCED WHEEL™ 54108

Wheeling 8 Numbers in 5 Games for a 4 of 5 Win

NUMBERS CORRECT	MAXIMUM WINS				MINIMUM WINS			
	5x	4x	3x	2x	5X	4X	3X	2X
5 (w/o Jackpot)	0	3	1	1				
5	1	2	1	1	0	1	2	2
4	—	2	2	0	—	0	2	2
3	—	—	4	0	—	—	0	4
2	—	—	—	4	—	—	—	1

Your 8 Numbers to Wheel

A	B	C	D	E	F	G	H

The 5 Games to Play

1. | A | B | D | G | H |

2. | A | C | D | E | H |

3. | A | C | D | F | H |

4. | A | D | E | F | H |

5. | B | C | E | F | G |

Copyright © 1988-1998 Gail Howard

For this example, let's presume that you have chosen the following group of eight numbers: 3, 8, 14, 15, 21, 28, 34, 39. Having selected your eight numbers, you could place them in any order, or from low to high under the eight letters, A-B-C-D-E-F-G-H, in the boxes below "Your 8 Numbers to Wheel," as I have done with the numbers chosen for this example. Those letters tell us which of your chosen numbers should be placed in which lettered box to make the right combinations.

Under "The 5 Games to Play," notice there is a tiny letter in the upper left hand corner of each box. As shown below, simply take the number you have placed under the letter 'A' and write that number in each box in this system where you see a little A.

- 5 -

BALANCED WHEEL™ 54108

Wheeling 8 Numbers in 5 Games for a 4 of 5 Win

NUMBERS CORRECT	MAXIMUM WINS				MINIMUM WINS			
	5x	4x	3x	2x	5X	4X	3X	2X
5 (w/o Jackpot)	0	3	1	1				
5	1	2	1	1	0	1	2	2
4	—	2	2	0	—	0	2	2
3	—	—	4	0	—	—	0	4
2	—	—	—	4	—	—	—	1

Your 8 Numbers to Wheel

A	B	C	D	E	F	G	H
3	8	14	15	21	28	34	39

The 5 Games to Play

1. ᴬ3 ᴮ8 ᴰ15 ᴳ34 ᴴ39
2. ᴬ3 ᶜ14 ᴰ15 ᴱ21 ᴴ39
3. ᴬ3 ᶜ14 ᴰ15 ꜰ28 ᴴ39
4. ᴬ3 ᴰ15 ᴱ21 ꜰ28 ᴴ39
5. ᴮ8 ᶜ14 ᴱ21 ꜰ28 ᴳ34

Copyright © 1988-1998 Gail Howard

In our example, we have designated Lotto number 3 as A. So, if you were using the numbers in this example, you would place a 3 in each box that has a little A in it. Then do the same with the number you have placed under the letter B, filling in all the little B boxes with that number, which in this example is an 8.

Continue with the rest of the numbers until you have filled in every box in the system. When you have finished, your eight number picks will be perfectly wheeled into the five correct combinations—ready to be transferred to your bet slips so you can buy your tickets. That is all there is to it. I told you it was easy!

For the minimum win guarantee to be effective, you must play every game in the system—and be careful not to make any mistakes when filling in your bet slips. One mistake could cost you your win guarantee. It's always possible that you may win much more than the guaranteed minimum. The maximum number of prizes you could hope to win are shown above each system in the book. **See page 21 to understand how to read the Minimum and Maximum Prize Charts.**

System 54108 wheels 8 Lotto numbers in five combinations at a ticket cost of $5. It has a 4 out of 5 win guarantee, which means, if you get all five winning numbers in your chosen group of eight, you are guaranteed to win at least one four-number prize. If only four of your numbers are winners, you are guaranteed to win two three-number prizes. But, as with all my Balanced Wheels™, you could win much more than the guaranteed minimum.

This is what the bet slip should look like after you have filled in all five games with the numbers used in the example.

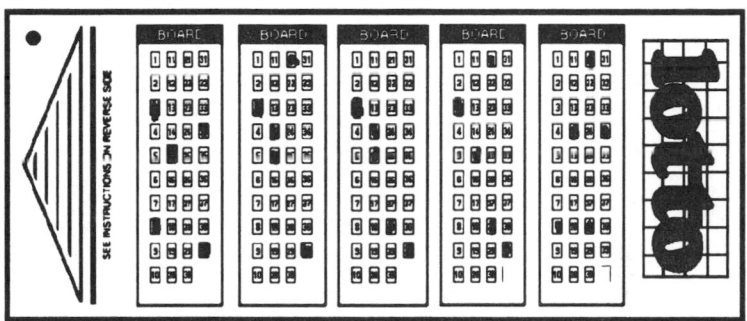

THE ODDS YOU MUST BEAT

In most pick-5 games you win with five, four or three correctly chosen numbers. Some, but not all pick-5 Lotto games, give a prize for two winning numbers. It's great when they do, because you win something almost every time you play. In most cases, the prize is a dollar or a free ticket. It's a welcome win—especially if the free ticket is not a Quick Pick. (The Big Game and Powerball have nine prize categories each.)

The pick-5 game with a 5/39 format is the most prevalent. It is played in seven states: California, Maryland, Michigan, Minnesota, New York, Pennsylvania, and Texas, which have a combined population of 100 million. Because of the large number of people playing it, I will feature the 5/39 Lotto in all the examples given in this book.

According to the lotteries' published odds, you have one chance in 575,757 of randomly getting all five of the winning numbers on one game panel in a 5/39 Lotto game. That is because there are 575,757 different combinations of five numbers one could make. The only way you can be sure of winning the five-number jackpot prize is if you spend $575,757 on tickets and buy all the possible combinations.

The lotteries' published odds of getting four of the five winning numbers on one game panel in the 5/39 game are one in 3,387. This means that, at $1 a game, you could expect to win one four-number prize for every $3,387 you spend on Lotto tickets—if you don't use a Balanced Wheeling System.

Or you could expect to win one three-number prize for every $103 you spend on Lotto tickets—if you don't use a Balanced Wheel. You could expect to win one two-number prize for every $10 you spend on Lotto tickets—if you don't use a Balanced Wheel.

Unless you know the odds you are bucking, you can't expect to understand the benefits of using these wheels, nor appreciate how dramatically they work to reduce the odds.

The wheeling systems in this book can be used for any pick-5 Lotto game in the world.

The field of numbers from which the five are chosen doesn't matter, as long as five numbers make a bet. Currently, the number fields from which the five are chosen range from 26 to 50 numbers. The Big Game and Powerball should be wheeled as a pick-5 game because the sixth number is chosen from a separate set of numbers.

The **PUBLISHED ODDS CHART** shows the actual odds of winning each of the prize categories in each of the existing number fields of the various state pick-5 Lotto games. Read the odds in this chart as "your chances are one in…(whatever the number)".

Or place a dollar sign in front of the odds and you will know the average amount of money you would have to spend on lottery tickets to win each of the prize categories in the various pick-5 Lotto games—if you don't use a Balanced Wheeling System™.

PUBLISHED ODDS CHART

PICK FIVE LOTTO GAMES

Lotto Game	5–Number Prize	4–Number Prize	3–Number Prize	2–Number Prize
5/26	65,780	626	31	5
5/30	142,506	1,140	47	6
5/31	169,911	1,307	52	7
5/32	201,376	1,492	57	7
5/34	276,256	1,919	68	8
5/35	324,632	2,164	75	8
5/36	376,992	2,432	81	8
5/37	435,897	2,724	88	9
5/38	501,942	3,042	95	9
5/39	575,757	3,387	103	10
5/40	658,008	3,760	111	10
5/42	850,668	4,598	128	11
5/45	1,221,759	6,109	157	12
*5/49	1,906,884	8,668	202	13
*5/50	2,118,760	9,417	214	14

HOW WHEELING REDUCES THE ODDS

The concept of wheeling is really quite simple to understand. "Wheeling" means using more numbers than you can play on any one game panel. For example, in a pick-5 game, you can wheel (play the combinations of) six numbers, seven numbers, eight, nine—or many more numbers. With each additional number you wheel, you increase your mathematical probability of winning one or more prizes.

In a pick-5 game, five numbers are marked on one panel of a bet slip. But let's say you have six favorite numbers, and you want to make every possible combination of those numbers so that no matter which five of the six are drawn, you are guaranteed to win the jackpot.

To cover every possible five-number combination of your six numbers—using the Full System Wheel—you would have to play six sets of five numbers (six game panels). That is because one additional number can be combined with all five other numbers exactly six times, as shown below.

FULL WHEEL #55006

Game 1. 1-2-3-4-5   **Game 4. 1-2-4-5-6**
Game 2. 1-2-3-4-6   **Game 5. 1-3-4-5-6**
Game 3. 1-2-3-5-6   **Game 6. 2-3-4-5-6**

By adding just one extra number and making combinations with the other five, the odds against you in a 5/39 game drop from one in 575,757 to one in 95,960. The more numbers you wheel, the lower the odds and the greater are your chances of winning.

When you play every possible combination of seven Lotto numbers in a 5/39 game, the odds against you drop from one in 575,757 to one in only 27,417. But now you would have to play 21 game panels to cover all possible five-number combinations in a seven-number wheel. That's because two extra numbers can be combined with the other five in exactly 21 sets.

When you wheel 12 numbers in a 5/39 Lotto game, the odds of getting all five winning numbers in your chosen group of 12 would be one in 727. This sharply reduces the odds from one chance in 575,757 to one chance in 727.

However, in a 12-number wheel there are 792 five-number combinations. And to play every possible five-number combination of 12 numbers (with the Full System), you must spend $792 on tickets.

If you were to wheel every possible five-number combination (the Full System) of 20 Lotto numbers, the odds of getting all five numbers correct are one in 37, but the tickets would cost $15,504 for just one drawing! And who would be willing to spend that much money on one drawing?

The secret is you don't have to! All of my Balanced Wheeling Systems™ are abbreviated, which means that just enough combinations are covered to give a minimum win guarantee. Most of the expensive combinations have been eliminated. That is one major advantage of using Balanced Wheels.

The Full System Chart shows how many sets of numbers you would have to play if you wanted to cover *every possible* combination of from six to 50 Lotto numbers. One quick glance at the chart immediately shows that the ticket cost would be prohibitive for wheeling more than just a few numbers when buying all possible combinations.

Place a dollar sign in front of each of the total Combinations and you will know how much the tickets would cost if you were to wheel every possible combination of up to 50 numbers.

This chart should answer the question I am so often asked: "How much would it cost to wheel all 39 numbers?" My answer is, "It would cost you over half a million dollars for just one drawing!"

FULL WHEEL CHART FOR PICK-5 GAMES

NUMBERS	COMBINATIONS	NUMBERS	COMBINATIONS	NUMBERS	COMBINATIONS
5	1	21	20,349	37	435,897
6	0	22	26,334	38	501,942
7	21	23	33,649	39	575,757
8	56	24	42,504	40	658,008
9	126	25	53,130	41	749,398
10	252	26	65,780	42	850,668
11	462	27	80,730	43	962,598
12	792	28	98,280	44	1,086,008
13	1,287	29	118,755	45	1,221,759
14	2,002	30	142,506	46	1,370,754
15	3,003	31	169,911	47	1,533,939
16	4,368	32	201,376	48	1,712,304
17	6,188	33	237,336	49	1,906,884
18	8,568	34	278,256	50	2,118,760
19	11,628	35	324,632		
20	15,504	36	376,992		

WIN GUARANTEES EXPLAINED

Wheeling is fun because winning is fun—especially when you win several prizes all at once. Although my systems guarantee just one minimum prize (which is the least you could win), it is possible to win much more than the guaranteed minimum prize. It is also possible to win prizes with *fewer* numbers than the win guarantee requires.

Wheeling systems can be divided into two basic categories: Full System Wheels and Balanced Wheels™. There also are the Power Number™ wheels, which can be either Full System Wheels or Balanced Wheels™.

FULL WHEELS buy every possible combination of a group of numbers, so every wheel has a jackpot win guarantee if you have all the winning numbers in your wheeled group. Full Wheels are the most expensive wheels to use, but you are generously rewarded when you trap some or all of the winning numbers. For example, if you wheel 7 numbers in 21 combinations and get all five winning numbers in your chosen group of 7, you are guaranteed to win the jackpot plus 10 second prizes and 10 third prizes—every ticket is a winner. However, Full Wheels have the worst odds improvement.

BALANCED WHEELS™ give the most number coverage for the money and the best odds improvement. They guarantee smaller (second and third) prizes, and can cost as little as $3 to use. **All Balanced Wheels are abbreviated.** The lower the win guarantee is, the greater the odds improvement. For most players, Balanced Wheels are the best bet.

POWER NUMBER WHEELS™ have all the same win guarantees as Full Wheels and Balanced Wheels, but cost much less to wheel the same size groups of numbers with the same win guarantees. The Power Number™ appears in every combination in the system, permitting you to give extra heavy play to your strongest number. However, the number you designate as the

Power Number (and place in the FIRST position in the wheel) MUST be a winning number, or there is no win guarantee—although it is still possible to win prize(s) without it. In addition to wheels with one Power Number, there are also wheels with two and three Power Numbers, which reduce the ticket cost even more dramatically.

In *Lotto Wheel Five to Win*, there are 305 pick-5 wheels to choose from. You can spend as little as $2.00, or you can play all 39 numbers—or more. The Table of Contents has a convenient listing of all the wheeling systems in this book.

With Balanced Wheeling Systems™ you can select your own win guarantee. The minimum win guarantee you choose determines the ticket cost and the number of combinations in the system. Every wheeling system in this book has a valid win guarantee for a specific prize. However, let me make this perfectly clear:

WARNING!!! WARNING!!! WARNING!!!

 If the required number of winning numbers are **NOT** in the group you have chosen, **THERE IS NO WIN GUARANTEE!** If all the numbers you choose are losers, the wheel cannot help you.

The six types of wheeling systems are categorized by their minimum win guarantees, meaning the least you could expect to win—if you meet the conditions of the wheel. The systems in this book are grouped together as separate chapters according to their minimum win guarantees.

Suppose you had 11 favorite numbers you wanted to wheel. If the tickets cost $1 a play, you could spend as little as $2 or as much as $462 for one drawing for wheeling the same 11 numbers. The fewer combinations covered, the lower the ticket cost .

Each Balanced Wheel™ has a minimum win guarantee that requires having a specific number of winning numbers in the chosen group—either three, four or five, depending on the win guarantee. The minimum prize guaranteed is the prize most easily won. But you could get lucky and win up to the maximum number of multiple prizes possible, or you could get very lucky and win the first prize jackpot with any wheel in this book.

In addition to the 5 out of 5 Full System Wheels, there are five categories of abbreviated Balanced Wheels™. They are distinguished by their minimum win guarantee, which is the largest prize the wheel *guarantees* .

There are 4 out of 4, 4 out of 5, 3 out of 3, 3 out of 4, and 3 out of 5 systems. Those numbers describe the various minimum win guarantees of the Balanced Wheeling Systems™ for pick-5 games.

The first number of the system category (on the left) tells the minimum prize it guarantees to win. The second number (on the right), tells how many winning numbers in the wheeled group must match the winning numbers drawn to win the minimum prize.

The **4** out of **4** Balanced Wheels™ guarantee at least one four-number prize if just four of the five winning numbers are in your wheeled group.

The **4** out of **5** Balanced Wheels™ guarantee at least one four-number prize if all five winning numbers are in your wheeled group.

The **3** out of **3** Balanced Wheels™ guarantee at least one three-number prize if just three of the five winning numbers are in your wheeled group.

The **3** out of **4** Balanced Wheels™ guarantee at least one three-number prize if just four of the five winning numbers are in your wheeled group.

The **3** out of **5** Balanced Wheels™ guarantee at least one three-number prize if all five winning numbers are in your wheeled group.

The lower the win guarantee, the more numbers that can be wheeled for the money. The 3 out of 5 systems cost the *least* to play for the amount of numbers wheeled, and give the *greatest* odds improvement because of the leverage. The 5 out of 5 Full Wheels cost the most to use, and have the worst odds improvement.

5 OUT OF 5 FULL WHEELS

The 5 out of 5 Full System Wheels guarantee that you will win the first prize jackpot plus many other prizes IF you have all five winning numbers in your chosen group. Every possible five-number combination is covered. You can win the greatest number of prizes with Full Wheels, although multiple prize wins are possible with almost every wheeling system in this book.

Full Wheels are generally not recommended because it's too hard to trap the winning numbers in a small affordable group. Wheeling more than seven or eight numbers is very expensive, as shown in The Full Wheel Chart™ on page 11. However, I have included in *Lotto Wheel Five to Win* Full Wheels for up to 11 numbers in 462 combinations for those who insist on using them.

My Full Wheel Generator™ software can make Full Wheels for every amount of numbers up to all the numbers in the game for all pick-5, pick-6, pick-7, pick-8, pick-9, and pick-10 games. See page 63 for details.

The 5 out of 5 Full Wheels give you the worst odds improvement benefits and the lowest rate of success if used consistently. You can't expect to win very often when you use them exclusively. Full Wheels should be used on those very rare occasions when you think you might have the winning Lotto numbers trapped within a very small group of numbers.

Because every possible combination of five numbers is covered, the Balanced Game™ feature does not apply to Full Wheels. All Full Wheels include unlikely-to-win combinations such as 1-2-3-4-5, all odd or all even numbers, all consecutive numbers, etc.

Both Minimum and Maximum Prizes are exactly the same in Full Wheel systems.

4 OUT OF 4 BALANCED WHEELS™

The 4 out of 4 systems are the most expensive abbreviated Balanced Wheels™ to use, but they give the most combination coverage to a group of numbers. If just four of the numbers in the wheeled group are winners, you are guaranteed to win at least one four-number prize. Five winning numbers guarantees more three-number prizes. The 4 out of 4 systems cost less to play than the 5 out of 5 Full Systems because they do not cover every possible five-number combination. For example, it costs $462 to wheel 11 numbers with the 5 out of 5 Full Systems, but with the 4 out of 4 abbreviated Balanced Wheels, you can wheel 11 numbers at a ticket cost of only $66.

4 OUT OF 5 BALANCED WHEELS™

The 4 out of 5 Balanced Wheels guarantee one four-number prize if all five of the winning numbers are in the wheeled group. Although you must have five winning numbers in the wheel to trap the four winning numbers, the ticket cost is considerably less than the 4 out of 4 wheels. Wheeling 11 numbers with the 4 out of 5 system costs only $26, rather than $66 with the 4 out of 4 system. And the odds improvement is greater with the 4 out of 5 wheels, than with the 4 out of 4 wheels.

3 OUT OF 3 BALANCED WHEELS™

The 3 out of 3 Balanced Wheels™ guarantee one three-number prize if just three of the numbers in the wheeled group are winners. With four or five winning numbers, you are guaranteed to win more three-number prizes. You can choose more numbers with 3 out of 3 systems for the same money you'd spend on tickets for the 4 out of 4, or the 4 out of 5 systems. The 11-number wheel can be played for just $20 with the 3 out of 3 Balanced Wheel.

3 OUT OF 4 BALANCED WHEELS™

With the 3 out of 4 Balanced Wheels™, you start seeing some real value for your playing dollar. If just four of your numbers are winners, you are guaranteed to win at least one three-number prize. As you cover more numbers in fewer combinations (for less money), you may not win as many multiple prizes. But by covering more numbers, you increase your chances of trapping the winning numbers in your wheeled group. The 11-number wheel costs only $10 with the 3 out of 4 Balanced Wheel.

3 OUT OF 5 BALANCED WHEELS™

The 3 out of 5 Balanced Wheels allow you to wheel the most pick-5 Lotto numbers for the smallest amount of money and still have a minimum win guarantee of at least a three-number prize. For players who spend small amounts on lottery tickets, the 3 out of 5 Balanced Wheels™ are the best way to go. Notice that 11 numbers can be wheeled for just $5, using the 3 out of 5 Balanced Wheel. The 3 out of 5 Balanced Wheels are the most economical to use, and also give the greatest odds improvement.

As the systems become more abbreviated, the cost of wheeling any particular set of numbers becomes more affordable. In our example, the 11-number wheel, which with the 5 out of 5 Full Wheel costs $462 in tickets, drops to $66 with the 4 out of 4 Balanced Wheel, and to $26 with the 4 out of 5 Balanced Wheel, and to $20 using the 3 out of 3 Balanced Wheel, and to $10 with the 3 out of 4 Balanced Wheel, and to $5 with the 3 out of 5 Balanced Wheel.

POWER NUMBER™ WHEELS

Power Number™ Wheels have all the same win guarantees as other Full and Balanced Wheels™, but they allow you to play the same amount of numbers at a much lower ticket cost. They also make higher win guarantees more affordable. That's because one fixed number appears in every game in the system and the other numbers are wheeled around it.

Do not confuse "Powerball" with "Power Number." My Power Number™ Wheels were trademarked, copyrighted and published in 1988—a full four years before the multi-state lottery dreamed up the name "Powerball" for their game, which started in 1992.

Power Number™ Wheels should be used only if you study the numbers and can find one strong number that has an outstanding chance of being drawn. A Power Number™ must be chosen carefully because it appears in every combination in the system. If the number you designate as the Power Number is not a winner, every combination in the wheel has at least one *losing* number.

Wheels with one Power Number cut the ticket cost by about half in most cases. But wheels with TWO Power Numbers reduce the cost much more. For example, a Full Wheel costs $462 to wheel 11 numbers. Using ONE Power Number reduces the cost of the Full Wheel for 11 numbers to $210. Using TWO Power Numbers reduces the cost to just $84 for the Full Wheel for wheeling 11 numbers. A THREE Power Number Full Wheel costs only $28 to wheel 11 numbers!

When using a wheel with TWO Power Numbers, BOTH numbers you designate as Power Numbers MUST be drawn for the win guarantee to be valid. And when using a wheel with THREE Power Numbers, all three numbers you designate as Power Numbers MUST be drawn for the win guarantee to be valid.

WARNING!!!

THIS IS VERY IMPORTANT: Power Number(s) MUST be placed in designated positions in the wheel, as follows, and anyone who does not read and understand the following three paragraphs should NOT use Power Number Wheels.

When using a **ONE** Power Number Wheel, the Power Number must be placed in the **A** box, which is the FIRST POSITION in the wheel. **If the number you place in the first position, the A box, is NOT a winning number, there is NO win guarantee.** I want to stress this point, so please read it again—AND AGAIN!!! Anyone who does not understand those two sentences SHOULD NOT USE Power Number Wheels.

When using a **TWO** Power Numbers Wheel, the Power Numbers must be placed in the **A** box and the **B** box, which are the FIRST TWO POSITIONS in the wheel. **If the TWO numbers you place in the first and second positions, the A box and the B box, are NOT BOTH winning numbers, there is NO win guarantee.** I want to stress this point, so please read it again—AND AGAIN!!! Anyone who does not understand those two sentences SHOULD NOT USE Power Number Wheels.

When using a **THREE** Power Number Wheel, the Power Numbers must be placed in the **A** box, the **B** box, and the **C** box, which are the FIRST THREE POSITIONS in the wheel. **If the THREE numbers you place in the first, second, and third positions, the 'A' box, the 'B' box, and the 'C' box, are NOT ALL THREE winning numbers, there is NO win guarantee.** I want to stress this point, so please read it again—AND AGAIN!!! Anyone who does not understand those two sentences SHOULD NOT USE Power Number Wheels.

If I seem a bit extreme in making my point, it's because I don't want some wise guy accusing me of selling a flawed system when he or she misses the Power Number. The win guarantees of all the wheeling systems in this book are mathematically correct, totally accurate, flawless, without holes.

Not to confuse the issue, but if the Power Number(s) is a losing number, it is still *possible* to win one or more prizes without it—but not the guaranteed minimum prize of the system wheel. Again, I repeat: **The Power Number(s) MUST ALL be winners for the minimum win guarantee to be valid.**

Power Number™ Wheels have the same types of win guarantees as other Balanced Wheels™ and Full Wheels, 5 out of 5, 4 out of 4, 4 out of 5, etc. Those with the 5 out of 5 win guarantees are the most expensive Power Number™ Systems to use for the amount of numbers wheeled.

As the Power Number Wheels become more abbreviated, the ticket cost is less for wheeling the same group of numbers. Power Number™ Systems should be used only if you have chosen your Power Number(s)™ carefully. Otherwise you might be disappointed with the results. **Power Number™ Wheels should NOT be used by people who pick their numbers randomly.**

Power Number Wheels work best for people who handicap the numbers, using proven, successful number selection methods. See the chapter "Lottery Products to Help You Win," on pages 51 to 68. *Lottery Master Guide* is the most thorough and complete book on lottery strategy ever written. My most basic to my most advanced strategies for picking numbers scientifically are explained in great detail. *Lottery Master Guide* is a book every lottery player should read—and use!.

All the Lottery Advantage® Charts described in *Lottery Master Guide* are available for any pick-5 or pick-6 game, updated through the latest drawing—25 pages of charts in all. People who have access to computers should get my Advantage Plus™ software rather than the printed Lottery Advantage charts. (See pages 59 and 60.)

MINIMUM AND MAXIMUM PRIZES

Shown above each of the wheeling systems in this book are the maximum number of multiple prizes **possible** to win, as well as the minimum number of prizes the system guarantees. **Maximum Prizes are *possible but not guaranteed*. Only Minimum Prizes are guaranteed.**

#54108 Win 4 with 5 Right, 8 Numbers in 5 Games

NUMBERS CORRECT	MAXIMUM WINS				MINIMUM WINS			
	5x	4x	3x	2x	5X	4X	3X	2X
5 (w/o Jackpot)	0	3	1	1				
5	1	2	1	1	0	1	2	2
4	—	2	2	0	—	0	2	2
3	—	—	4	0	—	—	0	4
2	—	—	—	4	—	—	—	1

Pay close attention while I explain how to read the Minimum and Maximum Prize listings. Once you understand how to read one listing, you can read all of them the same way. It's a simple, easy, convenient and practical way to see all the win information at a glance.

The Minimum and Maximum Prizes are given here for getting 5, 4, 3 or 2 winning numbers correct. (A 2-number prize applies only to games that have them.) Prize categories are listed in the column on the far left, and again across the top of the chart.

I'll use system #54108 as the example again, to tell you how to read the Minimum and Maximum Prizes. This is a 4 out of 5 Balanced Wheel, which means it guarantees one four-number prize if all five of the winning numbers are in the wheeled group. But, there is more to it than that.

The column on the left shows the number of correct (winning) pick-5 Lotto numbers required to produce the prizes shown across that line. The **5 w/o Jackpot** means "5 **without** a Jackpot win"—when five winning numbers do not win a jackpot.

If you have all five winning numbers but you *don't* win the first prize jackpot, you could win up to three 4-number prizes plus one 3-number prize and one 2-number prize. The reason I include this special "5 without jackpot" category is that more secondary prizes can be won when no first prize jackpot is won. Notice that under the Minimum Prizes, that line is left blank because it doesn't apply.

The second line shows that with 5 numbers correct, it is possible to win one 5-number first prize jackpot plus two 4-number prizes plus one 3-number prize and one 2-number prize. But, you are **guaranteed** with 5 numbers correct to win one 4-number prize plus two 3-number prizes and two 2-number prizes.

The third line shows that with 4 numbers correct, it is possible to win two 4-number prizes plus two 3-number prizes, but you are guaranteed to win two 3-number prizes plus two 2-number prizes.

The fourth line shows that with 3 numbers correct, it is possible to win four 3-number prizes, but you are guaranteed to win four 2-number prizes. The last line shows that with two numbers correct, you could win four 2-number prizes, but you are guaranteed to win just one 2-number prize.

TIMES IN THE WHEEL™ Handicapping Feature

The all-important TIMES IN THE WHEEL™ handicapping feature enables you to give extra heavy play to your strongest numbers. It tells how many times each number position is in the wheel, so you can place you best numbers in the system positions that appear most often in the wheel.

Those who use scientific tools to analyze Lotto numbers know that certain numbers in any given drawing are far more likely to win than others. Some numbers are best, second best, and so on, in varying degrees. You can give extra heavy play to your special number picks by placing them under the letters that appear more often in the wheel you are using.

When you find one particular number that stands out above *all* the rest as being the most likely number to win the next drawing, you should use a Power Number Wheel—and designate that number as your Power Number—because Power Numbers appear in every combination in the wheel.

Some Balanced Wheels have an equal distribution of the letters (number positions) within the wheel. In that case, each of your chosen numbers gets equal play. But in those wheels which have unequal distribution of the number positions, you can place your strongest numbers where they will appear most often, and your weakest numbers in the positions that appear least often.

Naturally, when you use this feature, your numbers will not appear in order from low to high. You can place your chosen numbers in any order you wish. Win guarantees can be destroyed only if you make an error when filling in your bet slips, or if you don't play every combination in the system.

BALANCED WHEEL™ 54108
Wheeling 8 Numbers in 5 Games for a 4 of 5 Win

NUMBERS CORRECT	MAXIMUM WINS				MINIMUM WINS			
	5x	4x	3x	2x	5X	4X	3X	2X
5 (w/o Jackpot)	0	3	1	1				
5	1	2	1	1	0	1	2	2
4	—	2	2	0	—	0	2	2
3	—	—	4	0	—	—	0	4
2	—	—	—	4	—	—	—	1

Your 8 Numbers to Wheel

A	B	C	D	E	F	G	H
4	2	3	4	3	3	2	4

The 5 Games to Play

1. | A | B | D | G | H |
2. | A | C | D | E | H |
3. | A | C | D | F | H |
4. | A | D | E | F | H |
5. | B | C | E | F | G |

Copyright © 1988-1998 Gail Howard

Notice that in Balanced Wheel #54108, the system positions **A** and **D** and **H** are in the wheel 4x (four times). But system positions **B** and **G** are in the wheel only 2 times. So, you would place your

- 23 -

strongest numbers in positions **A-D-H**, your second best numbers in positions **C-E-F**, and your weakest numbers in positions **B-G**.

THE BALANCED GAME™

American lottery players first learned about wheeling systems in 1983. It was entirely through my efforts—my books, newsletters, articles in national magazines, television appearances and especially my 30-minute television infomercial—that wheeling systems became known and recognized as mathematically valid systems that reduce the odds.

The first wheeling book I sold had only 65 wheeling systems in it. Several years after I popularized wheeling systems, others copied them and began selling them in pamphlets, books and share ware. Those primitive basic wheeling systems could not be copyrighted, and are still used in books and software by others.

In 1987, I improved on the wheeling concept by creating totally different wheeling systems. I combined my Balanced Game™ system with wheeling to produce the most Balanced Games™ possible within each wheel itself. This eliminated the unbalanced, wasted combinations that appear at the beginning and end of all other wheeling systems.

These unique copyrighted and trademarked Balanced Wheels™, were published in the 1988 edition of my book, *Lotto How to Wheel a Fortune*. Balanced Wheels™ can not be legally sold anywhere in the world, except in my own books and software.

In a July 24, 1988 article, the *New York Daily News* reported: "Wheeling systems like (Gail) Howard's have the most respectability among critics since they concede that the wheels offer a systematic way of reducing the odds."

The combinations that result from the built-in Balanced Game™ feature are patterned closest to the way the winning Lotto numbers are actually drawn. This unique feature has refined wheeling to a state-of-the-art science. No wonder my Balanced Wheels™ have produced so many winners!

The natural tendency of novice Lotto players is to bet the lower numbers, especially the calendar numbers of 1 to 31 because of the heavy play given to birth dates, anniversary dates and children's ages.

To convince my readers not to bet this, or other unlikely combinations, but to play the combinations that are more likely to be drawn as winners, I invented the Balanced Game™. My intention was to show my readers that to have a better chance of winning, the sum of a set of Lotto numbers should fall within a certain range similar to the range of sums of actual drawing results.

If you study the list of past winning numbers for your state's Lotto game, you'll see that randomly drawn numbers tend to be more or less evenly distributed over the entire number field. When you add up the five winning numbers in your state's Lotto game, you get a sum. (For example, a typical 5/39 game could be: 3 + 17 + 20 + 24 + 36 = 100.) Add up the five winning numbers for several of the drawings and you will find that most of the winning combinations tend to fall within the same range of sums.

A Balanced Game™ is a five-number combination that falls within the Most Probable Range of Sums™.

I discovered that randomly drawn numbers tend to have their sums distributed as a bell-shaped curve. The range of all possible sums in a pick-5 39-number game is from 15 to 185. If we were to plot the number of combinations that could be made with the various sums, we would see a perfect bell-shaped curve, with the sums 15 and 185 at either end.

In a pick-5 Lotto game with a 39-number field, there is only *one* five-number combination that adds up to 15:

$1 + 2 + 3 + 4 + 5 = 15.$

And, in the 5/39 Lotto game, only *one* five-number combination adds up to 185:

$35 + 36 + 37 + 38 + 39 = 185.$

Those two combinations have the smallest and largest possible sums. And they occur only *once*—at the tail ends of a bell curve, making it virtually impossible for either of those groups of numbers to be drawn as a winning combination.

In the 39-number pick-5 game, the most frequently occurring sum is 100. The greatest percentage of five-number combinations in a 5/39 game have sums of 100. There are 9,343 different ways to make a five number combination that adds up to 100. So theoretically, five-number combinations that add up to 100 are the most likely to occur in a randomly drawn 39-number game. The 100 sum would be at the top center point of the bell curve.

There are slightly fewer combinations (9,339) that add up to sums of 99 or 101, the numbers on either side of the top center point of the bell curve. Next, there are 9,314 combinations that add up to sums of 98 or 102. And there are 9,282 combinations that add up to sums of 97 or 103. As we move away from the center of the bell curve, the count for each sum becomes progressively lower until we reach the extreme ends, where the sums 15 and 185 appear only once.

Balanced Game Bell-Curve Distribution™

LOTTO 5/39 575,757 Total Combinations

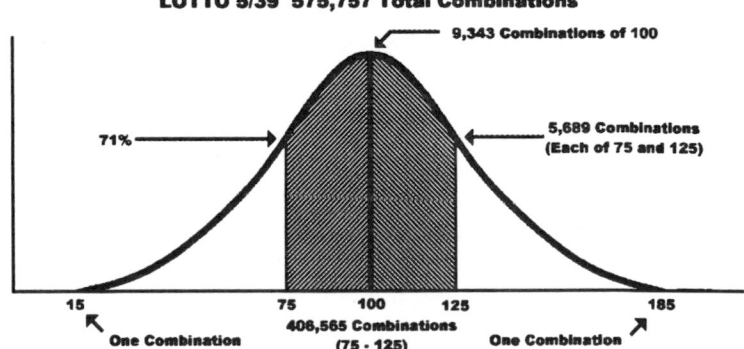

9,343 Combinations of 100

5,689 Combinations
(Each of 75 and 125)

71%

15   75   100   125   185

One Combination   406,565 Combinations
(75 - 125)   One Combination

The sums of Lotto combinations can be compared to the sums of combinations on a pair of dice. On either end of the Bell Curve, there is only one way to make a 12 (boxcars, 6 and 6), and there is only one way to make a 2 (snake eyes, 1 and 1). But there are six ways to make a 7 (the top center point of a Bell Curve for a pair of dice). They are 6 and 1, 1 and 6, 5 and 2, 2 and 5, 4 and 3, 3 and 4.

So, of course, it's much easier to throw a 7 in dice than any other number because there are more ways of getting the sum of 7.

SUM COUNTS FOR 5 OF 39 LOTTO GAMES
Sums for all 575,757 Combinations

SUM	GAMES	SUM	GAMES	SUM	GAMES	SUM	GAMES	SUM	GAMES
15	1	50	1,114	85	7,844	120	6,818	155	674
16	1	51	1,224	86	8,022	121	6,600	156	603
17	2	52	1,338	87	8,198	122	6,372	157	540
18	3	53	1,462	88	8,357	123	6,148	158	480
19	5	54	1,590	89	8,512	124	5,916	159	427
20	7	55	1,729	90	8,649	125	5,689	160	377
21	10	56	1,871	91	8,781	126	5,455	161	333
22	13	57	2,024	92	8,894	127	5,228	162	291
23	18	58	2,180	93	9,001	128	4,996	163	255
24	23	59	2,347	94	9,088	129	4,771	164	221
25	30	60	2,517	95	9,169	130	4,543	165	192
26	37	61	2,697	96	9,229	131	4,323	166	164
27	47	62	2,879	97	9,282	132	4,101	167	141
28	57	63	3,072	98	9,314	133	3,888	168	119
29	70	64	3,266	99	9,339	134	3,674	169	101
30	84	65	3,470	→100	9,343	135	3,470	170	84
31	101	66	3,674	101	9,339	136	3,266	171	70
32	119	67	3,888	102	9,314	137	3,072	172	57
33	141	68	4,101	103	9,282	138	2,879	173	47
34	164	69	4,323	104	9,229	139	2,697	174	37
35	192	70	4,543	105	9,169	140	2,517	175	30
36	221	71	4,771	106	9,088	141	2,347	176	23
37	255	72	4,996	107	9,001	142	2,180	177	18
38	291	73	5,228	108	8,894	143	2,024	178	13
39	333	74	5,455	109	8,781	144	1,871	179	10
40	377	75	5,689	110	8,649	145	1,729	180	7
41	427	76	5,916	111	8,512	146	1,590	181	5
42	480	77	6,148	112	8,357	147	1,462	182	3
43	540	78	6,372	113	8,198	148	1,338	183	2
44	603	79	6,600	114	8,022	149	1,224	184	1
45	674	80	6,818	115	7,844	150	1,114	185	1
46	748	81	7,038	116	7,650	151	1,014		
47	831	82	7,246	117	7,455	152	918		
48	918	83	7,455	118	7,246	153	831		
49	1,014	84	7,650	119	7,038	154	748		

After carefully analyzing all the pick-5 games currently in existence, I discovered that **more than 70 percent of the past sets of winning numbers are produced by only 32 percent or less of all the possible sums.**

For example, in the 5/39 game, there are 575,757 possible combinations of five numbers. Of those, 406,565 combinations have sums ranging from 75 to 125.

The range of sums varies with the number field of the Lotto game. For example, the 70 percent Most Probable Range of Sums for the 5/26 Fantasy 5 game is 51 to 84.

The 70 percent Most Probable Range of Sums for all pick-5 games are shown in the Balanced Game Bell-Curve Distribution Chart™ on page 29.

My Wheel Five Plus™ software makes instant wheeled combinations of your chosen numbers with the touch of a key, and displays the sum next to each combination in your wheel. To improve on your Balanced Game sums, simply touch the Optimizing Key to enhance the results.

If you want to give your odds more leverage, that is, play with the probabilities more in your favor, be sure that the sums of your five-number bets fall within the Most Probable Range™ for the Lotto game you are playing.

Because the vast majority of Lotto players still bet the lower (calendar) numbers, I recommend that you play the *higher* end of the Most Probable Range™. For example, in the 5/39 Lotto game, the sums at the higher end of the Most Probable Range are between 100 and 125. If your numbers do win, the prize payouts will be higher because fewer winners will be sharing the prize pool.

To use the following chart, locate the Lotto game with the number field you want to play. You are more likely to win if the sum of the numbers you play falls within the Most Probable Range™.

MOST PROBABLE RANGE OF SUMS™

Pick 5 Lotto Game	Most Probable Sum	Most Probable Range	Pick 5 Lotto Game	Most Probable Sum	Most Probable Range
5/50	128	95 - 160	5/36	93	69 - 116
5/49	125	93 - 157	5/35	90	68 - 112
5/45	115	86 - 144	5/34	88	66 - 109
5/42	108	80 - 135	5/32	83	61 - 103
5/40	102	77 - 128	5/31	80	60 - 100
5/39	100	75 - 125	5/30	77	59 - 96
5/38	98	73 - 122	5/26	68	51 - 84
5/37	95	71 - 119	Copyright © 1983-1998 Gail Howard		

The BALANCED GAME BELL-CURVE DISTRIBUTION CHART™ lists in the first column all the pick-5 game formats. Find the number field of the pick-5 game YOU play. The second column lists the Total Number of Combinations in each game. The third column shows the Most Probable Range of the most frequently drawn sums for 70 percent coverage for each pick-5 game. The fourth column shows the Percentage of Total Sums in the Most Probable Range. Next, in the fifth column is the Total Number of Combinations in the Most Probable Range. And last, the sixth column shows the Percentage of Total Combinations which fall within the Most Probable Range of sums.

This unique copyrighted chart is my proof that between 29 and 32 percent of the combinations account for more than 70 percent of the winning combinations in pick-5 games.

BALANCED GAME BELL-CURVE DISTRIBUTION CHART™

Lotto Game	Total Number of Combinations	Most Probable RANGE⁻	PERCENTAGE of TOTAL SUMS in Most Probable Range	TOTAL NUMBER of COMBINATIONS in Most Probable Range	PERCENTAGE of Total COMBINATIONS in Most Probable Range
5x26	65,780	51- 84	(32.1%)	47,470	72.16%
5x30	142,506	58- 97	(31.7%)	103,294	72.48%
5x31	169,911	60-100	(31.3%)	122,259	71.95%
5x32	201,376	62-103	(30.9%)	143,896	71.46%
5x33	237,336	64-106	(30.5%)	168,474	70.99%
5x34	278,256	66-109	(30.1%)	196,284	70.54%
5x35	324,632	68-112	(29.8%)	227,630	70.12%
5x36	376,992	69-116	(30.8%)	270,758	71.82%
5x37	435,807	71-119	(30.4%)	311,225	71.40%
5x38	501,942	73-122	(30.1%)	356,362	71.00%
5x39	575,757	75-125	(29.8%)	406,565	70.61%
5x40	658,008	77-128	(29.5%)	462,240	70.25%
5x42	850,668	80-135	(30.1%)	607,042	71.36%
5x45	1,221,759	86-144	(29.4%)	859,515	70.35%
5x49	1,906,884	93-157	(29.4%)	1,348,616	70.72%
5x50	2,118,760	95-160	(29.2%)	1,492,334	70.43%

MAXIMIZE BENEFITS OF BALANCED WHEELS™

Before I created my unique Balanced Wheeling Systems™, it was very difficult to both wheel the numbers and have Balanced Games™. All other wheeling systems sold in this country and elsewhere group the low numbers together in the first part of the system and group the high numbers together at the end of the system, leaving very few combinations with balanced games in the middle of the system.

The question of where to place one's chosen numbers in order to get Balanced Games was one my readers used to ask most often. To eliminate the confusion, I came up with a solution that structured wheeling systems internally to give the most balanced games possible within the wheel itself.

When using my Balanced Wheels, you can place your chosen numbers in ascending order from low to high, or in descending order from high to low, are you can mix them up. Actually, you can place your numbers in any order and it will not affect the win guarantee.

With Balanced Wheels™, a much smaller percentage of combinations falls outside the Balanced Game™ parameters. Given the nature of wheeling, this is not always possible to totally avoid. Do not eliminate those combinations. You must play every combination in a system or you will destroy the win guarantee. Besides, even an unbalanced combination is capable of winning a small prize—which may be your guaranteed minimum prize.

You will have Balanced Games™ when using my Balanced Wheeling Systems™ only if your chosen group of numbers is balanced to begin with. Now that you know the the Most Probable Range™ of sums for picking a five-number combination (one game panel), I'll show you how you can apply this Balanced Game probability rule when you wheel a *group* of numbers.

The easiest way to be sure that the number selection in your wheel is balanced, is to choose half of the Lotto numbers in your wheel that are higher than the mid point number and half that are lower than the midpoint number of your Lotto game.

For example, in a 5/39 game, half of the number picks in your wheel would be chosen from the numbers 1 to 18; and the other half would be chosen from 19 to 39.

Another way to have a balanced selection of numbers for your wheel is to choose a relatively equal amount of numbers from each of the number groups—from the single digits, the teens, the 20's, the 30's, etc.

TIME TABLE FOR WINNING

How often can you expect to win when you wheel your numbers? That depends on how often you *want* to win, because the wheeling system you use determines how often you can expect to have the winning numbers in your wheeled group. In other words, **YOU CHOOSE YOUR OWN TIMETABLE FOR WINNING.** If you play Lotto on a regular basis, you can expect to get the winning numbers in your wheeled group according to a specific mathematical frequency.

How often you can expect to win varies with the number field of the game you are playing. Naturally, you can expect to win more often in Lotto games with smaller number fields and lower odds.

Win Frequency Charts™ show the mathematical probability of trapping five, four, or three winning numbers in a wheeled group of from 6 to 30 numbers, for each of the pick-5 games now being played in every state. Notice how the odds melt away with each additional number wheeled.

The top line of the Win Frequency Chart™ for the 5/39 game shows that you have one chance in 575,757 of getting five winning numbers when choosing just five numbers. But when you choose six numbers, the odds of getting the five winning numbers drop dramatically—to one in 95,960. The odds of getting four of the five winning numbers out of 39 are one in 3,387. But when you wheel six numbers, those odds magically drop to one in 1,163. The odds of getting four winning numbers drop from the expected one in 103 to one in 55.

When you wheel 12 of the 39 numbers, your chance of trapping the five winning numbers drops to one in 727. But when you wheel 18 numbers, the odds drop to one in 67. The odds are really tamed when you wheel 24 numbers—dropping to a more manageable one in 14. Of course, the odds drop even more drastically for getting four or three of the winning numbers in your wheeled group. As you look at the various Win Frequency Charts™, it should become obvious that the more numbers you wheel, the easier it is to trap the winning numbers in your chosen group.

The number field of the Lotto game you play makes a significant difference, too. The fewer Lotto numbers you have to choose from, the lower the odds and the more frequently you will trap the winning numbers in your group.

Now that you have the Win Frequency Charts™ for the pick-5 game you play, you can see for yourself whether or not you are getting the winning numbers as often as probability says you should be. If you have been wheeling 12 numbers in a 5/39 game for several drawings, and have not had even four winning numbers in your wheeled group yet, you can see that the overall average time for trapping four numbers is once for every 42 times you wheel 12 numbers.

This does not mean you will have to wait for 42 drawings for that to happen. The purpose of the Win Frequency Charts™ is to give you some perspective of what you can expect time-wise when you wheel your numbers. If you want to wheel more numbers but can't afford the ticket cost of a more expensive system, you can always pool your money with others and spread the cost and share the wealth. It's better to win a small percent of something than 100 percent of nothing.

On pages 35 to 37, find the Win Frequency Chart™ for the number field of the game you play.

WARNING!!!

Keep in mind that the Win Frequency Chart™ tells you how often you can expect to trap the winning numbers in your chosen wheeled group. It does not guarantee any prize. The actual prize you could expect to win depends on the win guarantee of the wheeling system you use.

Notice that the most dramatic reduction of odds always occurs at the top of Win Frequency Charts™. The smaller the size of your chosen group, the more ways there are to make combinations of the *missing* numbers—for all the prize categories. As more numbers are chosen, the number of missed combinations decreases. As the size of the chosen group comes closer to the total numbers in the game, there is a crossover at some point, when it becomes easier to trap the winning numbers than to miss them.

I make the following explanation in the next three paragraphs—not because it has any value in helping you play Lotto better—but because I know I will be swamped with letters if I don't explain here why the odds *against* winning the lower prizes *increase*, as most of the numbers become used up. It is meant only to satisfy the curious.

On page 37, the Win Frequency Chart™ for Lotto 5/32 shows the crossover occurring at 24 for the THREE-number prize. When 24 numbers are chosen, there are only 8 numbers left. With 25 numbers chosen, there are only 7 numbers left to make missing combinations. With 26 of the 32 numbers chosen, there are only 6 missing numbers left.

As more of the remaining numbers are chosen, fewer ways remain to make missing combinations. And there also become *fewer* ways to trap *lower* prize combinations than the higher prize combinations—because the *higher* prize categories use the remaining possible combinations FIRST, leaving fewer ways to make the lower prize categories.

To illustrate how the higher prize categories use up the combinations first, let's look at a pick-5 Full Wheel that wheels 6 numbers in six-combinations. It guarantees one 5-number first prize jackpot plus five 4-number prizes. Every combination is a winner, but the higher tier prizes use all 6 combinations, leaving nothing to make a lower tier prize. So, in the Lotto Win Frequency Charts™, when nearly all the numbers are chosen, the odds *against* trapping the lowest prizes *increase*.

Gail Howard's LOTTO WIN FREQUENCY CHARTS™

LOTTO 5/50			
Nrs	Five	Four	Three
5	2,118,760	9.417	214
6	353,127	3,210	112
7	100,893	1,408	67
8	37,835	721	44
9	16,816	410	31
10	8.408	252	23
11	4,586	165	17
12	2,675	113	14
13	1,646	80	11
14	1,058	59	9
15	706	44	8
16	485	34	7
17	342	27	6
18	247	22	5
19	182	18	5
20	137	15	4
21	104	12	4
22	80	10	4
23	63	9	3
24	50	8	3
25	40	7	3
26	32	6	3
27	26	5	3
28	22	5	3
29	18	4	3
30	15	4	3

Copyright © 1983-1998 Gail Howard

LOTTO 5/49			
Nrs	Five	Four	Three
5	1,906,884	6,668	202
6	317,814	2,956	106
7	90,804	1,297	63
8	34,052	664	42
9	15,134	378	29
10	7,567	233	21
11	4,127	152	16
12	2,408	104	13
13	1,482	74	11
14	952	54	9
15	635	41	7
16	437	32	6
17	308	25	6
18	223	20	5
19	164	16	5
20	120	14	4
21	94	11	4
22	72	10	4
23	57	8	4
24	45	7	3
25	36	6	3
26	29	6	3
27	24	5	3
28	19	4	3
29	16	4	3
30	13	4	3

Copyright © 1983-1998 Gail Howard

LOTTO 5/45			
Nrs	Five	Four	Three
5	1,221,759	6,109	157
6	203,627	2,088	82
7	58,179	919	50
8	21,817	472	33
9	9,697	269	23
10	4,040	166	17
11	2,645	109	13
12	1,540	75	11
13	949	53	9
14	610	39	7
15	407	30	6
16	280	23	5
17	197	18	5
18	143	15	4
19	105	12	4
20	79	10	4
21	60	9	3
22	46	7	3
23	36	6	3
24	29	5	3
25	23	5	3
26	19	4	3
27	15	4	3
28	12	4	3
29	10	3	3
30	9	3	3

Copyright © 1983-1998 Gail Howard

LOTTO 5/39			
Nrs	Five	Four	Three
5	575,757	3,387	103
6	95,960	1,163	55
7	27,417	514	33
8	10,281	265	22
9	4,570	152	16
10	2,285	95	12
11	1,248	62	9
12	727	43	7
13	447	31	6
14	288	23	5
15	192	18	5
16	132	14	4
17	93	11	4
18	67	9	3
19	50	7	3
20	37	6	3
21	28	5	3
22	22	5	3
23	17	4	3
24	14	4	3
25	11	3	3
26	9	3	3
27	7	3	3
28	6	3	3
29	5	2	4
30	4	2	4

Copyright © 1983-1998 Gail Howard

Gail Howard's LOTTO WIN FREQUENCY CHARTS™

LOTTO 5/38			
Nrs	Five	Four	Three
5	501,942	3,042	95
6	83,657	1,046	51
7	23,902	463	31
8	8,963	239	21
9	3,984	137	15
10	1,992	85	11
11	1,086	56	9
12	634	39	7
13	390	28	6
14	251	21	5
15	167	16	4
16	115	13	4
17	81	10	4
18	59	8	3
19	43	7	3
20	32	6	3
21	25	5	3
22	19	4	3
23	15	4	3
24	12	3	3
25	9	3	3
26	8	3	3
27	6	3	3
28	5	2	3
29	4	2	4
30	4	2	4

Copyright © 1983-1998 Gail Howard

LOTTO 5/37			
Nrs	Five	Four	Three
5	435,897	2,724	88
6	72,650	937	47
7	20,757	415	29
8	7,784	215	19
9	3,460	124	14
10	1,730	77	10
11	944	51	8
12	550	35	7
13	339	25	6
14	218	19	5
15	145	15	4
16	100	11	4
17	70	9	3
18	51	8	3
19	37	6	3
20	28	5	3
21	21	5	3
22	17	4	3
23	13	4	3
24	10	3	3
25	8	3	3
26	7	3	3
27	5	2	3
28	4	2	4
29	4	2	4
30	3	2	5

Copyright © 1983-1998 Gail Howard

LOTTO 5/36			
Nrs	Five	Four	Three
5	376,992	2,432	81
6	62,832	838	43
7	17.952	371	27
8	6,732	192	18
9	2,992	111	13
10	1,496	69	10
11	816	46	8
12	476	32	6
13	293	23	5
14	188	17	4
15	126	13	4
16	86	10	4
17	61	8	3
18	44	7	3
19	32	6	3
20	24	5	3
21	19	4	3
22	14	4	3
23	11	3	3
24	9	3	3
25	7	3	3
26	6	3	3
27	5	3	4
28	4	2	4
29	3	3	5
30	3	2	6

Copyright © 1983-1998 Gail Howard

LOTTO 5/35			
Nrs	Five	Four	Three
5	324,632	2,164	75
6	54,105	746	40
7	15,459	331	25
8	5,797	172	17
9	2,576	99	12
10	1,288	62	9
11	703	41	7
12	410	29	6
13	252	21	5
14	162	15	4
15	108	12	4
16	74	9	3
17	52	8	3
18	38	6	3
19	28	5	3
20	21	4	3
21	16	4	3
22	12	3	3
23	10	3	3
24	8	3	3
25	6	3	3
26	5	2	3
27	4	2	4
28	3	2	5
29	3	2	6
30	2	2	8

Copyright © 1983-1998 Gail Howard

Gail Howard's LOTTO WIN FREQUENCY CHARTS™

LOTTO 5/34				LOTTO 5/32			
Nrs	Five	Four	Three	Nrs	Five	Four	Three
5	278,256	1,919	69	5	201,376	1,492	57
6	46,376	663	37	6	33,563	516	31
7	13,250	294	23	7	9,589	230	19
8	4,969	153	15	8	3,596	120	13
9	2,208	88	11	9	1,598	69	9
10	1,104	55	8	10	799	44	7
11	602	37	7	11	436	29	6
12	351	26	5	12	254	20	5
13	216	19	5	13	156	15	4
14	139	14	4	14	101	11	4
15	93	11	4	15	67	9	3
16	64	8	3	16	46	7	3
17	45	7	3	17	33	6	3
18	32	6	3	18	24	5	3
19	24	5	3	19	17	4	3
20	18	4	3	20	13	3	3
21	14	4	3	21	10	3	3
22	11	3	3	22	8	3	3
23	8	3	3	23	6	3	3
24	7	3	3	24	5	2	4
25	5	2	3	25	4	2	4
26	4	2	4	26	3	2	5
27	3	2	5	27	2	2	7
28	3	2	6	28	2	2	10
29	2	2	8	29	2	3	18
30	2	3	11	30	1	4	50

LOTTO 5/30				LOTTO 5/26			
Nrs	Five	Four	Three	Nrs	Five	Four	Three
5	142,506	1,140	48	5	65,780	626	31
6	23,751	396	26	6	10,963	219	17
7	6,786	177	16	7	3,132	99	11
8	2,545	93	11	8	1,176	62	9
9	1,131	54	8	9	522	31	6
10	566	34	6	10	261	20	5
11	308	23	5	11	142	13	4
12	180	16	4	12	83	9	3
13	111	12	4	13	51	7	3
14	71	9	3	14	32	5	3
15	48	7	3	15	22	4	3
16	33	6	3	16	15	4	3
17	23	5	3	17	11	3	3
18	17	4	3	18	8	3	3
19	12	3	3	19	6	2	3
20	9	3	3	20	4	2	4
21	7	3	3	21	3	2	5
22	5	2	3	22	3	2	7
23	4	2	4	23	2	2	12
24	3	2	5	24	2	3	33
25	3	2	6	25	1	5	Never
26	2	2	9	26	NA	NA	NA
27	2	3	16				
28	1	3	44				
29	1	6	Never				
30	N/A	N/A	N/A				

WHEELING GUIDELINES

RULE #1. It is more important to wheel MORE numbers than to choose a higher win guarantee. The Win Frequency Charts™ should make that abundantly clear. If it doesn't, then look carefully again at the chart for the game YOU play. Unless you use my number selection strategies before each drawing to find the best possible choices, you need to include as many numbers as your lottery budget allows. To win prizes, you must trap some winning numbers in your wheeled group. The more numbers you wheel, the easier it is to have winning numbers.

RULE #2. The optimum number of numbers to wheel is about HALF the numbers in your game—not to exceed 4 or 5 numbers over that. Otherwise you will be spending MORE money chasing a SMALLER guaranteed prize.

It's true that the more numbers you wheel, the easier it is to trap the winning numbers in your chosen group—but only up to a certain point is it cost effective. When wheeling most or all of the numbers in a game with an *affordable* wheel, the numbers will be too spread out, so that even when the minimum prize is won, it may not cover the cost of the wheel. Multiple prize wins are rare with such wheels.

RULE #3. Do NOT try to include ALL the numbers in your game in one wheel. There are many smarter ways to play all the numbers. When all the numbers in the game are played using SEVERAL wheels, your money does not lose leverage. On the contrary, by using several wheels at once, you have several minimum win guarantees, as opposed to using one large system that wheels ALL the numbers in the game and guarantees ONE minimum prize. Always keep in mind, you will have the most success if you do not wheel more than 4 or 5 numbers more than half the numbers in you game.

RULE #4. When using multiple wheels, do NOT give all Lotto numbers equal play. When wheeling all the numbers in the game, it's still important to carefully select a group of numbers, and wheel your strongest numbers with other groups of numbers. Placing Lotto numbers in multiple wheels an equal number of times will not bring the best results. You *must give a bias* to favored groups of numbers which appear in more wheels than other less favored numbers do.

RULE #5. Do not make many SMALL wheels just for the sake of using multiple wheels. It's a bad risk for a large investment of cash. When many small wheels are used, the winning numbers are less likely to come together in one wheel, resulting in a costly disappointment. Spending $6 on one 12-number wheel is not a big risk. But risking $60 on TEN 12-number wheels is a waste of money that could be put to better use with wheeling strategy. In a 5/39 Lotto game, the odds of getting the five winning numbers in a 12-number wheel are one in 727. A $60 budget would be better spent on two 20-number wheels, in which the odds of getting the five winning numbers are one in 37. (See the Lotto Win Frequency Charts™ for your game.)

RULE #6. Players with small budgets should use Balanced Wheels™ with the lowest win guarantees. To have the best chance of trapping the winning numbers, try to include as many numbers as your lottery budget allows. Most of the jackpot winners who won with my wheeling systems used Balanced Wheels™ with the lower win guarantees—which allowed them to wheel more numbers at an affordable ticket cost.

RULE #7. You do not have to be in *every* drawing. Just because the drawings for your favorite game increased from twice a week to daily, does not mean you have to be in every one. Many times I have heard people say they stopped playing a game because they can't afford it anymore now that it is drawn daily. Buy tickets only when you think you have some good numbers.

RULE #8. Cash in on Good Old Fashioned Dumb Luck. Luck does come in streaks. If you're on a losing streak, cut back on the amount you spend on tickets. You don't have to spend a fortune to wheel a fortune. For as little as $3 you can wheel 12 numbers and get a 3 out of 5 win guarantee using one Power Number. When you start winning, you can afford to spend more because you may be on a roll!

WHEELING STRATEGY FOR POOLS

By pooling your money with others, you can afford to wheel more numbers, play more expensive systems, or play several wheels. Whether your pool has a few dollars or a few thousand dollars to invest in Lotto tickets, there are strategies you can use to make the most of what you have.

If your pool's budget is very small, it would be better to play a wheeling system such as #53219 for $28 once a month—or when the numbers look especially promising—rather than using one very small wheel every drawing.

Pools with large budgets can use creative variations of the Rose Trap by Overlap method. For example, if you were to use several 20-number wheels, you could take the best 10 numbers and wheel them with three or four different sets of 10 numbers, so that all the numbers in your game are played.

For example, if your strongest numbers were: 2-4-7-11-13-16-25-29-33-34, you might wheel them with: 1-5-8-14-18-24-28-30-35-39 and 3-6-10-19-22-26-27-32-37-38 and 8-9-12-15-17-20-21-23-31-36.

Each of your three wheels could contain your ten best numbers, but you would be covering all the numbers in a 5/39 game.

Or, if you are not so sure of your number picks, you could rotate groups of 10 numbers with other groups of 10 numbers, not necessarily having one same set of 10 numbers appear in every wheel.

Consider the following options. For approximately the same amount of money it would cost to wheel 30 numbers in one wheel, you could wheel 23 numbers in each of two wheels—and you would be wheeling 46 number picks, not just 30. Or you could wheel 18 numbers in each of four wheels—and you would be wheeling 72 number picks. Or you could wheel 17 numbers in each of five wheels—and you would be wheeling 85 number picks—which means you could wheel each of 39 numbers at least twice).

Another variation is to use a combination of several wheeling systems with assorted win guarantees. Use one (or more) relatively large system(s) with a lower win guarantee that lets you wheel many numbers for the money, such as the 3 out of 5 and 3 out of 4 Balanced Wheels. Also use one (or more) Balanced Wheels with higher win guarantees such as the 3 out of 3 or 4 out of 5 Balanced Wheels.

The 3 out of 3 Balanced Wheels are particularly useful for pool play because while they guarantee one 3-number prize if just three of the five numbers are winners, they can win many multiple prizes.

For example, Balanced Wheel #53018, which wheels 18 numbers in 94 combinations, guarantees one 3-number prize and 15 2-number prizes if you get just three of the five winning numbers in your group. If four of your numbers are winners, you are guaranteed to win four 3-number prizes and 24 2-number prizes.

With five winning numbers, you are guaranteed to win 10 3-number prizes plus 30 2-number prizes. If the 3-number prize pays $20, you collect $200, which gives you double your money back. And this would be just the GUARANTEED MINIMUM. But, you could win three 4-number prizes plus six 3-number prizes and 29 2-number prizes—or you could win the first prize jackpot plus other prizes.

If your pool plays with $500 or less, or if you make multiple wheels of $500 or less, you can find every wheel you could possibly want in my Wheel Six Plus™ and Wheel Five Plus™ software. Buy both together and they cost only $99.95 plus shipping. However, if your pool spends thousands of dollars for a single drawing, then you might want to order a custom wheel. The custom wheels cost $100 per 1,000 combinations.

For example, a 30-number wheel in a pick-6 game with a 4 out of 4 win guarantee has 2,910 combinations, so that system would cost $291. If you own the Wheel Six Plus software, we would ship it on disk so you can use all the features for your custom wheel, such as viewing minimum and maximum prizes, win checking, testing through past histories for wins, etc. Or you could have an A-B-C's print out on paper, or a print out with your own chosen group of numbers.

THE JACKPOT BUSTER™

WIN THE JACKPOT WITH 3 NUMBERS!!

This is a dynamite pooling tool for pick-5 games. If you play in states with pick-5 number fields of 26, 30, 35 or 39 numbers, you can use the Jackpot Buster™ Wheels in this book.

All you have to do to win the first prize jackpot and many more prizes-is PICK THREE (NOT FIVE) numbers and have all three come up as winners. You are required to pick only three numbers because the other two winning numbers are bought and paid for built right into the ticket cost.

Jackpot Busters™ are actually Full Wheels with three Power Numbers™ that wheel all the numbers in the game. Your three number picks must be placed in the system positions A-B-C in the wheels. When filling in the bet slips, it is easier to mark the three chosen numbers first. Then go back and mark the two additional numbers, as shown in the system, to complete each of the game panels.

If the Jackpot Buster™ for your game is not included here, you will find it in my Full Wheel Generator™ software. In fact, if you use a computer, the software is much faster and easier to use. Instead of making hundreds of combinations by hand, a touch of a key will make all the combinations for you instantly. See page 63.

JACKPOT BUSTER ™ #55026-3 costs $253 to use in the 5/26 games played in Florida and Louisiana. Jackpot Buster Wheel #55026-3 starts on page 392.

WIN WITH THREE NUMBERS: Pick Just THREE Numbers Correctly (NOT FIVE) in the Florida and Louisiana 5/26 games and play just 253 Combinations (NOT the Full 65,780) and YOU WILL WIN THE JACKPOT—GUARANTEED! And that's not all. You also will WIN 42 SECOND PRIZES AND 210 THIRD PRIZES!! Every ticket is a winner!

WIN WITH TWO NUMBERS: If only TWO of your three chosen numbers are winners, you won't win the jackpot, but YOU WILL WIN THREE SECOND PRIZES AND 60 THIRD PRIZES. A total of 63 prizes for picking just TWO Winning Numbers!

WIN WITH ONE NUMBER: If only ONE of your three chosen numbers is a winner, you are guaranteed to win SIX THIRD PRIZES!

WARNING!!!

The Jackpot Buster™ WIN GUARANTEE is valid on these conditions:

(1) All three of your chosen numbers, placed in system positions A-B-C, must be winners.

(2) You must play ALL 253 combinations.

(3) You must not make any errors when filling in your play slips.

JACKPOT BUSTER™ #55030-3 costs $351 to use

in the 5/30 games played in Illinois, Missouri and Nebraska. Jackpot Buster Wheel #55030-3 starts on page 396.

WIN WITH THREE NUMBERS: Pick Just THREE Numbers Correctly (NOT FIVE) in the Illinois, Missouri or Nebraska 5/30 games and play just 351 combinations (NOT the Full 142,506) and YOU WILL WIN THE FIRST PRIZE JACKPOT— GUARANTEED! And that's not all. You also will WIN 50 SECOND PRIZES AND 300 THIRD PRIZES!! Every ticket is a winner!

WIN WITH TWO NUMBERS: If only TWO of your three chosen numbers are winners, you won't win the jackpot, but YOU WILL WIN THREE SECOND PRIZES AND 72 THIRD PRIZES. A total of 76 prizes for picking just TWO Winning Numbers!

WIN WITH ONE NUMBER: If only ONE of your three chosen numbers is a winner, you are guaranteed to win SIX THIRD PRIZES!

WARNING!!!

The Jackpot Buster™ WIN GUARANTEE is valid on these conditions:

(1) All three of your chosen numbers, placed in system positions A-B-C, must be winners.

(2) You must play ALL 351 combinations.

(3) You must not make any errors when filling in your play slips.

JACKPOT BUSTER ™ #55035-3 costs $496 to

use in the 5/35 games played in Arizona, Connecticut, Georgia, Kentucky, Massachusetts and South Dakota. Jackpot Buster Wheel #55035-3 starts on page 401.

WIN WITH THREE NUMBERS: Pick Just THREE Numbers Correctly (NOT FIVE) in the Arizona, Connecticut, Georgia, Kentucky, Massachusetts or South Dakota 5/35 games and play just 496 combinations (NOT the Full 324,632) and YOU WILL WIN THE FIRST PRIZE JACKPOT—GUARANTEED! And that's not all. You also will WIN 60 SECOND PRIZES AND 435 THIRD PRIZES!! Every ticket is a winner!

WIN WITH TWO NUMBERS: If only TWO of your three chosen numbers are winners, you won't win the jackpot, but YOU WILL WIN THREE SECOND PRIZES AND 87 THIRD PRIZES. A total of 90 prizes for picking just TWO Winning Numbers!

WIN WITH ONE NUMBER: If only ONE of your three chosen numbers is a winner, you are guaranteed to win SIX THIRD PRIZES!

WARNING!!!

The Jackpot Buster™ WIN GUARANTEE is valid on these conditions:

(1) All three of your chosen numbers, placed in system positions A-B-C, must be winners.

(2) You must play ALL 496 combinations.

(3) You must not make any errors when filling in your play slips.

JACKPOT BUSTER ™ #55039-3 costs $630 to

use in the 5/39 games played in California, Maryland, Michigan, Minnesota, New York, Pennsylvania and Texas. Jackpot Buster System #55039-3 starts on page 409.

WIN WITH THREE NUMBERS: Pick Just THREE Numbers Correctly (NOT FIVE) in California, Maryland, Michigan, Minnesota, New York, Pennsylvania or Texas 5/39 games and play just 630 combinations (NOT 575,757) and YOU WILL WIN THE FIRST PRIZE JACKPOT—GUARANTEED! And that's not all. You also will WIN 68 SECOND PRIZES AND 561 THIRD PRIZES!! Every ticket is a winner!

WIN WITH TWO NUMBERS: If only TWO of your three chosen numbers are winners, you won't win the jackpot, but YOU WILL WIN THREE SECOND PRIZES AND 99 THIRD PRIZES and 528 two-number prizes. A total of 630 prizes for picking just TWO Winning Numbers!

WIN WITH ONE NUMBER: If only ONE of your three chosen numbers is a winner, you are guaranteed to win SIX THIRD PRIZES and 128 two-number prizes!

WARNING!!!

The Jackpot Buster™ WIN GUARANTEE is valid on these conditions:

(1) All three of your chosen numbers, placed in system positions A-B-C, must be winners.

(2) You must play ALL 630 combinations.

(3) You must not make any errors when filling in your play slips.

SYSTEM NUMBERS EXPLAINED

Many of you who bought the first edition of *Lotto Wheel Five to Win* will find a different numbering system in the second edition. With more than three hundred wheeling systems available in the expanded second edition, a new numbering system had to be devised to simplify the listing. (Many of the wheels have remained the same, but where it was possible to shorten and still retain the win guarantee, some wheels have fewer combinations, making them more economical to use.

Each wheel now has a six-digit System Number, which not only identifies the wheel, but also describes what it does. From left to right, each of the six digits means: (1) Game Pick Size (pick-5); (2) Minimum Prize Guaranteed; (3) Numbers MORE than Minimum Guaranteed Prize Required to win it; (4 and 5) Numbers Wheeled; (6) Number of Power Numbers

For example, Balanced Wheel **#53214-1** has a first digit of **5**. This means it is a pick-5 wheel. Since this book contains only pick-5 wheels, all systems in *Lotto Wheel Five to Win* start with a 5.

The second digit is a **3**, which means this wheel guarantees a 3-number prize.

The third digit is a **2**, which means 2 additional winning numbers—beyond the guaranteed three-number prize—are required to meet the win guarantee. So, the first three digits tell us this is a pick-5 wheel with a 3 out of 5 win guarantee (win 3 with 5 right).

The fourth and fifth digit tell us the number of numbers to be wheeled. In this case, it is a **14**-number wheel. (A nine number wheel would also be two digits: 09.)

The sixth digit is the number of Power Numbers in the wheel. System #53214-1 has **one** Power Number. When the wheel has no power number, the sixth digit is omitted.

Here is another example. The old System #3401 has become System #54107. Once you get used to this numbering system, you'll instantly know that System #54107 is for a pick-5 game, guarantees a 4-number prize if the four plus one additional winning number (win 4 with 5 right) are in the chosen group, and that it wheels 7 numbers, and has no Power Number.

INSTANT WHEEL FINDER™

To help you get faster to the wheel you want to use, there are three types of listings of the 305 wheels in this book. The **Instant Wheel Finder™ on page 429** shows at a glance the number of combinations required to wheel each group of numbers for each specific win guarantee.

In columns on the extreme left and right sides of the Instant Wheel Finder are the quantity of numbers to be wheeled from 6 to 49. The win guarantees (5/5, 4/4, 4/5, 3/3, 3/4, 3/5) are at the top of the Wheel Index. The numbers within the chart (where the win guarantee meets the number of numbers to wheel) show how many combinations it takes to make that wheel.

The Instant Wheel Finder is divided into four sections. The first section on the left shows all the wheels in this book with NO POWER NUMBERS. The section to the right of it shows all the wheels with ONE POWER NUMBER. Further to the right, you see all the wheels with TWO POWER NUMBERS. The section on the extreme rights shows all the wheels with THREE POWER NUMBERS.

BUDGET WHEEL FINDER™ - BY GAMES

(How Much You Want to Spend on Tickets)

The **Budget Wheel Finder by GAMES on page 430**, makes it fast and easy to choose a wheel that matches the dollar amount you want to spend on tickets. The first column on the left tells you the ticket cost by number of GAMES to play. (Most pick-5 tickets cost a dollar a play.)

The second column (##-P) tells you the number of numbers in the wheel and how many Power Numbers (if any) are in the wheel. The third column (WIN) shows the win guarantee, and the fourth column (PAGE) tells you the page number in this book where the wheel is located.

For example, the first line tells you that the wheel has 2 games ($2 cost); and that 10 numbers are wheeled; no Power Number is used; it has a Win 3 with 5 Right win guarantee, and that you will find the wheel on page 177.

BUDGET WHEEL FINDER™ - BY NUMBERS

(How Many Numbers You Want to Wheel)

The **Budget Wheel Finder BY NUMBERS on page 432**, makes it fast and easy to choose a wheel that matches the number of numbers you want to wheel. The first column on the left (NRS.) tells you the number of numbers you want to wheel; the next column tells you the ticket cost or number of GAMES to play; the third column tells you the win guarantee; and the fourth column tells you the page on which to find the wheel you are looking for.

Let's say you have 15 numbers you want to wheel. When you come to 15 in the first column, you see you have a choice of 15 systems that wheel 15 numbers. Next decide how much money you want to invest in those 15 numbers by the number of games to be played, and whether or not you want to use Power Number(s). Then go right to the page for the wheel of your choice!

A FINAL WORD

When jackpots are won with my systems, it gives me enormous pleasure to hear from my winners—and makes my work more meaningful. In fact, the success of my jackpot winners is the force that drives me to create new and better ways to win.

Helping people win jackpots is my biggest thrill in this lottery business. If people weren't consistently winning with my systems — and TELLING ME about it — I would probably find something else to do with my life. (When I was a stock broker, I was also in the business of helping people make money!)

I never accept money or gifts from my winners. On the contrary, my first prize jackpot winners get all my latest products FREE. After all, it is THEY who inspire me with their success.

I appreciate it immensely when jackpot winners publicly acknowledge (to the lottery officials and to the press) that they used the Gail Howard system to win. Not only is it ethical, appropriate and fair to give credit where credit is due, but it establishes a life-long personal link, a bond, between us.

When you win your first prize jackpot with my systems and strategies, tell ME the happy news right after you tell your family! I love to hear from my winners no matter how small the jackpot. I won't publicize your name if you ask me not to. But I would like to have complete verifiable documentation about your win for my own personal files so I can claim another documented jackpot won with my systems. Your success is my success.

I hope you win a first prize jackpot soon. I'd love to share your joy and welcome another very special person to the exclusive Club of Gail Howard Lottery Jackpot Winners.

LOTTERY PRODUCTS TO HELP YOU WIN!

Smart people don't wait for Dumb Luck. Whether it's big jackpots you are after, or winning smaller prizes consistently, you can improve your "luck" by using knowledge and skill to zero in on winning Lotto numbers.

Wheeling is very important because it allows you to play with large groups of numbers. However, wheeling is only half the battle. Being armed with powerful number selection strategies, and knowing how to target numbers most likely to hit is equally important. Your best bet to beat the lottery is to use both weapons TOGETHER!

The following pages describe the lottery products currently available. I'll begin with books and charts which can be used by anyone without a computer. Keep in mind that this book was printed in 1998. In the future, prices are subject to change, and new products will be added. I am continually developing and testing new ideas and enhancing and improving my old original published methods. I have working ideas for several new books and software.

To get an updated list of my latest products, send a self-addressed, stamped envelop to the address near the bottom of the order form at the end of this chapter. If you are not on my current mailing list, or if you have moved since placing your last order, send us a change of address form so you won't miss out on exciting new products as they become available. Or visit my web site at: **www.gailhoward.com**.

Whether you have a computer or not, *Lottery Master Guide* is an absolute MUST read for EVERY serious Lotto player. It is the most complete book on lottery strategy ever written.

If you DO NOT use a computer, you can order a printed set of Lottery Advantage® Charts to scientifically select the best numbers for the Lotto game YOU play.

If you DO HAVE access to an IBM/compatible computer, for best results, you should order at least TWO Smart Luck®

programs: ADVANTAGE PLUS™ to scientifically select the numbers, and a Smart Luck® WHEEL program to wheel the numbers.

Advantage Plus™ programs contain no wheels. Wheel programs contain no game histories nor number selection methods.

LOTTERY BOOKS AND CHARTS

- **LOTTERY MASTER GUIDE** - the complete book on how to select numbers most likely to win in pick-5, pick-6, pick-10, Powerball, and The Big Game. A must read for everyone who plays Lotto. (See page 53)
- **LOTTO HOW TO WHEEL A FORTUNE** - wheeling systems for all pick-6 Lotto games. (See page 55)
- **LOTTO WHEEL FIVE TO WIN** - wheeling systems for all pick-5 Lotto games. (See page 56)
- **LOTTERY ADVANTAGE® CHARTS** - printed set of charts helps pick the best numbers for any pick-5 or pick-6 Lotto game of your choice. (See page 56)

LOTTERY SOFTWARE (IBM/Comp.)

ADVANTAGE PLUS™ has all of my original, unique, proven number selection methods for choosing Lotto numbers with the greatest probability of winning. Available in three different editions. (Read from page 59)

- **U.S.A. ADVANTAGE PLUS™** comes loaded with all past winning numbers for all 64 pick-5 and pick-6 Lotto games played in all 37 lottery states and D.C., including Powerball, The Big Game, PA Keystone and Puerto Rico. (See page 59)

- **INTERNATIONAL ADVANTAGE PLUS™** includes past winning numbers for lotto games outside the U.S.A—Canadian Lotto and Keno, and most European, Asian, and Australian Lotto games. (See page 60)

- **KENO ADVANTAGE PLUS™** includes past winning numbers for U.S.A. pick-10 Keno games—excluding Keno games drawn every five minutes. (See page 60)

SMART LUCK WHEELING PROGRAMS are available for pick-5 through pick-10 Lotto games in standard or deluxe versions. (Scc page 61)

- **COMPUTER WHEEL™** has 252 wheeling systems for pick-6 Lotto games. (See page 61)

- **COMPUTER WHEEL FIVE™** has 220 wheeling systems for pick-5 Lotto games. (See page 62)

- **FULL WHEEL GENERATOR™** has Full Wheels for all pick-5, pick-6, pick-7, pick-8, pick-9, and pick-10 Lotto or Keno games. Want to buy a guaranteed jackpot? This program will make ALL the combinations for you. (See page 63)

- **KENO WHEEL™** has 401 wheeling systems for pick-10 Keno. (See page 64)

DELUXE WHEELING PROGRAMS have many more features and provide many more wheels for pick-5, pick-6 and pick-7 Lotto games. (See page 65)

- **WHEEL SIX PLUS™** has 1,650 wheeling systems: 844 for pick-6 and 792 for pick-7 games. (See page 65)

- **WHEEL FIVE PLUS™** has 475 wheeling systems for pick-5 Lotto games. (See page 67)

LOTTERY MASTER GUIDE (3rd Edition)

Lottery Master Guide is the most comprehensive book on lottery strategy ever written. Once you apply the methods in this book, you will never look at Lotto numbers the same way again. By using the powerful and effective rules and tools in *Lottery*

Master Guide, you'll learn how to spot specific numbers for specific drawings, and make the best use of the dollars you spend on Lotto. You will learn how to recognize the winning patterns that produce winning numbers—and spot the Hot Numbers of tomorrow...TODAY!!!

Lottery Master Guide is a virtual library of indispensable lottery information—everything serious players need to know about pick-5, pick-6, pick-10, Powerball and The Big Game. It also lists state lottery addresses, telephone numbers, drawing result hot lines, odds, drawing days, etc. After you have read *Lottery Master Guide* from cover to cover, not only will you be on your way to winning more prizes, but you will be an authority on lotteries—and you will have the world's best strategies to beat them!

LOTTERY MASTER GUIDE REVEALS HOW YOU CAN:

- Turn a game of chance into a game of skill. (Page 2)
- Reduce the odds by millions. (Page 32)
- Buy fewer tickets yet have a greater chance to win. (Page 90)
- Discover the one thing ALL jackpot winners have in common. (Page 165)
- Tell if a number is about to start a long losing streak before it loses 15 or 20 games or more. (Page 53)
- Know when to play—or when not to play—a specific number for a specific drawing. (Page 68)
- See how often you can expect to trap the six, five, four or three winning numbers in your wheeled group. (Page 128)
- Tell which "cold" number is best to play. (No, it is not the number out the longest!) (Page 44)
- Detect at a glance which numbers are hot and which are not. (Page 53)
- Avoid playing Lotto numbers that are sure to lose. (Page 19)
- Cash in on the luck of others. (Page 152)
- Eliminate one quarter to one fifth of the Lotto numbers in your state's game and turn a 49-number game into a 39-number game. (Page 39)
- Know how many cold, lukewarm, and hot numbers to include on your tickets. (Page 41)
- Spot a Hot Number before it gets hot—so you can be on it when it starts its winning streak. (Page 53)

- Know which of last game's WINNING numbers has the best chance of winning in the next drawing. (Page 65)
- Know which of last game's LOSING numbers have the best chance of winning in the next drawing. (Page 68)
- Tell which numbers are hot and which are not. (Page 53)
- Tell which numbers have an affinity to win most often with your strongest numbers. (Page 71)
- Cash on the most predictable indicator—the balancing Bias Tracker™. (Page 34)
- Learn how to choose the best and eliminate the rest. (Page 45)

COST IS: $24.50 plus shipping.

LOTTO HOW TO WHEEL A FORTUNE (3rd edition)

This book could be worth millions! *Lotto How to Wheel a Fortune* has 397 pages of valuable information to help you win, including 162 wheeling systems with specific win guarantees. It contains my most successful Balanced Wheels™—including most of those used by my biggest Lotto jackpot winners.

You'll find a wide variety of Balanced Wheels™ to choose from in every price range, from $2 up to $100's, with dozens of wheels that cost $10 or less to play. They can be used for any pick-6 Lotto game in the world—from a pick-6 out of 25 numbers to a pick-6 out of 54 numbers. There is no faster, easier way to give your money leverage and dramatically improve your odds in Lotto than by using Balanced Wheels™.

Lotto How to Wheel a Fortune tells the maximum number of multiple prizes you could win with each system, as well as the minimum prize you are guaranteed to win. Winning several prizes all at once is fun, exciting—and lucrative! The book also gives TIMES IN THE WHEEL handicapping help, which tells the number of times each number position is in the wheel, so you can place your strongest numbers where they will appear most often.

It's easy to read—and easy to use as A-B-C. You'll use it every time you play Lotto. A MUST for all pick-6 games.

COST IS: $19.50 plus shipping.

LOTTO WHEEL FIVE TO WIN (2nd edition)

Lotto Wheel Five to Win has 305 wheeling systems for the low-odds, easy-to-win pick-5 games, now played in almost every Lotto state. Pick-5 games are known as Fantasy-5, Cash-5, Take-5, Lucky-5, Easy-5, Match-5, Little Lotto, etc. Pick-5 wheels should also be used for Power Ball and The Big Game. Forty-nine (49!) of the wheels cost $5 or less to use. Wheels up to 45 numbers. Has Instant Wheel Finder™, Budget Wheel Finder by Games™, and Budget Wheel Finder by Numbers.

At least thirty (37) first prize pick-5 jackpots (all fully documented) have been won with my pick-5 Balanced Wheels™. I say "at least" because so often I have heard only by accident from many of those winners. After placing an order, they say something to the effect of: "By the way, I really like Gail's systems. I won a pick-5 jackpot last month (or last year, or whatever the case may be). I was going to tell her when I won the Big One." So, there may be hundreds I don't know about. If YOU win a first prize jackpot with my systems—no matter how small it is—please let me know!!!

Lotto Wheel Five to Win is A MUST for ALL pick-5 games. COST IS: $19.95 plus shipping.

LOTTERY ADVANTAGE® CHARTS

Lottery Advantage® Charts are your key to making intelligent number selections. If you combine Balanced Wheeling Systems™ with my Lottery Advantage® number selection strategies, you have a winning combination!

Once you have read *Lottery Master Guide* from cover to cover, you will want to order a set of Lottery Advantage® Charts for the

Lotto game YOU play. You get 25 pages of charts to help zero in on the winning numbers, and an 8-page manual.

When ordering, you MUST tell us both the number field of the game, as well as the country or state, such as "Australia 6/45" or "New York 5/39." Charts for Lotto games with fewer than 100 drawings will not be as complete or useful as those of older games.

(If you have access to a computer, you can buy Advantage Plus™ software and print your own up-to-date Lottery Advantage® charts any time you want them.)

Lottery Advantage® Charts are custom printed just for you the day after the drawing and shipped by Priority Mail within the U.S.A.

A set of charts for ONE Lotto game of your choice costs $19.00 ($15.00 plus $4.00 for shipping & handling). Or get two sets of charts for TWO Lotto games of your choice for only $34.00 (shipping included). Or get three sets of charts for THREE Lotto games of your choice for only $49.00 (shipping included).

LOTTERY SOFTWARE

SOFTWARE REQUIREMENTS: Smart Luck® lottery software is available only for IBM/comp. computers. We ship 3.5" disks unless you specifically request 5.25 instead. Minimum memory requirement is 512 K, DOS 3.0 or higher. You can run it on a floppy or a hard disk drive. It can be installed in Windows 3.x, Windows 95 and Windows NT. Step-by-step install instructions show you how. Macintosh computers will not run my software unless you use a DOS Card, "Soft PC" or equivalent.

SHIPPING COST: For orders within the U.S.A. shipping is $3.00 per TOTAL software order. Shipping to Canada is $5.00 per total software order, and $10.00 to all other countries. ONLY U.S.A. $$ currency accepted. Canadian dollar checks will be returned. Books are shipped separately and have different postage rates.

TWO TYPES OF LOTTERY SOFTWARE: I have two types of lottery software, number selection software and wheeling software. For the best results, you should have BOTH. Advantage Plus™ is the number selection software—which helps you choose the best Lotto numbers. There are no wheeling systems in Advantage Plus™. And there are no number selection methods, nor data files of past winning numbers, in any of my wheeling programs.

SIX WHEELING PROGRAMS: I'll explain each of my six different wheeling programs in detail, so you will be able to decide which is best for you. I don't sell all my software as one unit because not everyone needs to own everything I sell.

GET DISCOUNTS when you buy two or more software packages at the same time—if they are shipped together. Read about the money saving package deals! Use the handy order forms on last pages of this book.

LOOK FOR THE WINNERS™. I get great satisfaction in knowing that I have the very best lottery software on the market—from the positive feedback I get from happy customers, from the high percentage of repeat customers who buy every new product and upgrade I put out, and from the joy I share with elated jackpot winners who win with my systems. To date, 59 Lotto jackpot winners have won $97.4 million dollars using my systems. And that's only the documented winners who have contacted me to say thank you.

Don't be fooled by imitations. Don't be misled by ads that claim to have "picked" or "wheeled" or "predicted" jackpots. "Picking" or "predicting" or "wheeling" OR "guessing" jackpots is entirely different from anyone actually winning money. It means that no jackpot was won, but that a large group of numbers predicted, wheeled or picked, contained within it the winning numbers. Anyone selling a system that has won a jackpot or two, would certainly boast about their first prize jackpot winners in their ads.

ADVANTAGE PLUS™

The easiest, fastest, most convenient way to use my proven jackpot winning number selection methods is by using Advantage Plus™ software.

Nowhere else will you find a more complete set of tools for picking winners. Advantage Plus™ is in a class by itself. Such great flexibility and wide variety of useful charts just doesn't exist in any other lottery software. It's fast and easy to use. Help menus are located throughout the entire program on every level. Florida's Lakeland Ledger said, "Gail Howard's Smart Luck software is so user friendly, it would hug you if it could."

ALL DATA FOR ALL STATES FREE. Advantage Plus™ comes loaded with ALL the drawing results for ALL pick-5 and pick-6 and pick-7 Lotto games played in all state lotteries (currently 38). It's the only lottery software that has all the past winning numbers from the very first drawing, complete through the latest drawing of the night before it's shipped. To keep it updated, you just enter the winning numbers. The drawing number, date and day come up automatically

LOTTERY BREAKTHROUGH. More than 50 charts and reports help you zero in on the winning Lotto numbers. And for players who want the numbers chosen for them, there is an automatic Smart Picks™ feature, which selects numbers scientifically from specific patterns in the charts. (No simplistic random number generators in this program!) Smart Picks™ are marked on the charts with asterisks. Winning numbers are marked with plus signs. You can view the past performance of Smart Picked™ numbers for any chart with just one key stroke, going back game by game, throughout the entire history of any Lotto game. This unique, exciting test that reveals the past accuracy of automatic number picks is a major lottery breakthrough!!

ULTIMATE LOTTERY TOOL. However, Advantage Plus™ is much more than a scientific number generator. Depending on how you want to use it, it's the fastest, easiest way to choose your numbers scientifically or the ultimate lottery software for the serious lottery player who wants to study Lotto numbers from every possible angle. I don't just throw statistics at you. A detailed 88-page manual explains how to use each chart and shows how to recognize the winning patterns that produce winning numbers.

Advantage Plus™ (Version 3.xx), written in Borland-pascal and assembler, is incredibly fast. Menu driven. Instant column sorts throughout. Context sensitive Help Menus at every level. Allows you to enter and track numbers as drawn, unsorted. Add new games in seconds. Includes or ignores bonus numbers—can turn bonus number on or off at the main menu. Separate set of charts for the Gold Ball and the powerball ball. Has charts for individual numbers. Summaries, Analyses and Projections for many charts. Can change game range throughout. Change sensitivity settings, group settings, etc. Powerful searches. Perpetual Calendar, Lottery Odds Calculator™.

COST: $82.95 ($79.95 plus $3.00 shipping & handling.)

INTERNATIONAL ADVANTAGE PLUS™

The international version of Advantage Plus™ has all the same charts and reports and Smart Picks™. The only difference is that the data is for the international Lotto games of AUSTRALIA (5), BELGIUM, CANADA (9 including Quebec 6/49, Banco, B.C. 6/49 and B.C. Keno, Lotario, Ontario 6/49, Pogo, Super 7, National 6/49 Lotto), ENGLAND, FRANCE, GERMANY, HONG KONG, IRELAND, MEXICO, NETHERLANDS, NEW ZEALAND, PORTUGAL, SINGAPORE, SWITZERLAND, TRINIDAD & TOBAGO. COST: $89.95 ($79.95 plus $10.00 shipping & handling to ALL countries other than U.S.A and Canada); $84.95 to Canada ($79.95 plus $5.00 shipping); $82.95 within the U.S.A. ($79.95 plus $3.00 shipping).

PICK-10 KENO ADVANTAGE™ PLUS

Has the same charts and reports as the other two versions of Advantage Plus™, but contains the data for all pick-10 keno games played in the U.S.A—excluding, of course, games played every five minutes. COST: $82.95 within the U.S.A. ($79.95 plus $3.00 shipping.)

SMART LUCK® WHEELING SOFTWARE

My wheel programs interface with Advantage Plus™ so you don't have to leave the program to wheel—which in itself is one good reason to buy my wheeling software. Every wheel is guaranteed flawless! No holes! You get DOUBLE your money back if you find one wheel that fails its stated win guarantee. It's the only software program on the market dares make this "no holes" iron clad guarantee!!! I can because I know that every one of my wheels is mathematically correct. They are all perfect!!

WHICH WHEEL PROGRAM SHOULD YOU BUY? You have a choice of two abbreviated Balanced Wheel programs for pick-6 games and two for pick-5 games. Most new customers start with the $99.95 package (plus shipping), which is Advantage Plus™ and Computer Wheel™.

Order Advantage Plus for $79.95 and get one wheel program for only $20, which is about half off—but ONLY if the two programs are ordered and shipped at the same time. Choose from Computer Wheel™, Wheel Five™, OR Full Wheel Generator™.

See this and other money saving discounts on the order forms on pages 69, 71, 441 and 443. The more programs you order at the same time, the greater the savings. And you save on shipping costs, too, by paying just one shipping charge. Generous discounts are also offered on the deluxe Wheel Six Plus™ and Wheel Five Plus™ programs, See the Deluxe Order Form on pages 71 and 443

COMPUTER WHEEL™ (Ver. 2)

- Has 252 wheeling systems and wheels up to 40 of the numbers in any pick-6 Lotto game in the world. Each wheeling system has a valid minimum win guarantee.
- Minimum and maximum number of MULTIPLE prizes that can be won with each wheel are shown on screen. Shows how many times each number position is in the wheel, so you can place your strongest numbers where they appear most often.

- Has unique copyrighted built-in Balanced Games™ feature, which reduces or eliminates wasted, unbalanced combinations found at the beginning and end of all other wheeling systems on the market. Optimizes the wheel to give the most Balanced Games™ (best range of sums) possible with the numbers you have entered.
- The sum of each combination is shown.
- Has a wide variety of Balanced Wheeling Systems™ in every price range from $2 up to $100's. Has Power Number systems for One Power Number™ that let you wheel more Lotto numbers for less money with the same win guarantees. Saves ups to 500 wheels for win checking. Can be used for any pick-6 Lotto game in the world—from pick-6 out of 25 numbers to pick-6 out of 54 numbers—or even 6 out of 100.
- Interfaces with Advantage Plus™ so you won't have to leave the program to wheel your numbers. Limitations: Lacks many of the features of the Wheel Six Plus™ program, and does not wheel all the numbers in the higher-numbered pick-6 games.

COST: $39.50 plus $3.00 shipping within the U.S.A.
(Shipping to Canada is $5. Shipping to other countries is $10.)

COMPUTER WHEEL FIVE™ (Ver. 2)

- 220 Balanced Wheeling™ Systems for pick-5 Lotto games, including Powerball and The Big Game. Wheels up to 39 of the numbers in any pick-5 Lotto game in the world—from pick-5 out of 26 numbers to pick-5 out of 50 numbers—or even 5 out of 100.
- Has all the same features of the Computer Wheel™ except that all the wheeling systems are for the pick-5 games. Limitations: Lacks many of the features of the Wheel Five Plus™ program, and does not wheel all the numbers in the higher-numbered pick-5 games.

COST: $37.50 plus $3.00 shipping within the U.S.A.
(Shipping to Canada is $5. Shipping to other countries is $10.)

FULL WHEEL GENERATOR™

- 2,590 Full Wheels with jackpot win guarantees* for ALL Lotto games: Pick-5, Pick-6, Pick-7, Pick-8, Pick-9 and Pick-10.
- Full Wheels guarantee the jackpot prize (plus loads of multiple prizes) *if you have the required number of winning numbers in your wheeled group.
- If you want to generate every possible combination of all the numbers in your Lotto game, this is the software that can do it for you!
- No limits to the size of wheels that can be generated for all the above games.
- Wheels your numbers in every possible combination, with as few or as many numbers as you wish.
- Has up to four Power Numbers™ which drastically reduce the cost, making larger Full Wheels more affordable.
- Shows on screen the exact number of MULTIPLE prizes you can win with each wheel.
- Shows minimum and maximum prizes even when you MISS one or more of the Power Numbers.
- Each Full Wheel has a valid win guarantee. Perfect!! Flawless! Guaranteed to be mathematically correct.
- Find one wheel that fails its stated win guarantee, and you get DOUBLE your money back!!
- The sum of each combination is shown.
- Saves up to 1,000 wheels for win checking.
- Allows you to test drive a wheel through any Advantage Plus™ history to get total number of wins for each prize category as well as game by game results.
- Printed manual comes with it.
- Interfaces with Advantage Plus™ so you won't have to leave the program to wheel your numbers.
- The negative: Costs more to use than my other wheeling programs.

COST: $34.50 plus $3.00 shipping within the U.S.A.
(Shipping to Canada is $5. Shipping to other countries is $10.)

PICK-10 KENO WHEEL™

- 401 Balanced Wheeling™ Systems for pick-10 Keno games.
- Wheels up to 43 of the numbers in any pick-10 game in the world.
- Wheels range from 2 plays to 400+.
- Has full set of wheels with one and two Power Numbers™, which can be eliminated to produce Balanced Wheels™ for pick-9 and pick-8 games.
- Each wheeling system has a valid minimum win guarantee. Every wheel is mathematically correct. Perfect!! Guaranteed flawless!
- Find one wheel that fails its stated win guarantee, and you get DOUBLE your money back!!!
- Lowest win guarantee is six numbers.
- Minimum and maximum number of MULTIPLE prizes that can be won with each wheel are shown on screen.
- Shows how many times each number position is in the wheel, so you can place your strongest numbers where they appear most often.
- Has unique copyrighted built-in Balanced Games™ feature, which reduces or eliminates wasted, unbalanced combinations found at the beginning and end of all other wheeling systems on the market.
- Optimizes the wheel to give the most Balanced Games™ (best range of sums) possible with the numbers you have entered.
- The sum of each combination is shown.
- Has a wide variety of Balanced Wheeling Systems™ in every price range from $2 up to $100's.
- Has full set of Balanced Power Number™ Systems that let you wheel more Lotto numbers for less money with the same win guarantees.
- Shows minimum and maximum prizes even when you MISS one or more of the Power Numbers.
- Saves ups to 660 wheels for win checking.
- Interfaces with Advantage Plus™ so you won't have to leave the program to wheel your numbers.

COST: $59.95 plus $3.00 shipping within the U.S.A.
(Shipping to Canada is $5. Shipping to other countries is $10.)

THE DELUXE (ROLLS ROYCE) WHEELS

The deluxe Wheel Six Plus™ and Wheel Five Plus™ Lotto wheeling programs contain many, many added features and more than two thousand abbreviated Balanced Wheeling Systems™. And with that you get almost a quarter of a million combinations! Nowhere else in the world can anyone get such a huge assortment of wheeling systems. All 2,125 wheels are guaranteed flawless, without holes. Find one wheel that fails its win guarantee and get DOUBLE YOUR MONEY BACK!

If all those wheels were published in book form, it would require TWENTY (20!) volumes the size of my 397-page book, *Lotto How to Wheel a Fortune*. (BOTH programs combined take only 368k.)

WHEEL SIX PLUS™

- Deluxe wheel program for pick-6 Lotto games has 1,650 Balanced Wheeling™ Systems, 844 wheels for pick-6 Lottos, 792 wheels for pick-7, and a sampling of 14 pick-5 wheels.
- Contains all the wheels (many shortened) and all the features of Computer Wheel™, but much more!
- Choose from three types of listings to quickly and easily select a wheel that 1) Matches your budget, or 2) The number of numbers you want to wheel, or 3) To see the complete index.
- At least a dozen wheels let you play ALL of the numbers in any pick-6 game in the world
- All win guarantees go up to 500+ combinations or up to 54 numbers, which ever comes first.
- Has 133 different wheels that cost $10 or less to play; 249 that cost $20 or less, 427 cost $50 or less.
- Shows how many times each number position is in the wheel, so you can place your strongest numbers where they appear most often.
- Shows how many times each PAIRED position, as well as TRIPLE positions appear in the wheel—so you can place your strongest numbers where they appear most often TOGETHER.
- Optimizes your numbers two ways. A bar chart of your sums instantly shows if your wheel is balanced.
- Zaps Smart Picks™ directly into the wheel from Advantage Plus™.

- Allows you to test drive a wheel through any Advantage Plus™ history to get the total number of wins for each prize category as well as game by game results.
- Each wheeling system has a valid minimum win guarantee. Every wheel is mathematically correct. Perfect!! Guaranteed flawless!
- Find one wheel that fails its stated win guarantee, and you get DOUBLE your money back!!!
- Minimum and maximum number of MULTIPLE prizes that can be won with each wheel are shown on screen.
- Has full set of Balanced Power Number™ Systems with up to THREE Power Numbers that let you wheel more numbers for less money with even higher win guarantees.
- Shows minimum and maximum prizes you could win, even when you MISS one, two or three of the Power Numbers.
- Has unique copyrighted built-in Balanced Games™ feature, which reduces or eliminates wasted, unbalanced combinations found at the beginning and end of all other wheeling systems on the market.
- Optimizes the wheel to give the most Balanced Games™ (best range of sums) possible with the numbers you have entered.
- The sum of each combination is shown.
- Has a wide variety of Balanced Wheeling Systems™ in every price range, up to over $500 for every win guarantee, or all the numbers in the game, whichever comes first. .
- Saves up to 660 wheels for win-checking.
- Can be used for any pick-6 Lotto game in the world_from pick-6 out of 25 numbers to pick-6 out of 54 numbers_or even 6 out of 100.
- Interfaces with Advantage Plus™ so you won't have to leave the program to wheel your numbers.
- Comes with detailed printed manual.

COST: $59.95 plus $3.00 shipping within the U.S.A.
(Shipping to Canada is $5. Shipping to other countries is $10.)

WHEEL FIVE PLUS™

- Deluxe wheel program for pick-5 Lotto games has 475 Balanced Wheeling™ Systems to use for all pick-5 games, including Powerball and The Big Game.

- Contains all the wheels (many shortened) and all the features of Wheel Five™, but much more!

- Choose from three types of listings to quickly and easily select a wheel that 1) Matches your budget, or 2) The number of numbers you want to wheel, or 3) To see the complete index.

- At least a dozen wheels let you play ALL of the numbers in any pick-5 game in the world.

- All win guarantees go up to 500+ combinations or up to 45 Lotto numbers, whichever comes first.

- Has 34 wheels that cost $5 or less to play; 90 wheels that cost $10 or less; 166 wheels cost $20 or less; 246 wheels cost $50 or less.

- Shows how many times each number position is in the wheel, so you can place your strongest numbers where they appear most often.

- Shows how many times each PAIRED positions, as well TRIPLE positions appear in the wheel—so you can place your strongest numbers where they appear most often TOGETHER.

- Optimizes your numbers two ways. A bar chart of your sums instantly shows if your wheel is balanced.

- Zaps Smart Picks™ directly into the wheel from Advantage Plus™.

- Allows you to test drive a wheel through any Advantage Plus history to get the total number of wins for each prize category as well as game by game results.

- Each wheeling system has a valid minimum win guarantee. Every wheel is mathematically correct. Perfect!! Guaranteed flawless!

- Find one wheel that fails its stated win guarantee, and you get DOUBLE your money back!!!

- Minimum and maximum number of MULTIPLE prizes that can be won with each wheel are shown on screen.

- Win check shows 2-number prizes WHEN desired.

- Has full set of Balanced Power Number™ Systems with up to THREE Power Numbers™ that let you wheel more numbers for less money with even higher win guarantees.
- Shows minimum and maximum prizes you could win, even when you MISS one, two or three of the Power Numbers.
- Has unique copyrighted built-in Balanced Games™ feature, which reduces or eliminates wasted, unbalanced combinations found at the beginning and end of all other wheeling systems on the market.
- Optimizes the wheel to give the most Balanced Games™ (best range of sums) possible with the numbers you have entered.
- The sum of each combination is shown.
- Has a wide variety of Balanced Wheeling Systems™ in every price range, up to over $500 for every win guarantee, or all the numbers in the game, whichever comes first.
- Saves up to 660 wheels for win-checking.
- Can be used for ANY pick-5 Lotto game in the world—from pick-5 out of 26 numbers to pick-5 out of 52 numbers—or even 5 out of 100.
- Interfaces with Advantage Plus™ so you won't have to leave the program to wheel your numbers.
- Comes with detailed printed manual.

COST: $57.95 plus $3.00 shipping within the U.S.A.
(Shipping to Canada is $5. Shipping to other countries is $10.)

DELUXE Lottery Software ORDER FORM

Fold here and tape or staple.

——————————
——————————
——————————

SMART LUCK Publishers
Dept. B-5, P.O. Box 81770
Las Vegas, Nevada 89180-1770

Gail Howard's Smart Luck® ORDER FORM

LOTTERY BOOKS

❑ LOTTO HOW TO WHEEL A FORTUNE .... $19.50+$4.50 S/H
❑ LOTTO WHEEL FIVE TO WIN .... $19.95+$4.50 S/H
❑ LOTTERY MASTER GUIDE .... $24.50+$4.50 S/H

Lottery Books S/H (Shipping/Handling) Costs
$$$ SAVE $$$ for Buying Two or More Shipped TOGETHER

	U.S.A	CANADA	OTHER
❑ Total S/H for ONE Book	$4.50	$5.00	$10.00
❑ Total S/H for TWO Books	$6.50	$8.00	$17.00
❑ Total S/H for THREE Books	$8.50	$11.00	$24.00

PRINTED CHARTS

❑ LOTTERY ADVANTAGE® Charts .... $15.00+$4.00 S/H
Printed for your Game Choice: State: _____ Nr.Field _____

$$$ SAVE $$$ GET DISCOUNTS for Buying Two or More

❑ TWO sets of LOTTERY ADVANTAGE® Charts $34.00
State: _____ Nr.Field _____ State: _____ Nr.Field _____

❑ THREE sets of LOTTERY ADVANTAGE® Charts $49.00
State: _____ Nr.Field _____ State: _____ Nr.Field _____
State: _____ Nr.Field _____

Books and Charts are mailed separately and require separate postage.

$ _____ TOTAL $ ENCLOSED (ONLY U.S.$ accepted.)

Make Checks or money orders payable to: **SMART LUCK PUBLISHERS**
VISA/ MASTERCARD Orders Call: **1-800-692-4245**

Or Call: 1-702-365-1818 or visit us at: **www.smartluck.com**

VISA

**SMART LUCK Publishers
Dept. B-5, P.O. Box 81770
Las Vegas, Nevada 89180-1770**

Name:		
Address:		
City:	State:	Zip:
Phone: ( )		
☐ VISA ☐ MC Card #:		Exp Date:
Signature:		

Fold here and tape or staple.

PLACE
STAMP
HERE

SMART LUCK Publishers
Dept. B-5, P.O. Box 81770
Las Vegas, Nevada 89180-1770

FULL WHEEL 55006
Wheeling 6 Numbers in 6 games for a 5 of 5 Win

NUMBERS CORRECT	MAXIMUM WINS				MINIMUM WINS			
	5x	4x	3x	2x	5x	4x	3x	2x
5 (w/o Jackpot)	0	0	0	0				
5	1	5	0	0	1	5	0	0
4	–	2	4	0	–	2	4	0
3	–	–	3	3	–	–	3	3
2	–	–	–	4	–	–	–	4

Your 6 Numbers to Wheel

A	B	C	D	E	F
5	5	5	5	5	5

The 6 Games to Play

1.	A	B	C	D	E
2.	A	D	C	D	F
3.	A	B	C	E	F

4.	A	B	D	E	F
5.	A	C	D	E	F
6.	B	C	D	E	F

Copyright © 1983-1998 Gail Howard

FULL WHEEL 55007
Wheeling 7 Numbers in 21 games for a 5 of 5 Win

NUMBERS CORRECT	MAXIMUM WINS				MINIMUM WINS			
	5x	4x	3x	2x	5x	4x	3x	2x
5 (w/o Jackpot)	0	0	0	0				
5	1	10	10	0	1	10	10	0
4	–	3	12	6	–	3	12	6
3	–	–	6	12	–	–	6	12
2	–	–	–	10	–	–	–	10

Your 7 Numbers to Wheel

A	B	C	D	E	F	G
15	15	15	15	15	15	15

The 21 Games to Play

1.	A	B	C	D	E
2.	A	B	C	D	F
3.	A	B	C	D	G
4.	A	B	C	E	F
5.	A	B	C	E	G
6.	A	B	C	F	G
7.	A	B	D	E	F
8.	A	B	D	E	G
9.	A	B	D	F	G
10.	A	B	E	F	G
11.	A	C	D	E	F

12.	A	C	D	E	G
13.	A	C	D	F	G
14.	A	C	E	F	G
15.	A	D	E	F	G
16.	B	C	D	E	F
17.	B	C	D	E	G
18.	B	C	D	F	G
19.	B	C	E	F	G
20.	B	D	E	F	G
21.	C	D	E	F	G

Copyright © 1983-1998 Gail Howard

FULL WHEEL 55008
Wheeling 8 Numbers in 56 games for a 5 of 5 Win

NUMBERS CORRECT	MAXIMUM WINS				MINIMUM WINS			
	5x	4x	3x	2x	5x	4x	3x	2x
5 (w/o Jackpot)	0	0	0	0				
5	1	15	30	10	1	15	30	10
4	–	4	24	24	–	4	24	24
3	–	–	10	30	–	–	10	30
2	–	–	–	20	–	–	–	20

Your 8 Numbers to Wheel

A	B	C	D	E	F	G	H
35	35	35	35	35	35	35	35

The 56 Games to Play

#						#					
1.	A	B	C	D	E	27.	A	C	E	F	G
2.	A	B	C	D	F	28.	A	C	E	F	H
3.	A	B	C	D	G	29.	A	C	E	G	H
4.	A	B	C	D	H	30.	A	C	F	G	H
5.	A	B	C	E	F	31.	A	D	E	F	G
6.	A	B	C	E	G	32.	A	D	E	F	H
7.	A	B	C	E	H	33.	A	D	E	G	H
8.	A	B	C	F	G	34.	A	D	F	G	H
9.	A	B	C	F	H	35.	A	E	F	G	H
10.	A	B	C	G	H	36.	B	C	D	E	F
11.	A	B	D	E	F	37.	B	C	D	E	G
12.	A	B	D	E	G	38.	B	C	D	E	H
13.	A	B	D	E	H	39.	B	C	D	F	G
14.	A	B	D	F	G	40.	B	C	D	F	H
15.	A	B	D	F	H	41.	B	C	D	G	H
16.	A	B	D	G	H	42.	B	C	E	F	G
17.	A	B	E	F	G	43.	B	C	E	F	H
18.	A	B	E	F	H	44.	B	C	E	G	H
19.	A	B	E	G	H	45.	B	C	F	G	H
20.	A	B	F	G	H	46.	B	D	E	F	G
21.	A	C	D	E	F	47.	B	D	E	F	H
22.	A	C	D	E	G	48.	B	D	E	G	H
23.	A	C	D	E	H	49.	B	D	F	G	H
24.	A	C	D	F	G	50.	B	E	F	G	H
25.	A	C	D	F	H	51.	C	D	E	F	G
26.	A	C	D	G	H	52.	C	D	E	F	H

     (Continued Next Page)

FULL WHEEL 55008 (Continued from previous page)

53.	C	D	E	G	H
54.	C	D	F	G	H

55.	C	E	F	G	H
56.	D	E	F	G	H

FULL WHEEL 55009
Wheeling 9 Numbers in 126 games for a 5 of 5 Win

NUMBERS CORRECT	MAXIMUM WINS				MINIMUM WINS			
	5x	4x	3x	2x	5x	4x	3x	2x
5 (w/o Jackpot)	0	0	0	0				
5	1	20	60	40	1	20	60	40
4	–	5	40	60	–	5	40	60
3	–	–	15	60	–	–	15	60
2	–	–	–	35	–	–	–	35

Your 9 Numbers to Wheel

A	B	C	D	E	F	G	H	I
70	70	70	70	70	70	70	70	70

The 126 Games to Play

1.	A	B	C	D	E
2.	A	B	C	D	F
3.	A	B	C	D	G
4.	A	B	C	D	H
5.	A	B	C	D	I
6.	A	B	C	E	F
7.	A	B	C	E	G
8.	A	B	C	E	H
9.	A	B	C	E	I
10.	A	B	C	F	G
11.	A	B	C	F	H
12.	A	B	C	F	I
13.	A	B	C	G	H
14.	A	B	C	G	I
15.	A	B	C	H	I
16.	A	B	D	E	F
17.	A	B	D	E	G
18.	A	B	D	E	H
19.	A	B	D	E	I
20.	A	B	D	F	G
21.	A	B	D	F	H
22.	A	B	D	F	I

23.	A	B	D	G	H
24.	A	B	D	G	I
25.	A	B	D	H	I
26.	A	B	E	F	G
27.	A	B	E	F	H
28.	A	B	E	F	I
29.	A	B	E	G	H
30.	A	B	E	G	I
31.	A	B	E	H	I
32.	A	B	F	G	H
33.	A	B	F	G	I
34.	A	B	F	H	I
35.	A	B	G	H	I
36.	A	C	D	E	F
37.	A	C	D	E	G
38.	A	C	D	E	H
39.	A	C	D	E	I
40.	A	C	D	F	G
41.	A	C	D	F	H
42.	A	C	D	F	I
43.	A	C	D	G	H
44.	A	C	D	G	I

 (Continued Next Page)

75

FULL WHEEL 55009 (Continued from previous page)

#	1	2	3	4	5	#	1	2	3	4	5
45.	A	C	D	H	I	80.	B	C	D	H	I
46.	A	C	E	F	G	81.	B	C	E	F	G
47.	A	C	E	F	H	82.	B	C	E	F	H
48.	A	C	E	F	I	83.	B	C	E	F	I
49.	A	C	E	G	H	84.	B	C	E	G	H
50.	A	C	E	G	I	85.	B	C	E	G	I
51.	A	C	E	H	I	86.	B	C	E	H	I
52.	A	C	F	G	H	87.	B	C	F	G	H
53.	A	C	F	G	I	88.	B	C	F	G	I
54.	A	C	F	H	I	89.	B	C	F	H	I
55.	A	C	G	H	I	90.	B	C	G	H	I
56.	A	D	E	F	G	91.	B	D	E	F	G
57.	A	D	E	F	H	92.	B	D	E	F	H
58.	A	D	E	F	I	93.	B	D	E	F	I
59.	A	D	E	G	H	94.	B	D	E	G	H
60.	A	D	E	G	I	95.	B	D	E	G	I
61.	A	D	E	H	I	96.	B	D	E	H	I
62.	A	D	F	G	H	97.	B	D	F	G	H
63.	A	D	F	G	I	98.	B	D	F	G	I
64.	A	D	F	H	I	99.	B	D	F	H	I
65.	A	D	G	H	I	100.	B	D	G	H	I
66.	A	E	F	G	H	101.	B	E	F	G	H
67.	A	E	F	G	I	102.	B	E	F	G	I
68.	A	E	F	H	I	103.	B	E	F	H	I
69.	A	E	G	H	I	104.	B	E	G	H	I
70.	A	F	G	H	I	105.	B	F	G	H	I
71.	B	C	D	E	F	106.	C	D	E	F	G
72.	B	C	D	E	G	107.	C	D	E	F	H
73.	B	C	D	E	H	108.	C	D	E	F	I
74.	B	C	D	E	I	109.	C	D	E	G	H
75.	B	C	D	F	G	110.	C	D	E	G	I
76.	B	C	D	F	H	111.	C	D	E	H	I
77.	B	C	D	F	I	112.	C	D	F	G	H
78.	B	C	D	G	H	113.	C	D	F	G	I
79.	B	C	D	G	I	114.	C	D	F	H	I

(Continued Next Page)

FULL WHEEL 55009 (Continued from previous page)

115.	C	D	G	H	I	121.	D	E	F	G	H
116.	C	E	F	G	H	122.	D	E	F	G	I
117.	C	E	F	G	I	123.	D	E	F	H	I
118.	C	E	F	H	I	124.	D	E	G	H	I
119.	C	E	G	H	I	125.	D	F	G	H	I
120.	C	F	G	H	I	126.	E	F	G	H	I

FULL WHEEL 55010

Wheeling 10 Numbers in 252 games for a 5 of 5 Win

NUMBERS CORRECT	MAXIMUM WINS				MINIMUM WINS			
	5x	4x	3x	2x	5x	4x	3x	2x
5 (w/o Jackpot)	0	0	0	0				
5	1	25	100	100	1	25	100	100
4	–	6	60	120	–	6	60	120
3	–	–	21	105	–	–	21	105
2	–	–	–	56	–	–	–	56

Your 10 Numbers to Wheel

A	B	C	D	E	F	G	H	I	J
126	126	126	126	126	126	126	126	126	126

The 252 Games to Play

1.	A	B	C	D	E	19.	A	B	C	H	I
2.	A	B	C	D	F	20.	A	B	C	H	J
3.	A	B	C	D	G	21.	A	B	C	I	J
4.	A	B	C	D	H	22.	A	B	D	E	F
5.	A	B	C	D	I	23.	A	B	D	E	G
6.	A	B	C	D	J	24.	A	B	D	E	H
7.	A	B	C	E	F	25.	A	B	D	E	I
8.	A	B	C	E	G	26.	A	B	D	E	J
9.	A	B	C	E	H	27.	A	B	D	F	G
10.	A	B	C	E	I	28.	A	B	D	F	H
11.	A	B	C	E	J	29.	A	B	D	F	I
12.	A	B	C	F	G	30.	A	B	D	F	J
13.	A	B	C	F	H	31.	A	B	D	G	H
14.	A	B	C	F	I	32.	A	B	D	G	I
15.	A	B	C	F	J	33.	A	B	D	G	J
16.	A	B	C	G	H	34.	A	B	D	H	I
17.	A	B	C	G	I	35.	A	B	D	H	J
18.	A	B	C	G	J	36.	A	B	D	I	J

(Continued Next Page)

FULL WHEEL 55010 (Continued from previous page)

#						#					
37.	A	B	E	F	G	72.	A	C	E	F	G
38.	A	B	E	F	H	73.	A	C	E	F	H
39.	A	B	E	F	I	74.	A	C	E	F	I
40.	A	B	E	F	J	75.	A	C	E	F	J
41.	A	B	E	G	H	76.	A	C	E	G	H
42.	A	B	E	G	I	77.	A	C	E	G	I
43.	A	B	E	G	J	78.	A	C	E	G	J
44.	A	B	E	H	I	79.	A	C	E	H	I
45.	A	B	E	H	J	80.	A	C	E	H	J
46.	A	B	E	I	J	81.	A	C	E	I	J
47.	A	B	F	G	H	82.	A	C	F	G	H
48.	A	B	F	G	I	83.	A	C	F	G	I
49.	A	B	F	G	J	84.	A	C	F	G	J
50.	A	B	F	H	I	85.	A	C	F	H	I
51.	A	B	F	H	J	86.	A	C	F	H	J
52.	A	B	F	I	J	87.	A	C	F	I	J
53.	A	B	G	H	I	88.	A	C	G	H	I
54.	A	B	G	H	J	89.	A	C	G	H	J
55.	A	B	G	I	J	90.	A	C	G	I	J
56.	A	B	H	I	J	91.	A	C	H	I	J
57.	A	C	D	E	F	92.	A	D	E	F	G
58.	A	C	D	E	G	93.	A	D	E	F	H
59.	A	C	D	E	H	94.	A	D	E	F	I
60.	A	C	D	E	I	95.	A	D	E	F	J
61.	A	C	D	E	J	96.	A	D	E	G	H
62.	A	C	D	F	G	97.	A	D	E	G	I
63.	A	C	D	F	H	98.	A	D	E	G	J
64.	A	C	D	F	I	99.	A	D	E	H	I
65.	A	C	D	F	J	100.	A	D	E	H	J
66.	A	C	D	G	H	101.	A	D	E	I	J
67.	A	C	D	G	I	102.	A	D	F	G	H
68.	A	C	D	G	J	103.	A	D	F	G	I
69.	A	C	D	H	I	104.	A	D	F	G	J
70.	A	C	D	H	J	105.	A	D	F	H	I
71.	A	C	D	I	J	106.	A	D	F	H	J

 (Continued Next Page)

FULL WHEEL 55010 (Continued from previous page)

#						#					
107.	A	D	F	I	J	142.	B	C	E	F	G
108.	A	D	G	H	I	143.	B	C	E	F	H
109.	A	D	G	H	J	144.	B	C	E	F	I
110.	A	D	G	I	J	145.	B	C	E	F	J
111.	A	D	H	I	J	146.	B	C	E	G	H
112.	A	E	F	G	H	147.	B	C	E	G	I
113.	A	E	F	G	I	148.	B	C	E	G	J
114.	A	E	F	G	J	149.	B	C	E	H	I
115.	A	E	F	H	I	150.	B	C	E	H	J
116.	A	E	F	H	J	151.	B	C	E	I	J
117.	A	E	F	I	J	152.	B	C	F	G	H
118.	A	E	G	H	I	153.	B	C	F	G	I
119.	A	E	G	H	J	154.	B	C	F	G	J
120.	A	E	G	I	J	155.	B	C	F	H	I
121.	A	E	H	I	J	156.	B	C	F	H	J
122.	A	F	G	H	I	157.	B	C	F	I	J
123.	A	F	G	H	J	158.	B	C	G	H	I
124.	A	F	G	I	J	159.	B	C	G	H	J
125.	A	F	H	I	J	160.	B	C	G	I	J
126.	A	G	H	I	J	161.	B	C	H	I	J
127.	B	C	D	E	F	162.	B	D	E	F	G
128.	B	C	D	E	G	163.	B	D	E	F	H
129.	B	C	D	E	H	164.	B	D	E	F	I
130.	B	C	D	E	I	165.	B	D	E	F	J
131.	B	C	D	E	J	166.	B	D	E	G	H
132.	B	C	D	F	G	167.	B	D	E	G	I
133.	B	C	D	F	H	168.	B	D	E	G	J
134.	B	C	D	F	I	169.	B	D	E	H	I
135.	B	C	D	F	J	170.	B	D	E	H	J
136.	B	C	D	G	H	171.	B	D	E	I	J
137.	B	C	D	G	I	172.	B	D	F	G	H
138.	B	C	D	G	J	173.	B	D	F	G	I
139.	B	C	D	H	I	174.	B	D	F	G	J
140.	B	C	D	H	J	175.	B	D	F	H	I
141.	B	C	D	I	J	176.	B	D	F	H	J

          (Continued Next Page)

FULL WHEEL 55010 (Continued from previous page)

#						#					
177.	B	D	F	I	J	212.	C	D	F	I	J
178.	B	D	G	H	I	213.	C	D	G	H	I
179.	B	D	G	H	J	214.	C	D	G	H	J
180.	B	D	G	I	J	215.	C	D	G	I	J
181.	B	D	H	I	J	216.	C	D	H	I	J
182.	B	E	F	G	H	217.	C	E	F	G	H
183.	B	E	F	G	I	218.	C	E	F	G	I
184.	B	E	F	G	J	219.	C	E	F	G	J
185.	B	E	F	H	I	220.	C	E	F	H	I
186.	B	E	F	H	J	221.	C	E	F	H	J
187.	B	E	F	I	J	222.	C	E	F	I	J
188.	B	E	G	H	I	223.	C	E	G	H	I
189.	B	E	G	H	J	224.	C	E	G	H	J
190.	B	E	G	I	J	225.	C	E	G	I	J
191.	B	E	H	I	J	226.	C	E	H	I	J
192.	B	F	G	H	I	227.	C	F	G	H	I
193.	B	F	G	H	J	228.	C	F	G	H	J
194.	B	F	G	I	J	229.	C	F	G	I	J
195.	B	F	H	I	J	230.	C	F	H	I	J
196.	B	G	H	I	J	231.	C	G	H	I	J
197.	C	D	E	F	G	232.	D	E	F	G	H
198.	C	D	E	F	H	233.	D	E	F	G	I
199.	C	D	E	F	I	234.	D	E	F	G	J
200.	C	D	E	F	J	235.	D	E	F	H	I
201.	C	D	E	G	H	236.	D	E	F	H	J
202.	C	D	E	G	I	237.	D	E	F	I	J
203.	C	D	E	G	J	238.	D	E	G	H	I
204.	C	D	E	H	I	239.	D	E	G	H	J
205.	C	D	E	H	J	240.	D	E	G	I	J
206.	C	D	E	I	J	241.	D	E	H	I	J
207.	C	D	F	G	H	242.	D	F	G	H	I
208.	C	D	F	G	I	243.	D	F	G	H	J
209.	C	D	F	G	J	244.	D	F	G	I	J
210.	C	D	F	H	I	245.	D	F	H	I	J
211.	C	D	F	H	J	246.	D	G	H	I	J

          (Continued Next Page)

FULL WHEEL 55010 (Continued from previous page)

247.	E	F	G	H	I
248.	E	F	G	H	J
249.	E	F	G	I	J

250.	E	F	H	I	J
251.	E	G	H	I	J
252.	F	G	H	I	J

FULL WHEEL 55011
Wheeling 11 Numbers in 462 games for a 5 of 5 Win

NUMBERS CORRECT	MAXIMUM WINS				MINIMUM WINS			
	5x	4x	3x	2x	5x	4x	3x	2x
5 (w/o Jackpot)	0	0	0	0				
5	1	30	150	200	1	30	150	200
4	–	7	84	210	–	7	84	210
3	–	–	28	168	–	–	28	168
2	–	–	–	84	–	–	–	84

Your 11 Numbers to Wheel

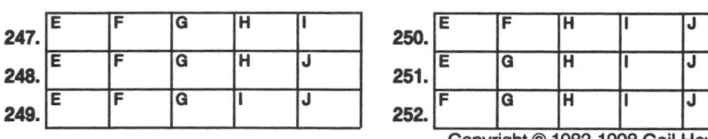

A	B	C	D	E	F	G	H	I	J	K
210	210	210	210	210	210	210	210	210	210	210

The 462 Games to Play

1.	A	B	C	D	E
2.	A	B	C	D	F
3.	A	B	C	D	G
4.	A	B	C	D	H
5.	A	B	C	D	I
6.	A	B	C	D	J
7.	A	B	C	D	K
8.	A	B	C	E	F
9.	A	B	C	E	G
10.	A	B	C	E	H
11.	A	B	C	E	I
12.	A	B	C	E	J
13.	A	B	C	E	K
14.	A	B	C	F	G
15.	A	B	C	F	H
16.	A	B	C	F	I
17.	A	B	C	F	J
18.	A	B	C	F	K
19.	A	B	C	G	H
20.	A	B	C	G	I
21.	A	B	C	G	J

22.	A	B	C	G	K
23.	A	B	C	H	I
24.	A	B	C	H	J
25.	A	B	C	H	K
26.	A	B	C	I	J
27.	A	B	C	I	K
28.	A	B	C	J	K
29.	A	B	D	E	F
30.	A	B	D	E	G
31.	A	B	D	E	H
32.	A	B	D	E	I
33.	A	B	D	E	J
34.	A	B	D	E	K
35.	A	B	D	F	G
36.	A	B	D	F	H
37.	A	B	D	F	I
38.	A	B	D	F	J
39.	A	B	D	F	K
40.	A	B	D	G	H
41.	A	B	D	G	I
42.	A	B	D	G	J

                     (Continued Next Page)

FULL WHEEL 55011 (Continued from previous page)

#	1	2	3	4	5	#	1	2	3	4	5
43.	A	B	D	G	K	78.	A	B	G	I	J
44.	A	B	D	H	I	79.	A	B	G	I	K
45.	A	B	D	H	J	80.	A	B	G	J	K
46.	A	B	D	H	K	81.	A	B	H	I	J
47.	A	B	D	I	J	82.	A	B	H	I	K
48.	A	B	D	I	K	83.	A	B	H	J	K
49.	A	B	D	J	K	84.	A	B	I	J	K
50.	A	B	E	F	G	85.	A	C	D	E	F
51.	A	B	E	F	H	86.	A	C	D	E	G
52.	A	B	E	F	I	87.	A	C	D	E	H
53.	A	B	E	F	J	88.	A	C	D	E	I
54.	A	B	E	F	K	89.	A	C	D	E	J
55.	A	B	E	G	H	90.	A	C	D	E	K
56.	A	B	E	G	I	91.	A	C	D	F	G
57.	A	B	E	G	J	92.	A	C	D	F	H
58.	A	B	E	G	K	93.	A	C	D	F	I
59.	A	B	E	H	I	94.	A	C	D	F	J
60.	A	B	E	H	J	95.	A	C	D	F	K
61.	A	B	E	H	K	96.	A	C	D	G	H
62.	A	B	E	I	J	97.	A	C	D	G	I
63.	A	B	E	I	K	98.	A	C	D	G	J
64.	A	B	E	J	K	99.	A	C	D	G	K
65.	A	B	F	G	H	100.	A	C	D	H	I
66.	A	B	F	G	I	101.	A	C	D	H	J
67.	A	B	F	G	J	102.	A	C	D	H	K
68.	A	B	F	G	K	103.	A	C	D	I	J
69.	A	B	F	H	I	104.	A	C	D	I	K
70.	A	B	F	H	J	105.	A	C	D	J	K
71.	A	B	F	H	K	106.	A	C	E	F	G
72.	A	B	F	I	J	107.	A	C	E	F	H
73.	A	B	F	I	K	108.	A	C	E	F	I
74.	A	B	F	J	K	109.	A	C	E	F	J
75.	A	B	G	H	I	110.	A	C	E	F	K
76.	A	B	G	H	J	111.	A	C	E	G	H
77.	A	B	G	H	K	112.	A	C	E	G	I

     (Continued Next Page)

82

FULL WHEEL 55011 (Continued from previous page)

#						#					
113.	A	C	E	G	J	148.	A	D	E	G	J
114.	A	C	E	G	K	149.	A	D	E	G	K
115.	A	C	E	H	I	150.	A	D	E	H	I
116.	A	C	E	H	J	151.	A	D	E	H	J
117.	A	C	E	H	K	152.	A	D	E	H	K
118.	A	C	E	I	J	153.	A	D	E	I	J
119.	A	C	E	I	K	154.	A	D	E	I	K
120.	A	C	E	J	K	155.	A	D	E	J	K
121.	A	C	F	G	H	156.	A	D	F	G	H
122.	A	C	F	G	I	157.	A	D	F	G	I
123.	A	C	F	G	J	158.	A	D	F	G	J
124.	A	C	F	G	K	159.	A	D	F	G	K
125.	A	C	F	H	I	160.	A	D	F	H	I
126.	A	C	F	H	J	161.	A	D	F	H	J
127.	A	C	F	H	K	162.	A	D	F	H	K
128.	A	C	F	I	J	163.	A	D	F	I	J
129.	A	C	F	I	K	164.	A	D	F	I	K
130.	A	C	F	J	K	165.	A	D	F	J	K
131.	A	C	G	H	I	166.	A	D	G	H	I
132.	A	C	G	H	J	167.	A	D	G	H	J
133.	A	C	G	H	K	168.	A	D	G	H	K
134.	A	C	G	I	J	169.	A	D	G	I	J
135.	A	C	G	I	K	170.	A	D	G	I	K
136.	A	C	G	J	K	171.	A	D	G	J	K
137.	A	C	H	I	J	172.	A	D	H	I	J
138.	A	C	H	I	K	173.	A	D	H	I	K
139.	A	C	H	J	K	174.	A	D	H	J	K
140.	A	C	I	J	K	175.	A	D	I	J	K
141.	A	D	E	F	G	176.	A	E	F	G	H
142.	A	D	E	F	H	177.	A	E	F	G	I
143.	A	D	E	F	I	178.	A	E	F	G	J
144.	A	D	E	F	J	179.	A	E	F	G	K
145.	A	D	E	F	K	180.	A	E	F	H	I
146.	A	D	E	G	H	181.	A	E	F	H	J
147.	A	D	E	G	I	182.	A	E	F	H	K

　　　　(Continued Next Page)

83

FULL WHEEL 55011 (Continued from previous page)

#						#					
183.	A	E	F	I	J	218.	B	C	D	F	H
184.	A	E	F	I	K	219.	B	C	D	F	I
185.	A	E	F	J	K	220.	B	C	D	F	J
186.	A	E	G	H	I	221.	B	C	D	F	K
187.	A	E	G	H	J	222.	B	C	D	G	H
188.	A	E	G	H	K	223.	B	C	D	G	I
189.	A	E	G	I	J	224.	B	C	D	G	J
190.	A	E	G	I	K	225.	B	C	D	G	K
191.	A	E	G	J	K	226.	B	C	D	H	I
192.	A	E	H	I	J	227.	B	C	D	H	J
193.	A	E	H	I	K	228.	B	C	D	H	K
194.	A	E	H	J	K	229.	B	C	D	I	J
195.	A	E	I	J	K	230.	B	C	D	I	K
196.	A	F	G	H	I	231.	B	C	D	J	K
197.	A	F	G	H	J	232.	B	C	E	F	G
198.	A	F	G	H	K	233.	B	C	E	F	H
199.	A	F	G	I	J	234.	B	C	E	F	I
200.	A	F	G	I	K	235.	B	C	E	F	J
201.	A	F	G	J	K	236.	B	C	E	F	K
202.	A	F	H	I	J	237.	B	C	E	G	H
203.	A	F	H	I	K	238.	B	C	E	G	I
204.	A	F	H	J	K	239.	B	C	E	G	J
205.	A	F	I	J	K	240.	B	C	E	G	K
206.	A	G	H	I	J	241.	B	C	E	H	I
207.	A	G	H	I	K	242.	B	C	E	H	J
208.	A	G	H	J	K	243.	B	C	E	H	K
209.	A	G	I	J	K	244.	B	C	E	I	J
210.	A	H	I	J	K	245.	B	C	E	I	K
211.	B	C	D	E	F	246.	B	C	E	J	K
212.	B	C	D	E	G	247.	B	C	F	G	H
213.	B	C	D	E	H	248.	B	C	F	G	I
214.	B	C	D	E	I	249.	B	C	F	G	J
215.	B	C	D	E	J	250.	B	C	F	G	K
216.	B	C	D	E	K	251.	B	C	F	H	I
217.	B	C	D	F	G	252.	B	C	F	H	J

     (Continued Next Page)

FULL WHEEL 55011 (Continued from previous page)

#						#					
253.	B	C	F	H	K	288.	B	D	F	H	K
254.	B	C	F	I	J	289.	B	D	F	I	J
255.	B	C	F	I	K	290.	B	D	F	I	K
256.	B	C	F	J	K	291.	B	D	F	J	K
257.	B	C	G	H	I	292.	B	D	G	H	I
258.	B	C	G	H	J	293.	B	D	G	H	J
259.	B	C	G	H	K	294.	B	D	G	H	K
260.	B	C	G	I	J	295.	B	D	G	I	J
261.	B	C	G	I	K	296.	B	D	G	I	K
262.	B	C	G	J	K	297.	B	D	G	J	K
263.	B	C	H	I	J	298.	B	D	H	I	J
264.	B	C	H	I	K	299.	B	D	H	I	K
265.	B	C	H	J	K	300.	B	D	H	J	K
266.	B	C	I	J	K	301.	B	D	I	J	K
267.	B	D	E	F	G	302.	B	E	F	G	H
268.	B	D	E	F	H	303.	B	E	F	G	I
269.	B	D	E	F	I	304.	B	E	F	G	J
270.	B	D	E	F	J	305.	B	E	F	G	K
271.	B	D	E	F	K	306.	B	E	F	H	I
272.	B	D	E	G	H	307.	B	E	F	H	J
273.	B	D	E	G	I	308.	B	E	F	H	K
274.	B	D	E	G	J	309.	B	E	F	I	J
275.	B	D	E	G	K	310.	B	E	F	I	K
276.	B	D	E	H	I	311.	B	E	F	J	K
277.	B	D	E	H	J	312.	B	E	G	H	I
278.	B	D	E	H	K	313.	B	E	G	H	J
279.	B	D	E	I	J	314.	B	E	G	H	K
280.	B	D	E	I	K	315.	B	E	G	I	J
281.	B	D	E	J	K	316.	B	E	G	I	K
282.	B	D	F	G	H	317.	B	E	G	J	K
283.	B	D	F	G	I	318.	B	E	H	I	J
284.	B	D	F	G	J	319.	B	E	H	I	K
285.	B	D	F	G	K	320.	B	E	H	J	K
286.	B	D	F	H	I	321.	B	E	I	J	K
287.	B	D	F	H	J	322.	B	F	G	H	I

                    (Continued Next Page)

FULL WHEEL 55011 (Continued from previous page)

#						#					
323.	B	F	G	H	J	358.	C	D	F	H	K
324.	B	F	G	H	K	359.	C	D	F	I	J
325.	B	F	G	I	J	360.	C	D	F	I	K
326.	B	F	G	I	K	361.	C	D	F	J	K
327.	B	F	G	J	K	362.	C	D	G	H	I
328.	B	F	H	I	J	363.	C	D	G	H	J
329.	B	F	H	I	K	364.	C	D	G	H	K
330.	B	F	H	J	K	365.	C	D	G	I	J
331.	B	F	I	J	K	366.	C	D	G	I	K
332.	B	G	H	I	J	367.	C	D	G	J	K
333.	B	G	H	I	K	368.	C	D	H	I	J
334.	B	G	H	J	K	369.	C	D	H	I	K
335.	B	G	I	J	K	370.	C	D	H	J	K
336.	B	H	I	J	K	371.	C	D	I	J	K
337.	C	D	E	F	G	372.	C	E	F	G	H
338.	C	D	E	F	H	373.	C	E	F	G	I
339.	C	D	E	F	I	374.	C	E	F	G	J
340.	C	D	E	F	J	375.	C	E	F	G	K
341.	C	D	E	F	K	376.	C	E	F	H	I
342.	C	D	E	G	H	377.	C	E	F	H	J
343.	C	D	E	G	I	378.	C	E	F	H	K
344.	C	D	E	G	J	379.	C	E	F	I	J
345.	C	D	E	G	K	380.	C	E	F	I	K
346.	C	D	E	H	I	381.	C	E	F	J	K
347.	C	D	E	H	J	382.	C	E	G	H	I
348.	C	D	E	H	K	383.	C	E	G	H	J
349.	C	D	E	I	J	384.	C	E	G	H	K
350.	C	D	E	I	K	385.	C	E	G	I	J
351.	C	D	E	J	K	386.	C	E	G	I	K
352.	C	D	F	G	H	387.	C	E	G	J	K
353.	C	D	F	G	I	388.	C	E	H	I	J
354.	C	D	F	G	J	389.	C	E	H	I	K
355.	C	D	F	G	K	390.	C	E	H	J	K
356.	C	D	F	H	I	391.	C	E	I	J	K
357.	C	D	F	H	J	392.	C	F	G	H	I

(Continued Next Page)

FULL WHEEL 55011 (Continued from previous page)

#						#					
393.	C	F	G	H	J	428.	D	F	G	H	J
394.	C	F	G	H	K	429.	D	F	G	H	K
395.	C	F	G	I	J	430.	D	F	G	I	J
396.	C	F	G	I	K	431.	D	F	G	I	K
397.	C	F	G	J	K	432.	D	F	G	J	K
398.	C	F	H	I	J	433.	D	F	H	I	J
399.	C	F	H	I	K	434.	D	F	H	I	K
400.	C	F	H	J	K	435.	D	F	H	J	K
401.	C	F	I	J	K	436.	D	F	I	J	K
402.	C	G	H	I	J	437.	D	G	H	I	J
403.	C	G	H	I	K	438.	D	G	H	I	K
404.	C	G	H	J	K	439.	D	G	H	J	K
405.	C	G	I	J	K	440.	D	G	I	J	K
406.	C	H	I	J	K	441.	D	H	I	J	K
407.	D	E	F	G	H	442.	E	F	G	H	I
408.	D	E	F	G	I	443.	E	F	G	H	J
409.	D	E	F	G	J	444.	E	F	G	H	K
410.	D	E	F	G	K	445.	E	F	G	I	J
411.	D	E	F	H	I	446.	E	F	G	I	K
412.	D	E	F	H	J	447.	E	F	G	J	K
413.	D	E	F	H	K	448.	E	F	H	I	J
414.	D	E	F	I	J	449.	E	F	H	I	K
415.	D	E	F	I	K	450.	E	F	H	J	K
416.	D	E	F	J	K	451.	E	F	I	J	K
417.	D	E	G	H	I	452.	E	G	H	I	J
418.	D	E	G	H	J	453.	E	G	H	I	K
419.	D	E	G	H	K	454.	E	G	H	J	K
420.	D	E	G	I	J	455.	E	G	I	J	K
421.	D	E	G	I	K	456.	E	H	I	J	K
422.	D	E	G	J	K	457.	F	G	H	I	J
423.	D	E	H	I	J	458.	F	G	H	I	K
424.	D	E	H	I	K	459.	F	G	H	J	K
425.	D	E	H	J	K	460.	F	G	I	J	K
426.	D	E	I	J	K	461.	F	H	I	J	K
427.	D	F	G	H	I	462.	G	H	I	J	K

87

BALANCED WHEEL™ 54006
Wheeling 6 Numbers in 5 games for a 4 of 4 Win

NUMBERS CORRECT	MAXIMUM WINS				MINIMUM WINS			
	5x	4x	3x	2x	5x	4x	3x	2x
5 (w/o Jackpot)	0	5	0	0				
5	1	4	0	0	0	5	0	0
4	–	2	3	0	–	1	4	0
3	–	–	3	2	–	–	2	3
2	–	–	–	4	–	–	–	3

Your 6 Numbers to Wheel

A	B	C	D	E	F
4	4	4	4	4	5

The 5 Games to Play

1.
A	B	C	D	F

2.
A	B	C	E	F

3.
A	B	D	E	F

4.
A	C	D	E	F

5.
B	C	D	E	F

Copyright © 1983-1998 Gail Howard

BALANCED WHEEL™ 54007
Wheeling 7 Numbers in 9 games for a 4 of 4 Win

NUMBERS CORRECT	MAXIMUM WINS				MINIMUM WINS			
	5x	4x	3x	2x	5x	4x	3x	2x
5 (w/o Jackpot)	0	5	4	0				
5	1	4	4	0	0	5	4	0
4	–	3	3	3	–	1	5	3
3	–	–	6	0	–	–	2	6
2	–	–	–	6	–	–	–	4

Your 7 Numbers to Wheel

A	B	C	D	E	F	G
7	6	6	7	6	6	7

The 9 Games to Play

1.
A	B	C	D	G

2.
A	B	C	E	F

3.
A	B	D	E	G

4.
A	B	D	F	G

5.
A	C	D	E	G

6.
A	C	D	F	G

7.
A	D	E	F	G

8.
B	C	D	E	F

9.
B	C	E	F	G

Copyright © 1983-1998 Gail Howard

BALANCED WHEEL™ 54008
Wheeling 8 Numbers in 20 games for a 4 of 4 Win

NUMBERS CORRECT	MAXIMUM WINS				MINIMUM WINS			
	5x	4x	3x	2x	5x	4x	3x	2x
5 (w/o Jackpot)	0	9	6	5				
5	1	6	8	5	0	5	12	3
4	–	4	4	11	–	1	8	10
3	–	–	7	5	–	–	3	10
2	–	–	–	10	–	–	–	6

Your 8 Numbers to Wheel

A	B	C	D	E	F	G	H
12	13	13	12	13	12	12	13

The 20 Games to Play

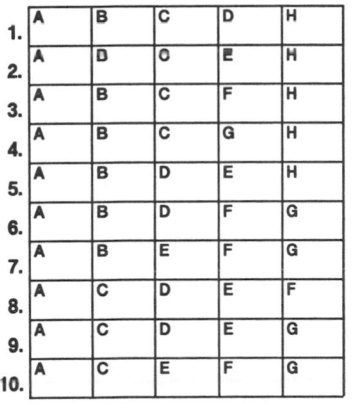

1. A B C D H
2. A D C E H
3. A B C F H
4. A B C G H
5. A B D E H
6. A B D F G
7. A B E F G
8. A C D E F
9. A C D E G
10. A C E F G
11. A D F G H
12. A E F G H
13. B C D E G
14. B C D F H
15. B C E F H
16. B C F G H
17. B D E F H
18. B D E G H
19. C D E F G
20. C D E G H

BALANCED WHEEL™ 54009
Wheeling 9 Numbers in 30 games for a 4 of 4 Win

NUMBERS CORRECT	MAXIMUM WINS				MINIMUM WINS			
	5x	4x	3x	2x	5x	4x	3x	2x
5 (w/o Jackpot)	0	7	14	8				
5	1	6	14	8	0	5	11	13
4	–	5	0	24	–	1	8	14
3	–	–	7	12	–	–	3	12
2	–	–	–	11	–	–	–	7

Your 9 Numbers to Wheel

A	B	C	D	E	F	G	H	I
17	18	17	17	14	14	18	18	17

The 30 Games to Play

1. A B C D I
2. A B C E H
3. A B C F H
4. A B C G H
5. A B D E G
6. A B D F G
7. A B D G H
8. A B E F I
9. A B G H I
10. A C D E I

          (Continued Next Page)

BALANCED WHEEL™ 54009 (Continued from previous page)

11.	A	C	D	F	I		21.	B	C	F	G	I
12.	A	C	D	G	I		22.	B	C	G	H	I
13.	A	C	D	H	I		23.	B	D	E	H	I
14.	A	C	E	F	G		24.	B	D	F	H	I
15.	A	D	E	F	H		25.	B	D	G	H	I
16.	A	E	G	H	I		26.	B	E	F	G	H
17.	A	F	G	H	I		27.	C	D	E	G	H
18.	B	C	D	E	F		28.	C	D	F	G	H
19.	B	C	D	G	H		29.	C	E	F	H	I
20.	B	C	E	G	I		30.	D	E	F	G	I

Copyright © 1983-1998 Gail Howard

BALANCED WHEEL™ 54010
Wheeling 10 Numbers in 51 games for a 4 of 4 Win

NUMBERS CORRECT	MAXIMUM WINS				MINIMUM WINS			
	5x	4x	3x	2x	5x	4x	3x	2x
5 (w/o Jackpot)	0	8	14	26				
5	1	5	20	21	0	5	20	20
4	–	6	0	40	–	1	12	24
3	–	–	6	20	–	–	4	21
2	–	–	–	14	–	–	–	11

Your 10 Numbers to Wheel

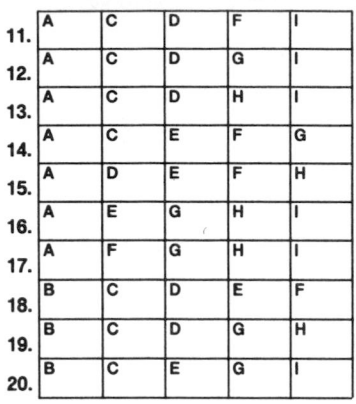

A	B	C	D	E	F	G	H	I	J
27	26	26	25	25	25	25	25	25	26

The 51 Games to Play

1.	A	B	C	D	J		15.	A	C	D	F	I
2.	A	B	C	E	J		16.	A	C	E	F	H
3.	A	B	C	F	J		17.	A	C	E	G	I
4.	A	B	C	G	J		18.	A	C	G	H	I
5.	A	B	C	H	J		19.	A	D	E	F	J
6.	A	B	C	I	J		20.	A	D	E	G	J
7.	A	B	D	E	I		21.	A	D	G	I	J
8.	A	B	D	F	H		22.	A	D	H	I	J
9.	A	B	D	G	H		23.	A	E	F	G	H
10.	A	B	E	F	G		24.	A	E	F	I	J
11.	A	B	E	H	I		25.	A	E	G	H	J
12.	A	B	F	G	I		26.	A	F	G	H	J
13.	A	C	D	E	H		27.	A	F	H	I	J
14.	A	C	D	F	G		28.	B	C	D	E	F

Copyright © 1983-1998 Gail Howard   (Continued Next Page)

BALANCED WHEEL™ 54010 (Continued from previous page)

29.	B	C	D	E	G		41.	B	G	H	I	J
30.	B	C	D	G	I		42.	C	D	E	I	J
31.	B	C	D	H	I		43.	C	D	F	H	J
32.	B	C	E	F	I		44.	C	D	G	H	J
33.	B	C	E	G	H		45.	C	E	F	G	J
34.	B	C	F	G	H		46.	C	E	H	I	J
35.	B	C	F	H	I		47.	C	F	G	I	J
36.	B	D	E	H	J		48.	D	E	F	G	I
37.	B	D	F	G	J		49.	D	E	F	H	I
38.	B	D	F	I	J		50.	D	E	G	H	I
39.	B	E	F	H	J		51.	D	F	G	H	I
40.	B	E	G	I	J							

BALANCED WHEEL™ 54011
Wheeling 11 Numbers in 66 games for a 4 of 4 Win

NUMBERS CORRECT	MAXIMUM WINS				MINIMUM WINS			
	5x	4x	3x	2x	5x	4x	3x	2x
5 (w/o Jackpot)	0	5	20	30				
5	1	0	30	20	0	5	20	30
4	–	1	12	30	–	1	12	30
3	–	–	4	24	–	–	4	24
2	–	–	–	12	–	–	–	12

Your 11 Numbers to Wheel

A	B	C	D	E	F	G	H	I	J	K
30	30	30	30	30	30	30	00	00	00	00

The 66 Games to Play

1.	A	B	C	D	K		13.	A	C	D	E	H
2.	A	B	C	E	I		14.	A	C	D	F	J
3.	A	B	C	F	G		15.	A	C	D	G	I
4.	A	B	C	H	J		16.	A	C	E	F	K
5.	A	B	D	E	G		17.	A	C	E	G	J
6.	A	B	D	F	H		18.	A	C	F	H	I
7.	A	B	D	I	J		19.	A	C	G	H	K
8.	A	B	E	F	J		20.	A	C	I	J	K
9.	A	B	E	H	K		21.	A	D	E	F	I
10.	A	B	F	I	K		22.	A	D	E	J	K
11.	A	B	G	H	I		23.	A	D	F	G	K
12.	A	B	G	J	K		24.	A	D	G	H	J

                    (Continued Next Page)

BALANCED WHEEL™ 54011 (Continued from previous page)

25.	A	D	H	I	K	46.	B	E	G	I	J
26.	A	E	F	G	H	47.	B	F	G	H	J
27.	A	E	G	I	K	48.	B	H	I	J	K
28.	A	E	H	I	J	49.	C	D	E	G	K
29.	A	F	G	I	J	50.	C	D	E	I	J
30.	A	F	H	J	K	51.	C	D	F	G	H
31.	B	C	D	E	F	52.	C	D	F	I	K
32.	B	C	D	G	J	53.	C	D	H	J	K
33.	B	C	D	H	I	54.	C	E	F	G	I
34.	B	C	E	G	H	55.	C	E	F	H	J
35.	B	C	E	J	K	56.	C	E	H	I	K
36.	B	C	F	H	K	57.	C	F	G	J	K
37.	B	C	F	I	J	58.	C	G	H	I	J
38.	B	C	G	I	K	59.	D	E	F	G	J
39.	B	D	E	H	J	60.	D	E	F	H	K
40.	B	D	E	I	K	61.	D	E	G	H	I
41.	B	D	F	G	I	62.	D	F	H	I	J
42.	B	D	F	J	K	63.	D	G	I	J	K
43.	B	D	G	H	K	64.	E	F	I	J	K
44.	B	E	F	G	K	65.	E	G	H	J	K
45.	B	E	F	H	I	66.	F	G	H	I	K

BALANCED WHEEL™ 54012
Wheeling 12 Numbers in 113 games for a 4 of 4 Win

NUMBERS CORRECT	MAXIMUM WINS				MINIMUM WINS			
	5x	4x	3x	2x	5x	4x	3x	2x
5 (w/o Jackpot)	0	8	24	54				
5	1	4	30	50	0	5	30	50
4	–	2	15	48	–	1	16	48
3	–	–	6	35	–	–	5	36
2	–	–	–	18	–	–	–	17

Your 12 Numbers to Wheel

A	B	C	D	E	F	G	H	I	J	K	L
47	47	47	47	47	47	47	48	47	47	47	47

The 113 Games to Play

1.	A	B	C	D	K	4.	A	B	C	F	L
2.	A	B	C	E	J	5.	A	B	C	G	H
3.	A	B	C	F	I	6.	A	B	D	E	L

     (Continued Next Page)

BALANCED WHEEL™ 54012 (Continued from previous page)

#						#					
7.	A	B	D	F	H	42.	A	E	I	J	L
8.	A	B	D	G	J	43.	A	F	G	H	J
9.	A	B	D	I	L	44.	A	F	G	I	L
10.	A	B	E	F	G	45.	A	F	H	K	L
11.	A	B	E	H	K	46.	A	F	I	J	K
12.	A	B	E	I	K	47.	A	G	H	I	K
13.	A	B	F	J	K	48.	B	C	D	E	F
14.	A	B	G	I	J	49.	B	C	D	F	I
15.	A	B	G	K	L	50.	B	C	D	G	L
16.	A	B	H	I	L	51.	B	C	D	H	J
17.	A	B	H	J	L	52.	B	C	E	G	K
18.	A	C	D	E	G	53.	B	C	E	H	L
19.	A	C	D	E	I	54.	B	C	E	I	J
20.	A	C	D	F	J	55.	B	C	F	G	J
21.	A	C	D	H	L	56.	B	C	F	H	K
22.	A	C	E	F	H	57.	B	C	G	I	L
23.	A	C	E	G	I	58.	B	C	H	I	K
24.	A	C	E	K	L	59.	B	C	J	K	L
25.	A	C	F	G	K	60.	B	D	E	G	H
26.	A	C	G	J	L	61.	B	D	E	H	I
27.	A	C	H	I	J	62.	B	D	E	J	K
28.	A	C	H	J	K	63.	B	D	F	G	K
29.	A	C	I	K	L	64.	B	D	F	J	L
30.	A	D	E	F	K	65.	B	D	G	I	K
31.	A	D	E	H	J	66.	B	D	H	I	J
32.	A	D	F	G	I	67.	B	D	H	K	L
33.	A	D	F	G	L	68.	B	E	F	H	J
34.	A	D	G	H	K	69.	B	E	F	I	L
35.	A	D	H	I	K	70.	B	E	F	K	L
36.	A	D	I	J	K	71.	B	E	G	H	I
37.	A	D	J	K	L	72.	B	E	G	J	L
38.	A	E	F	H	I	73.	B	F	G	H	L
39.	A	E	F	J	L	74.	B	F	G	I	K
40.	A	E	G	H	L	75.	B	F	H	I	J
41.	A	E	G	J	K	76.	B	G	H	J	K

                    (Continued Next Page)

BALANCED WHEEL™ 54012 (Continued from previous page)

77.	B	I	J	K	L
78.	C	D	E	H	K
79.	C	D	E	J	L
80.	C	D	F	G	H
81.	C	D	F	K	L
82.	C	D	G	H	I
83.	C	D	G	J	K
84.	C	D	I	J	L
85.	C	D	I	K	L
86.	C	E	F	G	L
87.	C	E	F	I	K
88.	C	E	F	J	K
89.	C	E	G	H	J
90.	C	E	H	I	L
91.	C	F	G	H	I
92.	C	F	H	J	L
93.	C	F	I	J	L
94.	C	G	H	K	L
95.	C	G	I	J	K

96.	D	E	F	G	J
97.	D	E	F	H	L
98.	D	E	F	I	K
99.	D	E	G	I	L
100.	D	E	G	K	L
101.	D	E	H	I	J
102.	D	F	G	I	J
103.	D	F	H	I	L
104.	D	F	H	J	K
105.	D	G	H	J	L
106.	E	F	G	H	K
107.	E	F	G	I	J
108.	E	G	I	K	L
109.	E	H	I	J	K
110.	E	H	J	K	L
111.	F	G	J	K	L
112.	F	H	I	K	L
113.	G	H	I	J	L

BALANCED WHEEL™ 54013
Wheeling 13 Numbers in 166 games for a 4 of 4 Win

NUMBERS CORRECT	MAXIMUM WINS				MINIMUM WINS			
	5x	4x	3x	2x	5x	4x	3x	2x
5 (w/o Jackpot)	0	9	27	85				
5	1	4	37	70	0	5	32	75
4	–	3	15	66	–	1	16	64
3	–	–	8	46	–	–	5	42
2	–	–	–	24	–	–	–	19

Your 13 Numbers to Wheel

A	B	C	D	E	F	G
62	65	65	64	65	64	57

H	I	J	K	L	M
63	65	65	65	65	65

The 166 Games to Play

1.	A	B	C	D	J
2.	A	B	C	E	M
3.	A	B	C	F	L

4.	A	B	C	G	M
5.	A	B	C	H	J
6.	A	B	C	I	K

                    (Continued Next Page)

BALANCED WHEEL™ 54013 (Continued from previous page)

#	1	2	3	4	5		#	1	2	3	4	5
7.	A	B	D	E	I		42.	A	D	F	I	L
8.	A	B	D	F	G		43.	A	D	G	I	K
9.	A	B	D	H	M		44.	A	D	G	J	L
10.	A	B	D	K	L		45.	A	D	H	J	L
11.	A	B	E	F	K		46.	A	D	I	J	K
12.	A	B	E	G	I		47.	A	D	J	L	M
13.	A	B	E	H	I		48.	A	E	F	G	J
14.	A	B	E	J	L		49.	A	E	F	H	J
15.	A	B	F	H	M		50.	A	E	F	L	M
16.	A	B	F	I	J		51.	A	E	G	K	M
17.	A	B	G	H	L		52.	A	F	H	K	L
18.	A	B	G	J	K		53.	A	E	I	J	M
19.	A	B	H	K	M		54.	A	E	I	K	L
20.	A	B	I	L	M		55.	A	F	G	H	I
21.	A	B	J	K	M		56.	A	F	G	K	L
22.	A	C	D	E	L		57.	A	F	I	K	M
23.	A	C	D	F	G		58.	A	F	J	K	L
24.	A	C	D	F	K		59.	A	G	H	J	M
25.	A	C	D	H	I		60.	A	G	I	L	M
26.	A	C	D	I	M		61.	A	H	I	J	K
27.	A	C	E	F	I		62.	A	H	I	L	M
28.	A	C	E	G	L		63.	D	O	D	E	F
29.	A	C	E	H	M		64.	B	C	D	G	M
30.	A	C	E	J	K		65.	B	C	D	H	J
31.	A	C	F	H	L		66.	B	C	D	I	L
32.	A	C	F	J	M		67.	B	C	D	K	M
33.	A	C	G	H	K		68.	B	C	E	G	K
34.	A	C	G	I	J		69.	B	C	E	H	K
35.	A	C	I	J	L		70.	B	C	E	I	M
36.	A	C	K	L	M		71.	B	C	E	J	L
37.	A	D	E	F	J		72.	B	C	F	G	M
38.	A	D	E	G	H		73.	B	C	F	H	I
39.	A	D	E	K	M		74.	B	C	F	J	M
40.	A	D	F	G	M		75.	B	C	F	K	L
41.	A	D	F	H	K		76.	B	C	G	H	J

(Continued Next Page)

BALANCED WHEEL™ 54013 (Continued from previous page)

#	1	2	3	4	5		#	1	2	3	4	5
77.	B	C	G	I	L		112.	C	D	F	I	J
78.	B	C	H	L	M		113.	C	D	F	L	M
79.	B	C	I	J	K		114.	C	D	G	H	I
80.	B	D	E	G	L		115.	C	D	G	K	L
81.	B	D	E	H	I		116.	C	D	H	I	M
82.	B	D	E	J	K		117.	C	D	J	K	L
83.	B	D	E	L	M		118.	C	E	F	G	I
84.	B	D	F	H	M		119.	C	E	F	H	M
85.	B	D	F	I	K		120.	C	E	F	I	L
86.	B	D	F	J	L		121.	C	E	F	J	K
87.	B	D	G	H	K		122.	C	E	G	H	M
88.	B	D	G	I	J		123.	C	E	H	I	J
89.	B	D	H	K	L		124.	C	E	K	L	M
90.	B	D	I	J	M		125.	C	F	G	H	L
91.	B	E	F	G	H		126.	C	F	G	J	K
92.	B	E	F	H	L		127.	C	F	H	J	L
93.	B	E	F	I	J		128.	C	F	I	K	M
94.	B	E	F	K	M		129.	C	G	I	K	M
95.	B	E	G	J	M		130.	C	G	J	L	M
96.	B	E	H	J	M		131.	C	H	I	K	L
97.	B	E	I	K	L		132.	C	H	J	K	M
98.	B	F	G	I	K		133.	C	I	J	L	M
99.	B	F	G	J	L		134.	D	E	F	G	K
100.	B	F	H	J	K		135.	D	E	F	H	J
101.	B	F	I	L	M		136.	D	E	F	I	M
102.	B	G	H	I	M		137.	D	E	F	K	L
103.	B	G	K	L	M		138.	D	E	G	I	M
104.	B	H	I	J	L		139.	D	E	H	K	M
105.	B	H	I	K	M		140.	D	E	I	J	L
106.	B	J	K	L	M		141.	D	F	G	H	J
107.	C	D	E	G	J		142.	D	F	G	I	L
108.	C	D	E	H	L		143.	D	F	H	I	L
109.	C	D	E	I	K		144.	D	F	J	K	M
110.	C	D	E	J	M		145.	D	G	H	L	M
111.	C	D	F	H	K		146.	D	G	J	K	M

    (Continued Next Page)

BALANCED WHEEL™ 54013 (Continued from previous page)

147.	D	H	I	J	K
148.	D	H	J	L	M
149.	D	I	K	L	M
150.	E	F	G	L	M
151.	E	F	H	I	K
152.	E	F	J	L	M
153.	E	G	H	I	L
154.	E	G	H	J	K
155.	E	G	I	J	K
156.	E	G	J	K	L

157.	E	H	I	L	M
158.	E	H	J	K	L
159.	E	I	J	K	M
160.	F	G	H	K	M
161.	F	G	I	J	M
162.	F	H	I	J	M
163.	F	H	K	L	M
164.	F	I	J	K	L
165.	G	H	I	J	L
166.	G	H	I	K	L

BALANCED WHEEL™ 54014
Wheeling 14 Numbers in 245 games for a 4 of 4 Win

NUMBERS CORRECT	MAXIMUM WINS				MINIMUM WINS			
	5x	4x	3x	2x	5x	4x	3x	2x
5 (w/o Jackpot)	0	10	35	117				
5	1	6	41	109	0	5	40	103
4	–	4	14	99	–	1	20	84
3	–	–	9	61	–	–	6	56
2	–	–	–	31	–	–	–	24

Your 14 Numbers to Wheel

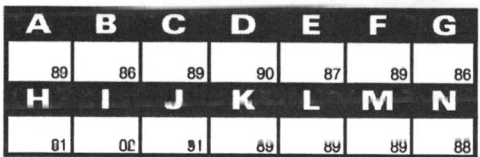

A	B	C	D	E	F	G
89	86	89	90	87	89	86

H	I	J	K	L	M	N
81	80	81	89	89	89	88

The 245 Games to Play

1.	A	B	C	D	M
2.	A	B	C	E	K
3.	A	B	C	F	N
4.	A	B	C	G	L
5.	A	B	C	H	N
6.	A	B	C	I	L
7.	A	B	C	J	L
8.	A	B	D	E	N
9.	A	B	D	F	H
10.	A	B	D	F	J
11.	A	B	D	G	I
12.	A	B	D	G	N

13.	A	B	D	H	I
14.	A	B	D	K	L
15.	A	B	E	F	G
16.	A	B	E	F	L
17.	A	B	E	H	M
18.	A	B	E	I	J
19.	A	B	F	I	K
20.	A	B	F	K	M
21.	A	B	G	H	K
22.	A	B	G	J	M
23.	A	B	H	J	L
24.	A	B	I	M	N

                     (Continued Next Page)

BALANCED WHEEL™ 54014 (Continued from previous page)

25.	A	B	J	K	N	60.	A	D	H	L	M
26.	A	B	L	M	N	61.	A	D	I	K	M
27.	A	C	D	E	H	62.	A	D	J	K	M
28.	A	C	D	E	J	63.	A	D	J	L	N
29.	A	C	D	F	L	64.	A	E	F	H	N
30.	A	C	D	G	M	65.	A	E	F	J	N
31.	A	C	D	H	J	66.	A	E	G	H	L
32.	A	C	D	H	K	67.	A	E	G	I	N
33.	A	C	D	I	N	68.	A	E	G	J	M
34.	A	C	D	K	N	69.	A	E	H	I	L
35.	A	C	E	F	I	70.	A	E	H	J	K
36.	A	C	E	F	M	71.	A	E	I	K	N
37.	A	C	E	G	I	72.	A	E	J	K	L
38.	A	C	E	G	K	73.	A	E	K	M	N
39.	A	C	E	I	M	74.	A	F	G	H	I
40.	A	C	E	L	N	75.	A	F	G	H	J
41.	A	C	F	G	J	76.	A	F	G	I	M
42.	A	C	F	H	L	77.	A	F	G	K	N
43.	A	C	F	J	K	78.	A	F	H	K	M
44.	A	C	G	H	M	79.	A	F	I	L	N
45.	A	C	G	M	N	80.	A	F	J	L	M
46.	A	C	H	I	J	81.	A	F	K	L	N
47.	A	C	H	I	N	82.	A	G	I	J	N
48.	A	C	I	J	K	83.	A	G	I	K	L
49.	A	C	J	M	N	84.	A	G	J	L	N
50.	A	C	K	L	M	85.	A	G	K	L	M
51.	A	D	E	F	K	86.	A	H	I	K	M
52.	A	D	E	G	J	87.	A	H	J	M	N
53.	A	D	E	I	L	88.	A	H	K	L	N
54.	A	D	E	L	M	89.	A	I	J	L	M
55.	A	D	F	G	L	90.	B	C	D	E	I
56.	A	D	F	I	J	91.	B	C	D	F	G
57.	A	D	F	M	N	92.	B	C	D	H	L
58.	A	D	G	H	N	93.	B	C	D	J	K
59.	A	D	G	J	K	94.	B	C	D	L	N

                    (Continued Next Page)

98

BALANCED WHEEL™ 54014 (Continued from previous page)

#						#					
95.	B	C	E	F	H	130.	B	E	H	J	N
96.	B	C	E	G	J	131.	B	E	H	K	L
97.	B	C	E	I	N	132.	B	E	I	K	M
98.	B	C	E	L	M	133.	B	E	K	L	N
99.	B	C	F	I	N	134.	B	F	G	H	L
100.	B	C	F	J	M	135.	B	F	G	H	M
101.	B	C	F	K	L	136.	B	F	G	H	N
102.	B	C	G	H	J	137.	B	F	G	I	J
103.	B	C	G	I	K	138.	B	F	G	J	K
104.	B	C	G	J	M	139.	B	F	H	I	J
105.	B	C	G	J	N	140.	B	F	H	J	K
106.	B	C	H	I	K	141.	B	F	J	L	N
107.	B	C	H	K	M	142.	B	G	H	I	N
108.	B	C	I	J	M	143.	B	G	I	L	M
109.	B	C	K	M	N	144.	B	G	K	L	N
110.	B	D	E	F	K	145.	B	H	I	L	M
111.	B	D	E	G	H	146.	B	H	L	M	N
112.	B	D	E	J	L	147.	B	I	J	K	N
113.	B	D	E	J	M	148.	B	I	J	L	N
114.	B	D	F	I	M	149.	B	J	K	L	M
115.	B	D	F	K	N	150.	C	D	E	F	G
116.	B	D	F	L	M	151.	C	D	E	K	L
117.	B	D	G	J	L	152.	C	D	E	M	N
118.	B	D	G	K	M	153.	C	D	F	G	H
119.	B	D	H	J	M	154.	C	D	F	I	K
120.	B	D	H	K	N	155.	C	D	F	J	N
121.	B	D	I	J	N	156.	C	D	F	K	M
122.	B	D	I	K	L	157.	C	D	G	H	I
123.	B	D	J	M	N	158.	C	D	G	I	J
124.	B	E	F	I	L	159.	C	D	G	K	N
125.	B	E	F	J	K	160.	C	D	G	L	M
126.	B	E	F	M	N	161.	C	D	H	M	N
127.	B	E	G	H	I	162.	C	D	I	L	M
128.	B	E	G	K	L	163.	C	D	J	L	M
129.	B	E	G	M	N	164.	C	E	F	J	L

          (Continued Next Page)

BALANCED WHEEL™ 54014 (Continued from previous page)

#	1	2	3	4	5		#	1	2	3	4	5
165.	C	E	F	K	N		200.	D	F	G	I	L
166.	C	E	G	H	N		201.	D	F	G	J	M
167.	C	E	G	L	M		202.	D	F	G	J	N
168.	C	E	H	I	M		203.	D	F	G	K	L
169.	C	E	H	J	K		204.	D	F	H	I	K
170.	C	E	H	L	M		205.	D	F	H	J	N
171.	C	E	I	J	N		206.	D	F	H	K	L
172.	C	E	I	K	L		207.	D	F	J	K	L
173.	C	E	J	K	M		208.	D	G	H	J	L
174.	C	F	G	I	M		209.	D	G	H	K	M
175.	C	F	G	K	M		210.	D	G	I	M	N
176.	C	F	G	L	N		211.	D	H	I	J	M
177.	C	F	H	I	L		212.	D	H	I	L	N
178.	C	F	H	J	M		213.	D	I	J	K	L
179.	C	F	H	K	N		214.	D	I	K	L	N
180.	C	F	I	J	L		215.	D	K	L	M	N
181.	C	F	L	M	N		216.	E	F	G	H	K
182.	C	G	H	K	L		217.	E	F	G	I	M
183.	C	G	I	L	N		218.	E	F	G	J	L
184.	C	G	J	K	L		219.	E	F	G	M	N
185.	C	H	J	L	N		220.	E	F	H	I	N
186.	C	I	K	M	N		221.	E	F	H	J	L
187.	C	J	K	L	N		222.	E	F	I	J	K
188.	D	E	F	H	M		223.	E	F	K	L	M
189.	D	E	F	I	N		224.	E	G	H	J	M
190.	D	E	F	J	M		225.	E	G	I	J	L
191.	D	E	F	L	N		226.	E	G	J	K	N
192.	D	E	G	I	K		227.	E	H	I	J	L
193.	D	E	G	K	M		228.	E	H	K	M	N
194.	D	E	G	L	N		229.	E	I	L	M	N
195.	D	E	H	I	K		230.	E	J	L	M	N
196.	D	E	H	J	K		231.	F	G	I	K	N
197.	D	E	H	L	N		232.	F	G	J	L	M
198.	D	E	I	J	M		233.	F	H	I	M	N
199.	D	E	J	K	N		234.	F	H	L	M	N

(Continued Next Page)

BALANCED WHEEL™ 54014 (Continued from previous page)

235.	F	I	J	M	N
236.	F	I	K	L	M
237.	F	J	K	M	N
238.	G	H	I	J	M
239.	G	H	I	K	L
240.	G	H	J	K	N

241.	G	H	L	M	N
242.	G	I	J	K	M
243.	G	J	K	M	N
244.	H	I	J	K	N
245.	H	J	K	L	M

BALANCED WHEEL™ 54015
Wheeling 15 Numbers in 311 games for a 4 of 4 Win

NUMBERS CORRECT	MAXIMUM WINS				MINIMUM WINS			
	5x	4x	3x	2x	5x	4x	3x	2x
5 (w/o Jackpot)	0	10	36	132				
5	1	5	50	121	0	5	41	129
4	–	3	27	91	–	1	20	102
3	–	–	18	48	–	–	6	66
2	–	–	–	34	–	–	–	28

Your 15 Numbers to Wheel

A	B	C	D	E	F	G	H
104	105	104	103	103	103	102	102

I	J	K	L	M	N	O	
102	102	105	105	105	105	105	

The 311 Games to Play

1.	A	B	C	D	L
2.	A	B	C	E	K
3.	A	B	C	F	J
4.	A	B	C	G	N
5.	A	B	C	H	O
6.	A	B	C	I	M
7.	A	B	D	E	J
8.	A	B	D	F	G
9.	A	B	D	H	I
10.	A	B	D	H	K
11.	A	B	D	H	N
12.	A	B	D	M	O
13.	A	B	E	F	I
14.	A	B	E	G	H
15.	A	B	E	L	M
16.	A	B	E	N	O

17.	A	B	F	H	J
18.	A	B	F	J	O
19.	A	B	F	K	M
20.	A	B	F	L	N
21.	A	B	G	I	M
22.	A	B	G	J	L
23.	A	B	G	K	O
24.	A	B	H	L	M
25.	A	B	I	J	K
26.	A	B	I	K	N
27.	A	B	I	L	O
28.	A	B	J	M	N
29.	A	B	K	L	N
30.	A	B	K	N	O
31.	A	C	D	E	G
32.	A	C	D	F	K

                (Continued Next Page)

BALANCED WHEEL™ 54015 (Continued from previous page)

#						#					
33.	A	C	D	H	M	68.	A	D	J	L	M
34.	A	C	D	I	O	69.	A	E	F	G	N
35.	A	C	D	J	N	70.	A	E	F	J	N
36.	A	C	E	F	L	71.	A	E	F	K	N
37.	A	C	E	H	N	72.	A	E	F	M	O
38.	A	C	E	I	K	73.	A	E	G	I	O
39.	A	C	E	J	M	74.	A	E	G	J	K
40.	A	C	E	K	O	75.	A	E	G	L	M
41.	A	C	F	G	M	76.	A	E	H	I	J
42.	A	C	F	H	J	77.	A	E	H	K	O
43.	A	C	F	I	N	78.	A	E	H	L	M
44.	A	C	F	J	O	79.	A	E	I	K	L
45.	A	C	G	H	K	80.	A	E	I	M	N
46.	A	C	G	I	J	81.	A	E	J	L	O
47.	A	C	G	L	N	82.	A	F	G	H	I
48.	A	C	G	N	O	83.	A	F	G	J	N
49.	A	C	H	I	L	84.	A	F	G	K	N
50.	A	C	J	K	L	85.	A	F	G	L	O
51.	A	C	K	M	N	86.	A	F	H	J	O
52.	A	C	L	M	O	87.	A	F	H	K	L
53.	A	D	E	F	H	88.	A	F	H	M	N
54.	A	D	E	G	I	89.	A	F	I	J	L
55.	A	D	E	G	O	90.	A	F	I	K	O
56.	A	D	E	K	M	91.	A	F	I	L	M
57.	A	D	E	L	N	92.	A	F	J	K	N
58.	A	D	F	I	L	93.	A	G	H	L	M
59.	A	D	F	J	M	94.	A	G	H	N	O
60.	A	D	F	N	O	95.	A	G	I	K	M
61.	A	D	G	H	J	96.	A	G	I	L	N
62.	A	D	G	K	L	97.	A	G	J	M	O
63.	A	D	G	M	N	98.	A	H	I	K	N
64.	A	D	H	L	O	99.	A	H	I	M	O
65.	A	D	I	J	M	100.	A	H	J	K	M
66.	A	D	I	K	N	101.	A	H	J	L	N
67.	A	D	J	K	O	102.	A	I	J	N	O

     (Continued Next Page)

BALANCED WHEEL™ 54015 (Continued from previous page)

#						#					
103.	A	K	L	M	O	138.	B	D	G	J	M
104.	A	L	M	N	O	139.	B	D	H	I	K
105.	B	C	D	E	H	140.	B	D	H	I	N
106.	B	C	D	F	I	141.	B	D	H	J	L
107.	B	C	D	G	K	142.	B	D	I	J	O
108.	B	C	D	J	M	143.	B	D	J	K	M
109.	B	C	D	N	O	144.	B	D	K	L	O
110.	B	C	E	F	G	145.	B	D	K	N	O
111.	B	C	E	I	N	146.	B	D	L	M	N
112.	B	C	E	J	N	147.	B	E	F	H	N
113.	B	C	E	L	N	148.	B	E	F	J	M
114.	B	C	E	M	O	149.	B	E	F	L	O
115.	B	C	F	H	O	150.	B	E	G	H	J
116.	B	C	F	K	N	151.	B	E	G	H	M
117.	B	C	F	L	M	152.	B	E	G	I	K
118.	B	C	G	H	I	153.	B	E	G	L	M
119.	B	C	G	J	K	154.	B	E	G	M	O
120.	B	C	G	K	M	155.	B	E	H	I	O
121.	B	C	G	L	O	156.	B	E	H	K	L
122.	B	C	H	J	O	157.	B	E	I	J	L
123.	B	C	H	K	L	158.	B	E	J	K	O
124.	B	C	H	M	N	159.	B	E	K	M	N
125.	B	C	I	J	N	160.	B	F	G	H	K
126.	B	C	I	K	O	161.	B	F	G	I	J
127.	B	C	I	L	N	162.	B	F	G	L	O
128.	B	C	J	L	N	163.	B	F	G	M	N
129.	B	D	E	F	K	164.	B	F	H	I	L
130.	B	D	E	G	N	165.	B	F	I	K	O
131.	B	D	E	I	M	166.	B	F	I	M	O
132.	B	D	E	L	O	167.	B	F	I	N	O
133.	B	D	F	H	M	168.	B	F	J	K	L
134.	B	D	F	J	N	169.	B	G	H	L	N
135.	B	D	F	L	O	170.	B	G	I	N	O
136.	B	D	G	H	O	171.	B	G	J	N	O
137.	B	D	G	I	L	172.	B	G	K	L	N

          (Continued Next Page)

103

BALANCED WHEEL™ 54015 (Continued from previous page)

#						#					
173.	B	H	I	J	M	208.	C	E	H	L	O
174.	B	H	J	K	N	209.	C	E	I	J	L
175.	B	H	K	M	O	210.	C	E	I	K	M
176.	B	H	L	N	O	211.	C	F	G	H	L
177.	B	I	K	L	M	212.	C	F	G	J	L
178.	B	I	M	N	O	213.	C	F	G	K	O
179.	B	J	L	M	O	214.	C	F	H	L	N
180.	C	D	E	F	J	215.	C	F	I	J	K
181.	C	D	E	I	O	216.	C	F	I	K	M
182.	C	D	E	K	N	217.	C	F	I	L	O
183.	C	D	E	L	M	218.	C	F	J	M	N
184.	C	D	F	G	N	219.	C	F	K	L	O
185.	C	D	F	H	L	220.	C	G	H	J	N
186.	C	D	F	M	O	221.	C	G	H	M	O
187.	C	D	G	H	L	222.	C	G	I	K	N
188.	C	D	G	I	O	223.	C	G	I	L	M
189.	C	D	G	J	M	224.	C	H	I	K	M
190.	C	D	H	I	J	225.	C	H	I	N	O
191.	C	D	H	K	N	226.	C	H	J	L	M
192.	C	D	H	K	O	227.	C	I	J	M	O
193.	C	D	H	L	N	228.	C	J	K	N	O
194.	C	D	I	K	L	229.	C	K	L	M	N
195.	C	D	I	M	N	230.	C	K	L	N	O
196.	C	D	J	K	M	231.	C	K	M	N	O
197.	C	D	J	L	O	232.	D	E	F	G	M
198.	C	E	F	G	I	233.	D	E	F	I	N
199.	C	E	F	H	I	234.	D	E	F	K	L
200.	C	E	F	H	K	235.	D	E	F	K	O
201.	C	E	F	H	M	236.	D	E	G	H	K
202.	C	E	F	N	O	237.	D	E	G	J	L
203.	C	E	G	H	L	238.	D	E	H	I	L
204.	C	E	G	J	O	239.	D	E	H	J	M
205.	C	E	G	K	L	240.	D	E	H	N	O
206.	C	E	G	M	N	241.	D	E	I	J	K
207.	C	E	H	J	K	242.	D	E	J	M	N

                    (Continued Next Page)

BALANCED WHEEL™ 54015 (Continued from previous page)

#						#					
243.	D	E	J	M	O	278.	E	H	I	K	M
244.	D	F	G	H	N	279.	E	H	J	N	O
245.	D	F	G	I	K	280.	E	H	K	L	N
246.	D	F	G	J	O	281.	E	H	M	N	O
247.	D	F	G	L	N	282.	E	I	J	L	N
248.	D	F	H	I	O	283.	E	I	K	N	O
249.	D	F	H	J	K	284.	E	I	L	M	O
250.	D	F	I	J	M	285.	E	J	K	L	M
251.	D	F	J	L	M	286.	E	K	L	N	O
252.	D	F	K	M	N	287.	F	G	H	J	M
253.	D	G	H	I	M	288.	F	G	I	M	N
254.	D	G	I	J	N	289.	F	G	I	M	O
255.	D	G	J	K	M	290.	F	G	K	L	M
256.	D	G	K	N	O	291.	F	G	M	N	O
257.	D	G	L	M	O	292.	F	H	I	J	N
258.	D	H	J	M	N	293.	F	H	I	K	M
259.	D	H	J	M	O	294.	F	H	K	N	O
260.	D	H	K	L	M	295.	F	H	L	M	O
261.	D	I	J	L	M	296.	F	I	K	L	N
262.	D	I	K	M	O	297.	F	J	K	M	O
263.	D	I	L	N	O	298.	F	J	L	N	O
264.	D	J	K	L	N	299.	G	H	I	J	K
265.	D	J	M	N	O	300.	G	H	I	L	O
266.	E	F	G	H	O	301.	G	H	J	L	O
267.	E	F	G	I	L	302.	G	H	K	L	O
268.	E	F	G	J	K	303.	G	H	K	M	N
269.	E	F	H	J	L	304.	G	I	J	K	L
270.	E	F	I	J	O	305.	G	I	J	K	O
271.	E	F	I	K	M	306.	G	J	L	M	N
272.	E	F	L	M	N	307.	H	I	J	L	O
273.	E	G	H	I	N	308.	H	I	K	L	O
274.	E	G	I	J	M	309.	H	I	L	M	N
275.	E	G	J	K	N	310.	H	J	K	L	O
276.	E	G	K	M	O	311.	I	J	K	M	N
277.	E	G	L	N	O						

BALANCED WHEEL™ 54107
Wheeling 7 Numbers in 3 games for a 4 of 5 Win

NUMBERS CORRECT	MAXIMUM WINS				MINIMUM WINS			
	5x	4x	3x	2x	5x	4x	3x	2x
5 (w/o Jackpot)	0	2	1	0				
5	1	0	2	0	0	1	2	0
4	–	1	1	1	–	0	2	1
3	–	–	2	0	–	–	0	3
2	–	–	–	2	–	–	–	1

Your 7 Numbers to Wheel

A	B	C	D	E	F	G
2	2	2	3	2	2	2

The 3 Games to Play

1.

A	B	D	F	G

2.

A	C	D	E	G

3.

B	C	D	E	F

Copyright © 1983-1998 Gail Howard

BALANCED WHEEL™ 54108
Wheeling 8 Numbers in 5 games for a 4 of 5 Win

NUMBERS CORRECT	MAXIMUM WINS				MINIMUM WINS			
	5x	4x	3x	2x	5x	4x	3x	2x
5 (w/o Jackpot)	0	3	1	1				
5	1	2	1	1	0	1	2	2
4	–	2	2	0	–	0	2	2
3	–	–	4	0	–	–	0	4
2	–	–	–	4	–	–	–	1

Your 8 Numbers to Wheel

A	B	C	D	E	F	G	H
4	2	3	4	3	3	2	4

The 5 Games to Play

1.

A	B	D	G	H

2.

A	C	D	E	H

3.

A	C	D	F	H

4.

A	D	E	F	H

5.

B	C	E	F	G

Copyright © 1983-1998 Gail Howard

BALANCED WHEEL™ 54109
Wheeling 9 Numbers in 9 games for a 4 of 5 Win

NUMBERS CORRECT	MAXIMUM WINS				MINIMUM WINS			
	5x	4x	3x	2x	5x	4x	3x	2x
5 (w/o Jackpot)	0	3	3	1				
5	1	1	2	5	0	1	5	3
4	–	2	1	3	–	0	3	5
3	–	–	3	1	–	–	0	6
2	–	–	–	4	–	–	–	2

Your 9 Numbers to Wheel

A	B	C	D	E	F	G	H	I
5	5	5	5	5	5	5	5	5

(Continued Next Page)

BALANCED WHEEL™ 54109 (Continued from previous page)
The 9 Games to Play

1.	A	B	D	F	I	6.	B	C	D	E	I
2.	A	B	E	F	H	7.	B	C	G	H	I
3.	A	C	D	G	H	8.	B	D	E	G	I
4.	A	C	E	F	G	9.	C	D	F	G	H
5.	A	E	F	H	I						

Copyright © 1983-1998 Gail Howard

BALANCED WHEEL™ 54110
Wheeling 10 Numbers in 14 games for a 4 of 5 Win

NUMBERS CORRECT	MAXIMUM WINS				MINIMUM WINS			
	5x	4x	3x	2x	5x	4x	3x	2x
5 (w/o Jackpot)	0	3	1	1				
5	1	0	6	6	0	1	6	6
4	–	1	4	4	–	0	3	8
3	–	–	3	4	–	–	0	7
2	–	–	–	7	–	–	–	0

Your 10 Numbers to Wheel

A	B	C	D	E	F	G	H	I	J
7	7	7	7	7	7	7	7	7	7

The 14 Games to Play

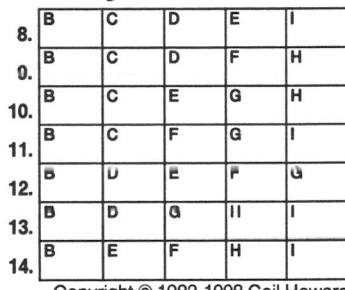

1.	A	C	D	G	J	8.	B	C	D	E	I
2.	A	C	E	F	J	9.	B	C	D	F	H
3.	A	C	H	I	J	10.	B	C	E	G	H
4.	A	D	E	H	J	11.	B	C	F	G	I
5.	A	D	F	I	J	12.	B	D	E	F	G
6.	A	E	G	I	J	13.	B	D	G	H	I
7.	A	F	G	H	J	14.	B	E	F	H	I

Copyright © 1983-1998 Gail Howard

BALANCED WHEEL™ 54111
Wheeling 11 Numbers in 26 games for a 4 of 5 Win

NUMBERS CORRECT	MAXIMUM WINS				MINIMUM WINS			
	5x	4x	3x	2x	5x	4x	3x	2x
5 (w/o Jackpot)	0	5	0	20				
5	1	0	10	10	0	1	10	10
4	–	1	4	12	–	0	5	12
3	–	–	4	0	–	–	1	10
2	–	–	–	5	–	–	–	4

Your 11 Numbers to Wheel

A	B	C	D	E	F	G	H	I	J	K
12	12	12	12	10	12	12	12	12	12	12

(Continued Next Page)

107

BALANCED WHEEL™ 54111 (Continued from previous page)
The 26 Games to Play

#							#					
1.	A	B	C	E	K		14.	B	C	D	G	H
2.	A	B	D	E	J		15.	B	C	F	H	J
3.	A	B	E	F	G		16.	B	C	G	I	J
4.	A	B	E	H	I		17.	B	D	F	H	K
5.	A	C	D	F	H		18.	B	D	G	I	K
6.	A	C	D	G	I		19.	B	F	I	J	K
7.	A	C	F	I	J		20.	B	G	H	J	K
8.	A	C	G	H	J		21.	C	D	E	J	K
9.	A	D	F	I	K		22.	C	E	F	G	K
10.	A	D	G	H	K		23.	C	E	H	I	K
11.	A	F	H	J	K		24.	D	E	F	G	J
12.	A	G	I	J	K		25.	D	E	H	I	J
13.	B	C	D	F	I		26.	E	F	G	H	I

Copyright © 1983-1998 Gail Howard

BALANCED WHEEL™ 54112
Wheeling 12 Numbers in 37 games for a 4 of 5 Win

NUMBERS CORRECT	MAXIMUM WINS				MINIMUM WINS			
	5x	4x	3x	2x	5x	4x	3x	2x
5 (w/o Jackpot)	0	4	7	18				
5	1	2	7	19	0	1	8	19
4	–	2	3	16	–	0	4	17
3	–	–	3	13	–	–	1	11
2	–	–	–	8	–	–	–	4

Your 12 Numbers to Wheel

A	B	C	D	E	F	G	H	I	J	K	L
15	16	15	17	15	15	15	14	15	16	16	16

The 37 Games to Play

#							#					
1.	A	B	C	G	I		12.	A	E	H	I	K
2.	A	B	D	G	J		13.	A	F	G	J	L
3.	A	B	D	I	L		14.	A	G	H	K	L
4.	A	B	D	J	K		15.	A	H	I	J	L
5.	A	B	E	F	I		16.	B	C	D	E	K
6.	A	B	F	H	L		17.	B	C	D	G	L
7.	A	C	D	F	H		18.	B	C	F	J	L
8.	A	C	E	H	J		19.	B	C	H	I	K
9.	A	C	E	K	L		20.	B	D	E	H	L
10.	A	C	F	I	K		21.	B	D	F	G	K
11.	A	D	E	G	K		22.	B	D	F	I	J

Copyright © 1983-1998 Gail Howard

108

(Continued Next Page)

BALANCED WHEEL™ 54112 (Continued from previous page)

23.	B	E	G	H	J
24.	B	E	G	I	L
25.	B	E	J	K	L
26.	C	D	E	I	J
27.	C	D	G	J	L
28.	C	D	H	J	K
29.	C	E	F	G	H
30.	C	F	H	I	L

31.	C	G	I	J	K
32.	D	E	F	J	L
33.	D	F	G	H	I
34.	D	F	G	K	L
35.	D	F	I	K	L
36.	E	F	H	J	K
37.	E	G	I	J	K

Copyright © 1983-1998 Gail Howard

BALANCED WHEEL™ 54113
Wheeling 13 Numbers in 58 games for a 4 of 5 Win

NUMBERS CORRECT	MAXIMUM WINS				MINIMUM WINS			
	5x	4x	3x	2x	5x	4x	3x	2x
5 (w/o Jackpot)	0	4	11	25				
5	1	3	7	34	0	1	9	34
4	–	2	5	23	–	0	5	23
3	–	–	4	14	–	–	1	16
2	–	–	–	9	–	–	–	6

Your 13 Numbers to Wheel

A	B	C	D	E	F	G
22	22	21	24	21	23	24

H	I	J	K	L	M
23	22	21	24	21	22

The 58 Games to Play

1.	A	B	C	G	L
2.	A	B	C	H	I
3.	A	B	D	H	K
4.	A	B	D	I	M
5.	A	B	E	F	M
6.	A	B	E	G	H
7.	A	B	G	J	K
8.	A	C	D	F	J
9.	A	C	D	K	L
10.	A	C	E	K	M
11.	A	C	G	H	I
12.	A	C	I	K	M
13.	A	D	E	G	K
14.	A	D	E	H	J

15.	A	D	F	I	M
16.	A	D	G	H	J
17.	A	E	F	I	L
18.	A	E	I	J	L
19.	A	F	G	I	M
20.	A	F	H	K	L
21.	A	G	J	L	M
22.	A	H	J	L	M
23.	B	C	D	E	I
24.	B	C	D	H	M
25.	B	C	E	J	M
26.	B	C	F	G	K
27.	B	C	G	I	J
28.	B	D	E	J	L

Copyright © 1983-1998 Gail Howard   (Continued Next Page)

BALANCED WHEEL™ 54113 (Continued from previous page)

29.	B	D	F	G	I	44.	C	F	I	L	M
30.	B	D	F	G	L	45.	C	G	H	J	L
31.	B	D	J	K	M	46.	C	H	I	J	K
32.	B	E	F	I	K	47.	D	E	G	L	M
33.	B	E	H	K	L	48.	D	E	H	I	K
34.	B	F	G	J	L	49.	D	F	H	L	M
35.	B	F	H	I	J	50.	D	F	I	J	K
36.	B	G	H	K	M	51.	D	F	J	K	L
37.	B	I	K	L	M	52.	D	G	H	I	L
38.	C	D	E	F	H	53.	D	G	I	J	M
39.	C	D	G	K	M	54.	E	F	G	H	K
40.	C	D	J	K	L	55.	E	F	J	K	M
41.	C	E	F	G	J	56.	E	G	H	I	M
42.	C	E	F	H	L	57.	E	G	I	K	L
43.	C	F	H	K	M	58.	F	G	H	K	M

Copyright © 1983-1998 Gail Howard

BALANCED WHEEL™ 54114
Wheeling 14 Numbers in 76 games for a 4 of 5 Win

NUMBERS CORRECT	MAXIMUM WINS				MINIMUM WINS			
	5x	4x	3x	2x	5x	4x	3x	2x
5 (w/o Jackpot)	0	7	13	19				
5	1	4	11	33	0	1	11	35
4	–	4	6	27	–	0	5	28
3	–	–	8	19	–	–	1	18
2	–	–	–	15	–	–	–	6

Your 14 Numbers to Wheel

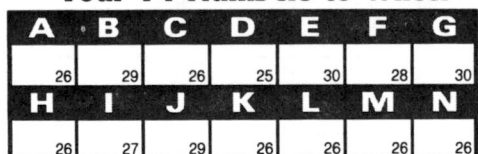

A	B	C	D	E	F	G
26	29	26	25	30	28	30

H	I	J	K	L	M	N
26	27	29	26	26	26	26

The 76 Games to Play

1.	A	B	C	G	L	8.	A	B	J	K	L
2.	A	B	D	F	N	9.	A	C	D	E	M
3.	A	B	E	F	L	10.	A	C	E	K	L
4.	A	B	E	J	N	11.	A	C	F	J	L
5.	A	B	G	H	N	12.	A	C	F	K	M
6.	A	B	G	I	J	13.	A	C	H	I	M
7.	A	B	G	J	M	14.	A	C	I	K	N

Copyright © 1983-1998 Gail Howard   (Continued Next Page)

BALANCED WHEEL™ 54114 (Continued from previous page)

#						#					
15.	A	D	E	G	N	46.	B	G	J	L	N
16.	A	D	F	H	M	47.	B	J	K	M	N
17.	A	D	H	I	L	48.	C	D	E	L	N
18.	A	D	H	J	N	49.	C	D	F	G	I
19.	A	D	I	K	M	50.	C	D	G	H	K
20.	A	E	F	H	N	51.	C	D	G	J	K
21.	A	E	F	I	M	52.	C	E	F	G	H
22.	A	E	G	J	L	53.	C	E	G	I	K
23.	A	E	H	K	M	54.	C	E	H	I	J
24.	A	F	G	J	N	55.	C	E	K	M	N
25.	A	F	G	K	L	56.	C	F	J	M	N
26.	A	I	L	M	N	57.	C	F	K	L	N
27.	B	C	D	H	K	58.	C	G	H	J	K
28.	B	C	D	I	J	59.	C	H	I	L	N
29.	B	C	E	F	I	60.	C	I	K	L	M
30.	B	C	E	G	H	61.	D	E	F	I	J
31.	B	C	F	H	J	62.	D	E	F	J	K
32.	B	C	G	M	N	63.	D	E	G	L	M
33.	B	D	E	G	J	64.	D	F	G	H	I
34.	B	D	E	G	K	65.	D	F	H	L	N
35.	B	D	E	H	I	66.	D	H	I	M	N
36.	B	D	F	L	M	67.	D	H	J	L	M
37.	B	E	F	M	N	68.	D	I	K	L	N
38.	B	E	I	J	K	69.	E	F	H	L	M
39.	B	E	J	L	M	70.	E	F	I	L	N
40.	B	F	G	J	K	71.	E	G	H	I	K
41.	B	F	H	I	K	72.	E	G	J	M	N
42.	B	G	H	L	M	73.	E	H	K	L	N
43.	B	G	I	J	L	74.	F	G	J	L	M
44.	B	G	I	J	M	75.	F	G	K	M	N
45.	B	G	I	J	N	76.	F	H	I	J	K

111

BALANCED WHEEL™ 54115
Wheeling 15 Numbers in 118 games for a 4 of 5 Win

NUMBERS CORRECT	MAXIMUM WINS				MINIMUM WINS			
	5x	4x	3x	2x	5x	4x	3x	2x
5 (w/o Jackpot)	0	8	16	42				
5	1	4	18	42	0	1	13	55
4	–	4	8	38	–	0	6	38
3	–	–	9	25	–	–	1	24
2	–	–	–	18	–	–	–	8

Your 15 Numbers to Wheel

A	B	C	D	E	F	G	H
38	38	41	36	38	38	38	38

I	J	K	L	M	N	O
43	38	42	40	39	43	40

The 118 Games to Play

#						#					
1.	A	B	C	G	O	26.	A	D	G	J	M
2.	A	B	D	J	K	27.	A	E	H	J	N
3.	A	B	D	J	L	28.	A	E	I	M	O
4.	A	B	E	F	L	29.	A	E	J	K	M
5.	A	B	E	K	L	30.	A	E	J	N	O
6.	A	B	F	H	I	31.	A	F	G	J	L
7.	A	B	F	J	M	32.	A	F	J	K	L
8.	A	B	G	I	J	33.	A	G	H	I	K
9.	A	B	G	M	N	34.	A	G	K	N	O
10.	A	B	H	K	O	35.	A	H	I	L	N
11.	A	B	I	K	N	36.	A	H	J	N	O
12.	A	C	D	F	O	37.	A	H	L	M	O
13.	A	C	D	K	M	38.	A	I	J	L	N
14.	A	C	E	H	J	39.	B	C	D	E	M
15.	A	C	E	I	N	40.	B	C	D	H	N
16.	A	C	F	K	M	41.	B	C	D	I	O
17.	A	C	G	I	K	42.	B	C	E	K	M
18.	A	C	H	L	M	43.	B	C	F	K	L
19.	A	C	I	L	O	44.	B	C	F	N	O
20.	A	C	K	L	N	45.	B	C	G	I	M
21.	A	D	E	F	K	46.	B	C	G	J	N
22.	A	D	E	G	L	47.	B	C	H	I	K
23.	A	D	F	I	J	48.	B	C	L	N	O
24.	A	D	F	M	N	49.	B	D	E	H	O
25.	A	D	G	H	I	50.	B	D	E	I	N

(Continued Next Page)
112

BALANCED WHEEL™ 54115 (Continued from previous page)

#							#					
51.	B	D	F	G	K		85.	C	I	K	N	O
52.	B	D	F	G	L		86.	C	J	M	N	O
53.	B	D	H	I	M		87.	D	E	F	H	L
54.	B	D	M	N	O		88.	D	E	G	H	M
55.	B	E	F	H	M		89.	D	E	G	I	J
56.	B	E	F	I	J		90.	D	E	I	K	L
57.	B	E	G	H	L		91.	D	F	I	N	O
58.	B	E	J	K	N		92.	D	F	J	M	O
59.	B	F	H	J	L		93.	D	F	K	M	N
60.	B	F	I	K	O		94.	D	G	H	J	L
61.	B	F	I	L	M		95.	D	G	H	K	N
62.	B	G	I	N	O		96.	D	G	I	L	M
63.	B	G	J	M	O		97.	D	I	J	K	O
64.	B	I	K	L	M		98.	D	K	L	M	O
65.	B	J	K	L	N		99.	E	F	G	H	O
66.	C	D	F	I	M		100.	E	F	G	I	K
67.	C	D	F	J	N		101.	E	F	G	I	N
68.	C	D	G	N	O		102.	E	F	H	K	O
69.	C	D	H	K	L		103.	E	F	H	L	M
70.	C	D	L	N	O		104.	E	G	K	L	O
71.	C	E	F	G	M		105.	E	H	L	M	N
72.	C	E	G	K	N		106.	E	I	K	N	O
73.	C	E	H	I	L		107.	E	I	L	M	O
74.	C	E	H	J	K		108.	E	J	L	M	N
75.	C	E	J	L	O		109.	F	G	H	I	M
76.	C	E	K	N	O		110.	F	G	M	N	O
77.	C	F	G	H	N		111.	F	H	I	J	K
78.	C	F	G	I	O		112.	F	H	K	L	N
79.	C	F	L	N	O		113.	G	H	J	K	M
80.	C	G	J	K	O		114.	G	I	K	L	M
81.	C	G	L	N	O		115.	G	J	K	N	O
82.	C	H	I	J	N		116.	H	I	J	L	O
83.	C	H	J	M	O		117.	H	I	J	M	N
84.	C	I	J	L	M		118.	H	I	K	M	N

BALANCED WHEEL™ 54116
Wheeling 16 Numbers in 159 games for a 4 of 5 Win

NUMBERS CORRECT	MAXIMUM WINS				MINIMUM WINS			
	5x	4x	3x	2x	5x	4x	3x	2x
5 (w/o Jackpot)	0	7	13	59				
5	1	3	29	44	0	1	15	66
4	–	4	4	58	–	0	6	51
3	–	–	8	40	–	–	0	31
2	–	–	–	22	–	–	–	9

Your 16 Numbers to Wheel

A	B	C	D	E	F	G	H
50	47	52	52	52	48	52	52

I	J	K	L	M	N	O	P
48	48	52	47	50	48	47	50

The 159 Games to Play

#						#					
1.	A	B	E	F	J	26.	A	D	G	H	N
2.	A	B	E	F	O	27.	A	D	G	M	P
3.	A	B	E	I	N	28.	A	D	H	J	P
4.	A	B	E	L	M	29.	A	D	J	K	M
5.	A	B	F	I	M	30.	A	D	K	N	P
6.	A	B	F	L	N	31.	A	E	F	I	J
7.	A	B	I	J	L	32.	A	E	F	L	M
8.	A	B	I	L	O	33.	A	E	F	N	O
9.	A	B	J	M	O	34.	A	E	G	K	M
10.	A	B	M	N	O	35.	A	E	G	N	P
11.	A	C	D	E	P	36.	A	E	H	J	N
12.	A	C	D	G	K	37.	A	E	H	M	P
13.	A	C	D	H	M	38.	A	E	I	J	O
14.	A	C	D	J	N	39.	A	E	I	L	M
15.	A	C	E	G	H	40.	A	E	J	K	P
16.	A	C	E	J	M	41.	A	E	L	M	O
17.	A	C	E	K	N	42.	A	F	I	L	N
18.	A	C	G	J	P	43.	A	F	I	M	O
19.	A	C	G	M	N	44.	A	F	J	L	O
20.	A	C	H	J	K	45.	A	G	H	J	M
21.	A	C	H	N	P	46.	A	G	H	K	P
22.	A	C	K	M	P	47.	A	G	J	K	N
23.	A	D	E	G	J	48.	A	H	K	M	N
24.	A	D	E	H	K	49.	A	I	L	N	O
25.	A	D	E	M	N	50.	A	J	M	N	P

114

(Continued Next Page)

BALANCED WHEEL™ 54116 (Continued from previous page)

#	1	2	3	4	5		#	1	2	3	4	5
51.	B	C	D	F	L		86.	B	I	L	M	N
52.	B	C	D	H	I		87.	B	J	L	N	O
53.	B	C	D	K	O		88.	C	D	E	G	N
54.	B	C	F	G	H		89.	C	D	E	H	J
55.	B	C	F	I	K		90.	C	D	E	K	M
56.	B	C	F	O	P		91.	C	D	F	G	I
57.	B	C	G	I	O		92.	C	D	F	H	O
58.	B	C	G	K	L		93.	C	D	G	H	P
59.	B	C	H	L	O		94.	C	D	G	J	M
60.	B	C	I	L	P		95.	C	D	G	L	O
61.	B	D	F	G	K		96.	C	D	H	K	N
62.	B	D	F	H	P		97.	C	D	I	K	L
63.	B	D	G	H	O		98.	C	D	I	O	P
64.	B	D	G	I	L		99.	C	D	J	K	P
65.	B	D	H	K	L		100.	C	D	M	N	P
66.	B	D	I	K	P		101.	C	E	G	J	K
67.	B	D	L	O	P		102.	C	E	G	M	P
68.	B	E	F	I	L		103.	C	E	H	K	P
69.	B	E	F	M	N		104.	C	E	H	M	N
70.	B	E	I	J	M		105.	C	E	J	N	P
71.	B	E	I	M	O		106.	C	F	G	K	O
72.	B	E	J	L	O		107.	C	F	G	L	P
73.	B	E	L	N	O		108.	C	F	H	I	P
74.	B	F	G	I	P		109.	C	F	H	K	L
75.	B	F	H	K	O		110.	C	G	H	I	L
76.	B	F	I	J	N		111.	C	G	H	J	N
77.	B	F	I	J	O		112.	C	G	H	K	M
78.	B	F	I	N	O		113.	C	G	K	N	P
79.	B	F	J	L	M		114.	C	H	I	K	O
80.	B	F	K	L	P		115.	C	H	J	M	P
81.	B	F	L	M	O		116.	C	J	K	M	N
82.	B	G	H	I	K		117.	C	K	L	O	P
83.	B	G	H	L	P		118.	D	E	G	H	M
84.	B	G	K	O	P		119.	D	E	G	K	P
85.	B	H	I	O	P		120.	D	E	H	N	P

          (Continued Next Page)

BALANCED WHEEL™ 54116 (Continued from previous page)

121.	D	E	J	K	N	141.	E	G	J	M	N

#						#					
121.	D	E	J	K	N	141.	E	G	J	M	N
122.	D	E	J	M	P	142.	E	H	J	K	M
123.	D	F	G	H	L	143.	E	I	J	L	N
124.	D	F	G	O	P	144.	E	I	M	N	O
125.	D	F	H	I	K	145.	E	K	M	N	P
126.	D	F	I	L	P	146.	F	G	H	I	O
127.	D	F	K	L	O	147.	F	G	I	K	L
128.	D	G	H	J	K	148.	F	H	L	O	P
129.	D	G	I	K	O	149.	F	I	J	L	M
130.	D	G	J	N	P	150.	F	I	J	N	O
131.	D	G	K	M	N	151.	F	I	K	O	P
132.	D	H	I	L	O	152.	F	L	M	N	O
133.	D	H	J	M	N	153.	G	H	K	L	O
134.	D	H	K	M	P	154.	G	H	M	N	P
135.	E	F	I	L	O	155.	G	I	L	O	P
136.	E	F	I	M	N	156.	G	J	K	M	P
137.	E	F	J	L	N	157.	H	I	K	L	P
138.	E	F	J	M	O	158.	H	J	K	N	P
139.	E	G	H	J	P	159.	I	J	L	M	O
140.	E	G	H	K	N						

BALANCED WHEEL™ 54117
Wheeling 17 Numbers in 217 games for a 4 of 5 Win

NUMBERS CORRECT	MAXIMUM WINS				MINIMUM WINS			
	5x	4x	3x	2x	5x	4x	3x	2x
5 (w/o Jackpot)	0	7	31	79				
5	1	3	36	76	0	1	17	82
4	–	2	20	78	–	0	7	57
3	–	–	8	51	–	–	0	37
2	–	–	–	26	–	–	–	10

Your 17 Numbers to Wheel

A	B	C	D	E	F	G	H	I
52	69	67	68	68	70	70	70	67

J	K	L	M	N	O	P	Q
70	70	52	52	52	52	68	68

The 217 Games to Play

#						#					
1.	A	B	C	E	L	3.	A	B	C	O	P
2.	A	B	C	M	N	4.	A	B	D	E	O

                    (Continued Next Page)

BALANCED WHEEL™ 54117 (Continued from previous page)

#						#					
5.	A	B	D	L	M	40.	A	G	J	L	N
6.	A	B	D	N	P	41.	A	G	K	L	O
7.	A	B	E	M	P	42.	A	H	I	K	L
8.	A	B	E	N	Q	43.	A	H	I	M	N
9.	A	B	L	P	Q	44.	A	H	J	K	O
10.	A	B	M	O	Q	45.	A	H	J	L	M
11.	A	C	D	E	N	46.	A	H	L	N	O
12.	A	C	D	L	O	47.	A	I	J	K	N
13.	A	C	D	M	P	48.	A	I	J	L	O
14.	A	C	E	M	O	49.	A	I	K	M	O
15.	A	C	L	M	Q	50.	A	J	M	N	O
16.	A	C	L	N	P	51.	A	K	L	M	N
17.	A	C	N	O	Q	52.	A	M	N	P	Q
18.	A	D	E	L	P	53.	B	C	D	E	Q
19.	A	D	E	M	Q	54.	B	C	D	F	K
20.	A	D	L	N	Q	55.	B	C	D	G	Q
21.	A	D	O	P	Q	56.	B	C	D	H	J
22.	A	E	L	O	Q	57.	B	C	D	I	P
23.	A	E	N	O	P	58.	B	C	D	N	O
24.	A	F	G	H	L	59.	B	C	E	F	I
25.	A	F	G	J	O	60.	B	C	E	G	K
26.	A	F	G	M	N	61.	B	C	E	H	J
27.	A	F	H	I	Q	62.	B	C	E	K	P
28.	A	F	H	J	N	63.	B	C	F	G	H
29.	A	F	H	K	M	64.	B	C	F	I	Q
30.	A	F	I	J	M	65.	B	C	F	J	P
31.	A	F	I	L	N	66.	B	C	G	I	J
32.	A	F	J	K	L	67.	B	C	G	K	P
33.	A	F	K	N	O	68.	B	C	H	I	K
34.	A	F	L	M	O	69.	B	C	H	P	Q
35.	A	G	H	K	N	70.	B	C	J	K	Q
36.	A	G	H	M	O	71.	B	C	L	M	O
37.	A	G	I	L	M	72.	B	C	L	N	Q
38.	A	G	I	N	O	73.	B	D	E	F	G
39.	A	G	J	K	M	74.	B	D	E	H	I

                (Continued Next Page)

BALANCED WHEEL™ 54117 (Continued from previous page)

#						#					
75.	B	D	E	I	P	110.	B	L	M	N	P
76.	B	D	E	J	K	111.	B	N	O	P	Q
77.	B	D	E	L	N	112.	C	D	E	F	J
78.	B	D	F	G	J	113.	C	D	E	G	I
79.	B	D	F	H	I	114.	C	D	E	H	K
80.	B	D	F	P	Q	115.	C	D	E	J	P
81.	B	D	G	H	P	116.	C	D	F	G	P
82.	B	D	G	I	K	117.	C	D	F	H	Q
83.	B	D	H	K	Q	118.	C	D	F	I	J
84.	B	D	I	J	Q	119.	C	D	G	H	I
85.	B	D	J	K	P	120.	C	D	G	J	K
86.	B	D	L	O	Q	121.	C	D	H	K	P
87.	B	D	M	N	Q	122.	C	D	I	K	Q
88.	B	D	M	O	P	123.	C	D	J	P	Q
89.	B	E	F	H	K	124.	C	D	L	M	N
90.	B	E	F	J	Q	125.	C	D	M	O	Q
91.	B	E	F	K	P	126.	C	E	F	G	H
92.	B	E	G	H	Q	127.	C	E	F	H	P
93.	B	E	G	I	J	128.	C	E	F	K	Q
94.	B	E	G	J	P	129.	C	E	G	J	Q
95.	B	E	H	P	Q	130.	C	E	G	P	Q
96.	B	E	I	K	Q	131.	C	E	H	I	Q
97.	B	E	L	M	Q	132.	C	E	I	J	K
98.	B	E	L	O	P	133.	C	E	I	J	P
99.	B	E	M	N	O	134.	C	E	L	M	P
100.	B	F	G	I	P	135.	C	E	L	N	O
101.	B	F	G	K	Q	136.	C	E	M	N	Q
102.	B	F	H	J	Q	137.	C	F	G	I	K
103.	B	F	H	K	P	138.	C	F	G	J	Q
104.	B	F	I	J	K	139.	C	F	H	I	P
105.	B	G	H	I	Q	140.	C	F	H	J	K
106.	B	G	H	J	K	141.	C	F	K	P	Q
107.	B	G	J	P	Q	142.	C	G	H	J	P
108.	B	H	I	J	P	143.	C	G	H	K	Q
109.	B	I	K	P	Q	144.	C	G	I	P	Q

     (Continued Next Page)

BALANCED WHEEL™ 54117 (Continued from previous page)

#						#					
145.	C	H	I	J	Q	180.	E	I	K	P	Q
146.	C	I	J	K	P	181.	E	L	N	P	Q
147.	C	L	O	P	Q	182.	E	M	O	P	Q
148.	C	M	N	O	P	183.	F	G	H	I	J
149.	D	E	F	H	P	184.	F	G	H	N	O
150.	D	E	F	H	Q	185.	F	G	H	P	Q
151.	D	E	F	I	K	186.	F	G	I	L	O
152.	D	E	G	H	J	187.	F	G	J	K	P
153.	D	E	G	K	P	188.	F	G	J	L	M
154.	D	E	G	K	Q	189.	F	G	K	L	N
155.	D	E	I	J	Q	190.	F	G	K	M	O
156.	D	E	L	M	O	191.	F	H	I	K	Q
157.	D	E	M	N	P	192.	F	H	J	M	O
158.	D	E	N	O	Q	193.	F	H	K	L	O
159.	D	F	G	H	K	194.	F	H	L	M	N
160.	D	F	G	I	Q	195.	F	I	J	P	Q
161.	D	F	H	J	P	196.	F	I	K	L	M
162.	D	F	I	K	P	197.	F	I	M	N	O
163.	D	F	J	K	Q	198.	F	J	K	M	N
164.	D	G	H	J	Q	199.	F	J	L	N	O
165.	D	G	I	J	P	200.	G	H	I	K	P
166.	D	G	K	L	Q	201.	G	H	I	L	N
167.	D	H	I	J	K	202.	G	H	J	L	O
168.	D	H	I	P	Q	203.	G	H	J	M	N
169.	D	L	M	P	Q	204.	G	H	K	L	M
170.	D	L	N	O	P	205.	G	I	J	K	Q
171.	E	F	G	I	P	206.	G	I	J	M	O
172.	E	F	G	I	Q	207.	G	I	K	M	N
173.	E	F	G	J	K	208.	G	J	K	N	O
174.	E	F	H	I	J	209.	G	L	M	N	O
175.	E	F	J	P	Q	210.	H	I	J	N	O
176.	E	G	H	I	K	211.	H	I	L	M	O
177.	E	G	H	I	P	212.	H	J	K	L	N
178.	E	H	J	K	P	213.	H	J	K	P	Q
179.	E	H	J	K	Q	214.	H	K	M	N	O

                    (Continued Next Page)

BALANCED WHEEL™ 54117 (Continued from previous page)

215.	I	J	L	M	N
216.	I	K	L	N	O

217.	J	K	L	M	O

BALANCED WHEEL™ 54118
Wheeling 18 Numbers in 285 games for a 4 of 5 Win

NUMBERS CORRECT	MAXIMUM WINS				MINIMUM WINS			
	5x	4x	3x	2x	5x	4x	3x	2x
5 (w/o Jackpot)	0	8	18	94				
5	1	5	23	85	0	1	19	101
4	–	3	11	68	–	0	7	71
3	–	–	9	62	–	–	0	43
2	–	–	–	31	–	–	–	13

Your 18 Numbers to Wheel

A	B	C	D	E	F	G	H	I
81	73	84	74	83	74	82	82	82

J	K	L	M	N	O	P	Q	R
82	81	75	70	79	81	76	83	83

The 285 Games to Play

1.	A	B	D	G	P
2.	A	B	D	H	O
3.	A	B	D	N	Q
4.	A	B	F	G	Q
5.	A	B	F	H	M
6.	A	B	F	H	P
7.	A	B	F	N	O
8.	A	B	G	L	O
9.	A	B	G	M	Q
10.	A	B	H	L	Q
11.	A	B	L	M	O
12.	A	B	L	N	P
13.	A	B	M	N	P
14.	A	B	O	P	Q
15.	A	C	E	G	K
16.	A	C	E	H	I
17.	A	C	E	I	N
18.	A	C	E	J	O
19.	A	C	E	Q	R
20.	A	C	G	H	R

21.	A	C	G	I	O
22.	A	C	G	J	Q
23.	A	C	G	K	N
24.	A	C	H	J	K
25.	A	C	H	N	R
26.	A	C	H	O	Q
27.	A	C	I	J	R
28.	A	C	I	K	Q
29.	A	C	J	N	Q
30.	A	C	K	N	O
31.	A	C	K	O	R
32.	A	D	F	G	H
33.	A	D	F	M	Q
34.	A	D	F	N	P
35.	A	D	F	O	Q
36.	A	D	G	L	Q
37.	A	D	G	M	O
38.	A	D	H	L	N
39.	A	D	H	M	N
40.	A	D	H	P	Q

          (Continued Next Page)

BALANCED WHEEL™ 54118 (Continued from previous page)

#						#					
41.	A	D	L	O	P	76.	A	H	M	P	Q
42.	A	E	G	H	O	77.	A	I	J	N	O
43.	A	E	G	I	Q	78.	A	I	J	O	Q
44.	A	E	G	J	R	79.	A	J	K	N	R
45.	A	E	G	N	R	80.	A	J	K	Q	R
46.	A	E	H	J	Q	81.	A	N	O	Q	R
47.	A	E	H	K	R	82.	B	C	D	E	P
48.	A	E	H	N	O	83.	B	C	D	F	L
49.	A	E	I	J	K	84.	B	C	D	I	J
50.	A	E	I	K	N	85.	B	C	D	K	R
51.	A	E	I	O	R	86.	B	C	D	M	R
52.	A	E	J	N	Q	87.	B	C	E	F	I
53.	A	E	K	O	Q	88.	B	C	E	I	M
54.	A	F	G	L	N	89.	B	C	E	L	R
55.	A	F	G	M	N	90.	B	C	F	J	R
56.	A	F	G	O	P	91.	B	C	F	K	P
57.	A	F	H	L	O	92.	B	C	I	K	L
58.	A	F	L	P	Q	93.	B	C	I	P	R
59.	A	F	M	O	P	94.	B	C	J	I	P
60.	A	G	H	I	J	95.	B	C	J	M	P
61.	A	G	H	J	N	96.	B	C	K	L	M
62.	A	G	H	K	Q	97.	B	D	E	F	R
63.	A	G	H	L	P	98.	B	D	E	I	K
64.	A	G	H	M	P	99.	B	D	E	J	L
65.	A	G	I	K	R	100.	B	D	E	J	M
66.	A	G	I	N	Q	101.	B	D	F	G	O
67.	A	G	J	K	O	102.	B	D	F	H	N
68.	A	G	L	M	N	103.	B	D	F	I	P
69.	A	G	O	Q	R	104.	B	D	F	J	K
70.	A	H	I	K	O	105.	B	D	G	H	Q
71.	A	H	I	N	R	106.	B	D	G	M	N
72.	A	H	I	Q	R	107.	B	D	H	M	Q
73.	A	H	J	O	R	108.	B	D	I	K	M
74.	A	H	K	N	Q	109.	B	D	I	L	R
75.	A	H	L	M	Q	110.	B	D	J	P	R

                    (Continued Next Page)

121

BALANCED WHEEL™ 54118 (Continued from previous page)

#						#					
111.	B	D	K	L	P	146.	C	D	I	K	P
112.	B	D	L	O	Q	147.	C	D	I	L	M
113.	B	D	N	O	P	148.	C	D	J	K	L
114.	B	E	F	J	P	149.	C	D	J	K	M
115.	B	E	F	K	L	150.	C	D	L	M	R
116.	B	E	I	L	P	151.	C	D	L	P	R
117.	B	E	K	M	P	152.	C	E	F	I	M
118.	B	E	K	P	R	153.	C	E	F	J	L
119.	B	E	L	M	R	154.	C	E	F	J	M
120.	B	F	G	H	L	155.	C	E	F	P	R
121.	B	F	G	M	O	156.	C	E	G	H	N
122.	B	F	G	N	P	157.	C	E	G	H	Q
123.	B	F	H	O	Q	158.	C	E	G	I	J
124.	B	F	I	J	L	159.	C	E	G	O	R
125.	B	F	I	K	R	160.	C	E	H	J	R
126.	B	F	L	P	R	161.	C	E	H	K	O
127.	B	F	M	N	Q	162.	C	E	I	N	Q
128.	B	G	H	L	M	163.	C	E	I	O	Q
129.	B	G	H	O	P	164.	C	E	J	K	Q
130.	B	G	L	N	Q	165.	C	E	J	L	M
131.	B	G	L	P	Q	166.	C	E	J	N	O
132.	B	H	L	N	O	167.	C	E	K	L	P
133.	B	H	M	N	O	168.	C	E	K	N	R
134.	B	H	N	P	Q	169.	C	F	I	L	P
135.	B	I	J	K	P	170.	C	F	I	M	P
136.	B	I	J	L	M	171.	C	F	K	L	M
137.	B	I	M	P	R	172.	C	F	L	M	R
138.	B	J	K	L	R	173.	C	G	H	I	K
139.	B	J	K	M	R	174.	C	G	H	J	O
140.	B	M	O	P	Q	175.	C	G	I	K	N
141.	C	D	E	F	K	176.	C	G	I	Q	R
142.	C	D	E	I	L	177.	C	G	J	K	R
143.	C	D	E	M	P	178.	C	G	J	N	Q
144.	C	D	F	I	R	179.	C	G	K	O	Q
145.	C	D	F	J	P	180.	C	G	N	O	R

    (Continued Next Page)

BALANCED WHEEL™ 54118 (Continued from previous page)

#						#					
181.	C	H	I	J	Q	216.	D	I	J	L	P
182.	C	H	I	N	O	217.	D	I	J	M	P
183.	C	H	I	O	R	218.	D	J	L	M	P
184.	C	H	J	K	N	219.	D	K	M	P	R
185.	C	H	K	Q	R	220.	D	M	N	P	Q
186.	C	H	N	Q	R	221.	E	F	I	K	P
187.	C	I	J	K	O	222.	E	F	I	L	R
188.	C	I	J	N	R	223.	E	F	J	K	M
189.	C	J	K	M	P	224.	E	F	L	M	R
190.	C	J	O	Q	R	225.	E	G	H	I	R
191.	C	K	N	O	Q	226.	F	G	H	J	K
192.	C	L	M	P	R	227.	E	G	I	K	O
193.	D	E	F	I	J	228.	E	G	I	N	O
194.	D	E	F	L	P	229.	E	G	J	N	R
195.	D	E	I	M	R	230.	E	G	J	O	Q
196.	D	E	I	P	R	231.	E	G	K	N	Q
197.	D	E	J	K	P	232.	E	G	K	Q	R
198.	D	E	K	L	M	233.	E	H	I	J	O
199.	D	E	K	L	R	234.	E	H	I	K	Q
200.	D	F	G	H	M	235.	E	H	I	N	R
201.	D	F	G	N	Q	236.	E	H	J	N	Q
202.	D	F	H	L	Q	237.	E	H	K	N	O
203.	D	F	H	O	P	238.	E	H	O	Q	R
204.	D	F	I	K	L	239.	E	I	J	K	N
205.	D	F	J	L	R	240.	E	I	J	Q	R
206.	D	F	J	M	R	241.	E	I	L	M	P
207.	D	F	K	P	R	242.	E	J	K	O	R
208.	D	F	L	N	O	243.	E	J	L	P	R
209.	D	F	M	N	O	244.	E	J	M	P	R
210.	D	G	H	L	O	245.	E	N	O	Q	R
211.	D	G	H	N	P	246.	F	G	H	P	Q
212.	D	G	L	N	Q	247.	F	G	L	O	Q
213.	D	G	M	O	Q	248.	F	G	M	P	Q
214.	D	G	O	P	Q	249.	F	H	L	N	P
215.	D	H	M	O	P	250.	F	H	M	N	P

　　　(Continued Next Page)

BALANCED WHEEL™ 54118 (Continued from previous page)

251.	F	H	M	O	Q	**269.**	G	J	K	N	O
252.	F	I	J	L	M	**270.**	G	L	M	O	Q
253.	F	I	J	P	R	**271.**	G	L	N	O	P
254.	F	I	K	M	R	**272.**	G	M	N	O	P
255.	F	J	K	L	P	**273.**	H	I	J	K	R
256.	F	K	L	P	R	**274.**	H	I	K	N	Q
257.	F	L	M	N	Q	**275.**	H	J	K	O	Q
258.	F	L	N	P	Q	**276.**	H	J	N	O	R
259.	F	N	O	P	Q	**277.**	H	L	M	N	O
260.	G	H	I	J	N	**278.**	H	L	O	P	Q
261.	G	H	I	O	Q	**279.**	I	J	N	O	Q
262.	G	H	J	Q	R	**280.**	I	K	L	M	P
263.	G	H	K	N	R	**281.**	I	K	N	O	R
264.	G	H	K	O	R	**282.**	I	K	O	Q	R
265.	G	H	N	O	Q	**283.**	I	L	M	P	R
266.	G	I	J	K	Q	**284.**	J	K	L	M	R
267.	G	I	J	O	R	**285.**	J	K	N	Q	R
268.	G	I	N	Q	R						

BALANCED WHEEL™ 53006
Wheeling 6 Numbers in 4 games for a 3 of 3 Win

NUMBERS CORRECT	MAXIMUM WINS				MINIMUM WINS			
	5x	4x	3x	2x	5x	4x	3x	2x
5 (w/o Jackpot)	0	4	0	0				
5	1	3	0	0	0	4	0	0
4	–	2	2	0	–	0	4	0
3	–	–	3	1	–	–	1	3
2	–	–	–	4	–	–	–	2

Your 6 Numbers to Wheel

A	B	C	D	E	F
4	3	3	3	3	4

The 4 Games to Play

1.	A	B	C	D	F
2.	A	B	C	E	F

3.	A	B	D	E	F
4.	A	C	D	E	F

BALANCED WHEEL™ 53007
Wheeling 7 Numbers in 5 games for a 3 of 3 Win

NUMBERS CORRECT	MAXIMUM WINS				MINIMUM WINS			
	5x	4x	3x	2x	5x	4x	3x	2x
5 (w/o Jackpot)	0	3	2	0				
5	1	2	2	0	0	2	3	0
4	–	3	0	2	–	0	4	1
3	–	–	3	1	–	–	1	3
2	–	–	–	4	–	–	–	2

Your 7 Numbers to Wheel

A	B	C	D	E	F	G
4	4	3	3	3	4	4

The 5 Games to Play

1. | A | B | C | F | G |

2. | A | B | D | F | G |

3. | A | B | E | F | G |

4. | A | C | D | E | G |

5. | B | C | D | E | F |

BALANCED WHEEL™ 53008
Wheeling 8 Numbers in 8 games for a 3 of 3 Win

NUMBERS CORRECT	MAXIMUM WINS				MINIMUM WINS			
	5x	4x	3x	2x	5x	4x	3x	2x
5 (w/o Jackpot)	0	3	3	2				
5	1	0	6	1	0	2	5	1
4	–	1	3	3	–	0	4	4
3	–	–	2	3	–	–	1	5
2	–	–	–	3	–	–	–	2

Your 8 Numbers to Wheel

A	B	C	D	E	F	G	H
5	5	5	5	5	5	5	5

The 8 Games to Play

1. | A | B | C | F | H |

2. | A | B | D | E | H |

3. | A | B | E | F | G |

4. | A | C | D | E | G |

5. | A | D | F | G | H |

6. | B | C | D | F | G |

7. | B | C | E | G | H |

8. | C | D | E | F | H |

BALANCED WHEEL™ 53009
Wheeling 9 Numbers in 12 games for a 3 of 3 Win

NUMBERS CORRECT	MAXIMUM WINS				MINIMUM WINS			
	5x	4x	3x	2x	5x	4x	3x	2x
5 (w/o Jackpot)	0	4	2	6				
5	1	1	5	5	0	0	10	1
4	–	2	2	6	–	0	4	6
3	–	–	3	4	–	–	1	6
2	–	–	–	5	–	–	–	3

(Continued Next Page)

BALANCED WHEEL™ 53009 (Continued from previous page)
Your 9 Numbers to Wheel

A	B	C	D	E	F	G	H	I
7	7	7	6	6	7	6	7	7

The 12 Games to Play

1.	A	B	C	G	I	7.	A	F	G	H	I
2.	A	B	D	F	H	8.	B	C	D	F	I
3.	A	B	E	F	H	9.	B	C	E	H	I
4.	A	C	D	H	I	10.	B	C	F	G	H
5.	A	C	E	F	I	11.	B	D	E	G	I
6.	A	D	E	G	H	12.	C	D	E	F	G

Copyright © 1983-1998 Gail Howard

BALANCED WHEEL™ 53010
Wheeling 10 Numbers in 17 games for a 3 of 3 Win

NUMBERS CORRECT	MAXIMUM WINS				MINIMUM WINS			
	5x	4x	3x	2x	5x	4x	3x	2x
5 (w/o Jackpot)	0	4	3	9				
5	1	2	4	8	0	0	10	5
4	–	2	3	6	–	0	4	8
3	–	–	4	2	–	–	1	6
2	–	–	–	6	–	–	–	3

Your 10 Numbers to Wheel

A	B	C	D	E	F	G	H	I	J
9	9	8	9	8	8	9	8	9	8

The 17 Games to Play

1.	A	B	C	G	H	10.	B	C	D	G	J
2.	A	B	D	E	H	11.	B	C	E	F	I
3.	A	B	F	H	I	12.	B	D	F	G	I
4.	A	B	G	I	J	13.	B	D	F	G	J
5.	A	C	D	E	I	14.	B	E	G	H	J
6.	A	C	F	I	J	15.	C	D	F	G	H
7.	A	D	E	F	G	16.	C	E	F	H	J
8.	A	D	E	I	J	17.	C	E	G	H	I
9.	A	D	H	I	J						

Copyright © 1983-1998 Gail Howard

BALANCED WHEEL™ 53011
Wheeling 11 Numbers in 20 games for a 3 of 3 Win

NUMBERS CORRECT	MAXIMUM WINS				MINIMUM WINS			
	5x	4x	3x	2x	5x	4x	3x	2x
5 (w/o Jackpot)	0	5	0	10				
5	1	0	6	10	0	0	10	6
4	–	1	4	6	–	0	4	8
3	–	–	4	0	–	–	1	7
2	–	–	–	4	–	–	–	3

Your 11 Numbers to Wheel

A	B	C	D	E	F	G	H	I	J	K
9	9	9	9	10	9	9	9	9	9	9

The 20 Games to Play

1.	A	B	C	H	J
2.	A	B	D	G	K
3.	A	B	E	F	I
4.	A	C	D	F	J
5.	A	C	E	G	I
6.	A	C	F	H	K
7.	A	D	E	H	I
8.	A	E	I	J	K
9.	A	F	G	H	J
10.	B	C	D	I	K

11.	B	C	E	F	G
12.	B	D	E	F	H
13.	B	D	G	I	J
14.	B	E	F	J	K
15.	B	G	H	I	K
16.	C	D	E	G	H
17.	C	E	G	J	K
18.	C	F	H	I	J
19.	D	E	H	J	K
20.	D	F	G	I	K

Copyright © 1983-1998 Gail Howard

BALANCED WHEEL™ 53012
Wheeling 12 Numbers in 30 games for a 3 of 3 Win

NUMBERS CORRECT	MAXIMUM WINS				MINIMUM WINS			
	5x	4x	3x	2x	5x	4x	3x	2x
5 (w/o Jackpot)	0	4	4	13				
5	1	1	7	12	0	0	10	11
4	–	2	3	11	–	0	4	12
3	–	–	5	1	–	–	1	9
2	–	–	–	6	–	–	–	4

Your 12 Numbers to Wheel

A	B	C	D	E	F	G	H	I	J	K	L
13	12	12	14	12	12	12	12	13	12	13	13

The 30 Games to Play

1.	A	B	C	K	L
2.	A	B	D	E	K
3.	A	B	D	I	J
4.	A	B	E	G	H
5.	A	B	F	G	K

6.	A	C	D	G	I
7.	A	C	E	F	H
8.	A	C	H	J	L
9.	A	D	F	I	L
10.	A	D	H	I	K

Copyright © 1983-1998 Gail Howard   (Continued Next Page)

BALANCED WHEEL™ 53012 (Continued from previous page)

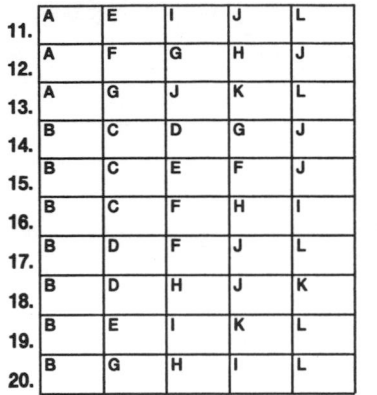

#						#					
11.	A	E	I	J	L	21.	C	D	E	G	L
12.	A	F	G	H	J	22.	C	D	F	G	L
13.	A	G	J	K	L	23.	C	D	G	H	K
14.	B	C	D	G	J	24.	C	E	I	K	L
15.	B	C	E	F	J	25.	C	F	I	J	K
16.	B	C	F	H	I	26.	D	E	F	G	I
17.	B	D	F	J	L	27.	D	E	H	I	J
18.	B	D	H	J	K	28.	D	F	H	K	L
19.	B	E	I	K	L	29.	E	F	H	K	L
20.	B	G	H	I	L	30.	E	G	I	J	K

Copyright © 1983-1998 Gail Howard

BALANCED WHEEL™ 53013
Wheeling 13 Numbers in 34 games for a 3 of 3 Win

NUMBERS CORRECT	MAXIMUM WINS				MINIMUM WINS			
	5x	4x	3x	2x	5x	4x	3x	2x
5 (w/o Jackpot)	0	2	10	6				
5	1	0	8	16	0	0	10	11
4	–	1	4	12	–	0	4	12
3	–	–	5	0	–	–	1	9
2	–	–	–	7	–	–	–	4

Your 13 Numbers to Wheel

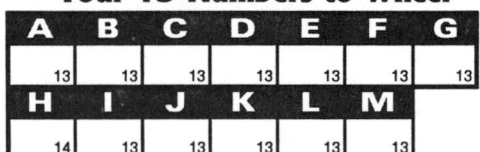

A	B	C	D	E	F	G
13	13	13	13	13	13	13

H	I	J	K	L	M
14	13	13	13	13	13

The 34 Games to Play

#						#					
1.	A	B	C	E	M	13.	A	F	G	J	K
2.	A	B	D	G	L	14.	B	C	D	F	I
3.	A	B	F	H	L	15.	B	C	G	K	L
4.	A	B	I	J	K	16.	B	C	H	J	L
5.	A	C	D	F	M	17.	B	D	E	H	K
6.	A	C	G	H	M	18.	B	D	J	L	M
7.	A	C	I	L	M	19.	B	E	F	G	J
8.	A	C	J	K	M	20.	B	E	H	I	L
9.	A	D	E	G	I	21.	B	F	K	L	M
10.	A	D	H	J	K	22.	B	G	H	I	M
11.	A	E	F	H	I	23.	C	D	E	F	L
12.	A	E	J	K	L	24.	C	D	F	G	J

Copyright © 1983-1998 Gail Howard   (Continued Next Page)

BALANCED WHEEL™ 53013 (Continued from previous page)

25.	C	D	F	H	K	30.	D	H	I	K	L
26.	C	E	G	I	K	31.	E	F	I	K	M
27.	C	E	H	I	J	32.	E	G	H	L	M
28.	D	E	I	J	M	33.	F	G	H	J	M
29.	D	G	H	K	M	34.	F	G	I	J	L

BALANCED WHEEL™ 53014
Wheeling 14 Numbers in 46 games for a 3 of 3 Win

NUMBERS CORRECT	MAXIMUM WINS				MINIMUM WINS			
	5x	4x	3x	2x	5x	4x	3x	2x
5 (w/o Jackpot)	0	4	9	15				
5	1	1	11	15	0	0	10	11
4	–	2	5	13	–	0	4	12
3	–	–	6	1	–	–	1	9
2	–	–	–	8	–	–	–	4

Your 14 Numbers to Wheel

A	B	C	D	E	F	G
18	17	18	14	13	13	18

H	I	J	K	L	M	N
18	13	17	18	18	17	18

The 46 Games to Play

1.	A	B	C	J	M	18.	A	H	L	M	N
2.	A	B	D	I	M	19.	B	C	D	K	N
3.	A	B	E	F	M	20.	B	C	E	H	L
4.	A	B	G	L	N	21.	B	C	F	K	N
5.	A	B	H	K	N	22.	B	C	G	H	K
6.	A	C	D	G	L	23.	B	C	H	I	L
7.	A	C	E	J	K	24.	B	D	E	G	J
8.	A	C	F	G	L	25.	B	D	F	H	L
9.	A	C	H	J	N	26.	B	E	I	K	N
10.	A	C	I	J	K	27.	B	F	G	I	J
11.	A	C	K	L	M	28.	B	G	H	L	M
12.	A	D	E	H	N	29.	B	H	J	K	L
13.	A	D	F	J	K	30.	B	J	K	M	N
14.	A	E	G	I	L	31.	C	D	E	F	I
15.	A	F	H	I	N	32.	C	D	H	J	M
16.	A	G	H	K	N	33.	C	E	G	M	N
17.	A	G	J	L	M	34.	C	F	H	J	M

(Continued Next Page)

129

BALANCED WHEEL™ 53014 (Continued from previous page)

35.	C	G	I	M	N
36.	C	G	J	L	N
37.	D	E	K	L	M
38.	D	F	G	M	N
39.	D	G	H	I	K
40.	D	G	K	L	N

41.	D	I	J	L	N
42.	E	F	G	H	K
43.	E	F	J	L	N
44.	E	H	I	J	M
45.	F	I	K	L	M
46.	G	H	J	K	M

BALANCED WHEEL™ 53015
Wheeling 15 Numbers in 57 games for a 3 of 3 Win

NUMBERS CORRECT	MAXIMUM WINS				MINIMUM WINS			
	5x	4x	3x	2x	5x	4x	3x	2x
5 (w/o Jackpot)	0	3	5	24				
5	1	0	10	18	0	0	10	22
4	–	1	6	12	–	0	4	19
3	–	–	6	2	–	–	1	12
2	–	–	–	7	–	–	–	5

Your 15 Numbers to Wheel

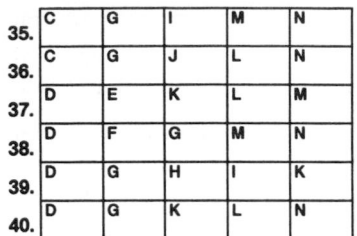

A	B	C	D	E	F	G	H
19	19	19	19	19	19	19	19

I	J	K	L	M	N	O
19	19	19	19	19	19	19

The 57 Games to Play

1.	A	B	C	H	N
2.	A	B	D	K	L
3.	A	B	E	I	J
4.	A	B	E	M	O
5.	A	B	F	G	L
6.	A	C	D	K	N
7.	A	C	E	F	O
8.	A	C	E	H	L
9.	A	C	G	H	I
10.	A	C	J	L	M
11.	A	D	E	K	M
12.	A	D	F	I	K
13.	A	D	G	J	K
14.	A	D	H	K	O
15.	A	E	G	M	N
16.	A	F	H	I	M

17.	A	F	J	L	N
18.	A	G	H	J	O
19.	A	I	L	N	O
20.	B	C	D	E	N
21.	B	C	F	J	N
22.	B	C	G	I	N
23.	B	C	K	L	N
24.	B	C	M	N	O
25.	B	D	F	G	H
26.	B	D	H	M	O
27.	B	D	I	J	L
28.	B	E	F	G	K
29.	B	E	H	L	N
30.	B	F	I	M	O
31.	B	G	J	M	O
32.	B	H	I	J	K

  (Continued Next Page)

BALANCED WHEEL™ 53015 (Continued from previous page)

#						#					
33.	B	K	L	M	O	46.	D	G	L	M	N
34.	C	D	F	L	O	47.	D	H	I	N	O
35.	C	D	G	I	L	48.	E	F	H	L	M
36.	C	D	H	J	M	49.	E	G	H	K	L
37.	C	E	G	I	K	50.	E	H	J	L	O
38.	C	E	J	K	M	51.	E	I	K	N	O
39.	C	F	G	I	M	52.	F	G	J	N	O
40.	C	F	H	K	O	53.	F	H	J	K	N
41.	C	G	I	J	O	54.	F	I	J	M	N
42.	D	E	F	I	M	55.	F	I	K	L	M
43.	D	E	F	J	N	56.	G	H	K	M	N
44.	D	E	G	J	O	57.	G	J	K	L	O
45.	D	E	H	I	L						

Copyright © 1983-1998 Gail Howard

BALANCED WHEEL™ 53016
Wheeling 16 Numbers in 67 games for a 3 of 3 Win

NUMBERS CORRECT	MAXIMUM WINS				MINIMUM WINS			
	5x	4x	3x	2x	5x	4x	3x	2x
5 (w/o Jackpot)	0	3	6	26				
5	1	0	7	31	0	0	10	20
4	–	1	5	18	–	0	4	18
3	–	–	3	11	–	–	1	12
2	–	–	–	8	–	–	–	5

Your 16 Numbers to Wheel

A	B	C	D	E	F	G	H
21	23	21	20	20	21	20	23

I	J	K	L	M	N	O	P
24	21	20	20	20	20	20	21

The 67 Games to Play

#						#					
1.	A	B	C	L	N	10.	A	C	F	G	K
2.	A	B	D	G	N	11.	A	C	H	I	K
3.	A	B	E	I	M	12.	A	D	E	I	K
4.	A	B	F	J	O	13.	A	D	F	H	J
5.	A	B	H	K	L	14.	A	D	L	O	P
6.	A	B	J	K	P	15.	A	E	F	N	P
7.	A	C	D	E	P	16.	A	E	G	J	L
8.	A	C	D	J	M	17.	A	F	I	L	M
9.	A	C	E	H	O	18.	A	G	H	M	P

Copyright © 1983-1998 Gail Howard   (Continued Next Page)

BALANCED WHEEL™ 53016 (Continued from previous page)

19.	A	G	I	O	P
20.	A	H	I	J	N
21.	A	K	M	N	O
22.	B	C	D	I	L
23.	B	C	D	K	O
24.	B	C	E	F	L
25.	B	C	G	J	P
26.	B	C	H	M	N
27.	B	D	E	H	J
28.	B	D	F	M	P
29.	B	D	G	K	M
30.	B	E	F	I	J
31.	B	E	G	K	P
32.	B	E	I	N	O
33.	B	F	G	H	I
34.	B	F	I	K	N
35.	B	G	L	M	O
36.	B	H	I	O	P
37.	B	H	J	L	M
38.	B	J	L	N	P
39.	C	D	F	I	N
40.	C	D	G	H	L
41.	C	E	G	I	M
42.	C	E	J	K	N
43.	C	F	H	J	P

44.	C	F	I	M	O
45.	C	G	N	O	P
46.	C	I	J	L	O
47.	C	I	M	N	P
48.	C	K	L	M	P
49.	D	E	F	G	O
50.	D	E	L	M	N
51.	D	F	J	K	L
52.	D	G	I	J	P
53.	D	H	I	M	O
54.	D	H	J	N	O
55.	D	H	K	N	P
56.	E	F	H	K	M
57.	E	F	K	L	O
58.	E	G	H	I	N
59.	E	H	I	L	P
60.	E	J	M	O	P
61.	F	G	H	L	P
62.	F	G	J	M	N
63.	F	H	L	N	O
64.	F	I	K	O	P
65.	G	H	J	K	O
66.	G	I	K	L	N
67.	H	I	J	K	M

Copyright © 1983-1998 Gail Howard

BALANCED WHEEL™ 53017
Wheeling 17 Numbers in 68 games for a 3 of 3 Win

NUMBERS CORRECT	MAXIMUM WINS				MINIMUM WINS			
	5x	4x	3x	2x	5x	4x	3x	2x
5 (w/o Jackpot)	0	1	6	26				
5	1	0	0	40	0	0	10	20
4	–	1	0	24	–	0	4	18
3	–	–	1	12	–	–	1	12
2	–	–	–	5	–	–	–	5

(Continued Next Page)

132

BALANCED WHEEL™ 53017 (Continued from previous page)
Your 17 Numbers to Wheel

A	B	C	D	E	F	G	H	I
20	20	20	20	20	20	20	20	20

J	K	L	M	N	O	P	Q
20	20	20	20	20	20	20	20

The 68 Games to Play

#						#					
1.	A	B	C	K	O	31.	B	F	H	I	J
2.	A	B	D	H	N	32.	B	G	I	O	P
3.	A	B	E	F	P	33.	B	H	K	L	P
4.	A	B	G	J	Q	34.	B	J	L	N	O
5.	A	B	I	L	M	35.	B	M	N	P	Q
6.	A	C	D	E	Q	36.	C	D	F	G	I
7.	A	C	F	J	M	37.	C	D	H	L	O
8.	A	C	G	L	N	38.	C	D	K	M	N
9.	A	C	H	I	P	39.	C	E	F	H	K
10.	A	D	F	K	L	40.	C	E	G	J	O
11.	A	D	G	M	P	41.	C	E	L	M	P
12.	A	D	I	J	O	42.	C	F	N	O	P
13.	A	E	G	I	K	43.	C	G	K	P	Q
14.	A	E	H	J	L	44.	C	H	J	N	Q
15.	A	E	M	N	O	45.	C	I	J	K	L
16.	A	F	G	H	O	46.	C	I	M	O	Q
17.	A	F	I	N	Q	47.	D	E	F	J	N
18.	A	H	K	M	Q	48.	D	E	H	I	M
19.	A	J	K	N	P	49.	D	E	K	O	P
20.	A	L	O	P	Q	50.	D	F	H	P	Q
21.	B	C	D	J	P	51.	D	G	H	J	K
22.	B	C	E	I	N	52.	D	G	N	O	Q
23.	B	C	F	L	Q	53.	D	I	L	N	P
24.	B	C	G	H	M	54.	D	J	L	M	Q
25.	B	D	E	G	L	55.	E	F	G	M	Q
26.	B	D	F	M	O	56.	E	F	I	L	O
27.	B	D	I	K	Q	57.	E	G	H	N	P
28.	B	E	H	O	Q	58.	E	I	J	P	Q
29.	B	E	J	K	M	59.	E	K	L	N	Q
30.	B	F	G	K	N	60.	F	G	J	L	P

(Continued Next Page)

BALANCED WHEEL™ 53017 (Continued from previous page)

61. F	H	L	M	N
62. F	I	K	M	P
63. F	J	K	O	Q
64. G	H	I	L	Q

65. G	I	J	M	N
66. G	K	L	M	O
67. H	I	K	N	O
68. H	J	M	O	P

Copyright © 1983-1998 Gail Howard

BALANCED WHEEL™ 53018
Wheeling 18 Numbers in 94 games for a 3 of 3 Win

NUMBERS CORRECT	MAXIMUM WINS				MINIMUM WINS			
	5x	4x	3x	2x	5x	4x	3x	2x
5 (w/o Jackpot)	0	3	6	29				
5	1	1	6	33	0	0	10	30
4	–	2	1	26	–	0	4	24
3	–	–	3	12	–	–	1	15
2	–	–	–	7	–	–	–	6

Your 18 Numbers to Wheel

A	B	C	D	E	F	G	H	I
26	26	26	26	26	26	26	26	26

J	K	L	M	N	O	P	Q	R
26	26	27	26	26	27	26	26	26

The 94 Games to Play

1.	A	B	C	H	N
2.	A	B	D	M	P
3.	A	B	E	I	O
4.	A	B	F	G	K
5.	A	B	F	G	Q
6.	A	B	J	L	R
7.	A	C	D	G	R
8.	A	C	E	J	K
9.	A	C	F	I	P
10.	A	C	I	M	Q
11.	A	C	L	M	O
12.	A	D	E	F	L
13.	A	D	H	K	O
14.	A	D	I	J	N
15.	A	D	J	O	Q
16.	A	E	G	M	N
17.	A	E	H	P	R
18.	A	E	K	Q	R
19.	A	F	H	J	M
20.	A	F	N	O	Q
21.	A	F	N	O	R
22.	A	G	H	I	L
23.	A	G	J	O	P
24.	A	H	L	P	Q
25.	A	I	K	M	R
26.	A	K	L	N	P
27.	B	C	D	E	Q
28.	B	C	D	K	L
29.	B	C	E	F	M
30.	B	C	G	I	J
31.	B	C	O	P	R
32.	B	D	E	H	J
33.	B	D	F	I	R
34.	B	D	G	N	O
35.	B	E	G	L	P
36.	B	E	K	N	R

Copyright © 1983-1998 Gail Howard   (Continued Next Page)

BALANCED WHEEL™ 53018 (Continued from previous page)

#						#					
37.	B	F	H	L	O	66.	D	F	M	P	Q
38.	B	F	J	N	P	67.	D	G	H	Q	R
39.	B	G	H	M	R	68.	D	G	J	L	M
40.	B	H	I	J	Q	69.	D	G	K	N	Q
41.	B	H	I	K	P	70.	D	H	L	N	R
42.	B	I	L	M	N	71.	D	I	K	L	Q
43.	B	I	N	P	Q	72.	D	I	L	O	P
44.	B	J	K	M	O	73.	D	J	K	P	R
45.	B	K	O	P	Q	74.	E	F	G	J	R
46.	B	L	M	Q	R	75.	E	F	H	I	N
47.	C	D	E	N	P	76.	E	F	J	L	Q
48.	C	D	F	J	O	77.	E	F	K	O	P
49.	C	D	H	I	M	78.	E	G	I	P	Q
50.	C	E	G	H	O	79.	E	H	K	L	M
51.	C	E	I	L	R	80.	E	H	M	O	Q
52.	C	F	G	L	N	81.	E	I	J	M	P
53.	C	F	H	K	Q	82.	E	J	L	N	O
54.	C	F	H	K	R	83.	E	J	N	Q	R
55.	C	G	K	M	P	84.	F	G	I	M	O
56.	C	G	L	O	Q	85.	F	I	J	K	L
57.	C	H	J	L	P	86.	F	I	O	Q	R
58.	C	I	K	N	O	87.	F	L	M	P	R
59.	C	J	M	N	R	88.	G	H	J	K	N
60.	C	J	P	Q	R	89.	G	I	N	P	R
61.	C	L	N	O	Q	90.	G	J	K	M	Q
62.	D	E	G	I	K	91.	G	K	L	O	R
63.	D	E	M	O	R	92.	H	I	J	O	R
64.	D	F	G	H	P	93.	H	L	M	N	Q
65.	D	F	K	M	N	94.	H	M	N	O	P

BALANCED WHEEL™ 53019
Wheeling 19 Numbers in 117 games for a 3 of 3 Win

NUMBERS CORRECT	MAXIMUM WINS				MINIMUM WINS			
	5x	4x	3x	2x	5x	4x	3x	2x
5 (w/o Jackpot)	0	5	10	31				
5	1	3	9	37	0	0	10	30
4	–	3	5	30	–	0	4	24
3	–	–	8	15	–	–	1	15
2	–	–	–	23	–	–	–	6

Your 19 Numbers to Wheel

A	B	C	D	E	F	G	H	I	J
29	28	36	32	29	31	30	31	30	30

K	L	M	N	O	P	Q	R	S
31	30	29	31	31	36	31	30	30

The 117 Games to Play

#						#					
1.	A	B	C	P	Q	26.	A	H	N	O	R
2.	A	B	D	G	O	27.	A	I	K	O	Q
3.	A	B	E	J	K	28.	A	J	M	O	S
4.	A	B	F	N	S	29.	A	K	L	M	N
5.	A	B	H	M	Q	30.	B	C	D	H	P
6.	A	B	I	L	R	31.	B	C	E	G	P
7.	A	C	D	J	P	32.	B	C	F	P	R
8.	A	C	E	I	P	33.	B	C	I	M	P
9.	A	C	F	G	S	34.	B	C	J	N	P
10.	A	C	H	P	S	35.	B	C	K	O	P
11.	A	C	K	P	R	36.	B	C	L	P	S
12.	A	C	L	M	P	37.	B	D	E	I	Q
13.	A	C	N	O	P	38.	B	D	F	L	M
14.	A	D	E	M	R	39.	B	D	H	J	S
15.	A	D	F	H	K	40.	B	D	K	N	R
16.	A	D	I	J	N	41.	B	E	F	H	R
17.	A	D	L	Q	S	42.	B	E	G	L	S
18.	A	E	F	L	O	43.	B	E	M	N	O
19.	A	E	G	N	Q	44.	B	F	G	K	Q
20.	A	E	H	I	S	45.	B	F	I	J	O
21.	A	F	G	I	M	46.	B	G	H	I	N
22.	A	F	G	P	S	47.	B	G	J	M	R
23.	A	F	J	Q	R	48.	B	H	K	L	O
24.	A	G	H	J	L	49.	B	I	K	M	S
25.	A	G	K	R	S	50.	B	J	L	N	Q

(Continued Next Page)

BALANCED WHEEL™ 53019 (Continued from previous page)

#						#					
51.	B	O	Q	R	S	85.	D	J	K	M	Q
52.	C	D	E	F	Q	86.	D	J	L	O	R
53.	C	D	F	H	I	87.	D	L	N	P	R
54.	C	D	G	J	K	88.	D	M	O	P	S
55.	C	D	L	N	R	89.	E	F	I	K	N
56.	C	D	M	O	S	90.	E	F	M	Q	S
57.	C	E	H	K	L	91.	E	G	H	K	M
58.	C	E	J	M	P	92.	E	G	I	O	R
59.	C	E	N	P	S	93.	E	H	J	O	Q
60.	C	E	O	P	R	94.	E	H	K	L	P
61.	C	F	J	L	O	95.	E	I	J	L	M
62.	C	F	K	M	N	96.	E	J	N	R	S
63.	C	G	H	N	O	97.	E	K	L	Q	R
64.	C	G	I	L	Q	98.	F	G	H	O	S
65.	C	G	M	P	R	99.	F	G	L	N	R
66.	C	H	J	Q	R	100.	F	H	I	L	Q
67.	C	H	M	P	Q	101.	F	H	J	M	N
68.	C	I	J	P	S	102.	F	J	K	L	S
69.	C	I	K	P	R	103.	F	J	L	O	P
70.	C	I	N	O	Q	104.	F	K	M	N	P
71.	C	K	P	Q	S	105.	F	K	M	O	R
72.	C	K	P	R	S	106.	G	H	N	O	P
73.	D	E	F	G	J	107.	G	I	J	Q	S
74.	D	E	F	P	Q	108.	G	I	L	P	Q
75.	D	E	H	L	N	109.	G	J	K	N	O
76.	D	E	K	O	S	110.	G	L	M	O	Q
77.	D	F	H	I	P	111.	H	I	J	K	R
78.	D	F	I	R	S	112.	H	J	P	Q	R
79.	D	F	N	O	Q	113.	H	K	N	Q	S
80.	D	G	H	Q	R	114.	H	L	M	R	S
81.	D	G	I	K	L	115.	I	L	N	O	S
82.	D	G	J	K	P	116.	I	M	N	Q	R
83.	D	G	M	N	S	117.	I	N	O	P	Q
84.	D	H	I	M	O						

BALANCED WHEEL™ 53020
Wheeling 20 Numbers in 146 games for a 3 of 3 Win

NUMBERS CORRECT	MAXIMUM WINS				MINIMUM WINS			
	5x	4x	3x	2x	5x	4x	3x	2x
5 (w/o Jackpot)	0	6	17	42				
5	1	2	21	45	0	0	10	36
4	–	3	13	39	–	0	4	27
3	–	–	9	40	–	–	1	16
2	–	–	–	47	–	–	–	6

Your 20 Numbers to Wheel

A	B	C	D	E	F	G	H	I	J
52	34	35	34	37	34	34	34	34	35

K	L	M	N	O	P	Q	R	S	T
34	35	37	32	35	52	37	34	34	37

The 146 Games to Play

#						#					
1.	A	B	C	J	P	26.	A	E	F	L	P
2.	A	B	D	L	P	27.	A	E	G	K	N
3.	A	B	E	I	P	28.	A	E	H	P	S
4.	A	B	F	P	R	29.	A	E	J	P	Q
5.	A	B	G	O	P	30.	A	E	K	P	T
6.	A	B	H	P	T	31.	A	F	G	H	P
7.	A	B	K	M	P	32.	A	F	I	K	P
8.	A	B	N	O	S	33.	A	F	J	M	P
9.	A	B	P	Q	S	34.	A	F	O	P	T
10.	A	C	D	P	T	35.	A	G	I	J	P
11.	A	C	E	M	P	36.	A	G	L	P	Q
12.	A	C	E	O	P	37.	A	G	M	P	S
13.	A	C	E	P	R	38.	A	G	P	R	T
14.	A	C	F	P	Q	39.	A	H	I	O	P
15.	A	C	G	K	P	40.	A	H	J	K	P
16.	A	C	H	J	N	41.	A	H	M	P	R
17.	A	C	H	L	P	42.	A	I	L	P	R
18.	A	C	I	P	S	43.	A	I	M	N	Q
19.	A	D	E	G	P	44.	A	I	P	Q	T
20.	A	D	F	N	P	45.	A	J	L	O	P
21.	A	D	F	P	S	46.	A	J	P	S	T
22.	A	D	H	P	Q	47.	A	K	L	P	S
23.	A	D	I	M	P	48.	A	K	P	Q	R
24.	A	D	J	P	R	49.	A	L	M	P	T
25.	A	D	K	O	P	50.	A	L	N	R	T

(Continued Next Page)

BALANCED WHEEL™ 53020 (Continued from previous page)

#						#					
51.	A	M	O	P	Q	86.	C	F	G	L	O
52.	A	O	P	R	S	87.	C	F	H	J	S
53.	B	C	D	I	N	88.	C	F	I	R	T
54.	B	C	D	J	O	89.	C	F	N	R	S
55.	B	C	E	L	R	90.	C	G	J	Q	R
56.	B	C	F	K	M	91.	C	G	M	N	O
57.	B	C	G	H	T	92.	C	H	L	M	Q
58.	B	C	I	Q	S	93.	C	I	J	K	L
59.	B	D	E	I	T	94.	C	K	L	N	T
60.	B	D	F	G	R	95.	C	K	O	Q	T
61.	B	D	H	M	S	96.	C	M	O	R	S
62.	B	D	K	L	Q	97.	D	E	G	H	L
63.	B	E	F	O	S	98.	D	E	J	R	S
64.	B	E	G	M	Q	99.	D	E	K	M	O
65.	B	E	H	J	K	100.	D	E	M	N	O
66.	B	E	H	L	N	101.	D	F	H	O	T
67.	B	F	H	I	L	102.	D	F	I	K	S
68.	B	F	J	K	N	103.	D	F	J	L	M
69.	B	F	J	Q	T	104.	D	G	J	K	T
70.	B	G	I	K	O	105.	D	G	L	N	S
71.	B	G	J	L	S	106.	D	G	O	Q	S
72.	B	G	N	P	R	107.	D	H	I	J	Q
73.	B	H	O	Q	R	108.	D	H	K	N	R
74.	B	I	J	M	R	109.	D	I	L	O	R
75.	B	K	R	S	T	110.	D	J	N	Q	T
76.	B	L	M	O	T	111.	D	M	Q	R	T
77.	B	M	N	Q	T	112.	E	F	G	I	J
78.	C	D	E	F	Q	113.	E	F	H	M	R
79.	C	D	G	I	M	114.	E	F	K	L	T
80.	C	D	H	K	R	115.	E	F	M	N	T
81.	C	D	L	S	T	116.	E	G	O	R	T
82.	C	E	G	K	S	117.	E	H	Q	S	T
83.	C	E	H	I	O	118.	E	I	K	Q	R
84.	C	E	J	M	T	119.	E	I	L	M	S
85.	C	E	N	P	Q	120.	E	I	L	N	T

　　　　(Continued Next Page)

139

BALANCED WHEEL™ 53020 (Continued from previous page)

121.	E	J	L	O	Q	**134.**	G	J	N	Q	T
122.	E	J	N	S	T	**135.**	G	K	L	M	R
123.	E	M	N	Q	R	**136.**	H	I	K	M	T
124.	F	G	H	I	N	**137.**	H	J	L	R	T
125.	F	G	H	K	Q	**138.**	H	K	L	O	S
126.	F	G	M	S	T	**139.**	H	M	N	Q	S
127.	F	I	M	O	Q	**140.**	H	N	O	P	T
128.	F	J	K	O	R	**141.**	I	J	N	O	R
129.	F	L	N	O	Q	**142.**	I	J	O	S	T
130.	F	L	Q	R	S	**143.**	I	K	N	P	S
131.	G	H	I	R	S	**144.**	J	K	M	Q	S
132.	G	H	J	M	O	**145.**	J	L	M	N	P
133.	G	I	L	Q	T	**146.**	K	M	N	O	Q

Copyright © 1983-1998 Gail Howard

BALANCED WHEEL™ 53021
Wheeling 21 Numbers in 173 games for a 3 of 3 Win

NUMBERS CORRECT	MAXIMUM WINS				MINIMUM WINS			
	5x	4x	3x	2x	5x	4x	3x	2x
5 (w/o Jackpot)	0	4	11	46				
5	1	2	8	49	0	0	10	42
4	–	2	6	31	–	0	4	30
3	–	–	8	11	–	–	1	18
2	–	–	–	16	–	–	–	7

Your 21 Numbers to Wheel

A	B	C	D	E	F	G	H	I	J	K
44	40	40	39	42	41	40	42	39	42	40

L	M	N	O	P	Q	R	S	T	U
41	38	41	43	41	41	43	45	41	42

The 173 Games to Play

1.	A	B	C	K	T	**10.**	A	C	E	P	T
2.	A	B	D	N	U	**11.**	A	C	F	O	T
3.	A	B	E	G	O	**12.**	A	C	G	M	U
4.	A	B	F	Q	U	**13.**	A	C	H	L	U
5.	A	B	H	M	S	**14.**	A	C	I	N	T
6.	A	B	I	L	P	**15.**	A	C	O	R	U
7.	A	B	J	Q	R	**16.**	A	C	S	T	U
8.	A	C	D	E	Q	**17.**	A	D	F	P	U
9.	A	C	E	J	U	**18.**	A	D	G	H	T

Copyright © 1983-1998 Gail Howard   (Continued Next Page)

BALANCED WHEEL™ 53021 (Continued from previous page)

#						#					
19.	A	D	I	K	U	54.	B	D	G	M	O
20.	A	D	J	L	T	55.	B	D	J	K	L
21.	A	D	J	R	S	56.	B	E	F	L	M
22.	A	D	M	O	U	57.	B	E	G	K	U
23.	A	D	O	R	T	58.	B	E	G	P	S
24.	A	E	F	I	R	59.	B	E	J	Q	R
25.	A	E	H	K	N	60.	B	F	G	N	Q
26.	A	E	I	L	T	61.	B	F	G	O	S
27.	A	E	M	S	T	62.	B	F	H	N	T
28.	A	F	G	M	S	63.	B	F	J	O	P
29.	A	F	H	J	K	64.	B	G	H	I	J
30.	A	F	L	N	S	65.	B	G	L	Q	T
31.	A	G	I	J	S	66.	B	H	I	N	S
32.	A	G	K	P	R	67.	B	H	L	O	Q
33.	A	G	L	R	S	68.	B	H	L	O	U
34.	A	G	N	Q	S	69.	B	H	P	R	T
35.	A	H	I	Q	T	70.	B	I	J	T	U
36.	A	H	O	P	R	71.	B	I	K	M	Q
37.	A	I	M	O	S	72.	B	I	L	N	P
38.	A	J	M	S	U	73.	B	J	L	Q	S
39.	A	J	N	O	S	74.	B	J	M	O	T
40.	A	J	N	P	S	75.	B	K	N	O	R
41.	A	K	L	M	O	76.	B	K	P	R	S
42.	A	K	L	O	Q	77.	B	M	P	R	U
43.	A	M	N	R	S	78.	C	D	F	J	U
44.	A	M	P	Q	S	79.	C	D	G	K	N
45.	B	C	D	P	Q	80.	C	D	H	O	R
46.	B	C	E	I	O	81.	C	D	I	L	M
47.	B	C	F	H	K	82.	C	D	M	S	T
48.	B	C	F	S	U	83.	C	D	Q	S	U
49.	B	C	G	L	R	84.	C	E	F	J	U
50.	B	C	J	M	N	85.	C	E	G	H	M
51.	B	D	E	H	N	86.	C	E	G	S	T
52.	B	D	E	S	T	87.	C	E	K	L	Q
53.	B	D	F	I	R	88.	C	E	N	P	R

   (Continued Next Page)

BALANCED WHEEL™ 53021 (Continued from previous page)

#						#					
89.	C	F	G	I	P	124.	E	F	I	Q	S
90.	C	F	L	N	O	125.	E	F	J	R	T
91.	C	F	M	Q	R	126.	E	G	J	L	N
92.	C	G	J	O	Q	127.	E	H	I	L	R
93.	C	H	I	N	Q	128.	E	H	J	O	T
94.	C	H	J	L	P	129.	E	H	L	N	S
95.	C	H	J	S	T	130.	E	I	J	M	P
96.	C	I	J	K	R	131.	E	I	L	Q	U
97.	C	I	P	S	U	132.	E	J	K	N	T
98.	C	K	M	O	P	133.	E	J	K	O	S
99.	C	K	N	S	U	134.	E	K	O	P	U
100.	C	L	R	S	T	135.	E	M	N	O	Q
101.	C	O	Q	S	T	136.	E	M	Q	T	U
102.	D	E	F	J	S	137.	F	G	J	K	M
103.	D	E	G	I	Q	138.	F	G	K	S	T
104.	D	E	K	M	R	139.	F	G	L	O	U
105.	D	E	L	O	P	140.	F	H	I	M	O
106.	D	E	R	S	U	141.	F	H	J	N	R
107.	D	F	G	H	L	142.	F	H	P	R	S
108.	D	F	K	O	Q	143.	F	I	J	L	Q
109.	D	F	M	N	P	144.	F	I	M	T	U
110.	D	F	Q	T	U	145.	F	K	L	P	T
111.	D	G	H	S	U	146.	F	K	L	R	U
112.	D	G	J	P	R	147.	G	H	K	Q	R
113.	D	H	I	K	P	148.	G	H	N	O	P
114.	D	H	J	M	Q	149.	G	I	K	L	O
115.	D	I	J	N	O	150.	G	I	M	N	R
116.	D	I	K	S	T	151.	G	I	R	T	U
117.	D	L	N	Q	R	152.	G	J	N	O	U
118.	D	L	O	S	U	153.	G	J	P	Q	T
119.	D	N	P	S	T	154.	G	L	M	P	Q
120.	E	F	G	O	R	155.	G	M	N	O	T
121.	E	F	H	N	U	156.	G	O	P	Q	U
122.	E	F	H	P	Q	157.	H	I	N	P	U
123.	E	F	I	K	N	158.	H	J	Q	R	U

     (Continued Next Page)

BALANCED WHEEL™ 53021 (Continued from previous page)

159.	H	K	L	M	N		167.	I	O	P	T	U
160.	H	K	L	O	T		168.	J	K	L	P	U
161.	H	K	M	T	U		169.	J	K	N	P	Q
162.	H	K	Q	R	S		170.	J	L	M	O	R
163.	H	M	P	R	T		171.	K	N	Q	R	T
164.	H	O	P	R	S		172.	K	N	Q	R	U
165.	I	L	P	R	S		173.	L	M	N	T	U
166.	I	O	P	Q	R							

BALANCED WHEEL™ 53022
Wheeling 22 Numbers in 205 games for a 3 of 3 Win

NUMBERS CORRECT	MAXIMUM WINS				MINIMUM WINS			
	5x	4x	3x	2x	5x	4x	3x	2x
5 (w/o Jackpot)	0	4	6	56				
5	1	1	10	49	0	0	10	49
4	–	2	5	34	–	0	4	34
3	–	–	5	16	–	–	1	19
2	–	–	–	11	–	–	–	7

Your 22 Numbers to Wheel

A	B	C	D	E	F	G	H	I	J	K
46	47	46	46	47	46	47	45	46	47	47

L	M	N	O	P	Q	R	S	T	U	V
48	47	46	47	45	49	49	46	46	46	46

The 205 Games to Play

1.	A	B	C	F	U		15.	A	C	H	K	O
2.	A	B	D	L	P		16.	A	O	I	Q	R
3.	A	B	E	F	T		17.	A	D	E	K	T
4.	A	B	G	L	R		18.	A	D	F	G	O
5.	A	B	G	M	N		19.	A	D	F	I	N
6.	A	B	H	Q	U		20.	A	D	H	P	S
7.	A	B	I	O	V		21.	A	D	J	M	P
8.	A	B	J	K	R		22.	A	D	M	S	U
9.	A	B	O	R	S		23.	A	D	Q	R	V
10.	A	C	D	N	P		24.	A	E	H	I	J
11.	A	C	E	G	T		25.	A	E	L	M	Q
12.	A	C	F	L	V		26.	A	E	N	U	V
13.	A	C	G	J	S		27.	A	E	O	P	R
14.	A	C	G	M	T		28.	A	E	O	S	V

     (Continued Next Page)

BALANCED WHEEL™ 53022 (Continued from previous page)

#						#					
29.	A	F	H	M	R	64.	B	E	K	S	V
30.	A	F	J	Q	T	65.	B	E	M	R	U
31.	A	F	K	S	V	66.	B	F	G	P	S
32.	A	F	P	R	T	67.	B	F	H	I	N
33.	A	G	H	N	T	68.	B	F	I	K	V
34.	A	G	H	Q	V	69.	B	F	I	L	M
35.	A	G	I	S	T	70.	B	F	L	N	R
36.	A	G	K	P	V	71.	B	F	O	Q	R
37.	A	G	L	T	U	72.	B	G	K	N	Q
38.	A	H	L	N	S	73.	B	G	M	U	V
39.	A	I	K	L	M	74.	B	H	I	S	U
40.	A	I	O	P	U	75.	B	H	J	N	V
41.	A	J	K	O	V	76.	B	H	P	Q	R
42.	A	J	K	R	U	77.	B	I	K	Q	T
43.	A	J	L	N	O	78.	B	J	L	O	P
44.	A	K	N	Q	R	79.	B	J	M	Q	S
45.	A	M	O	T	V	80.	B	K	M	O	U
46.	A	O	P	Q	S	81.	B	K	N	P	U
47.	B	C	D	M	T	82.	B	L	Q	U	V
48.	B	C	E	N	Q	83.	B	M	P	T	V
49.	B	C	G	H	R	84.	B	N	R	S	T
50.	B	C	G	O	T	85.	C	D	E	H	R
51.	B	C	H	K	M	86.	C	D	F	H	T
52.	B	C	I	R	V	87.	C	D	F	J	S
53.	B	C	J	T	U	88.	C	D	G	I	K
54.	B	C	L	P	S	89.	C	D	G	N	U
55.	B	D	E	O	U	90.	C	D	J	Q	T
56.	B	D	F	J	R	91.	C	D	L	M	N
57.	B	D	G	I	V	92.	C	D	O	P	V
58.	B	D	H	N	O	93.	C	E	F	K	O
59.	B	D	K	L	S	94.	C	E	H	P	U
60.	B	D	L	O	Q	95.	C	E	I	M	S
61.	B	E	G	J	Q	96.	C	E	J	L	V
62.	B	E	H	L	T	97.	C	E	K	R	T
63.	B	E	I	J	P	98.	C	F	G	P	Q

(Continued Next Page)

BALANCED WHEEL™ 53022 (Continued from previous page)

#						#					
99.	C	F	I	O	Q	134.	D	K	P	Q	U
100.	C	F	J	M	O	135.	D	M	O	R	T
101.	C	F	N	O	U	136.	D	O	R	U	V
102.	C	F	O	R	S	137.	E	F	G	R	V
103.	C	G	L	O	V	138.	E	F	H	L	S
104.	C	H	I	J	Q	139.	E	F	I	J	U
105.	C	H	L	N	R	140.	E	G	H	M	S
106.	C	H	S	T	V	141.	E	G	I	L	N
107.	C	I	K	L	U	142.	E	G	K	R	U
108.	C	I	N	P	T	143.	E	G	M	O	P
109.	C	J	K	N	S	144.	E	H	I	K	N
110.	C	J	M	P	R	145.	E	H	J	O	T
111.	C	K	P	Q	V	146.	E	H	J	R	S
112.	C	L	M	Q	T	147.	E	H	M	Q	V
113.	C	M	N	U	V	148.	E	I	L	Q	R
114.	C	Q	R	S	U	149.	E	I	T	U	V
115.	D	E	F	M	P	150.	E	J	K	Q	U
116.	D	E	F	N	Q	151.	E	J	M	N	T
117.	D	E	G	J	M	152.	E	K	L	M	P
118.	D	E	I	O	S	153.	E	L	M	O	Q
119.	D	E	J	L	V	154.	E	L	N	S	U
120.	D	F	I	S	T	155.	E	N	O	S	T
121.	D	F	J	K	N	156.	E	N	P	R	V
122.	D	F	L	T	U	157.	E	P	Q	S	T
123.	D	F	N	T	V	158.	F	G	H	J	K
124.	D	G	H	L	U	159.	F	G	H	P	S
125.	D	G	I	M	Q	160.	F	G	I	P	U
126.	D	G	N	R	S	161.	F	G	K	M	T
127.	D	G	P	R	T	162.	F	G	L	N	P
128.	D	G	Q	S	V	163.	F	H	O	Q	V
129.	D	H	I	J	Q	164.	F	H	Q	S	U
130.	D	H	K	M	V	165.	F	I	K	R	U
131.	D	I	J	O	U	166.	F	J	L	P	V
132.	D	I	L	P	R	167.	F	K	L	O	Q
133.	D	K	N	O	R	168.	F	K	O	P	T

(Continued Next Page)

BALANCED WHEEL™ 53022 (Continued from previous page)

169.	F	M	N	P	S	188.	H	N	Q	T	U
170.	F	M	Q	U	V	189.	I	J	K	M	V
171.	G	H	I	O	R	190.	I	J	L	S	T
172.	G	I	J	O	R	191.	I	J	N	R	U
173.	G	J	K	L	R	192.	I	K	M	N	O
174.	G	J	N	T	V	193.	I	K	P	R	S
175.	G	J	P	S	U	194.	I	L	O	R	T
176.	G	K	L	O	S	195.	I	M	P	Q	U
177.	G	L	M	Q	R	196.	I	N	Q	S	V
178.	G	N	O	Q	V	197.	J	L	N	P	Q
179.	G	O	Q	T	U	198.	J	M	O	Q	S
180.	H	I	L	P	V	199.	J	P	S	U	V
181.	H	I	M	R	T	200.	J	Q	R	T	V
182.	H	J	K	P	T	201.	K	L	N	T	V
183.	H	J	L	M	U	202.	K	M	N	Q	R
184.	H	K	L	Q	S	203.	K	M	S	T	U
185.	H	K	R	U	V	204.	L	M	R	S	V
186.	H	L	O	S	U	205.	L	P	R	T	U
187.	H	M	N	O	P						

Copyright © 1983-1998 Gail Howard

BALANCED WHEEL™ 53026
Wheeling 26 Numbers in 331 games for a 3 of 3 Win

NUMBERS CORRECT	MAXIMUM WINS				MINIMUM WINS			
	5x	4x	3x	2x	5x	4x	3x	2x
5 (w/o Jackpot)	0	4	11	60				
5	1	1	13	62	0	0	10	60
4	–	2	9	35	–	0	4	41
3	–	–	9	15	–	–	1	23
2	–	–	–	17	–	–	–	8

Your 26 Numbers to Wheel

A	B	C	D	E	F	G	H	I
62	63	65	60	63	65	64	63	65

J	K	L	M	N	O	P	Q	R
65	64	64	65	65	63	64	65	63

S	T	U	V	W	X	Y	Z
62	65	63	64	63	61	65	64

The 331 Games to Play

1.	A	B	C	M	Y		2.	A	B	D	O	P

Copyright © 1983-1998 Gail Howard

(Continued Next Page)

BALANCED WHEEL™ 53026 (Continued from previous page)

#						#					
3.	A	B	E	J	V	38.	A	F	J	K	U
4.	A	B	F	G	X	39.	A	F	L	U	Z
5.	A	B	F	H	U	40.	A	F	M	R	U
6.	A	B	I	P	X	41.	A	F	S	T	U
7.	A	B	K	N	S	42.	A	F	U	V	W
8.	A	B	L	Q	T	43.	A	G	H	I	O
9.	A	B	R	W	Z	44.	A	G	J	K	R
10.	A	C	D	T	Z	45.	A	G	J	Q	U
11.	A	C	E	G	U	46.	A	G	O	U	X
12.	A	C	F	N	U	47.	A	G	S	T	W
13.	A	C	G	L	N	48.	A	H	J	L	Y
14.	A	C	H	Q	W	49.	A	H	M	S	Z
15.	A	C	I	J	S	50.	A	H	N	R	V
16.	A	C	K	O	V	51.	A	I	K	L	W
17.	A	C	P	Q	R	52.	A	I	M	N	T
18.	A	C	R	T	X	53.	A	I	Q	V	Z
19.	A	D	E	M	W	54.	A	J	K	M	P
20.	A	D	F	P	U	55.	A	J	N	W	X
21.	A	D	G	J	N	56.	A	J	O	T	Z
22.	A	D	H	K	Q	57.	A	K	X	Y	Z
23.	A	D	H	P	X	58.	A	L	M	V	X
24.	A	D	I	N	X	59.	A	L	O	R	S
25.	A	D	L	M	S	60.	A	N	O	Q	Y
26.	A	D	Q	V	Y	61.	A	P	S	T	V
27.	A	D	S	U	Y	62.	A	P	T	W	Y
28.	A	E	F	G	Z	63.	B	C	D	T	Y
29.	A	E	G	L	P	64.	B	C	E	O	X
30.	A	E	H	K	T	65.	B	C	F	Q	V
31.	A	E	I	R	Y	66.	B	C	G	K	T
32.	A	E	M	O	W	67.	B	C	H	I	Z
33.	A	E	N	P	Z	68.	B	C	J	P	W
34.	A	E	Q	S	X	69.	B	C	L	N	O
35.	A	F	G	M	Q	70.	B	C	R	S	U
36.	A	F	G	V	Y	71.	B	D	E	H	U
37.	A	F	I	O	U	72.	B	D	F	I	S

(Continued Next Page)

BALANCED WHEEL™ 53026 (Continued from previous page)

73.	B	D	F	N	Z	108.	B	K	L	P	Y
74.	B	D	G	O	V	109.	B	K	M	R	X
75.	B	D	J	M	R	110.	B	K	U	V	Z
76.	B	D	K	L	Q	111.	B	L	M	U	W
77.	B	D	Q	W	X	112.	B	L	N	X	Z
78.	B	E	F	K	W	113.	B	M	N	P	V
79.	B	E	G	M	S	114.	B	O	S	T	W
80.	B	E	H	L	N	115.	B	O	S	X	Y
81.	B	E	I	O	Z	116.	B	P	Q	S	Z
82.	B	E	P	R	T	117.	C	D	E	F	T
83.	B	E	Q	U	Y	118.	C	D	E	G	X
84.	B	E	V	W	Z	119.	C	D	E	I	Y
85.	B	F	G	O	P	120.	C	D	H	I	L
86.	B	F	H	U	X	121.	C	D	H	J	M
87.	B	F	J	L	S	122.	C	D	K	N	P
88.	B	F	M	T	Z	123.	C	D	L	R	U
89.	B	F	N	R	Y	124.	C	D	O	Q	S
90.	B	G	H	I	U	125.	C	D	P	V	W
91.	B	G	H	T	X	126.	C	E	F	P	Z
92.	B	G	J	Y	Z	127.	C	E	H	N	X
93.	B	G	L	R	V	128.	C	E	J	M	Q
94.	B	G	N	Q	W	129.	C	E	K	L	R
95.	B	H	I	J	M	130.	C	E	L	T	W
96.	B	H	I	K	R	131.	C	E	S	V	Y
97.	B	H	I	S	V	132.	C	F	G	P	Z
98.	B	H	I	W	Y	133.	C	F	H	J	T
99.	B	H	O	P	U	134.	C	F	I	K	Y
100.	B	H	Q	R	Y	135.	C	F	L	N	P
101.	B	I	L	N	O	136.	C	F	M	S	X
102.	B	I	M	O	Q	137.	C	F	O	R	W
103.	B	I	O	V	Y	138.	C	G	H	R	Y
104.	B	I	T	V	X	139.	C	G	I	M	W
105.	B	J	K	O	R	140.	C	G	J	V	X
106.	B	J	N	T	U	141.	C	G	O	Q	S
107.	B	J	O	Q	X	142.	C	H	K	P	S

                          (Continued Next Page)

BALANCED WHEEL™ 53026 (Continued from previous page)

#	1	2	3	4	5		#	1	2	3	4	5
143.	C	H	L	X	Z		178.	D	H	I	O	W
144.	C	H	M	U	V		179.	D	H	N	S	Y
145.	C	H	N	O	Z		180.	D	H	R	V	Z
146.	C	I	N	O	X		181.	D	I	J	K	V
147.	C	I	P	R	V		182.	D	I	O	U	Z
148.	C	I	Q	T	U		183.	D	J	K	L	T
149.	C	J	K	N	Q		184.	D	J	K	O	Y
150.	C	J	L	M	N		185.	D	J	Q	V	W
151.	C	J	N	R	Z		186.	D	J	S	U	X
152.	C	J	O	U	Y		187.	D	K	L	X	Z
153.	C	K	M	R	Z		188.	D	L	M	P	Y
154.	C	K	U	W	X		189.	D	L	N	U	W
155.	C	L	N	S	V		190.	D	M	N	O	T
156.	C	L	P	U	Z		191.	D	M	N	V	X
157.	C	L	Q	R	Z		192.	D	M	Q	Y	Z
158.	C	L	W	Y	Z		193.	D	P	R	S	T
159.	C	M	O	P	T		194.	D	Q	T	U	V
160.	C	N	S	T	Y		195.	D	T	W	X	Y
161.	C	N	S	W	Z		196.	E	F	G	N	P
162.	C	P	Q	X	Y		197.	E	F	H	R	S
163.	C	T	V	W	Z		198.	E	F	I	M	V
164.	D	E	H	L	O		199.	E	F	J	X	Y
165.	D	E	J	P	Z		200.	E	F	L	M	U
166.	D	E	K	S	V		201.	E	F	O	Q	T
167.	D	E	N	Q	R		202.	E	G	H	Q	V
168.	D	F	G	L	V		203.	E	G	I	J	T
169.	D	F	H	O	X		204.	E	G	K	O	Y
170.	D	F	I	M	N		205.	E	G	N	P	U
171.	D	F	J	Q	Y		206.	E	G	R	W	X
172.	D	F	K	R	W		207.	E	H	I	N	Z
173.	D	G	H	I	T		208.	E	H	J	U	W
174.	D	G	I	P	Q		209.	E	H	M	P	Y
175.	D	G	K	M	U		210.	E	I	K	S	U
176.	D	G	O	R	Y		211.	E	I	L	X	Z
177.	D	G	S	W	Z		212.	E	I	P	Q	W

(Continued Next Page)

149

BALANCED WHEEL™ 53026 (Continued from previous page)

#	1	2	3	4	5		#	1	2	3	4	5
213.	E	J	K	L	Q		248.	F	L	Q	W	X
214.	E	J	L	N	R		249.	F	R	V	X	Z
215.	E	J	M	R	Z		250.	F	T	U	W	Y
216.	E	J	O	P	S		251.	G	H	J	N	S
217.	E	K	M	N	Z		252.	G	H	K	W	Z
218.	E	K	P	V	X		253.	G	H	L	M	T
219.	E	L	N	S	W		254.	G	I	K	N	V
220.	E	L	N	V	Y		255.	G	I	L	Q	Y
221.	E	M	T	U	X		256.	G	I	R	S	Z
222.	E	N	O	W	Y		257.	G	J	L	O	W
223.	E	N	Q	T	Z		258.	G	K	L	S	X
224.	E	O	R	U	V		259.	G	K	P	Q	R
225.	E	S	T	V	Z		260.	G	L	N	U	Z
226.	E	T	U	Y	Z		261.	G	M	N	X	Y
227.	F	G	H	I	P		262.	G	M	O	V	Z
228.	F	G	I	P	X		263.	G	M	Q	R	U
229.	F	G	J	M	P		264.	G	N	O	R	T
230.	F	G	K	R	U		265.	G	Q	T	X	Z
231.	F	G	P	S	V		266.	G	S	T	U	Y
232.	F	G	P	T	V		267.	G	U	V	W	Y
233.	F	G	P	W	Y		268.	H	I	K	M	Q
234.	F	H	K	L	V		269.	H	I	V	X	Y
235.	F	H	M	N	W		270.	H	J	K	M	O
236.	F	H	Q	Y	Z		271.	H	J	K	Q	X
237.	F	I	J	W	Z		272.	H	J	M	R	X
238.	F	I	L	R	T		273.	H	J	P	V	Z
239.	F	I	N	Q	S		274.	H	K	N	U	Y
240.	F	I	S	W	Y		275.	H	K	O	Q	R
241.	F	J	N	O	V		276.	H	L	P	R	W
242.	F	J	P	Q	R		277.	H	L	Q	S	U
243.	F	K	M	Q	W		278.	H	N	P	Q	T
244.	F	K	N	T	X		279.	H	O	S	T	V
245.	F	K	O	S	Z		280.	H	O	T	W	Y
246.	F	K	P	Q	U		281.	H	R	T	U	Z
247.	F	L	M	O	Y		282.	H	S	V	W	X

     (Continued Next Page)

BALANCED WHEEL™ 53026 (Continued from previous page)

283.	I	J	K	O	X	308.	K	L	M	N	R
284.	I	J	L	U	V	309.	K	L	O	T	U
285.	I	J	N	P	Y	310.	K	M	P	Q	T
286.	I	J	Q	R	T	311.	K	M	R	V	Y
287.	I	K	P	T	Z	312.	K	N	O	P	W
288.	I	L	M	P	S	313.	K	Q	R	S	W
289.	I	M	O	R	X	314.	K	Q	S	W	Y
290.	I	M	Q	R	X	315.	K	R	T	V	W
291.	I	M	U	Y	Z	316.	L	M	N	Q	Z
292.	I	N	R	U	W	317.	L	N	T	V	W
293.	I	O	P	U	X	318.	L	N	V	Y	Z
294.	I	O	S	T	X	319.	L	O	P	Q	V
295.	I	O	V	W	X	320.	L	R	U	X	Y
296.	I	Q	T	W	Y	321.	L	S	T	Y	Z
297.	J	K	M	S	W	322.	M	N	O	S	U
298.	J	K	Q	V	Z	323.	M	P	W	X	Z
299.	J	K	S	T	Y	324.	M	Q	S	T	V
300.	J	L	O	X	Z	325.	M	R	S	T	Y
301.	J	L	P	T	X	326.	N	P	R	S	X
302.	J	M	P	R	U	327.	N	Q	U	V	X
303.	J	M	R	W	Y	328.	O	P	R	Y	Z
304.	J	M	I	V	W	329.	O	Q	U	W	Z
305.	J	P	T	V	Y	330.	P	O	T	U	Y
306.	J	Q	R	S	V	331.	P	S	U	V	W
307.	J	S	U	X	Z						

BALANCED WHEEL™ 53108
Wheeling 8 Numbers in 3 games for a 3 of 4 Win

NUMBERS CORRECT	MAXIMUM WINS				MINIMUM WINS			
	5x	4x	3x	2x	5x	4x	3x	2x
5 (w/o Jackpot)	0	2	0	1				
5	1	0	1	1	0	0	3	0
4	–	1	1	0	–	0	1	2
3	–	–	2	0	–	–	0	2
2	–	–	–	2	–	–	–	0

Your 8 Numbers to Wheel

A	B	C	D	E	F	G	H
2	2	2	2	2	2	1	2

(Continued Next Page)

151

BALANCED WHEEL™ 53108 (Continued from previous page)
The 3 Games to Play

1.	A	B	E	F	G
2.	A	C	D	F	H

3.	B	C	D	E	H

Copyright © 1983-1998 Gail Howard

BALANCED WHEEL™ 53109
Wheeling 9 Numbers in 5 games for a 3 of 4 Win

NUMBERS CORRECT	MAXIMUM WINS				MINIMUM WINS			
	5x	4x	3x	2x	5x	4x	3x	2x
5 (w/o Jackpot)	0	3	0	1				
5	1	0	2	2	0	0	3	2
4	–	1	2	1	–	0	1	3
3	–	–	2	1	–	–	0	2
2	–	–	–	3	–	–	–	0

Your 9 Numbers to Wheel

A	B	C	D	E	F	G	H	I
3	3	2	3	3	3	2	3	3

The 5 Games to Play

1.	A	B	C	H	I
2.	A	D	E	F	H
3.	A	D	F	G	I

4.	B	C	E	G	H
5.	B	D	E	F	I

Copyright © 1983-1998 Gail Howard

BALANCED WHEEL™ 53110
Wheeling 10 Numbers in 7 games for a 3 of 4 Win

NUMBERS CORRECT	MAXIMUM WINS				MINIMUM WINS			
	5x	4x	3x	2x	5x	4x	3x	2x
5 (w/o Jackpot)	0	2	3	0				
5	1	1	1	4	0	0	3	3
4	–	2	0	3	–	0	1	4
3	–	–	2	3	–	–	0	3
2	–	–	–	4	–	–	–	0

Your 10 Numbers to Wheel

A	B	C	D	E	F	G	H	I	J
3	4	4	4	3	3	3	3	4	4

The 7 Games to Play

1.	A	C	F	H	I
2.	A	D	E	F	J
3.	A	D	F	G	J
4.	B	C	D	H	J

5.	B	C	D	I	J
6.	B	C	E	G	I
7.	B	E	G	H	I

Copyright © 1983-1998 Gail Howard

BALANCED WHEEL™ 53111
Wheeling 11 Numbers in 10 games for a 3 of 4 Win

NUMBERS CORRECT	MAXIMUM WINS				MINIMUM WINS			
	5x	4x	3x	2x	5x	4x	3x	2x
5 (w/o Jackpot)	0	3	2	2				
5	1	0	4	4	0	0	3	5
4	–	1	3	3	–	0	1	5
3	–	–	3	1	–	–	0	3
2	–	–	–	4	–	–	–	0

Your 11 Numbers to Wheel

A	B	C	D	E	F	G	H	I	J	K
4	5	5	5	5	4	4	4	4	4	6

The 10 Games to Play

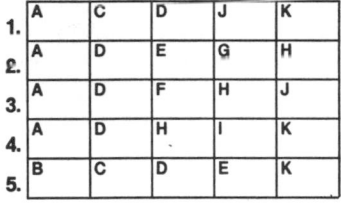

1.	A	C	D	J	K
2.	A	D	E	G	H
3.	A	D	F	H	J
4.	A	D	H	I	K
5.	B	C	D	E	K

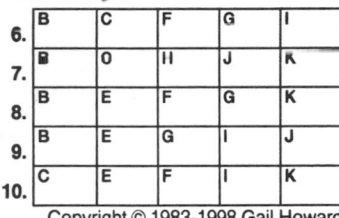

6.	B	C	F	G	I
7.	B	D	H	J	K
8.	B	E	F	G	K
9.	B	E	G	I	J
10.	C	E	F	I	K

BALANCED WHEEL™ 53112
Wheeling 12 Numbers in 12 games for a 3 of 4 Win

NUMBERS CORRECT	MAXIMUM WINS				MINIMUM WINS			
	5x	4x	3x	2x	5x	4x	3x	2x
5 (w/o Jackpot)	0	1	4	2				
5	1	0	0	9	0	0	3	7
4	–	1	0	6	–	0	1	6
3	–	–	1	3	–	–	0	4
2	–	–	–	2	–	–	–	1

Your 12 Numbers to Wheel

A	B	C	D	E	F	G	H	I	J	K	L
5	5	5	5	5	5	5	5	5	5	5	5

The 12 Games to Play

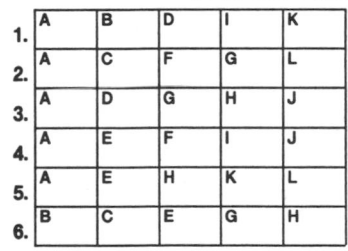

1.	A	B	D	I	K
2.	A	C	F	G	L
3.	A	D	G	H	J
4.	A	E	F	I	J
5.	A	E	H	K	L
6.	B	C	E	G	H

7.	B	C	I	J	L
8.	B	D	F	H	L
9.	B	F	G	J	K
10.	C	D	E	J	K
11.	C	F	H	I	K
12.	D	E	G	I	L

BALANCED WHEEL™ 53113
Wheeling 13 Numbers in 18 games for a 3 of 4 Win

NUMBERS CORRECT	MAXIMUM WINS				MINIMUM WINS			
	5x	4x	3x	2x	5x	4x	3x	2x
5 (w/o Jackpot)	0	3	1	5				
5	1	1	2	5	0	0	3	10
4	–	2	0	7	–	0	1	8
3	–	–	2	4	–	–	0	5
2	–	–	–	4	–	–	–	1

Your 13 Numbers to Wheel

A	B	C	D	E	F	G
7	7	7	7	7	7	6

H	I	J	K	L	M
7	7	7	7	7	7

The 18 Games to Play

1.	A	B	C	I	M
2.	A	C	G	J	L
3.	A	C	H	K	L
4.	A	D	F	L	M
5.	A	D	H	I	J
6.	A	E	F	J	K
7.	A	G	H	L	M
8.	B	C	F	H	J
9.	B	D	E	G	I

10.	B	D	E	H	K
11.	B	E	J	L	M
12.	B	F	G	I	K
13.	B	F	I	K	L
14.	C	D	E	I	L
15.	C	D	J	K	M
16.	C	G	H	J	M
17.	D	E	F	G	K
18.	E	F	H	I	M

Copyright © 1983-1998 Gail Howard

BALANCED WHEEL™ 53114
Wheeling 14 Numbers in 23 games for a 3 of 4 Win

NUMBERS CORRECT	MAXIMUM WINS				MINIMUM WINS			
	5x	4x	3x	2x	5x	4x	3x	2x
5 (w/o Jackpot)	0	3	4	8				
5	1	2	2	9	0	0	3	11
4	–	3	0	10	–	0	1	8
3	–	–	3	8	–	–	0	5
2	–	–	–	11	–	–	–	1

Your 14 Numbers to Wheel

A	B	C	D	E	F	G
11	8	8	7	8	8	8

H	I	J	K	L	M	N
8	8	7	8	8	11	7

The 23 Games to Play

1.	A	B	D	I	M
2.	A	B	I	J	M

3.	A	B	I	M	N
4.	A	C	E	G	M

Copyright © 1983-1998 Gail Howard   (Continued Next Page)

154

BALANCED WHEEL™ 53114 (Continued from previous page)

5.	A	C	F	H	M
6.	A	C	K	L	M
7.	A	D	J	M	N
8.	A	E	F	K	M
9.	A	E	H	L	M
10.	A	F	G	L	M
11.	A	G	H	K	M
12.	B	C	G	H	J
13.	B	C	I	K	L
14.	B	D	E	H	I

15.	B	D	J	K	N
16.	B	E	F	L	N
17.	C	D	F	J	L
18.	C	E	H	K	N
19.	C	F	G	I	N
20.	D	E	F	G	K
21.	D	G	H	L	N
22.	E	G	I	J	L
23.	F	H	I	J	K

Copyright © 1983-1998 Gail Howard

BALANCED WHEEL™ 53115
Wheeling 15 Numbers in 28 games for a 3 of 4 Win

NUMBERS CORRECT	MAXIMUM WINS				MINIMUM WINS			
	5x	4x	3x	2x	5x	4x	3x	2x
5 (w/o Jackpot)	0	3	4	8				
5	1	1	3	12	0	0	3	11
4	–	2	1	7	–	0	1	8
3	–	–	3	3	–	–	0	5
2	–	–	–	6	–	–	–	1

Your 15 Numbers to Wheel

A	B	C	D	E	F	G	H
11	8	10	8	9	9	10	9

I	J	K	L	M	N	O	
9	9	9	9	10	11	9	

The 28 Games to Play

1.	A	B	D	I	K
2.	A	B	E	G	L
3.	A	C	F	N	O
4.	A	C	H	L	O
5.	A	C	J	K	M
6.	A	D	E	N	O
7.	A	E	H	I	L
8.	A	F	K	M	N
9.	A	G	J	L	M
10.	A	G	L	M	N
11.	A	J	K	L	N
12.	B	C	G	K	O

13.	B	C	K	L	N
14.	B	D	H	J	M
15.	B	E	F	M	N
16.	B	F	H	J	N
17.	B	I	J	M	O
18.	C	D	E	F	J
19.	C	D	G	M	O
20.	C	E	G	H	I
21.	C	F	G	I	J
22.	C	F	H	M	N
23.	D	F	G	H	K
24.	D	F	I	L	O

Copyright © 1983-1998 Gail Howard   (Continued Next Page)

BALANCED WHEEL™ 53115 (Continued from previous page)

| 25. | D | G | H | I | N |
| 26. | E | G | I | N | O |

| 27. | E | H | J | K | O |
| 28. | E | I | K | L | M |

BALANCED WHEEL™ 53116
Wheeling 16 Numbers in 37 games for a 3 of 4 Win

NUMBERS CORRECT	MAXIMUM WINS				MINIMUM WINS			
	5x	4x	3x	2x	5x	4x	3x	2x
5 (w/o Jackpot)	0	3	5	11				
5	1	2	2	13	0	0	3	15
4	–	3	0	12	–	0	1	10
3	–	–	3	11	–	–	0	6
2	–	–	–	14	–	–	–	1

Your 16 Numbers to Wheel

A	B	C	D	E	F	G	H
14	10	10	11	11	14	11	11

I	J	K	L	M	N	O	P
11	11	11	11	11	14	14	10

The 37 Games to Play

1.	A	B	D	J	N
2.	A	B	L	M	N
3.	A	B	N	O	P
4.	A	C	E	K	N
5.	A	C	F	H	N
6.	A	C	G	I	N
7.	A	D	L	N	O
8.	A	D	M	N	P
9.	A	E	F	I	N
10.	A	E	G	H	N
11.	A	F	G	K	N
12.	A	H	I	K	N
13.	A	J	L	N	P
14.	A	J	M	N	O
15.	B	C	F	O	P
16.	B	C	G	I	J
17.	B	C	K	L	P
18.	B	D	J	M	P
19.	B	E	F	L	O

20.	B	E	H	I	L
21.	B	G	H	K	M
22.	C	D	E	G	M
23.	C	D	H	I	K
24.	C	E	F	L	O
25.	C	H	J	L	M
26.	D	E	J	K	L
27.	D	F	G	H	O
28.	D	F	I	M	O
29.	D	F	J	K	O
30.	D	G	I	L	P
31.	E	F	L	O	P
32.	E	G	H	J	P
33.	E	I	K	M	P
34.	F	G	I	K	O
35.	F	G	J	M	O
36.	F	H	I	J	O
37.	F	H	K	M	O

BALANCED WHEEL™ 53117
Wheeling 17 Numbers in 46 games for a 3 of 4 Win

NUMBERS CORRECT	MAXIMUM WINS				MINIMUM WINS			
	5x	4x	3x	2x	5x	4x	3x	2x
5 (w/o Jackpot)	0	12	0	0				
5	1	11	0	0	0	0	3	19
4	-	12	0	0	-	0	1	11
3	-	-	12	0	-	-	0	5
2	-	-	-	12	-	-	-	0

Your 17 Numbers to Wheel

A	B	C	D	E	F	G	H	I
12	12	14	14	14	13	14	14	14

J	K	L	M	N	O	P	Q
14	14	14	12	14	12	14	15

The 46 Games to Play

#						#					
1.	A	B	C	M	O	24.	C	G	K	N	Q
2.	A	B	D	M	O	25.	C	H	J	K	Q
3.	A	B	E	M	O	26.	D	E	F	G	N
4.	A	B	G	M	O	27.	D	E	F	H	J
5.	A	B	H	M	O	28.	D	E	I	K	L
6.	A	B	I	M	O	29.	D	F	L	P	Q
7.	A	B	J	M	O	30.	D	G	H	I	K
8.	A	B	K	M	O	31.	D	G	J	P	Q
9.	A	B	L	M	O	32.	D	H	N	P	Q
10.	A	B	M	N	O	33.	D	I	J	K	N
11.	A	B	M	O	P	34.	D	I	K	P	Q
12.	A	B	M	O	Q	35.	E	F	K	L	Q
13.	C	D	E	P	Q	36.	E	G	I	N	Q
14.	C	D	F	I	K	37.	E	G	J	K	L
15.	C	D	G	L	N	38.	E	H	I	J	Q
16.	C	D	H	J	L	39.	E	H	K	L	N
17.	C	E	F	I	P	40.	F	G	H	L	Q
18.	C	E	G	H	P	41.	F	G	K	N	P
19.	C	E	J	N	P	42.	F	H	J	K	P
20.	C	E	K	L	P	43.	F	J	L	N	Q
21.	C	F	G	I	J	44.	G	H	J	N	Q
22.	C	F	H	I	N	45.	G	I	L	N	P
23.	C	F	I	L	Q	46.	H	I	J	L	P

BALANCED WHEEL™ 53118
Wheeling 18 Numbers in 56 games for a 3 of 4 Win

NUMBERS CORRECT	MAXIMUM WINS				MINIMUM WINS			
	5x	4x	3x	2x	5x	4x	3x	2x
5 (w/o Jackpot)	0	3	8	16				
5	1	2	2	19	0	0	3	20
4	–	3	0	18	–	0	1	13
3	–	–	4	15	–	–	0	7
2	–	–	–	19	–	–	–	1

Your 18 Numbers to Wheel

A	B	C	D	E	F	G	H	I
17	19	15	17	15	14	15	17	15

J	K	L	M	N	O	P	Q	R
15	14	14	14	14	15	14	19	17

The 56 Games to Play

#						#					
1.	A	B	D	K	Q	26.	B	E	J	P	Q
2.	A	B	H	N	Q	27.	B	F	G	P	Q
3.	A	B	M	Q	R	28.	B	F	I	O	Q
4.	A	C	E	G	R	29.	B	G	I	J	Q
5.	A	C	I	M	R	30.	B	H	K	Q	R
6.	A	C	J	O	R	31.	B	I	L	P	Q
7.	A	D	F	H	P	32.	B	J	L	O	Q
8.	A	D	H	J	M	33.	B	K	M	N	Q
9.	A	D	H	N	O	34.	C	D	E	H	L
10.	A	E	I	O	R	35.	C	D	G	H	I
11.	A	E	J	M	R	36.	C	D	H	K	R
12.	A	F	K	N	R	37.	C	E	F	L	M
13.	A	F	L	P	R	38.	C	E	N	O	P
14.	A	G	I	J	R	39.	C	F	I	K	N
15.	A	G	M	O	R	40.	C	G	I	L	O
16.	A	K	L	N	R	41.	C	G	J	K	P
17.	A	K	N	P	R	42.	D	E	G	H	R
18.	B	C	E	I	Q	43.	D	E	H	I	K
19.	B	C	F	J	Q	44.	D	F	H	J	N
20.	B	C	G	L	Q	45.	D	F	H	M	O
21.	B	C	O	P	Q	46.	D	G	H	K	L
22.	B	D	H	M	Q	47.	D	H	I	L	R
23.	B	D	N	Q	R	48.	D	H	J	O	P
24.	B	E	F	L	Q	49.	D	H	M	N	P
25.	B	E	G	O	Q	50.	E	F	G	I	J

158
(Continued Next Page)

BALANCED WHEEL™ 53118 (Continued from previous page)

51.	E	I	K	M	P		**54.**	F	J	M	O	P
52.	E	J	K	L	O		**55.**	G	K	M	N	O
53.	F	G	L	N	P		**56.**	I	J	L	M	N

BALANCED WHEEL™ 53119
Wheeling 19 Numbers in 66 games for a 3 of 4 Win

NUMBERS CORRECT	MAXIMUM WINS				MINIMUM WINS			
	5x	4x	3x	2x	5x	4x	3x	2x
5 (w/o Jackpot)	0	10	0	12				
5	1	7	4	6	0	0	3	21
4	–	8	2	8	–	0	1	13
3	–	–	9	4	–	–	0	6
2				16				1

Your 19 Numbers to Wheel

A	B	C	D	E	F	G	H	I	J
20	19	17	18	17	17	19	17	18	17

K	L	M	N	O	P	Q	R	S
17	17	18	17	17	17	16	16	16

The 66 Games to Play

1.	A	B	C	F	Q		**20.**	A	G	J	M	N
2.	A	B	C	H	K		**21.**	B	C	D	E	I
3.	A	B	C	J	R		**22.**	B	O	D	II	M
4.	A	B	C	L	S		**23.**	B	F	H	I	M
5.	A	B	D	F	K		**24.**	C	E	F	G	M
6.	A	B	E	G	O		**25.**	C	E	F	H	J
7.	A	B	E	H	Q		**26.**	O	E	F	H	L
8.	A	B	E	J	K		**27.**	C	E	F	H	N
9.	A	B	E	L	M		**28.**	C	E	F	H	O
10.	A	B	E	N	P		**29.**	C	E	F	H	P
11.	A	B	F	G	N		**30.**	C	E	F	H	Q
12.	A	B	F	J	L		**31.**	C	E	F	H	R
13.	A	B	F	O	P		**32.**	C	E	F	H	S
14.	A	B	G	H	P		**33.**	D	G	I	J	R
15.	A	B	H	N	O		**34.**	D	G	J	Q	S
16.	A	B	H	R	S		**35.**	D	G	K	N	P
17.	A	C	D	G	I		**36.**	D	G	L	M	O
18.	A	C	F	I	M		**37.**	D	I	K	P	Q
19.	A	D	E	H	I		**38.**	D	I	L	O	S

                    (Continued Next Page)

BALANCED WHEEL™ 53119 (Continued from previous page)

39.	D	I	M	N	R	53.	G	L	N	Q	R
40.	D	J	K	M	P	54.	G	M	P	R	S
41.	D	J	L	N	O	55.	I	J	K	N	Q
42.	D	K	L	O	P	56.	I	J	M	O	S
43.	D	K	P	R	S	57.	I	K	L	Q	R
44.	D	L	O	Q	R	58.	I	K	O	Q	S
45.	D	M	N	Q	S	59.	I	L	M	N	P
46.	E	F	G	H	K	60.	I	O	P	R	S
47.	G	I	J	L	P	61.	J	L	M	Q	R
48.	G	I	K	M	Q	62.	J	N	P	R	S
49.	G	I	N	O	S	63.	K	L	M	N	S
50.	G	J	K	L	S	64.	K	M	N	O	R
51.	G	J	K	O	R	65.	L	P	Q	R	S
52.	G	J	O	P	Q	66.	M	N	O	P	Q

BALANCED WHEEL™ 53120
Wheeling 20 Numbers in 76 games for a 3 of 4 Win

NUMBERS CORRECT	MAXIMUM WINS				MINIMUM WINS			
	5x	4x	3x	2x	5x	4x	3x	2x
5 (w/o Jackpot)	0	2	6	5				
5	1	0	7	5	0	0	3	18
4	–	1	7	0	–	0	1	12
3	–	–	8	0	–	–	0	6
2	–	–	–	8	–	–	–	0

Your 20 Numbers to Wheel

A	B	C	D	E	F	G	H	I	J
8	21	21	21	21	21	21	21	21	21

K	L	M	N	O	P	Q	R	S	T
21	21	21	21	21	21	20	8	8	21

The 76 Games to Play

1.	A	B	F	R	S	9.	B	C	D	E	Q
2.	A	C	M	R	S	10.	B	C	F	K	L
3.	A	D	J	R	S	11.	B	C	G	J	N
4.	A	E	O	R	S	12.	B	C	H	M	T
5.	A	G	L	R	S	13.	B	C	I	O	P
6.	A	H	I	R	S	14.	B	D	F	M	O
7.	A	K	P	R	S	15.	B	D	G	H	P
8.	A	N	R	S	T	16.	B	D	I	K	N

          (Continued Next Page)

BALANCED WHEEL™ 53120 (Continued from previous page)

#						#					
17.	B	D	J	L	T	47.	D	E	M	P	T
18.	B	E	F	J	P	48.	D	F	G	J	Q
19.	B	E	G	K	M	49.	D	F	I	L	P
20.	B	E	H	I	L	50.	D	G	K	O	T
21.	B	E	N	O	T	51.	D	H	I	Q	T
22.	B	F	G	I	T	52.	D	H	J	M	N
23.	B	F	H	N	Q	53.	D	K	L	M	Q
24.	B	G	L	O	Q	54.	D	N	O	P	Q
25.	B	H	J	K	O	55.	E	F	I	M	N
26.	B	I	J	M	Q	56.	E	F	L	Q	T
27.	B	K	P	Q	T	57.	E	G	H	J	T
28.	B	L	M	N	P	58.	E	G	I	P	Q
29.	C	D	F	N	T	59.	E	H	M	O	Q
30.	C	D	G	I	M	60.	E	J	K	N	Q
31.	C	D	H	L	O	61.	E	K	L	O	P
32.	C	D	J	K	P	62.	F	G	H	L	M
33.	C	E	F	G	O	63.	F	G	K	N	P
34.	C	E	H	N	P	64.	F	H	O	P	T
35.	C	E	I	K	T	65.	F	I	K	O	Q
36.	C	E	J	L	M	66.	F	J	K	M	T
37.	C	F	H	I	J	67.	F	J	L	N	O
38.	C	F	M	P	Q	68.	G	H	I	N	O
39.	C	G	H	K	Q	69.	G	I	J	K	L
40.	C	G	L	P	T	70.	G	J	M	O	P
41.	C	I	L	N	Q	71.	G	M	N	Q	T
42.	C	J	O	Q	T	72.	H	I	K	M	P
43.	C	K	M	N	O	73.	H	J	L	P	Q
44.	D	E	F	H	K	74.	H	K	L	N	T
45.	D	E	G	L	N	75.	I	J	N	P	T
46.	D	E	I	J	O	76.	I	L	M	O	T

161

BALANCED WHEEL™ 53121
Wheeling 21 Numbers in 84 games for a 3 of 4 Win

NUMBERS CORRECT	MAXIMUM WINS				MINIMUM WINS			
	5x	4x	3x	2x	5x	4x	3x	2x
5 (w/o Jackpot)	0	12	3	1				
5	1	10	2	3	0	0	3	24
4	–	11	2	3	–	0	1	14
3	–	–	13	0	–	–	0	6
2	–	–	–	13	–	–	–	0

Your 21 Numbers to Wheel

A	B	C	D	E	F	G	H	I	J	K
14	14	21	21	21	21	21	21	21	21	21

L	M	N	O	P	Q	R	S	T	U
23	21	22	22	22	22	22	21	14	14

The 84 Games to Play

#						#					
1.	A	B	C	T	U	26.	C	F	G	K	R
2.	A	B	D	T	U	27.	C	F	H	J	O
3.	A	B	E	T	U	28.	C	F	I	N	P
4.	A	B	F	T	U	29.	C	F	L	M	Q
5.	A	B	G	T	U	30.	C	G	H	I	S
6.	A	B	H	T	U	31.	C	G	J	M	P
7.	A	B	I	T	U	32.	C	H	K	N	Q
8.	A	B	J	T	U	33.	C	I	L	O	R
9.	A	B	K	T	U	34.	C	J	K	L	S
10.	A	B	M	T	U	35.	C	M	N	O	S
11.	A	B	P	Q	R	36.	C	P	Q	R	S
12.	A	B	S	T	U	37.	D	E	G	H	K
13.	A	L	R	T	U	38.	D	E	I	P	R
14.	A	P	Q	T	U	39.	D	E	J	L	O
15.	B	L	N	O	T	40.	D	E	M	N	Q
16.	B	L	N	O	U	41.	D	F	G	I	J
17.	C	D	E	F	S	42.	D	F	H	Q	R
18.	C	D	G	O	Q	43.	D	F	K	L	N
19.	C	D	H	L	P	44.	D	F	M	O	P
20.	C	D	I	K	M	45.	D	G	L	M	R
21.	C	D	J	N	R	46.	D	G	N	P	S
22.	C	E	G	L	N	47.	D	H	I	N	O
23.	C	E	H	M	R	48.	D	H	J	M	S
24.	C	E	I	J	Q	49.	D	I	L	Q	S
25.	C	E	K	O	P	50.	D	J	K	P	Q

162

(Continued Next Page)

BALANCED WHEEL™ 53121 (Continued from previous page)

51.	D	K	O	R	S
52.	E	F	G	P	Q
53.	E	F	H	I	L
54.	E	F	J	K	M
55.	E	F	N	O	R
56.	E	G	I	M	O
57.	E	G	J	R	S
58.	E	H	J	N	P
59.	E	H	O	Q	S
60.	E	I	K	N	S
61.	E	K	L	Q	H
62.	E	L	M	P	S
63.	F	G	H	M	N
64.	F	G	L	O	S
65.	F	H	K	P	S
66.	F	I	K	O	Q
67.	F	I	M	R	S

68.	F	J	L	P	R
69.	F	J	N	Q	S
70.	G	H	J	L	Q
71.	G	H	O	P	R
72.	G	I	K	L	P
73.	G	I	N	Q	R
74.	G	J	K	N	O
75.	G	K	M	Q	S
76.	H	I	J	K	R
77.	H	I	M	P	Q
78.	H	K	L	M	O
79.	H	L	N	R	S
80.	I	J	L	M	N
81.	I	J	O	P	S
82.	J	M	O	Q	R
83.	K	M	N	P	R
84.	L	N	O	P	Q

Copyright © 1983-1998 Gail Howard

BALANCED WHEEL™ 53122
Wheeling 22 Numbers in 98 games for a 3 of 4 Win

NUMBERS CORRECT	MAXIMUM WINS				MINIMUM WINS			
	5x	4x	3x	2x	5x	4x	3x	2x
5 (w/o Jackpot)	0	4	8	15				
5	1	2	7	12	0	0	3	21
4	–	3	0	16	–	0	1	14
3	–	–	7	9	–	–	0	7
2	–	–	–	13	–	–	–	0

Your 22 Numbers to Wheel

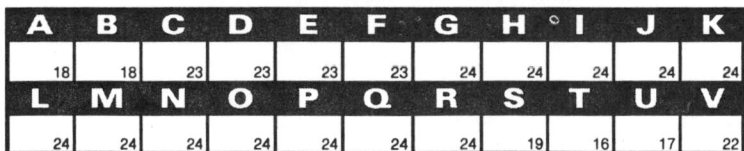

A	B	C	D	E	F	G	H	I	J	K
18	18	23	23	23	23	24	24	24	24	24

L	M	N	O	P	Q	R	S	T	U	V
24	24	24	24	24	24	24	19	16	17	22

The 98 Games to Play

1.	A	B	E	T	U
2.	A	B	F	T	U
3.	A	B	G	N	S
4.	A	B	H	J	U
5.	A	B	I	K	U

6.	A	B	L	P	U
7.	A	B	M	O	S
8.	A	B	Q	R	S
9.	A	E	F	S	T
10.	A	G	N	S	T

Copyright © 1983-1998 Gail Howard

(Continued Next Page)

BALANCED WHEEL™ 53122 (Continued from previous page)

#	1	2	3	4	5		#	1	2	3	4	5
11.	A	G	N	S	U		46.	C	H	K	O	P
12.	A	H	J	S	T		47.	C	J	K	N	R
13.	A	I	K	S	T		48.	C	M	N	O	Q
14.	A	L	P	S	T		49.	C	P	Q	R	V
15.	A	M	O	S	T		50.	D	E	F	K	O
16.	A	M	O	S	U		51.	D	E	G	I	L
17.	A	Q	R	S	T		52.	D	E	H	P	V
18.	A	Q	R	S	U		53.	D	E	M	N	R
19.	B	C	D	T	V		54.	D	F	G	J	N
20.	B	C	E	F	S		55.	D	F	I	M	V
21.	B	D	H	J	S		56.	D	F	L	P	Q
22.	B	G	N	T	U		57.	D	G	H	M	Q
23.	B	I	K	S	U		58.	D	G	K	P	R
24.	B	I	K	T	U		59.	D	H	I	J	K
25.	B	L	P	S	U		60.	D	H	L	N	O
26.	B	L	P	T	U		61.	D	I	O	Q	R
27.	B	M	O	T	U		62.	D	J	L	R	V
28.	B	Q	R	T	U		63.	D	J	M	O	P
29.	C	D	E	J	Q		64.	D	K	N	Q	V
30.	C	D	F	H	R		65.	E	F	G	R	V
31.	C	D	G	O	V		66.	E	F	H	J	L
32.	C	D	I	N	P		67.	E	F	I	N	Q
33.	C	D	K	L	M		68.	E	G	J	K	M
34.	C	D	S	U	V		69.	E	G	O	P	Q
35.	C	E	F	M	P		70.	E	H	I	M	O
36.	C	E	G	H	N		71.	E	H	K	Q	R
37.	C	E	I	K	V		72.	E	I	J	P	R
38.	C	E	L	O	R		73.	E	J	N	O	V
39.	C	F	G	K	Q		74.	E	K	L	N	P
40.	C	F	I	J	O		75.	E	L	M	Q	V
41.	C	F	L	N	V		76.	F	G	H	I	P
42.	C	G	I	M	R		77.	F	G	L	M	O
43.	C	G	J	L	P		78.	F	H	K	M	N
44.	C	H	I	L	Q		79.	F	H	O	Q	V
45.	C	H	J	M	V		80.	F	I	K	L	R

          (Continued Next Page)

BALANCED WHEEL™ 53122 (Continued from previous page)

81.	F	J	K	P	V
82.	F	J	M	Q	R
83.	F	N	O	P	R
84.	G	H	J	O	R
85.	G	H	K	L	V
86.	G	I	J	Q	V
87.	G	I	K	N	O
88.	G	L	N	Q	R
89.	G	M	N	P	V

90.	H	I	N	R	V
91.	H	J	N	P	Q
92.	H	J	S	T	U
93.	H	L	M	P	R
94.	I	J	L	M	N
95.	I	K	M	P	Q
96.	I	L	O	P	V
97.	J	K	L	O	Q
98.	K	M	O	R	V

BALANCED WHEEL™ 53124
Wheeling 24 Numbers in 132 games for a 3 of 4 Win

NUMBERS CORRECT	MAXIMUM WINS				MINIMUM WINS			
	5x	4x	3x	2x	5x	4x	3x	2x
5 (w/o Jackpot)	0	5	5	26				
5	1	3	6	21	0	0	3	29
4	–	3	3	15	–	0	1	19
3	–	–	5	21	–	–	0	9
2	–	–	–	14	–	–	–	1

Your 24 Numbers to Wheel

A	B	C	D	E	F	G	H	I	J	K	L
28	28	28	28	28	28	28	30	28	26	26	27

M	N	O	P	Q	R	S	T	U	V	W	X
27	27	27	27	27	27	27	27	27	28	28	28

The 132 Games to Play

1.	A	B	C	P	T
2.	A	B	D	I	V
3.	A	B	E	M	W
4.	A	B	K	N	R
5.	A	B	L	S	U
6.	A	C	D	S	W
7.	A	C	E	L	N
8.	A	C	I	K	M
9.	A	C	R	U	V
10.	A	D	E	R	T
11.	A	D	K	L	P
12.	A	D	M	N	U
13.	A	E	G	J	P

14.	A	E	I	P	U
15.	A	E	K	S	V
16.	A	F	G	O	S
17.	A	F	G	Q	W
18.	A	F	H	J	W
19.	A	F	I	J	X
20.	A	G	H	W	X
21.	A	H	O	Q	S
22.	A	I	L	R	W
23.	A	I	N	S	T
24.	A	J	Q	W	X
25.	A	K	T	U	W
26.	A	L	M	T	V

          (Continued Next Page)

BALANCED WHEEL™ 53124 (Continued from previous page)

#						#					
27.	A	M	P	R	S	62.	C	H	J	O	Q
28.	A	N	P	V	W	63.	C	H	J	Q	V
29.	B	C	D	M	R	64.	C	H	Q	V	X
30.	B	C	E	I	S	65.	C	I	N	P	R
31.	B	C	K	L	V	66.	C	I	T	V	W
32.	B	C	N	U	W	67.	C	K	P	S	U
33.	B	D	E	K	U	68.	C	L	M	P	W
34.	B	D	F	G	Q	69.	C	L	R	S	T
35.	B	D	F	G	X	70.	C	M	N	S	V
36.	B	D	L	T	W	71.	D	E	H	J	O
37.	B	D	N	P	S	72.	D	E	I	N	W
38.	B	E	F	O	X	73.	D	E	L	M	S
39.	B	E	H	Q	X	74.	D	F	G	J	X
40.	B	E	L	P	R	75.	D	F	H	J	P
41.	B	E	N	T	V	76.	D	G	L	O	X
42.	B	F	H	J	K	77.	D	H	K	O	W
43.	B	G	H	N	O	78.	D	H	Q	U	X
44.	B	H	J	N	O	79.	D	I	K	R	S
45.	B	I	K	P	W	80.	D	I	M	P	T
46.	B	I	L	M	N	81.	D	K	M	V	W
47.	B	I	R	T	U	82.	D	L	N	R	V
48.	B	J	M	P	X	83.	D	P	R	U	W
49.	B	K	M	S	T	84.	D	S	T	U	V
50.	B	M	P	U	V	85.	E	F	G	I	Q
51.	B	R	S	V	W	86.	E	F	H	M	X
52.	C	D	E	P	V	87.	E	G	H	M	Q
53.	C	D	I	L	U	88.	E	I	K	L	T
54.	C	D	K	N	T	89.	E	I	M	R	V
55.	C	E	K	R	W	90.	E	J	L	N	X
56.	C	E	M	T	U	91.	E	K	M	N	P
57.	C	F	G	J	V	92.	E	L	U	V	W
58.	C	F	H	Q	V	93.	E	N	R	S	U
59.	C	F	O	T	X	94.	E	P	S	T	W
60.	C	G	H	V	X	95.	F	G	H	J	S
61.	C	G	O	Q	V	96.	F	G	H	L	X

     (Continued Next Page)

BALANCED WHEEL™ 53124 (Continued from previous page)

97.	F	G	H	P	Q	**115.**	H	I	M	O	X
98.	F	G	H	T	U	**116.**	H	J	L	M	O
99.	F	G	I	J	R	**117.**	H	L	O	Q	W
100.	F	G	N	P	X	**118.**	H	N	O	R	X
101.	F	G	O	P	R	**119.**	H	O	P	Q	X
102.	F	H	J	T	U	**120.**	H	O	Q	T	X
103.	F	I	N	O	Q	**121.**	I	J	O	Q	R
104.	F	I	Q	R	X	**122.**	I	K	N	U	V
105.	F	K	M	O	Q	**123.**	I	L	P	S	V
106.	F	L	Q	S	X	**124.**	I	M	S	U	W
107.	F	O	U	V	X	**125.**	J	K	M	N	Q
108.	G	H	I	Q	R	**126.**	J	K	O	S	X
109.	G	J	L	Q	S	**127.**	J	O	Q	T	U
110.	G	J	O	V	W	**128.**	K	L	M	R	U
111.	G	J	R	S	X	**129.**	K	L	N	S	W
112.	G	J	T	U	X	**130.**	K	P	R	T	V
113.	G	K	O	W	X	**131.**	L	N	P	T	U
114.	G	O	Q	T	U	**132.**	M	N	R	T	W

BALANCED WHEEL™ 53126
Wheeling 26 Numbers in 174 games for a 3 of 4 Win

NUMBERS CORRECT	MAXIMUM WINS				MINIMUM WINS			
	5x	4x	3x	2x	5x	4x	3x	2x
5 (w/o Jackpot)	0	4	6	38				
5	1	2	7	30	0	0	3	30
4	–	2	6	32	–	0	1	19
3	–	–	6	14	–	–	0	10
2	–	–	–	13	–	–	–	2

Your 26 Numbers to Wheel

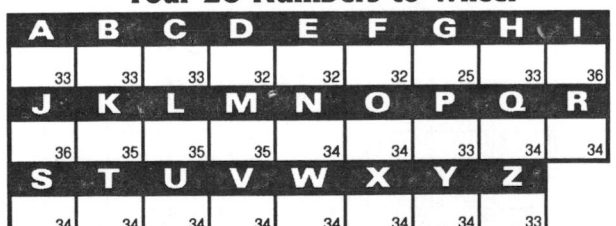

A	B	C	D	E	F	G	H	I
33	33	33	32	32	32	25	33	36

J	K	L	M	N	O	P	Q	R
36	35	35	35	34	34	33	34	34

S	T	U	V	W	X	Y	Z
34	34	34	34	34	34	34	33

The 174 Games to Play

1.	A	B	D	W	X	**3.**	A	B	I	L	N
2.	A	B	G	Y	Z	**4.**	A	B	J	R	X

    (Continued Next Page)

BALANCED WHEEL™ 53126 (Continued from previous page)

#						#					
5.	A	B	Q	W	X	40.	B	D	I	Q	T
6.	A	C	D	J	T	41.	B	E	F	X	Y
7.	A	C	I	Q	Z	42.	B	E	K	M	Z
8.	A	C	N	W	Z	43.	B	E	L	P	S
9.	A	D	E	Q	Z	44.	B	E	O	U	V
10.	A	D	H	Q	Y	45.	B	F	G	L	Z
11.	A	D	I	O	S	46.	B	F	H	V	Z
12.	A	D	K	L	W	47.	B	F	I	R	W
13.	A	D	N	P	V	48.	B	F	K	O	P
14.	A	D	N	U	W	49.	B	F	L	T	U
15.	A	D	Q	U	V	50.	B	G	M	S	U
16.	A	E	H	J	R	51.	B	G	N	O	X
17.	A	E	I	N	T	52.	B	H	K	L	X
18.	A	E	T	W	Y	53.	B	H	M	P	U
19.	A	F	G	M	O	54.	B	H	O	S	Y
20.	A	F	I	N	V	55.	B	I	J	N	O
21.	A	F	Q	V	W	56.	B	J	N	W	Y
22.	A	G	L	N	S	57.	B	K	S	T	V
23.	A	G	L	U	X	58.	B	L	M	V	Y
24.	A	H	I	N	W	59.	B	M	O	T	X
25.	A	I	M	N	X	60.	B	P	T	Y	Z
26.	A	I	R	S	Y	61.	B	S	U	X	Z
27.	A	J	K	P	Q	62.	C	D	E	G	T
28.	A	J	L	M	R	63.	C	D	I	Q	R
29.	A	J	M	Q	S	64.	C	D	I	W	Z
30.	A	J	O	R	V	65.	C	E	F	P	Z
31.	A	J	P	R	U	66.	C	E	I	R	W
32.	A	K	L	R	T	67.	C	E	K	O	X
33.	A	O	P	Q	W	68.	C	E	L	M	U
34.	B	C	E	H	T	69.	C	E	S	V	Y
35.	B	C	F	M	S	70.	C	F	H	U	X
36.	B	C	K	U	Y	71.	C	F	K	L	V
37.	B	C	L	O	Z	72.	C	F	N	Q	R
38.	B	C	P	V	X	73.	C	F	O	T	Y
39.	B	D	H	N	R	74.	C	G	H	Q	V

    (Continued Next Page)

168

BALANCED WHEEL™ 53126 (Continued from previous page)

#						#					
75.	C	G	I	J	K	110.	E	G	K	P	V
76.	C	G	P	R	W	111.	E	H	K	P	V
77.	C	H	K	S	Z	112.	E	H	M	S	X
78.	C	H	L	P	Y	113.	E	H	U	Y	Z
79.	C	H	M	O	V	114.	E	K	L	T	Y
80.	C	I	J	M	N	115.	E	L	V	X	Z
81.	C	J	Q	W	Z	116.	E	M	O	P	Y
82.	C	K	M	P	T	117.	E	N	Q	R	U
83.	C	L	S	T	X	118.	E	O	S	T	Z
84.	C	M	X	Y	Z	119.	E	P	T	U	X
85.	C	O	P	S	U	120.	F	G	N	U	Y
86.	C	T	U	V	Z	121.	F	G	S	X	Y
87.	D	E	I	Q	R	122.	F	H	J	N	W
88.	D	E	J	N	W	123.	F	H	K	M	Y
89.	D	F	I	Q	W	124.	F	H	P	S	T
90.	D	F	J	R	Z	125.	F	I	J	Q	Y
91.	D	G	H	J	P	126.	F	K	T	X	Z
92.	D	G	I	V	W	127.	F	L	M	P	X
93.	D	G	K	Q	R	128.	F	L	S	Y	Z
94.	D	I	J	K	U	129.	F	M	O	U	Z
95.	D	I	J	L	Q	130.	F	O	S	V	X
96.	D	I	M	W	Y	131.	F	P	U	V	Y
97.	D	I	O	Q	X	132.	G	H	K	T	W
98.	D	J	M	N	T	133.	G	I	P	Q	T
99.	D	J	R	S	V	134.	G	J	R	T	V
100.	D	J	R	X	Y	135.	G	L	M	O	Y
101.	D	K	N	O	Y	136.	G	M	N	X	Z
102.	D	L	N	S	X	137.	G	O	S	U	Z
103.	D	O	R	S	W	138.	H	I	R	V	W
104.	D	P	Q	R	T	139.	H	J	Q	T	W
105.	E	F	H	L	O	140.	H	K	M	Q	R
106.	E	F	K	S	U	141.	H	K	N	Q	S
107.	E	F	M	T	V	142.	H	K	O	T	U
108.	E	G	H	I	R	143.	H	L	M	T	Z
109.	E	G	J	Q	W	144.	H	L	S	U	V

     (Continued Next Page)

169

BALANCED WHEEL™ 53126 (Continued from previous page)

145.	H	O	P	X	Z	**160.**	K	L	M	R	U
146.	H	T	V	X	Y	**161.**	K	L	P	U	Z
147.	I	J	K	M	N	**162.**	K	M	U	V	X
148.	I	J	K	N	Y	**163.**	K	O	V	Y	Z
149.	I	J	K	W	X	**164.**	K	P	S	X	Y
150.	I	J	L	U	W	**165.**	L	M	N	Q	Z
151.	I	J	N	R	Z	**166.**	L	N	O	V	W
152.	I	J	P	S	U	**167.**	L	O	P	T	V
153.	I	J	Q	U	V	**168.**	L	O	U	X	Y
154.	I	O	R	W	X	**169.**	L	Q	R	W	Z
155.	I	P	R	T	W	**170.**	M	P	S	V	Z
156.	J	M	Q	U	W	**171.**	M	S	T	U	Y
157.	J	N	P	S	W	**172.**	N	O	Q	R	V
158.	J	N	R	T	X	**173.**	N	P	Q	R	S
159.	K	L	M	O	S	**174.**	N	Q	R	W	Y

BALANCED WHEEL™ 53135
Wheeling 35 Numbers in 470 games for a 3 of 4 Win

NUMBERS CORRECT	MAXIMUM WINS				MINIMUM WINS			
	5x	4x	3x	2x	5x	4x	3x	2x
5 (w/o Jackpot)	0	4	9	68				
5	1	1	10	50	0	0	3	48
4	–	2	6	42	–	0	1	28
3	–	–	6	17	–	–	0	14
2	–	–	–	15	–	–	–	3

Your 35 Numbers to Wheel

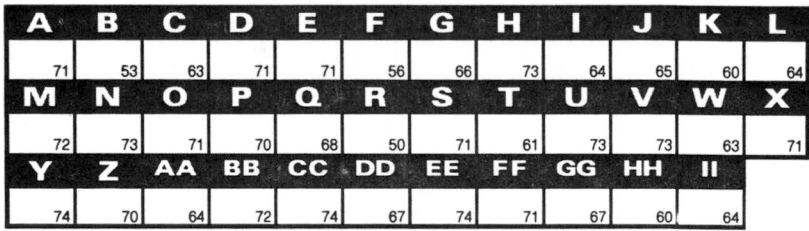

A	B	C	D	E	F	G	H	I	J	K	L
71	53	63	71	71	56	66	73	64	65	60	64

M	N	O	P	Q	R	S	T	U	V	W	X
72	73	71	70	68	50	71	61	73	73	63	71

Y	Z	AA	BB	CC	DD	EE	FF	GG	HH	II
74	70	64	72	74	67	74	71	67	60	64

The 470 Games to Play

1.	A	B	D	R	bb	**6.**	A	C	D	S	U
2.	A	B	E	J	ff	**7.**	A	C	E	Z	gg
3.	A	B	G	V	aa	**8.**	A	C	H	I	V
4.	A	B	I	L	dd	**9.**	A	C	J	L	ii
5.	A	B	N	W	Z	**10.**	A	D	F	O	S

　　　　　　　(Continued Next Page)

BALANCED WHEEL™ 53135 (Continued from previous page)

#						#				
11.	A	D	F	V	X	46.	A	K	O	Y	Z
12.	A	D	H	S	ii	47.	A	K	S	V	cc
13.	A	D	X	aa	ee	48.	A	K	aa	bb	ff
14.	A	D	ee	ff	gg	49.	A	L	N	Q	aa
15.	A	E	F	cc	ff	50.	A	L	O	W	cc
16.	A	E	G	J	Q	51.	A	M	N	V	cc
17.	A	E	I	N	bb	52.	A	M	O	bb	dd
18.	A	E	J	O	Z	53.	A	M	Q	S	Y
19.	A	E	M	U	W	54.	A	M	R	Z	ff
20.	A	E	N	R	S	55.	A	M	T	U	gg
21.	A	E	P	V	X	56.	A	N	O	P	S
22.	A	E	W	Y	Z	57.	A	N	O	V	hh
23.	A	E	Y	gg	hh	58.	A	N	T	X	ee
24.	A	E	cc	dd	ff	59.	A	O	Q	T	Z
25.	A	F	H	Z	ee	60.	A	O	R	V	Y
26.	A	F	M	N	P	61.	A	O	U	V	ee
27.	A	F	U	Y	bb	62.	A	P	U	Y	dd
28.	A	G	I	X	gg	63.	A	P	Z	bb	cc
29.	A	G	L	O	dd	64.	A	R	X	cc	ee
30.	A	G	Y	aa	cc	65.	A	S	T	bb	cc
31.	A	H	I	P	Q	66.	A	S	V	Z	dd
32.	A	H	J	W	X	67.	A	S	W	aa	ii
33.	A	H	K	M	N	68.	A	S	Z	bb	hh
34.	A	H	K	U	ff	69.	A	T	V	Y	ff
35.	A	H	L	X	ff	70.	A	U	X	cc	hh
36.	A	H	M	ff	hh	71.	A	V	ee	gg	ii
37.	A	H	R	U	bb	72.	B	C	F	Q	W
38.	A	I	K	X	ee	73.	B	C	H	T	ii
39.	A	I	L	cc	ee	74.	B	C	K	Y	hh
40.	A	I	U	Z	aa	75.	B	C	M	T	ee
41.	A	I	Y	Z	ii	76.	B	C	O	S	U
42.	A	J	M	P	ff	77.	B	C	P	X	gg
43.	A	J	N	X	dd	78.	B	C	Q	cc	ee
44.	A	J	S	U	cc	79.	B	D	E	G	dd
45.	A	J	V	Y	bb	80.	B	D	F	M	U

          (Continued Next Page)

BALANCED WHEEL™ 53135 (Continued from previous page)

#						#					
81.	B	D	I	V	Z	116.	B	S	X	ee	hh
82.	B	D	J	L	N	117.	B	T	U	Y	ee
83.	B	D	O	Q	W	118.	B	U	X	cc	ii
84.	B	D	W	aa	ff	119.	B	Z	bb	dd	ff
85.	B	E	I	R	W	120.	C	D	E	V	cc
86.	B	E	L	Z	aa	121.	C	D	G	P	hh
87.	B	E	N	V	bb	122.	C	D	H	J	gg
88.	B	F	G	dd	gg	123.	C	D	I	K	T
89.	B	F	I	K	ii	124.	C	D	I	L	Z
90.	B	F	J	aa	hh	125.	C	D	P	R	T
91.	B	F	L	R	T	126.	C	D	Y	gg	ii
92.	B	F	M	Q	X	127.	C	E	G	T	ii
93.	B	G	I	N	ff	128.	C	E	H	L	S
94.	B	G	J	R	Z	129.	C	E	I	N	U
95.	B	G	L	W	bb	130.	C	E	K	ee	hh
96.	B	H	K	S	cc	131.	C	E	Q	S	ii
97.	B	H	M	cc	ee	132.	C	F	G	I	R
98.	B	H	O	P	ee	133.	C	F	J	K	gg
99.	B	H	Q	X	Y	134.	C	F	L	aa	dd
100.	B	H	U	gg	hh	135.	C	F	T	hh	ii
101.	B	I	J	aa	bb	136.	C	G	H	S	ff
102.	B	J	V	W	dd	137.	C	G	J	R	aa
103.	B	K	M	S	Y	138.	C	G	K	P	gg
104.	B	K	O	T	X	139.	C	G	M	W	ii
105.	B	K	P	Q	U	140.	C	G	N	Z	bb
106.	B	K	ee	gg	ii	141.	C	G	U	V	ee
107.	B	L	R	V	ff	142.	C	H	U	Z	cc
108.	B	M	O	hh	ii	143.	C	I	J	P	T
109.	B	M	P	V	gg	144.	C	I	K	R	ii
110.	B	N	R	aa	dd	145.	C	I	L	X	hh
111.	B	O	Y	cc	gg	146.	C	I	S	cc	gg
112.	B	P	S	Y	ii	147.	C	J	K	W	dd
113.	B	P	T	cc	hh	148.	C	J	L	Q	cc
114.	B	Q	S	T	gg	149.	C	J	S	Z	bb
115.	B	Q	U	hh	ii	150.	C	J	T	W	hh

     (Continued Next Page)

BALANCED WHEEL™ 53135 (Continued from previous page)

#	1	2	3	4	5		#	1	2	3	4	5
151.	C	K	L	Q	ii		186.	D	G	R	hh	ii
152.	C	L	P	T	aa		187.	D	G	S	W	ee
153.	C	L	R	W	dd		188.	D	G	S	X	cc
154.	C	L	U	V	gg		189.	D	G	V	bb	ii
155.	C	M	N	P	Y		190.	D	G	W	Z	ii
156.	C	M	O	bb	ee		191.	D	H	I	Q	hh
157.	C	M	Q	X	ff		192.	D	H	J	Q	Y
158.	C	M	aa	dd	ee		193.	D	H	L	P	V
159.	C	N	O	X	aa		194.	D	H	M	aa	bb
160.	C	N	Q	W	bb		195.	D	H	O	T	Z
161.	C	N	dd	ee	ff		196.	D	H	U	cc	dd
162.	C	O	P	Q	dd		197.	D	I	J	R	dd
163.	C	O	W	Y	ff		198.	D	I	L	M	bb
164.	C	P	W	X	ee		199.	D	I	L	O	ff
165.	C	P	Z	ee	ii		200.	D	I	L	P	W
166.	C	P	aa	bb	ff		201.	D	I	S	Y	aa
167.	C	Q	R	gg	hh		202.	D	J	T	aa	ii
168.	C	Q	Y	aa	ee		203.	D	K	L	Q	R
169.	C	I	aa	dd	hh		204.	D	K	P	Q	dd
170.	C	V	Z	aa	ii		205.	D	K	W	ee	ii
171.	C	X	Y	bb	dd		206.	D	L	N	S	gg
172.	D	E	F	X	Z		207.	D	L	P	T	ii
173.	D	E	G	T	dd		208.	D	L	Y	dd	ii
174.	D	E	H	L	N		209.	D	L	aa	dd	hh
175.	D	E	K	L	gg		210.	D	M	Q	cc	gg
176.	D	E	Q	U	ee		211.	D	N	Q	X	ii
177.	D	F	H	cc	ff		212.	D	N	Y	Z	ee
178.	D	F	I	N	aa		213.	D	O	P	aa	gg
179.	D	F	J	Y	ee		214.	D	O	W	bb	ee
180.	D	F	P	X	bb		215.	D	Q	U	X	gg
181.	D	G	J	K	hh		216.	D	Q	V	Y	bb
182.	D	G	M	N	ee		217.	D	R	W	aa	gg
183.	D	G	N	V	W		218.	D	T	V	W	ff
184.	D	G	P	U	ff		219.	D	T	bb	ee	hh
185.	D	G	P	W	hh		220.	D	V	aa	cc	ee

          (Continued Next Page)

BALANCED WHEEL™ 53135 (Continued from previous page)

#						#					
221.	D	W	dd	ee	gg	256.	E	N	aa	ee	gg
222.	D	X	dd	ee	gg	257.	E	O	S	bb	ee
223.	E	F	H	S	V	258.	E	O	V	Y	dd
224.	E	F	K	M	O	259.	E	O	Z	ff	hh
225.	E	F	N	Y	ee	260.	E	P	S	cc	ff
226.	E	F	P	U	Z	261.	E	R	U	ee	ff
227.	E	F	Z	aa	bb	262.	E	R	V	X	Z
228.	E	G	I	ee	hh	263.	E	R	Y	bb	cc
229.	E	G	K	dd	ii	264.	E	S	U	X	dd
230.	E	G	L	cc	gg	265.	E	U	V	Z	cc
231.	E	G	O	X	Y	266.	E	V	bb	cc	hh
232.	E	G	Q	aa	hh	267.	F	G	J	T	W
233.	E	H	I	N	Q	268.	F	G	K	L	hh
234.	E	H	M	O	R	269.	F	G	Q	aa	ii
235.	E	H	N	X	hh	270.	F	H	M	V	Y
236.	E	H	P	T	ee	271.	F	H	N	X	cc
237.	E	H	S	cc	ee	272.	F	H	O	P	ee
238.	E	H	W	aa	cc	273.	F	H	O	S	bb
239.	E	H	X	bb	ii	274.	F	H	U	V	ee
240.	E	I	J	K	Q	275.	F	I	J	L	Q
241.	E	I	L	T	aa	276.	F	I	T	aa	gg
242.	E	I	N	ff	ii	277.	F	I	W	dd	hh
243.	E	J	M	X	cc	278.	F	J	P	V	ii
244.	E	J	N	S	V	279.	F	J	R	dd	ii
245.	E	J	P	bb	dd	280.	F	K	Q	T	dd
246.	E	J	S	W	X	281.	F	K	R	W	aa
247.	E	J	U	Y	ff	282.	F	L	W	gg	ii
248.	E	K	P	T	W	283.	F	M	O	Y	hh
249.	E	L	P	Q	gg	284.	F	M	S	Z	ff
250.	E	M	N	Z	dd	285.	F	M	bb	cc	ee
251.	E	M	O	P	Y	286.	F	N	O	X	Z
252.	E	M	O	U	ii	287.	F	N	S	U	X
253.	E	M	S	U	hh	288.	F	N	V	bb	ff
254.	E	M	V	bb	ff	289.	F	O	U	cc	ff
255.	E	N	P	Y	cc	290.	F	O	V	Z	cc

          (Continued Next Page)

BALANCED WHEEL™ 53135 (Continued from previous page)

#						#					
291.	F	P	S	Y	cc	326.	H	I	M	aa	gg
292.	F	P	Y	Z	ff	327.	H	I	O	Q	ii
293.	F	Q	R	gg	hh	328.	H	I	Q	X	bb
294.	F	Q	S	T	ee	329.	H	I	V	Z	gg
295.	F	X	Y	ee	ff	330.	H	K	O	V	bb
296.	G	H	J	Q	V	331.	H	K	S	Z	aa
297.	G	H	M	N	ii	332.	H	K	X	Y	cc
298.	G	H	M	U	Z	333.	H	L	M	Y	gg
299.	G	H	P	bb	ee	334.	H	L	O	ee	gg
300.	G	H	T	W	ii	335.	H	L	T	W	dd
301.	G	H	dd	hh	ii	336.	H	L	U	bb	gg
302.	G	I	J	L	Y	337.	H	L	aa	dd	gg
303.	G	I	K	L	W	338.	H	M	S	W	Z
304.	G	I	L	R	gg	339.	H	N	R	V	ee
305.	G	I	O	Q	cc	340.	H	O	P	aa	gg
306.	G	I	T	aa	dd	341.	H	O	U	bb	hh
307.	G	J	O	aa	gg	342.	H	Q	Y	ee	ff
308.	G	J	X	cc	dd	343.	H	R	S	Z	cc
309.	G	K	L	T	hh	344.	H	R	X	Y	ff
310.	G	K	P	R	W	345.	H	S	U	W	Y
311.	G	K	Q	T	ee	346.	H	S	V	Y	hh
312.	G	K	T	dd	ii	347.	H	U	cc	ff	ii
313.	G	L	O	X	aa	348.	H	Y	aa	ff	gg
314.	G	M	N	V	ff	349.	H	Z	cc	gg	hh
315.	G	M	P	S	bb	350.	I	J	T	hh	ii
316.	G	N	P	W	ii	351.	I	J	aa	ee	ff
317.	G	N	S	U	ii	352.	I	K	P	hh	ii
318.	G	P	S	V	Z	353.	I	K	dd	ee	gg
319.	G	P	T	W	aa	354.	I	M	X	cc	ii
320.	G	Q	R	T	dd	355.	I	M	Y	dd	ff
321.	G	Q	Y	dd	gg	356.	I	N	O	W	gg
322.	G	U	W	bb	ff	357.	I	P	Q	R	aa
323.	G	Z	ee	ff	ii	358.	I	P	cc	ee	gg
324.	H	I	J	T	aa	359.	I	Q	S	Z	ff
325.	H	I	M	Q	dd	360.	I	Q	V	W	ee

    (Continued Next Page)

BALANCED WHEEL™ 53135 (Continued from previous page)

#						#					
361.	I	R	T	W	hh	396.	K	Q	W	gg	hh
362.	I	S	U	ee	gg	397.	K	R	aa	dd	hh
363.	I	U	bb	dd	ii	398.	K	U	X	Y	Z
364.	I	W	aa	dd	hh	399.	K	U	Y	bb	cc
365.	I	W	bb	ff	gg	400.	K	V	X	aa	ff
366.	J	K	L	P	ee	401.	L	M	Q	X	ee
367.	J	K	L	T	dd	402.	L	N	V	W	bb
368.	J	K	L	ee	ii	403.	L	N	W	ee	ff
369.	J	K	R	T	gg	404.	L	O	Q	V	aa
370.	J	L	P	R	hh	405.	L	Q	S	Y	aa
371.	J	L	Z	gg	ii	406.	L	Q	U	aa	ff
372.	J	M	N	O	Y	407.	L	Q	Z	aa	cc
373.	J	M	O	S	Z	408.	L	R	T	aa	ii
374.	J	M	U	V	dd	409.	L	S	V	ee	ii
375.	J	M	W	aa	gg	410.	L	W	ee	hh	ii
376.	J	N	P	U	Z	411.	L	Y	bb	dd	ee
377.	J	N	bb	cc	ff	412.	M	N	P	U	X
378.	J	O	P	V	cc	413.	M	N	R	X	bb
379.	J	O	S	dd	ff	414.	M	N	S	T	Y
380.	J	O	U	X	bb	415.	M	N	bb	gg	hh
381.	J	P	S	X	Y	416.	M	O	S	V	X
382.	J	Q	R	W	ii	417.	M	O	T	X	bb
383.	J	Q	dd	ee	hh	418.	M	O	cc	ff	hh
384.	J	U	W	Z	cc	419.	M	P	S	cc	dd
385.	J	V	X	Z	ff	420.	M	P	V	Y	Z
386.	J	Y	Z	cc	dd	421.	M	Q	T	V	cc
387.	K	M	U	aa	cc	422.	M	Q	bb	ff	ii
388.	K	M	V	Y	ff	423.	M	R	S	Y	ee
389.	K	M	X	Z	bb	424.	M	R	U	V	cc
390.	K	N	O	Y	aa	425.	M	T	Z	ee	ff
391.	K	N	S	X	bb	426.	M	V	X	Z	hh
392.	K	N	U	V	Z	427.	M	W	X	Y	cc
393.	K	N	Z	cc	ff	428.	N	O	R	cc	ff
394.	K	O	S	U	Z	429.	N	O	T	V	gg
395.	K	O	S	cc	ff	430.	N	O	U	cc	dd

     (Continued Next Page)

BALANCED WHEEL™ 53135 (Continued from previous page)

431.	N	O	bb	cc	ii	451.	P	Q	bb	dd	hh
432.	N	P	V	dd	ff	452.	P	R	dd	gg	ii
433.	N	Q	T	bb	ff	453.	P	S	U	V	bb
434.	N	Q	bb	ee	gg	454.	P	U	X	cc	ff
435.	N	R	U	Y	Z	455.	P	aa	ee	hh	ii
436.	N	S	Y	bb	dd	456.	Q	T	U	X	Y
437.	N	S	cc	ff	hh	457.	Q	W	cc	dd	ii
438.	N	T	U	Z	cc	458.	R	S	V	bb	ff
439.	N	U	V	X	Y	459.	S	T	V	X	Z
440.	N	U	Y	Z	hh	460.	S	V	W	gg	ii
441.	N	U	aa	bb	gg	461.	T	U	V	bb	ee
442.	O	P	U	Y	bb	462.	T	X	cc	ff	gg
443.	O	P	X	Z	dd	463.	T	Y	Z	bb	gg
444.	O	R	S	U	X	464.	U	V	ff	gg	hh
445.	O	R	Z	bb	ee	465.	U	W	X	Z	aa
446.	O	S	T	U	ff	466.	U	Z	bb	dd	ee
447.	O	S	X	gg	hh	467.	V	X	bb	cc	dd
448.	O	T	Y	cc	ee	468.	V	Y	cc	ff	hh
449.	O	X	dd	ff	ii	469.	W	Y	aa	gg	ii
450.	P	Q	W	ff	gg	470.	X	Y	bb	ff	hh

BALANCED WHEEL™ 53210
Wheeling 10 Numbers in 2 games for a 3 of 5 Win

NUMBERS CORRECT	MAXIMUM WINS				MINIMUM WINS			
	5x	4x	3x	2x	5x	4x	3x	2x
5 (w/o Jackpot)	0	1	0	0				
5	1	0	0	0	0	0	1	1
4	–	1	0	0	–	0	0	2
3	–	–	1	0	–	–	0	1
2	–	–	–	1	–	–	–	0

Your 10 Numbers to Wheel

A	B	C	D	E	F	G	H	I	J
1	1	1	1	1	1	1	1	1	1

The 2 Games to Play

1.
A	B	F	I	J

2.
C	D	E	G	H

177

BALANCED WHEEL™ 53211
Wheeling 11 Numbers in 5 games for a 3 of 5 Win

NUMBERS CORRECT	MAXIMUM WINS				MINIMUM WINS			
	5x	4x	3x	2x	5x	4x	3x	2x
5 (w/o Jackpot)	0	3	1	0				
5	1	2	0	1	0	0	1	2
4	–	2	1	0	–	0	0	3
3	–	–	3	0	–	–	0	1
2	–	–	–	3	–	–	–	0

Your 11 Numbers to Wheel

A	B	C	D	E	F	G	H	I	J	K
2	3	1	2	3	3	3	3	3	1	1

The 5 Games to Play

1. | A | C | D | J | K |

2. | A | D | G | H | I |

3. | B | E | F | G | H |

4. | B | E | F | G | I |

5. | B | E | F | H | I |

Copyright © 1983-1998 Gail Howard

BALANCED WHEEL™ 53212
Wheeling 12 Numbers in 6 games for a 3 of 5 Win

NUMBERS CORRECT	MAXIMUM WINS				MINIMUM WINS			
	5x	4x	3x	2x	5x	4x	3x	2x
5 (w/o Jackpot)	0	3	0	0				
5	1	1	1	0	0	0	1	3
4	–	2	1	0	–	0	0	3
3	–	–	3	0	–	–	0	1
2	–	–	–	3	–	–	–	0

Your 12 Numbers to Wheel

A	B	C	D	E	F	G	H	I	J	K	L
3	2	2	3	2	3	2	3	3	2	2	3

The 6 Games to Play

1. | A | C | G | J | K |

2. | A | D | F | H | L |

3. | A | D | H | I | L |

4. | B | D | E | H | L |

5. | B | F | G | I | J |

6. | C | E | F | I | K |

Copyright © 1983-1998 Gail Howard

BALANCED WHEEL™ 53213
Wheeling 13 Numbers in 9 games for a 3 of 5 Win

NUMBERS CORRECT	MAXIMUM WINS				MINIMUM WINS			
	5x	4x	3x	2x	5x	4x	3x	2x
5 (w/o Jackpot)	0	3	2	1				
5	1	1	1	2	0	0	1	5
4	–	2	1	2	–	0	0	4
3	–	–	3	1	–	–	0	1
2	–	–	–	4	–	–	–	0

(Continued Next Page)

BALANCED WHEEL™ 53213 (Continued from previous page)
Your 13 Numbers to Wheel

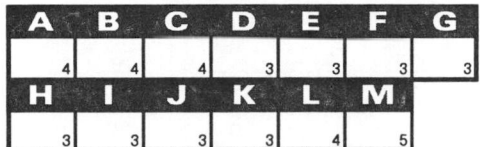

A	B	C	D	E	F	G
4	4	4	3	3	3	3

H	I	J	K	L	M
3	3	3	3	4	5

The 9 Games to Play

1.	A	B	D	L	M
2.	A	B	G	K	M
3.	A	C	E	L	M
4.	A	C	H	L	M
5.	B	C	F	J	M

6.	B	F	I	J	L
7.	C	D	G	I	K
8.	D	E	F	H	J
9.	E	G	H	I	K

Copyright © 1983-1998 Gail Howard

BALANCED WHEEL™ 53214
Wheeling 14 Numbers in 10 games for a 3 of 5 Win

NUMBERS CORRECT	MAXIMUM WINS				MINIMUM WINS			
	5x	4x	3x	2x	5x	4x	3x	2x
5 (w/o Jackpot)	0	3	2	0				
5	1	2	2	0	0	0	1	5
4	–	3	0	2	–	0	0	4
3	–	–	3	1	–	–	0	2
2	–	–	–	4	–	–	–	0

Your 14 Numbers to Wheel

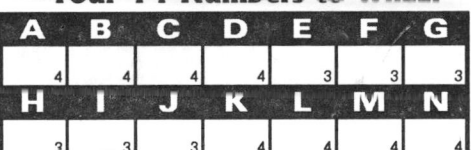

A	B	C	D	E	F	G
4	4	4	4	3	3	3

H	I	J	K	L	M	N
3	3	3	4	4	4	4

The 10 Games to Play

1.	A	C	H	K	M
2.	A	C	I	K	M
3.	A	C	J	K	M
4.	A	H	I	J	M
5.	B	D	E	L	N

6.	B	D	F	L	N
7.	B	D	G	L	N
8.	B	E	F	G	N
9.	C	H	I	J	K
10.	D	E	F	G	L

Copyright © 1983-1998 Gail Howard

BALANCED WHEEL™ 53215
Wheeling 15 Numbers in 13 games for a 3 of 5 Win

NUMBERS CORRECT	MAXIMUM WINS				MINIMUM WINS			
	5x	4x	3x	2x	5x	4x	3x	2x
5 (w/o Jackpot)	0	2	3	3				
5	1	1	0	6	0	0	1	5
4	–	2	0	6	–	0	0	4
3	–	–	2	3	–	–	0	2
2	–	–	–	5	–	–	–	0

Your 15 Numbers to Wheel

A	B	C	D	E	F	G	H
5	5	4	4	5	4	4	4

I	J	K	L	M	N	O	
4	4	4	3	5	5	5	

The 13 Games to Play

1. A	B	C	N	O
2. A	B	K	N	O
3. A	D	E	M	O
4. A	E	J	M	O
5. A	G	I	L	O
6. B	E	G	I	N
7. B	F	H	L	N
8. B	G	I	M	N
9. C	D	J	K	L
10. C	E	F	K	M
11. C	E	H	K	M
12. D	F	G	H	J
13. D	F	H	I	J

Copyright © 1983-1998 Gail Howard

BALANCED WHEEL™ 53216
Wheeling 16 Numbers in 16 games for a 3 of 5 Win

NUMBERS CORRECT	MAXIMUM WINS				MINIMUM WINS			
	5x	4x	3x	2x	5x	4x	3x	2x
5 (w/o Jackpot)	0	3	3	2				
5	1	0	6	1	0	0	1	7
4	–	1	3	3	–	0	0	4
3	–	–	2	3	–	–	0	2
2	–	–	–	3	–	–	–	0

Your 16 Numbers to Wheel

A	B	C	D	E	F	G	H
5	5	5	5	5	5	5	5

I	J	K	L	M	N	O	P
5	5	5	5	5	5	5	5

The 16 Games to Play

1. A	B	E	K	P
2. A	B	F	L	N
3. A	E	F	L	P
4. A	E	K	L	N
5. A	F	K	N	P
6. B	E	F	K	N
7. B	E	L	N	P
8. B	F	K	L	P

Copyright © 1983-1998 Gail Howard   (Continued Next Page)

BALANCED WHEEL™ 53216 (Continued from previous page)

9.	C	D	G	H	O

C	D	G	H	O
C	D	I	J	M
C	G	H	I	M
C	G	I	J	O

9.
10.
11.
12.

C	H	J	M	O
D	G	H	J	M
D	G	I	M	O
D	H	I	J	O

13.
14.
15.
16.

BALANCED WHEEL™ 53217
Wheeling 17 Numbers in 20 games for a 3 of 5 Win

NUMBERS CORRECT	MAXIMUM WINS				MINIMUM WINS			
	5x	4x	3x	2x	5x	4x	3x	2x
5 (w/o Jackpot)	0	4	1	3				
5	1	1	4	2	0	0	1	8
4	–	2	2	2	–	0	0	6
3	–	–	3	3	–	–	0	2
2	–	–	–	5	–	–	–	0

Your 17 Numbers to Wheel

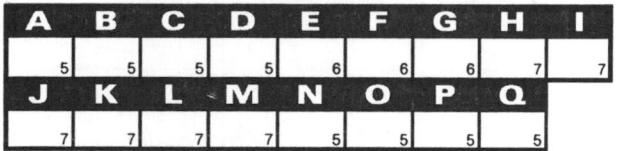

A	B	C	D	E	F	G	H	I
5	5	5	5	6	6	6	7	7

J	K	L	M	N	O	P	Q
7	7	7	7	5	5	5	5

The 20 Games to Play

A	B	C	P	Q
A	B	D	N	O
A	C	D	O	Q
A	C	N	P	Q
A	D	O	P	Q
B	C	D	N	P
B	C	N	O	P
B	D	N	O	Q
E	F	G	H	J
E	F	G	I	M

1.
2.
3.
4.
5.
6.
7.
8.
9.
10.

E	F	G	K	L
E	H	I	J	L
E	H	K	L	M
E	I	J	K	M
F	H	I	L	M
F	H	J	K	M
F	I	J	K	L
G	H	I	J	M
G	H	I	K	L
G	J	K	L	M

11.
12.
13.
14.
15.
16.
17.
18.
19.
20.

BALANCED WHEEL™ 53218
Wheeling 18 Numbers in 24 games for a 3 of 5 Win

NUMBERS CORRECT	MAXIMUM WINS				MINIMUM WINS			
	5x	4x	3x	2x	5x	4x	3x	2x
5 (w/o Jackpot)	0	4	3	5				
5	1	1	6	3	0	0	1	9
4	–	2	3	4	–	0	0	6
3	–	–	3	4	–	–	0	3
2	–	–	–	6	–	–	–	0

(Continued Next Page)

BALANCED WHEEL™ 53218 (Continued from previous page)
Your 18 Numbers to Wheel

A	B	C	D	E	F	G	H	I
6	6	7	6	7	7	7	6	7

J	K	L	M	N	O	P	Q	R
7	7	7	7	7	7	7	6	6

The 24 Games to Play

1.	A	D	F	M	Q
2.	A	D	G	L	O
3.	A	D	I	L	Q
4.	A	F	G	I	O
5.	A	F	I	L	M
6.	A	G	M	O	Q
7.	B	C	E	J	P
8.	B	C	H	J	R
9.	B	C	J	K	N
10.	B	E	H	P	R
11.	B	E	K	N	P
12.	B	H	K	N	R
13.	C	E	H	J	K
14.	C	E	N	P	R
15.	C	H	K	N	P
16.	C	J	K	P	R
17.	D	F	G	L	M
18.	D	F	I	M	O
19.	D	G	I	O	Q
20.	E	H	J	N	P
21.	E	J	K	N	R
22.	F	G	L	O	Q
23.	F	I	L	M	Q
24.	G	I	L	M	O

BALANCED WHEEL™ 53219
Wheeling 19 Numbers in 28 games for a 3 of 5 Win

NUMBERS CORRECT	MAXIMUM WINS				MINIMUM WINS			
	5x	4x	3x	2x	5x	4x	3x	2x
5 (w/o Jackpot)	0	5	0	10				
5	1	0	6	10	0	0	1	8
4	–	1	4	6	–	0	0	5
3	–	–	4	0	–	–	0	2
2	–	–	–	4	–	–	–	0

Your 19 Numbers to Wheel

A	B	C	D	E	F	G	H	I	J
5	10	5	9	9	5	5	9	9	5

K	L	M	N	O	P	Q	R	S
9	9	9	5	9	9	5	9	5

The 28 Games to Play

1.	A	C	F	G	S
2.	A	C	F	N	Q
3.	A	C	G	J	Q
4.	A	F	G	J	N
5.	A	J	N	Q	S
6.	B	D	E	I	P
7.	B	D	H	I	K
8.	B	D	I	L	O
9.	B	D	I	M	R
10.	B	E	H	K	P

          (Continued Next Page)

BALANCED WHEEL™ 53219 (Continued from previous page)

11.	B	E	L	O	P	20.	D	H	M	O	P
12.	R	F	M	P	R	21.	D	K	L	M	P
13.	B	H	K	L	O	22.	D	K	O	P	R
14.	B	H	K	M	R	23.	E	H	I	L	M
15.	B	L	M	O	R	24.	E	H	I	O	R
16.	C	F	J	N	S	25.	E	I	K	L	R
17.	C	G	N	Q	S	26.	F	G	J	Q	S
18.	D	E	H	L	R	27.	H	I	L	P	R
19.	D	E	K	M	O	28.	I	K	M	O	P

BALANCED WHEEL™ 53220
Wheeling 20 Numbers in 32 games for a 3 of 5 Win

NUMBERS CORRECT	MAXIMUM WINS				MINIMUM WINS			
	5x	4x	3x	2x	5x	4x	3x	2x
5 (w/o Jackpot)	0	5	0	10				
5	1	1	5	5	0	0	1	9
4	–	2	2	6	–	0	0	6
3	–	–	4	0	–	–	0	3
2	–	–	–	5	–	–	–	0

Your 20 Numbers to Wheel

A	B	C	D	E	F	G	H	I	J
7	6	6	7	10	9	9	9	9	9

K	L	M	N	O	P	Q	R	S	T
9	6	9	0	0	0	0	7	7	7

The 32 Games to Play

1.	A	B	C	L	I	14.	E	F	H	J	N
2.	A	B	D	Q	R	15.	E	F	I	M	N
3.	A	B	Q	S	T	16.	E	F	K	N	P
4.	A	C	D	Q	R	17.	E	G	H	J	O
5.	A	C	R	S	T	18.	E	G	I	M	O
6.	A	D	L	S	T	19.	E	G	K	O	P
7.	A	L	Q	R	S	20.	E	H	I	J	M
8.	B	C	D	L	R	21.	E	H	J	K	P
9.	B	C	L	Q	S	22.	E	I	K	M	P
10.	B	D	R	S	T	23.	F	G	H	I	K
11.	C	D	Q	S	T	24.	F	G	H	M	P
12.	D	L	Q	R	T	25.	F	G	J	K	M
13.	E	F	G	N	O	26.	F	H	K	M	O

(Continued Next Page)

BALANCED WHEEL™ 53220 (Continued from previous page)

27.	F	I	J	O	P
28.	G	H	K	M	N
29.	G	I	J	N	P

30.	H	I	N	O	P
31.	I	J	K	N	O
32.	J	M	N	O	P

Copyright © 1983-1998 Gail Howard

BALANCED WHEEL™ 53221
Wheeling 21 Numbers in 37 games for a 3 of 5 Win

NUMBERS CORRECT	MAXIMUM WINS				MINIMUM WINS			
	5x	4x	3x	2x	5x	4x	3x	2x
5 (w/o Jackpot)	0	5	0	10				
5	1	2	4	8	0	0	1	9
4	–	2	3	6	–	0	0	6
3	–	–	4	2	–	–	0	3
2	–	–	–	6	–	–	–	0

Your 21 Numbers to Wheel

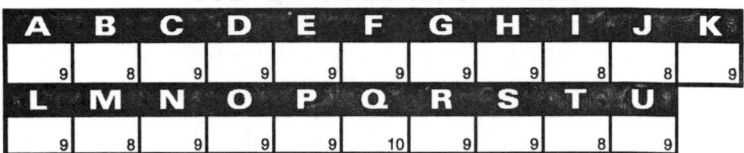

A	B	C	D	E	F	G	H	I	J	K
9	8	9	9	9	9	9	9	8	8	9

L	M	N	O	P	Q	R	S	T	U
9	8	9	9	9	10	9	9	8	9

The 37 Games to Play

1.	A	B	F	M	T
2.	A	B	H	J	R
3.	A	B	I	R	S
4.	A	F	H	I	S
5.	A	F	J	R	S
6.	A	H	J	M	R
7.	A	H	M	R	T
8.	A	I	J	R	T
9.	A	I	M	S	T
10.	B	F	H	I	T
11.	B	F	J	M	S
12.	B	F	R	S	T
13.	B	H	M	R	S
14.	B	I	J	M	T
15.	C	D	E	L	U
16.	C	D	G	K	N
17.	C	D	O	P	Q
18.	C	E	G	P	U
19.	C	E	K	L	P

20.	C	E	N	O	Q
21.	C	G	L	O	Q
22.	C	K	O	Q	U
23.	C	L	N	P	U
24.	D	E	G	K	O
25.	D	E	N	P	Q
26.	D	G	L	P	Q
27.	D	G	N	O	U
28.	D	K	L	N	O
29.	D	K	P	Q	U
30.	E	G	L	N	Q
31.	E	K	N	Q	U
32.	E	L	O	P	U
33.	F	H	I	J	S
34.	F	H	I	M	R
35.	F	H	J	S	T
36.	G	K	L	Q	U
37.	G	K	N	O	P

Copyright © 1983-1998 Gail Howard

184

BALANCED WHEEL™ 53222
Wheeling 22 Numbers in 40 games for a 3 of 5 Win

NUMBERS CORRECT	MAXIMUM WINS				MINIMUM WINS			
	5x	4x	3x	2x	5x	4x	3x	2x
5 (w/o Jackpot)	0	5	0	10				
5	1	0	6	10	0	0	1	10
4	–	1	4	6	–	0	0	6
3	–	–	4	0	–	–	0	3
2	–	–	–	4	–	–	–	0

Your 22 Numbers to Wheel

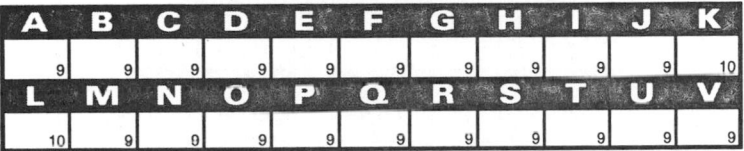

A	B	C	D	E	F	G	H	I	J	K
9	9	9	9	9	9	9	9	9	9	10

L	M	N	O	P	Q	R	S	T	U	V
10	9	9	9	9	9	9	9	9	9	9

The 40 Games to Play

#						#					
1.	A	B	F	O	S	21.	C	G	H	N	T
2.	A	B	I	J	S	22.	C	G	R	T	U
3.	A	B	I	O	P	23.	C	H	Q	T	U
4.	A	B	L	M	V	24.	D	E	G	N	R
5.	A	F	I	L	V	25.	D	E	H	N	Q
6.	A	F	J	M	P	26.	D	E	Q	R	U
7.	A	I	M	O	S	27.	D	G	H	T	U
8.	A	J	L	O	V	28.	D	N	Q	R	T
9.	A	L	P	S	V	29.	E	G	K	Q	T
10.	B	F	I	L	M	30.	E	H	K	R	T
11.	B	I	J	P	V	31.	E	K	N	T	U
12.	B	I	O	S	V	32.	F	I	J	L	O
13.	B	J	L	M	O	33.	F	I	L	P	S
14.	B	L	M	P	S	34.	F	J	M	S	V
15.	C	D	E	K	T	35.	F	M	O	P	V
16.	C	D	G	K	Q	36.	G	H	K	Q	R
17.	C	D	H	K	R	37.	G	K	N	Q	U
18.	C	D	K	N	U	38.	H	K	N	R	U
19.	C	E	G	H	U	39.	I	J	M	P	V
20.	C	E	N	Q	R	40.	J	L	O	P	S

BALANCED WHEEL™ 53223
Wheeling 23 Numbers in 50 games for a 3 of 5 Win

NUMBERS CORRECT	MAXIMUM WINS				MINIMUM WINS			
	5x	4x	3x	2x	5x	4x	3x	2x
5 (w/o Jackpot)	0	5	0	10				
5	1	1	7	12	0	0	1	11
4	–	2	3	11	–	0	0	7
3	–	–	5	1	–	–	0	3
2	–	–	–	6	–	–	–	0

Your 23 Numbers to Wheel

A	B	C	D	E	F	G	H	I	J	K	L
9	9	9	9	9	9	14	13	13	13	13	12

M	N	O	P	Q	R	S	T	U	V	W	
12	12	12	12	12	12	10	9	9	9	9	

The 50 Games to Play

#						#					
1.	A	B	C	F	W	26.	G	H	O	P	R
2.	A	B	D	S	T	27.	G	I	K	L	O
3.	A	B	E	U	V	28.	G	I	M	N	O
4.	A	C	D	E	V	29.	G	I	O	Q	R
5.	A	C	S	T	U	30.	G	I	P	Q	R
6.	A	D	E	F	U	31.	G	J	K	N	P
7.	A	D	U	V	W	32.	G	K	L	M	N
8.	A	E	S	T	W	33.	G	K	L	Q	R
9.	A	F	S	T	V	34.	G	M	N	Q	R
10.	B	C	D	S	U	35.	H	I	J	M	P
11.	B	C	E	F	T	36.	H	I	K	N	P
12.	B	C	T	V	W	37.	H	I	K	P	Q
13.	B	D	E	S	W	38.	H	I	L	N	R
14.	B	D	F	S	V	39.	H	K	M	O	Q
15.	B	F	T	U	W	40.	H	K	M	P	R
16.	C	D	F	T	W	41.	H	L	N	O	Q
17.	C	E	S	U	W	42.	I	J	K	M	R
18.	C	F	S	U	V	43.	I	J	K	N	Q
19.	D	E	T	U	V	44.	I	J	L	M	Q
20.	E	F	S	V	W	45.	I	K	L	O	P
21.	G	H	I	J	O	46.	J	K	N	O	R
22.	G	H	J	K	L	47.	J	L	M	O	R
23.	G	H	J	M	N	48.	J	L	N	P	R
24.	G	H	J	Q	R	49.	J	L	O	P	Q
25.	G	H	L	M	P	50.	M	N	O	P	Q

BALANCED WHEEL™ 53224
Wheeling 24 Numbers in 54 games for a 3 of 5 Win

NUMBERS CORRECT	MAXIMUM WINS				MINIMUM WINS			
	5x	4x	3x	2x	5x	4x	3x	2x
5 (w/o Jackpot)	0	5	0	10				
5	1	0	8	16	0	0	1	11
4	–	1	4	12	–	0	0	7
3	–	–	5	0	–	–	0	3
2	–	–	–	7	–	–	–	0

Your 24 Numbers to Wheel

A	B	C	D	E	F	G	H	I	J	K	L
9	13	13	9	13	9	13	13	13	9	9	13

M	N	O	P	Q	R	S	T	U	V	W	X
9	9	13	13	13	13	10	9	13	9	14	9

The 54 Games to Play

#						#					
1.	A	D	F	J	T	26.	C	G	H	U	W
2.	A	D	F	M	V	27.	C	G	L	P	R
3.	A	D	J	M	N	28.	C	H	L	P	Q
4.	A	D	K	S	X	29.	C	I	O	U	W
5.	A	F	J	M	X	30.	C	L	P	U	W
6.	A	F	K	N	S	31.	C	Q	R	U	W
7.	A	J	K	S	V	32.	D	F	J	K	M
8.	A	K	M	S	T	33.	D	F	N	S	X
9.	A	N	T	V	X	34.	D	J	S	V	X
10.	B	C	E	U	W	35.	D	K	N	T	V
11.	B	C	G	O	Q	36.	D	M	S	T	X
12.	B	C	H	O	R	37.	E	Q	U	L	O
13.	B	C	I	L	P	38.	E	G	P	Q	W
14.	B	E	G	R	U	39.	E	H	P	R	W
15.	B	E	H	Q	U	40.	E	I	L	O	W
16.	B	E	I	P	U	41.	E	L	O	Q	R
17.	B	E	L	O	U	42.	F	J	N	S	V
18.	B	G	H	I	P	43.	F	K	T	V	X
19.	B	G	L	Q	W	44.	F	M	N	S	T
20.	B	H	L	R	W	45.	G	H	Q	R	W
21.	B	I	O	P	W	46.	G	I	L	Q	U
22.	B	I	P	Q	R	47.	G	I	O	R	W
23.	C	E	G	I	Q	48.	G	O	P	Q	U
24.	C	E	H	I	R	49.	H	I	L	R	U
25.	C	E	L	O	P	50.	H	I	O	Q	W

187

(Continued Next Page)

BALANCED WHEEL™ 53224 (Continued from previous page)

51.	H	O	P	R	U
52.	J	K	N	T	X

53.	J	M	S	T	V
54.	K	M	N	V	X

Copyright © 1983-1998 Gail Howard

BALANCED WHEEL™ 53225
Wheeling 25 Numbers in 64 games for a 3 of 5 Win

NUMBERS CORRECT	MAXIMUM WINS				MINIMUM WINS			
	5x	4x	3x	2x	5x	4x	3x	2x
5 (w/o Jackpot)	0	4	4	13				
5	1	1	7	12	0	0	1	13
4	–	2	3	11	–	0	0	8
3	–	–	5	1	–	–	0	4
2	–	–	–	7	–	–	–	0

Your 25 Numbers to Wheel

A	B	C	D	E	F	G	H	I
13	12	13	13	13	12	13	13	12

J	K	L	M	N	O	P	Q	R
13	14	12	12	13	13	13	12	13

S	T	U	V	W	X	Y
14	13	13	13	12	13	13

The 64 Games to Play

1.	A	B	E	M	X
2.	A	B	F	S	V
3.	A	B	I	L	W
4.	A	B	I	Q	X
5.	A	B	L	S	X
6.	A	E	F	I	X
7.	A	E	F	L	V
8.	A	E	F	M	W
9.	A	E	Q	S	V
10.	A	F	I	Q	W
11.	A	I	M	S	V
12.	A	L	M	Q	W
13.	A	S	V	W	X
14.	B	E	F	Q	S
15.	B	E	I	V	W
16.	B	E	L	V	X
17.	B	F	I	M	S
18.	B	F	L	M	Q

19.	B	F	S	W	X
20.	B	M	Q	V	W
21.	C	D	G	O	U
22.	C	D	H	T	U
23.	C	D	J	R	U
24.	C	D	K	P	U
25.	C	D	N	U	Y
26.	C	G	H	K	R
27.	C	G	J	N	Y
28.	C	G	P	R	T
29.	C	H	J	K	O
30.	C	H	N	P	Y
31.	C	J	O	P	T
32.	C	K	N	T	Y
33.	C	N	O	R	Y
34.	D	G	H	R	Y
35.	D	G	J	K	P
36.	D	G	N	R	T

Copyright © 1983-1998 Gail Howard   (Continued Next Page)

BALANCED WHEEL™ 53225 (Continued from previous page)

37.	D	H	J	O	Y
38.	D	H	K	N	P
39.	D	J	N	O	T
40.	D	K	O	P	R
41.	D	K	P	T	Y
42.	E	I	L	M	S
43.	E	I	M	Q	S
44.	E	L	M	V	X
45.	E	L	Q	W	X
46.	E	Q	S	W	X
47.	F	I	L	V	X
48.	F	L	S	V	W
49.	F	M	Q	V	X
50.	G	H	J	T	U

51.	G	H	N	O	P
52.	G	J	K	O	R
53.	G	K	N	R	U
54.	G	K	O	T	Y
55.	G	P	R	U	Y
56.	H	J	N	P	R
57.	H	K	T	U	Y
58.	H	N	P	T	U
59.	H	O	R	T	U
60.	I	L	Q	S	V
61.	I	M	S	W	X
62.	J	K	N	O	U
63.	J	K	R	T	Y
64.	J	O	P	U	Y

BALANCED WHEEL™ 53226
Wheeling 26 Numbers in 68 games for a 3 of 5 Win

NUMBERS CORRECT	MAXIMUM WINS				MINIMUM WINS			
	5x	4x	3x	2x	5x	4x	3x	2x
5 (w/o Jackpot)	0	2	10	6	0	0	1	13
5	1	0	8	16	0	0	1	13
4	–	1	4	12	–	0	0	8
3	–	–	5	0	–	–	0	4
2	–	–	–	7	–	–	–	0

Your 26 Numbers to Wheel

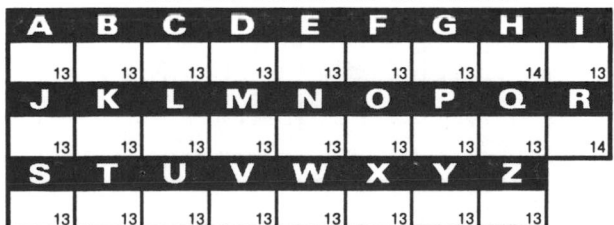

A	B	C	D	E	F	G	H	I
13	13	13	13	13	13	13	14	13

J	K	L	M	N	O	P	Q	R
13	13	13	13	13	13	13	13	14

S	T	U	V	W	X	Y	Z
13	13	13	13	13	13	13	13

The 68 Games to Play

1.	A	B	C	Q	Y
2.	A	B	F	Q	V
3.	A	B	J	Q	S
4.	A	B	K	P	Q
5.	A	B	Q	R	U
6.	A	C	F	P	R

7.	A	C	J	S	U
8.	A	C	K	R	V
9.	A	F	J	K	S
10.	A	F	P	U	Y
11.	A	J	P	S	V
12.	A	J	R	S	Y

 (Continued Next Page)

BALANCED WHEEL™ 53226 (Continued from previous page)

#						#					
13.	A	K	U	V	Y	41.	E	G	H	N	X
14.	B	C	F	P	S	42.	E	G	H	O	W
15.	B	C	J	R	U	43.	E	G	L	M	Z
16.	B	C	K	S	V	44.	E	H	I	M	W
17.	B	F	J	P	Y	45.	E	H	O	T	Z
18.	B	F	K	R	U	46.	E	I	L	N	O
19.	B	J	K	V	Y	47.	E	I	O	X	Z
20.	B	P	R	U	V	48.	E	L	T	W	X
21.	B	R	S	U	Y	49.	E	M	N	O	T
22.	C	F	J	U	V	50.	F	J	P	Q	R
23.	C	F	K	Q	Y	51.	F	K	P	R	V
24.	C	J	K	P	U	52.	F	P	Q	S	U
25.	C	J	Q	U	Y	53.	F	R	S	V	Y
26.	C	P	Q	V	Y	54.	G	H	I	M	O
27.	C	Q	R	S	Y	55.	G	H	T	W	Z
28.	D	E	G	I	T	56.	G	I	L	N	W
29.	D	E	H	L	O	57.	G	I	W	X	Z
30.	D	E	M	O	X	58.	G	L	O	T	X
31.	D	E	N	W	Z	59.	G	M	N	T	W
32.	D	G	H	L	W	60.	H	I	L	M	Z
33.	D	G	M	W	X	61.	H	I	M	N	X
34.	D	G	N	O	Z	62.	H	L	N	T	X
35.	D	H	I	M	T	63.	H	N	O	W	X
36.	D	H	N	X	Z	64.	J	K	Q	R	V
37.	D	I	L	T	X	65.	K	P	R	S	Y
38.	D	I	N	T	Z	66.	K	Q	S	U	V
39.	D	I	O	T	W	67.	L	M	O	W	Z
40.	D	L	M	N	Z	68.	L	M	T	X	Z

190

BALANCED WHEEL™ 53230 (Continued from previous page)
The 102 Games to Play

#						#					
1.	A	B	C	cc	dd	36.	G	H	K	N	W
2.	A	B	D	E	bb	37.	G	H	L	M	V
3.	A	B	F	Y	Z	38.	G	H	O	P	Q
4.	A	B	X	Y	aa	39.	G	H	R	T	U
5.	A	C	D	Z	aa	40.	G	I	K	O	T
6.	A	C	E	F	X	41.	G	I	L	U	W
7.	A	C	F	Y	bb	42.	G	I	M	N	Q
8.	A	D	F	Y	cc	43.	G	I	P	R	V
9.	A	D	X	Y	dd	44.	G	J	K	L	P
10.	A	E	Y	Z	dd	45.	G	J	M	O	U
11.	A	E	Y	aa	cc	46.	G	J	N	T	V
12.	A	F	aa	bb	dd	47.	G	J	Q	R	W
13.	A	X	Z	bb	cc	48.	G	K	M	R	S
14.	B	C	D	E	Y	49.	G	K	Q	U	V
15.	B	C	F	Z	bb	50.	G	L	N	O	R
16.	B	C	X	aa	bb	51.	G	L	Q	S	T
17.	B	D	E	F	X	52.	G	M	P	T	W
18.	B	D	E	Z	aa	53.	G	N	P	S	U
19.	B	D	E	cc	dd	54.	G	O	S	V	W
20.	B	F	aa	cc	dd	55.	H	I	K	L	R
21.	B	X	Z	cc	dd	56.	H	I	M	P	U
22.	B	Y	bb	cc	dd	57.	H	I	N	O	V
23.	C	D	F	bb	cc	58.	H	I	Q	T	W
24.	C	D	X	bb	dd	59.	H	J	K	M	Q
25.	C	E	Z	bb	dd	60.	H	J	L	O	T
26.	C	E	aa	bb	cc	61.	H	J	N	P	R
27.		F	Y	aa	dd	62.	H	J	U	V	W
28.		X	Y	Z	cc	63.	H	K	O	S	U
29.		F	Z	aa	dd	64.	H	K	P	T	V
30.		X	Z	aa	cc	65.	H	L	N	Q	U
31.	D	Y	Z	aa	bb	66.	H	L	P	S	W
32.	E	F	X	Y	bb	67.	H	M	N	S	T
33.	E	F	X	Z	cc	68.	H	M	O	R	W
34.	E		X	aa	dd	69.	H	Q	R	S	V
35.	G		I	J	S	70.	I	J	K	N	U

Copyr   1983-1998 Gail Howard   (Continued Next Page)

193

BALANCED WHEEL™ 53230 (Continued from previous page)

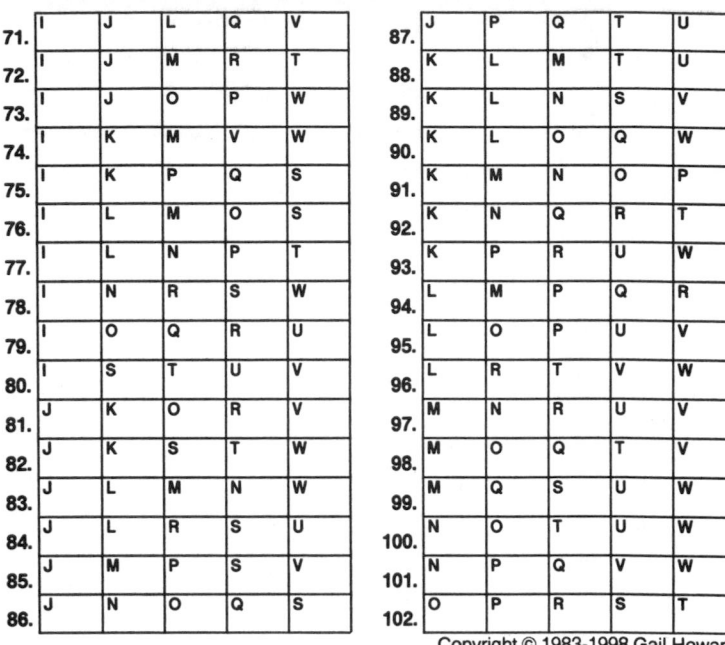

71.	I	J	L	Q	V
72.	I	J	M	R	T
73.	I	J	O	P	W
74.	I	K	M	V	W
75.	I	K	P	Q	S
76.	I	L	M	O	S
77.	I	L	N	P	T
78.	I	N	R	S	W
79.	I	O	Q	R	U
80.	I	S	T	U	V
81.	J	K	O	R	V
82.	J	K	S	T	W
83.	J	L	M	N	W
84.	J	L	R	S	U
85.	J	M	P	S	V
86.	J	N	O	Q	S

87.	J	P	Q	T	U
88.	K	L	M	T	U
89.	K	L	N	S	V
90.	K	L	O	Q	W
91.	K	M	N	O	P
92.	K	N	Q	R	T
93.	K	P	R	U	W
94.	L	M	P	Q	R
95.	L	O	P	U	V
96.	L	R	T	V	W
97.	M	N	R	U	V
98.	M	O	Q	T	V
99.	M	Q	S	U	W
100.	N	O	T	U	W
101.	N	P	Q	V	W
102.	O	P	R	S	T

BALANCED WHEEL™ 53235
Wheeling 35 Numbers in 162 games for a 3 of 5 Win

NUMBERS CORRECT	MAXIMUM WINS				MINIMUM WINS			
	5x	4x	3x	2x	5x	4x	3x	2x
5 (w/o Jackpot)	0	3	6	29				
5	1	1	6	33	0	0	1	18
4	–	2	1	26	–	0	0	11
3	–	–	3	12	–	–	0	5
2	–	–	–	7	–	–	–	0

Your 35 Numbers to Wheel

A	B	C	D	E	F	G	H	I	J	K	L
26	20	20	20	20	26	26	26	27	26	20	27

M	N	O	P	Q	R	S	T	U	V	W	X
26	20	20	26	20	26	26	26	20	20	26	20

Y	Z	AA	BB	CC	DD	EE	FF	GG	HH	II
26	20	20	20	26	20	20	26	26	26	20

The 162 Games to Play

1.	A	F	G	S	hh
2.	A	F	H	L	Y
3.	A	F	I	J	gg
4.	A	F	M	P	hh

5.	A	F	R	W	ff
6.	A	F	S	T	cc
7.	A	G	H	L	T
8.	A	G	I	P	R

            (Continued Next Page)

BALANCED WHEEL™ 53235 (Continued from previous page)

#						#					
9.	A	G	J	W	cc	44.	B	O	Q	aa	ee
10.	A	G	L	P	Y	45.	B	O	V	X	Z
11.	A	G	M	ff	gg	46.	B	Z	bb	ee	ii
12.	A	H	I	W	cc	47.	C	D	E	Q	aa
13.	A	H	J	P	T	48.	C	D	K	O	V
14.	A	H	M	S	ff	49.	C	D	U	X	Z
15.	A	H	R	gg	hh	50.	C	D	bb	dd	ii
16.	A	I	L	S	hh	51.	C	E	K	U	dd
17.	A	I	M	R	T	52.	C	E	N	X	ii
18.	A	I	P	Y	ff	53.	C	E	V	Z	ee
19.	A	J	L	M	W	54.	C	K	N	Z	bb
20.	A	J	R	S	Y	55.	C	K	aa	ee	ii
21.	A	J	cc	ff	hh	56.	C	N	O	U	aa
22.	A	L	P	R	cc	57.	C	N	Q	V	dd
23.	A	L	T	ff	gg	58.	C	O	Q	Z	ii
24.	A	M	Y	cc	gg	59.	C	O	X	dd	ee
25.	A	P	S	W	gg	60.	C	Q	U	bb	ee
26.	A	T	W	Y	hh	61.	C	V	X	aa	bb
27.	B	C	D	N	ee	62.	D	E	N	U	bb
28.	B	C	E	O	bb	63.	D	E	O	ee	ii
29.	B	C	K	Q	X	64.	D	E	V	X	dd
30.	B	C	ii	V	ii	65.	D	K	N	aa	dd
31.	B	C	Z	aa	dd	66.	D	K	Q	U	ii
32.	B	D	E	K	Z	67.	D	K	X	bb	ee
33.	B	D	O	U	dd	68.	D	N	O	Q	X
34.	B	D	Q	V	bb	69.	D	N	V	Z	ii
35.	B	D	X	aa	ii	70.	D	O	Z	aa	bb
36.	B	E	N	V	aa	71.	D	Q	Z	dd	ee
37.	B	E	Q	dd	ii	72.	D	U	V	aa	ee
38.	B	E	U	X	ee	73.	E	K	N	Q	ee
39.	B	K	N	O	ii	74.	E	K	O	X	aa
40.	B	K	U	aa	bb	75.	E	K	V	bb	ii
41.	B	K	V	dd	ee	76.	E	N	O	Z	dd
42.	B	N	Q	U	Z	77.	E	O	Q	U	V
43.	B	N	X	bb	dd	78.	E	Q	X	Z	bb

                    (Continued Next Page)

BALANCED WHEEL™ 53235 (Continued from previous page)

#						#					
79.	E	U	Z	aa	ii	114.	G	R	T	W	Y
80.	E	aa	bb	dd	ee	115.	G	T	W	ff	hh
81.	F	G	H	P	W	116.	H	I	J	M	Y
82.	F	G	H	Y	ff	117.	H	I	L	P	gg
83.	F	G	I	T	gg	118.	H	I	T	ff	hh
84.	F	G	J	R	ff	119.	H	J	L	R	ff
85.	F	G	L	M	cc	120.	H	J	S	cc	gg
86.	F	H	I	R	S	121.	H	L	M	cc	hh
87.	F	H	J	W	hh	122.	H	L	S	T	W
88.	F	H	M	T	gg	123.	H	M	P	R	W
89.	F	H	P	cc	ff	124.	H	P	S	Y	hh
90.	F	I	L	M	ff	125.	H	R	T	Y	cc
91.	F	I	P	T	W	126.	H	W	Y	ff	gg
92.	F	I	Y	cc	hh	127.	I	J	L	T	cc
93.	F	J	L	P	S	128.	I	J	P	R	hh
94.	F	J	M	R	cc	129.	I	J	S	W	ff
95.	F	J	T	Y	ff	130.	I	L	R	W	Y
96.	F	L	R	T	hh	131.	I	M	P	S	cc
97.	F	L	W	cc	gg	132.	I	M	W	gg	hh
98.	F	M	S	W	Y	133.	I	R	cc	ff	gg
99.	F	P	R	Y	gg	134.	I	S	T	Y	gg
100.	F	S	ff	gg	hh	135.	J	L	Y	gg	hh
101.	G	H	I	cc	ff	136.	J	M	P	ff	gg
102.	G	H	J	S	gg	137.	J	M	S	T	hh
103.	G	H	M	R	hh	138.	J	P	W	Y	cc
104.	G	I	J	L	hh	139.	J	R	T	W	gg
105.	G	I	L	Y	hh	140.	K	N	U	V	X
106.	G	I	M	S	W	141.	K	O	Q	bb	dd
107.	G	I	S	Y	gg	142.	K	O	U	Z	ee
108.	G	J	M	P	T	143.	K	Q	V	Z	aa
109.	G	J	M	Y	cc	144.	K	X	Z	dd	ii
110.	G	L	P	S	ff	145.	L	M	P	T	Y
111.	G	L	R	W	gg	146.	L	M	R	S	gg
112.	G	P	cc	gg	hh	147.	L	P	W	ff	hh
113.	G	R	S	T	cc	148.	L	S	Y	cc	ff

                    (Continued Next Page)

BALANCED WHEEL™ 53235 (Continued from previous page)

149.	M	R	Y	ff	hh
150.	M	T	W	cc	ff
151.	N	O	V	bb	ee
152.	N	Q	aa	bb	ii
153.	N	U	dd	ee	ii
154.	N	X	Z	aa	ee
155.	O	U	X	bb	ii

156.	O	V	aa	dd	ii
157.	P	R	S	T	ff
158.	P	T	cc	gg	hh
159.	Q	U	X	aa	dd
160.	Q	V	X	ee	ii
161.	R	S	W	cc	hh
162.	U	V	Z	bb	dd

Copyright © 1983-1998 Gail Howard

BALANCED WHEEL™ 53239
Wheeling 39 Numbers in 263 games for a 3 of 5 Win

NUMBERS CORRECT	MAXIMUM WINS				MINIMUM WINS			
	5x	4x	3x	2x	5x	4x	3x	2x
5 (w/o Jackpot)	0	6	17	42				
5	1	3	9	37	0	0	1	21
4	–	3	13	39	–	0	0	12
3	–	–	9	40	–	–	0	6
2	–	–	–	47	–	–	–	0

Your 39 Numbers to Wheel

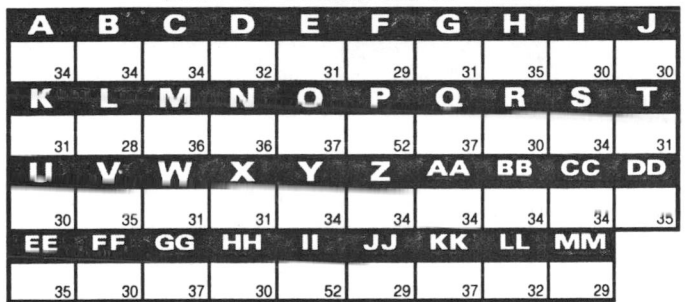

A	B	C	D	E	F	G	H	I	J
34	34	34	32	31	29	31	35	30	30

K	L	M	N	O	P	Q	R	S	T
31	28	36	36	37	52	37	30	34	31

U	V	W	X	Y	Z	AA	BB	CC	DD
30	35	31	31	34	34	34	34	34	35

EE	FF	GG	HH	II	JJ	KK	LL	MM
35	30	37	30	52	29	37	32	29

The 263 Games to Play

1.	A	B	C	V	ee
2.	A	B	D	cc	ii
3.	A	B	H	bb	kk
4.	A	B	O	Y	Z
5.	A	B	P	ee	ii
6.	A	B	Q	dd	gg
7.	A	B	S	aa	cc
8.	A	C	D	Z	aa
9.	A	C	H	Z	aa
10.	A	C	O	cc	gg
11.	A	C	P	dd	ii

12.	A	C	Q	S	bb
13.	A	C	Y	dd	kk
14.	A	D	H	O	ee
15.	A	D	P	bb	kk
16.	A	D	Q	V	gg
17.	A	D	S	Y	dd
18.	A	H	O	Q	V
19.	A	H	P	bb	ii
20.	A	H	S	Y	gg
21.	A	H	cc	dd	ee
22.	A	O	P	ii	kk

Copyright © 1983-1998 Gail Howard

(Continued Next Page)

197

BALANCED WHEEL™ 53239 (Continued from previous page)

#						#					
23.	A	O	S	ee	kk	58.	B	S	V	Y	kk
24.	A	O	aa	bb	dd	59.	B	Y	bb	dd	ee
25.	A	P	Q	Z	ii	60.	B	Z	aa	dd	kk
26.	A	P	S	cc	ii	61.	B	cc	ee	gg	kk
27.	A	P	V	aa	ii	62.	C	D	H	P	dd
28.	A	P	Y	gg	ii	63.	C	D	O	V	ii
29.	A	Q	Y	aa	ee	64.	C	D	S	bb	cc
30.	A	Q	Z	cc	kk	65.	C	D	Y	ee	kk
31.	A	S	V	Z	dd	66.	C	H	O	Y	bb
32.	A	V	Y	bb	cc	67.	C	H	P	ee	ii
33.	A	V	aa	gg	kk	68.	C	H	Q	ee	gg
34.	A	Z	bb	ee	gg	69.	C	H	V	cc	kk
35.	B	C	D	Q	gg	70.	C	O	P	Y	ii
36.	B	C	H	S	dd	71.	C	O	S	V	aa
37.	B	C	O	Q	kk	72.	C	O	Z	dd	ee
38.	B	C	P	ii	kk	73.	C	P	Q	aa	ii
39.	B	C	Y	aa	gg	74.	C	P	S	bb	ii
40.	B	C	Z	bb	cc	75.	C	P	V	cc	ii
41.	B	D	H	S	Z	76.	C	P	Z	gg	ii
42.	B	D	O	dd	kk	77.	C	Q	V	Y	Z
43.	B	D	P	V	Y	78.	C	Q	aa	cc	dd
44.	B	D	aa	bb	ee	79.	C	S	Y	cc	ee
45.	B	H	O	aa	ee	80.	C	S	Z	gg	kk
46.	B	H	P	cc	ii	81.	C	V	bb	dd	gg
47.	B	H	Q	Y	cc	82.	C	aa	bb	ee	kk
48.	B	H	V	Z	gg	83.	D	H	Q	ii	kk
49.	B	O	P	dd	ii	84.	D	H	V	bb	gg
50.	B	O	S	bb	gg	85.	D	H	Y	aa	cc
51.	B	O	V	cc	dd	86.	D	O	P	Z	ee
52.	B	P	Q	Y	ii	87.	D	O	Q	Y	gg
53.	B	P	S	aa	ii	88.	D	O	Q	aa	dd
54.	B	P	V	Z	ii	89.	D	O	Q	bb	dd
55.	B	P	bb	gg	ii	90.	D	O	S	gg	kk
56.	B	Q	S	Z	ee	91.	D	O	cc	ee	kk
57.	B	Q	V	aa	bb	92.	D	P	Q	cc	gg

     (Continued Next Page)

BALANCED WHEEL™ 53239 (Continued from previous page)

#					
93.	D	P	S	aa	ii
94.	D	Q	S	V	ee
95.	D	Q	Z	gg	kk
96.	D	V	Z	cc	dd
97.	D	V	aa	gg	kk
98.	D	Y	Z	bb	ii
99.	D	dd	ee	gg	ll
100.	E	F	G	M	X
101.	E	F	G	N	X
102.	E	F	G	T	ff
103.	E	F	I	W	X
104.	E	F	J	K	mm
105.	E	F	L	hh	ll
106.	E	F	R	U	jj
107.	E	G	I	U	hh
108.	E	G	J	L	jj
109.	E	G	K	W	ll
110.	E	G	R	X	mm
111.	E	I	J	R	ii
112.	E	I	K	ff	jj
113.	E	I	L	M	N
114.	E	I	L	T	mm
115.	E	J	M	U	jj
116.	E	J	N	U	jj
117.	E	J	T	U	W
118.	E	J	X	ff	hh
119.	E	K	L	U	X
120.	E	K	M	ll	mm
121.	E	K	N	ll	mm
122.	E	K	R	T	hh
123.	E	L	R	W	ff
124.	E	M	R	T	ll
125.	E	M	W	ff	hh
126.	E	N	R	T	ll
127.	E	N	W	ff	hh
128.	E	T	X	jj	ll
129.	E	U	ff	ll	mm
130.	E	W	hh	jj	mm
131.	F	G	I	K	R
132.	F	G	J	U	ll
133.	F	G	L	W	mm
134.	F	G	X	hh	jj
135.	F	I	J	T	hh
136.	F	I	L	U	ff
137.	F	I	M	N	U
138.	F	I	jj	ll	mm
139.	F	J	L	R	X
140.	F	J	M	W	ll
141.	F	J	N	W	ll
142.	F	J	W	ff	jj
143.	F	K	L	T	jj
144.	F	K	M	N	T
145.	F	K	U	W	hh
146.	F	K	X	ff	ll
147.	F	L	M	N	R
148.	F	M	N	ff	mm
149.	F	M	N	hh	jj
150.	F	R	T	W	ll
151.	F	R	ff	hh	mm
152.	F	T	U	X	mm
153.	G	I	J	ff	mm
154.	G	I	L	X	ll
155.	G	I	M	hh	ll
156.	G	I	N	hh	ll
157.	G	I	T	W	jj
158.	G	J	K	T	X
159.	G	J	M	N	mm
160.	G	J	R	W	hh
161.	G	K	L	ff	hh
162.	G	K	M	R	W

                    (Continued Next Page)

BALANCED WHEEL™ 53239 (Continued from previous page)

#						#					
163.	G	K	N	R	W	198.	I	R	T	X	ff
164.	G	K	U	jj	mm	199.	I	R	U	W	mm
165.	G	L	M	N	ff	200.	I	W	ff	hh	ll
166.	G	L	R	T	U	201.	J	K	M	N	X
167.	G	M	N	W	jj	202.	J	K	R	U	ff
168.	G	M	T	U	W	203.	J	K	hh	jj	ll
169.	G	N	T	U	W	204.	J	L	M	N	hh
170.	G	R	ff	jj	ll	205.	J	L	T	ff	ll
171.	G	T	hh	ll	mm	206.	J	L	U	hh	mm
172.	G	U	W	X	ff	207.	J	M	N	R	ff
173.	H	O	P	aa	ii	208.	J	M	N	T	jj
174.	H	O	S	Z	cc	209.	J	R	T	jj	mm
175.	H	O	dd	gg	kk	210.	J	W	X	ll	mm
176.	H	P	Q	S	ii	211.	K	L	M	N	jj
177.	H	P	V	ii	kk	212.	K	L	R	ll	mm
178.	H	P	Y	dd	ii	213.	K	M	R	U	hh
179.	H	P	Z	ii	kk	214.	K	N	R	U	hh
180.	H	P	gg	ii	kk	215.	K	R	W	X	jj
181.	H	Q	S	aa	kk	216.	K	T	W	ff	mm
182.	H	Q	Z	bb	dd	217.	L	M	N	T	ll
183.	H	S	V	bb	ee	218.	L	M	N	U	mm
184.	H	V	Y	aa	dd	219.	L	M	N	W	X
185.	H	Y	Z	ee	kk	220.	L	T	W	X	hh
186.	H	aa	bb	cc	gg	221.	L	U	W	jj	ll
187.	I	J	K	L	W	222.	L	X	ff	jj	mm
188.	I	J	M	N	X	223.	M	N	R	jj	mm
189.	I	J	U	X	jj	224.	M	N	ff	jj	ll
190.	I	K	M	T	ff	225.	M	T	X	hh	mm
191.	I	K	N	T	ff	226.	M	U	X	ff	ll
192.	I	K	T	U	ll	227.	N	T	X	hh	mm
193.	I	K	X	hh	mm	228.	N	U	X	ff	ll
194.	I	L	R	hh	jj	229.	O	P	Q	cc	ii
195.	I	M	N	R	X	230.	O	P	S	V	ii
196.	I	M	N	W	mm	231.	O	P	Z	bb	ii
197.	I	M	N	X	jj	232.	O	P	ee	gg	ii

     (Continued Next Page)

BALANCED WHEEL™ 53239 (Continued from previous page)

233.	O	Q	S	Y	dd
234.	O	Q	Z	aa	gg
235.	O	Q	bb	cc	ee
236.	O	V	Y	ee	gg
237.	O	V	Z	bb	kk
238.	O	Y	aa	cc	kk
239.	P	Q	V	gg	ii
240.	P	Q	bb	ee	ii
241.	P	Q	dd	ii	kk
242.	P	S	Y	Z	ii
243.	P	S	dd	gg	ii
244.	P	S	ee	ii	kk
245.	P	V	Y	bb	ii
246.	P	V	dd	ee	ii
247.	P	Y	aa	ee	ii
248.	P	Y	cc	ii	kk

249.	P	Z	aa	dd	ii
250.	P	Z	cc	ee	ii
251.	P	aa	bb	ii	kk
252.	P	aa	cc	gg	ii
253.	P	bb	cc	dd	ii
254.	Q	S	V	cc	gg
255.	Q	V	dd	ee	kk
256.	Q	Y	bb	gg	kk
257.	R	U	X	hh	ll
258.	S	Y	Z	aa	bb
259.	S	aa	dd	ee	gg
260.	S	bb	cc	dd	kk
261.	T	U	ff	hh	jj
262.	V	Z	aa	cc	ee
263.	Y	Z	cc	dd	gg

POWER NUMBER™WHEEL 55006-1
Wheeling 6 Numbers in 5 games for a 5 of 5 Win

NUMBERS CORRECT***	MAXIMUM WINS				MINIMUM WINS			
	5x	4x	3x	2x	5x	4x	3x	2x
5 (w/o Jackpot)	0	0	0	0				
5	1	4	0	0	1	4	0	0
4	–	2	3	0	–	2	3	0
3	–	–	3	2	–	–	3	2
2	–	–	–	4	–	–	–	4

*** POWER NUMBER POSITION A* MUST BE A WINNER.

Your 6 Numbers to Wheel

A*	B	C	D	E	F
5	4	4	4	4	4

The 5 Games to Play

1.	A*	B	C	D	E
2.	A*	B	C	D	F
3.	A*	B	C	E	F

| 4. | A* | B | D | E | F |
| 5. | A* | C | D | E | F |

POWER NUMBER™WHEEL 55007-1
Wheeling 7 Numbers in 15 games for a 5 of 5 Win

NUMBERS CORRECT***	MAXIMUM WINS				MINIMUM WINS			
	5x	4x	3x	2x	5x	4x	3x	2x
5 (w/o Jackpot)	0	0	0	0				
5	1	8	6	0	1	8	6	0
4	-	3	9	3	-	3	9	3
3	-	-	6	8	-	-	6	8
2	-	-	-	10	-	-	-	10

*** POWER NUMBER POSITION A* MUST BE A WINNER.

Your 7 Numbers to Wheel

A*	B	C	D	E	F	G
15	10	10	10	10	10	10

The 15 Games to Play

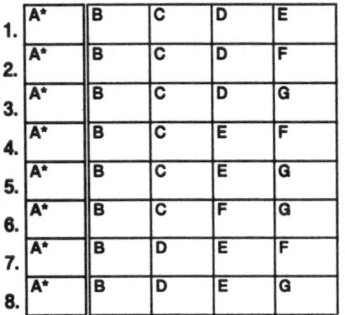

1. A* B C D E
2. A* B C D F
3. A* B C D G
4. A* B C E F
5. A* B C E G
6. A* B C F G
7. A* B D E F
8. A* B D E G
9. A* B D F G
10. A* B E F G
11. A* C D E F
12. A* C D E G
13. A* C D F G
14. A* C E F G
15. A* D E F G

Copyright © 1983-1998 Gail Howard

POWER NUMBER™WHEEL 55008-1
Wheeling 8 Numbers in 35 games for a 5 of 5 Win

NUMBERS CORRECT***	MAXIMUM WINS				MINIMUM WINS			
	5x	4x	3x	2x	5x	4x	3x	2x
5 (w/o Jackpot)	0	0	0	0				
5	1	12	18	4	1	12	18	4
4	-	4	18	12	-	4	18	12
3	-	-	10	20	-	-	10	20
2	-	-	-	20	-	-	-	20

*** POWER NUMBER POSITION A* MUST BE A WINNER.

Your 8 Numbers to Wheel

A*	B	C	D	E	F	G	H
35	20	20	20	20	20	20	20

The 35 Games to Play

1. A* B C D E
2. A* B C D F
3. A* B C D G
4. A* B C D H
5. A* B C E F
6. A* B C E G
7. A* B C E H
8. A* B C F G
9. A* B C F H
10. A* B C G H
11. A* B D E F
12. A* B D E G

Copyright © 1983-1998 Gail Howard

(Continued Next Page)

POWER NUMBER™ WHEEL 55008-1 (Continued from previous page)

13. A*	B	D	E	H
14. A*	B	D	F	G
15. A*	B	D	F	H
16. A*	B	D	G	H
17. A*	B	E	F	G
18. A*	B	E	F	H
19. A*	B	E	G	H
20. A*	B	F	G	H
21. A*	C	D	E	F
22. A*	C	D	E	G
23. A*	C	D	E	H
24. A*	C	D	F	G
25. A*	C	D	F	H
26. A*	C	D	G	H
27. A*	C	E	F	G
28. A*	C	E	F	H
29. A*	C	E	G	H
30. A*	C	F	G	H
31. A*	D	E	F	G
32. A*	D	E	F	H
33. A*	D	E	G	H
34. A*	D	F	G	H
35. A*	E	F	G	H

POWER NUMBER™ WHEEL 55009-1
Wheeling 9 Numbers in 70 games for a 5 of 5 Win

NUMBERS CORRECT***	MAXIMUM WINS				MINIMUM WINS			
	5x	4x	3x	2x	5x	4x	3x	2x
5 (w/o Jackpot)	0	0	0	0				
5	1	16	36	16	1	16	36	16
4	–	5	30	30	–	5	30	30
3	–	–	15	40	–	–	15	40
2	–	–	–	35	–	–	–	35

*** POWER NUMBER POSITION A* MUST BE A WINNER.

Your 9 Numbers to Wheel

A*	B	C	D	E	F	G	H	I
70	35	35	35	36	35	35	35	35

The 70 Games to Play

1. A*	B	C	D	E
2. A*	B	C	D	F
3. A*	B	C	D	G
4. A*	B	C	D	H
5. A*	B	C	D	I
6. A*	B	C	E	F
7. A*	B	C	E	G
8. A*	B	C	E	H
9. A*	B	C	E	I
10. A*	B	C	F	G
11. A*	B	C	F	H
12. A*	B	C	F	I
13. A*	B	C	G	H
14. A*	B	C	G	I
15. A*	B	C	H	I
16. A*	B	D	E	F
17. A*	B	D	E	G
18. A*	B	D	E	H
19. A*	B	D	E	I
20. A*	B	D	F	G
21. A*	B	D	F	H
22. A*	B	D	F	I
23. A*	B	D	G	H
24. A*	B	D	G	I

          (Continued Next Page)

POWER NUMBER™ WHEEL 55009-1 (Continued from previous page)

	A*	B	D	H	I
25.	A*	B	D	H	I
26.	A*	B	E	F	G
27.	A*	B	E	F	H
28.	A*	B	E	F	I
29.	A*	B	E	G	H
30.	A*	B	E	G	I
31.	A*	B	E	H	I
32.	A*	B	F	G	H
33.	A*	B	F	G	I
34.	A*	B	F	H	I
35.	A*	B	G	H	I
36.	A*	C	D	E	F
37.	A*	C	D	E	G
38.	A*	C	D	E	H
39.	A*	C	D	E	I
40.	A*	C	D	F	G
41.	A*	C	D	F	H
42.	A*	C	D	F	I
43.	A*	C	D	G	H
44.	A*	C	D	G	I
45.	A*	C	D	H	I
46.	A*	C	E	F	G
47.	A*	C	E	F	H

	A*	C	E	F	I
48.	A*	C	E	F	I
49.	A*	C	E	G	H
50.	A*	C	E	G	I
51.	A*	C	E	H	I
52.	A*	C	F	G	H
53.	A*	C	F	G	I
54.	A*	C	F	H	I
55.	A*	C	G	H	I
56.	A*	D	E	F	G
57.	A*	D	E	F	H
58.	A*	D	E	F	I
59.	A*	D	E	G	H
60.	A*	D	E	G	I
61.	A*	D	E	H	I
62.	A*	D	F	G	H
63.	A*	D	F	G	I
64.	A*	D	F	H	I
65.	A*	D	G	H	I
66.	A*	E	F	G	H
67.	A*	E	F	G	I
68.	A*	E	F	H	I
69.	A*	E	G	H	I
70.	A*	F	G	H	I

POWER NUMBER™WHEEL 55010-1
Wheeling 10 Numbers in 126 games for a 5 of 5 Win

NUMBERS CORRECT***	MAXIMUM WINS				MINIMUM WINS			
	5x	4x	3x	2x	5x	4x	3x	2x
5 (w/o Jackpot)	0	0	0	0				
5	1	20	60	40	1	20	60	40
4	–	6	45	60	–	6	45	60
3	–	–	21	70	–	–	21	70
2	–	–	–	56	–	–	–	56

*** POWER NUMBER POSITION A* MUST BE A WINNER.

Your 10 Numbers to Wheel

A*	B	C	D	E	F	G	H	I	J
126	56	56	56	56	56	56	56	56	56

The 126 Games to Play

1.	A*	B	C	D	E

2.	A*	B	C	D	F

(Continued Next Page)

POWER NUMBER™ WHEEL 55010-1 (Continued from previous page)

#							#					
3.	A*	B	C	D	G		38.	A*	B	E	F	H
4.	A*	B	C	D	H		39.	A*	B	E	F	I
5.	A*	B	C	D	I		40.	A*	B	E	F	J
6.	A*	B	C	D	J		41.	A*	B	E	G	H
7.	A*	B	C	E	F		42.	A*	B	E	G	I
8.	A*	B	C	E	G		43.	A*	B	E	G	J
9.	A*	B	C	E	H		44.	A*	B	E	H	I
10.	A*	B	C	E	I		45.	A*	B	E	H	J
11.	A*	B	C	E	J		46.	A*	B	E	I	J
12.	A*	B	C	F	G		47.	A*	B	F	G	H
13.	A*	B	C	F	H		48.	A*	B	F	G	I
14.	A*	B	C	F	I		49.	A*	B	F	G	J
15.	A*	B	C	F	J		50.	A*	B	F	H	I
16.	A*	B	C	G	H		51.	A*	B	F	H	J
17.	A*	B	C	G	I		52.	A*	B	F	I	J
18.	A*	B	C	G	J		53.	A*	B	G	H	I
19.	A*	B	C	H	I		54.	A*	B	G	H	J
20.	A*	B	C	H	J		55.	A*	B	G	I	J
21.	A*	B	C	I	J		56.	A*	B	H	I	J
22.	A*	B	D	E	F		57.	A*	C	D	E	F
23.	A*	B	D	E	G		58.	A*	C	D	E	G
24.	A*	B	D	E	H		59.	A*	C	D	E	H
25.	A*	B	D	E	I		60.	A*	C	D	E	I
26.	A*	B	D	E	J		61.	A*	C	D	E	J
27.	A*	B	D	F	G		62.	A*	C	D	F	G
28.	A*	B	D	F	H		63.	A*	C	D	F	H
29.	A*	B	D	F	I		64.	A*	C	D	F	I
30.	A*	B	D	F	J		65.	A*	C	D	F	J
31.	A*	B	D	G	H		66.	A*	C	D	G	H
32.	A*	B	D	G	I		67.	A*	C	D	G	I
33.	A*	B	D	G	J		68.	A*	C	D	G	J
34.	A*	B	D	H	I		69.	A*	C	D	H	I
35.	A*	B	D	H	J		70.	A*	C	D	H	J
36.	A*	B	D	I	J		71.	A*	C	D	I	J
37.	A*	B	E	F	G		72.	A*	C	E	F	G

(Continued Next Page)

205

POWER NUMBER™ WHEEL 55010-1 (Continued from previous page)

#						#					
73.	A*	C	E	F	H	100.	A*	D	E	H	J
74.	A*	C	E	F	I	101.	A*	D	E	I	J
75.	A*	C	E	F	J	102.	A*	D	F	G	H
76.	A*	C	E	G	H	103.	A*	D	F	G	I
77.	A*	C	E	G	I	104.	A*	D	F	G	J
78.	A*	C	E	G	J	105.	A*	D	F	H	I
79.	A*	C	E	H	I	106.	A*	D	F	H	J
80.	A*	C	E	H	J	107.	A*	D	F	I	J
81.	A*	C	E	I	J	108.	A*	D	G	H	I
82.	A*	C	F	G	H	109.	A*	D	G	H	J
83.	A*	C	F	G	I	110.	A*	D	G	I	J
84.	A*	C	F	G	J	111.	A*	D	H	I	J
85.	A*	C	F	H	I	112.	A*	E	F	G	H
86.	A*	C	F	H	J	113.	A*	E	F	G	I
87.	A*	C	F	I	J	114.	A*	E	F	G	J
88.	A*	C	G	H	I	115.	A*	E	F	H	I
89.	A*	C	G	H	J	116.	A*	E	F	H	J
90.	A*	C	G	I	J	117.	A*	E	F	I	J
91.	A*	C	H	I	J	118.	A*	E	G	H	I
92.	A*	D	E	F	G	119.	A*	E	G	H	J
93.	A*	D	E	F	H	120.	A*	E	G	I	J
94.	A*	D	E	F	I	121.	A*	E	H	I	J
95.	A*	D	E	F	J	122.	A*	F	G	H	I
96.	A*	D	E	G	H	123.	A*	F	G	H	J
97.	A*	D	E	G	I	124.	A*	F	G	I	J
98.	A*	D	E	G	J	125.	A*	F	H	I	J
99.	A*	D	E	H	I	126.	A*	G	H	I	J

POWER NUMBER™WHEEL 55011-1
Wheeling 11 Numbers in 210 games for a 5 of 5 Win

NUMBERS CORRECT***	MAXIMUM WINS				MINIMUM WINS			
	5x	4x	3x	2x	5x	4x	3x	2x
5 (w/o Jackpot)	0	0	0	0				
5	1	24	90	80	1	24	90	80
4	–	7	63	105	–	7	63	105
3	–	–	28	112	–	–	28	112
2	–	–	–	84	–	–	–	84

*** POWER NUMBER POSITION A* MUST BE A WINNER.
(Continued Next Page)

POWER NUMBER™ WHEEL 55011-1 (Continued from previous page)
Your 11 Numbers to Wheel

A*	B	C	D	E	F	G	H	I	J	K
210	84	84	84	84	84	84	84	84	84	84

The 210 Games to Play

#						#					
1.	A*	B	C	D	E	33.	A*	B	D	E	J
2.	A*	B	C	D	F	34.	A*	B	D	E	K
3.	A*	B	C	D	G	35.	A*	B	D	F	G
4.	A*	B	C	D	H	36.	A*	B	D	F	H
5.	A*	B	C	D	I	37.	A*	B	D	F	I
6.	A*	B	C	D	J	38.	A*	B	D	F	J
7.	A*	B	C	D	K	39.	A*	B	D	F	K
8.	A*	B	C	E	F	40.	A*	B	D	G	H
9.	A*	B	C	E	G	41.	A*	B	D	G	I
10.	A*	B	C	E	H	42.	A*	B	D	G	J
11.	A*	B	C	E	I	43.	A*	B	D	G	K
12.	A*	B	C	E	J	44.	A*	B	D	H	I
13.	A*	B	C	E	K	45.	A*	B	D	H	J
14.	A*	B	C	F	G	46.	A*	B	D	H	K
15.	A*	B	C	F	H	47.	A*	B	D	I	J
16.	A*	B	C	F	I	48.	A*	B	D	I	K
17.	A*	B	C	F	J	49.	A*	B	D	J	K
18.	A*	B	C	F	K	50.	A*	B	E	F	G
19.	A*	B	C	G	H	51.	A*	B	E	F	H
20.	A*	B	C	G	I	52.	A*	B	E	F	I
21.	A*	B	C	G	J	53.	A*	B	E	F	J
22.	A*	B	C	G	K	54.	A*	B	E	F	K
23.	A*	B	C	H	I	55.	A*	B	E	G	H
24.	A*	B	C	H	J	56.	A*	B	E	G	I
25.	A*	B	C	H	K	57.	A*	B	E	G	J
26.	A*	B	C	I	J	58.	A*	B	E	G	K
27.	A*	B	C	I	K	59.	A*	B	E	H	I
28.	A*	B	C	J	K	60.	A*	B	E	H	J
29.	A*	B	D	E	F	61.	A*	B	E	H	K
30.	A*	B	D	E	G	62.	A*	B	E	I	J
31.	A*	B	D	E	H	63.	A*	B	E	I	K
32.	A*	B	D	E	I	64.	A*	B	E	J	K

(Continued Next Page)

POWER NUMBER™ WHEEL 55011-1 (Continued from previous page)

#						#					
65.	A*	B	F	G	H	100.	A*	C	D	H	I
66.	A*	B	F	G	I	101.	A*	C	D	H	J
67.	A*	B	F	G	J	102.	A*	C	D	H	K
68.	A*	B	F	G	K	103.	A*	C	D	I	J
69.	A*	B	F	H	I	104.	A*	C	D	I	K
70.	A*	B	F	H	J	105.	A*	C	D	J	K
71.	A*	B	F	H	K	106.	A*	C	E	F	G
72.	A*	B	F	I	J	107.	A*	C	E	F	H
73.	A*	B	F	I	K	108.	A*	C	E	F	I
74.	A*	B	F	J	K	109.	A*	C	E	F	J
75.	A*	B	G	H	I	110.	A*	C	E	F	K
76.	A*	B	G	H	J	111.	A*	C	E	G	H
77.	A*	B	G	H	K	112.	A*	C	E	G	I
78.	A*	B	G	I	J	113.	A*	C	E	G	J
79.	A*	B	G	I	K	114.	A*	C	E	G	K
80.	A*	B	G	J	K	115.	A*	C	E	H	I
81.	A*	B	H	I	J	116.	A*	C	E	H	J
82.	A*	B	H	I	K	117.	A*	C	E	H	K
83.	A*	B	H	J	K	118.	A*	C	E	I	J
84.	A*	B	I	J	K	119.	A*	C	E	I	K
85.	A*	C	D	E	F	120.	A*	C	E	J	K
86.	A*	C	D	E	G	121.	A*	C	F	G	H
87.	A*	C	D	E	H	122.	A*	C	F	G	I
88.	A*	C	D	E	I	123.	A*	C	F	G	J
89.	A*	C	D	E	J	124.	A*	C	F	G	K
90.	A*	C	D	E	K	125.	A*	C	F	H	I
91.	A*	C	D	F	G	126.	A*	C	F	H	J
92.	A*	C	D	F	H	127.	A*	C	F	H	K
93.	A*	C	D	F	I	128.	A*	C	F	I	J
94.	A*	C	D	F	J	129.	A*	C	F	I	K
95.	A*	C	D	F	K	130.	A*	C	F	J	K
96.	A*	C	D	G	H	131.	A*	C	G	H	I
97.	A*	C	D	G	I	132.	A*	C	G	H	J
98.	A*	C	D	G	J	133.	A*	C	G	H	K
99.	A*	C	D	G	K	134.	A*	C	G	I	J

(Continued Next Page)

POWER NUMBER™ WHEEL 55011-1 (Continued from previous page)

#						#				
135.	A*	C	G	I	K	170.	A*	D	G	I	K
136.	A*	C	G	J	K	171.	A*	D	G	J	K
137.	A*	C	H	I	J	172.	A*	D	H	I	J
138.	A*	C	H	I	K	173.	A*	D	H	I	K
139.	A*	C	H	J	K	174.	A*	D	H	J	K
140.	A*	C	I	J	K	175.	A*	D	I	J	K
141.	A*	D	E	F	G	176.	A*	E	F	G	H
142.	A*	D	E	F	H	177.	A*	E	F	G	I
143.	A*	D	E	F	I	178.	A*	E	F	G	J
144.	A*	D	E	F	J	179.	A*	E	F	G	K
145.	A*	D	E	F	K	180.	A*	E	F	H	I
146.	A*	D	E	G	H	181.	A*	E	F	H	J
147.	A*	D	E	G	I	182.	A*	E	F	H	K
148.	A*	D	E	G	J	183.	A*	E	F	I	J
149.	A*	D	E	G	K	184.	A*	E	F	I	K
150.	A*	D	E	H	I	185.	A*	E	F	J	K
151.	A*	D	E	H	J	186.	A*	E	G	H	I
152.	A*	D	E	H	K	187.	A*	E	G	H	J
153.	A*	D	E	I	J	188.	A*	E	G	H	K
154.	A*	D	E	I	K	189.	A*	E	G	I	J
155.	A*	D	E	J	K	190.	A*	E	G	I	K
156.	A*	D	F	G	H	191.	A*	E	G	J	K
157.	A*	D	F	G	I	192.	A*	E	H	I	J
158.	A*	D	F	G	J	193.	A*	E	H	I	K
159.	A*	D	F	G	K	194.	A*	E	H	J	K
160.	A*	D	F	H	I	195.	A*	E	I	J	K
161.	A*	D	F	H	J	196.	A*	F	G	H	I
162.	A*	D	F	H	K	197.	A*	F	G	H	J
163.	A*	D	F	I	J	198.	A*	F	G	H	K
164.	A*	D	F	I	K	199.	A*	F	G	I	J
165.	A*	D	F	J	K	200.	A*	F	G	I	K
166.	A*	D	G	H	I	201.	A*	F	G	J	K
167.	A*	D	G	H	J	202.	A*	F	H	I	J
168.	A*	D	G	H	K	203.	A*	F	H	I	K
169.	A*	D	G	I	J	204.	A*	F	H	J	K

          (Continued Next Page)

POWER NUMBER™ WHEEL 55011-1 (Continued from previous page)

205.	A*	F	I	J	K

206.	A*	G	H	I	J

207.	A*	G	H	I	K

208.	A*	G	H	J	K

209.	A*	G	I	J	K

210.	A*	H	I	J	K

POWER NUMBER™WHEEL 54006-1
Wheeling 6 Numbers in 4 games for a 4 of 4 Win

NUMBERS CORRECT***	MAXIMUM WINS 5x	4x	3x	2x	MINIMUM WINS 5x	4x	3x	2x
5 (w/o Jackpot)	0	4	0	0				
5	1	3	0	0	0	4	0	0
4	–	2	2	0	–	1	3	0
3	–	–	3	1	–	–	2	2
2	–	–	–	4	–	–	–	3

*** POWER NUMBER POSITION A* MUST BE A WINNER.

Your 6 Numbers to Wheel

A*	B	C	D	E	F
4	3	3	3	3	4

The 4 Games to Play

1.	A*	B	C	D	F

2.	A*	B	C	E	F

3.	A*	B	D	E	F

4.	A*	C	D	E	F

POWER NUMBER™WHEEL 54007-1
Wheeling 7 Numbers in 6 games for a 4 of 4 Win

NUMBERS CORRECT***	MAXIMUM WINS 5x	4x	3x	2x	MINIMUM WINS 5x	4x	3x	2x
5 (w/o Jackpot)	0	4	2	0				
5	1	2	3	0	0	4	2	0
4	–	3	0	3	–	1	4	1
3	–	–	3	2	–	–	2	4
2	–	–	–	4	–	–	–	4

*** POWER NUMBER POSITION A* MUST BE A WINNER.

Your 7 Numbers to Wheel

A*	B	C	D	E	F	G
6	4	4	4	4	4	4

The 6 Games to Play

1.	A*	B	C	D	G

2.	A*	B	C	E	F

3.	A*	B	D	E	F

4.	A*	B	E	F	G

5.	A*	C	D	E	G

6.	A*	C	D	F	G

POWER NUMBER™WHEEL 54008-1

Wheeling 8 Numbers in 12 games for a 4 of 4 Win

NUMBERS CORRECT***	MAXIMUM WINS				MINIMUM WINS			
	5x	4x	3x	2x	5x	4x	3x	2x
5 (w/o Jackpot)	0	7	1	4				
5	1	4	5	2	0	4	7	1
4	-	4	1	7	-	1	6	5
3	-	-	5	4	-	-	3	7
2	-	-	-	7	-	-	-	6

*** POWER NUMBER POSITION A* MUST BE A WINNER.

Your 8 Numbers to Wheel

A*	B	C	D	E	F	G	H
12	7	7	6	7	7	7	7

The 12 Games to Play

1.	A*	B	C	D	H		7.	A*	B	F	G	H
2.	A*	B	C	E	G		8.	A*	C	D	E	G
3.	A*	B	C	F	H		9.	A*	C	D	F	G
4.	A*	B	D	E	F		10.	A*	C	E	F	G
5.	A*	B	D	G	H		11.	A*	C	E	G	H
6.	A*	B	E	F	H		12.	A*	D	E	F	H

Copyright © 1983-1998 Gail Howard

POWER NUMBER™WHEEL 54009-1

Wheeling 9 Numbers in 14 games for a 4 of 4 Win

NUMBERS CORRECT***	MAXIMUM WINS				MINIMUM WINS			
	5x	4x	3x	2x	5x	4x	3x	2x
5 (w/o Jackpot)	0	4	6	4				
5	1	0	12	0	0	4	6	4
4	-	1	6	6	-	1	6	6
3	-	-	3	8	-	-	3	8
2	-	-	-	7	-	-	-	7

*** POWER NUMBER POSITION A* MUST BE A WINNER.

Your 9 Numbers to Wheel

A*	B	C	D	E	F	G	H	I
14	7	7	7	7	7	7	7	7

The 14 Games to Play

1.	A*	B	C	D	I		8.	A*	C	D	E	F
2.	A*	B	C	E	H		9.	A*	C	D	G	H
3.	A*	B	C	F	G		10.	A*	C	E	G	I
4.	A*	B	D	E	G		11.	A*	C	F	H	I
5.	A*	B	D	F	H		12.	A*	D	E	H	I
6.	A*	B	E	F	I		13.	A*	D	F	G	I
7.	A*	B	G	H	I		14.	A*	E	F	G	H

Copyright © 1983-1998 Gail Howard

211

POWER NUMBER™WHEEL 54010-1
Wheeling 10 Numbers in 25 games for a 4 of 4 Win

NUMBERS CORRECT***	MAXIMUM WINS				MINIMUM WINS			
	5x	4x	3x	2x	5x	4x	3x	2x
5 (w/o Jackpot)	0	6	9	9				
5	1	3	12	8	0	4	12	8
4	–	2	8	12	–	1	9	12
3	–	–	5	13	–	–	4	14
2	–	–	–	12	–	–	–	11

*** POWER NUMBER POSITION A* MUST BE A WINNER.

Your 10 Numbers to Wheel

A*	B	C	D	E	F	G	H	I	J
25	11	11	11	11	11	11	11	11	12

The 25 Games to Play

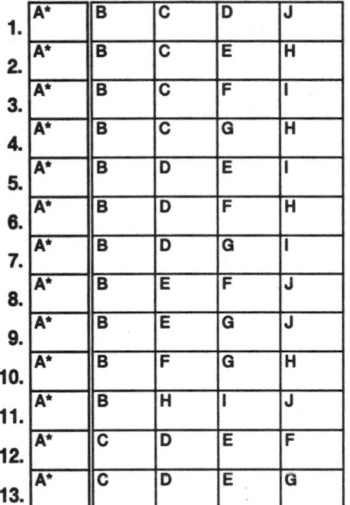

1. A* B C D J
2. A* B C E H
3. A* B C F I
4. A* B C G H
5. A* B D E I
6. A* B D F H
7. A* B D G I
8. A* B E F J
9. A* B E G J
10. A* B F G H
11. A* B H I J
12. A* C D E F
13. A* C D E G
14. A* C D H I
15. A* C E I J
16. A* C F G J
17. A* C F H J
18. A* C G I J
19. A* D E H J
20. A* D F G I
21. A* D F I J
22. A* D G H J
23. A* E F G J
24. A* E F H I
25. A* E G H I

Copyright © 1983-1998 Gail Howard

POWER NUMBER™WHEEL 54011-1
Wheeling 11 Numbers in 30 games for a 4 of 4 Win

NUMBERS CORRECT***	MAXIMUM WINS				MINIMUM WINS			
	5x	4x	3x	2x	5x	4x	3x	2x
5 (w/o Jackpot)	0	4	12	12				
5	1	0	18	8	0	4	12	12
4	–	1	9	15	–	1	9	15
3	–	–	4	16	–	–	4	16
2	–	–	–	12	–	–	–	12

*** POWER NUMBER POSITION A* MUST BE A WINNER.

Your 11 Numbers to Wheel

A*	B	C	D	E	F	G	H	I	J	K
30	12	12	12	12	12	12	12	12	12	12

The 30 Games to Play

1. A* B C D K
2. A* B C E J

Copyright © 1983-1998 Gail Howard

(Continued Next Page)

POWER NUMBER™ WHEEL 54011-1 (Continued from previous page)

3.	A*	B	C	F	I	17.	A*	C	E	G	K
4.	A*	B	C	G	H	18.	A*	C	F	J	K
5.	A*	B	D	E	H	19.	A*	C	G	I	J
6.	A*	B	D	F	J	20.	A*	C	H	I	K
7.	A*	B	D	G	I	21.	A*	D	E	F	K
8.	A*	B	E	F	G	22.	A*	D	E	G	J
9.	A*	B	E	I	K	23.	A*	D	F	H	I
10.	A*	B	F	H	K	24.	A*	D	G	H	K
11.	A*	B	G	J	K	25.	A*	D	I	J	K
12.	A*	B	H	I	J	26.	A*	E	F	I	J
13.	A*	C	D	E	I	27.	A*	E	G	H	I
14.	A*	C	D	F	G	28.	A*	E	H	J	K
15.	A*	C	D	H	J	29.	A*	F	G	H	J
16.	A*	C	E	F	H	30.	A*	F	G	I	K

POWER NUMBER™WHEEL 54012-1
Wheeling 12 Numbers in 47 games for a 4 of 4 Win

NUMBERS CORRECT***	MAXIMUM WINS				MINIMUM WINS			
	5x	4x	3x	2x	5x	4x	3x	2x
5 (w/o Jackpot)	0	7	12	24				
5	1	3	18	20	0	4	18	20
4	–	2	11	24	–	1	12	24
3	–	–	6	23	–	–	5	24
2	–	–	–	18	–	–	–	17

POWER NUMBER POSITION A* MUST BE A WINNER.

Your 12 Numbers to Wheel

A*	B	C	D	E	F	G	H	I	J	K	L
47	17	17	18	17	17	17	17	17	17	17	17

The 47 Games to Play

1.	A*	B	C	D	K	11.	A*	B	E	F	I
2.	A*	B	C	E	L	12.	A*	B	E	J	K
3.	A*	B	C	F	H	13.	A*	B	F	K	L
4.	A*	B	C	G	J	14.	A*	B	G	H	K
5.	A*	B	C	I	J	15.	A*	B	G	I	K
6.	A*	B	D	E	H	16.	A*	B	H	I	L
7.	A*	B	D	F	J	17.	A*	B	H	J	L
8.	A*	B	D	G	L	18.	A*	C	D	E	G
9.	A*	B	D	H	I	19.	A*	C	D	E	I
10.	A*	B	E	F	G	20.	A*	C	D	F	L

  (Continued Next Page)

213

POWER NUMBER™ WHEEL 54012-1 (Continued from previous page)

21.	A*	C	D	H	J	35.	A*	D	G	I	J
22.	A*	C	E	F	J	36.	A*	D	G	J	K
23.	A*	C	E	H	K	37.	A*	D	H	K	L
24.	A*	C	F	G	I	38.	A*	D	I	K	L
25.	A*	C	F	G	K	39.	A*	E	F	H	L
26.	A*	C	G	H	L	40.	A*	E	G	H	I
27.	A*	C	H	I	K	41.	A*	E	G	H	J
28.	A*	C	I	J	L	42.	A*	E	G	I	L
29.	A*	C	J	K	L	43.	A*	E	G	K	L
30.	A*	D	E	F	K	44.	A*	E	I	J	K
31.	A*	D	E	J	L	45.	A*	F	G	J	L
32.	A*	D	F	G	H	46.	A*	F	H	I	J
33.	A*	D	F	I	K	47.	A*	F	H	J	K
34.	A*	D	F	I	L						

Copyright © 1983-1998 Gail Howard

POWER NUMBER™WHEEL 54013-1
Wheeling 13 Numbers in 57 games for a 4 of 4 Win

NUMBERS CORRECT***	MAXIMUM WINS				MINIMUM WINS			
	5x	4x	3x	2x	5x	4x	3x	2x
5 (w/o Jackpot)	0	6	15	28				
5	1	2	21	24	0	4	18	28
4	–	3	9	30	–	1	12	30
3	–	–	6	26	–	–	5	28
2	–	–	–	19	–	–	–	19

*** POWER NUMBER POSITION A* MUST BE A WINNER.

Your 13 Numbers to Wheel

A*	B	C	D	E	F	G
57	19	19	19	19	19	19

H	I	J	K	L	M
19	19	19	19	19	19

The 57 Games to Play

1.	A*	B	C	D	K	9.	A*	B	D	H	J
2.	A*	B	C	E	M	10.	A*	B	E	F	I
3.	A*	B	C	F	H	11.	A*	B	E	G	H
4.	A*	B	C	G	I	12.	A*	B	E	I	L
5.	A*	B	C	J	L	13.	A*	B	E	J	K
6.	A*	B	D	E	I	14.	A*	B	F	G	J
7.	A*	B	D	F	L	15.	A*	B	F	K	M
8.	A*	B	D	G	M	16.	A*	B	G	K	L

Copyright © 1983-1998 Gail Howard   (Continued Next Page)

POWER NUMBER™ WHEEL 54013-1 (Continued from previous page)

17.	A*	B	H	I	K	38.	A*	D	F	I	L
18.	A*	B	H	L	M	39.	A*	D	F	J	M
19.	A*	B	I	J	M	40.	A*	D	G	H	I
20.	A*	C	D	E	J	41.	A*	D	G	J	L
21.	A*	C	D	F	G	42.	A*	D	I	J	K
22.	A*	C	D	H	L	43.	A*	D	K	L	M
23.	A*	C	D	I	M	44.	A*	E	F	G	M
24.	A*	C	E	F	K	45.	A*	E	F	H	J
25.	A*	C	E	G	L	46.	A*	E	G	I	J
26.	A*	C	E	H	I	47.	A*	E	H	K	L
27.	A*	C	F	I	J	48.	A*	E	I	K	M
28.	A*	C	F	L	M	49.	A*	E	J	L	M
29.	A*	C	G	H	M	50.	A*	F	G	H	L
30.	A*	C	G	J	K	51.	A*	F	G	I	K
31.	A*	C	H	J	M	52.	A*	F	H	I	M
32.	A*	C	H	K	M	53.	A*	F	J	K	L
33.	A*	C	I	K	L	54.	A*	G	H	J	K
34.	A*	D	E	F	L	55.	A*	G	I	L	M
35.	A*	D	E	G	K	56.	A*	G	J	K	M
36.	A*	D	E	H	M	57.	A*	H	I	J	L
37.	A*	D	F	H	K						

POWER NUMBER™WHEEL 54014-1
Wheeling 14 Numbers in 81 games for a 4 of 4 Win

NUMBERS CORRECT***	MAXIMUM WINS				MINIMUM WINS			
	5x	4x	3x	2x	5x	4x	3x	2x
5 (w/o Jackpot)	0	7	19	41				
5		1	3	25	37	0	4	24	39
4		–	3	13	40	–	1	15	41
3		–	–	8	34	–	–	6	37
2		–	–	–	25	–	–	–	24

*** POWER NUMBER POSITION A* MUST BE A WINNER.

Your 14 Numbers to Wheel

A*	B	C	D	E	F	G
81	25	25	25	25	24	25

H	I	J	K	L	M	N
25	25	25	25	25	25	25

The 81 Games to Play

1.	A*	B	C	D	M	2.	A*	B	C	E	L

    (Continued Next Page)

POWER NUMBER™ WHEEL 54014-1 (Continued from previous page)

#						#				
3.	A*	B	C	F	M	38.	A*	C	F	J	K
4.	A*	B	C	G	K	39.	A*	C	G	H	N
5.	A*	B	C	H	J	40.	A*	C	G	J	M
6.	A*	B	C	I	N	41.	A*	C	H	I	L
7.	A*	B	D	E	K	42.	A*	C	I	J	K
8.	A*	B	D	F	J	43.	A*	C	J	L	N
9.	A*	B	D	G	H	44.	A*	C	K	L	M
10.	A*	B	D	I	N	45.	A*	D	E	F	M
11.	A*	B	D	J	L	46.	A*	D	E	G	N
12.	A*	B	E	F	I	47.	A*	D	E	H	I
13.	A*	B	E	G	M	48.	A*	D	E	L	M
14.	A*	B	E	H	N	49.	A*	D	F	G	I
15.	A*	B	E	I	J	50.	A*	D	F	H	N
16.	A*	B	F	G	L	51.	A*	D	F	I	K
17.	A*	B	F	H	K	52.	A*	D	G	I	J
18.	A*	B	F	M	N	53.	A*	D	G	K	M
19.	A*	B	G	I	L	54.	A*	D	H	J	M
20.	A*	B	G	J	N	55.	A*	D	H	L	N
21.	A*	B	H	I	K	56.	A*	D	I	K	L
22.	A*	B	H	L	M	57.	A*	D	J	K	N
23.	A*	B	I	M	N	58.	A*	E	F	J	N
24.	A*	B	J	K	M	59.	A*	E	F	K	L
25.	A*	B	K	L	N	60.	A*	E	G	H	L
26.	A*	C	D	E	J	61.	A*	E	G	J	K
27.	A*	C	D	F	L	62.	A*	E	H	J	L
28.	A*	C	D	G	L	63.	A*	E	H	K	L
29.	A*	C	D	H	K	64.	A*	E	I	K	M
30.	A*	C	D	I	M	65.	A*	E	I	L	N
31.	A*	C	D	M	N	66.	A*	E	J	M	N
32.	A*	C	E	F	G	67.	A*	F	G	H	J
33.	A*	C	E	F	H	68.	A*	F	G	K	N
34.	A*	C	E	G	I	69.	A*	F	G	L	M .
35.	A*	C	E	H	M	70.	A*	F	H	I	M
36.	A*	C	E	K	N	71.	A*	F	H	L	N
37.	A*	C	F	I	N	72.	A*	F	I	J	L

    (Continued Next Page)

POWER NUMBER™ WHEEL 54014-1 (Continued from previous page)

73.	A*	F	J	K	M
74.	A*	G	H	I	M
75.	A*	G	H	J	K
76.	A*	G	I	K	N
77.	A*	G	J	K	L

78.	A*	G	L	M	N
79.	A*	H	I	J	N
80.	A*	H	K	M	N
81.	A*	I	J	L	M

Copyright © 1983-1998 Gail Howard

POWER NUMBER™WHEEL 54015-1
Wheeling 15 Numbers in 100 games for a 4 of 4 Win

NUMBERS CORRECT***	MAXIMUM WINS				MINIMUM WINS			
	5x	4x	3x	2x	5x	4x	3x	2x
5 (w/o Jackpot)	0	9	19	53				
5	1	4	27	47	0	4	24	52
4	–	3	15	50	–	1	15	51
3	–	–	9	43	–	–	6	44
2	–	–	–	31	–	–	–	28

*** POWER NUMBER POSITION A* MUST BE A WINNER.

Your 15 Numbers to Wheel

A*	B	C	D	E	F	G	H
100	30	28	28	28	29	28	28

I	J	K	L	M	N	O
28	28	28	29	31	28	29

The 100 Games to Play

1.	A*	B	C	D	M
2.	A*	B	C	E	N
3.	A*	B	C	F	J
4.	A*	B	C	G	K
5.	A*	B	C	H	L
6.	A*	B	C	I	O
7.	A*	B	D	E	L
8.	A*	B	D	F	I
9.	A*	B	D	G	O
10.	A*	B	D	H	J
11.	A*	B	D	K	N
12.	A*	B	E	F	J
13.	A*	B	E	G	L
14.	A*	B	E	H	M
15.	A*	B	E	I	M
16.	A*	B	E	K	M
17.	A*	B	E	L	O

18.	A*	B	F	G	H
19.	A*	B	F	J	N
20.	A*	B	F	K	L
21.	A*	B	F	M	O
22.	A*	B	G	I	J
23.	A*	B	G	M	N
24.	A*	B	H	I	N
25.	A*	B	H	K	O
26.	A*	B	I	K	M
27.	A*	B	I	L	M
28.	A*	B	J	K	O
29.	A*	B	J	L	M
30.	A*	B	L	N	O
31.	A*	C	D	E	I
32.	A*	C	D	F	H
33.	A*	C	D	G	J
34.	A*	C	D	H	K

POWER NUMBER™ WHEEL 54015-1 (Continued from previous page)

#						#					
35.	A*	C	D	H	O	68.	A*	D	M	N	O
36.	A*	C	D	L	N	69.	A*	E	F	G	K
37.	A*	C	E	F	N	70.	A*	E	F	H	L
38.	A*	C	E	G	H	71.	A*	E	F	I	O
39.	A*	C	E	J	N	72.	A*	E	G	I	N
40.	A*	C	E	K	L	73.	A*	E	G	J	M
41.	A*	C	E	M	O	74.	A*	E	H	I	K
42.	A*	C	F	G	M	75.	A*	E	H	J	O
43.	A*	C	F	I	L	76.	A*	E	I	J	L
44.	A*	C	F	K	O	77.	A*	E	K	N	O
45.	A*	C	G	I	M	78.	A*	E	L	M	N
46.	A*	C	G	L	M	79.	A*	F	G	I	L
47.	A*	C	G	N	O	80.	A*	F	G	J	O
48.	A*	C	H	I	J	81.	A*	F	H	I	M
49.	A*	C	H	M	N	82.	A*	F	H	J	M
50.	A*	C	I	K	N	83.	A*	F	H	K	M
51.	A*	C	J	K	M	84.	A*	F	H	N	O
52.	A*	C	J	L	O	85.	A*	F	I	J	K
53.	A*	D	E	F	M	86.	A*	F	I	L	N
54.	A*	D	E	G	O	87.	A*	F	K	M	N
55.	A*	D	E	H	N	88.	A*	F	L	M	O
56.	A*	D	E	J	K	89.	A*	G	H	I	O
57.	A*	D	F	G	N	90.	A*	G	H	J	L
58.	A*	D	F	J	L	91.	A*	G	H	K	N
59.	A*	D	F	K	O	92.	A*	G	J	K	N
60.	A*	D	G	H	M	93.	A*	G	K	L	N
61.	A*	D	G	I	K	94.	A*	G	K	M	O
62.	A*	D	G	L	O	95.	A*	H	J	K	L
63.	A*	D	H	I	L	96.	A*	H	J	L	N
64.	A*	D	I	J	M	97.	A*	H	L	M	O
65.	A*	D	I	N	O	98.	A*	I	J	M	N
66.	A*	D	J	N	O	99.	A*	I	J	M	O
67.	A*	D	K	L	M	100.	A*	I	K	L	O

218

POWER NUMBER™WHEEL 54016-1
Wheeling 16 Numbers in 130 games for a 4 of 4 Win

NUMBERS CORRECT***	MAXIMUM WINS				MINIMUM WINS			
	5x	4x	3x	2x	5x	4x	3x	2x
5 (w/o Jackpot)	0	8	25	65				
5	1	4	34	57	0	4	30	65
4	–	4	14	66	–	1	18	63
3	–	–	13	44	–	–	7	54
2	–	–	–	36	–	–	–	34

*** POWER NUMBER POSITION A* MUST BE A WINNER.

Your 16 Numbers to Wheel

A*	B	C	D	E	F	G	H
130	35	35	35	35	34	34	34

I	J	K	L	M	N	O	P
34	34	34	35	36	35	35	35

The 130 Games to Play

#						#					
1.	A*	B	C	D	M		25.	A*	B	G	K	N
2.	A*	B	C	E	L		26.	A*	B	G	O	P
3.	A*	B	C	F	I		27.	A*	B	H	I	N
4.	A*	B	C	G	P		28.	A*	B	H	K	L
5.	A*	B	C	H	J		29.	A*	B	H	M	P
6.	A*	B	C	K	P		30.	A*	B	I	J	O
7.	A*	B	C	N	O		31.	A*	B	I	M	P
8.	A*	B	D	E	O		32.	A*	B	J	L	P
9.	A*	B	D	F	P		33.	A*	B	K	O	P
10.	A*	B	D	G	H		34.	A*	B	L	M	O
11.	A*	B	D	I	K		35.	A*	B	M	N	P
12.	A*	B	D	J	P		36.	A*	C	D	E	G
13.	A*	B	D	L	N		37.	A*	C	D	E	P
14.	A*	B	E	F	G		38.	A*	C	D	F	O
15.	A*	B	E	H	P		39.	A*	C	D	H	N
16.	A*	B	E	I	P		40.	A*	C	D	I	J
17.	A*	B	E	J	K		41.	A*	C	D	K	L
18.	A*	B	E	M	N		42.	A*	C	E	F	N
19.	A*	B	F	H	O		43.	A*	C	E	G	I
20.	A*	B	F	J	N		44.	A*	C	E	G	J
21.	A*	B	F	K	M		45.	A*	C	E	H	O
22.	A*	B	F	L	P		46.	A*	C	E	K	M
23.	A*	B	G	I	L		47.	A*	C	F	G	L
24.	A*	B	G	J	M		48.	A*	C	F	H	L

          (Continued Next Page)

POWER NUMBER™ WHEEL 54016-1 (Continued from previous page)

#						#					
49.	A*	C	F	H	P	84.	A*	D	L	N	P
50.	A*	C	F	J	K	85.	A*	D	M	O	P
51.	A*	C	F	L	M	86.	A*	E	F	H	J
52.	A*	C	G	H	M	87.	A*	E	F	I	L
53.	A*	C	G	K	O	88.	A*	E	F	K	L
54.	A*	C	G	N	O	89.	A*	E	F	K	P
55.	A*	C	H	I	K	90.	A*	E	F	L	O
56.	A*	C	I	J	P	91.	A*	E	G	H	K
57.	A*	C	I	L	N	92.	A*	E	G	J	P
58.	A*	C	I	M	O	93.	A*	E	G	L	N
59.	A*	C	J	L	O	94.	A*	E	G	M	O
60.	A*	C	J	M	N	95.	A*	E	H	I	M
61.	A*	C	K	N	O	96.	A*	E	H	M	N
62.	A*	C	L	M	P	97.	A*	E	I	K	O
63.	A*	C	N	O	P	98.	A*	E	I	M	N
64.	A*	D	E	F	M	99.	A*	E	J	L	M
65.	A*	D	E	H	L	100.	A*	E	J	N	O
66.	A*	D	E	I	J	101.	A*	E	L	O	P
67.	A*	D	E	K	N	102.	A*	E	M	N	P
68.	A*	D	F	G	K	103.	A*	F	G	H	M
69.	A*	D	F	H	I	104.	A*	F	G	I	N
70.	A*	D	F	J	L	105.	A*	F	G	J	O
71.	A*	D	F	L	N	106.	A*	F	G	M	P
72.	A*	D	G	I	J	107.	A*	F	H	K	N
73.	A*	D	G	I	P	108.	A*	F	I	J	M
74.	A*	D	G	L	O	109.	A*	F	I	K	O
75.	A*	D	G	M	N	110.	A*	F	I	O	P
76.	A*	D	H	J	M	111.	A*	F	J	N	P
77.	A*	D	H	K	M	112.	A*	F	M	N	O
78.	A*	D	H	K	P	113.	A*	G	H	I	O
79.	A*	D	H	M	O	114.	A*	G	H	J	N
80.	A*	D	I	L	M	115.	A*	G	H	L	M
81.	A*	D	I	N	O	116.	A*	G	H	L	P
82.	A*	D	J	K	O	117.	A*	G	I	K	M
83.	A*	D	J	L	N	118.	A*	G	J	K	L

(Continued Next Page)

POWER NUMBER™ WHEEL 54016-1 (Continued from previous page)

119.	A*	G	K	N	P	125.	A*	I	J	K	N
120.	A*	H	I	J	L	126.	A*	I	K	L	O
121.	A*	H	I	N	P	127.	A*	I	K	L	P
122.	A*	H	J	K	O	128.	A*	J	K	M	O
123.	A*	H	J	O	P	129.	A*	J	K	M	P
124.	A*	H	L	N	O	130.	A*	K	L	M	N

Copyright © 1983-1998 Gail Howard

POWER NUMBER™ WHEEL 54017-1
Wheeling 17 Numbers in 140 games for a 4 of 4 Win

NUMBERS CORRECT***	MAXIMUM WINS				MINIMUM WINS			
	5x	4x	3x	2x	5x	4x	3x	2x
5 (w/o Jackpot)	0	4	30	68				
5	1	0	36	64	0	4	30	68
4	–	1	18	66	–	1	18	66
3	–	–	7	56	–	–	7	56
2	–	–	–	35	–	–	–	35

*** POWER NUMBER POSITION A* MUST BE A WINNER.

Your 17 Numbers to Wheel

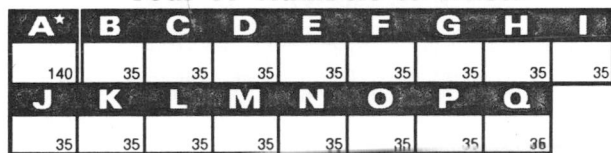

A*	B	C	D	E	F	G	H	I
140	35	35	35	35	35	35	35	35

J	K	L	M	N	O	P	Q
35	35	35	35	35	35	35	36

The 140 Games to Play

1.	A*	B	C	D	N	17.	A*	B	E	J	O
2.	A*	B	G	F	K	18.	A*	B	E	M	Q
3.	A*	B	C	F	J	19.	A*	B	F	G	I
4.	A*	B	C	G	Q	20.	A*	B	F	H	N
5.	A*	B	C	H	M	21.	A*	B	F	K	O
6.	A*	B	C	I	L	22.	A*	B	F	L	Q
7.	A*	B	C	O	P	23.	A*	B	G	J	L
8.	A*	B	D	E	L	24.	A*	B	G	K	M
9.	A*	B	D	F	M	25.	A*	B	G	N	P
10.	A*	B	D	G	O	26.	A*	B	H	I	P
11.	A*	B	D	H	J	27.	A*	B	H	K	Q
12.	A*	B	D	I	K	28.	A*	B	H	L	O
13.	A*	B	D	P	Q	29.	A*	B	I	J	Q
14.	A*	B	E	F	P	30.	A*	B	I	M	O
15.	A*	B	E	G	H	31.	A*	B	J	K	P
16.	A*	B	E	I	N	32.	A*	B	J	M	N

Copyright © 1983-1998 Gail Howard   (Continued Next Page)

POWER NUMBER™ WHEEL 54017-1 (Continued from previous page)

33.	A*	B	K	L	N	68.	A*	D	E	M	P
34.	A*	B	L	M	P	69.	A*	D	F	G	K
35.	A*	B	N	O	Q	70.	A*	D	F	I	O
36.	A*	C	D	E	I	71.	A*	D	F	J	N
37.	A*	C	D	F	H	72.	A*	D	F	L	P
38.	A*	C	D	G	P	73.	A*	D	G	H	L
39.	A*	C	D	J	M	74.	A*	D	G	I	M
40.	A*	C	D	K	L	75.	A*	D	G	N	Q
41.	A*	C	D	O	Q	76.	A*	D	H	I	Q
42.	A*	C	E	F	O	77.	A*	D	H	K	P
43.	A*	C	E	G	M	78.	A*	D	H	M	N
44.	A*	C	E	H	Q	79.	A*	D	I	J	P
45.	A*	C	E	J	P	80.	A*	D	I	L	N
46.	A*	C	E	L	N	81.	A*	D	J	K	Q
47.	A*	C	F	G	L	82.	A*	D	J	L	O
48.	A*	C	F	I	Q	83.	A*	D	K	M	O
49.	A*	C	F	K	P	84.	A*	D	L	M	Q
50.	A*	C	F	M	N	85.	A*	D	N	O	P
51.	A*	C	G	H	K	86.	A*	E	F	G	N
52.	A*	C	G	I	J	87.	A*	E	F	H	I
53.	A*	C	G	N	O	88.	A*	E	F	J	K
54.	A*	C	H	I	O	89.	A*	E	F	L	M
55.	A*	C	H	J	N	90.	A*	E	G	I	P
56.	A*	C	H	L	P	91.	A*	E	G	K	Q
57.	A*	C	I	K	N	92.	A*	E	G	L	O
58.	A*	C	I	M	P	93.	A*	E	H	J	L
59.	A*	C	J	K	O	94.	A*	E	H	K	M
60.	A*	C	J	L	Q	95.	A*	E	H	N	P
61.	A*	C	K	M	Q	96.	A*	E	I	J	M
62.	A*	C	L	M	O	97.	A*	E	I	K	L
63.	A*	C	N	P	Q	98.	A*	E	I	O	Q
64.	A*	D	E	F	Q	99.	A*	E	J	N	Q
65.	A*	D	E	G	J	100.	A*	E	K	O	P
66.	A*	D	E	H	O	101.	A*	E	L	P	Q
67.	A*	D	E	K	N	102.	A*	E	M	N	O

          (Continued Next Page)

POWER NUMBER™ WHEEL 54017-1 (Continued from previous page)

103.	A*	F	G	H	P
104.	A*	F	G	J	Q
105.	A*	F	G	M	O
106.	A*	F	H	J	M
107.	A*	F	H	K	L
108.	A*	F	H	O	Q
109.	A*	F	I	J	L
110.	A*	F	I	K	M
111.	A*	F	I	N	P
112.	A*	F	J	O	P
113.	A*	F	K	N	Q
114.	A*	F	L	N	O
115.	A*	F	M	P	Q
116.	A*	G	H	I	N
117.	A*	G	H	J	O
118.	A*	G	H	M	Q
119.	A*	G	I	K	O
120.	A*	G	I	L	Q
121.	A*	G	J	K	N

122.	A*	G	J	M	P
123.	A*	G	K	L	P
124.	A*	G	L	M	N
125.	A*	G	O	P	Q
126.	A*	H	I	J	K
127.	A*	H	I	L	M
128.	A*	H	J	P	Q
129.	A*	H	K	N	O
130.	A*	H	L	N	Q
131.	A*	H	M	O	P
132.	A*	I	J	N	O
133.	A*	I	K	P	Q
134.	A*	I	L	O	P
135.	A*	I	M	N	Q
136.	A*	J	K	L	M
137.	A*	J	L	N	P
138.	A*	J	M	O	Q
139.	A*	K	L	O	Q
140.	A*	K	M	N	P

Copyright © 1983-1998 Gail Howard

POWER NUMBER™ WHEEL 54018-1
Wheeling 18 Numbers in 183 games for a 4 of 4 Win

NUMBERS CORRECT***	MAXIMUM WINS				MINIMUM WINS			
	5x	4x	3x	2x	5x	4x	3x	2x
5 (w/o Jackpot)	0	6	31	92				
5	1	3	36	88	0	4	36	88
4	–	2	20	84	–	1	21	84
3	–	–	9	69	–	–	8	70
2	–	–	–	44	–	–	–	43

*** POWER NUMBER POSITION A* MUST BE A WINNER.

Your 18 Numbers to Wheel

A*	B	C	D	E	F	G	H	I
183	43	43	43	43	43	43	43	43

J	K	L	M	N	O	P	Q	R
44	43	43	43	43	43	43	43	43

The 183 Games to Play

1.	A*	B	C	D	R
2.	A*	B	C	E	P
3.	A*	B	C	F	L

4.	A*	B	C	G	N
5.	A*	B	C	H	M
6.	A*	B	C	I	Q

Copyright © 1983-1998 Gail Howard

(Continued Next Page)

POWER NUMBER™ WHEEL 54018-1 (Continued from previous page)

#	1	2	3	4	5	#	1	2	3	4	5
7.	A*	B	C	J	O	42.	A*	B	N	O	R
8.	A*	B	C	K	Q	43.	A*	B	O	P	Q
9.	A*	B	D	E	M	44.	A*	C	D	E	P
10.	A*	B	D	F	Q	45.	A*	C	D	F	M
11.	A*	B	D	G	O	46.	A*	C	D	G	H
12.	A*	B	D	H	P	47.	A*	C	D	I	Q
13.	A*	B	D	I	K	48.	A*	C	D	J	K
14.	A*	B	D	I	L	49.	A*	C	D	L	R
15.	A*	B	D	J	N	50.	A*	C	D	N	O
16.	A*	B	E	F	N	51.	A*	C	E	F	J
17.	A*	B	E	G	L	52.	A*	C	E	G	Q
18.	A*	B	E	H	R	53.	A*	C	E	H	I
19.	A*	B	E	I	O	54.	A*	C	E	K	M
20.	A*	B	E	J	Q	55.	A*	C	E	L	N
21.	A*	B	E	K	O	56.	A*	C	E	O	R
22.	A*	B	F	G	P	57.	A*	C	F	G	L
23.	A*	B	F	H	O	58.	A*	C	F	H	R
24.	A*	B	F	I	R	59.	A*	C	F	I	O
25.	A*	B	F	J	K	60.	A*	C	F	K	P
26.	A*	B	F	J	M	61.	A*	C	F	N	Q
27.	A*	B	G	H	K	62.	A*	C	G	I	P
28.	A*	B	G	H	Q	63.	A*	C	G	J	N
29.	A*	B	G	I	M	64.	A*	C	G	K	O
30.	A*	B	G	J	R	65.	A*	C	G	M	R
31.	A*	B	H	I	N	66.	A*	C	H	J	O
32.	A*	B	H	J	L	67.	A*	C	H	K	N
33.	A*	B	I	J	P	68.	A*	C	H	L	M
34.	A*	B	J	K	M	69.	A*	C	H	P	Q
35.	A*	B	K	L	N	70.	A*	C	I	J	R
36.	A*	B	K	P	R	71.	A*	C	I	K	L
37.	A*	B	L	M	O	72.	A*	C	I	M	N
38.	A*	B	L	N	P	73.	A*	C	J	L	Q
39.	A*	B	L	Q	R	74.	A*	C	J	M	P
40.	A*	B	M	N	Q	75.	A*	C	K	Q	R
41.	A*	B	M	P	R	76.	A*	C	L	O	P

     (Continued Next Page)

POWER NUMBER™ WHEEL 54018-1 (Continued from previous page)

#						#				
77.	A*	C	M	O	Q	112.	A*	E	G	H	P
78.	A*	C	N	P	R	113.	A*	E	G	J	L
79.	A*	D	E	F	K	114.	A*	E	G	K	R
80.	A*	D	E	G	I	115.	A*	E	G	M	O
81.	A*	D	E	H	Q	116.	A*	E	H	J	R
82.	A*	D	E	J	M	117.	A*	E	H	K	L
83.	A*	D	E	L	O	118.	A*	E	H	M	N
84.	A*	D	E	N	R	119.	A*	E	I	J	O
85.	A*	D	F	G	R	120.	A*	E	I	K	N
86.	A*	D	F	H	L	121.	A*	E	I	L	M
87.	A*	D	F	I	N	122.	A*	E	I	P	Q
88.	A*	D	F	J	P	123.	A*	E	J	K	P
89.	A*	D	F	O	Q	124.	A*	E	J	N	Q
90.	A*	D	G	J	O	125.	A*	E	K	O	Q
91.	A*	D	G	K	N	126.	A*	E	L	P	R
92.	A*	D	G	L	M	127.	A*	E	M	Q	R
93.	A*	D	G	P	Q	128.	A*	E	N	O	P
94.	A*	D	H	I	P	129.	A*	F	G	H	M
95.	A*	D	H	J	N	130.	A*	F	G	I	K
96.	A*	D	H	K	O	131.	A*	F	G	J	Q
97.	A*	D	H	M	R	132.	A*	F	G	O	P
98.	A*	D	I	J	L	133.	A*	F	H	I	J
99.	A*	D	I	K	R	134.	A*	F	H	K	Q
100.	A*	D	I	M	O	135.	A*	F	H	N	P
101.	A*	D	J	Q	R	136.	A*	F	I	L	P
102.	A*	D	K	L	Q	137.	A*	F	I	M	Q
103.	A*	D	K	M	P	138.	A*	F	J	K	M
104.	A*	D	L	N	P	139.	A*	F	J	L	N
105.	A*	D	M	N	Q	140.	A*	F	J	O	R
106.	A*	D	O	P	R	141.	A*	F	K	L	O
107.	A*	E	F	G	N	142.	A*	F	K	N	R
108.	A*	E	F	H	O	143.	A*	F	L	M	R
109.	A*	E	F	I	R	144.	A*	F	M	N	O
110.	A*	E	F	L	Q	145.	A*	F	P	Q	R
111.	A*	E	F	M	P	146.	A*	G	H	I	Q

　　　　(Continued Next Page)

POWER NUMBER™ WHEEL 54018-1 (Continued from previous page)

	A*	G	H	J	K
147.					

	A*	G	H	L	R
148.					

	A*	G	H	N	O
149.					

	A*	G	I	J	M
150.					

	A*	G	I	L	O
151.					

	A*	G	I	N	R
152.					

	A*	G	J	P	R
153.					

	A*	G	K	L	P
154.					

	A*	G	K	M	Q
155.					

	A*	G	L	N	Q
156.					

	A*	G	M	N	P
157.					

	A*	G	O	Q	R
158.					

	A*	H	I	K	M
159.					

	A*	H	I	L	N
160.					

	A*	H	I	O	R
161.					

	A*	H	J	L	P
162.					

	A*	H	J	M	Q
163.					

	A*	H	K	P	R
164.					

	A*	H	L	O	Q
165.					

	A*	H	M	O	P
166.					

	A*	H	N	Q	R
167.					

	A*	I	J	K	Q
168.					

	A*	I	J	N	P
169.					

	A*	I	K	O	P
170.					

	A*	I	L	Q	R
171.					

	A*	I	M	P	R
172.					

	A*	I	N	O	Q
173.					

	A*	J	K	L	R
174.					

	A*	J	K	N	O
175.					

	A*	J	L	M	O
176.					

	A*	J	M	N	R
177.					

	A*	J	O	P	Q
178.					

	A*	K	L	M	N
179.					

	A*	K	M	O	R
180.					

	A*	K	N	P	Q
181.					

	A*	L	M	P	Q
182.					

	A*	L	N	O	R
183.					

POWER NUMBER™WHEEL 54020-1
Wheeling 20 Numbers in 274 games for a 4 of 4 Win

NUMBERS CORRECT***	MAXIMUM WINS				MINIMUM WINS			
	5x	4x	3x	2x	5x	4x	3x	2x
5 (w/o Jackpot)	0	8	41	130				
5	1	4	45	130	0	4	42	129
4	–	3	25	119	–	1	24	117
3	–	–	12	95	–	–	9	94
2	–	–	–	60	–	–	–	56

*** POWER NUMBER POSITION A* MUST BE A WINNER.

Your 20 Numbers to Wheel

A*	B	C	D	E	F	G	H	I	J
274	57	57	56	56	56	60	60	60	59

K	L	M	N	O	P	Q	R	S	T
59	58	58	58	57	57	57	57	57	57

The 274 Games to Play

	A*	B	C	D	T
1.					

	A*	B	C	E	L
2.					

	A*	B	C	F	M
3.					

	A*	B	C	G	O
4.					

	A*	B	C	H	P
5.					

	A*	B	C	I	K
6.					

     (Continued Next Page)

POWER NUMBER™ WHEEL 54020-1 (Continued from previous page)

#	A*	B	C	J	Q		#	A*	B	I	N	Q
7.	A*	B	C	J	Q		42.	A*	B	I	N	Q
8.	A*	B	C	M	R		43.	A*	B	J	K	L
9.	A*	B	C	N	S		44.	A*	B	J	M	S
10.	A*	B	D	E	R		45.	A*	B	J	P	R
11.	A*	B	D	F	J		46.	A*	B	K	M	P
12.	A*	B	D	G	Q		47.	A*	B	K	N	Q
13.	A*	B	D	H	L		48.	A*	B	K	Q	S
14.	A*	B	D	I	P		49.	A*	B	K	R	T
15.	A*	B	D	K	O		50.	A*	B	L	N	P
16.	A*	B	D	M	N		51.	A*	B	L	O	S
17.	A*	B	D	O	S		52.	A*	B	L	Q	R
18.	A*	B	E	F	S		53.	A*	B	M	O	Q
19.	A*	B	E	G	M		54.	A*	B	N	O	P
20.	A*	B	E	G	T		55.	A*	B	O	R	T
21.	A*	B	E	H	O		56.	A*	B	P	Q	T
22.	A*	B	E	I	K		57.	A*	B	P	S	T
23.	A*	B	E	J	N		58.	A*	C	D	E	L
24.	A*	B	E	P	Q		59.	A*	C	D	F	I
25.	A*	B	F	G	P		60.	A*	C	D	G	H
26.	A*	B	F	H	Q		61.	A*	C	D	G	N
27.	A*	B	F	I	L		62.	A*	C	D	I	Q
28.	A*	B	F	I	R		63.	A*	C	D	J	S
29.	A*	B	F	K	O		64.	A*	C	D	K	M
30.	A*	B	F	N	T		65.	A*	C	D	O	P
31.	A*	B	G	H	K		66.	A*	C	D	O	R
32.	A*	B	G	I	J		67.	A*	C	E	F	T
33.	A*	B	G	L	T		68.	A*	C	E	G	R
34.	A*	B	G	M	N		69.	A*	C	E	H	I
35.	A*	B	G	R	S		70.	A*	C	E	J	M
36.	A*	B	H	I	S		71.	A*	C	E	K	Q
37.	A*	B	H	J	T		72.	A*	C	E	N	O
38.	A*	B	H	L	M		73.	A*	C	E	P	S
39.	A*	B	H	N	R		74.	A*	C	F	G	M
40.	A*	B	I	J	O		75.	A*	C	F	H	J
41.	A*	B	I	M	T		76.	A*	C	F	K	R

 (Continued Next Page)

227

POWER NUMBER™ WHEEL 54020-1 (Continued from previous page)

#	1	2	3	4	5		#	1	2	3	4	5
77.	A*	C	F	L	N		112.	A*	D	E	N	T
78.	A*	C	F	O	Q		113.	A*	D	F	G	P
79.	A*	C	F	P	S		114.	A*	D	F	H	N
80.	A*	C	G	I	Q		115.	A*	D	F	I	T
81.	A*	C	G	J	O		116.	A*	D	F	L	S
82.	A*	C	G	K	L		117.	A*	D	F	M	R
83.	A*	C	G	M	P		118.	A*	D	F	O	Q
84.	A*	C	G	S	T		119.	A*	D	G	I	O
85.	A*	C	H	K	S		120.	A*	D	G	J	R
86.	A*	C	H	L	O		121.	A*	D	G	K	S
87.	A*	C	H	M	T		122.	A*	D	G	L	R
88.	A*	C	H	N	Q		123.	A*	D	G	M	T
89.	A*	C	H	N	R		124.	A*	D	H	I	L
90.	A*	C	I	J	L		125.	A*	D	H	J	P
91.	A*	C	I	M	O		126.	A*	D	H	K	R
92.	A*	C	I	N	T		127.	A*	D	H	O	T
93.	A*	C	I	P	T		128.	A*	D	H	Q	S
94.	A*	C	I	R	S		129.	A*	D	I	J	K
95.	A*	C	J	K	O		130.	A*	D	I	M	S
96.	A*	C	J	N	P		131.	A*	D	I	N	R
97.	A*	C	J	R	T		132.	A*	D	J	K	T
98.	A*	C	K	M	N		133.	A*	D	J	L	M
99.	A*	C	K	P	T		134.	A*	D	J	N	Q
100.	A*	C	L	M	S		135.	A*	D	K	L	Q
101.	A*	C	L	P	R		136.	A*	D	K	N	P
102.	A*	C	L	Q	T		137.	A*	D	L	N	O
103.	A*	C	M	Q	S		138.	A*	D	L	P	T
104.	A*	C	O	S	T		139.	A*	D	M	O	R
105.	A*	C	P	Q	R		140.	A*	D	M	P	Q
106.	A*	D	E	F	K		141.	A*	D	N	S	T
107.	A*	D	E	G	Q		142.	A*	D	P	R	S
108.	A*	D	E	H	M		143.	A*	D	Q	R	T
109.	A*	D	E	I	P		144.	A*	E	F	G	J
110.	A*	D	E	J	O		145.	A*	E	F	H	O
111.	A*	D	E	K	S		146.	A*	E	F	I	R

                    (Continued Next Page)

POWER NUMBER™ WHEEL 54020-1 (Continued from previous page)

#						#					
147.	A*	E	F	J	P	182.	A*	F	H	L	S
148.	A*	E	F	L	M	183.	A*	F	H	M	N
149.	A*	E	F	N	Q	184.	A*	F	H	P	R
150.	A*	E	G	H	S	185.	A*	F	I	J	N
151.	A*	E	G	I	M	186.	A*	F	I	K	M
152.	A*	E	G	K	N	187.	A*	F	I	O	S
153.	A*	E	G	L	P	188.	A*	F	I	P	Q
154.	A*	E	G	M	O	189.	A*	F	J	K	S
155.	A*	E	H	J	K	190.	A*	F	J	L	O
156.	A*	E	H	L	N	191.	A*	F	J	M	T
157.	A*	E	H	P	Q	192.	A*	F	J	Q	R
158.	A*	E	H	R	T	193.	A*	F	K	L	R
159.	A*	E	I	J	S	194.	A*	F	K	N	P
160.	A*	E	I	L	Q	195.	A*	F	K	Q	T
161.	A*	E	I	N	P	196.	A*	F	L	P	T
162.	A*	E	I	O	T	197.	A*	F	M	O	P
163.	A*	E	J	L	T	198.	A*	F	M	Q	S
164.	A*	E	J	N	R	199.	A*	F	N	O	T
165.	A*	E	J	O	Q	200.	A*	F	N	Q	R
166.	A*	E	K	L	T	201.	A*	F	R	S	T
167.	A*	E	K	M	O	202.	A*	G	H	I	N
168.	A*	E	K	P	R	203.	A*	G	H	J	M
169.	A*	E	L	O	P	204.	A*	G	H	K	R
170.	A*	E	L	R	S	205.	A*	G	H	L	O
171.	A*	E	M	N	S	206.	A*	G	H	M	P
172.	A*	E	M	P	T	207.	A*	G	H	Q	T
173.	A*	E	M	Q	R	208.	A*	G	I	J	P
174.	A*	E	O	R	S	209.	A*	G	I	K	S
175.	A*	E	Q	S	T	210.	A*	G	I	L	R
176.	A*	F	G	H	K	211.	A*	G	J	K	Q
177.	A*	F	G	I	T	212.	A*	G	J	L	S
178.	A*	F	G	L	Q	213.	A*	G	J	N	T
179.	A*	F	G	N	S	214.	A*	G	K	L	M
180.	A*	F	G	O	R	215.	A*	G	K	O	T
181.	A*	F	H	I	T	216.	A*	G	K	P	Q

                    (Continued Next Page)

POWER NUMBER™ WHEEL 54020-1 (Continued from previous page)

#						#					
217.	A*	G	L	M	Q	246.	A*	I	J	N	S
218.	A*	G	L	N	R	247.	A*	I	J	Q	T
219.	A*	G	M	R	S	248.	A*	I	K	L	O
220.	A*	G	N	O	Q	249.	A*	I	K	N	T
221.	A*	G	N	P	Q	250.	A*	I	L	M	N
222.	A*	G	O	P	S	251.	A*	I	L	S	T
223.	A*	G	P	R	T	252.	A*	I	M	P	S
224.	A*	G	Q	R	S	253.	A*	I	M	R	T
225.	A*	H	I	J	M	254.	A*	I	O	P	R
226.	A*	H	I	K	Q	255.	A*	I	O	Q	S
227.	A*	H	I	L	P	256.	A*	J	K	L	N
228.	A*	H	I	M	Q	257.	A*	J	K	M	Q
229.	A*	H	I	N	O	258.	A*	J	L	M	P
230.	A*	H	I	Q	R	259.	A*	J	L	M	R
231.	A*	H	J	K	N	260.	A*	J	M	N	O
232.	A*	H	J	L	Q	261.	A*	J	N	O	R
233.	A*	H	J	O	S	262.	A*	J	O	P	T
234.	A*	H	J	R	S	263.	A*	J	P	Q	S
235.	A*	H	J	S	T	264.	A*	K	L	P	S
236.	A*	H	K	L	T	265.	A*	K	M	S	T
237.	A*	H	K	M	R	266.	A*	K	N	O	S
238.	A*	H	K	O	P	267.	A*	K	N	R	S
239.	A*	H	L	O	R	268.	A*	K	O	Q	R
240.	A*	H	M	O	S	269.	A*	L	M	O	T
241.	A*	H	N	P	S	270.	A*	L	N	Q	S
242.	A*	H	N	P	T	271.	A*	L	N	R	T
243.	A*	H	O	Q	T	272.	A*	L	O	P	Q
244.	A*	I	J	K	P	273.	A*	M	N	P	R
245.	A*	I	J	K	R	274.	A*	M	N	Q	T

230

POWER NUMBER™ WHEEL 54107-1
Wheeling 7 Numbers in 3 games for a 4 of 5 Win

NUMBERS CORRECT***	MAXIMUM WINS				MINIMUM WINS			
	5x	4x	3x	2x	5x	4x	3x	2x
5 (w/o Jackpot)	0	3	0	0				
5	1	1	1	0	0	1	2	0
4	–	2	0	1	–	0	2	1
3	–	–	2	1	–	–	0	3
2	–	–	–	3	–	–	–	1

*** POWER NUMBER POSITION A* MUST BE A WINNER.

Your 7 Numbers to Wheel

A*	B	C	D	E	F	G
3	2	1	2	2	2	3

The 3 Games to Play

1.

A*	B	D	F	G

2.

A*	B	E	F	G

3.

A*	C	D	E	G

POWER NUMBER™ WHEEL 54108-1
Wheeling 8 Numbers in 4 games for a 4 of 5 Win

NUMBERS CORRECT***	MAXIMUM WINS				MINIMUM WINS			
	5x	4x	3x	2x	5x	4x	3x	2x
5 (w/o Jackpot)	0	3	0	1				
5	1	1	1	1	0	1	2	1
4	–	2	1	0	–	0	2	2
3	–	–	3	0	–	–	0	4
2	–	–	–	3	–	–	–	2

*** POWER NUMBER POSITION A* MUST BE A WINNER.

Your 8 Numbers to Wheel

A*	B	C	D	E	F	G	H
4	3	2	2	2	3	2	2

The 4 Games to Play

1.

A*	B	C	F	H

2.

A*	B	D	F	H

3.

A*	B	E	F	G

4.

A*	C	D	E	G

POWER NUMBER™ WHEEL 54109-1
Wheeling 9 Numbers in 6 games for a 4 of 5 Win

NUMBERS CORRECT***	MAXIMUM WINS				MINIMUM WINS			
	5x	4x	3x	2x	5x	4x	3x	2x
5 (w/o Jackpot)	0	3	1	1				
5	1	1	1	3	0	1	4	1
4	–	2	1	1	–	0	3	3
3	–	–	3	0	–	–	0	6
2	–	–	–	3	–	–	–	3

*** POWER NUMBER POSITION A* MUST BE A WINNER.

(Continued Next Page)

POWER NUMBER™ WHEEL 54109-1 (Continued from previous page)

Your 9 Numbers to Wheel

A*	B	C	D	E	F	G	H	I
6	3	3	3	3	3	3	3	3

The 6 Games to Play

1.	A*	B	D	F	G
2.	A*	B	D	H	I
3.	A*	B	F	G	H
4.	A*	C	D	E	H
5.	A*	C	E	F	I
6.	A*	C	E	G	I

POWER NUMBER™ WHEEL 54110-1

Wheeling 10 Numbers in 10 games for a 4 of 5 Win

NUMBERS CORRECT***	MAXIMUM WINS 5x	4x	3x	2x	MINIMUM WINS 5x	4x	3x	2x
5 (w/o Jackpot)	0	4	2	3				
5	1	2	2	5	0	1	4	5
4	–	2	3	1	–	0	3	6
3	–	–	4	2	–	–	1	6
2	–	–	–	5	–	–	–	4

*** POWER NUMBER POSITION A* MUST BE A WINNER.

Your 10 Numbers to Wheel

A*	B	C	D	E	F	G	H	I	J
10	5	5	4	4	4	4	4	5	5

The 10 Games to Play

1.	A*	B	C	G	J
2.	A*	B	C	H	J
3.	A*	B	D	F	I
4.	A*	B	E	F	I
5.	A*	B	G	H	I
6.	A*	C	D	E	I
7.	A*	C	F	G	J
8.	A*	C	F	H	J
9.	A*	D	E	G	H
10.	A*	D	E	I	J

POWER NUMBER™ WHEEL 54111-1

Wheeling 11 Numbers in 14 games for a 4 of 5 Win

NUMBERS CORRECT***	MAXIMUM WINS 5x	4x	3x	2x	MINIMUM WINS 5x	4x	3x	2x
5 (w/o Jackpot)	0	4	4	3				
5	1	2	4	6	0	1	6	6
4	–	2	3	6	–	0	4	8
3	–	–	3	6	–	–	1	8
2	–	–	–	6	–	–	–	5

*** POWER NUMBER POSITION A* MUST BE A WINNER.

Your 11 Numbers to Wheel

A*	B	C	D	E	F	G	H	I	J	K
14	5	6	5	6	6	6	6	5	5	6

(Continued Next Page)

POWER NUMBER™ WHEEL 54111-1 (Continued from previous page)
The 14 Games to Play

1.	A*	B	C	E	K		8.	A*	C	E	G	H
2.	A*	B	D	G	K		9.	A*	C	F	G	J
3.	A*	B	E	F	H		10.	A*	C	H	I	K
4.	A*	B	F	J	K		11.	A*	D	E	I	J
5.	A*	B	G	I	J		12.	A*	D	F	H	I
6.	A*	C	D	F	I		13.	A*	E	F	G	K
7.	A*	C	D	H	J		14.	A*	E	G	H	K

POWER NUMBER™WHEEL 54112-1
Wheeling 12 Numbers in 20 games for a 4 of 5 Win

NUMBERS CORRECT***	MAXIMUM WINS				MINIMUM WINS			
	5x	4x	3x	2x	5x	4x	3x	2x
5 (w/o Jackpot)	0	4	4	11				
5	1	1	9	7	0	1	7	10
4	–	2	3	12	–	0	4	13
3	–	–	3	10	–	–	1	11
2	–	–	–	8	–	–	–	6

*** POWER NUMBER POSITION A* MUST BE A WINNER.
Your 12 Numbers to Wheel

A*	B	C	D	E	F	G	H	I	J	K	L
20	6	8	7	7	7	7	7	8	8	7	8

The 20 Games to Play

1.	A*	B	C	E	L		11.	A*	C	F	I	L
2.	A*	B	D	F	K		12.	A*	C	G	H	K
3.	A*	B	D	H	I		13.	A*	C	I	J	L
4.	A*	B	E	G	J		14.	A*	D	E	F	H
5.	A*	B	G	I	L		15.	A*	D	E	K	L
6.	A*	B	J	K	L		16.	A*	D	G	I	J
7.	A*	C	D	G	J		17.	A*	D	H	J	L
8.	A*	C	E	I	K		18.	A*	E	F	I	J
9.	A*	C	F	G	K		19.	A*	E	H	I	K
10.	A*	C	F	H	J		20.	A*	F	G	H	L

POWER NUMBER™WHEEL 54113-1
Wheeling 13 Numbers in 28 games for a 4 of 5 Win

NUMBERS CORRECT***	MAXIMUM WINS				MINIMUM WINS			
	5x	4x	3x	2x	5x	4x	3x	2x
5 (w/o Jackpot)	0	4	8	13				
5	1	2	7	16	0	1	8	14
4	-	2	5	14	-	0	5	14
3	-	-	4	13	-	-	1	14
2	-	-	-	11	-	-	-	8

*** POWER NUMBER POSITION A* MUST BE A WINNER.

Your 13 Numbers to Wheel

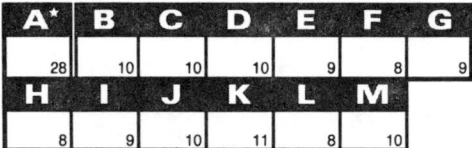

A*	B	C	D	E	F	G
28	10	10	10	9	8	9

H	I	J	K	L	M
8	9	10	11	8	10

The 28 Games to Play

1.	A*	B	C	D	M
2.	A*	B	C	E	M
3.	A*	B	C	H	L
4.	A*	B	D	H	I
5.	A*	B	D	I	K
6.	A*	B	E	F	J
7.	A*	B	E	G	K
8.	A*	B	F	G	M
9.	A*	B	F	J	L
10.	A*	B	J	K	M
11.	A*	C	D	F	I
12.	A*	C	E	F	K
13.	A*	C	E	G	H
14.	A*	C	G	I	J

15.	A*	C	H	J	K
16.	A*	C	I	J	M
17.	A*	C	K	L	M
18.	A*	D	E	G	L
19.	A*	D	E	J	L
20.	A*	D	F	H	M
21.	A*	D	G	J	K
22.	A*	D	G	K	L
23.	A*	D	I	K	M
24.	A*	E	F	H	K
25.	A*	E	I	L	M
26.	A*	F	G	I	L
27.	A*	G	H	J	M
28.	A*	H	I	J	K

POWER NUMBER™WHEEL 54114-1
Wheeling 14 Numbers in 37 games for a 4 of 5 Win

NUMBERS CORRECT***	MAXIMUM WINS				MINIMUM WINS			
	5x	4x	3x	2x	5x	4x	3x	2x
5 (w/o Jackpot)	0	5	7	20				
5	1	2	9	20	0	1	10	20
4	-	2	6	19	-	0	6	20
3	-	-	5	16	-	-	2	17
2	-	-	-	13	-	-	-	10

*** POWER NUMBER POSITION A* MUST BE A WINNER.
(Continued Next Page)

POWER NUMBER™ WHEEL 54114-1 (Continued from previous page)

Your 14 Numbers to Wheel

A*	B	C	D	E	F	G
37	12	11	11	11	13	11

H	I	J	K	L	M	N
11	13	10	11	11	11	12

The 37 Games to Play

#						#					
1.	A*	B	C	F	M	20.	A*	D	E	G	I
2.	A*	B	C	F	N	21.	A*	D	E	H	N
3.	A*	B	C	H	I	22.	A*	D	F	I	L
4.	A*	B	C	I	K	23.	A*	D	F	I	M
5.	A*	B	D	F	J	24.	A*	D	G	K	N
6.	A*	B	D	L	M	25.	A*	D	I	J	L
7.	A*	B	E	G	J	26.	A*	D	J	K	M
8.	A*	B	E	J	M	27.	A*	E	F	G	H
9.	A*	B	G	K	N	28.	A*	E	F	I	N
10.	A*	B	H	K	L	29.	A*	E	F	K	L
11.	A*	B	H	L	M	30.	A*	E	H	I	J
12.	A*	B	I	L	N	31.	A*	E	K	L	M
13.	A*	C	D	E	K	32.	A*	F	G	H	L
14.	A*	C	D	G	H	33.	A*	F	G	I	K
15.	A*	C	E	L	N	34.	A*	F	H	I	K
16.	A*	C	F	J	N	35.	A*	F	J	M	N
17.	A*	C	G	H	M	36.	A*	G	I	M	N
18.	A*	C	G	J	L	37.	A*	H	J	K	N
19.	A*	C	I	M	N						

POWER NUMBER™WHEEL 54115-1

Wheeling 15 Numbers in 49 games for a 4 of 5 Win

NUMBERS CORRECT***	MAXIMUM WINS				MINIMUM WINS			
	5x	4x	3x	2x	5x	4x	3x	2x
5 (w/o Jackpot)	0	6	10	23				
5	1	4	10	24	0	1	12	24
4	–	4	5	25	–	0	7	24
3	–	–	6	20	–	–	2	21
2	–	–	–	17	–	–	–	12

*** POWER NUMBER POSITION A* MUST BE A WINNER.

(Continued Next Page)

235

POWER NUMBER™ WHEEL 54115-1 (Continued from previous page)
Your 15 Numbers to Wheel

A*	B	C	D	E	F	G	H
49	13	13	12	13	17	15	15

I	J	K	L	M	N	O
15	13	14	14	14	14	14

The 49 Games to Play

#						#					
1.	A*	B	C	F	J	26.	A*	D	E	H	M
2.	A*	B	C	L	N	27.	A*	D	F	L	O
3.	A*	B	D	G	I	28.	A*	D	G	I	J
4.	A*	B	D	G	M	29.	A*	D	G	L	N
5.	A*	B	D	H	K	30.	A*	D	J	K	M
6.	A*	B	E	F	H	31.	A*	D	K	N	O
7.	A*	B	E	I	O	32.	A*	E	F	H	K
8.	A*	B	E	J	O	33.	A*	E	F	J	N
9.	A*	B	F	G	L	34.	A*	E	F	L	M
10.	A*	B	H	K	M	35.	A*	E	G	N	O
11.	A*	B	J	L	N	36.	A*	E	I	K	L
12.	A*	B	K	N	O	37.	A*	F	G	H	I
13.	A*	B	M	N	O	38.	A*	F	G	K	N
14.	A*	C	D	E	L	39.	A*	F	G	M	O
15.	A*	C	D	F	O	40.	A*	F	H	I	J
16.	A*	C	E	G	K	41.	A*	F	H	I	N
17.	A*	C	E	K	M	42.	A*	F	I	M	O
18.	A*	C	F	H	I	43.	A*	G	H	J	M
19.	A*	C	F	I	K	44.	A*	G	H	L	N
20.	A*	C	G	H	O	45.	A*	G	I	L	M
21.	A*	C	H	J	N	46.	A*	G	J	K	L
22.	A*	C	I	J	M	47.	A*	H	I	L	O
23.	A*	C	I	M	N	48.	A*	H	J	L	O
24.	A*	C	K	L	M	49.	A*	I	J	K	O
25.	A*	D	E	F	N						

POWER NUMBER™WHEEL 54116-1
Wheeling 16 Numbers in 61 games for a 4 of 5 Win

NUMBERS CORRECT***	MAXIMUM WINS				MINIMUM WINS			
	5x	4x	3x	2x	5x	4x	3x	2x
5 (w/o Jackpot)	0	7	8	32				
5	1	3	12	29	0	1	14	30
4	–	3	6	28	–	0	8	29
3	–	–	6	24	–	–	2	26
2	–	–	–	18	–	–	–	15

*** POWER NUMBER POSITION A* MUST BE A WINNER.

Your 16 Numbers to Wheel

A*	B	C	D	E	F	G	H
61	16	16	16	15	15	15	15

I	J	K	L	M	N	O	P
16	18	18	17	17	17	17	16

The 61 Games to Play

#						#					
1.	A*	B	C	D	N	25.	A*	C	F	J	P
2.	A*	B	C	H	J	26.	A*	C	G	H	K
3.	A*	B	C	I	P	27.	A*	C	H	M	P
4.	A*	B	D	H	P	28.	A*	C	I	J	K
5.	A*	B	E	F	K	29.	A*	C	K	O	P
6.	A*	B	E	G	O	30.	A*	D	E	F	I
7.	A*	B	F	G	H	31.	A*	D	E	H	M
8.	A*	B	F	I	J	32.	A*	D	E	I	L
9.	A*	B	F	M	O	33.	A*	D	E	J	N
10.	A*	B	G	I	K	34.	A*	D	E	K	N
11.	A*	B	G	I	M	35.	A*	D	F	K	L
12.	A*	B	I	J	M	36.	A*	D	G	H	J
13.	A*	B	J	K	L	37.	A*	D	G	L	P
14.	A*	B	J	L	P	38.	A*	D	G	M	P
15.	A*	B	K	M	N	39.	A*	D	I	K	O
16.	A*	B	L	N	O	40.	A*	D	J	N	O
17.	A*	C	D	I	O	41.	A*	E	G	J	O
18.	A*	C	D	L	N	42.	A*	E	G	K	P
19.	A*	C	D	M	N	43.	A*	E	H	I	N
20.	A*	C	E	G	M	44.	A*	E	H	J	L
21.	A*	C	E	L	N	45.	A*	E	M	N	P
22.	A*	C	E	O	P	46.	A*	F	G	N	O
23.	A*	C	F	G	L	47.	A*	F	H	O	P
24.	A*	C	F	H	N	48.	A*	F	I	K	M

(Continued Next Page)

POWER NUMBER™ WHEEL 54116-1 (Continued from previous page)

49. A*	F	J	K	M
50. A*	F	L	M	O
51. A*	F	L	N	P
52. A*	G	H	J	N
53. A*	G	I	N	P
54. A*	H	I	L	O
55. A*	H	I	M	O

56. A*	H	K	O	P
57. A*	I	J	K	P
58. A*	I	J	L	M
59. A*	J	K	L	O
60. A*	J	K	M	O
61. A*	K	L	M	N

POWER NUMBER™ WHEEL 54117-1
Wheeling 17 Numbers in 77 games for a 4 of 5 Win

NUMBERS CORRECT***	MAXIMUM WINS				MINIMUM WINS			
	5x	4x	3x	2x	5x	4x	3x	2x
5 (w/o Jackpot)	0	6	13	35				
5	1	3	14	36	0	1	16	38
4	–	3	7	36	–	0	9	36
3	–	–	6	29	–	–	2	32
2	–	–	–	21	–	–	–	18

*** POWER NUMBER POSITION A* MUST BE A WINNER.

Your 17 Numbers to Wheel

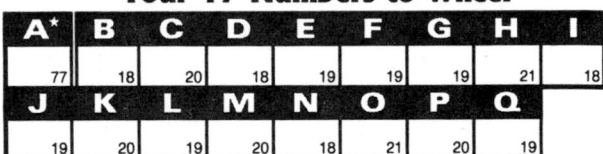

A*	B	C	D	E	F	G	H	I
77	18	20	18	19	19	19	21	18

J	K	L	M	N	O	P	Q
19	20	19	20	18	21	20	19

The 77 Games to Play

1. A*	B	C	E	Q
2. A*	B	C	I	K
3. A*	B	C	J	O
4. A*	B	C	N	O
5. A*	B	C	O	P
6. A*	B	D	H	I
7. A*	B	D	J	K
8. A*	B	E	F	O
9. A*	B	E	G	L
10. A*	B	F	G	N
11. A*	B	F	G	Q
12. A*	B	F	I	J
13. A*	B	H	J	P
14. A*	B	H	L	M
15. A*	B	K	L	P

16. A*	B	K	M	N
17. A*	B	M	N	P
18. A*	B	M	O	Q
19. A*	C	D	F	L
20. A*	C	D	G	J
21. A*	C	D	G	M
22. A*	C	E	G	H
23. A*	C	E	K	O
24. A*	C	F	H	M
25. A*	C	F	H	P
26. A*	C	F	K	N
27. A*	C	G	H	K
28. A*	C	G	N	P
29. A*	C	I	L	Q
30. A*	C	J	K	P

(Continued Next Page)

POWER NUMBER™ WHEEL 54117-1 (Continued from previous page)

#						#					
31.	A*	C	J	M	P	55.	A*	E	J	O	Q
32.	A*	C	K	O	Q	56.	A*	E	L	M	O
33.	A*	C	M	N	O	57.	A*	F	G	I	O
34.	A*	D	E	H	M	58.	A*	F	G	M	N
35.	A*	D	E	H	Q	59.	A*	F	H	J	Q
36.	A*	D	E	I	P	60.	A*	F	H	K	Q
37.	A*	D	E	N	Q	61.	A*	F	I	L	O
38.	A*	D	F	G	P	62.	A*	F	N	O	P
39.	A*	D	F	M	O	63.	A*	G	H	L	O
40.	A*	D	G	K	L	64.	A*	G	I	M	Q
41.	A*	D	G	L	O	65.	A*	G	I	P	Q
42.	A*	D	H	I	O	66.	A*	G	J	K	M
43.	A*	D	H	J	N	67.	A*	G	K	N	O
44.	A*	D	I	K	Q	68.	A*	H	I	J	L
45.	A*	D	I	L	N	69.	A*	H	K	M	O
46.	A*	D	L	P	Q	70.	A*	H	K	N	P
47.	A*	E	F	I	K	71.	A*	H	L	N	Q
48.	A*	E	F	J	L	72.	A*	H	M	O	P
49.	A*	E	F	P	Q	73.	A*	I	J	M	P
50.	A*	E	G	L	P	74.	A*	I	J	N	Q
51.	A*	E	H	I	N	75.	A*	J	K	O	P
52.	A*	E	H	K	Q	76.	A*	J	L	M	Q
53.	A*	E	I	J	M	77.	A*	K	L	M	P
54.	A*	E	J	L	N						

POWER NUMBER™WHEEL 54118-1
Wheeling 18 Numbers in 95 games for a 4 of 5 Win

NUMBERS CORRECT***	MAXIMUM WINS				MINIMUM WINS			
	5x	4x	3x	2x	5x	4x	3x	2x
5 (w/o Jackpot)	0	6	12	52				
5	1	3	19	47	0	1	16	50
4	–	3	9	48	–	0	9	45
3	–	–	7	36	–	–	2	40
2	–	–	–	25	–	–	–	19

*** POWER NUMBER POSITION A* MUST BE A WINNER.
(Continued Next Page)

POWER NUMBER™ WHEEL 54118-1 (Continued from previous page)
Your 18 Numbers to Wheel

A*	B	C	D	E	F	G	H	I
95	20	19	21	25	22	22	22	25

J	K	L	M	N	O	P	Q	R
23	22	25	23	24	21	23	22	21

The 95 Games to Play

#						#					
1.	A*	B	C	F	N	31.	A*	C	H	N	R
2.	A*	B	C	G	R	32.	A*	C	I	J	O
3.	A*	B	C	H	Q	33.	A*	C	I	K	L
4.	A*	B	D	E	Q	34.	A*	C	J	L	M
5.	A*	B	D	F	L	35.	A*	C	K	M	P
6.	A*	B	D	G	M	36.	A*	C	L	O	P
7.	A*	B	D	M	N	37.	A*	D	E	G	P
8.	A*	B	E	I	R	38.	A*	D	E	M	P
9.	A*	B	E	J	O	39.	A*	D	F	H	K
10.	A*	B	F	O	P	40.	A*	D	F	I	J
11.	A*	B	G	J	R	41.	A*	D	G	I	K
12.	A*	B	G	K	L	42.	A*	D	G	P	R
13.	A*	B	G	O	Q	43.	A*	D	H	I	R
14.	A*	B	H	I	N	44.	A*	D	H	J	O
15.	A*	B	H	M	P	45.	A*	D	I	L	O
16.	A*	B	I	J	P	46.	A*	D	J	K	Q
17.	A*	B	J	L	Q	47.	A*	D	J	L	N
18.	A*	B	K	M	O	48.	A*	D	M	Q	R
19.	A*	B	K	P	R	49.	A*	D	N	O	R
20.	A*	B	L	N	R	50.	A*	E	F	G	O
21.	A*	C	D	E	L	51.	A*	E	F	H	I
22.	A*	C	D	I	M	52.	A*	E	F	J	M
23.	A*	C	D	J	P	53.	A*	E	F	K	R
24.	A*	C	D	K	O	54.	A*	E	F	L	N
25.	A*	C	E	I	P	55.	A*	E	G	H	K
26.	A*	C	E	J	K	56.	A*	E	G	K	N
27.	A*	C	E	M	O	57.	A*	E	H	L	Q
28.	A*	C	F	G	H	58.	A*	E	H	N	P
29.	A*	C	F	Q	R	59.	A*	E	I	J	L
30.	A*	C	G	N	Q	60.	A*	E	I	L	M

          (Continued Next Page)

240

POWER NUMBER™ WHEEL 54118-1 (Continued from previous page)

#						#					
61.	A*	E	I	L	P	79.	A*	G	K	M	Q
62.	A*	E	I	N	Q	80.	A*	G	L	Q	R
63.	A*	E	J	Q	R	81.	A*	G	M	N	P
64.	A*	E	K	O	P	82.	A*	H	I	J	K
65.	A*	E	M	N	R	83.	A*	H	J	M	R
66.	A*	F	G	I	N	84.	A*	H	K	N	Q
67.	A*	F	G	L	P	85.	A*	H	L	M	N
68.	A*	F	G	N	Q	86.	A*	H	L	M	O
69.	A*	F	H	J	P	87.	A*	H	L	P	Q
70.	A*	F	H	O	R	88.	A*	I	J	M	Q
71.	A*	F	I	K	Q	89.	A*	I	K	N	P
72.	A*	F	I	M	R	90.	A*	I	M	O	R
73.	A*	F	J	K	N	91.	A*	I	O	P	Q
74.	A*	F	M	O	Q	92.	A*	J	L	N	O
75.	A*	F	N	P	Q	93.	A*	J	L	N	R
76.	A*	G	H	I	Q	94.	A*	K	L	M	P
77.	A*	G	H	L	N	95.	A*	K	L	O	R
78.	A*	G	J	O	P						

POWER NUMBER™WHEEL 54119-1
Wheeling 19 Numbers in 116 games for a 4 of 5 Win

NUMBERS CORRECT***	MAXIMUM WINS				MINIMUM WINS			
	5x	4x	3x	2x	5x	4x	3x	2x
5 (w/o Jackpot)	0	6	16	56				
5	1	3	15	60	0	1	19	55
4	–	3	8	55	–	0	10	53
3	–	–	7	38	–	–	3	43
2	–	–	–	28	–	–	–	23

*** POWER NUMBER POSITION A* MUST BE A WINNER.

Your 19 Numbers to Wheel

A*	B	C	D	E	F	G	H	I	J
116	27	27	23	27	26	23	26	27	25

K	L	M	N	O	P	Q	R	S
28	26	26	26	26	24	26	24	27

The 116 Games to Play

#						#					
1.	A*	B	C	G	Q	5.	A*	B	C	O	S
2.	A*	B	C	J	K	6.	A*	B	D	G	O
3.	A*	B	C	L	P	7.	A*	B	D	H	Q
4.	A*	B	C	O	R	8.	A*	B	D	K	R

          (Continued Next Page)

POWER NUMBER™ WHEEL 54119-1 (Continued from previous page)

#	1	2	3	4	5		#	1	2	3	4	5
9.	A*	B	D	P	S		44.	A*	C	H	Q	S
10.	A*	B	E	F	K		45.	A*	C	I	J	N
11.	A*	B	E	G	J		46.	A*	C	J	K	P
12.	A*	B	E	H	S		47.	A*	C	J	L	Q
13.	A*	B	E	M	N		48.	A*	C	M	N	O
14.	A*	B	F	G	I		49.	A*	C	M	P	S
15.	A*	B	F	H	M		50.	A*	D	E	F	J
16.	A*	B	F	L	O		51.	A*	D	E	I	L
17.	A*	B	F	N	P		52.	A*	D	E	I	M
18.	A*	B	G	H	K		53.	A*	D	F	J	M
19.	A*	B	G	J	M		54.	A*	D	F	L	N
20.	A*	B	H	J	N		55.	A*	D	G	H	P
21.	A*	B	I	L	R		56.	A*	D	G	K	S
22.	A*	B	I	M	Q		57.	A*	D	G	Q	R
23.	A*	B	I	O	P		58.	A*	D	H	K	O
24.	A*	B	J	Q	R		59.	A*	D	H	R	S
25.	A*	B	K	O	P		60.	A*	D	I	J	N
26.	A*	B	K	Q	S		61.	A*	D	K	P	Q
27.	A*	B	N	R	S		62.	A*	D	L	M	N
28.	A*	C	D	E	M		63.	A*	D	O	P	R
29.	A*	C	D	E	N		64.	A*	D	O	Q	S
30.	A*	C	D	F	I		65.	A*	E	F	G	R
31.	A*	C	D	J	L		66.	A*	E	F	J	S
32.	A*	C	E	F	P		67.	A*	E	G	P	S
33.	A*	C	E	H	N		68.	A*	E	H	I	L
34.	A*	C	E	I	R		69.	A*	E	H	K	M
35.	A*	C	E	K	N		70.	A*	E	H	O	Q
36.	A*	C	F	G	H		71.	A*	E	I	K	O
37.	A*	C	F	I	S		72.	A*	E	I	N	Q
38.	A*	C	F	K	Q		73.	A*	E	J	N	O
39.	A*	C	F	Q	R		74.	A*	E	K	L	S
40.	A*	C	G	L	O		75.	A*	E	K	M	Q
41.	A*	C	G	R	S		76.	A*	E	L	M	O
42.	A*	C	H	I	M		77.	A*	E	L	P	Q
43.	A*	C	H	L	M		78.	A*	E	P	R	S

                    (Continued Next Page)

POWER NUMBER™ WHEEL 54119-1 (Continued from previous page)

#						#				
79.	A*	F	G	N	O	98.	A*	H	I	O	R
80.	A*	F	H	J	Q	99.	A*	H	I	O	S
81.	A*	F	I	K	L	100.	A*	H	J	L	R
82.	A*	F	I	K	P	101.	A*	H	J	O	P
83.	A*	F	I	L	M	102.	A*	H	K	N	S
84.	A*	F	J	K	O	103.	A*	H	K	Q	R
85.	A*	F	J	M	P	104.	A*	H	L	P	S
86.	A*	F	L	N	R	105.	A*	H	M	P	R
87.	A*	F	O	R	S	106.	A*	I	J	M	R
88.	A*	F	Q	R	S	107.	A*	I	J	P	S
89.	A*	G	I	J	K	108.	A*	I	K	N	S
90.	A*	G	I	P	Q	109.	A*	I	L	O	Q
91.	A*	G	J	L	S	110.	A*	J	K	O	R
92.	A*	G	K	M	S	111.	A*	J	M	Q	S
93.	A*	G	L	N	P	112.	A*	K	L	M	R
94.	A*	G	L	N	Q	113.	A*	K	L	N	O
95.	A*	G	M	O	Q	114.	A*	K	M	N	Q
96.	A*	G	N	P	R	115.	A*	L	M	N	S
97.	A*	H	I	M	N	116.	A*	N	O	P	Q

Copyright © 1983-1998 Gail Howard

POWER NUMBER™ WHEEL 54120-1
Wheeling 20 Numbers in 138 games for a 4 of 5 Win

NUMBERS CORRECT***	MAXIMUM WINS				MINIMUM WINS			
	5x	4x	3x	2x	5x	4x	3x	2x
5 (w/o Jackpot)	0	7	17	64				
5	1	3	22	61	0	1	20	64
4	–	3	10	67	–	0	10	64
3	–	–	8	48	–	–	2	56
2	–	–	–	34	–	–	–	24

*** POWER NUMBER POSITION A* MUST BE A WINNER.

Your 20 Numbers to Wheel

A*	B	C	D	E	F	G	H	I	J
138	27	28	30	32	34	30	30	30	28

K	L	M	N	O	P	Q	R	S	T
29	30	28	29	30	28	27	30	28	24

The 138 Games to Play

#					#				
1.	A*	B	C	G	N	4.	A*	B	C	R	T
2.	A*	B	C	K	M	5.	A*	B	D	G	S
3.	A*	B	C	O	S	6.	A*	B	D	I	M

Copyright © 1983-1998 Gail Howard   (Continued Next Page)

243

POWER NUMBER™ WHEEL 54120-1 (Continued from previous page)

7.	A*	B	D	L	O	42.	A*	C	G	K	T
8.	A*	B	D	N	P	43.	A*	C	G	M	O
9.	A*	B	D	Q	R	44.	A*	C	G	M	Q
10.	A*	B	E	F	S	45.	A*	C	H	J	L
11.	A*	B	E	I	R	46.	A*	C	H	P	Q
12.	A*	B	E	M	P	47.	A*	C	I	J	T
13.	A*	B	F	G	K	48.	A*	C	I	P	Q
14.	A*	B	F	I	J	49.	A*	C	K	N	O
15.	A*	B	F	K	T	50.	A*	C	L	P	R
16.	A*	B	G	H	P	51.	A*	C	M	N	S
17.	A*	B	G	I	T	52.	A*	D	E	F	H
18.	A*	B	H	J	K	53.	A*	D	E	F	I
19.	A*	B	H	L	R	54.	A*	D	E	F	J
20.	A*	B	H	O	P	55.	A*	D	E	G	N
21.	A*	B	I	O	S	56.	A*	D	E	K	O
22.	A*	B	J	L	S	57.	A*	D	E	M	T
23.	A*	B	J	N	R	58.	A*	D	F	P	R
24.	A*	B	J	Q	T	59.	A*	D	G	I	P
25.	A*	B	L	O	Q	60.	A*	D	G	I	R
26.	A*	B	M	O	R	61.	A*	D	G	I	S
27.	A*	B	N	Q	S	62.	A*	D	H	J	L
28.	A*	C	D	E	P	63.	A*	D	H	K	R
29.	A*	C	D	F	L	64.	A*	D	H	O	T
30.	A*	C	D	H	I	65.	A*	D	J	K	M
31.	A*	C	D	J	R	66.	A*	D	J	L	Q
32.	A*	C	E	F	Q	67.	A*	D	L	P	T
33.	A*	C	E	H	R	68.	A*	D	L	R	S
34.	A*	C	E	I	L	69.	A*	D	M	O	S
35.	A*	C	E	J	O	70.	A*	D	N	O	Q
36.	A*	C	F	H	I	71.	A*	D	N	S	T
37.	A*	C	F	I	R	72.	A*	D	Q	R	S
38.	A*	C	F	J	P	73.	A*	E	F	G	M
39.	A*	C	F	K	Q	74.	A*	E	F	K	N
40.	A*	C	F	Q	T	75.	A*	E	G	H	Q
41.	A*	C	G	K	S	76.	A*	E	G	J	K

     (Continued Next Page)

POWER NUMBER™ WHEEL 54120-1 (Continued from previous page)

#	1	2	3	4	5		#	1	2	3	4	5
77.	A*	E	G	L	O		108.	A*	G	H	J	O
78.	A*	E	H	I	N		109.	A*	G	H	K	O
79.	A*	E	H	J	P		110.	A*	G	H	M	S
80.	A*	E	H	L	T		111.	A*	G	I	L	N
81.	A*	E	H	N	R		112.	A*	G	J	M	N
82.	A*	E	I	M	S		113.	A*	G	K	L	M
83.	A*	E	I	P	Q		114.	A*	G	K	P	Q
84.	A*	E	J	L	R		115.	A*	G	P	R	S
85.	A*	E	K	L	O		116.	A*	G	Q	R	T
86.	A*	E	K	M	Q		117.	A*	H	I	K	S
87.	A*	E	L	N	S		118.	A*	H	I	M	Q
88.	A*	E	N	O	R		119.	A*	H	L	M	O
89.	A*	E	N	P	T		120.	A*	H	M	N	T
90.	A*	E	O	S	T		121.	A*	H	P	S	T
91.	A*	F	G	I	Q		122.	A*	I	J	K	N
92.	A*	F	G	J	L		123.	A*	I	J	O	R
93.	A*	F	G	J	T		124.	A*	I	K	P	R
94.	A*	F	G	N	O		125.	A*	I	K	Q	T
95.	A*	F	H	K	Q		126.	A*	I	L	M	P
96.	A*	F	H	M	P		127.	A*	J	K	R	T
97.	A*	F	H	N	S		128.	A*	J	N	Q	R
98.	A*	F	H	N	O		129.	A*	J	O	P	O
99.	A*	F	I	K	L		130.	A*	J	O	Q	S
100.	A*	F	I	N	P		131.	A*	K	L	N	P
101.	A*	F	I	R	T		132.	A*	K	N	R	S
102.	A*	F	J	M	R		133.	A*	L	M	S	T
103.	A*	F	K	M	O		134.	A*	L	N	O	T
104.	A*	F	K	P	S		135.	A*	L	N	Q	S
105.	A*	F	L	M	N		136.	A*	L	O	Q	R
106.	A*	F	L	O	P		137.	A*	M	N	O	R
107.	A*	F	M	P	Q		138.	A*	M	O	P	T

245

POWER NUMBER™ WHEEL 54121-1
Wheeling 21 Numbers in 164 games for a 4 of 5 Win

NUMBERS CORRECT***	MAXIMUM WINS				MINIMUM WINS			
	5x	4x	3x	2x	5x	4x	3x	2x
5 (w/o Jackpot)	0	7	19	77				
5	1	4	22	76	0	1	21	80
4	–	3	12	74	–	0	11	71
3	–	–	9	50	–	–	3	59
2	–	–	–	37	–	–	–	28

*** POWER NUMBER POSITION A* MUST BE A WINNER.

Your 21 Numbers to Wheel

A*	B	C	D	E	F	G	H	I	J	K
164	35	33	35	33	34	33	32	32	32	32

L	M	N	O	P	Q	R	S	T	U
31	31	31	34	31	28	34	37	35	33

The 164 Games to Play

#						#					
1.	A*	B	C	E	R	25.	A*	B	I	K	S
2.	A*	B	C	H	K	26.	A*	B	I	L	O
3.	A*	B	C	I	T	27.	A*	B	I	M	P
4.	A*	B	C	J	Q	28.	A*	B	I	R	U
5.	A*	B	D	G	M	29.	A*	B	J	M	R
6.	A*	B	D	I	L	30.	A*	B	J	P	R
7.	A*	B	D	J	O	31.	A*	B	L	S	T
8.	A*	B	D	K	N	32.	A*	B	M	Q	U
9.	A*	B	D	P	T	33.	A*	B	N	O	T
10.	A*	B	E	H	U	34.	A*	B	N	P	Q
11.	A*	B	E	I	M	35.	A*	B	N	S	T
12.	A*	B	E	K	U	36.	A*	C	D	F	U
13.	A*	B	E	S	T	37.	A*	C	D	G	O
14.	A*	B	F	G	P	38.	A*	C	D	H	S
15.	A*	B	F	J	S	39.	A*	C	D	K	R
16.	A*	B	F	R	T	40.	A*	C	E	H	T
17.	A*	B	G	H	J	41.	A*	C	E	J	L
18.	A*	B	G	L	U	42.	A*	C	E	K	S
19.	A*	B	G	O	R	43.	A*	C	E	N	U
20.	A*	B	H	L	R	44.	A*	C	F	G	S
21.	A*	B	H	N	S	45.	A*	C	F	I	J
22.	A*	B	H	O	P	46.	A*	C	F	L	M
23.	A*	B	H	Q	S	47.	A*	C	F	M	O
24.	A*	B	I	J	N	48.	A*	C	F	N	P

    (Continued Next Page)

POWER NUMBER™ WHEEL 54121-1 (Continued from previous page)

#						#					
49.	A*	C	G	I	O	84.	A*	D	I	K	Q
50.	A*	C	G	N	R	85.	A*	D	I	N	S
51.	A*	C	G	T	U	86.	A*	D	J	N	T
52.	A*	C	H	J	R	87.	A*	D	J	S	U
53.	A*	C	H	M	Q	88.	A*	D	L	O	U
54.	A*	C	J	O	U	89.	A*	D	L	R	U
55.	A*	C	J	P	T	90.	A*	D	O	Q	T
56.	A*	C	K	L	P	91.	A*	E	F	H	O
57.	A*	C	K	M	U	92.	A*	E	F	L	P
58.	A*	C	L	N	Q	93.	A*	E	F	N	R
59.	A*	C	M	N	O	94.	A*	E	F	R	T
60.	A*	C	M	S	T	95.	A*	E	F	T	U
61.	A*	C	N	Q	U	96.	A*	E	G	H	P
62.	A*	C	O	R	S	97.	A*	E	G	J	K
63.	A*	C	P	Q	S	98.	A*	E	G	J	M
64.	A*	C	P	S	U	99.	A*	E	G	N	P
65.	A*	D	E	F	I	100.	A*	E	G	O	Q
66.	A*	D	E	F	Q	101.	A*	E	H	I	L
67.	A*	D	E	J	P	102.	A*	E	I	P	U
68.	A*	D	E	M	R	103.	A*	E	I	Q	R
09.	A*	D	E	O	R	104.	A*	E	K	L	N
70.	A	D	F	Q	T	105.	A*	E	K	O	T
71.	A*	D	F	H	K	106.	A*	E	L	M	Q
72.	A*	D	F	R	S	107.	A*	E	L	R	S
73.	A*	D	G	I	P	108.	A*	E	M	P	R
74.	A*	D	G	K	S	109.	A*	E	O	P	S
75.	A*	D	G	L	T	110.	A*	F	G	K	Q
76.	A*	D	G	M	P	111.	A*	F	G	L	R
77.	A*	D	G	O	U	112.	A*	F	G	N	U
78.	A*	D	G	Q	R	113.	A*	F	H	I	P
79.	A*	D	H	L	S	114.	A*	F	H	M	T
80.	A*	D	H	N	O	115.	A*	F	I	O	Q
81.	A*	D	H	R	S	116.	A*	F	J	L	N
82.	A*	D	I	J	M	117.	A*	F	J	R	U
83.	A*	D	I	J	T	118.	A*	F	K	L	Q

    (Continued Next Page)

247

POWER NUMBER™ WHEEL 54121-1 (Continued from previous page)

119.	A*	F	K	M	S	142.	A*	H	P	Q	U
120.	A*	F	K	O	P	143.	A*	H	R	S	T
121.	A*	F	K	S	T	144.	A*	I	J	O	S
122.	A*	F	M	N	U	145.	A*	I	K	N	O
123.	A*	F	O	S	U	146.	A*	I	K	P	R
124.	A*	F	Q	R	T	147.	A*	I	L	R	T
125.	A*	G	H	L	O	148.	A*	I	L	S	U
126.	A*	G	I	L	S	149.	A*	I	O	S	T
127.	A*	G	I	M	R	150.	A*	J	K	L	M
128.	A*	G	I	Q	T	151.	A*	J	K	N	S
129.	A*	G	J	N	O	152.	A*	J	K	O	T
130.	A*	G	J	T	U	153.	A*	J	L	P	Q
131.	A*	G	K	P	T	154.	A*	J	M	P	Q
132.	A*	G	R	S	U	155.	A*	J	Q	S	U
133.	A*	H	I	K	U	156.	A*	K	M	N	T
134.	A*	H	I	N	T	157.	A*	K	O	Q	R
135.	A*	H	J	N	Q	158.	A*	K	P	T	U
136.	A*	H	J	P	S	159.	A*	L	M	N	P
137.	A*	H	K	M	N	160.	A*	L	M	O	S
138.	A*	H	K	M	O	161.	A*	L	O	R	T
139.	A*	H	K	O	R	162.	A*	M	N	Q	S
140.	A*	H	L	T	U	163.	A*	M	O	T	U
141.	A*	H	M	S	U	164.	A*	N	P	R	U

POWER NUMBER™ WHEEL 54122-1
Wheeling 22 Numbers in 188 games for a 4 of 5 Win

NUMBERS CORRECT***	MAXIMUM WINS				MINIMUM WINS			
	5x	4x	3x	2x	5x	4x	3x	2x
5 (w/o Jackpot)	0	7	17	91				
5	1	4	22	85	0	1	22	87
4	–	3	12	81	–	0	12	78
3	–	–	9	62	–	–	3	65
2	–	–	–	40	–	–	–	31

*** POWER NUMBER POSITION A* MUST BE A WINNER.

Your 22 Numbers to Wheel

A*	B	C	D	E	F	G	H	I	J	K
188	32	35	35	34	36	40	36	40	36	37

L	M	N	O	P	Q	R	S	T	U	V
35	37	37	37	36	35	35	36	37	35	31

(Continued Next Page)

POWER NUMBER™ WHEEL 54122-1 (Continued from previous page)
The 188 Games to Play

#						#					
1.	A*	B	C	E	P	36.	A*	C	D	M	U
2.	A*	B	C	F	Q	37.	A*	C	D	N	O
3.	A*	B	C	H	P	38.	A*	C	D	S	T
4.	A*	B	C	I	S	39.	A*	C	E	J	Q
5.	A*	B	C	J	V	40.	A*	C	E	L	N
6.	A*	B	C	K	M	41.	A*	C	E	R	U
7.	A*	B	D	G	O	42.	A*	C	F	G	P
8.	A*	B	D	J	R	43.	A*	C	F	H	L
9.	A*	B	D	L	T	44.	A*	C	F	J	U
10.	A*	B	D	N	U	45.	A*	C	F	L	T
11.	A*	B	D	S	V	46.	A*	C	F	M	R
12.	A*	B	E	J	N	47.	A*	C	G	H	I
13.	A*	B	E	L	R	48.	A*	C	G	J	R
14.	A*	B	E	Q	U	49.	A*	C	G	N	Q
15.	A*	B	E	R	V	50.	A*	C	G	O	S
16.	A*	B	F	H	S	51.	A*	C	G	P	U
17.	A*	B	F	I	M	52.	A*	C	H	Q	R
18.	A*	B	F	K	P	53.	A*	C	I	J	O
19.	A*	B	G	J	U	54.	A*	C	I	K	N
20.	A*	B	G	L	N	55.	A*	C	J	M	S
21.	A*	B	G	R	T	56.	A*	C	K	I	S
22.	A*	B	H	I	K	57.	A*	C	L	M	P
23.	A*	B	H	M	Q	58.	A*	C	L	S	V
24.	A*	B	I	P	Q	59.	A*	C	N	T	U
25.	A*	B	J	L	O	60.	A*	C	O	Q	T
26.	A*	B	J	N	T	61.	A*	C	R	U	V
27.	A*	B	K	Q	S	62.	A*	D	E	F	T
28.	A*	B	L	R	U	63.	A*	D	E	G	I
29.	A*	B	L	U	V	64.	A*	D	E	H	M
30.	A*	B	M	P	S	65.	A*	D	E	K	O
31.	A*	B	N	O	R	66.	A*	D	E	Q	S
32.	A*	B	O	T	U	67.	A*	D	F	G	K
33.	A*	C	D	E	V	68.	A*	D	F	J	S
34.	A*	C	D	I	P	69.	A*	D	F	N	Q
35.	A*	C	D	J	K	70.	A*	D	F	P	U

  (Continued Next Page)

POWER NUMBER™ WHEEL 54122-1 (Continued from previous page)

#						#				
71.	A*	D	G	I	N	106.	A*	F	G	I	V
72.	A*	D	G	J	O	107.	A*	F	G	J	Q
73.	A*	D	G	L	R	108.	A*	F	G	M	S
74.	A*	D	G	T	U	109.	A*	F	G	N	U
75.	A*	D	H	L	Q	110.	A*	F	H	P	V
76.	A*	D	H	O	R	111.	A*	F	H	R	T
77.	A*	D	I	J	M	112.	A*	F	I	J	R
78.	A*	D	I	K	U	113.	A*	F	I	L	O
79.	A*	D	J	U	V	114.	A*	F	I	R	S
80.	A*	D	K	L	M	115.	A*	F	J	M	O
81.	A*	D	K	N	R	116.	A*	F	K	N	V
82.	A*	D	L	P	S	117.	A*	F	K	O	Q
83.	A*	D	L	R	V	118.	A*	F	L	N	R
84.	A*	D	M	P	Q	119.	A*	F	M	O	V
85.	A*	D	O	Q	T	120.	A*	F	M	T	U
86.	A*	E	F	G	O	121.	A*	F	N	O	S
87.	A*	E	F	H	I	122.	A*	F	P	Q	S
88.	A*	E	F	K	M	123.	A*	F	Q	T	V
89.	A*	E	F	S	T	124.	A*	G	H	K	T
90.	A*	E	G	H	S	125.	A*	G	H	M	P
91.	A*	E	G	K	S	126.	A*	G	H	N	V
92.	A*	E	G	M	T	127.	A*	G	I	J	S
93.	A*	E	H	K	P	128.	A*	G	I	K	P
94.	A*	E	H	O	T	129.	A*	G	I	L	T
95.	A*	E	I	K	T	130.	A*	G	I	M	V
96.	A*	E	I	M	N	131.	A*	G	I	O	V
97.	A*	E	I	O	S	132.	A*	G	J	M	U
98.	A*	E	J	L	U	133.	A*	G	K	M	N
99.	A*	E	J	L	V	134.	A*	G	K	Q	V
100.	A*	E	J	P	R	135.	A*	G	K	S	T
101.	A*	E	L	P	Q	136.	A*	G	L	M	Q
102.	A*	E	M	O	S	137.	A*	G	M	R	S
103.	A*	E	N	P	U	138.	A*	G	O	P	R
104.	A*	E	N	Q	R	139.	A*	G	P	T	V
105.	A*	E	S	U	V	140.	A*	H	I	K	V

 (Continued Next Page)

POWER NUMBER™ WHEEL 54122-1 (Continued from previous page)

141.	A*	H	I	L	S
142.	A*	H	I	L	U
143.	A*	H	I	N	P
144.	A*	H	I	N	T
145.	A*	H	I	O	U
146.	A*	H	J	K	N
147.	A*	H	J	L	Q
148.	A*	H	J	M	R
149.	A*	H	J	P	T
150.	A*	H	K	M	O
151.	A*	H	K	S	U
152.	A*	H	L	O	P
153.	A*	H	M	N	S
154.	A*	H	M	T	V
155.	A*	H	O	Q	V
156.	A*	H	Q	R	U
157.	A*	I	K	M	Q
158.	A*	I	L	Q	R
159.	A*	I	M	O	R
160.	A*	I	M	R	T
161.	A*	I	N	P	T
162.	A*	I	N	T	V
163.	A*	I	P	Q	V
164.	A*	I	Q	S	U
165.	A*	I	R	S	U
166.	A*	J	K	L	T
167.	A*	J	K	P	Q
168.	A*	J	L	N	P
169.	A*	J	N	Q	T
170.	A*	J	N	T	U
171.	A*	J	O	R	S
172.	A*	J	P	T	U
173.	A*	J	R	S	V
174.	A*	K	L	O	R
175.	A*	K	L	Q	U
176.	A*	K	M	P	V
177.	A*	K	O	P	T
178.	A*	K	O	R	U
179.	A*	K	O	T	V
180.	A*	K	P	R	T
181.	A*	L	O	S	U
182.	A*	L	Q	S	T
183.	A*	M	N	O	T
184.	A*	M	N	P	U
185.	A*	M	N	Q	V
186.	A*	N	O	P	V
187.	A*	N	O	Q	U
188.	A*	N	P	R	S

POWER NUMBER™ WHEEL 54126-1

Wheeling 26 Numbers in 337 games for a 4 of 5 Win

NUMBERS CORRECT***	MAXIMUM WINS 5x	4x	3x	2x	MINIMUM WINS 5x	4x	3x	2x
5 (w/o Jackpot)	0	8	26	145				
5	1	5	25	147	0	1	30	144
4	–	4	14	122	–	0	15	128
3	–	–	11	89	–	–	4	97
2	–	–	–	60	–	–	–	49

*** POWER NUMBER POSITION A* MUST BE A WINNER.

(Continued Next Page)

POWER NUMBER™ WHEEL 54126-1 (Continued from previous page)
Your 26 Numbers to Wheel

A*	B	C	D	E	F	G	H	I
337	54	54	54	54	57	54	56	56

J	K	L	M	N	O	P	Q	R
56	53	54	53	53	51	50	50	51

S	T	U	V	W	X	Y	Z
49	56	60	55	54	55	55	54

The 337 Games to Play

#	1	2	3	4	5
1.	A*	B	C	D	R
2.	A*	B	C	H	Z
3.	A*	B	C	J	K
4.	A*	B	C	L	U
5.	A*	B	C	N	X
6.	A*	B	C	R	S
7.	A*	B	C	V	Z
8.	A*	B	C	W	Y
9.	A*	B	D	F	Q
10.	A*	B	D	G	W
11.	A*	B	D	I	Y
12.	A*	B	D	K	U
13.	A*	B	E	H	W
14.	A*	B	E	H	X
15.	A*	B	E	J	R
16.	A*	B	E	L	Z
17.	A*	B	E	M	V
18.	A*	B	E	N	Y
19.	A*	B	F	K	L
20.	A*	B	F	M	W
21.	A*	B	F	O	Y
22.	A*	B	F	Q	U
23.	A*	B	F	T	Z
24.	A*	B	G	I	X
25.	A*	B	G	K	N
26.	A*	B	G	L	T
27.	A*	B	G	N	Q
28.	A*	B	G	S	X
29.	A*	B	H	P	Q
30.	A*	B	H	P	V
31.	A*	B	H	Q	S
32.	A*	B	I	J	W
33.	A*	B	I	P	U
34.	A*	B	I	S	Z
35.	A*	B	I	T	V
36.	A*	B	J	L	O
37.	A*	B	J	M	Z
38.	A*	B	J	N	R
39.	A*	B	J	P	Y
40.	A*	B	J	R	S
41.	A*	B	K	O	V
42.	A*	B	K	S	Y
43.	A*	B	K	T	U
44.	A*	B	L	V	X
45.	A*	B	M	O	X
46.	A*	B	M	P	T
47.	A*	B	N	U	Z
48.	A*	B	N	V	W
49.	A*	B	O	R	V
50.	A*	B	O	R	X
51.	A*	B	O	W	Z
52.	A*	B	Q	V	W
53.	A*	B	R	U	Y
54.	A*	B	U	X	Y
55.	A*	C	D	E	V
56.	A*	C	D	G	M

                    (Continued Next Page)

POWER NUMBER™ WHEEL 54126-1 (Continued from previous page)

#	1	2	3	4	5		#	1	2	3	4	5
57.	A*	C	D	H	K		92.	A*	C	N	O	R
58.	A*	C	D	O	T		93.	A*	C	N	R	Y
59.	A*	C	D	P	W		94.	A*	C	N	W	X
60.	A*	C	E	F	Y		95.	A*	C	N	W	Z
61.	A*	C	E	G	L		96.	A*	C	O	Q	U
62.	A*	C	E	I	U		97.	A*	C	Q	X	Y
63.	A*	C	E	N	R		98.	A*	C	R	U	V
64.	A*	C	E	O	P		99.	A*	C	S	X	Y
65.	A*	C	E	P	Z		100.	A*	C	U	W	Z
66.	A*	C	E	Q	T		101.	A*	D	E	F	P
67.	A*	C	F	G	P		102.	A*	D	E	J	U
68.	A*	C	F	I	M		103.	A*	D	E	O	R
69.	A*	C	F	I	Z		104.	A*	D	E	P	S
70.	A*	C	F	L	V		105.	A*	D	E	T	W
71.	A*	C	G	H	O		106.	A*	D	E	Y	Z
72.	A*	C	G	N	V		107.	A*	D	F	J	X
73.	A*	C	G	Q	S		108.	A*	D	F	M	N
74.	A*	C	H	I	K		109.	A*	D	F	M	Z
75.	A*	C	H	S	Z		110.	A*	D	F	S	W
76.	A*	C	H	T	U		111.	A*	D	F	U	V
77.	A*	C	H	U	X		112.	A*	D	G	H	X
78.	A*	C	H	V	W		113.	A*	D	G	I	J
79.	A*	C	I	K	Q		114.	A*	D	G	I	O
80.	A*	C	I	K	S		115.	A*	D	G	K	P
81.	A*	C	I	N	O		116.	A*	D	G	Q	V
82.	A*	C	J	M	Q		117.	A*	D	H	I	N
83.	A*	C	J	R	X		118.	A*	D	H	J	V
84.	A*	C	J	S	W		119.	A*	D	H	L	M
85.	A*	C	J	Y	Z		120.	A*	D	H	O	P
86.	A*	C	K	M	T		121.	A*	D	H	O	Q
87.	A*	C	K	N	U		122.	A*	D	H	T	U
88.	A*	C	K	P	X		123.	A*	D	I	L	W
89.	A*	C	L	Q	Z		124.	A*	D	I	T	X
90.	A*	C	L	T	X		125.	A*	D	I	V	W
91.	A*	C	M	U	Z		126.	A*	D	J	K	L

(Continued Next Page)

253

POWER NUMBER™ WHEEL 54126-1 (Continued from previous page)

127.	A*	D	J	N	U		162.	A*	E	K	P	W
128.	A*	D	J	R	V		163.	A*	E	K	Q	X
129.	A*	D	J	T	Z		164.	A*	E	L	O	Q
130.	A*	D	K	V	Y		165.	A*	E	L	T	V
131.	A*	D	L	N	S		166.	A*	E	L	X	Y
132.	A*	D	L	N	T		167.	A*	E	M	Q	X
133.	A*	D	L	P	Y		168.	A*	E	M	S	W
134.	A*	D	M	O	S		169.	A*	E	N	O	T
135.	A*	D	M	W	X		170.	A*	E	N	S	W
136.	A*	D	N	O	U		171.	A*	E	N	U	V
137.	A*	D	N	P	Q		172.	A*	E	N	X	Z
138.	A*	D	N	R	U		173.	A*	E	O	S	U
139.	A*	D	N	S	V		174.	A*	E	R	U	X
140.	A*	D	P	X	Z		175.	A*	E	R	V	Y
141.	A*	D	Q	U	W		176.	A*	E	S	T	V
142.	A*	D	R	X	Y		177.	A*	E	T	V	Y
143.	A*	D	S	T	U		178.	A*	E	V	W	Z
144.	A*	D	T	U	Y		179.	A*	F	G	J	T
145.	A*	E	F	G	H		180.	A*	F	G	L	R
146.	A*	E	F	I	K		181.	A*	F	G	P	Q
147.	A*	E	F	I	M		182.	A*	F	G	Q	R
148.	A*	E	F	J	V		183.	A*	F	G	U	Y
149.	A*	E	F	L	S		184.	A*	F	G	V	X
150.	A*	E	F	L	U		185.	A*	F	H	I	X
151.	A*	E	G	H	J		186.	A*	F	H	J	N
152.	A*	E	G	M	U		187.	A*	F	H	J	U
153.	A*	E	G	N	W		188.	A*	F	H	P	R
154.	A*	E	G	O	U		189.	A*	F	H	Q	V
155.	A*	E	G	P	X		190.	A*	F	H	W	Y
156.	A*	E	H	I	O		191.	A*	F	I	L	N
157.	A*	E	H	K	M		192.	A*	F	I	M	U
158.	A*	E	I	Q	Z		193.	A*	F	I	R	Z
159.	A*	E	J	Q	Y		194.	A*	F	J	M	O
160.	A*	E	J	T	X		195.	A*	F	K	L	O
161.	A*	E	K	N	W		196.	A*	F	K	M	R

    (Continued Next Page)

POWER NUMBER™ WHEEL 54126-1 (Continued from previous page)

No.						No.				
197.	A*	F	K	P	Z	232.	A*	G	O	Q	T
198.	A*	F	K	T	W	233.	A*	G	P	R	T
199.	A*	F	L	R	W	234.	A*	G	P	W	Z
200.	A*	F	L	S	U	235.	A*	G	Q	S	Y
201.	A*	F	L	U	X	236.	A*	G	R	S	Z
202.	A*	F	L	V	Z	237.	A*	G	T	V	Z
203.	A*	F	M	R	T	238.	A*	H	I	L	R
204.	A*	F	M	S	V	239.	A*	H	I	M	P
205.	A*	F	N	P	T	240.	A*	H	I	S	Y
206.	A*	F	N	Q	W	241.	A*	H	I	U	Z
207.	A*	F	N	S	T	242.	A*	H	J	L	W
208.	A*	F	O	P	S	243.	A*	H	J	P	T
209.	A*	F	O	V	Z	244.	A*	H	J	S	X
210.	A*	F	O	W	X	245.	A*	H	K	L	Y
211.	A*	F	P	W	X	246.	A*	H	K	R	S
212.	A*	F	U	X	Y	247.	A*	H	L	N	P
213.	A*	G	H	I	R	248.	A*	H	L	R	T
214.	A*	G	H	K	S	249.	A*	H	M	N	T
215.	A*	G	H	M	Y	250.	A*	H	M	Q	R
216.	A*	G	H	Q	U	251.	A*	H	M	T	V
217.	A*	G	H	Q	W	252.	A*	H	M	U	W
218.	A*	G	I	I	S	253.	A*	H	N	O	Q
219.	A*	G	I	T	W	254.	A*	H	O	T	U
220.	A*	G	I	V	Y	255.	A*	H	P	U	Y
221.	A*	G	J	K	V	256.	A*	H	R	W	Z
222.	A*	G	J	U	X	257.	A*	H	T	Y	Z
223.	A*	G	K	R	W	258.	A*	H	U	V	X
224.	A*	G	K	T	Y	259.	A*	I	J	L	Y
225.	A*	G	K	U	Z	260.	A*	I	J	N	T
226.	A*	G	L	U	V	261.	A*	I	J	P	V
227.	A*	G	L	X	Z	262.	A*	I	J	Q	T
228.	A*	G	M	R	W	263.	A*	I	J	V	X
229.	A*	G	N	O	P	264.	A*	I	K	L	P
230.	A*	G	N	U	X	265.	A*	I	K	M	Z
231.	A*	G	N	Y	Z	266.	A*	I	K	P	R

(Continued Next Page)

POWER NUMBER™ WHEEL 54126-1 (Continued from previous page)

#						#				
267.	A*	I	K	Q	Y	302.	A*	K	N	V	Z
268.	A*	I	K	U	Y	303.	A*	K	N	X	Y
269.	A*	I	L	M	Q	304.	A*	K	O	X	Z
270.	A*	I	M	N	P	305.	A*	K	R	T	Z
271.	A*	I	M	R	Z	306.	A*	K	S	X	Z
272.	A*	I	O	P	Q	307.	A*	K	T	W	X
273.	A*	I	O	T	U	308.	A*	L	M	O	Z
274.	A*	I	P	T	Y	309.	A*	L	M	P	R
275.	A*	I	Q	R	S	310.	A*	L	M	S	T
276.	A*	I	Q	T	X	311.	A*	L	O	S	V
277.	A*	I	R	S	X	312.	A*	L	O	V	X
278.	A*	I	R	T	W	313.	A*	L	O	W	Y
279.	A*	I	W	X	Y	314.	A*	L	P	R	Z
280.	A*	J	K	O	Y	315.	A*	L	P	S	W
281.	A*	J	K	Q	S	316.	A*	L	Q	T	Y
282.	A*	J	K	Q	Z	317.	A*	L	T	U	Z
283.	A*	J	K	W	Z	318.	A*	M	N	S	U
284.	A*	J	L	M	N	319.	A*	M	O	V	Y
285.	A*	J	L	M	Y	320.	A*	M	P	S	U
286.	A*	J	L	N	P	321.	A*	M	P	V	Y
287.	A*	J	L	Q	X	322.	A*	M	Q	Y	Z
288.	A*	J	M	P	U	323.	A*	M	T	X	Z
289.	A*	J	M	W	Y	324.	A*	N	O	P	S
290.	A*	J	O	R	U	325.	A*	N	Q	U	V
291.	A*	J	O	R	Y	326.	A*	N	R	V	X
292.	A*	J	O	V	W	327.	A*	N	U	W	Y
293.	A*	J	O	X	Y	328.	A*	N	V	Y	Z
294.	A*	J	O	Y	Z	329.	A*	O	P	T	U
295.	A*	J	S	Y	Z	330.	A*	O	S	T	W
296.	A*	J	T	U	V	331.	A*	P	Q	R	W
297.	A*	K	L	M	W	332.	A*	P	Q	U	V
298.	A*	K	L	Q	R	333.	A*	P	S	T	V
299.	A*	K	M	O	W	334.	A*	Q	R	T	Z
300.	A*	K	M	Q	T	335.	A*	Q	S	X	Z
301.	A*	K	M	V	X	336.	A*	R	S	X	Y

    (Continued Next Page)

POWER NUMBER™ WHEEL 54126-1 (Continued from previous page)

337. | A* | S | U | V | W |

POWER NUMBER™WHEEL 53007-1
Wheeling 7 Numbers in 3 games for a 3 of 3 Win

NUMBERS CORRECT***	MAXIMUM WINS				MINIMUM WINS			
	5x	4x	3x	2x	5x	4x	3x	2x
5 (w/o Jackpot)	0	2	1	0				
5	1	0	2	0	0	2	1	0
4	-	1	1	1	-	0	3	0
3	-	-	2	0	-	-	1	2
2	-	-	-	2	-	-	-	2

*** POWER NUMBER POSITION A* MUST BE A WINNER.

Your 7 Numbers to Wheel

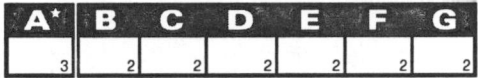

A*	B	C	D	E	F	G
3	2	2	2	2	2	2

The 3 Games to Play

1. | A* | B | C | F | G |

2. | A* | B | D | E | G |

3. | A* | C | D | E | F |

POWER NUMBER™WHEEL 53008-1
Wheeling 8 Numbers in 5 games for a 3 of 3 Win

NUMBERS CORRECT***	MAXIMUM WINS				MINIMUM WINS			
	5x	4x	3x	2x	5x	4x	3x	2x
5 (w/o Jackpot)	0	3	1	1				
5	1	1	2	1	0	1	4	0
4	-	2	1	1	-	0	0	2
3	-	-	3	0	-	-	1	0
2	-	-	-	3	-	-	-	2

*** POWER NUMBER POSITION A* MUST BE A WINNER.

Your 8 Numbers to Wheel

A*	B	C	D	E	F	G	H
5	3	3	3	2	3	3	3

The 5 Games to Play

1. | A* | B | C | F | H |

2. | A* | B | D | E | H |

3. | A* | B | D | G | H |

4. | A* | C | D | F | G |

5. | A* | C | E | F | G |

POWER NUMBER™WHEEL 53009-1
Wheeling 9 Numbers in 6 games for a 3 of 3 Win

NUMBERS CORRECT***	MAXIMUM WINS				MINIMUM WINS			
	5x	4x	3x	2x	5x	4x	3x	2x
5 (w/o Jackpot)	0	2	3	0				
5	1	0	3	2	0	0	6	0
4	–	1	2	2	–	0	3	3
3	–	–	3	0	–	–	1	4
2	–	–	–	3	–	–	–	3

*** POWER NUMBER POSITION A* MUST BE A WINNER.

Your 9 Numbers to Wheel

A*	B	C	D	E	F	G	H	I
6	3	3	3	3	3	3	3	3

The 6 Games to Play

1. | A* | B | C | G | I |

2. | A* | B | D | H | I |

3. | A* | B | E | F | I |

4. | A* | C | D | F | H |

5. | A* | C | E | G | H |

6. | A* | D | E | F | G |

Copyright © 1983-1998 Gail Howard

POWER NUMBER™WHEEL 53010-1
Wheeling 10 Numbers in 8 games for a 3 of 3 Win

NUMBERS CORRECT***	MAXIMUM WINS				MINIMUM WINS			
	5x	4x	3x	2x	5x	4x	3x	2x
5 (w/o Jackpot)	0	3	3	1				
5	1	1	3	2	0	0	6	1
4	–	2	2	2	–	0	3	3
3	–	–	4	0	–	–	1	4
2	–	–	–	4	–	–	–	3

*** POWER NUMBER POSITION A* MUST BE A WINNER.

Your 10 Numbers to Wheel

A*	B	C	D	E	F	G	H	I	J
8	4	4	3	3	3	3	4	4	4

The 8 Games to Play

1. | A* | B | C | I | J |

2. | A* | B | D | H | J |

3. | A* | B | E | H | J |

4. | A* | B | F | G | J |

5. | A* | C | D | G | H |

6. | A* | C | E | G | I |

7. | A* | C | F | H | I |

8. | A* | D | E | F | I |

Copyright © 1983-1998 Gail Howard

POWER NUMBER™WHEEL 53011-1
Wheeling 11 Numbers in 9 games for a 3 of 3 Win

NUMBERS CORRECT***	MAXIMUM WINS				MINIMUM WINS			
	5x	4x	3x	2x	5x	4x	3x	2x
5 (w/o Jackpot)	0	4	0	4				
5	1	0	3	5	0	0	6	2
4	–	1	3	3	–	0	3	4
3	–	–	4	0	–	–	1	4
2	–	–	–	4	–	–	–	3

*** POWER NUMBER POSITION A* MUST BE A WINNER.

Your 11 Numbers to Wheel

A*	B	C	D	E	F	G	H	I	J	K
9	4	4	4	3	3	3	3	4	4	4

The 9 Games to Play

1.	A*	B	C	H	K
2.	A*	B	D	G	K
3.	A*	B	E	J	K
4.	A*	B	F	I	K
5.	A*	C	D	E	I

6.	A*	C	D	F	J
7.	A*	C	G	I	J
8.	A*	D	H	I	J
9.	A*	E	F	G	H

Copyright © 1983-1998 Gail Howard

POWER NUMBER™WHEEL 53012-1
Wheeling 12 Numbers in 11 games for a 3 of 3 Win

NUMBERS CORRECT***	MAXIMUM WINS				MINIMUM WINS			
	5x	4x	3x	2x	5x	4x	3x	2x
5 (w/o Jackpot)	0	2	3	4				
5	1	1	0	9	0	0	6	4
4	–	2	0	6	–	0	3	6
3	–	–	3	2	–	–	1	6
2	–	–	–	4	–	–	–	4

*** POWER NUMBER POSITION A* MUST BE A WINNER.

Your 12 Numbers to Wheel

A*	B	C	D	E	F	G	H	I	J	K	L
11	4	4	4	4	4	4	4	4	4	4	4

The 11 Games to Play

1.	A*	B	C	G	L
2.	A*	B	D	I	J
3.	A*	B	E	J	K
4.	A*	B	F	H	J
5.	A*	C	D	F	K
6.	A*	C	E	H	I

7.	A*	C	G	J	L
8.	A*	D	E	G	H
9.	A*	D	H	K	L
10.	A*	E	F	I	L
11.	A*	F	G	I	K

Copyright © 1983-1998 Gail Howard

259

POWER NUMBER™ WHEEL 53013-1
Wheeling 13 Numbers in 12 games for a 3 of 3 Win

NUMBERS CORRECT***	MAXIMUM WINS				MINIMUM WINS			
	5x	4x	3x	2x	5x	4x	3x	2x
5 (w/o Jackpot)	0	2	2	6				
5	1	0	1	10	0	0	6	4
4	–	1	1	7	–	0	3	6
3	–	–	2	4	–	–	1	6
2	–	–	–	4	–	–	–	4

*** POWER NUMBER POSITION A* MUST BE A WINNER.

Your 13 Numbers to Wheel

A*	B	C	D	E	F	G
12	4	4	4	4	4	4

H	I	J	K	L	M
4	4	4	4	4	4

The 12 Games to Play

1.	A*	B	C	F	K
2.	A*	B	D	L	M
3.	A*	B	E	H	M
4.	A*	B	G	I	J
5.	A*	C	D	G	H
6.	A*	C	E	J	L

7.	A*	C	I	K	M
8.	A*	D	E	F	I
9.	A*	D	H	J	K
10.	A*	E	G	K	L
11.	A*	F	G	J	M
12.	A*	F	H	I	L

Copyright © 1983-1998 Gail Howard

POWER NUMBER™ WHEEL 53014-1
Wheeling 14 Numbers in 13 games for a 3 of 3 Win

NUMBERS CORRECT***	MAXIMUM WINS				MINIMUM WINS			
	5x	4x	3x	2x	5x	4x	3x	2x
5 (w/o Jackpot)	0	1	3	7				
5	1	0	0	12	0	0	6	4
4	–	1	0	9	–	0	3	6
3	–	–	1	6	–	–	1	6
2	–	–	–	4	–	–	–	4

*** POWER NUMBER POSITION A* MUST BE A WINNER.

Your 14 Numbers to Wheel

A*	B	C	D	E	F	G
13	4	4	4	4	4	4

H	I	J	K	L	M	N
4	4	4	4	4	4	4

The 13 Games to Play

1.	A*	B	C	F	K
2.	A*	B	D	G	I
3.	A*	B	E	L	M
4.	A*	B	H	J	N

5.	A*	C	D	L	N
6.	A*	C	E	G	H
7.	A*	C	I	J	M
8.	A*	D	E	F	J

Copyright © 1983-1998 Gail Howard   (Continued Next Page)

POWER NUMBER™ WHEEL 53014-1 (Continued from previous page)

9.	A*	D	H	K	M
10.	A*	E	I	K	N
11.	A*	F	G	M	N

12.	A*	F	H	I	L
13.	A*	G	J	K	L

Copyright © 1983-1998 Gail Howard

POWER NUMBER™ WHEEL 53015-1
Wheeling 15 Numbers in 18 games for a 3 of 3 Win

NUMBERS CORRECT***	MAXIMUM WINS				MINIMUM WINS			
	5x	4x	3x	2x	5x	4x	3x	2x
5 (w/o Jackpot)	0	3	0	12				
5	1	0	4	9	0	0	6	8
4	–	1	3	7	–	0	3	9
3	–	–	3	5	–	–	1	8
2	–	–	–	6	–	–	–	5

*** POWER NUMBER POSITION A* MUST BE A WINNER.

Your 15 Numbers to Wheel

A*	B	C	D	E	F	G	H
18	5	5	6	5	5	5	5

I	J	K	L	M	N	O
5	5	6	5	5	5	5

The 18 Games to Play

1.	A*	B	C	H	K
2.	A*	B	D	G	M
3.	A*	B	E	L	M
4.	A*	B	F	I	N
5.	A*	B	J	L	O
6.	A*	C	D	G	I
7.	A*	C	E	F	O
8.	A*	C	I	K	L
9.	A*	C	J	M	N

10.	A*	D	E	N	O
11.	A*	D	F	J	K
12.	A*	D	H	L	N
13.	A*	D	I	M	O
14.	A*	F	G	K	N
15.	A*	E	H	I	J
16.	A*	F	G	J	L
17.	A*	F	H	K	M
18.	A*	G	H	K	O

Copyright © 1983-1998 Gail Howard

POWER NUMBER™ WHEEL 53016-1
Wheeling 16 Numbers in 20 games for a 3 of 3 Win

NUMBERS CORRECT***	MAXIMUM WINS				MINIMUM WINS			
	5x	4x	3x	2x	5x	4x	3x	2x
5 (w/o Jackpot)	0	2	4	11				
5	1	0	4	13	0	0	6	8
4	–	1	3	11	–	0	3	9
3	–	–	3	9	–	–	1	8
2	–	–	–	9	–	–	–	5

*** POWER NUMBER POSITION A* MUST BE A WINNER.

(Continued Next Page)

POWER NUMBER™ WHEEL 53016-1 (Continued from previous page)

Your 16 Numbers to Wheel

A*	B	C	D	E	F	G	H
20	5	5	5	5	5	5	5

I	J	K	L	M	N	O	P
5	9	5	5	5	5	6	5

The 20 Games to Play

1.	A*	B	C	H	O	11.	A*	D	G	H	M
2.	A*	B	D	E	P	12.	A*	D	K	N	O
3.	A*	B	F	G	K	13.	A*	E	F	H	I
4.	A*	B	I	L	N	14.	A*	E	G	J	N
5.	A*	B	J	M	O	15.	A*	E	L	M	O
6.	A*	C	D	I	J	16.	A*	F	J	O	P
7.	A*	C	E	J	K	17.	A*	G	I	J	O
8.	A*	C	F	M	N	18.	A*	H	J	K	L
9.	A*	C	G	L	P	19.	A*	H	J	N	P
10.	A*	D	F	J	L	20.	A*	I	K	M	P

Copyright © 1983-1998 Gail Howard

POWER NUMBER™ WHEEL 53017-1
Wheeling 17 Numbers in 20 games for a 3 of 3 Win

NUMBERS CORRECT***	MAXIMUM WINS				MINIMUM WINS			
	5x	4x	3x	2x	5x	4x	3x	2x
5 (w/o Jackpot)	0	1	3	11				
5	1	0	0	16	0	0	6	8
4	–	1	0	12	–	0	3	9
3	–	–	1	8	–	–	1	8
2	–	–	–	5	–	–	–	5

*** POWER NUMBER POSITION A* MUST BE A WINNER.

Your 17 Numbers to Wheel

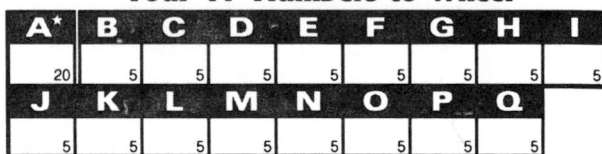

A*	B	C	D	E	F	G	H	I
20	5	5	5	5	5	5	5	5

J	K	L	M	N	O	P	Q
5	5	5	5	5	5	5	5

The 20 Games to Play

1.	A*	B	C	H	O	7.	A*	C	E	F	N
2.	A*	B	D	G	P	8.	A*	C	G	I	J
3.	A*	B	E	J	M	9.	A*	C	M	P	Q
4.	A*	B	F	I	K	10.	A*	D	E	I	Q
5.	A*	B	L	N	Q	11.	A*	D	F	H	M
6.	A*	C	D	K	L	12.	A*	D	J	N	O

Copyright © 1983-1998 Gail Howard (Continued Next Page)

POWER NUMBER™ WHEEL 53017-1 (Continued from previous page)

	A*	E	G	H	L
13.					

	A*	E	K	O	P
14.					

	A*	F	G	O	Q
15.					

	A*	F	J	L	P
16.					

	A*	G	K	M	N
17.					

	A*	H	I	N	P
18.					

	A*	H	J	K	Q
19.					

	A*	I	L	M	O
20.					

POWER NUMBER™WHEEL 53018-1
Wheeling 18 Numbers in 26 games for a 3 of 3 Win

NUMBERS CORRECT***	MAXIMUM WINS				MINIMUM WINS			
	5x	4x	3x	2x	5x	4x	3x	2x
5 (w/o Jackpot)	0	3	2	12				
5	1	0	3	16	0	0	6	12
4	–	1	3	10	–	0	3	12
3	–	–	3	7	–	–	1	10
2	–	–	–	7	–	–	–	6

*** POWER NUMBER POSITION A* MUST BE A WINNER.

Your 18 Numbers to Wheel

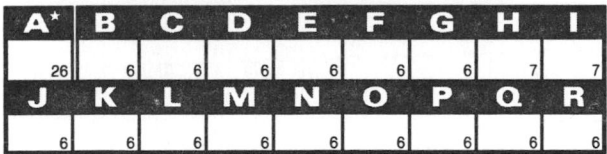

A*	B	C	D	E	F	G	H	I
26	6	6	6	6	6	6	7	7

J	K	L	M	N	O	P	Q	R
6	6	6	6	6	6	6	6	6

The 26 Games to Play

	A*	B	C	H	O
1.					

	A*	B	D	G	L
2.					

	A*	B	E	M	P
3.					

	A*	B	F	N	O
4.					

	A*	B	I	K	Q
5.					

	A*	B	J	Q	R
6.					

	A*	C	D	P	Q
7.					

	A*	C	E	G	J
8.					

	A*	C	F	K	L
9.					

	A*	C	I	P	R
10.					

	A*	C	M	N	Q
11.					

	A*	D	E	F	N
12.					

	A*	D	E	H	I
13.					

	A*	D	H	K	M
14.					

	A*	D	J	O	R
15.					

	A*	E	H	K	R
16.					

	A*	E	L	O	Q
17.					

	A*	F	G	H	Q
18.					

	A*	F	I	J	P
19.					

	A*	F	L	M	R
20.					

	A*	G	I	M	O
21.					

	A*	G	I	N	R
22.					

	A*	G	K	O	P
23.					

	A*	H	J	K	N
24.					

	A*	H	L	N	P
25.					

	A*	I	J	L	M
26.					

POWER NUMBER™WHEEL 53019-1
Wheeling 19 Numbers in 28 games for a 3 of 3 Win

NUMBERS CORRECT***	MAXIMUM WINS				MINIMUM WINS			
	5x	4x	3x	2x	5x	4x	3x	2x
5 (w/o Jackpot)	0	2	5	10				
5	1	0	4	15	0	0	6	12
4	–	1	4	9	–	0	3	12
3	–	–	4	6	–	–	1	10
2	–	–	–	7	–	–	–	6

*** POWER NUMBER POSITION A* MUST BE A WINNER.

Your 19 Numbers to Wheel

A*	B	C	D	E	F	G	H	I	J
28	7	7	7	6	6	6	6	6	6

K	L	M	N	O	P	Q	R	S
6	6	6	6	6	6	6	7	6

The 28 Games to Play

1.	A*	B	C	K	L	15.	A*	D	F	G	N
2.	A*	B	D	F	O	16.	A*	D	H	J	Q
3.	A*	B	D	I	M	17.	A*	D	L	P	S
4.	A*	B	E	R	S	18.	A*	E	H	I	L
5.	A*	B	G	J	P	19.	A*	E	J	K	O
6.	A*	B	H	N	S	20.	A*	E	N	O	P
7.	A*	B	M	P	Q	21.	A*	F	H	K	P
8.	A*	C	D	K	R	22.	A*	F	I	J	S
9.	A*	C	E	F	M	23.	A*	F	L	Q	R
10.	A*	C	G	H	R	24.	A*	G	I	L	O
11.	A*	C	I	P	R	25.	A*	G	K	M	S
12.	A*	C	J	N	R	26.	A*	H	M	O	R
13.	A*	C	O	Q	S	27.	A*	I	K	N	Q
14.	A*	D	E	G	Q	28.	A*	J	L	M	N

Copyright © 1983-1998 Gail Howard

POWER NUMBER™WHEEL 53020-1
Wheeling 20 Numbers in 32 games for a 3 of 3 Win

NUMBERS CORRECT***	MAXIMUM WINS				MINIMUM WINS			
	5x	4x	3x	2x	5x	4x	3x	2x
5 (w/o Jackpot)	0	3	9	8				
5	1	0	7	15	0	0	6	12
4	–	1	7	10	–	0	3	12
3	–	–	5	8	–	–	1	10
2	–	–	–	9	–	–	–	6

*** POWER NUMBER POSITION A* MUST BE A WINNER.

(Continued Next Page)

POWER NUMBER™ WHEEL 53020-1 (Continued from previous page)
Your 20 Numbers to Wheel

A*	B	C	D	E	F	G	H	I	J
32	6	6	6	7	7	6	9	6	6

K	L	M	N	O	P	Q	R	S	T
6	9	6	9	8	6	7	6	6	6

The 32 Games to Play

#						#					
1.	A*	B	C	G	S	17.	A*	E	G	P	T
2.	A*	B	D	R	T	18.	A*	E	I	R	S
3.	A*	B	E	H	N	19.	A*	E	K	L	N
4.	A*	B	F	K	M	20.	A*	E	M	N	O
5.	A*	B	I	J	P	21.	A*	F	G	N	R
6.	A*	D	L	O	Q	22.	A*	F	L	P	Q
7.	A*	C	D	E	Q	23.	A*	F	O	S	T
8.	A*	C	F	I	N	24.	A*	G	H	L	Q
9.	A*	C	H	L	O	25.	A*	G	I	K	O
10.	A*	C	J	K	T	26.	A*	H	K	Q	R
11.	A*	C	M	P	R	27.	A*	H	L	M	S
12.	A*	D	F	N	O	28.	A*	H	L	N	T
13.	A*	D	G	J	M	29.	A*	H	N	O	P
14.	A*	D	H	I	L	30.	A*	I	M	Q	T
15.	A*	D	K	P	S	31.	A*	J	L	O	R
16.	A*	E	F	H	J	32.	A*	J	N	Q	S

POWER NUMBER™WHEEL 53021-1
Wheeling 21 Numbers in 36 games for a 3 of 3 Win

NUMBERS CORRECT***	MAXIMUM WINS				MINIMUM WINS			
	5x	4x	3x	2x	5x	4x	3x	2x
5 (w/o Jackpot)	0	2	5	15				
5	1	0	4	18	0	0	6	16
4	–	1	4	12	–	0	3	15
3	–	–	3	10	–	–	1	12
2	–	–	–	8	–	–	–	7

*** POWER NUMBER POSITION A* MUST BE A WINNER.

Your 21 Numbers to Wheel

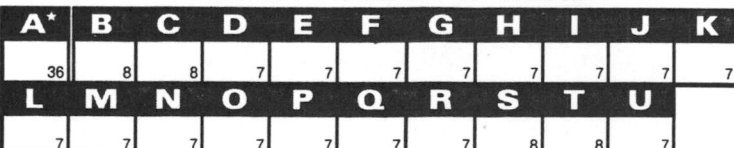

A*	B	C	D	E	F	G	H	I	J	K
36	8	8	7	7	7	7	7	7	7	7

L	M	N	O	P	Q	R	S	T	U
7	7	7	7	7	7	7	8	8	7

(Continued Next Page)

POWER NUMBER™ WHEEL 53021-1 (Continued from previous page)
The 36 Games to Play

1.	A*	B	C	J	Q	19.	A*	D	J	M	U
2.	A*	B	D	I	T	20.	A*	D	L	O	Q
3.	A*	B	E	F	R	21.	A*	E	H	Q	U
4.	A*	B	E	L	T	22.	A*	E	I	J	K
5.	A*	B	G	H	M	23.	A*	E	M	O	S
6.	A*	B	G	S	U	24.	A*	F	G	I	Q
7.	A*	B	K	P	U	25.	A*	F	J	S	T
8.	A*	B	N	O	T	26.	A*	F	L	M	U
9.	A*	C	D	H	N	27.	A*	F	N	P	S
10.	A*	C	E	G	T	28.	A*	G	J	L	N
11.	A*	C	F	I	O	29.	A*	G	K	O	P
12.	A*	C	I	M	P	30.	A*	H	I	L	S
13.	A*	C	K	L	S	31.	A*	H	J	O	R
14.	A*	C	O	T	U	32.	A*	H	P	Q	T
15.	A*	C	Q	R	S	33.	A*	I	N	R	U
16.	A*	D	E	N	P	34.	A*	J	L	P	R
17.	A*	D	F	H	K	35.	A*	K	M	N	Q
18.	A*	D	G	R	S	36.	A*	K	M	R	T

POWER NUMBER™WHEEL 53022-1
Wheeling 22 Numbers in 39 games for a 3 of 3 Win

NUMBERS CORRECT***	MAXIMUM WINS				MINIMUM WINS			
	5x	4x	3x	2x	5x	4x	3x	2x
5 (w/o Jackpot)	0	2	7	13				
5	1	0	4	21	0	0	6	16
4	–	1	4	14	–	0	3	15
3	–	–	3	11	–	–	1	12
2	–	–	–	9	–	–	–	7

*** POWER NUMBER POSITION A* MUST BE A WINNER.

Your 22 Numbers to Wheel

A*	B	C	D	E	F	G	H	I	J	K
39	7	8	8	7	7	9	7	7	7	8

L	M	N	O	P	Q	R	S	T	U	V
7	7	8	8	7	7	8	7	7	8	7

The 39 Games to Play

1.	A*	B	C	Q	S	4.	A*	B	G	I	N
2.	A*	B	D	R	U	5.	A*	B	H	K	M
3.	A*	B	E	F	T	6.	A*	B	J	L	V

(Continued Next Page)

POWER NUMBER™ WHEEL 53022-1 (Continued from previous page)

	A*	B	O	P	U			A*	E	R	S	V
7.	A*	B	O	P	U	24.	A*	E	R	S	V
8.	A*	C	D	I	T	25.	A*	F	G	J	Q
9.	A*	C	E	L	M	26.	A*	F	H	I	V
10.	A*	C	F	O	R	27.	A*	F	M	S	U
11.	A*	C	G	U	V	28.	A*	G	H	L	N
12.	A*	C	H	J	R	29.	A*	G	H	O	T
13.	A*	C	K	N	U	30.	A*	G	I	M	P
14.	A*	C	L	P	R	31.	A*	G	K	N	S
15.	A*	D	E	J	N	32.	A*	I	K	Q	R
16.	A*	D	F	K	L	33.	A*	I	L	O	S
17.	A*	D	F	N	P	34.	A*	J	K	M	O
18.	A*	D	G	O	R	35.	A*	J	P	S	T
19.	A*	D	H	S	U	36.	A*	K	P	T	V
20.	A*	D	M	Q	V	37.	A*	L	Q	T	U
21.	A*	E	G	K	O	38.	A*	M	N	R	T
22.	A*	E	H	P	Q	39.	A*	N	O	Q	V
23.	A*	E	I	J	U						

POWER NUMBER™WHEEL 53023-1
Wheeling 23 Numbers in 44 games for a 3 of 3 Win

NUMBERS CORRECT***	MAXIMUM WINS				MINIMUM WINS			
	5x	4x	3x	2x	5x	4x	3x	2x
5 (w/o Jackpot)	0	3	0	24				
5	1	0	5	20	0	0	6	17
4	–	1	3	17	–	0	3	15
3	–	–	3	11	–	–	1	12
2	–	–	–	9	–	–	–	7

*** POWER NUMBER POSITION A* MUST BE A WINNER.

Your 23 Numbers to Wheel

A*	B	C	D	E	F	G	H	I	J	K	L
44	8	8	7	8	8	8	9	8	8	7	8

M	N	O	P	Q	R	S	T	U	V	W	
8	8	7	8	8	9	9	8	8	8	8	

The 44 Games to Play

	A*	B	C	R	V			A*	B	H	I	S
1.	A*	B	C	R	V	6.	A*	B	H	I	S
2.	A*	B	D	L	U	7.	A*	B	N	O	T
3.	A*	B	E	K	M	8.	A*	B	N	R	W
4.	A*	B	F	J	S	9.	A*	C	D	J	Q
5.	A*	B	G	P	Q	10.	A*	C	E	P	T

          (Continued Next Page)

POWER NUMBER™ WHEEL 53023-1 (Continued from previous page)

11.	A*	C	F	M	O
12.	A*	C	G	K	N
13.	A*	C	H	M	W
14.	A*	C	I	V	W
15.	A*	C	L	S	U
16.	A*	D	E	O	R
17.	A*	D	F	I	N
18.	A*	D	G	M	T
19.	A*	D	H	P	W
20.	A*	D	K	S	V
21.	A*	E	F	H	R
22.	A*	E	G	I	R
23.	A*	E	G	J	V
24.	A*	E	L	N	S
25.	A*	E	Q	U	W
26.	A*	F	G	S	W
27.	A*	F	H	K	U

28.	A*	F	H	L	Q
29.	A*	F	P	T	V
30.	A*	G	H	O	U
31.	A*	G	L	T	W
32.	A*	H	J	R	T
33.	A*	H	N	Q	V
34.	A*	I	J	L	M
35.	A*	I	K	Q	T
36.	A*	I	O	P	S
37.	A*	I	S	T	U
38.	A*	J	K	O	W
39.	A*	J	M	N	P
40.	A*	J	M	U	V
41.	A*	K	L	P	R
42.	A*	L	O	Q	V
43.	A*	M	Q	R	S
44.	A*	N	P	R	U

POWER NUMBER™ WHEEL 53024-1
Wheeling 24 Numbers in 47 games for a 3 of 3 Win

NUMBERS CORRECT***	MAXIMUM WINS				MINIMUM WINS			
	5x	4x	3x	2x	5x	4x	3x	2x
5 (w/o Jackpot)	0	3	1	24				
5	1	0	4	23	0	0	6	20
4	–	1	3	18	–	0	3	18
3	–	–	3	12	–	–	1	14
2	–	–	–	9	–	–	–	8

*** POWER NUMBER POSITION A* MUST BE A WINNER.

Your 24 Numbers to Wheel

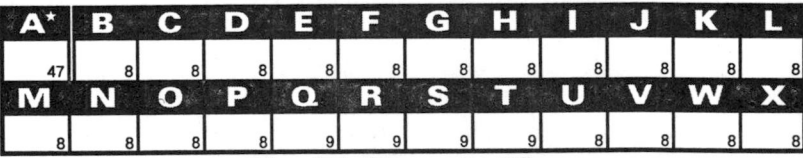

A*	B	C	D	E	F	G	H	I	J	K	L
47	8	8	8	8	8	8	8	8	8	8	8

M	N	O	P	Q	R	S	T	U	V	W	X
8	8	8	8	9	9	9	9	8	8	8	8

The 47 Games to Play

1.	A*	B	C	G	V
2.	A*	B	D	K	T
3.	A*	B	E	N	U
4.	A*	B	F	P	Q
5.	A*	B	H	M	Q

6.	A*	B	I	T	W
7.	A*	B	J	L	O
8.	A*	B	R	S	X
9.	A*	C	D	E	S
10.	A*	C	D	M	X

 (Continued Next Page)

POWER NUMBER™ WHEEL 53024-1 (Continued from previous page)

	A*	C	F	L	R
11.					

	A*	C	H	K	O
12.					

	A*	C	I	J	Q
13.					

	A*	C	N	P	T
14.					

	A*	C	Q	U	W
15.					

	A*	D	F	J	U
16.					

	A*	D	G	N	Q
17.					

	A*	D	H	P	W
18.					

	A*	D	I	L	P
19.					

	A*	D	O	R	V
20.					

	A*	E	F	I	X
21.					

	A*	E	G	H	J
22.					

	A*	E	G	M	W
23.					

	A*	E	K	L	R
24.					

	A*	E	O	P	T
25.					

	A*	E	Q	T	V
26.					

	A*	F	G	K	W
27.					

	A*	F	H	S	T
28.					

	A*	F	M	N	O
29.					

	A*	F	N	V	X
30.					

	A*	G	I	O	U
31.					

	A*	G	L	T	X
32.					

	A*	G	P	R	S
33.					

	A*	H	I	N	R
34.					

	A*	H	L	U	V
35.					

	A*	H	O	W	X
36.					

	A*	I	K	S	V
37.					

	A*	I	M	S	U
38.					

	A*	J	K	N	T
39.					

	A*	J	M	P	V
40.					

	A*	J	Q	S	X
41.					

	A*	J	R	V	W
42.					

	A*	K	L	M	Q
43.					

	A*	K	P	U	X
44.					

	A*	L	N	S	W
45.					

	A*	M	R	T	U
46.					

	A*	O	Q	R	S
47.					

Copyright © 1983 1000 Gail Howard

POWER NUMBER™ WHEEL 53025-1
Wheeling 25 Numbers in 51 games for a 3 of 3 Win

NUMBERS CORRECT***	MAXIMUM WINS				MINIMUM WINS			
	5x	4x	3x	2x	5x	4x	3x	2x
5 (w/o Jackpot)	0	2	6	19				
5	1	0	4	24	0	0	6	20
4	–	1	4	17	–	0	3	18
3	–	–	3	13	–	–	1	14
2	–	–	–	10	–	–	–	8

*** POWER NUMBER POSITION A* MUST BE A WINNER.

Your 25 Numbers to Wheel

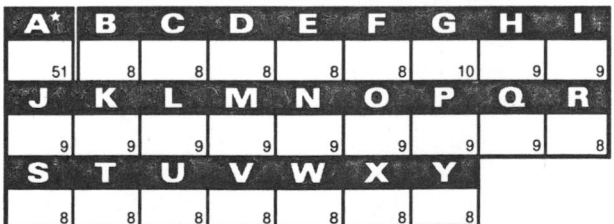

A*	B	C	D	E	F	G	H	I
51	8	8	8	8	8	10	9	9

J	K	L	M	N	O	P	Q	R
9	9	9	9	9	9	9	9	8

S	T	U	V	W	X	Y
8	8	8	8	8	8	8

The 51 Games to Play

	A*	B	C	G	T
1.					

	A*	B	D	E	X
2.					

Copyright © 1983-1998 Gail Howard   (Continued Next Page)

POWER NUMBER™ WHEEL 53025-1 (Continued from previous page)

3.	A*	B	D	I	U		28.	A*	F	K	L	U
4.	A*	B	F	N	Q		29.	A*	F	Q	S	V
5.	A*	B	H	K	R		30.	A*	F	T	W	X
6.	A*	B	J	W	Y		31.	A*	G	H	N	O
7.	A*	B	L	P	S		32.	A*	G	I	J	V
8.	A*	B	M	O	V		33.	A*	G	I	M	W
9.	A*	C	D	O	S		34.	A*	G	J	S	X
10.	A*	C	E	I	N		35.	A*	G	K	Q	Y
11.	A*	C	F	J	R		36.	A*	G	O	R	U
12.	A*	C	H	K	P		37.	A*	H	I	S	X
13.	A*	C	L	V	W		38.	A*	H	J	T	U
14.	A*	C	M	Q	U		39.	A*	H	L	P	Y
15.	A*	C	U	X	Y		40.	A*	H	M	Q	W
16.	A*	D	F	H	M		41.	A*	I	L	R	T
17.	A*	D	G	L	Q		42.	A*	I	N	O	Y
18.	A*	D	J	K	P		43.	A*	J	L	M	N
19.	A*	D	N	R	W		44.	A*	J	O	Q	T
20.	A*	D	T	V	Y		45.	A*	K	M	V	X
21.	A*	E	F	O	Y		46.	A*	K	N	S	T
22.	A*	E	G	J	L		47.	A*	K	O	P	W
23.	A*	E	H	R	V		48.	A*	L	N	O	X
24.	A*	E	I	K	Q		49.	A*	M	R	S	Y
25.	A*	E	M	P	T		50.	A*	N	P	U	V
26.	A*	E	S	U	W		51.	A*	P	Q	R	X
27.	A*	F	G	I	P							

POWER NUMBER™ WHEEL 53026-1
Wheeling 26 Numbers in 56 games for a 3 of 3 Win

NUMBERS CORRECT***	MAXIMUM WINS				MINIMUM WINS			
	5x	4x	3x	2x	5x	4x	3x	2x
5 (w/o Jackpot)	0	2	5	22				
5	1	0	3	28	0	0	6	21
4	–	1	3	20	–	0	3	18
3	–	–	3	13	–	–	1	14
2	–	–	–	10	–	–	–	8

*** POWER NUMBER POSITION A* MUST BE A WINNER.
(Continued Next Page)

270

POWER NUMBER™ WHEEL 53026-1 (Continued from previous page)
Your 26 Numbers to Wheel

A*	B	C	D	E	F	G	H	I
56	8	8	10	10	8	9	9	9

J	K	L	M	N	O	P	Q	R
9	9	9	9	9	9	9	9	9

S	T	U	V	W	X	Y	Z
9	9	9	9	9	9	9	9

The 56 Games to Play

#						#				
1.	A*	B	C	Q	T	29.	A*	E	Q	S	Y
2.	A*	B	D	M	U	30.	A*	F	I	T	X
3.	A*	B	E	S	X	31.	A*	F	M	W	Y
4.	A*	B	F	L	O	32.	A*	F	P	S	U
5.	A*	B	G	K	Z	33.	A*	F	R	V	Z
6.	A*	B	H	N	Y	34.	A*	G	H	P	X
7.	A*	B	I	P	R	35.	A*	G	J	L	U
8.	A*	B	J	V	W	36.	A*	G	M	R	S
9.	A*	C	D	J	P	37.	A*	G	O	R	T
10.	A*	C	E	I	M	38.	A*	H	I	L	V
11.	A*	C	F	G	N	39.	A*	H	J	M	N
12.	A*	C	H	U	V	40.	A*	H	K	M	Z
13.	A*	C	K	R	Y	41.	A*	H	O	R	W
14.	A*	C	L	O	S	42.	A*	I	J	S	Z
15.	A*	C	W	X	Z	43.	A*	I	K	N	O
16.	A*	D	E	G	W	44.	A*	I	P	W	Y
17.	A*	D	E	O	U	45.	A*	I	T	U	Y
18.	A*	D	F	J	K	46.	A*	J	O	X	Y
19.	A*	D	G	I	Q	47.	A*	J	Q	R	U
20.	A*	D	G	V	Y	48.	A*	K	P	Q	V
21.	A*	D	H	S	T	49.	A*	K	S	T	V
22.	A*	D	L	Y	Z	50.	A*	K	U	W	X
23.	A*	D	N	R	X	51.	A*	L	M	P	T
24.	A*	E	F	H	Q	52.	A*	L	M	Q	X
25.	A*	E	J	T	Z	53.	A*	L	N	Q	W
26.	A*	E	K	L	R	54.	A*	M	O	V	X
27.	A*	E	N	P	V	55.	A*	N	S	T	W
28.	A*	E	N	U	Z	56.	A*	O	P	Q	Z

POWER NUMBER™WHEEL 53030-1
Wheeling 30 Numbers in 76 games for a 3 of 3 Win

NUMBERS CORRECT***	MAXIMUM WINS				MINIMUM WINS			
	5x	4x	3x	2x	5x	4x	3x	2x
5 (w/o Jackpot)	0	3	2	32				
5	1	1	2	35	0	0	6	28
4	–	2	1	27	–	0	3	24
3	–	–	3	18	–	–	1	18
2	–	–	–	12	–	–	–	10

*** POWER NUMBER POSITION A* MUST BE A WINNER.

Your 30 Numbers to Wheel

A*	B	C	D	E	F	G	H	I	J
76	12	11	11	11	11	11	11	11	11

K	L	M	N	O	P	Q	R	S	T
10	11	10	10	10	10	10	10	11	10

U	V	W	X	Y	Z	AA	BB	CC	DD
10	10	10	10	10	10	10	10	10	12

The 76 Games to Play

#						#					
1.	A*	B	C	F	dd	23.	A*	D	E	N	Y
2.	A*	B	D	K	dd	24.	A*	D	F	W	aa
3.	A*	B	E	T	U	25.	A*	D	G	S	X
4.	A*	B	F	O	dd	26.	A*	D	H	J	L
5.	A*	B	G	L	M	27.	A*	D	J	L	R
6.	A*	B	H	I	S	28.	A*	D	J	Q	U
7.	A*	B	H	I	W	29.	A*	D	M	P	S
8.	A*	B	H	Q	V	30.	A*	D	O	V	Y
9.	A*	B	J	N	bb	31.	A*	D	T	Z	bb
10.	A*	B	N	P	V	32.	A*	E	F	I	V
11.	A*	B	R	Y	cc	33.	A*	E	G	P	R
12.	A*	B	X	Z	aa	34.	A*	E	H	Z	dd
13.	A*	C	D	I	cc	35.	A*	E	K	O	Z
14.	A*	C	E	J	X	36.	A*	E	K	S	cc
15.	A*	C	E	L	bb	37.	A*	E	M	aa	bb
16.	A*	C	F	K	Y	38.	A*	E	Q	S	W
17.	A*	C	G	W	Y	39.	A*	F	G	L	Q
18.	A*	C	H	N	O	40.	A*	F	G	M	U
19.	A*	C	H	P	U	41.	A*	F	H	T	cc
20.	A*	C	M	V	Z	42.	A*	F	J	S	Z
21.	A*	C	Q	R	T	43.	A*	F	N	R	S
22.	A*	C	S	V	aa	44.	A*	F	P	X	bb

(Continued Next Page)

272

POWER NUMBER™ WHEEL 53030-1 (Continued from previous page)

45.	A*	G	H	K	bb
46.	A*	G	I	bb	dd
47.	A*	G	J	V	cc
48.	A*	G	N	T	aa
49.	A*	G	O	W	Z
50.	A*	H	M	X	Y
51.	A*	H	R	aa	dd
52.	A*	I	J	O	P
53.	A*	I	K	Q	aa
54.	A*	I	L	T	Y
55.	A*	I	M	N	X
56.	A*	I	R	U	Z
57.	A*	I	S	T	dd
58.	A*	J	K	M	R
59.	A*	J	P	T	W
60.	A*	J	Y	aa	dd

61.	A*	K	L	P	dd
62.	A*	K	N	U	W
63.	A*	K	T	V	X
64.	A*	L	N	Z	cc
65.	A*	L	O	S	aa
66.	A*	L	U	V	dd
67.	A*	L	W	X	cc
68.	A*	M	O	Q	T
69.	A*	M	W	cc	dd
70.	A*	N	Q	X	dd
71.	A*	O	Q	bb	cc
72.	A*	O	R	U	X
73.	A*	P	Q	Y	Z
74.	A*	P	U	aa	cc
75.	A*	R	V	W	bb
76.	A*	S	U	Y	bb

Copyright © 1983-1998 Gail Howard

POWER NUMBER™ WHEEL 53035-1
Wheeling 35 Numbers in 106 games for a 3 of 3 Win

NUMBERS CORRECT***	MAXIMUM WINS				MINIMUM WINS			
	5x	4x	3x	2x	5x	4x	3x	2x
5 (w/o Jackpot)	0	3	1	41				
5	1	0	6	37	0	0	6	36
4	–	1	5	28	–	0	3	30
3	–	–	5	16	–	–	1	22
2	–	–	–	15	–	–	–	12

*** POWER NUMBER POSITION A* MUST BE A WINNER.

Your 35 Numbers to Wheel

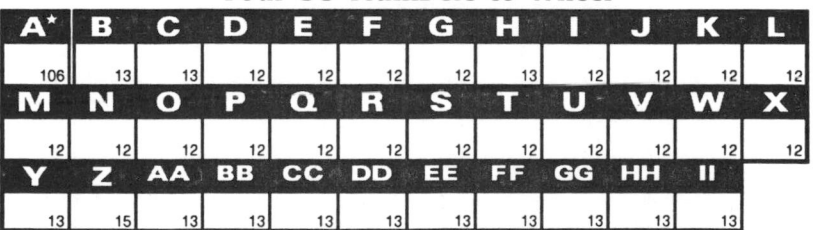

A*	B	C	D	E	F	G	H	I	J	K	L
106	13	13	12	12	12	12	13	12	12	12	12

M	N	O	P	Q	R	S	T	U	V	W	X
12	12	12	12	12	12	12	12	12	12	12	12

Y	Z	AA	BB	CC	DD	EE	FF	GG	HH	II
13	15	13	13	13	13	13	13	13	13	13

The 106 Games to Play

1.	A*	B	C	P	Q
2.	A*	B	D	K	W
3.	A*	B	E	I	ff
4.	A*	B	F	G	Y

5.	A*	B	H	X	Z
6.	A*	B	H	aa	ee
7.	A*	B	J	L	U
8.	A*	B	M	Z	cc

Copyright © 1983-1998 Gail Howard   (Continued Next Page)

POWER NUMBER™ WHEEL 53035-1 (Continued from previous page)

#						#				
9.	A*	B	N	V	cc	44.	A*	E	V	bb	ii
10.	A*	B	O	gg	ii	45.	A*	F	H	J	ii
11.	A*	B	R	cc	ii	46.	A*	F	I	Q	aa
12.	A*	B	S	aa	hh	47.	A*	F	K	X	ff
13.	A*	B	T	bb	dd	48.	A*	F	M	R	dd
14.	A*	C	D	ff	ii	49.	A*	F	O	P	S
15.	A*	C	E	O	ee	50.	A*	F	V	W	ee
16.	A*	C	F	N	X	51.	A*	F	Z	bb	hh
17.	A*	C	G	K	cc	52.	A*	G	I	V	Z
18.	A*	C	H	I	Y	53.	A*	G	J	P	T
19.	A*	C	J	S	W	54.	A*	G	K	R	aa
20.	A*	C	J	V	Z	55.	A*	G	L	gg	ii
21.	A*	C	L	S	ee	56.	A*	G	M	N	ee
22.	A*	C	M	U	ii	57.	A*	G	N	bb	dd
23.	A*	C	R	Y	hh	58.	A*	G	O	U	X
24.	A*	C	T	Y	gg	59.	A*	G	W	ff	hh
25.	A*	C	aa	bb	dd	60.	A*	H	I	L	P
26.	A*	D	E	cc	hh	61.	A*	H	K	S	bb
27.	A*	D	F	L	T	62.	A*	H	M	T	hh
28.	A*	D	G	H	S	63.	A*	H	N	O	ff
29.	A*	D	I	J	O	64.	A*	H	Q	U	ee
30.	A*	D	M	X	Y	65.	A*	H	V	gg	hh
31.	A*	D	N	R	gg	66.	A*	H	W	cc	dd
32.	A*	D	P	Z	aa	67.	A*	I	K	T	U
33.	A*	D	Q	ff	gg	68.	A*	I	M	bb	gg
34.	A*	D	U	V	dd	69.	A*	I	N	W	Z
35.	A*	D	Y	bb	ee	70.	A*	I	Q	R	hh
36.	A*	E	F	T	cc	71.	A*	I	S	dd	ii
37.	A*	E	F	U	gg	72.	A*	I	X	cc	ee
38.	A*	E	G	K	Q	73.	A*	J	K	M	ff
39.	A*	E	H	R	Z	74.	A*	J	P	hh	ii
40.	A*	E	J	N	aa	75.	A*	J	Q	Y	cc
41.	A*	E	L	W	bb	76.	A*	J	R	X	bb
42.	A*	E	M	S	X	77.	A*	J	dd	ee	gg
43.	A*	E	P	Y	dd	78.	A*	K	L	dd	gg

(Continued Next Page)

274

POWER NUMBER™ WHEEL 53035-1 (Continued from previous page)

79.	A*	K	N	P	hh
80.	A*	K	O	V	Y
81.	A*	K	Z	ee	ii
82.	A*	L	M	O	R
83.	A*	L	N	Y	Z
84.	A*	L	Q	V	Z
85.	A*	L	X	dd	hh
86.	A*	L	aa	cc	ff
87.	A*	M	O	Q	W
88.	A*	M	P	V	aa
89.	A*	N	Q	S	T
90.	A*	N	U	Y	ii
91.	A*	O	T	Z	cc
92.	A*	O	Z	bb	dd

93.	A*	O	aa	ee	hh
94.	A*	P	R	ee	ff
95.	A*	P	U	bb	cc
96.	A*	P	W	X	gg
97.	A*	Q	X	aa	ii
98.	A*	Q	bb	dd	ff
99.	A*	R	S	U	W
100.	A*	R	T	V	X
101.	A*	S	V	Y	ff
102.	A*	S	Z	cc	gg
103.	A*	T	W	ff	ii
104.	A*	T	aa	ee	gg
105.	A*	U	W	Y	aa
106.	A*	U	Z	ff	hh

POWER NUMBER™WHEEL 53039-1
Wheeling 39 Numbers in 130 games for a 3 of 3 Win

NUMBERS CORRECT***	MAXIMUM WINS				MINIMUM WINS			
	5x	4x	3x	2x	5x	4x	3x	2x
5 (w/o Jackpot)	0	2	6	40				
5	1	0	5	42	0	0	6	40
4	–	1	4	33	–	0	3	33
3	–	–	4	21	–	–	1	24
2	–	–	–	16	–			10

*** POWER NUMBER POSITION A MUST BE A WINNER.

Your 39 Numbers to Wheel

A*	B	C	D	E	F	G	H	I	J
130	14	14	14	14	14	14	14	14	14

K	L	M	N	O	P	Q	R	S	T
14	14	14	14	14	14	14	14	14	14

U	V	W	X	Y	Z	AA	BB	CC	DD
13	13	13	13	13	13	13	13	13	13

EE	FF	GG	HH	II	JJ	KK	LL	MM
13	13	13	13	13	14	16	15	14

The 130 Games to Play

1.	A*	B	C	ee	hh
2.	A*	B	D	K	jj
3.	A*	B	E	ll	mm
4.	A*	B	F	M	U

5.	A*	B	G	P	R
6.	A*	B	H	L	S
7.	A*	B	I	Y	ff
8.	A*	B	J	N	jj

    (Continued Next Page)

POWER NUMBER™ WHEEL 53039-1 (Continued from previous page)

	A*	B	O	W	Z		A*	E	K	T	mm
9.	A*	B	O	W	Z	44.	A*	E	K	T	mm
10.	A*	B	Q	V	aa	45.	A*	E	N	S	V
11.	A*	B	S	X	kk	46.	A*	E	O	X	bb
12.	A*	B	T	bb	dd	47.	A*	E	P	Z	ii
13.	A*	B	cc	ii	mm	48.	A*	E	R	ee	ff
14.	A*	B	ee	gg	kk	49.	A*	E	dd	gg	jj
15.	A*	C	D	S	Z	50.	A*	F	G	K	V
16.	A*	C	E	Y	cc	51.	A*	F	H	ff	kk
17.	A*	C	E	aa	hh	52.	A*	F	I	N	Q
18.	A*	C	F	H	jj	53.	A*	F	J	X	ll
19.	A*	C	G	O	kk	54.	A*	F	O	ee	ll
20.	A*	C	I	K	R	55.	A*	F	O	gg	ii
21.	A*	C	J	ff	ll	56.	A*	F	P	R	bb
22.	A*	C	K	N	bb	57.	A*	F	P	S	mm
23.	A*	C	L	M	X	58.	A*	F	Z	cc	jj
24.	A*	C	P	W	ll	59.	A*	F	aa	dd	hh
25.	A*	C	Q	T	ii	60.	A*	G	H	J	T
26.	A*	C	U	gg	mm	61.	A*	G	I	aa	gg
27.	A*	C	V	dd	ee	62.	A*	G	J	V	ll
28.	A*	D	E	V	kk	63.	A*	G	L	Y	bb
29.	A*	D	F	T	Y	64.	A*	G	M	dd	kk
30.	A*	D	G	N	ii	65.	A*	G	S	U	ee
31.	A*	D	H	M	ee	66.	A*	G	W	ff	jj
32.	A*	D	I	T	kk	67.	A*	G	X	cc	hh
33.	A*	D	J	Q	U	68.	A*	G	Z	aa	mm
34.	A*	D	L	dd	ll	69.	A*	H	I	W	bb
35.	A*	D	N	X	mm	70.	A*	H	K	P	Q
36.	A*	D	O	P	R	71.	A*	H	N	R	hh
37.	A*	D	W	aa	cc	72.	A*	H	O	cc	gg
38.	A*	D	bb	gg	ll	73.	A*	H	Q	dd	ii
39.	A*	D	ff	hh	mm	74.	A*	H	V	X	Z
40.	A*	E	F	L	W	75.	A*	H	Y	dd	mm
41.	A*	E	G	M	Q	76.	A*	H	aa	kk	ll
42.	A*	E	H	I	U	77.	A*	I	J	cc	ee
43.	A*	E	J	L	O	78.	A*	I	K	X	gg

          (Continued Next Page)

POWER NUMBER™ WHEEL 53039-1 (Continued from previous page)

#	A*					#	A*				
79.	A*	I	L	Z	dd	105.	A*	M	S	T	ff
80.	A*	I	M	ii	ll	106.	A*	M	T	W	gg
81.	A*	I	O	V	mm	107.	A*	M	V	bb	jj
82.	A*	I	P	hh	jj	108.	A*	N	O	dd	ff
83.	A*	I	R	S	cc	109.	A*	N	P	Y	gg
84.	A*	J	K	Y	ll	110.	A*	N	Q	W	ee
85.	A*	J	M	N	aa	111.	A*	N	T	cc	ll
86.	A*	J	P	R	dd	112.	A*	N	U	jj	kk
87.	A*	J	S	bb	mm	113.	A*	O	Q	Z	ll
88.	A*	J	W	ii	kk	114.	A*	O	T	U	jj
89.	A*	J	Z	gg	hh	115.	A*	P	T	X	ee
90.	A*	K	L	ff	ii	116.	A*	P	V	cc	ff
91.	A*	K	M	P	kk	117.	A*	Q	R	jj	ll
92.	A*	K	O	S	aa	118.	A*	Q	S	ff	gg
93.	A*	K	U	cc	dd	119.	A*	Q	X	Y	kk
94.	A*	K	W	hh	kk	120.	A*	R	T	Y	aa
95.	A*	K	Y	Z	ee	121.	A*	R	U	X	ii
96.	A*	L	N	T	Z	122.	A*	R	W	kk	mm
97.	A*	L	P	U	aa	123.	A*	S	U	hh	ii
98.	A*	L	Q	bb	hh	124.	A*	S	W	X	dd
99.	A*	L	R	V	gg	125.	A*	S	Y	ii	jj
100.	A*	L	bb	cc	kk	126.	A*	T	V	hh	ll
101.	A*	L	ee	jj	mm	127.	A*	U	V	W	Y
102.	A*	M	O	Y	hh	128.	A*	U	Z	bb	ff
103.	A*	M	Q	cc	mm	129.	A*	X	aa	ff	jj
104.	A*	M	R	Z	kk	130.	A*	aa	bb	ee	ii

POWER NUMBER™WHEEL 53109-1
Wheeling 9 Numbers in 2 games for a 3 of 4 Win

NUMBERS CORRECT***	MAXIMUM WINS				MINIMUM WINS			
	5x	4x	3x	2x	5x	4x	3x	2x
5 (w/o Jackpot)	0	1	0	1				
5	1	0	0	0	0	0	2	0
4	–	1	0	0	–	0	1	1
3	–	–	1	0	–	–	0	2
2	–	–	–	1	–	–	–	1

*** POWER NUMBER POSITION A* MUST BE A WINNER.
(Continued Next Page)

POWER NUMBER™ WHEEL 53109-1 (Continued from previous page)
Your 9 Numbers to Wheel

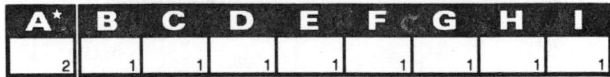

A*	B	C	D	E	F	G	H	I
2	1	1	1	1	1	1	1	1

The 2 Games to Play

1. | A* | B | E | G | H |

2. | A* | C | D | F | I |

POWER NUMBER™WHEEL 53111-1
Wheeling 11 Numbers in 4 games for a 3 of 4 Win

NUMBERS CORRECT***	MAXIMUM WINS				MINIMUM WINS			
	5x	4x	3x	2x	5x	4x	3x	2x
5 (w/o Jackpot)	0	2	1	0				
5	1	0	2	0	0	0	2	2
4	–	1	1	1	–	0	1	2
3	–	–	2	0	–	–	0	3
2	–	–	–	2	–	–	–	1

*** POWER NUMBER POSITION A* MUST BE A WINNER.
Your 11 Numbers to Wheel

A*	B	C	D	E	F	G	H	I	J	K
4	1	2	2	2	1	2	1	2	1	2

The 4 Games to Play

1. | A* | B | F | H | J |

2. | A* | C | D | I | K |

3. | A* | C | E | G | K |

4. | A* | D | E | G | I |

POWER NUMBER™WHEEL 53112-1
Wheeling 12 Numbers in 6 games for a 3 of 4 Win

NUMBERS CORRECT***	MAXIMUM WINS				MINIMUM WINS			
	5x	4x	3x	2x	5x	4x	3x	2x
5 (w/o Jackpot)	0	3	1	1				
5	1	1	2	1	0	0	2	3
4	–	2	1	1	–	0	1	2
3	–	–	3	0	–	–	0	3
2	–	–	–	3	–	–	–	1

*** POWER NUMBER POSITION A* MUST BE A WINNER.
Your 12 Numbers to Wheel

A*	B	C	D	E	F	G	H	I	J	K	L
6	1	3	3	3	1	2	3	1	3	1	3

The 6 Games to Play

1. | A* | B | F | I | K |

2. | A* | C | D | G | L |

3. | A* | C | D | J | L |

4. | A* | C | E | H | L |

5. | A* | D | E | H | J |

6. | A* | E | G | H | J |

POWER NUMBER™ WHEEL 53113-1
Wheeling 13 Numbers in 6 games for a 3 of 4 Win

NUMBERS CORRECT***	MAXIMUM WINS				MINIMUM WINS			
	5x	4x	3x	2x	5x	4x	3x	2x
5 (w/o Jackpot)	0	2	1	0				
5	1	0	2	0	0	0	2	4
4	–	1	1	1	–	0	1	4
3	–	–	2	0	–	–	0	4
2	–	–	–	2	–	–	–	2

*** POWER NUMBER POSITION A* MUST BE A WINNER.

Your 13 Numbers to Wheel

A*	B	C	D	E	F	G
6	2	2	2	2	2	2

H	I	J	K	L	M
2	2	2	2	2	2

The 6 Games to Play

1. A* B D K M
2. A* B F I M
3. A* C E J L
4. A* C G H L
5. A* D F I K
6. A* E G H J

Copyright © 1983-1998 Gail Howard

POWER NUMBER™ WHEEL 53114-1
Wheeling 14 Numbers in 8 games for a 3 of 4 Win

NUMBERS CORRECT***	MAXIMUM WINS				MINIMUM WINS			
	5x	4x	3x	2x	5x	4x	3x	2x
5 (w/o Jackpot)	0	3	1	1				
5	1	1	2	1	0	0	2	5
4	–	2	1	1	–	0	1	4
3	–	–	3	0	–	–	0	4
2	–	–	–	3	–	–	–	2

*** POWER NUMBER POSITION A* MUST BE A WINNER.

Your 14 Numbers to Wheel

A*	B	C	D	E	F	G
8	3	3	2	2	2	3

H	I	J	K	L	M	N
2	2	2	2	3	3	3

The 8 Games to Play

1. A* B C L N
2. A* B G L M
3. A* B I L M
4. A* C G I N
5. A* C G M N
6. A* D E J K
7. A* D F H J
8. A* E F H K

Copyright © 1983-1998 Gail Howard

279

POWER NUMBER™WHEEL 53115-1
Wheeling 15 Numbers in 9 games for a 3 of 4 Win

NUMBERS CORRECT***	MAXIMUM WINS				MINIMUM WINS			
	5x	4x	3x	2x	5x	4x	3x	2x
5 (w/o Jackpot)	0	2	3	0				
5	1	0	4	0	0	0	2	6
4	–	1	2	2	–	0	1	5
3	–	–	3	0	–	–	0	5
2	–	–	–	3	–	–	–	2

*** POWER NUMBER POSITION A* MUST BE A WINNER.

Your 15 Numbers to Wheel

A*	B	C	D	E	F	G	H
9	3	3	3	3	2	2	2

I	J	K	L	M	N	O
2	2	2	3	3	3	3

The 9 Games to Play

1.	A*	B	C	L	O	6.	A*	D	E	L	N
2.	A*	B	D	L	M	7.	A*	F	G	H	I
3.	A*	B	E	M	N	8.	A*	F	G	J	K
4.	A*	C	D	M	O	9.	A*	H	I	J	K
5.	A*	C	E	N	O						

Copyright © 1983-1998 Gail Howard

POWER NUMBER™WHEEL 53116-1
Wheeling 16 Numbers in 11 games for a 3 of 4 Win

NUMBERS CORRECT***	MAXIMUM WINS				MINIMUM WINS			
	5x	4x	3x	2x	5x	4x	3x	2x
5 (w/o Jackpot)	0	3	1	1				
5	1	1	1	2	0	0	2	6
4	–	2	1	1	–	0	1	5
3	–	–	3	0	–	–	0	5
2	–	–	–	4	–	–	–	2

*** POWER NUMBER POSITION A* MUST BE A WINNER.

Your 16 Numbers to Wheel

A*	B	C	D	E	F	G	H
11	3	3	3	3	3	3	3

I	J	K	L	M	N	O	P
4	2	2	3	3	3	3	3

The 11 Games to Play

1.	A*	B	D	I	O	6.	A*	C	G	I	M
2.	A*	B	H	O	P	7.	A*	D	H	J	P
3.	A*	B	J	K	O	8.	A*	D	H	K	P
4.	A*	C	E	M	N	9.	A*	E	F	I	L
5.	A*	C	F	L	M	10.	A*	E	G	I	N

Copyright © 1983-1998 Gail Howard   (Continued Next Page)

POWER NUMBER™ WHEEL 53116-1 (Continued from previous page)

11.

A*	F	G	L	N

Copyright © 1983-1998 Gail Howard

POWER NUMBER™ WHEEL 53117-1
Wheeling 17 Numbers in 12 games for a 3 of 4 Win

NUMBERS CORRECT***	MAXIMUM WINS				MINIMUM WINS			
	5x	4x	3x	2x	5x	4x	3x	2x
5 (w/o Jackpot)	0	2	3	0				
5	1	0	4	0	0	0	2	8
4	–	1	2	2	–	0	1	7
3	–	–	3	0	–	–	0	6
2	–	–	–	3	–	–	–	3

*** POWER NUMBER POSITION A* MUST BE A WINNER.

Your 17 Numbers to Wheel

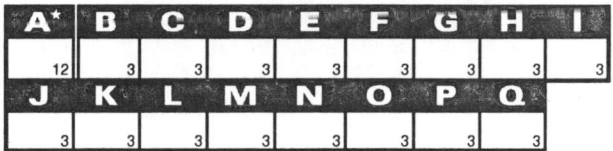

A*	B	C	D	E	F	G	H	I
12	3	3	3	3	3	3	3	3

J	K	L	M	N	O	P	Q
3	3	3	3	3	3	3	3

The 12 Games to Play

1.
A*	B	F	H	Q

2.
A*	B	I	J	Q

3.
A*	B	K	N	Q

4.
A*	C	D	O	P

5.
A*	C	E	L	O

6.
A*	C	G	L	M

7.
A*	D	E	L	P

8.
A*	D	G	M	P

9.
A*	E	G	M	O

10.
A*	F	H	I	J

11.
A*	F	I	K	N

12.
A*	H	J	K	N

Copyright © 1983-1998 Gail Howard

POWER NUMBER™ WHEEL 53118-1
Wheeling 18 Numbers in 14 games for a 3 of 4 Win

NUMBERS CORRECT***	MAXIMUM WINS				MINIMUM WINS			
	5x	4x	3x	2x	5x	4x	3x	2x
5 (w/o Jackpot)	0	3	2	3				
5	1	1	4	1	0	0	2	8
4	–	2	2	2	–	0	1	7
3	–	–	4	0	–	–	0	6
2	–	–	–	4	–	–	–	3

*** POWER NUMBER POSITION A* MUST BE A WINNER.

Your 18 Numbers to Wheel

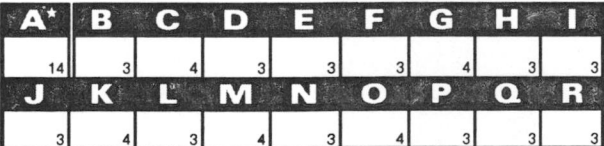

A*	B	C	D	E	F	G	H	I
14	3	4	3	3	3	4	3	3

J	K	L	M	N	O	P	Q	R
3	4	3	4	3	4	3	3	3

The 14 Games to Play

1.
A*	B	D	N	Q

2.
A*	B	E	Q	R

Copyright © 1983-1998 Gail Howard

(Continued Next Page)

POWER NUMBER™ WHEEL 53118-1 (Continued from previous page)

3.	A*	B	I	J	N
4.	A*	C	F	H	O
5.	A*	C	G	K	O
6.	A*	C	G	L	O
7.	A*	C	M	O	P
8.	A*	D	E	N	R

9.	A*	D	I	J	Q
10.	A*	E	I	J	R
11.	A*	F	G	K	M
12.	A*	F	L	M	P
13.	A*	G	H	K	P
14.	A*	H	K	L	M

Copyright © 1983-1998 Gail Howard

POWER NUMBER™ WHEEL 53119-1
Wheeling 19 Numbers in 15 games for a 3 of 4 Win

NUMBERS CORRECT***	MAXIMUM WINS				MINIMUM WINS			
	5x	4x	3x	2x	5x	4x	3x	2x
5 (w/o Jackpot)	0	2	3	4				
5	1	0	6	0	0	0	2	8
4	–	1	3	3	–	0	1	7
3	–	–	4	0	–	–	0	6
2	–	–	–	4	–	–	–	3

*** POWER NUMBER POSITION A* MUST BE A WINNER.

Your 19 Numbers to Wheel

A*	B	C	D	E	F	G	H	I	J
15	3	3	3	3	3	3	3	4	4

K	L	M	N	O	P	Q	R	S
4	3	4	4	4	3	3	3	3

The 15 Games to Play

1.	A*	B	C	P	Q
2.	A*	B	D	R	S
3.	A*	B	H	P	S
4.	A*	C	D	Q	R
5.	A*	C	H	Q	S
6.	A*	D	H	P	R
7.	A*	E	F	K	N
8.	A*	E	G	I	O

9.	A*	E	J	L	M
10.	A*	F	G	J	M
11.	A*	F	I	L	O
12.	A*	G	K	L	N
13.	A*	I	J	M	O
14.	A*	I	K	N	O
15.	A*	J	K	M	N

Copyright © 1983-1998 Gail Howard

282

POWER NUMBER™WHEEL 53120-1
Wheeling 20 Numbers in 17 games for a 3 of 4 Win

NUMBERS CORRECT***	MAXIMUM WINS				MINIMUM WINS			
	5x	4x	3x	2x	5x	4x	3x	2x
5 (w/o Jackpot)	0	3	3	1				
5	1	1	4	2	0	0	2	8
4	–	2	2	3	–	0	1	7
3	–	–	4	1	–	–	0	6
2	–	–	–	5	–	–	–	3

*** POWER NUMBER POSITION A* MUST BE A WINNER.

Your 20 Numbers to Wheel

A*	B	C	D	E	F	G	H	I	J
17	4	5	4	4	3	4	3	3	3

K	L	M	N	O	P	Q	R	S	T
3	3	3	3	3	4	4	4	4	4

The 17 Games to Play

#						#					
1.	A*	B	D	Q	T	10.	A*	D	E	Q	R
2.	A*	B	E	R	T	11.	A*	D	J	N	Q
3.	A*	B	J	L	T	12.	A*	D	L	O	Q
4.	A*	B	N	O	T	13.	A*	E	J	O	R
5.	A*	C	F	H	S	14.	A*	E	L	N	R
6.	A*	C	G	P	S	15.	A*	F	G	I	M
7.	A*	C	H	K	M	16.	A*	F	G	K	P
8.	A*	C	I	K	S	17.	A*	G	H	I	P
9.	A*	C	M	P	S						

Copyright © 1983-1998 Gail Howard

POWER NUMBER™WHEEL 53121-1
Wheeling 21 Numbers in 18 games for a 3 of 4 Win

NUMBERS CORRECT***	MAXIMUM WINS				MINIMUM WINS			
	5x	4x	3x	2x	5x	4x	3x	2x
5 (w/o Jackpot)	0	4	0	4				
5	1	0	6	0	0	0	2	8
4	–	1	3	3	–	0	1	7
3	–	–	4	0	–	–	0	6
2	–	–	–	4	–	–	–	3

*** POWER NUMBER POSITION A* MUST BE A WINNER.

Your 21 Numbers to Wheel

A*	B	C	D	E	F	G	H	I	J	K
18	4	4	4	4	4	4	3	3	3	3

L	M	N	O	P	Q	R	S	T	U
3	3	3	3	4	4	4	4	4	4

The 18 Games to Play

#						#					
1.	A*	B	E	K	T	2.	A*	B	F	I	T

Copyright © 1983-1998 Gail Howard

(Continued Next Page)

POWER NUMBER™ WHEEL 53121-1 (Continued from previous page)

	A*	B	L	Q	T
3.					

	A*	B	M	T	U
4.					

	A*	C	D	P	R
5.					

	A*	C	G	P	S
6.					

	A*	C	H	J	P
7.					

	A*	C	N	O	P
8.					

	A*	D	G	R	S
9.					

	A*	D	H	O	R
10.					

	A*	D	J	N	R
11.					

	A*	E	F	L	U
12.					

	A*	E	F	M	Q
13.					

	A*	E	I	Q	U
14.					

	A*	F	K	Q	U
15.					

	A*	G	H	N	S
16.					

	A*	G	J	O	S
17.					

	A*	I	K	L	M
18.					

POWER NUMBER™ WHEEL 53122-1
Wheeling 22 Numbers in 20 games for a 3 of 4 Win

NUMBERS CORRECT***	MAXIMUM WINS				MINIMUM WINS			
	5x	4x	3x	2x	5x	4x	3x	2x
5 (w/o Jackpot)	0	4	0	4				
5	1	1	0	9	0	0	2	10
4	–	2	0	6	–	0	1	8
3	–	–	4	0	–	–	0	7
2	–	–	–	4	–	–	–	3

*** POWER NUMBER POSITION A* MUST BE A WINNER.

Your 22 Numbers to Wheel

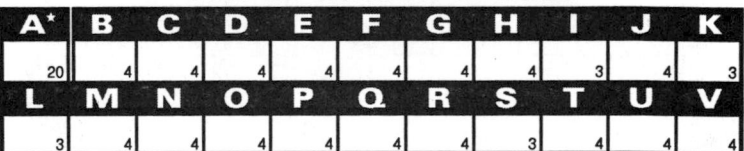

A*	B	C	D	E	F	G	H	I	J	K
20	4	4	4	4	4	4	4	3	4	3

L	M	N	O	P	Q	R	S	T	U	V
3	4	4	4	4	4	4	3	4	4	4

The 20 Games to Play

	A*	B	C	N	T
1.					

	A*	B	E	N	P
2.					

	A*	B	G	O	Q
3.					

	A*	B	J	N	U
4.					

	A*	C	E	O	U
5.					

	A*	C	G	J	P
6.					

	A*	C	P	Q	U
7.					

	A*	D	F	K	V
8.					

	A*	D	H	S	V
9.					

	A*	D	I	R	V
10.					

	A*	D	L	M	V
11.					

	A*	E	G	T	U
12.					

	A*	E	J	Q	T
13.					

	A*	F	H	I	M
14.					

	A*	F	H	L	R
15.					

	A*	F	M	R	S
16.					

	A*	G	N	O	Q
17.					

	A*	H	K	M	R
18.					

	A*	I	K	L	S
19.					

	A*	J	O	P	T
20.					

POWER NUMBER™WHEEL 53123-1
Wheeling 23 Numbers in 21 games for a 3 of 4 Win

NUMBERS CORRECT***	MAXIMUM WINS				MINIMUM WINS			
	5x	4x	3x	2x	5x	4x	3x	2x
5 (w/o Jackpot)	0	2	5	0				
5	1	0	4	4	0	0	2	10
4	-	1	3	3	-	0	1	8
3	-	-	3	2	-	-	0	7
2	-	-	-	4	-	-	-	3

*** POWER NUMBER POSITION A* MUST BE A WINNER.

Your 23 Numbers to Wheel

A*	B	C	D	E	F	G	H	I	J	K	L
21	4	3	3	4	4	4	4	4	4	4	4

M	N	O	P	Q	R	S	T	U	V	W
3	3	4	4	4	4	4	4	4	4	4

The 21 Games to Play

1.	A*	B	C	N	T		12.	A*	F	H	J	L
2.	A*	B	D	M	T		13.	A*	F	J	K	S
3.	A*	B	G	T	U		14.	A*	F	P	R	V
4.	A*	B	I	U	W		15.	A*	G	I	T	W
5.	A*	C	D	G	W		16.	A*	G	M	N	W
6.	A*	C	I	M	U		17.	A*	H	O	R	S
7.	A*	D	I	N	U		18.	A*	H	P	Q	S
8.	A*	E	F	O	Q		19.	A*	J	O	Q	V
9.	A*	E	H	K	V		20.	A*	K	L	O	P
10.	A*	E	J	P	R		21.	A*	K	L	Q	R
11.	A*	E	L	S	V							

Copyright © 1983-1998 Gail Howard

POWER NUMBER™WHEEL 53124-1
Wheeling 24 Numbers in 22 games for a 3 of 4 Win

NUMBERS CORRECT***	MAXIMUM WINS				MINIMUM WINS			
	5x	4x	3x	2x	5x	4x	3x	2x
5 (w/o Jackpot)	0	2	5	0				
5	1	0	4	4	0	0	2	10
4	-	1	3	3	-	0	1	8
3	-	-	3	2	-	-	0	7
2	-	-	-	4	-	-	-	3

*** POWER NUMBER POSITION A* MUST BE A WINNER.

Your 24 Numbers to Wheel

A*	B	C	D	E	F	G	H	I	J	K	L
22	4	3	4	4	4	4	4	4	4	4	4

M	N	O	P	Q	R	S	T	U	V	W	X
3	4	3	4	4	4	4	4	4	4	4	3

(Continued Next Page)

285

POWER NUMBER™ WHEEL 53124-1 (Continued from previous page)
The 22 Games to Play

1.	A*	B	C	M	U	12.	A*	E	N	Q	R
2.	A*	B	D	J	V	13.	A*	F	G	H	N
3.	A*	B	O	U	X	14.	A*	F	I	L	Q
4.	A*	B	P	U	V	15.	A*	F	R	T	W
5.	A*	C	D	V	X	16.	A*	G	I	K	R
6.	A*	C	J	O	P	17.	A*	G	Q	S	T
7.	A*	D	J	P	U	18.	A*	H	K	Q	W
8.	A*	D	M	O	V	19.	A*	H	L	R	S
9.	A*	E	F	K	S	20.	A*	I	N	S	W
10.	A*	E	G	L	W	21.	A*	J	M	P	X
11.	A*	E	H	I	T	22.	A*	K	L	N	T

POWER NUMBER™ WHEEL 53125-1
Wheeling 25 Numbers in 24 games for a 3 of 4 Win

NUMBERS CORRECT***	MAXIMUM WINS				MINIMUM WINS			
	5x	4x	3x	2x	5x	4x	3x	2x
5 (w/o Jackpot)	0	2	3	4				
5	1	1	0	9	0	0	2	12
4	–	2	0	6	–	0	1	10
3	–	–	3	2	–	–	0	8
2	–	–	–	4	–	–	–	4

*** POWER NUMBER POSITION A* MUST BE A WINNER.

Your 25 Numbers to Wheel

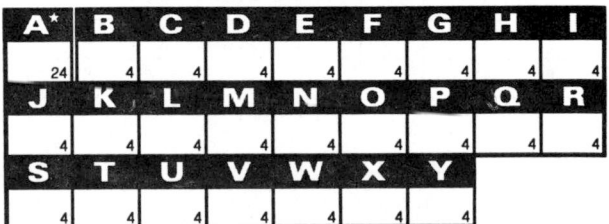

The 24 Games to Play

1.	A*	B	G	N	Y	9.	A*	D	E	J	W
2.	A*	B	H	O	X	10.	A*	D	F	R	U
3.	A*	B	K	L	P	11.	A*	D	M	Q	S
4.	A*	B	P	T	X	12.	A*	E	F	I	Q
5.	A*	C	D	I	V	13.	A*	E	S	U	V
6.	A*	C	E	M	R	14.	A*	F	M	V	W
7.	A*	C	F	J	S	15.	A*	G	H	P	Y
8.	A*	C	Q	U	W	16.	A*	G	K	X	Y

     (Continued Next Page)

POWER NUMBER™ WHEEL 53125-1 (Continued from previous page)

17.	A*	G	L	O	T
18.	A*	H	K	N	T
19.	A*	H	L	N	X
20.	A*	I	J	M	U

21.	A*	I	R	S	W
22.	A*	J	Q	R	V
23.	A*	K	N	O	P
24.	A*	L	O	T	Y

POWER NUMBER™ WHEEL 53126-1
Wheeling 26 Numbers in 25 games for a 3 of 4 Win

NUMBERS CORRECT***	MAXIMUM WINS				MINIMUM WINS			
	5x	4x	3x	2x	5x	4x	3x	2x
5 (w/o Jackpot)	0	2	2	6				
5	1	0	1	10	0	0	2	12
4	–	1	1	7	–	0	1	10
3	–	–	2	4	–		0	8
2	–	–	–	4	–	–	–	4

*** POWER NUMBER POSITION A* MUST BE A WINNER.

Your 26 Numbers to Wheel

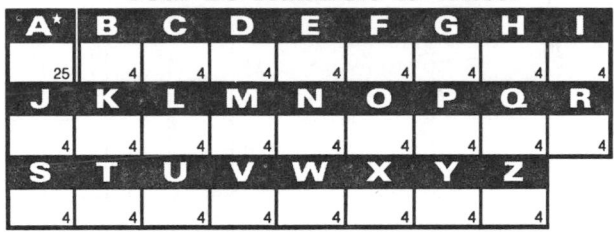

A*	B	C	D	E	F	G	H	I
25	4	4	4	4	4	4	4	4

J	K	L	M	N	O	P	Q	R
4	4	4	4	4	4	4	4	4

S	T	U	V	W	X	Y	Z
4	4	4	4	4	4	4	4

The 25 Games to Play

1.	A*	B	D	Y	Z
2.	A*	B	F	H	X
3.	A*	B	G	I	T
4.	A*	B	H	P	S
5.	A*	C	E	Q	V
6.	A*	C	J	L	N
7.	A*	C	K	U	W
8.	A*	C	M	O	R
9.	A*	D	F	I	S
10.	A*	D	G	H	Z
11.	A*	D	P	T	X
12.	A*	E	J	K	O
13.	A*	E	L	R	U

14.	A*	E	M	N	W
15.	A*	F	G	P	Y
16.	A*	F	S	T	Z
17.	A*	G	S	X	Y
18.	A*	H	I	T	Y
19.	A*	I	P	X	Z
20.	A*	J	M	U	V
21.	A*	J	Q	R	W
22.	A*	K	L	M	Q
23.	A*	K	N	R	V
24.	A*	L	O	V	W
25.	A*	N	O	Q	U

POWER NUMBER™ WHEEL 53128-1
Wheeling 28 Numbers in 31 games for a 3 of 4 Win

NUMBERS CORRECT***	MAXIMUM WINS				MINIMUM WINS			
	5x	4x	3x	2x	5x	4x	3x	2x
5 (w/o Jackpot)	0	2	4	7				
5	1	0	4	9	0	0	2	14
4	–	1	3	7	–	0	1	11
3	–	–	2	7	–	–	0	9
2	–	–	–	6	–	–	–	4

*** POWER NUMBER POSITION A* MUST BE A WINNER.

Your 28 Numbers to Wheel

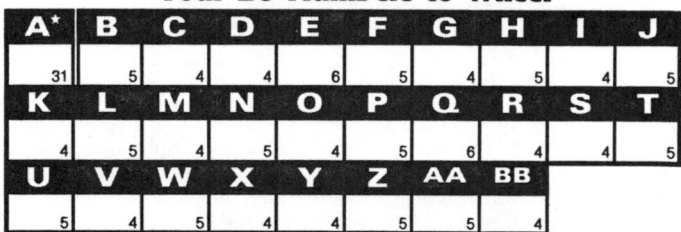

A*	B	C	D	E	F	G	H	I	J
31	5	4	4	6	5	4	5	4	5

K	L	M	N	O	P	Q	R	S	T
4	5	4	5	4	5	6	4	4	5

U	V	W	X	Y	Z	AA	BB
5	4	5	4	4	5	5	4

The 31 Games to Play

1.	A*	B	E	L	Z	17.	A*	E	Q	T	W
2.	A*	B	F	U	aa	18.	A*	F	J	W	Z
3.	A*	B	H	J	T	19.	A*	F	L	N	Q
4.	A*	B	N	P	W	20.	A*	F	P	Q	T
5.	A*	B	Q	Z	aa	21.	A*	G	I	R	X
6.	A*	C	D	G	Y	22.	A*	G	K	M	S
7.	A*	C	I	K	V	23.	A*	G	O	V	bb
8.	A*	C	M	X	bb	24.	A*	H	L	U	W
9.	A*	C	O	R	S	25.	A*	H	N	Q	aa
10.	A*	D	I	M	O	26.	A*	I	S	Y	bb
11.	A*	D	K	R	bb	27.	A*	J	P	Q	U
12.	A*	D	S	V	X	28.	A*	K	O	X	Y
13.	A*	E	F	H	U	29.	A*	L	P	T	aa
14.	A*	E	H	P	Z	30.	A*	M	R	V	Y
15.	A*	E	J	L	N	31.	A*	N	T	U	Z
16.	A*	E	J	W	aa						

Copyright © 1983-1998 Gail Howard

POWER NUMBER™WHEEL 53130-1
Wheeling 30 Numbers in 36 games for a 3 of 4 Win

NUMBERS CORRECT***	MAXIMUM WINS				MINIMUM WINS			
	5x	4x	3x	2x	5x	4x	3x	2x
5 (w/o Jackpot)	0	2	4	6				
5	1	0	4	8	0	0	2	15
4	–	1	3	6	–	0	1	12
3	–	–	3	4	–	–	0	9
2	–	–	–	5	–	–	–	4

*** POWER NUMBER POSITION A* MUST BE A WINNER.

Your 30 Numbers to Wheel

A*	B	C	D	E	F	G	H	I	J
36	4	5	5	5	5	5	5	5	5

K	L	M	N	O	P	Q	R	S	T
5	5	5	5	5	5	5	5	5	5

U	V	W	X	Y	Z	AA	BB	CC	DD
5	5	5	5	5	5	5	5	5	5

The 36 Games to Play

#						#				
1.	A*	B	D	R	S	19.	A*	F	J	Q	U
2.	A*	B	E	L	aa	20.	A*	F	K	T	W
3.	A*	B	M	O	X	21.	A*	G	H	P	W
4.	A*	B	Z	bb	cc	22.	A*	G	J	K	V
5.	A*	C	F	P	Y	23.	A*	G	T	U	Y
6.	A*	C	G	N	Q	24.	A*	H	I	Q	T
7.	A*	C	H	K	U	25.	A*	H	J	Y	dd
8.	A*	C	I	J	W	26.	A*	I	K	N	Y
9.	A*	C	T	V	dd	27.	A*	I	P	U	V
10.	A*	D	E	R	bb	28.	A*	J	N	P	T
11.	A*	D	L	R	cc	29.	A*	K	P	Q	dd
12.	A*	D	M	Z	aa	30.	A*	L	M	X	bb
13.	A*	D	O	S	X	31.	A*	L	O	S	aa
14.	A*	E	M	S	cc	32.	A*	L	S	Z	bb
15.	A*	E	O	Z	cc	33.	A*	M	R	X	Z
16.	A*	E	X	aa	cc	34.	A*	N	U	W	dd
17.	A*	F	G	I	dd	35.	A*	O	R	aa	bb
18.	A*	F	H	N	V	36.	A*	Q	V	W	Y

Copyright © 1983-1998 Gail Howard

POWER NUMBER™ WHEEL 53132-1
Wheeling 32 Numbers in 40 games for a 3 of 4 Win

NUMBERS CORRECT***	MAXIMUM WINS				MINIMUM WINS			
	5x	4x	3x	2x	5x	4x	3x	2x
5 (w/o Jackpot)	0	2	4	11				
5	1	0	4	12	0	0	2	16
4	–	1	3	10	–	0	1	13
3	–	–	3	6	–	–	0	10
2	–	–	–	7	–	–	–	5

*** POWER NUMBER POSITION A* MUST BE A WINNER.

Your 32 Numbers to Wheel

A*	B	C	D	E	F	G	H	I	J	K
40	5	5	5	5	5	5	5	5	5	5

L	M	N	O	P	Q	R	S	T	U	V
5	5	5	5	6	6	6	7	5	5	5

W	X	Y	Z	AA	BB	CC	DD	EE	FF
5	5	5	5	5	5	5	5	5	5

The 40 Games to Play

#						#					
1.	A*	B	C	T	cc	21.	A*	I	M	R	U
2.	A*	B	D	L	bb	22.	A*	I	P	W	Y
3.	A*	B	E	G	aa	23.	A*	I	Q	V	ee
4.	A*	B	F	H	Z	24.	A*	J	K	W	ee
5.	A*	B	O	dd	ff	25.	A*	J	M	P	Q
6.	A*	C	D	O	aa	26.	A*	J	N	R	Y
7.	A*	C	E	H	bb	27.	A*	J	P	U	V
8.	A*	C	F	L	dd	28.	A*	K	M	P	X
9.	A*	C	G	Z	ff	29.	A*	K	Q	U	Y
10.	A*	D	E	Z	dd	30.	A*	K	R	S	V
11.	A*	D	F	G	T	31.	A*	L	Z	aa	cc
12.	A*	D	H	cc	ff	32.	A*	M	N	V	W
13.	A*	E	F	O	cc	33.	A*	M	S	Y	ee
14.	A*	E	L	T	ff	34.	A*	N	P	Q	S
15.	A*	F	aa	bb	ff	35.	A*	N	U	X	ee
16.	A*	G	H	L	O	36.	A*	O	T	Z	bb
17.	A*	G	bb	cc	dd	37.	A*	P	Q	R	ee
18.	A*	H	T	aa	dd	38.	A*	Q	S	W	X
19.	A*	I	J	S	X	39.	A*	R	S	U	W
20.	A*	I	K	N	S	40.	A*	R	V	X	Y

POWER NUMBER™WHEEL 53135-1
Wheeling 35 Numbers in 50 games for a 3 of 4 Win

NUMBERS CORRECT***	MAXIMUM WINS				MINIMUM WINS			
	5x	4x	3x	2x	5x	4x	3x	2x
5 (w/o Jackpot)	0	3	3	13				
5	1	1	1	19	0	0	2	18
4	–	2	1	13	–	0	1	14
3	–	–	3	8	–	–	0	11
2	–	–	–	7	–	–	–	5

*** POWER NUMBER POSITION A* MUST BE A WINNER.

Your 35 Numbers to Wheel

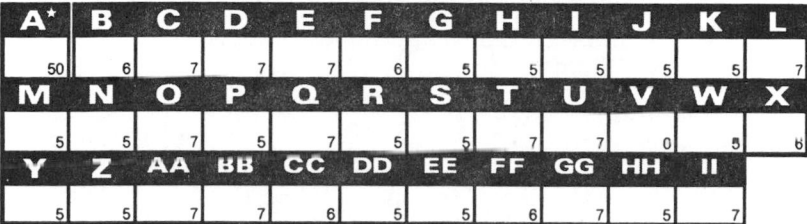

A*	B	C	D	E	F	G	H	I	J	K	L
50	6	7	7	7	6	5	5	5	5	5	7

M	N	O	P	Q	R	S	T	U	V	W	X
5	5	7	5	7	5	5	7	7	0	5	6

Y	Z	AA	BB	CC	DD	EE	FF	GG	HH	II
5	5	7	7	6	5	5	6	7	5	7

The 50 Games to Play

1.	A*	B	C	Q	ii	23.	A*	F	V	cc	ff
2.	A*	B	D	U	aa	24.	A*	G	H	R	Y
3.	A*	B	E	O	T	25.	A*	G	I	M	S
4.	A*	B	F	V	X	26.	A*	G	J	N	W
5.	A*	B	L	bb	gg	27.	A*	G	K	dd	ee
6.	A*	B	X	cc	ff	28.	A*	G	P	Z	hh
7.	A*	C	D	T	cc	29.	A*	H	I	N	ee
8.	A*	C	E	L	ff	30.	A*	H	J	dd	hh
9.	A*	C	E	V	aa	31.	A*	H	K	M	r
10.	A*	C	F	O	U	32.	A*	H	S	W	Z
11.	A*	C	Q	X	bb	33.	A*	I	J	P	R
12.	A*	C	aa	gg	ii	34.	A*	I	K	W	hh
13.	A*	D	E	F	aa	35.	A*	I	Y	Z	dd
14.	A*	D	L	Q	U	36.	A*	J	K	S	Y
15.	A*	D	L	V	gg	37.	A*	J	M	Z	ee
16.	A*	D	O	X	gg	38.	A*	K	N	R	Z
17.	A*	D	bb	ff	ii	39.	A*	L	O	cc	ii
18.	A*	E	O	T	bb	40.	A*	L	T	X	aa
19.	A*	E	Q	cc	gg	41.	A*	M	N	Y	hh
20.	A*	E	U	X	ii	42.	A*	M	R	W	dd
21.	A*	F	L	bb	gg	43.	A*	N	P	S	dd
22.	A*	F	Q	T	ii	44.	A*	O	Q	aa	ff

          (Continued Next Page)

POWER NUMBER™ WHEEL 53135-1 (Continued from previous page)

45.	A*	O	T	U	V
46.	A*	P	W	Y	ee
47.	A*	Q	V	bb	ii

48.	A*	R	S	ee	hh
49.	A*	T	U	ff	gg
50.	A*	U	aa	bb	cc

POWER NUMBER™ WHEEL 53139-1
Wheeling 39 Numbers in 64 games for a 3 of 4 Win

NUMBERS CORRECT***	MAXIMUM WINS				MINIMUM WINS			
	5x	4x	3x	2x	5x	4x	3x	2x
5 (w/o Jackpot)	0	3	9	8				
5	1	0	7	15	0	0	2	20
4	-	1	7	10	-	0	1	16
3	-	-	5	8	-	-	0	12
2	-	-	-	9	-	-	-	6

*** POWER NUMBER POSITION A* MUST BE A WINNER.

Your 39 Numbers to Wheel

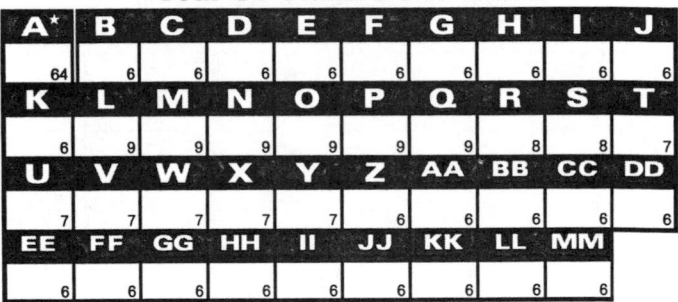

The 64 Games to Play

1.	A*	B	C	R	cc
2.	A*	B	F	G	ii
3.	A*	B	J	W	ll
4.	A*	B	M	X	dd
5.	A*	B	N	P	Y
6.	A*	B	Z	bb	jj
7.	A*	C	F	J	Z
8.	A*	C	G	N	W
9.	A*	C	M	P	jj
10.	A*	C	X	ii	ll
11.	A*	C	Y	bb	dd
12.	A*	D	E	H	aa
13.	A*	D	I	hh	mm
14.	A*	D	K	Q	T
15.	A*	D	L	S	kk

16.	A*	D	O	U	V
17.	A*	D	ee	ff	gg
18.	A*	E	I	ff	kk
19.	A*	E	K	ee	hh
20.	A*	E	L	O	S
21.	A*	E	Q	U	mm
22.	A*	E	T	V	gg
23.	A*	F	M	W	Y
24.	A*	F	N	X	bb
25.	A*	F	P	R	dd
26.	A*	F	cc	jj	ll
27.	A*	G	J	bb	cc
28.	A*	G	M	P	R
29.	A*	G	X	Y	jj
30.	A*	G	Z	dd	ll

          (Continued Next Page)

POWER NUMBER™ WHEEL 53139-1 (Continued from previous page)

31.	A*	H	I	V	ee	48.	A*	M	N	P	ii
32.	A*	H	K	S	U	49.	A*	M	N	R	Z
33.	A*	H	L	O	Q	50.	A*	M	P	X	cc
34.	A*	H	T	ff	mm	51.	A*	M	P	bb	ll
35.	A*	H	gg	hh	kk	52.	A*	N	R	W	jj
36.	A*	I	K	aa	gg	53.	A*	N	R	Y	ll
37.	A*	I	L	T	U	54.	A*	N	W	cc	dd
38.	A*	I	O	Q	S	55.	A*	O	Q	V	hh
39.	A*	J	M	N	Y	56.	A*	O	T	aa	kk
40.	A*	J	P	R	X	57.	A*	P	W	X	Z
41.	A*	J	dd	ii	jj	58.	A*	Q	S	U	gg
42.	A*	K	L	O	ff	59.	A*	Q	S	V	ff
43.	A*	K	V	kk	mm	60.	A*	Q	U	ee	kk
44.	A*	L	O	T	ee	61.	A*	R	W	bb	ii
45.	A*	L	O	gg	mm	62.	A*	S	aa	ee	mm
46.	A*	L	Q	V	aa	63.	A*	U	aa	ff	hh
47.	A*	L	S	T	hh	64.	A*	Y	Z	cc	ii

POWER NUMBER™ WHEEL 53210-1
Wheeling 10 Numbers in 2 games for a 3 of 5 Win

NUMBERS CORRECT***	MAXIMUM WINS				MINIMUM WINS			
	5x	4x	3x	?v	5H	4A	3X	2x
5 (w/o Jackpot)	0	1	0	1				
5	1	0	0	0	0	0	1	1
4	-	1	0	0	-	0	0	2
3	-	-	1	0	-	-	0	1
2	-	-	-	1	-	-	-	0

*** POWER NUMBER POSITION A* MUST BE A WINNER.

Your 10 Numbers to Wheel

A*	B	C	D	E	F	G	H	I	J
2	1	1	0	1	1	1	1	1	1

The 2 Games to Play

1.	A*	B	F	G	J
2.	A*	C	E	H	I

POWER NUMBER™WHEEL 53211-1
Wheeling 11 Numbers in 3 games for a 3 of 5 Win

NUMBERS CORRECT***	MAXIMUM WINS				MINIMUM WINS			
	5x	4x	3x	2x	5x	4x	3x	2x
5 (w/o Jackpot)	0	2	0	0				
5	1	0	1	0	0	0	1	2
4	–	1	1	0	–	0	0	3
3	–	–	2	0	–	–	0	2
2	–	–	–	2	–	–	–	1

*** POWER NUMBER POSITION A* MUST BE A WINNER.

Your 11 Numbers to Wheel

A*	B	C	D	E	F	G	H	I	J	K
3	1	1	1	1	1	1	1	2	2	1

The 3 Games to Play

1. | A* | B | G | I | J |

2. | A* | C | F | I | J |

3. | A* | D | E | H | K |

Copyright © 1983-1998 Gail Howard

POWER NUMBER™WHEEL 53212-1
Wheeling 12 Numbers in 3 games for a 3 of 5 Win

NUMBERS CORRECT***	MAXIMUM WINS				MINIMUM WINS			
	5x	4x	3x	2x	5x	4x	3x	2x
5 (w/o Jackpot)	0	1	1	0				
5	1	0	0	1	0	0	1	2
4	–	1	0	1	–	0	0	3
3	–	–	1	1	–	–	0	2
2	–	–	–	2	–	–	–	1

*** POWER NUMBER POSITION A* MUST BE A WINNER.

Your 12 Numbers to Wheel

A*	B	C	D	E	F	G	H	I	J	K	L
3	1	1	1	1	2	1	1	1	1	1	1

The 3 Games to Play

1. | A* | B | C | K | L |

2. | A* | D | F | G | J |

3. | A* | E | F | H | I |

Copyright © 1983-1998 Gail Howard

POWER NUMBER™WHEEL 53213-1
Wheeling 13 Numbers in 3 games for a 3 of 5 Win

NUMBERS CORRECT***	MAXIMUM WINS				MINIMUM WINS			
	5x	4x	3x	2x	5x	4x	3x	2x
5 (w/o Jackpot)	0	1	0	1				
5	1	0	0	0	0	0	1	2
4	–	1	0	0	–	0	0	3
3	–	–	1	0	–	–	0	2
2	–	–	–	1	–	–	–	1

*** POWER NUMBER POSITION A* MUST BE A WINNER.
(Continued Next Page)

POWER NUMBER™ WHEEL 53213-1 (Continued from previous page)

Your 13 Numbers to Wheel

A*	B	C	D	E	F	G
3	1	1	1	1	1	1

H	I	J	K	L	M
1	1	1	1	1	1

The 3 Games to Play

1. | A* | B | G | H | M |

2. | A* | C | E | J | L |

3. | A* | D | F | I | K |

Copyright © 1983-1998 Gail Howard

POWER NUMBER™WHEEL 53214-1

Wheeling 14 Numbers in 5 games for a 3 of 5 Win

NUMBERS CORRECT***	MAXIMUM WINS				MINIMUM WINS			
	5x	4x	3x	2x	5x	4x	3x	2x
5 (w/o Jackpot)	0	2	1	0				
5	1	0	2	0	0	0	1	3
4	–	1	1	1	–	0	0	4
3	–	–	2	0	–	–	0	2
2	–	–	–	2	–	–	–	1

*** POWER NUMBER POSITION A* MUST BE A WINNER.

Your 14 Numbers to Wheel

A*	B	C	D	E	F	G
5	1	2	1	2	2	1

H	I	J	K	L	M	N
1	2	2	2	1	1	2

The 5 Games to Play

1. | A* | B | H | I | M |

2. | A* | C | E | K | N |

3. | A* | C | F | J | N |

4. | A* | D | G | J | L |

5. | A* | E | F | I | K |

Copyright © 1983-1998 Gail Howard

POWER NUMBER™WHEEL 53215-1

Wheeling 15 Numbers in 5 games for a 3 of 5 Win

NUMBERS CORRECT***	MAXIMUM WINS				MINIMUM WINS			
	5x	4x	3x	2x	5x	4x	3x	2x
5 (w/o Jackpot)	0	2	1	0				
5	1	0	2	0	0	0	1	3
4	–	1	1	1	–	0	0	4
3	–	–	2	0	–	–	0	2
2	–	–	–	2	–	–	–	1

*** POWER NUMBER POSITION A* MUST BE A WINNER.

(Continued Next Page)

POWER NUMBER™ WHEEL 53215-1 (Continued from previous page)
Your 15 Numbers to Wheel

A*	B	C	D	E	F	G	H
5	1	1	1	2	2	1	2

I	J	K	L	M	N	O	
2	1	2	2	1	1	1	

The 5 Games to Play

1.	A*	B	C	N	O
2.	A*	D	G	J	M
3.	A*	E	F	K	L

4.	A*	E	H	I	K
5.	A*	F	H	I	L

Copyright © 1983-1998 Gail Howard

POWER NUMBER™WHEEL 53216-1
Wheeling 16 Numbers in 7 games for a 3 of 5 Win

NUMBERS CORRECT***	MAXIMUM WINS				MINIMUM WINS			
	5x	4x	3x	2x	5x	4x	3x	2x
5 (w/o Jackpot)	0	3	1	1				
5	1	1	1	2	0	0	1	3
4	–	2	1	1	–	0	0	4
3	–	–	3	0	–	–	0	2
2	–	–	–	3	–	–	–	1

*** POWER NUMBER POSITION A* MUST BE A WINNER.

Your 16 Numbers to Wheel

A*	B	C	D	E	F	G	H
7	1	1	1	1	3	3	3

I	J	K	L	M	N	O	P
3	3	2	2	2	1	1	1

The 7 Games to Play

1.	A*	B	D	N	O
2.	A*	C	E	L	P
3.	A*	F	G	I	J
4.	A*	F	H	J	L

5.	A*	F	J	K	M
6.	A*	G	H	I	K
7.	A*	G	H	I	M

Copyright © 1983-1998 Gail Howard

POWER NUMBER™WHEEL 53217-1
Wheeling 17 Numbers in 8 games for a 3 of 5 Win

NUMBERS CORRECT***	MAXIMUM WINS				MINIMUM WINS			
	5x	4x	3x	2x	5x	4x	3x	2x
5 (w/o Jackpot)	0	2	1	0				
5	1	1	0	1	0	0	1	6
4	–	2	0	0	–	0	0	6
3	–	–	2	0	–	–	0	4
2	–	–	–	2	–	–	–	2

*** POWER NUMBER POSITION A* MUST BE A WINNER.
(Continued Next Page)

POWER NUMBER™ WHEEL 53220-1 (Continued from previous page)

11. | A* | I | K | L | M |

Copyright © 1983-1998 Gail Howard

POWER NUMBER™WHEEL 53221-1
Wheeling 21 Numbers in 12 games for a 3 of 5 Win

NUMBERS CORRECT***	MAXIMUM WINS				MINIMUM WINS			
	5x	4x	3x	2x	5x	4x	3x	2x
5 (w/o Jackpot)	0	2	3	0				
5	1	0	4	0	0	0	1	7
4	–	1	2	2	–	0	0	7
3	–	–	3	0	–	–	0	4
2	–	–	–	3	–	–	–	2

*** POWER NUMBER POSITION A* MUST BE A WINNER.

Your 21 Numbers to Wheel

A*	B	C	D	E	F	G	H	I	J	K
12	2	3	2	2	3	2	2	2	3	3

L	M	N	O	P	Q	R	S	T	U
3	2	2	3	2	2	2	3	3	2

The 12 Games to Play

1. | A* | B | G | Q | U |
2. | A* | B | I | M | U |
3. | A* | C | F | S | T |
4. | A* | C | J | K | S |
5. | A* | C | L | O | S |
6. | A* | D | E | N | R |

7. | A* | D | H | P | R |
8. | A* | E | H | N | P |
9. | A* | F | J | L | T |
10. | A* | F | K | O | T |
11. | A* | G | I | M | Q |
12. | A* | J | K | L | O |

Copyright © 1983-1998 Gail Howard

POWER NUMBER™WHEEL 53222-1
Wheeling 22 Numbers in 14 games for a 3 of 5 Win

NUMBERS CORRECT***	MAXIMUM WINS				MINIMUM WINS			
	5x	4x	3x	2x	5x	4x	3x	2x
5 (w/o Jackpot)	0	4	0	3				
5	1	3	0	1	0	0	1	7
4	–	4	0	0	–	0	0	7
3	–	–	4	0	–	–	0	4
2	–	–	–	4	–	–	–	2

*** POWER NUMBER POSITION A* MUST BE A WINNER.

Your 22 Numbers to Wheel

A*	B	C	D	E	F	G	H	I	J	K
14	2	2	3	3	3	4	3	4	2	2

L	M	N	O	P	Q	R	S	T	U	V
2	3	2	2	4	2	3	3	3	2	2

The 14 Games to Play

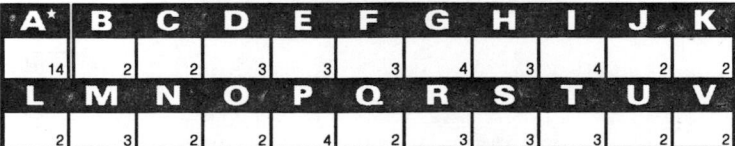

1. | A* | B | C | U | V |
2. | A* | B | K | O | V |

Copyright © 1983-1998 Gail Howard   (Continued Next Page)

POWER NUMBER™ WHEEL 53222-1 (Continued from previous page)

3.	A*	C	K	O	U
4.	A*	D	E	R	T
5.	A*	D	F	M	S
6.	A*	D	H	S	T
7.	A*	E	F	M	T
8.	A*	E	H	R	S

9.	A*	F	H	M	R
10.	A*	G	I	J	P
11.	A*	G	I	L	P
12.	A*	G	I	N	P
13.	A*	G	I	P	Q
14.	A*	J	L	N	Q

POWER NUMBER™WHEEL 53223-1
Wheeling 23 Numbers in 16 games for a 3 of 5 Win

NUMBERS CORRECT***	MAXIMUM WINS				MINIMUM WINS			
	5x	4x	3x	2x	5x	4x	3x	2x
5 (w/o Jackpot)	0	3	2	2				
5	1	1	2	4	0	0	1	7
4	–	2	2	2	–	0	0	7
3	–	–	4	0	–	–	0	4
2	–	–	–	4	–	–	–	2

*** POWER NUMBER POSITION A* MUST BE A WINNER.

Your 23 Numbers to Wheel

A*	B	C	D	E	F	G	H	I	J	K	L
16	3	3	2	3	3	3	2	3	3	4	2

M	N	O	P	Q	R	S	T	U	V	W
3	4	3	3	4	2	3	3	3	2	3

The 16 Games to Play

1.	A*	B	G	I	T
2.	A*	B	I	L	U
3.	A*	B	P	T	U
4.	A*	C	F	J	S
5.	A*	C	K	N	Q
6.	A*	C	O	S	W
7.	A*	D	E	M	V
8.	A*	D	H	R	V

9.	A*	E	F	Q	W
10.	A*	E	H	M	R
11.	A*	F	K	N	O
12.	A*	G	I	P	U
13.	A*	G	L	P	T
14.	A*	J	K	N	W
15.	A*	J	M	O	Q
16.	A*	K	N	Q	S

POWER NUMBER™ WHEEL 53224-1
Wheeling 24 Numbers in 17 games for a 3 of 5 Win

NUMBERS CORRECT***	MAXIMUM WINS				MINIMUM WINS			
	5x	4x	3x	2x	5x	4x	3x	2x
5 (w/o Jackpot)	0	3	1	1				
5	1	0	6	0	0	0	1	7
4	–	1	3	3	–	0	0	7
3	–	–	4	0	–	–	0	4
2	–	–	–	4	–	–	–	2

*** POWER NUMBER POSITION A* MUST BE A WINNER.

Your 24 Numbers to Wheel

A*	B	C	D	E	F	G	H	I	J	K	L
17	3	2	4	2	2	3	4	3	2	4	3

M	N	O	P	Q	R	S	T	U	V	W	X
3	2	3	4	3	3	3	2	2	3	4	4

The 17 Games to Play

1.	A*	B	D	L	X
2.	A*	B	H	O	W
3.	A*	B	K	P	V
4.	A*	C	G	M	S
5.	A*	C	I	Q	R
6.	A*	D	H	W	X
7.	A*	D	K	P	W
8.	A*	D	O	V	X
9.	A*	E	F	N	T

10.	A*	E	J	T	U
11.	A*	F	J	N	U
12.	A*	G	I	M	Q
13.	A*	G	Q	R	S
14.	A*	H	K	P	X
15.	A*	H	L	V	W
16.	A*	I	M	R	S
17.	A*	K	L	O	P

POWER NUMBER™ WHEEL 53225-1
Wheeling 25 Numbers in 19 games for a 3 of 5 Win

NUMBERS CORRECT***	MAXIMUM WINS				MINIMUM WINS			
	5x	4x	3x	2x	5x	4x	3x	2x
5 (w/o Jackpot)	0	3	1	1				
5	1	0	6	0	0	0	1	8
4	–	1	3	3	–	0	0	7
3	–	–	4	0	–	–	0	4
2	–	–	–	4	–	–	–	2

*** POWER NUMBER POSITION A* MUST BE A WINNER.

Your 25 Numbers to Wheel

A*	B	C	D	E	F	G	H	I
19	4	4	4	3	3	3	3	3

J	K	L	M	N	O	P	Q	R
3	3	3	3	3	3	3	3	3

S	T	U	V	W	X	Y
3	3	2	2	4	4	4

(Continued Next Page)

POWER NUMBER™ WHEEL 53225-1 (Continued from previous page)
The 19 Games to Play

1. A*	B	C	W	X
2. A*	B	D	X	Y
3. A*	B	E	P	W
4. A*	B	J	L	W
5. A*	C	D	W	Y
6. A*	C	E	J	X
7. A*	C	L	P	X
8. A*	D	E	L	Y
9. A*	D	J	P	Y
10. A*	F	I	N	O
11. A*	F	M	O	R
12. A*	F	N	R	V
13. A*	G	H	S	T
14. A*	G	K	Q	T
15. A*	G	K	S	U
16. A*	H	K	Q	S
17. A*	H	Q	T	U
18. A*	I	M	N	R
19. A*	I	M	O	V

Copyright © 1983-1998 Gail Howard

POWER NUMBER™ WHEEL 53226-1
Wheeling 26 Numbers in 21 games for a 3 of 5 Win

NUMBERS CORRECT***	MAXIMUM WINS				MINIMUM WINS			
	5x	4x	3x	2x	5x	4x	3x	2x
5 (w/o Jackpot)	0	4	0	1				
5	1	1	4	2	0	0	1	8
4	-	2	2	3	-	0	0	8
3	-	-	4	0	-	-	0	5
2	-	-	-	5	-	-	-	2

*** POWER NUMBER POSITION A* MUST BE A WINNER.

Your 26 Numbers to Wheel

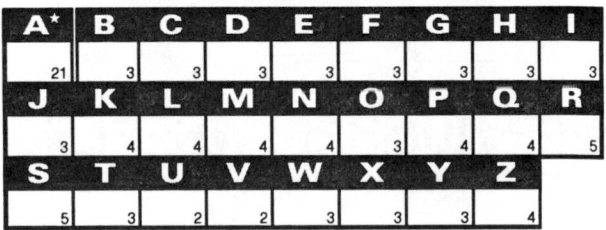

A*	B	C	D	E	F	G	H	I
21	3	3	3	3	3	3	3	3

J	K	L	M	N	O	P	Q	R
3	4	4	4	4	3	4	4	5

S	T	U	V	W	X	Y	Z
5	3	2	2	3	3	3	4

The 21 Games to Play

1. A*	B	C	W	Z
2. A*	B	D	W	Z
3. A*	B	U	V	W
4. A*	C	D	U	Z
5. A*	C	D	V	Z
6. A*	E	I	R	Y
7. A*	E	J	K	R
8. A*	E	L	Q	X
9. A*	F	G	N	S
10. A*	F	H	O	S
11. A*	F	M	P	T
12. A*	G	H	M	P
13. A*	G	O	S	T
14. A*	H	N	S	T
15. A*	I	J	L	Q
16. A*	I	K	R	X
17. A*	J	K	X	Y
18. A*	K	L	Q	R

Copyright © 1983-1998 Gail Howard

(Continued Next Page)

302

POWER NUMBER™ WHEEL 53226-1 (Continued from previous page)

19.	A*	L	Q	R	Y
20.	A*	M	N	O	P

21.	A*	M	N	P	S

POWER NUMBER™WHEEL 53230-1
Wheeling 30 Numbers in 26 games for a 3 of 5 Win

NUMBERS CORRECT***	MAXIMUM WINS				MINIMUM WINS			
	5x	4x	3x	2x	5x	4x	3x	2x
5 (w/o Jackpot)	0	4	0	4				
5	1	1	4	2	0	0	1	10
4	-	2	2	3	-	0	0	9
3	-	-	4	0	-	-	0	6
2	-	-	-	5	-	-	-	3

*** POWER NUMBER POSITION A* MUST BE A WINNER.

Your 30 Numbers to Wheel

A*	B	C	D	E	F	G	H	I	J
26	4	4	4	4	4	4	3	3	3

K	L	M	N	O	P	Q	R	S	T
4	3	3	3	3	3	3	3	3	3

U	V	W	X	Y	Z	AA	BB	CC	DD
3	4	5	4	4	4	4	4	4	4

The 26 Games to Play

#						#					
1.	A*	B	C	O	cc	14.	A*	E	P	V	Z
2.	A*	B	I	K	Y	15.	A*	F	H	S	bb
3.	A*	B	K	Q	dd	16.	A*	F	J	N	bb
4.	A*	B	M	Y	dd	17.	A*	F	U	W	bb
5.	A*	C	I	cc	dd	18.	A*	F	W	X	bb
6.	A*	C	K	M	cc	19.	A*	G	R	Z	aa
7.	A*	C	Q	Y	cc	20.	A*	H	J	W	X
8.	A*	D	E	R	V	21.	A*	H	N	U	X
9.	A*	D	G	L	Z	22.	A*	I	M	O	Q
10.	A*	D	G	P	aa	23.	A*	J	S	U	W
11.	A*	D	T	Z	aa	24.	A*	K	O	Y	dd
12.	A*	E	G	T	V	25.	A*	L	P	R	T
13.	A*	E	L	V	aa	26.	A*	N	S	W	X

303

POWER NUMBER™ WHEEL 53233-1
Wheeling 33 Numbers in 32 games for a 3 of 5 Win

NUMBERS CORRECT***	MAXIMUM WINS				MINIMUM WINS			
	5x	4x	3x	2x	5x	4x	3x	2x
5 (w/o Jackpot)	0	4	0	4				
5	1	0	5	7	0	0	1	11
4	–	1	5	3	–	0	0	10
3	–	–	4	3	–	–	0	6
2	–	–	–	6	–	–	–	3

*** POWER NUMBER POSITION A* MUST BE A WINNER.

Your 33 Numbers to Wheel

A*	B	C	D	E	F	G	H	I	J	K
32	5	4	3	4	5	3	6	3	5	3

L	M	N	O	P	Q	R	S	T	U	V
3	4	4	3	4	4	4	4	4	4	5

W	X	Y	Z	AA	BB	CC	DD	EE	FF	GG
4	5	4	4	4	4	3	4	3	5	4

The 32 Games to Play

#						#					
1.	A*	B	F	U	ff	17.	A*	F	J	W	ff
2.	A*	B	H	J	Q	18.	A*	F	Q	V	X
3.	A*	B	H	W	X	19.	A*	F	Q	dd	ff
4.	A*	B	J	bb	ff	20.	A*	G	I	L	ee
5.	A*	B	U	V	dd	21.	A*	H	J	U	X
6.	A*	C	E	I	S	22.	A*	H	V	X	ff
7.	A*	C	G	S	T	23.	A*	H	X	bb	dd
8.	A*	C	L	S	gg	24.	A*	I	T	Z	gg
9.	A*	C	S	Z	ee	25.	A*	J	V	W	dd
10.	A*	D	K	O	cc	26.	A*	K	M	N	P
11.	A*	D	M	N	aa	27.	A*	K	R	Y	aa
12.	A*	D	P	R	Y	28.	A*	M	N	O	R
13.	A*	E	G	Z	gg	29.	A*	M	N	Y	cc
14.	A*	E	L	T	Z	30.	A*	O	P	Y	aa
15.	A*	E	T	ee	gg	31.	A*	P	R	aa	cc
16.	A*	F	H	V	bb	32.	A*	Q	U	W	bb

POWER NUMBER™WHEEL 53235-1
Wheeling 35 Numbers in 37 games for a 3 of 5 Win

NUMBERS CORRECT***	MAXIMUM WINS				MINIMUM WINS			
	5x	4x	3x	2x	5x	4x	3x	2x
5 (w/o Jackpot)	0	4	1	6				
5	1	1	3	7	0	0	1	12
4	–	2	3	4	–	0	0	11
3	–	–	5	0	–	–	0	7
2	–	–	–	6	–	–	–	3

*** POWER NUMBER POSITION A* MUST BE A WINNER.

Your 35 Numbers to Wheel

A*	B	C	D	E	F	G	H	I	J	K	L
37	5	6	4	4	5	5	5	4	5	5	3

M	N	O	P	Q	R	S	T	U	V	W	X
4	3	4	4	4	4	4	4	5	4	5	3

Y	Z	AA	BB	CC	DD	EE	FF	GG	HH	II
5	4	4	4	5	4	5	5	5	3	5

The 37 Games to Play

#						#					
1.	A*	B	G	I	ee	20.	A*	F	H	U	Z
2.	A*	B	I	M	ii	21.	A*	F	P	Q	U
3.	A*	B	J	W	cc	22.	A*	F	U	V	aa
4.	A*	B	S	bb	ii	23.	A*	G	J	ee	gg
5.	A*	B	cc	gg	ii	24.	A*	G	M	bb	ee
6.	A*	C	F	U	Y	25.	A*	G	S	cc	ee
7.	A*	C	H	P	Y	26.	A*	G	W	gg	ii
8.	A*	C	H	Q	V	27.	A*	I	J	S	W
9.	A*	C	H	Y	aa	28.	A*	I	bb	cc	gg
10.	A*	C	K	Z	ff	29.	A*	J	M	W	bb
11.	A*	C	V	Y	Z	30.	A*	J	W	ee	ii
12.	A*	D	E	N	dd	31.	A*	K	P	V	ff
13.	A*	D	L	R	dd	32.	A*	K	Q	Y	ff
14.	A*	D	O	dd	hh	33.	A*	K	U	aa	ff
15.	A*	D	T	X	dd	34.	A*	L	N	X	hh
16.	A*	E	L	O	T	35.	A*	M	S	cc	gg
17.	A*	E	O	R	X	36.	A*	N	O	R	T
18.	A*	E	R	T	hh	37.	A*	P	Q	Z	aa
19.	A*	F	H	K	ff						

Copyright © 1983-1998 Gail Howard

POWER NUMBER™ WHEEL 53239-1
Wheeling 39 Numbers in 47 games for a 3 of 5 Win

NUMBERS CORRECT***	MAXIMUM WINS				MINIMUM WINS			
	5x	4x	3x	2x	5x	4x	3x	2x
5 (w/o Jackpot)	0	4	0	4				
5	1	1	4	11	0	0	1	13
4	–	2	2	10	–	0	0	12
3	–	–	4	6	–	–	0	7
2	–	–	–	7	–	–	–	3

*** POWER NUMBER POSITION A* MUST BE A WINNER.

Your 39 Numbers to Wheel

A*	B	C	D	E	F	G	H	I	J
47	3	6	4	4	4	6	5	3	6

K	L	M	N	O	P	Q	R	S	T
6	6	4	6	6	5	5	3	5	5

U	V	W	X	Y	Z	AA	BB	CC	DD
7	5	7	4	4	6	6	5	5	4

EE	FF	GG	HH	II	JJ	KK	LL	MM
5	6	4	5	6	3	4	4	6

The 47 Games to Play

#						#				
1.	A*	B	D	F	ii	21.	A*	G	L	N	Z
2.	A*	B	I	R	jj	22.	A*	G	L	O	mm
3.	A*	B	X	Y	dd	23.	A*	G	bb	ff	ii
4.	A*	C	G	U	aa	24.	A*	H	M	hh	kk
5.	A*	C	J	cc	mm	25.	A*	H	P	T	hh
6.	A*	C	K	L	U	26.	A*	H	Q	S	ee
7.	A*	C	N	bb	mm	27.	A*	H	S	V	hh
8.	A*	C	O	U	W	28.	A*	J	K	O	bb
9.	A*	C	Z	ff	ii	29.	A*	J	K	Z	mm
10.	A*	D	F	R	Y	30.	A*	J	L	W	ff
11.	A*	D	I	Y	ii	31.	A*	J	N	U	ii
12.	A*	D	X	dd	jj	32.	A*	K	N	W	ii
13.	A*	E	H	gg	hh	33.	A*	K	aa	ii	mm
14.	A*	E	M	S	T	34.	A*	L	O	cc	ii
15.	A*	E	P	Q	kk	35.	A*	L	Z	aa	bb
16.	A*	E	P	V	ee	36.	A*	M	P	Q	gg
17.	A*	F	I	X	dd	37.	A*	M	V	ee	kk
18.	A*	F	Y	jj	ii	38.	A*	N	O	aa	ff
19.	A*	G	J	W	aa	39.	A*	N	Z	aa	cc
20.	A*	G	K	cc	ff	40.	A*	O	U	W	Z

(Continued Next Page)

POWER NUMBER™ WHEEL 53239-1 (Continued from previous page)

41.	A*	P	Q	S	T	45.	A*	T	V	ee	gg
42.	A*	Q	V	ee	hh	46.	A*	U	W	bb	cc
43.	A*	R	X	dd	ll	47.	A*	U	W	ff	mm
44.	A*	S	T	gg	kk						

POWER NUMBER™WHEEL 55006-2
Wheeling 6 Numbers in 4 games for a 5 of 5 Win

NUMBERS CORRECT***	MAXIMUM WINS				MINIMUM WINS			
	5x	4x	3x	2x	5x	4x	3x	2x
5 (w/o Jackpot)	0	0	0	0				
5	1	3	0	0	1	3	0	0
4	-	2	2	0	-	2	2	0
3	-	-	3	1	-	-	3	1
2	-	-	-	4	-	-	-	4

*** POWER NUMBER POSITIONS A* & B* MUST BE WINNERS.

Your 6 Numbers to Wheel

A*	B*	C	D	E	F
4	4	3	3	3	3

The 4 Games to Play

1.	A*	B*	C	D	E
2.	A*	B*	C	D	F
3.	A*	B*	C	E	F
4.	A*	B*	D	E	F

POWER NUMBER™WHEEL 55007-2
Wheeling 7 Numbers in 10 games for a 5 of 5 Win

NUMBERS CORRECT***	MAXIMUM WINS				MINIMUM WINS			
	5x	4x	3x	2x	5x	4x	3x	2x
5 (w/o Jackpot)	0	0	0	0				
5	1	6	3	0	1	6	3	0
4	-	3	6	1	-	3	6	1
3	-	-	6	4	-	-	6	4
2	-	-	-	10	-	-	-	10

*** POWER NUMBER POSITIONS A* & B* MUST BE WINNERS.

Your 7 Numbers to Wheel

A*	B*	C	D	E	F	G
10	10	6	6	6	6	6

The 10 Games to Play

1.	A*	B*	C	D	E
2.	A*	B*	C	D	F
3.	A*	B*	C	D	G
4.	A*	B*	C	E	F
5.	A*	B*	C	E	G
6.	A*	B*	C	F	G
7.	A*	B*	D	E	F
8.	A*	B*	D	E	G
9.	A*	B*	D	F	G
10.	A*	B*	E	F	G

POWER NUMBER™WHEEL 55008-2
Wheeling 8 Numbers in 20 games for a 5 of 5 Win

NUMBERS CORRECT***	MAXIMUM WINS				MINIMUM WINS			
	5x	4x	3x	2x	5x	4x	3x	2x
5 (w/o Jackpot)	0	0	0	0				
5	1	9	9	1	1	9	9	1
4	–	4	12	4	–	4	12	4
3	–	–	10	10	–	–	10	10
2	–	–	–	20	–	–	–	20

*** POWER NUMBER POSITIONS A* & B* MUST BE WINNERS.

Your 8 Numbers to Wheel

A*	B*	C	D	E	F	G	H
20	20	10	10	10	10	10	10

The 20 Games to Play

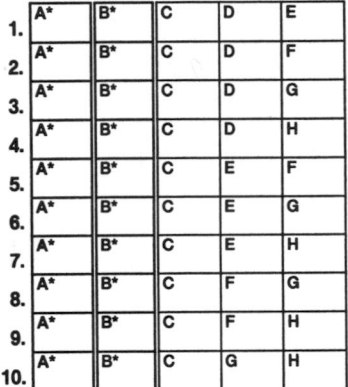

1.	A*	B*	C	D	E	11.	A*	B*	D	E	F
2.	A*	B*	C	D	F	12.	A*	B*	D	E	G
3.	A*	B*	C	D	G	13.	A*	B*	D	E	H
4.	A*	B*	C	D	H	14.	A*	B*	D	F	G
5.	A*	B*	C	E	F	15.	A*	B*	D	F	H
6.	A*	B*	C	E	G	16.	A*	B*	D	G	H
7.	A*	B*	C	E	H	17.	A*	B*	E	F	G
8.	A*	B*	C	F	G	18.	A*	B*	E	F	H
9.	A*	B*	C	F	H	19.	A*	B*	E	G	H
10.	A*	B*	C	G	H	20.	A*	B*	F	G	H

POWER NUMBER™WHEEL 55009-2
Wheeling 9 Numbers in 35 games for a 5 of 5 Win

NUMBERS CORRECT***	MAXIMUM WINS				MINIMUM WINS			
	5x	4x	3x	2x	5x	4x	3x	2x
5 (w/o Jackpot)	0	0	0	0				
5	1	12	18	4	1	12	18	4
4	–	5	20	10	–	5	20	10
3	–	–	15	20	–	–	15	20
2	–	–	–	35	–	–	–	35

*** POWER NUMBER POSITIONS A* & B* MUST BE WINNERS.

Your 9 Numbers to Wheel

A*	B*	C	D	E	F	G	H	I
35	35	15	15	15	15	15	15	15

The 35 Games to Play

1.	A*	B*	C	D	E	5.	A*	B*	C	D	I
2.	A*	B*	C	D	F	6.	A*	B*	C	E	F
3.	A*	B*	C	D	G	7.	A*	B*	C	E	G
4.	A*	B*	C	D	H	8.	A*	B*	C	E	H

 (Continued Next Page)

POWER NUMBER™ WHEEL 55009-2 (Continued from previous page)

#						#					
9.	A*	B*	C	E	I	23.	A*	B*	D	G	H
10.	A*	B*	C	F	G	24.	A*	B*	D	G	I
11.	A*	B*	C	F	H	25.	A*	B*	D	H	I
12.	A*	B*	C	F	I	26.	A*	B*	E	F	G
13.	A*	B*	C	G	H	27.	A*	B*	E	F	H
14.	A*	B*	C	G	I	28.	A*	B*	E	F	I
15.	A*	B*	C	H	I	29.	A*	B*	E	G	H
16.	A*	B*	D	E	F	30.	A*	B*	E	G	I
17.	A*	B*	D	E	G	31.	A*	B*	E	H	I
18.	A*	B*	D	E	H	32.	A*	B*	F	G	H
19.	A*	B*	D	E	I	33.	A*	B*	F	G	I
20.	A*	B*	D	F	G	34.	A*	B*	F	H	I
21.	A*	B*	D	F	H	35.	A*	B*	G	H	I
22.	A*	B*	D	F	I						

POWER NUMBER™ WHEEL 55010-2
Wheeling 10 Numbers in 56 games for a 5 of 5 Win

NUMBERS CORRECT***	MAXIMUM WINS				MINIMUM WINS			
	5x	4x	3x	2x	5x	4x	3x	2x
5 (w/o Jackpot)	0	0	0	0				
5	1	15	30	10	1	15	30	10
4	–	6	30	20	–	6	30	20
3	–	–	21	35	–	–	21	35
2	–	–	–	56	–	–	–	56

*** POWER NUMBER POSITIONS A* & B* MUST BE WINNERS.

Your 10 Numbers to Wheel

A*	B*	C	D	E	F	G	H	I	J
56	56	21	21	21	21	21	21	21	

The 56 Games to Play

#						#					
1.	A*	B*	C	D	E	11.	A*	B*	C	E	J
2.	A*	B*	C	D	F	12.	A*	B*	C	F	G
3.	A*	B*	C	D	G	13.	A*	B*	C	F	H
4.	A*	B*	C	D	H	14.	A*	B*	C	F	I
5.	A*	B*	C	D	I	15.	A*	B*	C	F	J
6.	A*	B*	C	D	J	16.	A*	B*	C	G	H
7.	A*	B*	C	E	F	17.	A*	B*	C	G	I
8.	A*	B*	C	E	G	18.	A*	B*	C	G	J
9.	A*	B*	C	E	H	19.	A*	B*	C	H	I
10.	A*	B*	C	E	I	20.	A*	B*	C	H	J

(Continued Next Page)

POWER NUMBER™ WHEEL 55010-2 (Continued from previous page)

#						#					
21.	A*	B*	C	I	J	39.	A*	B*	E	F	I
22.	A*	B*	D	E	F	40.	A*	B*	E	F	J
23.	A*	B*	D	E	G	41.	A*	B*	E	G	H
24.	A*	B*	D	E	H	42.	A*	B*	E	G	I
25.	A*	B*	D	E	I	43.	A*	B*	E	G	J
26.	A*	B*	D	E	J	44.	A*	B*	E	H	I
27.	A*	B*	D	F	G	45.	A*	B*	E	H	J
28.	A*	B*	D	F	H	46.	A*	B*	E	I	J
29.	A*	B*	D	F	I	47.	A*	B*	F	G	H
30.	A*	B*	D	F	J	48.	A*	B*	F	G	I
31.	A*	B*	D	G	H	49.	A*	B*	F	G	J
32.	A*	B*	D	G	I	50.	A*	B*	F	H	I
33.	A*	B*	D	G	J	51.	A*	B*	F	H	J
34.	A*	B*	D	H	I	52.	A*	B*	F	I	J
35.	A*	B*	D	H	J	53.	A*	B*	G	H	I
36.	A*	B*	D	I	J	54.	A*	B*	G	H	J
37.	A*	B*	E	F	G	55.	A*	B*	G	I	J
38.	A*	B*	E	F	H	56.	A*	B*	H	I	J

Copyright © 1983-1998 Gail Howard

POWER NUMBER™WHEEL 55011-2
Wheeling 11 Numbers in 84 games for a 5 of 5 Win

NUMBERS CORRECT***	MAXIMUM WINS				MINIMUM WINS			
	5x	4x	3x	2x	5x	4x	3x	2x
5 (w/o Jackpot)	0	0	0	0				
5	1	18	45	20	1	18	45	20
4	–	7	42	35	–	7	42	35
3	–	–	28	56	–	–	28	56
2	–	–	–	84	–	–	–	84

*** POWER NUMBER POSITIONS A* & B* MUST BE WINNERS.

Your 11 Numbers to Wheel

A*	B*	C	D	E	F	G	H	I	J	K
84	84	28	28	28	28	28	28	28	28	28

The 84 Games to Play

#						#					
1.	A*	B*	C	D	E	7.	A*	B*	C	D	K
2.	A*	B*	C	D	F	8.	A*	B*	C	E	F
3.	A*	B*	C	D	G	9.	A*	B*	C	E	G
4.	A*	B*	C	D	H	10.	A*	B*	C	E	H
5.	A*	B*	C	D	I	11.	A*	B*	C	E	I
6.	A*	B*	C	D	J	12.	A*	B*	C	E	J

Copyright © 1983-1998 Gail Howard

(Continued Next Page)

POWER NUMBER™ WHEEL 55011-2 (Continued from previous page)

#						#					
13.	A*	B*	C	E	K	48.	A*	B*	D	I	K
14.	A*	B*	C	F	G	49.	A*	B*	D	J	K
15.	A*	B*	C	F	H	50.	A*	B*	E	F	G
16.	A*	B*	C	F	I	51.	A*	B*	E	F	H
17.	A*	B*	C	F	J	52.	A*	B*	E	F	I
18.	A*	B*	C	F	K	53.	A*	B*	E	F	J
19.	A*	B*	C	G	H	54.	A*	B*	E	F	K
20.	A*	B*	C	G	I	55.	A*	B*	E	G	H
21.	A*	B*	C	G	J	56.	A*	B*	E	G	I
22.	A*	B*	C	G	K	57.	A*	B*	E	G	J
23.	A*	B*	C	H	I	58.	A*	B*	E	G	K
24.	A*	B*	C	H	J	59.	A*	B*	E	H	I
25.	A*	B*	C	H	K	60.	A*	B*	E	H	J
26.	A*	B*	C	I	J	61.	A*	B*	E	H	K
27.	A*	B*	C	I	K	62.	A*	B*	E	I	J
28.	A*	B*	C	J	K	63.	A*	B*	E	I	K
29.	A*	B*	D	E	F	64.	A*	B*	E	J	K
30.	A*	B*	D	E	G	65.	A*	B*	F	G	H
31.	A*	B*	D	E	H	66.	A*	B*	F	G	I
32.	A*	B*	D	E	I	67.	A*	B*	F	G	J
33.	A*	B*	D	E	J	68.	A*	B*	F	G	K
34.	A*	B*	D	E	K	69.	A*	B*	F	H	I
35.	A*	B*	D	F	G	70.	A*	B*	F	H	J
36.	A*	B*	D	F	H	71.	A*	B*	F	H	K
37.	A*	B*	D	F	I	72.	A*	B*	F	I	J
38.	A*	B*	D	F	J	73.	A*	B*	F	I	K
39.	A*	B*	D	F	K	74.	A*	B*	F	J	K
40.	A*	B*	D	G	H	75.	A*	B*	G	H	I
41.	A*	B*	D	G	I	76.	A*	B*	G	H	J
42.	A*	B*	D	G	J	77.	A*	B*	G	H	K
43.	A*	B*	D	G	K	78.	A*	B*	G	I	J
44.	A*	B*	D	H	I	79.	A*	B*	G	I	K
45.	A*	B*	D	H	J	80.	A*	B*	G	J	K
46.	A*	B*	D	H	K	81.	A*	B*	H	I	J
47.	A*	B*	D	I	J	82.	A*	B*	H	I	K

(Continued Next Page)

POWER NUMBER™ WHEEL 55011-2 (Continued from previous page)

83.

A*	B*	H	J	K

84.

A*	B*	I	J	K

POWER NUMBER™ WHEEL 55012-2
Wheeling 12 Numbers in 120 games for a 5 of 5 Win

NUMBERS CORRECT***	MAXIMUM WINS				MINIMUM WINS			
	5x	4x	3x	2x	5x	4x	3x	2x
5 (w/o Jackpot)	0	0	0	0				
5	1	21	63	35	1	21	63	35
4	–	8	56	56	–	8	56	56
3	–	–	36	84	–	–	36	84
2	–	–	–	120	–	–	–	120

*** POWER NUMBER POSITIONS A* & B* MUST BE WINNERS.

Your 12 Numbers to Wheel

A*	B*	C	D	E	F	G	H	I	J	K	L
120	120	36	36	36	36	36	36	36	36	36	36

The 120 Games to Play

1.

A*	B*	C	D	E

2.

A*	B*	C	D	F

3.

A*	B*	C	D	G

4.

A*	B*	C	D	H

5.

A*	B*	C	D	I

6.

A*	B*	C	D	J

7.

A*	B*	C	D	K

8.

A*	B*	C	D	L

9.

A*	B*	C	E	F

10.

A*	B*	C	E	G

11.

A*	B*	C	E	H

12.

A*	B*	C	E	I

13.

A*	B*	C	E	J

14.

A*	B*	C	E	K

15.

A*	B*	C	E	L

16.

A*	B*	C	F	G

17.

A*	B*	C	F	H

18.

A*	B*	C	F	I

19.

A*	B*	C	F	J

20.

A*	B*	C	F	K

21.

A*	B*	C	F	L

22.

A*	B*	C	G	H

23.

A*	B*	C	G	I

24.

A*	B*	C	G	J

25.

A*	B*	C	G	K

26.

A*	B*	C	G	L

27.

A*	B*	C	H	I

28.

A*	B*	C	H	J

29.

A*	B*	C	H	K

30.

A*	B*	C	H	L

31.

A*	B*	C	I	J

32.

A*	B*	C	I	K

33.

A*	B*	C	I	L

34.

A*	B*	C	J	K

35.

A*	B*	C	J	L

36.

A*	B*	C	K	L

37.

A*	B*	D	E	F

38.

A*	B*	D	E	G

39.

A*	B*	D	E	H

40.

A*	B*	D	E	I

41.

A*	B*	D	E	J

42.

A*	B*	D	E	K

43.

A*	B*	D	E	L

44.

A*	B*	D	F	G

45.

A*	B*	D	F	H

46.

A*	B*	D	F	I

 (Continued Next Page)

POWER NUMBER™ WHEEL 55012-2 (Continued from previous page)

#						#					
47.	A*	B*	D	F	J	82.	A*	B*	E	I	L
48.	A*	B*	D	F	K	83.	A*	B*	E	J	K
49.	A*	B*	D	F	L	84.	A*	B*	E	J	L
50.	A*	B*	D	G	H	85.	A*	B*	E	K	L
51.	A*	B*	D	G	I	86.	A*	B*	F	G	H
52.	A*	B*	D	G	J	87.	A*	B*	F	G	I
53.	A*	B*	D	G	K	88.	A*	B*	F	G	J
54.	A*	B*	D	G	L	89.	A*	B*	F	G	K
55.	A*	B*	D	H	I	90.	A*	B*	F	G	L
56.	A*	B*	D	H	J	91.	A*	B*	F	H	I
57.	A*	B*	D	H	K	92.	A*	B*	F	H	J
58.	A*	B*	D	H	L	93.	A*	B*	F	H	K
59.	A*	B*	D	I	J	94.	A*	B*	F	H	L
60.	A*	B*	D	I	K	95.	A*	B*	F	I	J
61.	A*	B*	D	I	L	96.	A*	B*	F	I	K
62.	A*	B*	D	J	K	97.	A*	B*	F	I	L
63.	A*	B*	D	J	L	98.	A*	B*	F	J	K
64.	A*	B*	D	K	L	99.	A*	B*	F	J	L
65.	A*	B*	E	F	G	100.	A*	B*	F	K	L
66.	A*	B*	E	F	H	101.	A*	B*	G	H	I
67.	A*	B*	E	F	I	102.	A*	B*	G	H	J
68.	A*	B*	E	F	J	103.	A*	B*	G	H	K
69.	A*	B*	E	F	K	104.	A*	B*	G	H	L
70.	A*	B*	E	F	L	105.	A*	B*	G	I	J
71.	A*	B*	E	G	H	106.	A*	B*	G	I	K
72.	A*	B*	E	G	I	107.	A*	B*	G	I	L
73.	A*	B*	E	G	J	108.	A*	B*	G	J	K
74.	A*	B*	E	G	K	109.	A*	B*	G	J	L
75.	A*	B*	E	G	L	110.	A*	B*	G	K	L
76.	A*	B*	E	H	I	111.	A*	B*	H	I	J
77.	A*	B*	E	H	J	112.	A*	B*	H	I	K
78.	A*	B*	E	H	K	113.	A*	B*	H	I	L
79.	A*	B*	E	H	L	114.	A*	B*	H	J	K
80.	A*	B*	E	I	J	115.	A*	B*	H	J	L
81.	A*	B*	E	I	K	116.	A*	B*	H	K	L

            (Continued Next Page)

POWER NUMBER™ WHEEL 55012-2 (Continued from previous page)

117.	A*	B*	I	J	K

118.	A*	B*	I	J	L

119.	A*	B*	I	K	L

120.	A*	B*	J	K	L

POWER NUMBER™WHEEL 54006-2
Wheeling 6 Numbers in 3 games for a 4 of 4 Win

NUMBERS CORRECT***	MAXIMUM WINS				MINIMUM WINS			
	5x	4x	3x	2x	5x	4x	3x	2x
5 (w/o Jackpot)	0	3	0	0				
5	1	2	0	0	0	3	0	0
4	–	2	1	0	–	1	2	0
3	–	–	3	0	–	–	2	1
2	–	–	–	3	–	–	–	3

*** POWER NUMBER POSITIONS A* & B* MUST BE WINNERS.

Your 6 Numbers to Wheel

A*	B*	C	D	E	F
3	3	3	2	2	2

The 3 Games to Play

1.	A*	B*	C	D	E

2.	A*	B*	C	D	F

3.	A*	B*	C	E	F

POWER NUMBER™WHEEL 54007-2
Wheeling 7 Numbers in 4 games for a 4 of 4 Win

NUMBERS CORRECT***	MAXIMUM WINS				MINIMUM WINS			
	5x	4x	3x	2x	5x	4x	3x	2x
5 (w/o Jackpot)	0	3	1	0				
5	1	2	1	0	0	3	1	0
4	–	3	0	1	–	1	2	1
3	–	–	3	1	–	–	2	2
2	–	–	–	4	–	–	–	4

*** POWER NUMBER POSITIONS A* & B* MUST BE WINNERS.

Your 7 Numbers to Wheel

A*	B*	C	D	E	F	G
4	4	3	2	2	2	3

The 4 Games to Play

1.	A*	B*	C	D	G

2.	A*	B*	C	E	G

3.	A*	B*	C	F	G

4.	A*	B*	D	E	F

POWER NUMBER™ WHEEL 54008-2
Wheeling 8 Numbers in 6 games for a 4 of 4 Win

NUMBERS CORRECT***	MAXIMUM WINS				MINIMUM WINS			
	5x	4x	3x	2x	5x	4x	3x	2x
5 (w/o Jackpot)	0	4	1	1				
5	1	1	4	0	0	3	3	0
4	–	2	2	2	–	1	4	1
3	–	–	3	3	–	–	3	3
2	–	–	–	6	–	–	–	6

*** POWER NUMBER POSITIONS A* & B* MUST BE WINNERS.

Your 8 Numbers to Wheel

A*	B*	C	D	E	F	G	H
6	6	3	3	3	3	3	3

The 6 Games to Play

1. | A* | B* | C | D | G |

2. | A* | B* | C | E | F |

3. | A* | B* | C | G | H |

4. | A* | B* | D | E | H |

5. | A* | B* | D | F | H |

6. | A* | B* | E | F | G |

Copyright © 1983-1998 Gail Howard

POWER NUMBER™ WHEEL 54009-2
Wheeling 9 Numbers in 7 games for a 4 of 4 Win

NUMBERS CORRECT***	MAXIMUM WINS				MINIMUM WINS			
	5x	4x	3x	2x	5x	4x	3x	2x
5 (w/o Jackpot)	0	3	3	1				
5	1	0	6	0	0	3	3	1
4	–	1	4	2	–	1	4	2
3	–	–	3	4	–	–	3	4
2	–	–	–	7	–	–	–	7

*** POWER NUMBER POSITIONS A* & B* MUST BE WINNERS.

Your 9 Numbers to Wheel

A*	B*	C	D	E	F	G	H	I
7	7	3	3	3	3	3	3	3

The 7 Games to Play

1. | A* | B* | C | D | I |

2. | A* | B* | C | E | G |

3. | A* | B* | C | F | H |

4. | A* | B* | D | E | F |

5. | A* | B* | D | G | H |

6. | A* | B* | E | H | I |

7. | A* | B* | F | G | I |

Copyright © 1983-1998 Gail Howard

POWER NUMBER™ WHEEL 54010-2
Wheeling 10 Numbers in 11 games for a 4 of 4 Win

NUMBERS CORRECT***	MAXIMUM WINS 5x	4x	3x	2x	MINIMUM WINS 5x	4x	3x	2x
5 (w/o Jackpot)	0	5	3	3				
5	1	2	6	2	0	3	6	2
4	–	2	5	4	–	1	6	4
3	–	–	5	6	–	–	4	7
2	–	–	–	11	–	–	–	11

*** POWER NUMBER POSITIONS A* & B* MUST BE WINNERS.

Your 10 Numbers to Wheel

A*	B*	C	D	E	F	G	H	I	J
11	11	4	4	4	4	4	4	4	5

The 11 Games to Play

1. A* B* C D J
2. A* B* C E H
3. A* B* C F I
4. A* B* C G J
5. A* B* D E G
6. A* B* D F H
7. A* B* D I J
8. A* B* E F G
9. A* B* E I J
10. A* B* F H J
11. A* B* G H I

Copyright © 1983-1998 Gail Howard

POWER NUMBER™ WHEEL 54011-2
Wheeling 11 Numbers in 12 games for a 4 of 4 Win

NUMBERS CORRECT***	MAXIMUM WINS 5x	4x	3x	2x	MINIMUM WINS 5x	4x	3x	2x
5 (w/o Jackpot)	0	3	6	3				
5	1	0	9	2	0	3	6	3
4	–	1	6	5	–	1	6	5
3	–	–	4	8	–	–	4	8
2	–	–	–	12	–	–	–	12

*** POWER NUMBER POSITIONS A* & B* MUST BE WINNERS.

Your 11 Numbers to Wheel

A*	B*	C	D	E	F	G	H	I	J	K
12	12	4	4	4	4	4	4	4	4	4

The 12 Games to Play

1. A* B* C D I
2. A* B* C E K
3. A* B* C F G
4. A* B* C H J
5. A* B* D E G
6. A* B* D F H
7. A* B* D J K
8. A* B* E F J
9. A* B* E H I
10. A* B* F I K
11. A* B* G H K
12. A* B* G I J

Copyright © 1983-1998 Gail Howard

POWER NUMBER™WHEEL 54012-2
Wheeling 12 Numbers in 17 games for a 4 of 4 Win

NUMBERS CORRECT***	MAXIMUM WINS				MINIMUM WINS			
	5x	4x	3x	2x	5x	4x	3x	2x
5 (w/o Jackpot)	0	5	6	6				
5	1	2	9	5	0	3	9	5
4	–	2	7	8	–	1	8	8
3	–	–	6	11	–	–	5	12
2	–	–	–	17	–	–	–	17

*** POWER NUMBER POSITIONS A* & B* MUST BE WINNERS.

Your 12 Numbers to Wheel

A*	B*	C	D	E	F	G	H	I	J	K	L
17	17	5	5	5	5	5	5	5	5	5	6

The 17 Games to Play

1.	A*	B*	C	D	J		10.	A*	B*	E	F	L
2.	A*	B*	C	E	J		11.	A*	B*	E	G	H
3.	A*	B*	C	F	H		12.	A*	B*	E	H	K
4.	A*	B*	C	G	I		13.	A*	B*	F	I	K
5.	A*	B*	C	K	L		14.	A*	B*	F	J	L
6.	A*	B*	D	E	I		15.	A*	B*	G	I	L
7.	A*	B*	D	F	G		16.	A*	B*	G	J	K
8.	A*	B*	D	H	L		17.	A*	B*	H	I	J
9.	A*	B*	D	K	L							

Copyright © 1983-1998 Gail Howard

POWER NUMBER™WHEEL 54013-2
Wheeling 13 Numbers in 21 games for a 4 of 4 Win

NUMBERS CORRECT***	MAXIMUM WINS				MINIMUM WINS			
	5x	4x	3x	2x	5x	4x	3x	2x
5 (w/o Jackpot)	0	7	7	7				
5	1	4	8	8	0	3	9	9
4	–	5	4	12	–	1	8	12
3	–	–	7	14	–	–	5	16
2	–	–	–	21	–	–	–	21

*** POWER NUMBER POSITIONS A* & B* MUST BE WINNERS.

Your 13 Numbers to Wheel

A*	B*	C	D	E	F	G
21	21	5	5	7	5	7

H	I	J	K	L	M
5	5	5	7	5	7

The 21 Games to Play

1.	A*	B*	C	D	L		4.	A*	B*	C	G	K
2.	A*	B*	C	E	M		5.	A*	B*	C	H	J
3.	A*	B*	C	F	I		6.	A*	B*	D	E	K

Copyright © 1983-1998 Gail Howard   (Continued Next Page)

POWER NUMBER™ WHEEL 54013-2 (Continued from previous page)

	A*	B*	D	F	H
7.					

	A*	B*	D	G	M
8.					

	A*	B*	D	I	J
9.					

	A*	B*	E	F	G
10.					

	A*	B*	E	H	M
11.					

	A*	B*	E	I	M
12.					

	A*	B*	E	J	M
13.					

	A*	B*	E	L	M
14.					

	A*	B*	F	J	L
15.					

	A*	B*	F	K	M
16.					

	A*	B*	G	H	K
17.					

	A*	B*	G	I	K
18.					

	A*	B*	G	J	K
19.					

	A*	B*	G	K	L
20.					

	A*	B*	H	I	L
21.					

POWER NUMBER™WHEEL 54014-2
Wheeling 14 Numbers in 24 games for a 4 of 4 Win

NUMBERS CORRECT***	MAXIMUM WINS				MINIMUM WINS			
	5x	4x	3x	2x	5x	4x	3x	2x
5 (w/o Jackpot)	0	4	10	10				
5	1	1	13	9	0	3	12	9
4	–	2	8	14	–	1	10	13
3	–	–	6	18	–	–	6	18
2	–	–	–	24	–	–	–	24

*** POWER NUMBER POSITIONS A* & B* MUST BE WINNERS.

Your 14 Numbers to Wheel

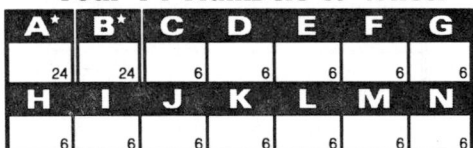

A*	B*	C	D	E	F	G
24	24	6	6	6	6	6
H	I	J	K	L	M	N
6	6	6	6	6	6	6

The 24 Games to Play

	A*	B*	C	D	L
1.					

	A*	B*	C	E	N
2.					

	A*	B*	C	F	K
3.					

	A*	B*	C	G	J
4.					

	A*	B*	C	H	I
5.					

	A*	B*	C	M	N
6.					

	A*	B*	D	E	J
7.					

	A*	B*	D	F	M
8.					

	A*	B*	D	G	N
9.					

	A*	B*	D	H	L
10.					

	A*	B*	D	I	K
11.					

	A*	B*	E	F	M
12.					

	A*	B*	E	G	H
13.					

	A*	B*	E	G	K
14.					

	A*	B*	E	I	L
15.					

	A*	B*	F	G	I
16.					

	A*	B*	F	H	J
17.					

	A*	B*	F	L	N
18.					

	A*	B*	G	L	M
19.					

	A*	B*	H	J	M
20.					

	A*	B*	H	K	N
21.					

	A*	B*	I	J	N
22.					

	A*	B*	I	K	M
23.					

	A*	B*	J	K	L
24.					

POWER NUMBER™WHEEL 54015-2
Wheeling 15 Numbers in 28 games for a 4 of 4 Win

NUMBERS CORRECT***	MAXIMUM WINS				MINIMUM WINS			
	5x	4x	3x	2x	5x	4x	3x	2x
5 (w/o Jackpot)	0	7	9	12				
5	1	4	12	11	0	3	12	13
4	–	3	10	15	–	1	10	17
3	–	–	8	20	–	–	6	22
2	–	–	–	28	–	–	–	28

*** POWER NUMBER POSITIONS A* & B* MUST BE WINNERS.

Your 15 Numbers to Wheel

A*	B*	C	D	E	F	G	H
28	28	6	6	8	7	6	6

I	J	K	L	M	N	O	
0	7	0	0	8	8	8	

The 28 Games to Play

	A*	B*	C	D	L
1.	A*	B*	C	D	L
2.	A*	B*	C	E	N
3.	A*	B*	C	F	J
4.	A*	B*	C	G	K
5.	A*	B*	C	H	O
6.	A*	B*	C	I	M
7.	A*	B*	D	E	J
8.	A*	B*	D	F	K
9.	A*	B*	D	G	O
10.	A*	B*	D	H	I
11.	A*	B*	D	M	N
12.	A*	B*	E	F	H
13.	A*	B*	E	G	M
14.	A*	B*	E	I	J
15.	A*	B*	E	J	O
16.	A*	B*	E	K	O
17.	A*	B*	E	L	O
18.	A*	B*	F	G	L
19.	A*	B*	F	I	O
20.	A*	B*	F	M	O
21.	A*	B*	F	N	O
22.	A*	B*	G	H	J
23.	A*	B*	G	I	N
24.	A*	B*	H	K	M
25.	A*	B*	H	L	N
26.	A*	B*	I	K	L
27.	A*	B*	J	K	N
28.	A*	B*	J	L	M

Copyright © 1983-1998 Gail Howard

POWER NUMBER™WHEEL 54016-2
Wheeling 16 Numbers in 33 games for a 4 of 4 Win

NUMBERS CORRECT***	MAXIMUM WINS				MINIMUM WINS			
	5x	4x	3x	2x	5x	4x	3x	2x
5 (w/o Jackpot)	0	5	12	16				
5	1	2	15	15	0	3	15	15
4	–	2	11	20	–	1	12	20
3	–	–	8	25	–	–	7	26
2	–	–	–	33	–	–	–	33

*** POWER NUMBER POSITIONS A* & B* MUST BE WINNERS.

(Continued Next Page)

POWER NUMBER™ WHEEL 54016-2 (Continued from previous page)
Your 16 Numbers to Wheel

A*	B*	C	D	E	F	G	H
33	33	7	7	7	7	7	7

I	J	K	L	M	N	O	P
7	7	7	7	7	7	8	7

The 33 Games to Play

#						#					
1.	A*	B*	C	D	L	18.	A*	B*	F	G	N
2.	A*	B*	C	E	M	19.	A*	B*	F	H	I
3.	A*	B*	C	F	K	20.	A*	B*	F	J	L
4.	A*	B*	C	G	I	21.	A*	B*	F	M	O
5.	A*	B*	C	H	N	22.	A*	B*	G	H	L
6.	A*	B*	C	J	O	23.	A*	B*	G	J	M
7.	A*	B*	C	N	P	24.	A*	B*	G	O	P
8.	A*	B*	D	E	I	25.	A*	B*	H	K	O
9.	A*	B*	D	E	N	26.	A*	B*	H	M	P
10.	A*	B*	D	F	P	27.	A*	B*	I	J	P
11.	A*	B*	D	G	J	28.	A*	B*	I	K	M
12.	A*	B*	D	H	M	29.	A*	B*	I	L	N
13.	A*	B*	D	K	O	30.	A*	B*	I	N	O
14.	A*	B*	E	F	P	31.	A*	B*	J	K	N
15.	A*	B*	E	G	K	32.	A*	B*	K	L	P
16.	A*	B*	E	H	J	33.	A*	B*	L	M	N
17.	A*	B*	E	L	O						

POWER NUMBER™ WHEEL 54017-2
Wheeling 17 Numbers in 35 games for a 4 of 4 Win

NUMBERS CORRECT***	MAXIMUM WINS				MINIMUM WINS			
	5x	4x	3x	2x	5x	4x	3x	2x
5 (w/o Jackpot)	0	3	15	17				
5	1	0	18	16	0	3	15	17
4	–	1	12	22	–	1	12	22
3	–	–	7	28	–	–	7	28
2	–	–	–	35	–	–	–	35

*** POWER NUMBER POSITIONS A* & B* MUST BE WINNERS.
Your 17 Numbers to Wheel

A*	B*	C	D	E	F	G	H	I
35	35	7	7	7	7	7	7	7

J	K	L	M	N	O	P	Q	
7	7	7	7	7	7	7	7	

(Continued Next Page)

POWER NUMBER™ WHEEL 54017-2 (Continued from previous page)
The 35 Games to Play

#						#					
1.	A*	B*	C	D	N	19.	A*	B*	F	G	N
2.	A*	B*	C	E	O	20.	A*	B*	F	J	L
3.	A*	B*	C	F	P	21.	A*	B*	F	K	M
4.	A*	B*	C	G	H	22.	A*	B*	F	O	Q
5.	A*	B*	C	I	Q	23.	A*	B*	G	I	M
6.	A*	B*	C	J	K	24.	A*	B*	G	J	O
7.	A*	B*	C	L	M	25.	A*	B*	G	L	Q
8.	A*	B*	D	E	L	26.	A*	B*	H	I	L
9.	A*	B*	D	F	H	27.	A*	B*	H	K	O
10.	A*	B*	D	G	P	28.	A*	B*	H	M	Q
11.	A*	B*	D	I	J	29.	A*	B*	H	N	P
12.	A*	B*	D	K	Q	30.	A*	B*	I	K	N
13.	A*	B*	D	M	O	31.	A*	B*	I	O	P
14.	A*	B*	E	F	I	32.	A*	B*	J	M	P
15.	A*	B*	E	G	K	33.	A*	B*	J	N	Q
16.	A*	B*	E	H	J	34.	A*	B*	K	L	P
17.	A*	B*	E	M	N	35.	A*	B*	L	N	O
18.	A*	B*	E	P	Q						

Copyright © 1983-1998 Gail Howard

POWER NUMBER™ WHEEL 54018-2
Wheeling 18 Numbers in 43 games for a 4 of 4 Win

NUMBERS CORRECT***	MAXIMUM WINS				MINIMUM WINS			
	5x	4x	3x	2x	5x	4x	3x	2x
5 (w/o Jackpot)	0	5	15	23				
5	1	2	18	22	0	3	18	22
4	–	2	13	28	–	1	14	28
3	–	–	9	34	–	–	8	35
2	–	–	–	43	–	–	–	43

*** POWER NUMBER POSITIONS A* & B* MUST BE WINNERS.

Your 18 Numbers to Wheel

A*	B*	C	D	E	F	G	H	I
43	43	8	8	8	8	8	8	8

J	K	L	M	N	O	P	Q	R
9	8	8	8	8	8	8	8	8

The 43 Games to Play

#						#					
1.	A*	B*	C	D	M	4.	A*	B*	C	G	O
2.	A*	B*	C	E	R	5.	A*	B*	C	H	J
3.	A*	B*	C	F	L	6.	A*	B*	C	I	J

Copyright © 1983-1998 Gail Howard

(Continued Next Page)

321

POWER NUMBER™ WHEEL 54018-2 (Continued from previous page)

#							#					
7.	A*	B*	C	K	Q		26.	A*	B*	F	N	Q
8.	A*	B*	C	N	P		27.	A*	B*	G	I	N
9.	A*	B*	D	E	N		28.	A*	B*	G	J	P
10.	A*	B*	D	F	O		29.	A*	B*	G	Q	R
11.	A*	B*	D	G	H		30.	A*	B*	H	K	L
12.	A*	B*	D	G	L		31.	A*	B*	H	M	R
13.	A*	B*	D	I	K		32.	A*	B*	H	N	O
14.	A*	B*	D	J	Q		33.	A*	B*	H	P	Q
15.	A*	B*	D	P	R		34.	A*	B*	I	M	Q
16.	A*	B*	E	F	J		35.	A*	B*	I	O	P
17.	A*	B*	E	G	K		36.	A*	B*	J	K	M
18.	A*	B*	E	H	I		37.	A*	B*	J	L	R
19.	A*	B*	E	I	L		38.	A*	B*	J	N	O
20.	A*	B*	E	M	P		39.	A*	B*	K	L	N
21.	A*	B*	E	O	Q		40.	A*	B*	K	O	R
22.	A*	B*	F	G	M		41.	A*	B*	L	M	O
23.	A*	B*	F	H	J		42.	A*	B*	L	P	Q
24.	A*	B*	F	I	R		43.	A*	B*	M	N	R
25.	A*	B*	F	K	P							

POWER NUMBER™WHEEL 54019-2
Wheeling 19 Numbers in 47 games for a 4 of 4 Win

NUMBERS CORRECT***	MAXIMUM WINS				MINIMUM WINS			
	5x	4x	3x	2x	5x	4x	3x	2x
5 (w/o Jackpot)	0	6	16	25				
5	1	2	20	24	0	3	18	26
4	–	3	13	31	–	1	14	32
3	–	–	10	37	–	–	8	39
2	–	–	–	47	–	–	–	47

*** POWER NUMBER POSITIONS A* & B* MUST BE WINNERS.

Your 19 Numbers to Wheel

A*	B*	C	D	E	F	G	H	I	J
47	47	8	8	8	8	8	8	8	8

K	L	M	N	O	P	Q	R	S
10	9	9	9	8	8	8	8	8

The 47 Games to Play

#							#					
1.	A*	B*	C	D	O		4.	A*	B*	C	G	N
2.	A*	B*	C	E	P		5.	A*	B*	C	H	L
3.	A*	B*	C	F	R		6.	A*	B*	C	I	M

(Continued Next Page)

322

POWER NUMBER™ WHEEL 54019-2 (Continued from previous page)

	A*	B*	C	J	K
7.					

	A*	B*	C	Q	S
8.					

	A*	B*	D	E	J
9.					

	A*	B*	D	F	S
10.					

	A*	B*	D	G	I
11.					

	A*	B*	D	H	M
12.					

	A*	B*	D	K	N
13.					

	A*	B*	D	L	P
14.					

	A*	B*	D	Q	R
15.					

	A*	B*	E	F	H
16.					

	A*	B*	E	G	O
17.					

	A*	B*	E	I	Q
18.					

	A*	B*	E	K	M
19.					

	A*	B*	E	L	R
20.					

	A*	B*	E	N	S
21.					

	A*	B*	F	G	J
22.					

	A*	B*	F	I	N
23.					

	A*	B*	F	K	L
24.					

	A*	B*	F	M	P
25.					

	A*	B*	F	O	Q
26.					

	A*	B*	G	H	K
27.					

	A*	B*	G	L	M
28.					

	A*	B*	G	P	Q
29.					

	A*	B*	G	R	S
30.					

	A*	B*	H	I	O
31.					

	A*	B*	H	J	S
32.					

	A*	B*	H	N	Q
33.					

	A*	B*	H	P	R
34.					

	A*	B*	I	J	R
35.					

	A*	B*	I	K	L
36.					

	A*	B*	I	P	S
37.					

	A*	B*	J	L	Q
38.					

	A*	B*	J	M	N
39.					

	A*	B*	J	O	P
40.					

	A*	B*	K	M	Q
41.					

	A*	B*	K	N	P
42.					

	A*	B*	K	N	R
43.					

	A*	B*	K	O	S
44.					

	A*	B*	L	M	S
45.					

	A*	B*	L	N	O
46.					

	A*	B*	M	O	R
47.					

POWER NUMBER™WHEEL 54020-2
Wheeling 20 Numbers in 54 games for a 4 of 4 Win

NUMBERS CORRECT***	MAXIMUM WINS				MINIMUM WINS			
	5x	4x	3x	2x	5x	4x	3x	2x
5 (w/o Jackpot)	0	4	19	31				
5	1	1	22	30	0	3	21	30
4	–	2	14	38	–	1	16	37
3	–	–	9	45	–	–	9	45
2	–	–	–	54	–	–	–	54

*** POWER NUMBER POSITIONS A* & B* MUST BE WINNERS.

Your 20 Numbers to Wheel

A*	B*	C	D	E	F	G	H	I	J
54	54	9	9	9	9	9	9	9	9

K	L	M	N	O	P	Q	R	S	T
9	9	9	9	9	9	9	9	9	9

The 54 Games to Play

	A*	B*	C	D	Q
1.					

	A*	B*	C	E	L
2.					

       (Continued Next Page)

POWER NUMBER™ WHEEL 54020-2 (Continued from previous page)

3.	A*	B*	C	F	T	29.	A*	B*	F	K	N
4.	A*	B*	C	G	R	30.	A*	B*	F	R	S
5.	A*	B*	C	H	N	31.	A*	B*	G	H	M
6.	A*	B*	C	I	K	32.	A*	B*	G	K	O
7.	A*	B*	C	J	S	33.	A*	B*	G	N	Q
8.	A*	B*	C	M	P	34.	A*	B*	G	S	T
9.	A*	B*	C	O	T	35.	A*	B*	H	J	L
10.	A*	B*	D	E	N	36.	A*	B*	H	K	S
11.	A*	B*	D	F	O	37.	A*	B*	H	O	P
12.	A*	B*	D	G	I	38.	A*	B*	H	R	T
13.	A*	B*	D	G	J	39.	A*	B*	I	J	N
14.	A*	B*	D	H	S	40.	A*	B*	I	L	R
15.	A*	B*	D	K	L	41.	A*	B*	I	P	S
16.	A*	B*	D	M	R	42.	A*	B*	I	Q	T
17.	A*	B*	D	P	T	43.	A*	B*	J	M	O
18.	A*	B*	E	F	R	44.	A*	B*	J	N	T
19.	A*	B*	E	G	P	45.	A*	B*	J	Q	R
20.	A*	B*	E	H	I	46.	A*	B*	K	L	T
21.	A*	B*	E	I	O	47.	A*	B*	K	M	Q
22.	A*	B*	E	J	K	48.	A*	B*	K	P	R
23.	A*	B*	E	M	T	49.	A*	B*	L	M	Q
24.	A*	B*	E	Q	S	50.	A*	B*	L	N	P
25.	A*	B*	F	G	L	51.	A*	B*	L	O	S
26.	A*	B*	F	H	Q	52.	A*	B*	M	N	S
27.	A*	B*	F	I	M	53.	A*	B*	N	O	R
28.	A*	B*	F	J	P	54.	A*	B*	O	P	Q

POWER NUMBER™WHEEL 54022-2
Wheeling 22 Numbers in 67 games for a 4 of 4 Win

NUMBERS CORRECT***	MAXIMUM WINS				MINIMUM WINS			
	5x	4x	3x	2x	5x	4x	3x	2x
5 (w/o Jackpot)	0	5	21	41				
5	1	2	24	40	0	3	24	40
4	–	2	17	48	–	1	18	48
3	–	–	11	56	–	–	10	57
2	–	–	–	67	–	–	–	67

*** POWER NUMBER POSITIONS A* & B* MUST BE WINNERS.
(Continued Next Page)

POWER NUMBER™ WHEEL 54022-2 (Continued from previous page)
Your 22 Numbers to Wheel

A*	B*	C	D	E	F	G	H	I	J	K
67	67	10	10	10	10	10	10	10	10	11

L	M	N	O	P	Q	R	S	T	U	V
10	10	10	10	10	10	10	10	10	10	10

The 67 Games to Play

#						#					
1.	A*	B*	C	D	O	31.	A*	B*	F	J	M
2.	A*	B*	C	E	V	32.	A*	B*	F	K	R
3.	A*	B*	C	F	Q	33.	A*	B*	F	L	S
4.	A*	B*	C	G	R	34.	A*	B*	F	U	V
5.	A*	B*	C	H	L	35.	A*	B*	G	H	K
6.	A*	B*	C	I	M	36.	A*	B*	G	I	Q
7.	A*	B*	C	J	U	37.	A*	B*	G	J	O
8.	A*	B*	C	K	N	38.	A*	B*	G	L	N
9.	A*	B*	C	N	T	39.	A*	B*	G	M	V
10.	A*	B*	C	P	S	40.	A*	B*	G	T	U
11.	A*	B*	D	E	M	41.	A*	B*	H	J	Q
12.	A*	B*	D	F	T	42.	A*	B*	H	M	O
13.	A*	B*	D	G	S	43.	A*	B*	H	S	U
14.	A*	B*	D	H	R	44.	A*	B*	H	T	V
15.	A*	B*	D	I	Q	45.	A*	B*	I	J	V
16.	A*	B*	D	J	K	46.	A*	B*	I	K	U
17.	A*	B*	D	L	U	47.	A*	B*	I	L	P
18.	A*	B*	D	N	U	48.	A*	B*	I	N	O
19.	A*	B*	D	P	V	49.	A*	B*	I	R	T
20.	A*	B*	E	F	O	50.	A*	B*	J	L	T
21.	A*	B*	E	G	T	51.	A*	B*	J	N	S
22.	A*	B*	E	H	P	52.	A*	B*	J	P	R
23.	A*	B*	E	I	S	53.	A*	B*	K	L	M
24.	A*	B*	E	J	K	54.	A*	B*	K	O	P
25.	A*	B*	E	L	Q	55.	A*	B*	K	Q	T
26.	A*	B*	E	M	U	56.	A*	B*	K	R	S
27.	A*	B*	E	N	R	57.	A*	B*	K	S	V
28.	A*	B*	F	G	P	58.	A*	B*	L	O	V
29.	A*	B*	F	H	I	59.	A*	B*	L	R	V
30.	A*	B*	F	H	N	60.	A*	B*	M	N	P

(Continued Next Page)

POWER NUMBER™ WHEEL 54022-2 (Continued from previous page)

	A*	B*	M	Q	R
61.					

	A*	B*	M	S	T
62.					

	A*	B*	N	Q	V
63.					

	A*	B*	O	P	T
64.					

	A*	B*	O	Q	S
65.					

	A*	B*	O	R	U
66.					

	A*	B*	P	Q	U
67.					

Copyright © 1983-1998 Gail Howard

POWER NUMBER™ WHEEL 54024-2
Wheeling 24 Numbers in 81 games for a 4 of 4 Win

NUMBERS CORRECT***	MAXIMUM WINS				MINIMUM WINS			
	5x	4x	3x	2x	5x	4x	3x	2x
5 (w/o Jackpot)	0	5	24	52				
5	1	1	29	50	0	3	27	51
4	–	2	19	60	–	1	20	60
3	–	–	12	69	–	–	11	70
2	–	–	–	81	–	–	–	81

*** POWER NUMBER POSITIONS A* & B* MUST BE WINNERS.

Your 24 Numbers to Wheel

A*	B*	C	D	E	F	G	H	I	J	K	L
81	81	11	11	11	11	11	11	11	11	11	11

M	N	O	P	Q	R	S	T	U	V	W	X
11	11	11	11	11	11	11	11	11	12	11	11

The 81 Games to Play

	A*	B*	C	D	O
1.					

	A*	B*	C	E	Q
2.					

	A*	B*	C	F	T
3.					

	A*	B*	C	G	M
4.					

	A*	B*	C	H	X
5.					

	A*	B*	C	I	K
6.					

	A*	B*	C	J	K
7.					

	A*	B*	C	L	V
8.					

	A*	B*	C	N	W
9.					

	A*	B*	C	P	U
10.					

	A*	B*	C	R	S
11.					

	A*	B*	D	E	U
12.					

	A*	B*	D	F	V
13.					

	A*	B*	D	G	L
14.					

	A*	B*	D	H	W
15.					

	A*	B*	D	I	T
16.					

	A*	B*	D	J	Q
17.					

	A*	B*	D	K	S
18.					

	A*	B*	D	M	X
19.					

	A*	B*	D	N	P
20.					

	A*	B*	D	R	T
21.					

	A*	B*	E	F	J
22.					

	A*	B*	E	G	P
23.					

	A*	B*	E	H	K
24.					

	A*	B*	E	I	Q
25.					

	A*	B*	E	L	W
26.					

	A*	B*	E	M	V
27.					

	A*	B*	E	N	T
28.					

	A*	B*	E	O	S
29.					

	A*	B*	E	R	X
30.					

	A*	B*	F	G	H
31.					

	A*	B*	F	I	S
32.					

	A*	B*	F	K	N
33.					

	A*	B*	F	L	O
34.					

	A*	B*	F	M	P
35.					

	A*	B*	F	Q	U
36.					

 (Continued Next Page)

POWER NUMBER™ WHEEL 54024-2 (Continued from previous page)

37.	A*	B*	F	R	W	60.	A*	B*	J	S	T
38.	A*	B*	F	V	X	61.	A*	B*	J	S	U
39.	A*	B*	G	H	J	62.	A*	B*	J	V	W
40.	A*	B*	G	I	R	63.	A*	B*	K	L	Q
41.	A*	B*	G	K	O	64.	A*	B*	K	M	W
42.	A*	B*	G	N	V	65.	A*	B*	K	P	V
43.	A*	B*	G	Q	T	66.	A*	B*	K	R	U
44.	A*	B*	G	S	X	67.	A*	B*	K	T	X
45.	A*	B*	G	U	W	68.	A*	B*	L	M	R
46.	A*	B*	H	I	M	69.	A*	B*	L	N	S
47.	A*	B*	H	L	T	70.	A*	B*	L	U	X
48.	A*	B*	H	N	R	71.	A*	B*	M	N	Q
49.	A*	B*	H	O	U	72.	A*	B*	M	S	V
50.	A*	B*	H	P	S	73.	A*	B*	M	T	U
51.	A*	B*	H	Q	V	74.	A*	B*	N	U	X
52.	A*	B*	I	J	L	75.	A*	B*	O	P	W
53.	A*	B*	I	L	P	76.	A*	B*	O	Q	X
54.	A*	B*	I	N	O	77.	A*	B*	O	R	V
55.	A*	B*	I	U	V	78.	A*	B*	O	T	W
56.	A*	B*	I	W	X	79.	A*	B*	P	Q	R
57.	A*	B*	J	M	O	80.	A*	B*	P	T	V
58.	A*	B*	J	N	R	81.	A*	B*	Q	S	W
59.	A*	B*	J	P	X						

POWER NUMBER™WHEEL 54026-2
Wheeling 26 Numbers in 96 games for a 4 of 4 Win

NUMBERS CORRECT***	MAXIMUM WINS				MINIMUM WINS			
	5x	4x	3x	2x	5x	4x	3x	2x
5 (w/o Jackpot)	0	4	28	64				
5	1	1	31	63	0	3	30	63
4	–	2	20	74	–	1	22	73
3	–	–	12	84	–	–	12	84
2	–	–	–	96	–	–	–	96

*** POWER NUMBER POSITIONS A* & B* MUST BE WINNERS.
(Continued Next Page)

327

POWER NUMBER™ WHEEL 54026-2 (Continued from previous page)
Your 26 Numbers to Wheel

A*	B*	C	D	E	F	G	H	I
96	96	12	12	12	12	12	12	12

J	K	L	M	N	O	P	Q	R
12	12	12	12	12	12	12	12	12

S	T	U	V	W	X	Y	Z
12	12	12	12	12	12	12	12

The 96 Games to Play

#						#				
1.	A*	B*	C	D	R	29.	A*	B*	E	O	U
2.	A*	B*	C	D	U	30.	A*	B*	E	R	V
3.	A*	B*	C	E	Q	31.	A*	B*	E	S	W
4.	A*	B*	C	F	Z	32.	A*	B*	E	U	Z
5.	A*	B*	C	G	J	33.	A*	B*	F	G	Y
6.	A*	B*	C	H	P	34.	A*	B*	F	H	V
7.	A*	B*	C	I	O	35.	A*	B*	F	I	M
8.	A*	B*	C	K	N	36.	A*	B*	F	J	Q
9.	A*	B*	C	L	M	37.	A*	B*	F	L	R
10.	A*	B*	C	S	Y	38.	A*	B*	F	N	S
11.	A*	B*	C	T	V	39.	A*	B*	F	O	X
12.	A*	B*	C	W	X	40.	A*	B*	F	P	T
13.	A*	B*	D	E	T	41.	A*	B*	F	U	Y
14.	A*	B*	D	F	W	42.	A*	B*	G	H	N
15.	A*	B*	D	G	I	43.	A*	B*	G	K	R
16.	A*	B*	D	H	L	44.	A*	B*	G	L	V
17.	A*	B*	D	J	K	45.	A*	B*	G	M	W
18.	A*	B*	D	M	O	46.	A*	B*	G	O	Z
19.	A*	B*	D	N	Q	47.	A*	B*	G	Q	T
20.	A*	B*	D	P	Y	48.	A*	B*	G	S	X
21.	A*	B*	D	S	V	49.	A*	B*	G	U	X
22.	A*	B*	D	X	Z	50.	A*	B*	H	I	J
23.	A*	B*	E	F	K	51.	A*	B*	H	I	U
24.	A*	B*	E	G	P	52.	A*	B*	H	K	T
25.	A*	B*	E	H	X	53.	A*	B*	H	M	Q
26.	A*	B*	E	I	L	54.	A*	B*	H	O	R
27.	A*	B*	E	J	N	55.	A*	B*	H	S	Z
28.	A*	B*	E	M	Y	56.	A*	B*	H	W	Y

          (Continued Next Page)

POWER NUMBER™ WHEEL 54026-2 (Continued from previous page)

#	A*	B*					#	A*	B*			
57.	A*	B*	I	K	S		77.	A*	B*	L	P	Z
58.	A*	B*	I	N	X		78.	A*	B*	L	Q	X
59.	A*	B*	I	P	Q		79.	A*	B*	L	S	T
60.	A*	B*	I	R	Y		80.	A*	B*	M	N	T
61.	A*	B*	I	T	Z		81.	A*	B*	M	N	U
62.	A*	B*	I	V	W		82.	A*	B*	M	P	R
63.	A*	B*	J	L	U		83.	A*	B*	M	V	X
64.	A*	B*	J	L	W		84.	A*	B*	N	O	P
65.	A*	B*	J	M	S		85.	A*	B*	N	R	W
66.	A*	B*	J	O	V		86.	A*	B*	N	V	Z
67.	A*	B*	J	P	X		87.	A*	B*	O	Q	S
68.	A*	B*	J	R	T		88.	A*	B*	O	T	Y
69.	A*	B*	J	Y	Z		89.	A*	B*	O	W	Z
70.	A*	B*	K	L	O		90.	A*	B*	P	S	W
71.	A*	B*	K	M	Z		91.	A*	B*	P	U	V
72.	A*	B*	K	P	V		92.	A*	B*	Q	R	Z
73.	A*	B*	K	Q	U		93.	A*	B*	Q	V	Y
74.	A*	B*	K	Q	W		94.	A*	B*	R	S	U
75.	A*	B*	K	X	Y		95.	A*	B*	R	T	X
76.	A*	B*	L	N	Y		96.	A*	B*	T	U	W

POWER NUMBER™WHEEL 54030-2
Wheeling 30 Numbers in 131 games for a 4 of 4 Win

NUMBERS CORRECT***	MAXIMUM WINS				MINIMUM WINS			
	5x	4x	3x	2x	5x	4x	3x	2x
5 (w/o Jackpot)	0	5	33	93				
5	1	1	38	91	0	3	36	92
4	–	2	25	104	–	1	26	104
3	–	–	15	116	–	–	14	117
2	–	–	–	131	–	–	–	131

*** POWER NUMBER POSITIONS A* & B* MUST BE WINNERS.

Your 30 Numbers to Wheel

A*	B*	C	D	E	F	G	H	I	J
131	131	14	14	14	14	14	14	14	14

K	L	M	N	O	P	Q	R	S	T
14	14	14	14	14	14	14	14	14	14

U	V	W	X	Y	Z	AA	BB	CC	DD
14	14	14	15	14	14	14	14	14	14

(Continued Next Page)

POWER NUMBER™ WHEEL 54030-2 (Continued from previous page)
The 131 Games to Play

#						#					
1.	A*	B*	C	D	Z	36.	A*	B*	E	R	W
2.	A*	B*	C	E	X	37.	A*	B*	E	S	V
3.	A*	B*	C	F	S	38.	A*	B*	E	T	dd
4.	A*	B*	C	G	cc	39.	A*	B*	E	X	Y
5.	A*	B*	C	H	P	40.	A*	B*	F	G	Y
6.	A*	B*	C	I	Q	41.	A*	B*	F	H	J
7.	A*	B*	C	J	aa	42.	A*	B*	F	I	K
8.	A*	B*	C	K	V	43.	A*	B*	F	I	T
9.	A*	B*	C	L	R	44.	A*	B*	F	L	O
10.	A*	B*	C	M	U	45.	A*	B*	F	M	bb
11.	A*	B*	C	N	Y	46.	A*	B*	F	N	W
12.	A*	B*	C	O	W	47.	A*	B*	F	P	U
13.	A*	B*	C	T	cc	48.	A*	B*	F	Q	V
14.	A*	B*	C	bb	dd	49.	A*	B*	F	X	dd
15.	A*	B*	D	E	bb	50.	A*	B*	F	Z	cc
16.	A*	B*	D	F	R	51.	A*	B*	G	H	W
17.	A*	B*	D	G	K	52.	A*	B*	G	I	aa
18.	A*	B*	D	H	X	53.	A*	B*	G	J	R
19.	A*	B*	D	I	O	54.	A*	B*	G	L	dd
20.	A*	B*	D	J	Q	55.	A*	B*	G	M	P
21.	A*	B*	D	L	P	56.	A*	B*	G	N	U
22.	A*	B*	D	M	N	57.	A*	B*	G	O	X
23.	A*	B*	D	S	U	58.	A*	B*	G	S	bb
24.	A*	B*	D	T	aa	59.	A*	B*	G	T	Z
25.	A*	B*	D	V	W	60.	A*	B*	G	V	X
26.	A*	B*	D	Y	aa	61.	A*	B*	H	I	bb
27.	A*	B*	D	cc	dd	62.	A*	B*	H	K	M
28.	A*	B*	E	F	aa	63.	A*	B*	H	L	N
29.	A*	B*	E	G	Q	64.	A*	B*	H	M	T
30.	A*	B*	E	H	O	65.	A*	B*	H	Q	cc
31.	A*	B*	E	I	J	66.	A*	B*	H	R	Y
32.	A*	B*	E	K	P	67.	A*	B*	H	S	Z
33.	A*	B*	E	L	U	68.	A*	B*	H	U	aa
34.	A*	B*	E	M	cc	69.	A*	B*	H	V	dd
35.	A*	B*	E	N	Z	70.	A*	B*	I	L	cc

    (Continued Next Page)

POWER NUMBER™ WHEEL 54030-2 (Continued from previous page)

	A*	B*			
71.	A*	B*	I	M	X
72.	A*	B*	I	N	V
73.	A*	B*	I	P	S
74.	A*	B*	I	R	U
75.	A*	B*	I	W	Z
76.	A*	B*	I	Y	dd
77.	A*	B*	J	K	W
78.	A*	B*	J	L	M
79.	A*	B*	J	N	P
80.	A*	B*	J	O	bb
81.	A*	B*	J	S	Y
82.	A*	B*	J	T	V
83.	A*	B*	J	U	dd
84.	A*	B*	J	V	cc
85.	A*	B*	J	X	Z
86.	A*	B*	K	L	S
87.	A*	B*	K	N	aa
88.	A*	B*	K	O	R
89.	A*	B*	K	Q	U
90.	A*	B*	K	T	bb
91.	A*	B*	K	X	bb
92.	A*	B*	K	Y	cc
93.	A*	B*	K	Z	dd
94.	A*	B*	L	O	T
95.	A*	B*	L	Q	X
96.	A*	B*	L	V	bb
97.	A*	B*	L	W	Y
98.	A*	B*	L	Z	aa
99.	A*	B*	M	O	V
100.	A*	B*	M	Q	R
101.	A*	B*	M	S	aa

	A*	B*			
102.	A*	B*	M	W	dd
103.	A*	B*	M	Y	Z
104.	A*	B*	N	O	Q
105.	A*	B*	N	R	dd
106.	A*	B*	N	S	X
107.	A*	B*	N	T	W
108.	A*	B*	N	bb	cc
109.	A*	B*	O	P	Z
110.	A*	B*	O	S	dd
111.	A*	B*	O	U	Y
112.	A*	B*	O	aa	cc
113.	A*	B*	P	Q	dd
114.	A*	B*	P	R	X
115.	A*	B*	P	S	T
116.	A*	B*	P	V	Y
117.	A*	B*	P	W	cc
118.	A*	B*	P	aa	bb
119.	A*	B*	Q	S	W
120.	A*	B*	Q	T	Z
121.	A*	B*	Q	Y	bb
122.	A*	B*	Q	aa	dd
123.	A*	B*	R	S	cc
124.	A*	B*	R	T	Y
125.	A*	B*	R	V	aa
126.	A*	B*	R	Z	bb
127.	A*	B*	T	U	X
128.	A*	B*	U	V	Z
129.	A*	B*	U	W	bb
130.	A*	B*	U	X	cc
131.	A*	B*	W	X	aa

POWER NUMBER™WHEEL 54035-2
Wheeling 35 Numbers in 185 games for a 4 of 4 Win

NUMBERS CORRECT***	MAXIMUM WINS				MINIMUM WINS			
	5x	4x	3x	2x	5x	4x	3x	2x
5 (w/o Jackpot)	0	7	40	138				
5	1	4	43	137	0	3	42	140
4	–	5	26	154	–	1	30	154
3	–	–	18	167	–	–	16	169
2	–	–	–	185	–	–	–	185

*** POWER NUMBER POSITIONS A* & B* MUST BE WINNERS.

Your 35 Numbers to Wheel

A*	B*	C	D	E	F	G	H	I	J	K	L
185	185	16	16	16	16	16	16	16	16	18	18

M	N	O	P	Q	R	S	T	U	V	W	X
18	18	17	18	17	17	17	17	17	17	17	17

Y	Z	AA	BB	CC	DD	EE	FF	GG	HH	II	
17	16	17	16	17	17	17	17	18	16	16	

The 185 Games to Play

#							#					
1.	A*	B*	C	D	W		23.	A*	B*	D	K	L
2.	A*	B*	C	E	U		24.	A*	B*	D	N	hh
3.	A*	B*	C	F	Y		25.	A*	B*	D	P	gg
4.	A*	B*	C	G	gg		26.	A*	B*	D	R	dd
5.	A*	B*	C	H	R		27.	A*	B*	D	S	V
6.	A*	B*	C	I	N		28.	A*	B*	D	U	cc
7.	A*	B*	C	J	S		29.	A*	B*	D	X	ii
8.	A*	B*	C	K	ii		30.	A*	B*	D	Y	ff
9.	A*	B*	C	L	M		31.	A*	B*	D	Z	bb
10.	A*	B*	C	O	cc		32.	A*	B*	E	F	Z
11.	A*	B*	C	P	ee		33.	A*	B*	E	G	N
12.	A*	B*	C	Q	ff		34.	A*	B*	E	H	M
13.	A*	B*	C	T	dd		35.	A*	B*	E	I	W
14.	A*	B*	C	V	aa		36.	A*	B*	E	J	Q
15.	A*	B*	C	X	bb		37.	A*	B*	E	K	V
16.	A*	B*	C	Z	hh		38.	A*	B*	E	L	R
17.	A*	B*	D	E	O		39.	A*	B*	E	P	gg
18.	A*	B*	D	F	aa		40.	A*	B*	E	S	dd
19.	A*	B*	D	G	ee		41.	A*	B*	E	T	Y
20.	A*	B*	D	H	T		42.	A*	B*	E	X	hh
21.	A*	B*	D	I	Q		43.	A*	B*	E	aa	ii
22.	A*	B*	D	J	M		44.	A*	B*	E	bb	ee

　　　　(Continued Next Page)

332

POWER NUMBER™ WHEEL 54035-2 (Continued from previous page)

#						#					
45.	A*	B*	E	cc	ff	80.	A*	B*	H	W	ee
46.	A*	B*	F	G	O	81.	A*	B*	H	X	gg
47.	A*	B*	F	H	Q	82.	A*	B*	I	K	hh
48.	A*	B*	F	I	dd	83.	A*	B*	I	L	P
49.	A*	B*	F	J	T	84.	A*	B*	I	M	U
50.	A*	B*	F	K	R	85.	A*	B*	I	O	ee
51.	A*	B*	F	L	S	86.	A*	B*	I	R	aa
52.	A*	B*	F	M	X	87.	A*	B*	I	S	gg
53.	A*	B*	F	N	P	88.	A*	B*	I	T	cc
54.	A*	B*	F	U	hh	89.	A*	B*	I	V	bb
55.	A*	B*	F	V	ee	90.	A*	B*	I	X	ff
56.	A*	B*	F	W	cc	91.	A*	B*	I	Y	ii
57.	A*	B*	F	bb	gg	92.	A*	B*	J	K	ee
58.	A*	B*	F	ff	ii	93.	A*	B*	J	L	U
59.	A*	B*	G	H	bb	94.	A*	B*	J	N	gg
60.	A*	B*	G	I	J	95.	A*	B*	J	O	ii
61.	A*	B*	G	K	M	96.	A*	B*	J	P	hh
62.	A*	B*	G	L	hh	97.	A*	B*	J	R	ff
63.	A*	B*	G	P	U	98.	A*	B*	J	W	bb
64.	A*	B*	G	Q	V	99.	A*	B*	J	X	aa
65.	A*	B*	G	R	S	100.	A*	B*	J	Y	dd
66.	A*	B*	G	T	Z	101.	A*	B*	J	Z	cc
67.	A*	B*	G	W	ii	102.	A*	B*	K	L	O
68.	A*	B*	G	X	Y	103.	A*	B*	K	L	Z
69.	A*	B*	G	aa	ff	104.	A*	B*	K	L	bb
70.	A*	B*	G	cc	dd	105.	A*	B*	K	L	gg
71.	A*	B*	H	I	Z	106.	A*	B*	K	N	dd
72.	A*	B*	H	J	V	107.	A*	B*	K	P	aa
73.	A*	B*	H	K	cc	108.	A*	B*	K	Q	W
74.	A*	B*	H	L	Y	109.	A*	B*	K	S	X
75.	A*	B*	H	N	aa	110.	A*	B*	K	T	Y
76.	A*	B*	H	O	hh	111.	A*	B*	K	U	ff
77.	A*	B*	H	P	ii	112.	A*	B*	L	N	ee
78.	A*	B*	H	S	ff	113.	A*	B*	L	Q	dd
79.	A*	B*	H	U	dd	114.	A*	B*	L	T	ff

     (Continued Next Page)

POWER NUMBER™ WHEEL 54035-2 (Continued from previous page)

#						#					
115.	A*	B*	L	V	ii	150.	A*	B*	P	V	Y
116.	A*	B*	L	W	aa	151.	A*	B*	P	Z	gg
117.	A*	B*	L	X	cc	152.	A*	B*	P	bb	dd
118.	A*	B*	M	N	P	153.	A*	B*	P	cc	ff
119.	A*	B*	M	O	W	154.	A*	B*	Q	R	Z
120.	A*	B*	M	Q	T	155.	A*	B*	Q	R	bb
121.	A*	B*	M	R	Y	156.	A*	B*	Q	U	Y
122.	A*	B*	M	S	U	157.	A*	B*	Q	aa	gg
123.	A*	B*	M	U	aa	158.	A*	B*	Q	cc	ee
124.	A*	B*	M	V	X	159.	A*	B*	Q	hh	ii
125.	A*	B*	M	Z	ii	160.	A*	B*	R	T	U
126.	A*	B*	M	bb	cc	161.	A*	B*	R	cc	hh
127.	A*	B*	M	dd	ff	162.	A*	B*	R	ee	ii
128.	A*	B*	M	ee	ff	163.	A*	B*	S	T	W
129.	A*	B*	M	gg	hh	164.	A*	B*	S	W	Z
130.	A*	B*	N	O	T	165.	A*	B*	S	aa	bb
131.	A*	B*	N	Q	S	166.	A*	B*	S	cc	ii
132.	A*	B*	N	Q	X	167.	A*	B*	S	ee	hh
133.	A*	B*	N	R	V	168.	A*	B*	T	V	ee
134.	A*	B*	N	U	Z	169.	A*	B*	T	aa	hh
135.	A*	B*	N	W	Y	170.	A*	B*	T	gg	ii
136.	A*	B*	N	aa	cc	171.	A*	B*	U	W	X
137.	A*	B*	N	bb	ff	172.	A*	B*	U	bb	ii
138.	A*	B*	N	dd	ii	173.	A*	B*	U	ee	gg
139.	A*	B*	O	P	Q	174.	A*	B*	V	W	cc
140.	A*	B*	O	R	X	175.	A*	B*	V	Z	ee
141.	A*	B*	O	R	gg	176.	A*	B*	V	dd	hh
142.	A*	B*	O	S	Y	177.	A*	B*	V	ff	gg
143.	A*	B*	O	T	bb	178.	A*	B*	W	dd	gg
144.	A*	B*	O	U	V	179.	A*	B*	W	ff	hh
145.	A*	B*	O	Z	ff	180.	A*	B*	X	Y	Z
146.	A*	B*	O	aa	dd	181.	A*	B*	X	dd	ee
147.	A*	B*	P	R	W	182.	A*	B*	Y	aa	ee
148.	A*	B*	P	S	gg	183.	A*	B*	Y	bb	hh
149.	A*	B*	P	T	X	184.	A*	B*	Y	cc	gg

    (Continued Next Page)

334

POWER NUMBER™ WHEEL 54035-2 (Continued from previous page)

185.

A*	B*	Z	aa	dd

POWER NUMBER™ WHEEL 54039-2
Wheeling 39 Numbers in 230 games for a 4 of 4 Win

NUMBERS CORRECT***	MAXIMUM WINS				MINIMUM WINS			
	5x	4x	3x	2x	5x	4x	3x	2x
5 (w/o Jackpot)	0	6	46	178				
5	1	2	51	176	0	3	48	179
4	–	3	33	194	–	1	34	195
3	–	–	20	210	–	–	18	212
2	–	–	–	230	–	–	–	230

*** POWER NUMBER POSITIONS A* & B* MUST BE WINNERS.

Your 39 Numbers to Wheel

A*	B*	C	D	E	F	G	H	I	J
230	230	19	19	19	19	19	19	19	19

K	L	M	N	O	P	Q	R	S	T
19	19	19	19	19	19	19	19	19	19

U	V	W	X	Y	Z	AA	BB	CC	DD
18	18	18	18	18	18	18	18	18	18

EE	FF	GG	HH	II	JJ	KK	LL	MM
18	18	18	18	19	20	19	19	19

The 230 Games to Play

#						#				
1.	A*	B*	C	D	ii	18.	A*	B*	C	gg	hh
2.	A*	B*	C	E	bb	19.	A*	B*	C	ll	mm
3.	A*	B*	C	F	Y	20.	A*	B*	D	E	V
4.	A*	B*	C	F	cc	21.	A*	B*	D	F	U
5.	A*	B*	C	F	dd	22.	A*	B*	D	G	J
6.	A*	B*	C	G	Z	23.	A*	B*	D	H	aa
7.	A*	B*	C	H	W	24.	A*	B*	D	H	cc
8.	A*	B*	C	I	T	25.	A*	B*	D	I	kk
9.	A*	B*	C	J	K	26.	A*	B*	D	J	bb
10.	A*	B*	C	L	aa	27.	A*	B*	D	K	L
11.	A*	B*	C	M	ee	28.	A*	B*	D	M	jj
12.	A*	B*	C	N	V	29.	A*	B*	D	N	mm
13.	A*	B*	C	O	Q	30.	A*	B*	D	O	Y
14.	A*	B*	C	P	jj	31.	A*	B*	D	P	dd
15.	A*	B*	C	R	X	32.	A*	B*	D	Q	ll
16.	A*	B*	C	S	U	33.	A*	B*	D	R	gg
17.	A*	B*	C	ff	kk	34.	A*	B*	D	S	T

(Continued Next Page)

POWER NUMBER™ WHEEL 54039-2 (Continued from previous page)

#	1	2	3	4	5	#	1	2	3	4	5
35.	A*	B*	D	W	ee	70.	A*	B*	G	I	ee
36.	A*	B*	D	X	Z	71.	A*	B*	G	K	T
37.	A*	B*	D	ff	hh	72.	A*	B*	G	K	dd
38.	A*	B*	E	F	hh	73.	A*	B*	G	M	Q
39.	A*	B*	E	G	L	74.	A*	B*	G	M	bb
40.	A*	B*	E	H	mm	75.	A*	B*	G	N	O
41.	A*	B*	E	I	N	76.	A*	B*	G	R	V
42.	A*	B*	E	J	W	77.	A*	B*	G	S	hh
43.	A*	B*	E	K	Q	78.	A*	B*	G	U	ll
44.	A*	B*	E	M	ll	79.	A*	B*	G	W	gg
45.	A*	B*	E	O	U	80.	A*	B*	G	X	cc
46.	A*	B*	E	P	Y	81.	A*	B*	G	Y	aa
47.	A*	B*	E	R	kk	82.	A*	B*	G	ff	mm
48.	A*	B*	E	S	X	83.	A*	B*	G	ii	jj
49.	A*	B*	E	T	gg	84.	A*	B*	H	I	ll
50.	A*	B*	E	Z	ii	85.	A*	B*	H	J	T
51.	A*	B*	E	aa	ee	86.	A*	B*	H	K	ee
52.	A*	B*	E	cc	ll	87.	A*	B*	H	L	ii
53.	A*	B*	E	dd	ff	88.	A*	B*	H	M	U
54.	A*	B*	E	jj	ll	89.	A*	B*	H	M	Z
55.	A*	B*	F	G	kk	90.	A*	B*	H	N	hh
56.	A*	B*	F	H	R	91.	A*	B*	H	O	ff
57.	A*	B*	F	I	S	92.	A*	B*	H	Q	S
58.	A*	B*	F	J	N	93.	A*	B*	H	V	bb
59.	A*	B*	F	K	ll	94.	A*	B*	H	X	gg
60.	A*	B*	F	L	ff	95.	A*	B*	H	Y	dd
61.	A*	B*	F	M	X	96.	A*	B*	H	jj	kk
62.	A*	B*	F	O	Z	97.	A*	B*	I	J	hh
63.	A*	B*	F	P	V	98.	A*	B*	I	K	P
64.	A*	B*	F	Q	ee	99.	A*	B*	I	L	U
65.	A*	B*	F	T	aa	100.	A*	B*	I	M	ii
66.	A*	B*	F	W	jj	101.	A*	B*	I	O	jj
67.	A*	B*	F	bb	mm	102.	A*	B*	I	Q	R
68.	A*	B*	F	gg	ii	103.	A*	B*	I	V	gg
69.	A*	B*	G	H	P	104.	A*	B*	I	W	dd

          (Continued Next Page)

POWER NUMBER™ WHEEL 54039-2 (Continued from previous page)

#						#					
105.	A*	B*	I	X	Y	140.	A*	B*	L	Y	hh
106.	A*	B*	I	Z	ff	141.	A*	B*	L	Z	jj
107.	A*	B*	I	aa	mm	142.	A*	B*	L	cc	mm
108.	A*	B*	I	bb	jj	143.	A*	B*	L	kk	ll
109.	A*	B*	I	cc	jj	144.	A*	B*	M	N	cc
110.	A*	B*	J	L	M	145.	A*	B*	M	O	R
111.	A*	B*	J	O	mm	146.	A*	B*	M	P	S
112.	A*	B*	J	P	ee	147.	A*	B*	M	T	mm
113.	A*	B*	J	Q	Z	148.	A*	B*	M	V	Y
114.	A*	B*	J	R	S	149.	A*	B*	M	W	hh
115.	A*	B*	J	U	Y	150.	A*	B*	M	dd	kk
116.	A*	B*	J	V	X	151.	A*	B*	M	ff	gg
117.	A*	B*	J	aa	ll	152.	A*	B*	N	P	jj
118.	A*	B*	J	cc	gg	153.	A*	B*	N	Q	W
119.	A*	B*	J	dd	jj	154.	A*	B*	N	Q	bb
120.	A*	B*	J	ff	ii	155.	A*	B*	N	R	ee
121.	A*	B*	J	kk	mm	156.	A*	B*	N	S	Z
122.	A*	B*	K	L	bb	157.	A*	B*	N	T	U
123.	A*	B*	K	M	aa	158.	A*	B*	N	X	kk
124.	A*	B*	K	N	S	159.	A*	B*	N	Y	ii
125.	A*	B*	K	O	kk	160.	A*	B*	N	aa	ff
126.	A*	B*	K	R	hh	161.	A*	B*	N	dd	ll
127.	A*	B*	K	U	jj	162.	A*	B*	O	P	ii
128.	A*	B*	K	V	ii	163.	A*	B*	O	T	X
129.	A*	B*	K	W	Z	164.	A*	B*	O	T	cc
130.	A*	B*	K	X	mm	165.	A*	B*	O	T	hh
131.	A*	B*	K	Y	gg	166.	A*	B*	O	V	ee
132.	A*	B*	K	cc	ff	167.	A*	B*	O	W	ll
133.	A*	B*	L	N	gg	168.	A*	B*	O	aa	bb
134.	A*	B*	L	O	S	169.	A*	B*	O	dd	gg
135.	A*	B*	L	P	kk	170.	A*	B*	P	Q	hh
136.	A*	B*	L	Q	V	171.	A*	B*	P	R	T
137.	A*	B*	L	R	dd	172.	A*	B*	P	R	aa
138.	A*	B*	L	T	W	173.	A*	B*	P	U	cc
139.	A*	B*	L	X	ee	174.	A*	B*	P	W	ff

     (Continued Next Page)

POWER NUMBER™ WHEEL 54039-2 (Continued from previous page)

#	A*	B*					#	A*	B*			
175.	A*	B*	P	X	bb		203.	A*	B*	T	ii	jj
176.	A*	B*	P	Z	ll		204.	A*	B*	U	V	aa
177.	A*	B*	P	gg	mm		205.	A*	B*	U	W	X
178.	A*	B*	Q	T	ff		206.	A*	B*	U	Z	dd
179.	A*	B*	Q	U	gg		207.	A*	B*	U	bb	ii
180.	A*	B*	Q	X	aa		208.	A*	B*	U	ee	kk
181.	A*	B*	Q	Y	jj		209.	A*	B*	U	hh	mm
182.	A*	B*	Q	cc	kk		210.	A*	B*	V	W	mm
183.	A*	B*	Q	dd	mm		211.	A*	B*	V	Z	cc
184.	A*	B*	Q	ii	kk		212.	A*	B*	V	ff	jj
185.	A*	B*	R	U	ff		213.	A*	B*	V	hh	ll
186.	A*	B*	R	W	ii		214.	A*	B*	W	Y	bb
187.	A*	B*	R	Y	cc		215.	A*	B*	W	aa	kk
188.	A*	B*	R	Z	bb		216.	A*	B*	X	dd	ii
189.	A*	B*	R	ii	ll		217.	A*	B*	X	ff	ll
190.	A*	B*	R	jj	mm		218.	A*	B*	X	hh	jj
191.	A*	B*	S	V	dd		219.	A*	B*	Y	Z	mm
192.	A*	B*	S	W	cc		220.	A*	B*	Y	ee	ff
193.	A*	B*	S	Y	kk		221.	A*	B*	Z	aa	gg
194.	A*	B*	S	aa	jj		222.	A*	B*	Z	hh	kk
195.	A*	B*	S	bb	ff		223.	A*	B*	aa	cc	dd
196.	A*	B*	S	ee	mm		224.	A*	B*	aa	hh	ii
197.	A*	B*	S	gg	ll		225.	A*	B*	bb	cc	hh
198.	A*	B*	S	ii	mm		226.	A*	B*	bb	ee	ll
199.	A*	B*	T	V	kk		227.	A*	B*	bb	gg	kk
200.	A*	B*	T	Y	ll		228.	A*	B*	cc	ee	ii
201.	A*	B*	T	Z	ee		229.	A*	B*	dd	ee	hh
202.	A*	B*	T	bb	dd		230.	A*	B*	ee	gg	jj

POWER NUMBER™WHEEL 54107-2
Wheeling 7 Numbers in 2 games for a 4 of 5 Win

NUMBERS CORRECT***	MAXIMUM WINS				MINIMUM WINS			
	5x	4x	3x	2x	5x	4x	3x	2x
5 (w/o Jackpot)	0	2	0	0				
5	1	0	1	0	0	1	1	0
4	–	1	1	0	–	0	2	0
3	–	–	2	0	–	–	1	1
2	–	–	–	2	–	–	–	2

*** POWER NUMBER POSITIONS A* & B* MUST BE WINNERS.

Your 7 Numbers to Wheel

A*	B*	C	D	E	F	G
2	2	1	1	1	1	2

The 2 Games to Play

1. | A* | B* | C | F | G |

2. | A* | B* | D | E | G |

POWER NUMBER™WHEEL 54108-2
Wheeling 8 Numbers in 2 games for a 4 of 5 Win

NUMBERS CORRECT***	MAXIMUM WINS				MINIMUM WINS			
	5x	4x	3x	2x	5x	4x	3x	2x
5 (w/o Jackpot)	0	1	1	0				
5	1	0	0	1	0	1	1	0
4	–	1	0	1	–	0	2	0
3	–	–	1	1	–	–	1	1
2	–	–	–	2	–	–	–	2

*** POWER NUMBER POSITIONS A* & B* MUST BE WINNERS.

Your 8 Numbers to Wheel

A*	B*	C	D	E	F	G	H
2	2	1	1	1	1	1	1

The 2 Games to Play

1. | A* | B* | C | F | H |

2. | A* | B* | D | E | G |

POWER NUMBER™WHEEL 54109-2
Wheeling 9 Numbers in 4 games for a 4 of 5 Win

NUMBERS CORRECT***	MAXIMUM WINS				MINIMUM WINS			
	5x	4x	3x	2x	5x	4x	3x	2x
5 (w/o Jackpot)	0	3	0	1				
5	1	2	0	1	0	1	2	1
4	–	2	1	1	–	0	3	1
3	–	–	3	1	–	–	1	3
2	–	–	–	4	–	–	–	4

*** POWER NUMBER POSITIONS A* & B* MUST BE WINNERS.

Your 9 Numbers to Wheel

A*	B*	C	D	E	F	G	H	I
4	4	1	2	2	2	1	3	1

(Continued Next Page)

POWER NUMBER™ WHEEL 54109-2 (Continued from previous page)
The 4 Games to Play

1.	A*	B*	C	G	I
2.	A*	B*	D	E	H

3.	A*	B*	D	F	H
4.	A*	B*	E	F	H

POWER NUMBER™ WHEEL 54110-2
Wheeling 10 Numbers in 5 games for a 4 of 5 Win

NUMBERS CORRECT***	MAXIMUM WINS 5x	4x	3x	2x	MINIMUM WINS 5x	4x	3x	2x
5 (w/o Jackpot)	0	3	1	1				
5	1	2	1	1	0	1	2	2
4	–	3	0	2	–	0	3	2
3	–	–	3	2	–	–	1	4
2	–	–	–	5	–	–	–	5

*** POWER NUMBER POSITIONS A* & B* MUST BE WINNERS.

Your 10 Numbers to Wheel

A*	B*	C	D	E	F	G	H	I	J
5	5	1	3	2	1	2	2	3	1

The 5 Games to Play

1.	A*	B*	C	F	J
2.	A*	B*	D	E	I
3.	A*	B*	D	G	I

4.	A*	B*	D	H	I
5.	A*	B*	E	G	H

POWER NUMBER™ WHEEL 54111-2
Wheeling 11 Numbers in 7 games for a 4 of 5 Win

NUMBERS CORRECT***	MAXIMUM WINS 5x	4x	3x	2x	MINIMUM WINS 5x	4x	3x	2x
5 (w/o Jackpot)	0	3	3	1				
5	1	2	1	3	0	1	4	2
4	–	3	0	4	–	0	4	3
3	–	–	3	4	–	–	2	5
2	–	–	–	7	–	–	–	7

*** POWER NUMBER POSITIONS A* & B* MUST BE WINNERS.

Your 11 Numbers to Wheel

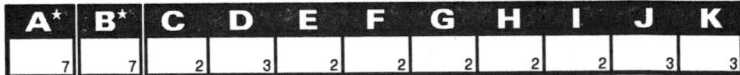

A*	B*	C	D	E	F	G	H	I	J	K
7	7	2	3	2	2	2	2	2	3	3

The 7 Games to Play

1.	A*	B*	C	E	K
2.	A*	B*	C	H	K
3.	A*	B*	D	F	J
4.	A*	B*	D	G	J

5.	A*	B*	D	I	J
6.	A*	B*	E	H	K
7.	A*	B*	F	G	I

POWER NUMBER™WHEEL 54112-2
Wheeling 12 Numbers in 8 games for a 4 of 5 Win

NUMBERS CORRECT***	MAXIMUM WINS				MINIMUM WINS			
	5x	4x	3x	2x	5x	4x	3x	2x
5 (w/o Jackpot)	0	3	3	2				
5	1	2	1	4	0	1	4	3
4	-	3	0	5	-	0	4	4
3	-	-	3	5	-	-	2	6
2	-	-	-	8	-	-	-	8

*** POWER NUMBER POSITIONS A* & B* MUST BE WINNERS.

Your 12 Numbers to Wheel

A*	B*	C	D	E	F	G	H	I	J	K	L
8	8	3	3	2	2	2	2	2	2	3	3

The 8 Games to Play

1.	A*	B*	C	F	L
2.	A*	B*	C	G	L
3.	A*	B*	C	J	L
4.	A*	B*	D	E	K

5.	A*	B*	D	H	K
6.	A*	B*	D	I	K
7.	A*	B*	E	H	I
8.	A*	B*	F	G	J

Copyright © 1983-1998 Gail Howard

POWER NUMBER™WHEEL 54113-2
Wheeling 13 Numbers in 10 games for a 4 of 5 Win

NUMBERS CORRECT***	MAXIMUM WINS				MINIMUM WINS			
	5x	4x	3x	2x	5x	4x	3x	2x
5 (w/o Jackpot)	0	4	1	5				
5	1	2	1	6	0	1	5	4
4	-	3	0	7	-	0	5	5
3	=		3	7	-	-	2	8
2	-	-	-	10	-	-	-	10

*** POWER NUMBER POSITIONS A* & B* MUST BE WINNERS.

Your 13 Numbers to Wheel

A*	B*	C	D	E	F	G
10	10	3	2	3	3	3

H	I	J	K	L	M
2	3	3	3	2	3

The 10 Games to Play

1.	A*	B*	C	D	M
2.	A*	B*	C	H	M
3.	A*	B*	C	L	M
4.	A*	B*	D	H	L
5.	A*	B*	E	F	J

6.	A*	B*	E	G	K
7.	A*	B*	E	I	J
8.	A*	B*	F	G	I
9.	A*	B*	F	I	K
10.	A*	B*	G	J	K

Copyright © 1983-1998 Gail Howard

POWER NUMBER™ WHEEL 54114-2
Wheeling 14 Numbers in 12 games for a 4 of 5 Win

NUMBERS CORRECT***	MAXIMUM WINS				MINIMUM WINS			
	5x	4x	3x	2x	5x	4x	3x	2x
5 (w/o Jackpot)	0	4	1	7				
5	1	1	4	6	0	1	7	4
4	-	2	2	8	-	0	6	6
3	-	-	3	9	-	-	3	9
2	-	-	-	12	-	-	-	12

*** POWER NUMBER POSITIONS A* & B* MUST BE WINNERS.

Your 14 Numbers to Wheel

A*	B*	C	D	E	F	G
12	12	3	3	3	3	3

H	I	J	K	L	M	N
3	3	3	3	3	3	3

The 12 Games to Play

1.	A*	B*	C	D	N
2.	A*	B*	C	G	K
3.	A*	B*	C	L	N
4.	A*	B*	D	G	L
5.	A*	B*	D	K	L
6.	A*	B*	E	F	J

7.	A*	B*	E	H	M
8.	A*	B*	E	I	M
9.	A*	B*	F	H	I
10.	A*	B*	F	J	M
11.	A*	B*	G	K	N
12.	A*	B*	H	I	J

Copyright © 1983-1998 Gail Howard

POWER NUMBER™ WHEEL 54115-2
Wheeling 15 Numbers in 13 games for a 4 of 5 Win

NUMBERS CORRECT***	MAXIMUM WINS				MINIMUM WINS			
	5x	4x	3x	2x	5x	4x	3x	2x
5 (w/o Jackpot)	0	4	1	8				
5	1	1	4	7	0	1	7	5
4	-	2	2	9	-	0	6	7
3	-	-	3	10	-	-	3	10
2	-	-	-	13	-	-	-	13

*** POWER NUMBER POSITIONS A* & B* MUST BE WINNERS.

Your 15 Numbers to Wheel

A*	B*	C	D	E	F	G	H
13	13	3	3	3	3	3	3

I	J	K	L	M	N	O
3	3	3	3	3	3	3

The 13 Games to Play

1.	A*	B*	C	E	O
2.	A*	B*	C	G	N
3.	A*	B*	C	L	N
4.	A*	B*	D	F	K

5.	A*	B*	D	H	I
6.	A*	B*	D	J	M
7.	A*	B*	E	G	L
8.	A*	B*	E	N	O

Copyright © 1983-1998 Gail Howard   (Continued Next Page)

POWER NUMBER™ WHEEL 54115-2 (Continued from previous page)

9.	A*	B*	F	H	J
10.	A*	B*	F	I	M
11.	A*	B*	G	L	O

12.	A*	B*	H	K	M
13.	A*	B*	I	J	K

POWER NUMBER™ WHEEL 54116-2
Wheeling 16 Numbers in 14 games for a 4 of 5 Win

NUMBERS CORRECT***	MAXIMUM WINS				MINIMUM WINS			
	5x	4x	3x	2x	5x	4x	3x	2x
5 (w/o Jackpot)	0	3	3	8				
5	1	0	6	7	0	1	7	6
4	–	1	4	9	–	0	6	8
3	–	–	3	11	–	–	3	11
2	–	–	–	14	–	–	–	14

*** POWER NUMBER POSITIONS A* & B* MUST BE WINNERS.

Your 16 Numbers to Wheel

A*	B*	C	D	E	F	G	H
14	14	3	3	3	3	3	3

I	J	K	L	M	N	O	P
3	3	3	3	3	3	3	3

The 14 Games to Play

1.	A*	B*	C	E	N
2.	A*	B*	C	I	J
3.	A*	B*	C	L	M
4	A*	B*	D	F	K
5.	A*	B*	D	G	O
6.	A*	B*	D	H	P
7.	A*	B*	E	I	L

8.	A*	B*	E	J	M
9.	A*	B*	F	G	H
10.	A*	B*	F	O	P
11.	A*	B*	G	K	P
12.	A*	B*	H	K	O
13.	A*	B*	I	M	N
14.	A*	B*	J	L	N

POWER NUMBER™ WHEEL 54117-2
Wheeling 17 Numbers in 18 games for a 4 of 5 Win

NUMBERS CORRECT***	MAXIMUM WINS				MINIMUM WINS			
	5x	4x	3x	2x	5x	4x	3x	2x
5 (w/o Jackpot)	0	5	3	10				
5	1	2	6	9	0	1	8	9
4	–	2	5	11	–	0	7	11
3	–	–	5	13	–	–	3	15
2	–	–	–	18	–	–	–	18

*** POWER NUMBER POSITIONS A* & B* MUST BE WINNERS.

(Continued Next Page)

POWER NUMBER™ WHEEL 54117-2 (Continued from previous page)
Your 17 Numbers to Wheel

A*	B*	C	D	E	F	G	H	I
18	18	4	3	3	4	3	5	4

J	K	L	M	N	O	P	Q
3	3	4	4	3	4	4	3

The 18 Games to Play

#						#					
1.	A*	B*	C	F	M	10.	A*	B*	F	H	I
2.	A*	B*	C	H	I	11.	A*	B*	F	L	M
3.	A*	B*	C	H	O	12.	A*	B*	F	O	P
4.	A*	B*	C	L	P	13.	A*	B*	G	K	N
5.	A*	B*	D	E	K	14.	A*	B*	H	L	O
6.	A*	B*	D	G	J	15.	A*	B*	H	M	P
7.	A*	B*	D	N	Q	16.	A*	B*	I	L	P
8.	A*	B*	E	G	Q	17.	A*	B*	I	M	O
9.	A*	B*	E	J	N	18.	A*	B*	J	K	Q

POWER NUMBER™ WHEEL 54118-2
Wheeling 18 Numbers in 21 games for a 4 of 5 Win

NUMBERS CORRECT***	MAXIMUM WINS				MINIMUM WINS			
	5x	4x	3x	2x	5x	4x	3x	2x
5 (w/o Jackpot)	0	5	5	11				
5	1	2	8	10	0	1	8	12
4	–	3	4	14	–	0	7	14
3	–	–	5	16	–	–	3	18
2	–	–	–	21	–	–	–	21

*** POWER NUMBER POSITIONS A* & B* MUST BE WINNERS.

Your 18 Numbers to Wheel

A*	B*	C	D	E	F	G	H	I
21	21	3	5	4	3	5	3	3

J	K	L	M	N	O	P	Q	R
5	5	4	5	3	3	5	3	4

The 21 Games to Play

#						#					
1.	A*	B*	C	F	N	8.	A*	B*	D	P	R
2.	A*	B*	C	H	O	9.	A*	B*	E	G	J
3.	A*	B*	C	I	Q	10.	A*	B*	E	K	P
4.	A*	B*	D	E	M	11.	A*	B*	E	L	R
5.	A*	B*	D	G	K	12.	A*	B*	F	H	I
6.	A*	B*	D	J	M	13.	A*	B*	F	O	Q
7.	A*	B*	D	L	M	14.	A*	B*	G	J	L

 (Continued Next Page)

POWER NUMBER™ WHEEL 54118-2 (Continued from previous page)

15.	A*	B*	G	J	P		19.	A*	B*	J	K	R

15.	A*	B*	G	J	P
16.	A*	B*	G	M	R
17.	A*	B*	H	N	Q
18.	A*	B*	I	N	O

19.	A*	B*	J	K	R
20.	A*	B*	K	L	P
21.	A*	B*	K	M	P

Copyright © 1983-1998 Gail Howard

POWER NUMBER™ WHEEL 54119-2
Wheeling 19 Numbers in 23 games for a 4 of 5 Win

NUMBERS CORRECT***	MAXIMUM WINS				MINIMUM WINS			
	5x	4x	3x	2x	5x	4x	3x	2x
5 (w/o Jackpot)	0	5	3	15				
5	1	2	6	14	0	1	10	12
4	–	2	5	16	–	0	8	15
3	–	–	5	18	–	–	4	19
2	–	–	–	23	–	–	–	23

*** POWER NUMBER POSITIONS A* & B* MUST BE WINNERS.

Your 19 Numbers to Wheel

A*	B*	C	D	E	F	G	H	I	J
23	23	4	4	4	4	4	4	4	4

K	L	M	N	O	P	Q	R	S
4	4	4	4	4	4	5	4	4

The 23 Games to Play

1.	A*	B*	C	F	K
2.	A*	B*	C	G	J
3.	A*	B*	C	M	P
4.	A*	B*	C	N	S
5.	A*	B*	D	E	R
6.	A*	B*	D	H	O
7.	A*	B*	D	I	Q
8.	A*	B*	D	L	Q
9.	A*	B*	E	H	I
10.	A*	B*	E	L	O
11.	A*	B*	E	O	Q
12.	A*	B*	F	G	M

13.	A*	B*	F	J	N
14.	A*	B*	F	P	S
15.	A*	B*	G	K	S
16.	A*	B*	G	N	P
17.	A*	B*	H	L	Q
18.	A*	B*	H	Q	R
19.	A*	B*	I	L	R
20.	A*	B*	I	O	R
21.	A*	B*	J	K	P
22.	A*	B*	J	M	S
23.	A*	B*	K	M	N

Copyright © 1983-1998 Gail Howard

POWER NUMBER™WHEEL 54120-2
Wheeling 20 Numbers in 24 games for a 4 of 5 Win

NUMBERS CORRECT***	MAXIMUM WINS				MINIMUM WINS			
	5x	4x	3x	2x	5x	4x	3x	2x
5 (w/o Jackpot)	0	3	6	15				
5	1	0	9	14	0	1	10	13
4	–	1	6	17	–	0	8	16
3	–	–	4	20	–	–	4	20
2	–	–	–	24	–	–	–	24

*** POWER NUMBER POSITIONS A* & B* MUST BE WINNERS.

Your 20 Numbers to Wheel

A★	B★	C	D	E	F	G	H	I	J
24	24	4	4	4	4	4	4	4	4

K	L	M	N	O	P	Q	R	S	T
4	4	4	4	4	4	4	4	4	4

The 24 Games to Play

	A*	B*	C	E	T
1.					

	A*	B*	C	G	O
2.					

	A*	B*	C	I	L
3.					

	A*	B*	C	K	S
4.					

	A*	B*	D	F	N
5.					

	A*	B*	D	H	Q
6.					

	A*	B*	D	J	M
7.					

	A*	B*	D	P	R
8.					

	A*	B*	E	G	L
9.					

	A*	B*	E	I	S
10.					

	A*	B*	E	K	O
11.					

	A*	B*	F	H	J
12.					

	A*	B*	F	M	P
13.					

	A*	B*	F	Q	R
14.					

	A*	B*	G	I	K
15.					

	A*	B*	G	S	T
16.					

	A*	B*	H	M	R
17.					

	A*	B*	H	N	P
18.					

	A*	B*	I	O	T
19.					

	A*	B*	J	N	R
20.					

	A*	B*	J	P	Q
21.					

	A*	B*	K	L	T
22.					

	A*	B*	L	O	S
23.					

	A*	B*	M	N	Q
24.					

POWER NUMBER™WHEEL 54122-2
Wheeling 22 Numbers in 31 games for a 4 of 5 Win

NUMBERS CORRECT***	MAXIMUM WINS				MINIMUM WINS			
	5x	4x	3x	2x	5x	4x	3x	2x
5 (w/o Jackpot)	0	5	7	19				
5	1	2	10	18	0	1	11	19
4	–	3	6	22	–	0	9	22
3	–	–	6	25	–	–	4	27
2	–	–	–	31	–	–	–	31

*** POWER NUMBER POSITIONS A* & B* MUST BE WINNERS.

(Continued Next Page)

POWER NUMBER™ WHEEL 54122-2 (Continued from previous page)
Your 22 Numbers to Wheel

A*	B*	C	D	E	F	G	H	I	J	K
31	31	5	4	5	4	6	5	4	4	5

L	M	N	O	P	Q	R	S	T	U	V
4	5	5	6	5	5	4	4	5	4	4

The 31 Games to Play

#						#					
1.	A*	B*	C	E	P	17.	A*	B*	G	H	K
2.	A*	B*	C	G	O	18.	A*	B*	G	N	O
3.	A*	B*	C	H	T	19.	A*	B*	G	O	Q
4.	A*	B*	C	K	M	20.	A*	B*	G	P	T
5.	A*	B*	C	N	Q	21.	A*	B*	H	M	O
6.	A*	B*	D	F	R	22.	A*	B*	H	N	P
7.	A*	B*	D	I	L	23.	A*	B*	I	R	V
8.	A*	B*	D	J	S	24.	A*	B*	I	S	U
9.	A*	B*	D	U	V	25.	A*	B*	J	L	V
10.	A*	B*	E	G	M	26.	A*	B*	J	R	U
11.	A*	B*	E	H	Q	27.	A*	B*	K	O	P
12.	A*	B*	E	K	N	28.	A*	B*	K	Q	T
13.	A*	B*	E	O	T	29.	A*	B*	L	R	S
14.	A*	B*	F	I	J	30.	A*	B*	M	N	T
15.	A*	B*	F	L	U	31.	A*	B*	M	P	Q
16.	A*	B*	F	S	V						

Copyright © 1000 1008 Gail Howard

POWER NUMBER™WHEEL 54124-2
Wheeling 24 Numbers in 38 games for a 4 of 5 Win

NUMBERS CORRECT***	MAXIMUM WINS				MINIMUM WINS			
	5x	4x	3x	2x	5x	4x	3x	2x
5 (w/o Jackpot)	0	5	7	26				
5	1	2	10	25	0	1	13	24
4	–	3	6	29	–	0	10	28
3	–	–	6	32	–	–	5	33
2	–	–	–	38	–	–	–	38

*** POWER NUMBER POSITIONS A* & B* MUST BE WINNERS.

Your 24 Numbers to Wheel

A*	B*	C	D	E	F	G	H	I	J	K	L
38	38	6	5	5	5	5	5	5	5	5	5

M	N	O	P	Q	R	S	T	U	V	W	X
5	5	5	6	5	5	5	6	5	5	5	6

(Continued Next Page)

347

POWER NUMBER™ WHEEL 54124-2 (Continued from previous page)
The 38 Games to Play

1.	A*	B*	C	E	X
2.	A*	B*	C	H	O
3.	A*	B*	C	I	X
4.	A*	B*	C	J	S
5.	A*	B*	C	K	N
6.	A*	B*	C	V	X
7.	A*	B*	D	F	P
8.	A*	B*	D	G	R
9.	A*	B*	D	L	U
10.	A*	B*	D	M	Q
11.	A*	B*	D	T	W
12.	A*	B*	E	H	N
13.	A*	B*	E	I	S
14.	A*	B*	E	J	K
15.	A*	B*	E	O	V
16.	A*	B*	F	G	W
17.	A*	B*	F	L	Q
18.	A*	B*	F	M	T
19.	A*	B*	F	R	U

20.	A*	B*	G	L	M
21.	A*	B*	G	P	T
22.	A*	B*	G	Q	U
23.	A*	B*	H	I	K
24.	A*	B*	H	J	V
25.	A*	B*	H	S	X
26.	A*	B*	I	J	O
27.	A*	B*	I	N	V
28.	A*	B*	J	N	X
29.	A*	B*	K	O	X
30.	A*	B*	K	S	V
31.	A*	B*	L	P	W
32.	A*	B*	L	R	T
33.	A*	B*	M	P	R
34.	A*	B*	M	U	W
35.	A*	B*	N	O	S
36.	A*	B*	P	Q	T
37.	A*	B*	P	T	U
38.	A*	B*	Q	R	W

POWER NUMBER™ WHEEL 54126-2
Wheeling 26 Numbers in 48 games for a 4 of 5 Win

NUMBERS CORRECT***	MAXIMUM WINS				MINIMUM WINS			
	5x	4x	3x	2x	5x	4x	3x	2x
5 (w/o Jackpot)	0	4	10	34				
5	1	1	13	33	0	1	16	31
4	–	2	8	38	–	0	12	36
3	–	–	6	42	–	–	6	42
2	–	–	–	48	–	–	–	48

*** POWER NUMBER POSITIONS A* & B* MUST BE WINNERS.

Your 26 Numbers to Wheel

A*	B*	C	D	E	F	G	H	I
48	48	6	6	6	6	6	6	6

J	K	L	M	N	O	P	Q	R
6	6	6	6	6	6	6	6	6

S	T	U	V	W	X	Y	Z
6	6	6	6	6	6	6	6

(Continued Next Page)

POWER NUMBER™ WHEEL 54126-2 (Continued from previous page)
The 48 Games to Play

#						#					
1.	A*	B*	C	D	O	25.	A*	B*	H	S	W
2.	A*	B*	C	F	S	26.	A*	B*	H	X	Y
3.	A*	B*	C	G	Z	27.	A*	B*	I	J	K
4.	A*	B*	C	H	L	28.	A*	B*	I	N	T
5.	A*	B*	C	S	X	29.	A*	B*	I	P	R
6.	A*	B*	C	W	Y	30.	A*	B*	I	Q	U
7.	A*	B*	D	F	L	31.	A*	B*	I	U	V
8.	A*	B*	D	F	Y	32.	A*	B*	J	K	P
9.	A*	B*	D	G	S	33.	A*	B*	J	M	N
10.	A*	B*	D	H	X	34.	A*	B*	J	Q	T
11.	A*	B*	D	W	Z	35.	A*	B*	J	R	U
12.	A*	B*	E	I	M	36.	A*	B*	K	M	R
13.	A*	B*	E	J	V	37.	A*	B*	K	N	U
14.	A*	B*	E	K	Q	38.	A*	B*	K	T	V
15.	A*	B*	E	N	P	39.	A*	B*	L	S	Z
16.	A*	B*	E	R	V	40.	A*	B*	L	W	X
17.	A*	B*	E	T	U	41.	A*	B*	L	Y	Z
18.	A*	B*	F	G	H	42.	A*	B*	M	N	V
19.	A*	B*	F	O	W	43.	A*	B*	M	P	U
20.	A*	B*	F	X	Z	44.	A*	B*	M	Q	T
21.	A*	B*	G	L	O	45.	A*	B*	N	Q	R
22.	A*	B*	G	O	X	46.	A*	B*	O	S	Y
23.	A*	B*	G	W	Y	47.	A*	B*	P	Q	V
24.	A*	B*	H	O	Z	48.	A*	B*	P	R	T

POWER NUMBER™WHEEL 54130-2
Wheeling 30 Numbers in 63 games for a 4 of 5 Win

NUMBERS CORRECT***	MAXIMUM WINS				MINIMUM WINS			
	5x	4x	3x	2x	5x	4x	3x	2x
5 (w/o Jackpot)	0	5	11	47				
5	1	2	14	46	0	1	17	45
4	–	3	8	52	–	0	13	50
3	–	–	7	56	–	–	6	57
2	–	–	–	63	–	–	–	63

*** POWER NUMBER POSITIONS A* & B* MUST BE WINNERS.
(Continued Next Page)

POWER NUMBER™ WHEEL 54130-2 (Continued from previous page)
Your 30 Numbers to Wheel

A*	B*	C	D	E	F	G	H	I	J
63	63	7	7	7	7	7	7	7	7

K	L	M	N	O	P	Q	R	S	T
7	7	7	7	7	7	7	6	6	6

U	V	W	X	Y	Z	AA	BB	CC	DD
6	6	6	6	7	7	7	7	7	7

The 63 Games to Play

#						#					
1.	A*	B*	C	F	S	29.	A*	B*	G	W	cc
2.	A*	B*	C	G	T	30.	A*	B*	H	I	Y
3.	A*	B*	C	M	Q	31.	A*	B*	H	J	K
4.	A*	B*	C	Q	W	32.	A*	B*	H	N	bb
5.	A*	B*	C	Q	X	33.	A*	B*	H	O	dd
6.	A*	B*	C	R	U	34.	A*	B*	H	P	aa
7.	A*	B*	C	V	cc	35.	A*	B*	I	J	L
8.	A*	B*	D	E	P	36.	A*	B*	I	N	P
9.	A*	B*	D	H	L	37.	A*	B*	I	Z	dd
10.	A*	B*	D	I	K	38.	A*	B*	I	aa	bb
11.	A*	B*	D	J	Y	39.	A*	B*	J	N	Z
12.	A*	B*	D	N	O	40.	A*	B*	J	O	aa
13.	A*	B*	D	Z	aa	41.	A*	B*	J	P	dd
14.	A*	B*	D	bb	dd	42.	A*	B*	K	L	Y
15.	A*	B*	E	H	Z	43.	A*	B*	K	O	P
16.	A*	B*	E	I	O	44.	A*	B*	K	Z	bb
17.	A*	B*	E	J	bb	45.	A*	B*	K	aa	dd
18.	A*	B*	E	K	N	46.	A*	B*	L	N	dd
19.	A*	B*	E	L	aa	47.	A*	B*	L	O	bb
20.	A*	B*	E	Y	dd	48.	A*	B*	L	P	Z
21.	A*	B*	F	G	Q	49.	A*	B*	M	R	V
22.	A*	B*	F	G	U	50.	A*	B*	M	S	cc
23.	A*	B*	F	G	V	51.	A*	B*	M	T	cc
24.	A*	B*	F	M	W	52.	A*	B*	M	U	cc
25.	A*	B*	F	R	T	53.	A*	B*	N	Y	aa
26.	A*	B*	F	X	cc	54.	A*	B*	O	Y	Z
27.	A*	B*	G	M	X	55.	A*	B*	P	Y	bb
28.	A*	B*	G	R	S	56.	A*	B*	Q	R	cc

    (Continued Next Page)

POWER NUMBER™ WHEEL 54130-2 (Continued from previous page)

57.	A*	B*	Q	S	T
58.	A*	B*	Q	U	V
59.	A*	B*	R	W	X
60.	A*	B*	S	U	W

61.	A*	B*	S	V	X
62.	A*	B*	T	U	X
63.	A*	B*	T	V	W

Copyright © 1983-1998 Gail Howard

POWER NUMBER™ WHEEL 54133-2
Wheeling 33 Numbers in 78 games for a 4 of 5 Win

NUMBERS CORRECT***	MAXIMUM WINS				MINIMUM WINS			
	5x	4x	3x	2x	5x	4x	3x	2x
5 (w/o Jackpot)	0	5	15	58				
5	1	2	18	57	0	1	20	57
4	–	2	13	63	–	0	15	63
3	–	–	9	69	–	–	7	71
2	–	–	–	78	–	–	–	78

*** POWER NUMBER POSITIONS A* & B* MUST BE WINNERS.

Your 33 Numbers to Wheel

A*	B*	C	D	E	F	G	H	I	J	K
78	78	8	8	7	7	8	7	8	7	7

L	M	N	O	P	Q	R	S	T	U	V
7	7	8	8	8	8	8	7	7	8	7

W	X	Y	Z	AA	BB	CC	DD	EE	FF	GG
8	8	0	7	8	7	7	9	8	7	7

The 78 Games to Play

1.	A*	B*	C	D	aa
2.	A*	B*	C	G	U
3.	A*	B*	C	I	Y
4.	A*	B*	C	N	R
5.	A*	B*	C	O	P
6.	A*	B*	C	Q	W
7.	A*	B*	C	Q	dd
8.	A*	B*	C	X	ee
9.	A*	B*	D	G	dd
10.	A*	B*	D	I	R
11.	A*	B*	D	N	Y
12.	A*	B*	D	O	ee
13.	A*	B*	D	P	X
14.	A*	B*	D	Q	U
15.	A*	B*	D	W	aa
16.	A*	B*	E	F	Z

17.	A*	B*	E	H	cc
18.	A*	B*	E	J	dd
19.	A*	B*	E	K	M
20.	A*	B*	E	L	V
21.	A*	B*	E	S	gg
22.	A*	B*	E	T	ff
23.	A*	B*	F	H	T
24.	A*	B*	F	J	S
25.	A*	B*	F	K	L
26.	A*	B*	F	M	V
27.	A*	B*	F	bb	gg
28.	A*	B*	F	cc	ff
29.	A*	B*	G	I	O
30.	A*	B*	G	I	W
31.	A*	B*	G	N	X
32.	A*	B*	G	P	R

Copyright © 1983-1998 Gail Howard

(Continued Next Page)

POWER NUMBER™ WHEEL 54133-2 (Continued from previous page)

33.	A*	B*	G	Q	aa	56.	A*	B*	M	T	gg
34.	A*	B*	G	Y	ee	57.	A*	B*	N	O	Q
35.	A*	B*	H	J	K	58.	A*	B*	N	P	U
36.	A*	B*	H	L	S	59.	A*	B*	N	W	X
37.	A*	B*	H	M	bb	60.	A*	B*	N	dd	ee
38.	A*	B*	H	V	gg	61.	A*	B*	O	R	U
39.	A*	B*	H	Z	ff	62.	A*	B*	O	R	W
40.	A*	B*	I	N	aa	63.	A*	B*	O	X	aa
41.	A*	B*	I	P	dd	64.	A*	B*	O	Y	dd
42.	A*	B*	I	Q	X	65.	A*	B*	P	Q	Y
43.	A*	B*	I	U	ee	66.	A*	B*	P	W	dd
44.	A*	B*	J	L	T	67.	A*	B*	P	aa	ee
45.	A*	B*	J	M	cc	68.	A*	B*	Q	R	ee
46.	A*	B*	J	V	ff	69.	A*	B*	R	X	dd
47.	A*	B*	J	Z	gg	70.	A*	B*	R	Y	aa
48.	A*	B*	K	S	T	71.	A*	B*	S	V	cc
49.	A*	B*	K	V	Z	72.	A*	B*	S	Z	bb
50.	A*	B*	K	bb	cc	73.	A*	B*	T	V	bb
51.	A*	B*	K	ff	gg	74.	A*	B*	T	Z	cc
52.	A*	B*	L	M	Z	75.	A*	B*	U	W	ee
53.	A*	B*	L	bb	ff	76.	A*	B*	U	X	Y
54.	A*	B*	L	cc	gg	77.	A*	B*	U	aa	dd
55.	A*	B*	M	S	ff	78.	A*	B*	W	Y	dd

POWER NUMBER™ WHEEL 54135-2
Wheeling 35 Numbers in 89 games for a 4 of 5 Win

NUMBERS CORRECT***	MAXIMUM WINS				MINIMUM WINS			
	5x	4x	3x	2x	5x	4x	3x	2x
5 (w/o Jackpot)	0	5	17	67				
5	1	2	19	67	0	1	22	66
4	–	3	12	74	–	0	16	73
3	–	–	9	80	–	–	8	81
2	–	–	–	89	–	–	–	89

*** POWER NUMBER POSITIONS A* & B* MUST BE WINNERS.
(Continued Next Page)

POWER NUMBER™ WHEEL 54135-2 (Continued from previous page)
Your 35 Numbers to Wheel

A*	B*	C	D	E	F	G	H	I	J	K	L
89	89	8	8	9	8	8	8	8	8	8	8

M	N	O	P	Q	R	S	T	U	V	W	X
8	9	8	8	8	8	8	8	8	8	8	8

Y	Z	AA	BB	CC	DD	EE	FF	GG	HH	II
8	8	8	8	9	8	8	8	8	8	8

The 89 Games to Play

#						#					
1.	A*	B*	C	D	dd	29.	A*	B*	F	O	ff
2.	A*	B*	C	I	R	30.	A*	B*	F	P	gg
3.	A*	B*	C	Q	T	31.	A*	B*	F	W	ii
4.	A*	B*	C	S	bb	32.	A*	B*	G	H	cc
5.	A*	B*	C	U	hh	33.	A*	B*	G	J	ii
6.	A*	B*	C	V	aa	34.	A*	B*	G	K	M
7.	A*	B*	C	X	Z	35.	A*	B*	G	N	gg
8.	A*	B*	C	Y	hh	36.	A*	B*	G	P	ee
9.	A*	B*	D	I	S	37.	A*	B*	G	W	ff
10.	A*	B*	D	Q	X	38.	A*	B*	H	J	O
11.	A*	B*	D	R	T	39.	A*	B*	H	K	W
12.	A*	B*	D	U	Y	40.	A*	B*	H	L	ee
13.	A*	B*	D	V	Z	41.	A*	B*	H	P	ii
14.	A*	B*	D	Y	bb	42.	A*	B*	H	ff	gg
15.	A*	B*	D	aa	hh	43.	A*	B*	I	Q	U
16.	A*	B*	E	F	N	44.	A*	B*	I	Q	hh
17.	A*	B*	E	G	O	45.	A*	B*	I	T	X
18.	A*	B*	E	H	N	46.	A*	B*	I	V	dd
19.	A*	B*	E	J	K	47.	A*	B*	I	Y	Z
20.	A*	B*	E	L	ii	48.	A*	B*	I	aa	bb
21.	A*	B*	E	M	cc	49.	A*	B*	J	L	gg
22.	A*	B*	E	N	ee	50.	A*	B*	J	M	N
23.	A*	B*	E	P	ff	51.	A*	B*	J	P	W
24.	A*	B*	E	W	gg	52.	A*	B*	J	ee	ff
25.	A*	B*	F	G	L	53.	A*	B*	K	L	O
26.	A*	B*	F	H	M	54.	A*	B*	K	N	P
27.	A*	B*	F	J	cc	55.	A*	B*	K	cc	ff
28.	A*	B*	F	K	ee	56.	A*	B*	K	gg	ii

          (Continued Next Page)

353

POWER NUMBER™ WHEEL 54135-2 (Continued from previous page)

#	A*	B*			
57.	A*	B*	L	M	W
58.	A*	B*	L	N	ff
59.	A*	B*	L	P	cc
60.	A*	B*	M	O	P
61.	A*	B*	M	ee	gg
62.	A*	B*	M	ff	ii
63.	A*	B*	N	O	W
64.	A*	B*	N	cc	ii
65.	A*	B*	O	cc	gg
66.	A*	B*	O	ee	ii
67.	A*	B*	Q	R	aa
68.	A*	B*	Q	S	V
69.	A*	B*	Q	Y	dd
70.	A*	B*	Q	Z	bb
71.	A*	B*	R	S	X
72.	A*	B*	R	T	U
73.	A*	B*	R	V	Y

#	A*	B*			
74.	A*	B*	R	Z	dd
75.	A*	B*	R	bb	hh
76.	A*	B*	S	T	Y
77.	A*	B*	S	U	V
78.	A*	B*	S	Z	aa
79.	A*	B*	S	dd	hh
80.	A*	B*	T	V	bb
81.	A*	B*	T	Z	hh
82.	A*	B*	T	aa	dd
83.	A*	B*	U	X	dd
84.	A*	B*	U	Z	aa
85.	A*	B*	U	bb	dd
86.	A*	B*	V	X	hh
87.	A*	B*	W	cc	ee
88.	A*	B*	X	Y	aa
89.	A*	B*	X	bb	cc

POWER NUMBER™ WHEEL 54139-2
Wheeling 39 Numbers in 112 games for a 4 of 5 Win

NUMBERS CORRECT***	MAXIMUM WINS				MINIMUM WINS			
	5x	4x	3x	2x	5x	4x	3x	2x
5 (w/o Jackpot)	0	6	18	88				
5	1	1	24	86	0	1	25	86
4	–	2	16	94	–	0	18	94
3	–	–	10	102	–	–	9	103
2	–	–	–	112	–	–	–	112

*** POWER NUMBER POSITIONS A* & B* MUST BE WINNERS.

Your 39 Numbers to Wheel

A*	B*	C	D	E	F	G	H	I	J
112	112	9	9	9	9	9	9	9	9

K	L	M	N	O	P	Q	R	S	T
9	9	9	9	9	9	9	9	9	9

U	V	W	X	Y	Z	AA	BB	CC	DD
9	9	9	9	9	9	9	9	9	9

EE	FF	GG	HH	II	JJ	KK	LL	MM
9	9	9	9	9	9	10	10	10

The 112 Games to Play

1.	A*	B*	C	D	ii

2.	A*	B*	C	F	U

     (Continued Next Page)

POWER NUMBER™ WHEEL 54139-2 (Continued from previous page)

#						#					
3.	A*	B*	C	G	bb	38.	A*	B*	G	Y	ee
4.	A*	B*	C	H	gg	39.	A*	B*	G	bb	ii
5.	A*	B*	C	I	W	40.	A*	B*	H	I	K
6.	A*	B*	C	K	ff	41.	A*	B*	H	U	bb
7.	A*	B*	C	U	ee	42.	A*	B*	H	Y	ff
8.	A*	B*	C	Y	dd	43.	A*	B*	H	dd	ii
9.	A*	B*	C	hh	jj	44.	A*	B*	H	ee	hh
10.	A*	B*	D	F	jj	45.	A*	B*	I	Y	ii
11.	A*	B*	D	G	gg	46.	A*	B*	I	ee	jj
12.	A*	B*	D	H	ee	47.	A*	B*	I	ff	gg
13.	A*	B*	D	I	U	48.	A*	B*	I	gg	hh
14.	A*	B*	D	K	W	49.	A*	B*	J	L	T
15.	A*	B*	D	K	Y	50.	A*	B*	J	M	mm
16.	A*	B*	D	bb	dd	51.	A*	B*	J	N	aa
17.	A*	B*	D	ff	hh	52.	A*	B*	J	O	S
18.	A*	B*	E	J	P	53.	A*	B*	J	Q	cc
19.	A*	B*	E	L	mm	54.	A*	B*	J	R	V
20.	A*	B*	E	M	N	55.	A*	B*	J	X	Z
21.	A*	B*	E	O	aa	56.	A*	B*	J	kk	ll
22.	A*	B*	E	Q	S	57.	A*	B*	K	bb	ee
23.	A*	B*	E	R	T	58.	A*	B*	K	gg	jj
24.	A*	B*	E	V	X	59.	A*	B*	K	hh	ii
25.	A*	B*	E	Z	cc	60.	A*	B*	L	M	Q
26.	A*	B*	E	kk	ll	61.	A*	B*	L	N	R
27.	A*	B*	F	G	ff	62.	A*	B*	L	O	P
28.	A*	B*	F	H	W	63.	A*	B*	L	S	X
29.	A*	B*	F	I	bb	64.	A*	B*	L	V	aa
30.	A*	B*	F	K	dd	65.	A*	B*	L	Z	ll
31.	A*	B*	F	W	ii	66.	A*	B*	L	cc	kk
32.	A*	B*	F	Y	hh	67.	A*	B*	M	O	Z
33.	A*	B*	F	ee	gg	68.	A*	B*	M	P	R
34.	A*	B*	G	H	jj	69.	A*	B*	M	S	T
35.	A*	B*	G	I	dd	70.	A*	B*	M	V	cc
36.	A*	B*	G	K	U	71.	A*	B*	M	X	kk
37.	A*	B*	G	W	hh	72.	A*	B*	M	aa	ll

    (Continued Next Page)

POWER NUMBER™ WHEEL 54139-2 (Continued from previous page)

	A*	B*	N	O	ll
73.					

	A*	B*	N	P	Z
74.					

	A*	B*	N	Q	T
75.					

	A*	B*	N	S	V
76.					

	A*	B*	N	X	cc
77.					

	A*	B*	N	kk	mm
78.					

	A*	B*	O	Q	V
79.					

	A*	B*	O	R	kk
80.					

	A*	B*	O	T	X
81.					

	A*	B*	O	cc	mm
82.					

	A*	B*	P	Q	kk
83.					

	A*	B*	P	S	ll
84.					

	A*	B*	P	T	V
85.					

	A*	B*	P	X	mm
86.					

	A*	B*	P	aa	cc
87.					

	A*	B*	Q	R	Z
88.					

	A*	B*	Q	X	aa
89.					

	A*	B*	Q	ll	mm
90.					

	A*	B*	R	S	cc
91.					

	A*	B*	R	X	ll
92.					

	A*	B*	R	aa	mm
93.					

	A*	B*	S	Z	aa
94.					

	A*	B*	S	kk	mm
95.					

	A*	B*	T	Z	mm
96.					

	A*	B*	T	aa	kk
97.					

	A*	B*	T	cc	ll
98.					

	A*	B*	U	W	ff
99.					

	A*	B*	U	Y	gg
100.					

	A*	B*	U	dd	hh
101.					

	A*	B*	U	ii	jj
102.					

	A*	B*	V	Z	kk
103.					

	A*	B*	V	ll	mm
104.					

	A*	B*	W	Y	jj
105.					

	A*	B*	W	bb	gg
106.					

	A*	B*	W	dd	ee
107.					

	A*	B*	Y	bb	jj
108.					

	A*	B*	bb	ff	hh
109.					

	A*	B*	dd	ff	jj
110.					

	A*	B*	dd	gg	ll
111.					

	A*	B*	ee	ff	ii
112.					

POWER NUMBER™WHEEL 53011-2
Wheeling 11 Numbers in 3 games for a 3 of 3 Win

NUMBERS CORRECT***	MAXIMUM WINS				MINIMUM WINS			
	5x	4x	3x	2x	5x	4x	3x	2x
5 (w/o Jackpot)	0	1	1	1				
5	1	0	0	2	0	0	3	0
4	–	1	0	2	–	0	2	1
3	–	–	1	2	–	–	1	2
2	–	–	–	3	–	–	–	3

*** POWER NUMBER POSITIONS A* & B* MUST BE WINNERS.

Your 11 Numbers to Wheel

A*	B*	C	D	E	F	G	H	I	J	K
3	3	1	1	1	1	1	1	1	1	1

The 3 Games to Play

	A*	B*	C	G	K
1.					

	A*	B*	D	H	I
2.					

	A*	B*	E	F	J
3.					

POWER NUMBER™WHEEL 53012-2
Wheeling 12 Numbers in 4 games for a 3 of 3 Win

NUMBERS CORRECT***	MAXIMUM WINS				MINIMUM WINS			
	5x	4x	3x	2x	5x	4x	3x	2x
5 (w/o Jackpot)	0	2	1	1				
5	1	1	0	2	0	0	3	1
4	-	2	0	2	-	0	2	2
3	-	-	2	2	-	-	1	3
2	-	-	-	4	-	-	-	4

*** POWER NUMBER POSITIONS A* & B* MUST BE WINNERS.

Your 12 Numbers to Wheel

A*	B*	C	D	E	F	G	H	I	J	K	L
4	4	1	2	1	1	1	2	1	1	1	1

The 4 Games to Play

| 1. | A* | D* | O | G | L |
| 2. | A* | B* | D | H | I |

| 3. | A* | B* | D | H | J |
| 4. | A* | B* | E | F | K |

Copyright © 1983-1998 Gail Howard

POWER NUMBER™WHEEL 53013-2
Wheeling 13 Numbers in 4 games for a 3 of 3 Win

NUMBERS CORRECT***	MAXIMUM WINS				MINIMUM WINS			
	5x	4x	3x	2x	5x	4x	3x	2x
5 (w/o Jackpot)	0	2	0	2				
5	1	0	1	2	0	0	3	1
4	-	1	1	2	-	0	2	2
3	-	-	2	2	-	-	1	3
2	-	-	-	4	-	-	-	4

*** POWER NUMBER POSITIONS A* & B* MUST BE WINNERS.

Your 13 Numbers to Wheel

A*	B*	C	D	E	F	G
4	4	1	2	1	1	1

H	I	J	K	L	M
1	1	1	1	1	1

The 4 Games to Play

| 1. | A* | B* | C | H | L |
| 2. | A* | B* | D | F | M |

| 3. | A* | B* | D | I | J |
| 4. | A* | B* | E | G | K |

Copyright © 1983-1998 Gail Howard

POWER NUMBER™WHEEL 53014-2
Wheeling 14 Numbers in 4 games for a 3 of 3 Win

NUMBERS CORRECT***	MAXIMUM WINS				MINIMUM WINS			
	5x	4x	3x	2x	5x	4x	3x	2x
5 (w/o Jackpot)	0	1	1	2				
5	1	0	0	3	0	0	3	1
4	-	1	0	3	-	0	2	2
3	-	-	1	3	-	-	1	3
2	-	-	-	4	-	-	-	4

*** POWER NUMBER POSITIONS A* & B* MUST BE WINNERS.

(Continued Next Page)

357

POWER NUMBER™ WHEEL 53014-2 (Continued from previous page)
Your 14 Numbers to Wheel

A*	B*	C	D	E	F	G
4	4	1	1	1	1	1

H	I	J	K	L	M	N
1	1	1	1	1	1	1

The 4 Games to Play

1. | A* | B* | C | J | L |

2. | A* | B* | D | G | N |

3. | A* | B* | E | H | M |

4. | A* | B* | F | I | K |

POWER NUMBER™WHEEL 53016-2
Wheeling 16 Numbers in 5 games for a 3 of 3 Win

NUMBERS CORRECT***	MAXIMUM WINS				MINIMUM WINS			
	5x	4x	3x	2x	5x	4x	3x	2x
5 (w/o Jackpot)	0	2	0	3				
5	1	0	1	3	0	0	3	2
4	–	1	1	3	–	0	2	3
3	–	–	2	3	–	–	1	4
2	–	–	–	5	–	–	–	5

*** POWER NUMBER POSITIONS A* & B* MUST BE WINNERS.

Your 16 Numbers to Wheel

A*	B*	C	D	E	F	G	H
5	5	1	2	1	1	1	1

I	J	K	L	M	N	O	P
1	1	1	1	1	1	1	1

The 5 Games to Play

1. | A* | B* | C | K | M |

2. | A* | B* | D | G | P |

3. | A* | B* | D | H | O |

4. | A* | B* | E | I | N |

5. | A* | B* | F | J | L |

POWER NUMBER™WHEEL 53018-2
Wheeling 18 Numbers in 6 games for a 3 of 3 Win

NUMBERS CORRECT***	MAXIMUM WINS				MINIMUM WINS			
	5x	4x	3x	2x	5x	4x	3x	2x
5 (w/o Jackpot)	0	2	1	3				
5	1	1	0	4	0	0	3	3
4	–	2	0	4	–	0	2	4
3	–	–	2	4	–	–	1	5
2	–	–	–	6	–	–	–	6

*** POWER NUMBER POSITIONS A* & B* MUST BE WINNERS.
(Continued Next Page)

POWER NUMBER™ WHEEL 53018-2 (Continued from previous page)
Your 18 Numbers to Wheel

A*	B*	C	D	E	F	G	H	I
6	6	2	1	1	1	1	1	1

J	K	L	M	N	O	P	Q	R
1	1	1	1	1	1	1	1	2

The 6 Games to Play

1. | A* | B* | C | I | R |

2. | A* | B* | C | J | R |

3. | A* | B* | D | K | O |

4. | A* | B* | E | L | P |

5. | A* | B* | F | M | N |

6. | A* | B* | G | H | Q |

Copyright © 1983-1998 Gail Howard

POWER NUMBER™ WHEEL 53020-2
Wheeling 20 Numbers in 6 games for a 3 of 3 Win

NUMBERS CORRECT***	MAXIMUM WINS				MINIMUM WINS			
	5x	4x	3x	2x	5x	4x	3x	2x
5 (w/o Jackpot)	0	1	1	4				
5	1	0	0	5	0	0	3	3
4	–	1	0	5	–	0	2	4
3	–	–	1	5	–	–	1	5
2	–	–	–	6	–	–	–	6

*** POWER NUMBER POSITIONS A* & B* MUST BE WINNERS.

Your 20 Numbers to Wheel

A*	B*	C	D	E	F	G	H	I	J
6	6	1	1	1	1	1	1	1	1

K	L	M	N	O	P	Q	R	S	T
1	1	1	1	1	1	1	1	1	1

The 6 Games to Play

1. | A* | B* | C | M | R |

2. | A* | B* | D | N | S |

3. | A* | B* | E | L | T |

4. | A* | B* | F | K | O |

5. | A* | B* | G | I | P |

6. | A* | B* | H | J | Q |

Copyright © 1983-1998 Gail Howard

POWER NUMBER™ WHEEL 53022-2
Wheeling 22 Numbers in 7 games for a 3 of 3 Win

NUMBERS CORRECT***	MAXIMUM WINS				MINIMUM WINS			
	5x	4x	3x	2x	5x	4x	3x	2x
5 (w/o Jackpot)	0	2	0	5				
5	1	0	1	5	0	0	3	4
4	–	1	1	5	–	0	2	5
3	–	–	2	5	–	–	1	6
2	–	–	–	7	–	–	–	7

*** POWER NUMBER POSITIONS A* & B* MUST BE WINNERS.
(Continued Next Page)

POWER NUMBER™ WHEEL 53022-2 (Continued from previous page)
Your 22 Numbers to Wheel

A*	B*	C	D	E	F	G	H	I	J	K
7	7	1	1	1	2	1	1	1	1	1

L	M	N	O	P	Q	R	S	T	U	V
1	1	1	1	1	1	1	1	1	1	1

The 7 Games to Play

1. | A* | B* | C | O | S |

2. | A* | B* | D | M | T |

3. | A* | B* | E | N | P |

4. | A* | B* | F | I | U |

5. | A* | B* | F | J | V |

6. | A* | B* | G | L | Q |

7. | A* | B* | H | K | R |

Copyright © 1983-1998 Gail Howard

POWER NUMBER™WHEEL 53024-2
Wheeling 24 Numbers in 8 games for a 3 of 3 Win

NUMBERS CORRECT***	MAXIMUM WINS 5x	4x	3x	2x	MINIMUM WINS 5x	4x	3x	2x
5 (w/o Jackpot)	0	2	1	5				
5	1	1	0	6	0	0	3	5
4	–	2	0	6	–	0	2	6
3	–	–	2	6	–	–	1	7
2	–	–	–	8	–	–	–	8

*** POWER NUMBER POSITIONS A* & B* MUST BE WINNERS.

Your 24 Numbers to Wheel

A*	B*	C	D	E	F	G	H	I	J	K	L
8	8	1	1	1	1	2	1	1	1	1	1

M	N	O	P	Q	R	S	T	U	V	W	X
1	1	1	1	1	1	1	1	1	1	1	2

The 8 Games to Play

1. | A* | B* | C | Q | V |

2. | A* | B* | D | P | U |

3. | A* | B* | E | N | R |

4. | A* | B* | F | G | X |

5. | A* | B* | G | L | X |

6. | A* | B* | H | K | W |

7. | A* | B* | I | O | T |

8. | A* | B* | J | M | S |

Copyright © 1983-1998 Gail Howard

POWER NUMBER™WHEEL 53026-2
Wheeling 26 Numbers in 8 games for a 3 of 3 Win

NUMBERS CORRECT***	MAXIMUM WINS 5x	4x	3x	2x	MINIMUM WINS 5x	4x	3x	2x
5 (w/o Jackpot)	0	1	1	6				
5	1	0	0	7	0	0	3	5
4	–	1	0	7	–	0	2	6
3	–	–	1	7	–	–	1	7
2	–	–	–	8	–	–	–	8

*** POWER NUMBER POSITIONS A* & B* MUST BE WINNERS.
(Continued Next Page)

POWER NUMBER™ WHEEL 53026-2 (Continued from previous page)
Your 26 Numbers to Wheel

A*	B*	C	D	E	F	G	H	I
8	8	1	1	1	1	1	1	1

J	K	L	M	N	O	P	Q	R
1		1	1	1	1	1	1	1

S	T	U	V	W	X	Y	Z
1	1	1	1	1	1	1	

The 8 Games to Play

1.	A*	B*	C	U	X
2.	A*	B*	D	Q	V
3.	A*	B*	E	O	R
4.	A*	B*	F	N	W

5.	A*	B*	G	K	Z
6.	A*	B*	H	M	S
7.	A*	B*	I	L	Y
8.	A*	B*	J	P	T

POWER NUMBER™WHEEL 53028-2
Wheeling 28 Numbers in 9 games for a 3 of 3 Win

NUMBERS CORRECT***	MAXIMUM WINS				MINIMUM WINS			
	5x	4x	3x	2x	5x	4x	3x	2x
5 (w/o Jackpot)	0	2	0	7				
5	1	0	1	7	0	0	3	6
4	–	1	1	7	–	0	2	7
3	–	–	2	7	–	–	1	8
2	–	–	–	9	–	–	–	9

*** POWER NUMBER POSITIONS A* & B* MUST BE WINNERS.

Your 28 Numbers to Wheel

A*	B*	C	D	E	F	G	H	I	J
9	9	1	1	1	1	1	2	1	1

K	L	M	N	O	P	Q	R	S	T
1	1	1	1	1	1	1	1	1	1

U	V	W	X	Y	Z	AA	BB
1	1	1	1	1	1	1	1

The 9 Games to Play

1.	A*	B*	C	O	bb
2.	A*	B*	D	R	aa
3.	A*	B*	E	N	X
4.	A*	B*	F	M	U
5.	A*	B*	G	K	W

6.	A*	B*	H	L	T
7.	A*	B*	H	P	Z
8.	A*	B*	I	Q	Y
9.	A*	B*	J	S	V

POWER NUMBER™WHEEL 53030-2
Wheeling 30 Numbers in 10 games for a 3 of 3 Win

NUMBERS CORRECT***	MAXIMUM WINS				MINIMUM WINS			
	5x	4x	3x	2x	5x	4x	3x	2x
5 (w/o Jackpot)	0	2	1	7				
5	1	1	0	8	0	0	3	7
4	–	2	0	8	–	0	2	8
3	–	–	2	8	–	–	1	9
2	–	–	–	10	–	–	–	10

*** POWER NUMBER POSITIONS A* & B* MUST BE WINNERS.

Your 30 Numbers to Wheel

A*	B*	C	D	E	F	G	H	I	J
10	10	1	1	1	1	2	1	1	1

K	L	M	N	O	P	Q	R	S	T
1	1	1	1	1	1	2	1	1	1

U	V	W	X	Y	Z	AA	BB	CC	DD
1	1	1	1	1	1	1	1	1	1

The 10 Games to Play

1.	A*	B*	C	W	cc
2.	A*	B*	D	M	bb
3.	A*	B*	E	S	aa
4.	A*	B*	F	O	Z
5.	A*	B*	G	Q	X

6.	A*	B*	G	Q	Y
7.	A*	B*	H	P	T
8.	A*	B*	I	R	U
9.	A*	B*	J	L	dd
10.	A*	B*	K	N	V

Copyright © 1983-1998 Gail Howard

POWER NUMBER™WHEEL 53034-2
Wheeling 34 Numbers in 11 games for a 3 of 3 Win

NUMBERS CORRECT***	MAXIMUM WINS				MINIMUM WINS			
	5x	4x	3x	2x	5x	4x	3x	2x
5 (w/o Jackpot)	0	2	0	9				
5	1	0	1	9	0	0	3	8
4	–	1	1	9	–	0	2	9
3	–	–	2	9	–	–	1	10
2	–	–	–	11	–	–	–	11

*** POWER NUMBER POSITIONS A* & B* MUST BE WINNERS.

Your 34 Numbers to Wheel

A*	B*	C	D	E	F	G	H	I	J	K	L
11	11	1	1	1	1	1	1	1	1	1	1

M	N	O	P	Q	R	S	T	U	V	W	X
1	1	1	1	2	1	1	1	1	1	1	1

Y	Z	AA	BB	CC	DD	EE	FF	GG	HH
1	1	1	1	1	1	1	1	1	1

The 11 Games to Play

1.	A*	B*	C	X	gg
2.	A*	B*	D	W	cc

3.	A*	B*	E	O	hh
4.	A*	B*	F	Q	dd

Copyright © 1983-1998 Gail Howard

(Continued Next Page)

POWER NUMBER™ WHEEL 53034-2 (Continued from previous page)

	A*	B*	G	Z	ee
5.					

	A*	B*	H	S	U
6.					

	A*	B*	I	P	bb
7.					

	A*	B*	J	N	aa
8.					

	A*	B*	K	R	V
9.					

	A*	B*	L	Y	ff
10.					

	A*	B*	M	R	T
11.					

Copyright © 1983-1998 Gail Howard

POWER NUMBER™WHEEL 53035-2
Wheeling 35 Numbers in 11 games for a 3 of 3 Win

NUMBERS CORRECT***	MAXIMUM WINS				MINIMUM WINS			
	5x	4x	3x	2x	5x	4x	3x	2x
5 (w/o Jackpot)	0	1	1	9				
5	1	0	0	10	0	0	3	8
4	–	1	0	10	–	0	2	9
3	–	–	1	10	–	–	1	10
2	–	–	–	11	–	–	–	11

*** POWER NUMBER POSITIONS A* & B* MUST BE WINNERS.

Your 35 Numbers to Wheel

A*	B*	C	D	E	F	G	H	I	J	K	L
11	11	1	1	1	1	1	1	1	1	1	1

M	N	O	P	Q	R	S	T	U	V	W	X
1	1	1	1	1	1	1	1	1	1	1	1

Y	Z	AA	BB	CC	DD	EE	FF	GG	HH	II
1	1	1	1	1	1	1	1	1	1	1

The 11 Games to Play

	A*	B*	C	Z	ee
1.					

	A*	B*	D	N	hh
2.					

	A*	B*	E	P	dd
3.					

	A*	B*	F	R	gg
4.					

	A*	B*	G	X	aa
5.					

	A*	B*	H	U	W
6.					

	A*	B*	I	S	Y
7.					

	A*	B*	J	T	ff
8.					

	A*	B*	K	V	cc
9.					

	A*	B*	L	O	ii
10.					

	A*	B*	M	Q	bb
11.					

Copyright © 1983-1998 Gail Howard

POWER NUMBER™WHEEL 53038-2
Wheeling 38 Numbers in 12 games for a 3 of 3 Win

NUMBERS CORRECT***	MAXIMUM WINS				MINIMUM WINS			
	5x	4x	3x	2x	5x	4x	3x	2x
5 (w/o Jackpot)	0	1	1	10				
5	1	0	0	11	0	0	3	9
4	–	1	0	11	–	0	2	10
3	–	–	1	11	–	–	1	11
2	–	–	–	12	–	–	–	12

*** POWER NUMBER POSITIONS A* & B* MUST BE WINNERS.
(Continued Next Page)

POWER NUMBER™ WHEEL 53038-2 (Continued from previous page)
Your 38 Numbers to Wheel

A*	B*	C	D	E	F	G	H	I	J
12	12	1	1	1	1	1	1	1	1

K	L	M	N	O	P	Q	R	S	T
1	1	1	1	1	1	1	1	1	1

U	V	W	X	Y	Z	AA	BB	CC	DD
1	1	1	1	1	1	1	1	1	1

EE	FF	GG	HH	II	JJ	KK	LL
1	1	1	1	1	1	1	1

The 12 Games to Play

1.	A*	B*	C	X	ll	7.	A*	B*	I	S	ii
2.	A*	B*	D	Y	jj	8.	A*	B*	J	O	ff
3.	A*	B*	E	Z	hh	9.	A*	B*	K	Q	bb
4.	A*	B*	F	W	aa	10.	A*	B*	L	T	ee
5.	A*	B*	G	U	dd	11.	A*	B*	M	R	gg
6.	A*	B*	H	P	kk	12.	A*	B*	N	V	cc

Copyright © 1983-1998 Gail Howard

POWER NUMBER™ WHEEL 53039-2
Wheeling 39 Numbers in 13 games for a 3 of 3 Win

NUMBERS CORRECT***	MAXIMUM WINS				MINIMUM WINS			
	5x	4x	3x	2x	5x	4x	3x	2x
5 (w/o Jackpot)	0	2	1	10				
5	1	1	0	11	0	0	3	10
4	–	2	0	11	–	0	2	11
3	–	–	2	11	–	–	1	12
2	–	–	–	13	–	–	–	13

*** POWER NUMBER POSITIONS A* & B* MUST BE WINNERS.

Your 39 Numbers to Wheel

A*	B*	C	D	E	F	G	H	I	J
13	13	1	1	1	1	1	1	1	1

K	L	M	N	O	P	Q	R	S	T
1	2	1	1	1	1	1	1	1	2

U	V	W	X	Y	Z	AA	BB	CC	DD
1	1	1	1	1	1	1	1	1	1

EE	FF	GG	HH	II	JJ	KK	LL	MM
1	1	1	1	1	1	1	1	1

The 13 Games to Play

1.	A*	B*	C	Y	ll	4.	A*	B*	F	Z	jj
2.	A*	B*	D	P	kk	5.	A*	B*	G	Q	dd
3.	A*	B*	E	aa	bb	6.	A*	B*	H	O	ff

Copyright © 1983-1998 Gail Howard

(Continued Next Page)

POWER NUMBER™ WHEEL 53039-2 (Continued from previous page)

7.	A*	B*	I	U	ii
8.	A*	B*	J	V	X
9.	A*	B*	K	R	gg
10.	A*	B*	L	T	ee

11.	A*	B*	L	T	mm
12.	A*	B*	M	S	hh
13.	A*	B*	N	W	cc

Copyright © 1983-1998 Gail Howard

POWER NUMBER™WHEEL 53042-2
Wheeling 42 Numbers in 14 games for a 3 of 3 Win

NUMBERS CORRECT***	MAXIMUM WINS				MINIMUM WINS			
	5x	4x	3x	2x	5x	4x	3x	2x
5 (w/o Jackpot)	0	2	1	11				
5	1	1	0	12	0	0	3	11
4	–	2	0	12	–	0	2	12
3	–	–	2	12	–	–	1	13
2	–	–	–	14	–	–	–	14

*** POWER NUMBER POSITIONS A* & B* MUST BE WINNERS.

Your 42 Numbers to Wheel

A*	B*	C	D	E	F	G	H	I	J	K
14	14	1	1	1	1	1	2	1	1	1

L	M	N	O	P	Q	R	S	T	U	V
1	1	1	1	1	1	1	1	1	1	1

W	X	Y	Z	AA	BB	CC	DD	EE	FF	GG
1	1	1	1	1	1	1	1	1	1	2

HH	II	JJ	KK	LL	MM	NN	OO	PP
1	1	1	1	1	1	1	1	1

The 14 Games to Play

1.	A*	B*	C	Z	mm
2.	A*	B*	D	Y	oo
3.	A*	B*	E	aa	kk
4.	A*	B*	F	P	pp
5.	A*	B*	G	T	ee
6.	A*	B*	H	bb	gg
7.	A*	B*	H	dd	gg

8.	A*	B*	I	Q	ii
9.	A*	B*	J	W	ll
10.	A*	B*	K	U	nn
11.	A*	B*	L	V	cc
12.	A*	B*	M	X	jj
13.	A*	B*	N	R	ff
14.	A*	B*	O	S	hh

Copyright © 1983-1998 Gail Howard

POWER NUMBER™ WHEEL 53112-2
Wheeling 12 Numbers in 3 games for a 3 of 4 Win

NUMBERS CORRECT***	MAXIMUM WINS				MINIMUM WINS			
	5x	4x	3x	2x	5x	4x	3x	2x
5 (w/o Jackpot)	0	1	1	1				
5	1	0	0	2	0	0	2	1
4	–	1	0	2	–	0	1	2
3	–	–	1	2	–	–	0	3
2	–	–	–	3	–	–	–	3

*** POWER NUMBER POSITIONS A* & B* MUST BE WINNERS.

Your 12 Numbers to Wheel

A*	B*	C	D	E	F	G	H	I	J	K	L
3	3	1	1	1	1	1	1	1	1	0	1

The 3 Games to Play

1. | A* | B* | C | F | L |

2. | A* | B* | D | H | I |

3. | A* | B* | E | G | J |

Copyright © 1983-1998 Gail Howard

POWER NUMBER™ WHEEL 53113-2
Wheeling 13 Numbers in 4 games for a 3 of 4 Win

NUMBERS CORRECT***	MAXIMUM WINS				MINIMUM WINS			
	5x	4x	3x	2x	5x	4x	3x	2x
5 (w/o Jackpot)	0	2	1	1				
5	1	0	2	1	0	0	2	2
4	–	1	2	1	–	0	1	3
3	–	–	3	1	–	–	0	4
2	–	–	–	4	–	–	–	4

*** POWER NUMBER POSITIONS A* & B* MUST BE WINNERS.

Your 13 Numbers to Wheel

A*	B*	C	D	E	F	G
4	4	1	1	0	1	1

H	I	J	K	L	M
1	1	1	3	1	1

The 4 Games to Play

1. | A* | B* | C | J | M |

2. | A* | B* | D | K | L |

3. | A* | B* | F | I | K |

4. | A* | B* | G | H | K |

Copyright © 1983-1998 Gail Howard

POWER NUMBER™ WHEEL 53114-2
Wheeling 14 Numbers in 4 games for a 3 of 4 Win

NUMBERS CORRECT***	MAXIMUM WINS				MINIMUM WINS			
	5x	4x	3x	2x	5x	4x	3x	2x
5 (w/o Jackpot)	0	2	0	2				
5	1	0	1	2	0	0	2	2
4	–	1	1	2	–	0	1	3
3	–	–	2	2	–	–	0	4
2	–	–	–	4	–	–	–	4

*** POWER NUMBER POSITIONS A* & B* MUST BE WINNERS.

(Continued Next Page)

POWER NUMBER™ WHEEL 53114-2 (Continued from previous page)

Your 14 Numbers to Wheel

A*	B*	C	D	E	F	G
4	4	1	2	1	1	1

H	I	J	K	L	M	N
0	1	1	1	1	1	1

The 4 Games to Play

1. | A* | B* | C | G | N |

2. | A* | B* | D | I | L |

3. | A* | B* | D | J | K |

4. | A* | B* | E | F | M |

Copyright © 1983-1998 Gail Howard

POWER NUMBER™ WHEEL 53115-2

Wheeling 15 Numbers in 4 games for a 3 of 4 Win

NUMBERS CORRECT***	MAXIMUM WINS				MINIMUM WINS			
	5x	4x	3x	2x	5x	4x	3x	2x
5 (w/o Jackpot)	0	1	1	2				
5	1	0	0	3	0	0	2	2
4	–	1	0	3	–	0	1	3
3	–	–	1	3	–	–	0	4
2	–	–	–	4	–	–	–	4

*** POWER NUMBER POSITIONS A* & B* MUST BE WINNERS.

Your 15 Numbers to Wheel

A*	B*	C	D	E	F	G	H
4	4	1	1	0	1	1	1

I	J	K	L	M	N	O
1	1	1	1	1	1	1

The 4 Games to Play

1. | A* | B* | C | J | O |

2. | A* | B* | D | K | N |

3. | A* | B* | F | I | M |

4. | A* | B* | G | H | L |

Copyright © 1983-1998 Gail Howard

POWER NUMBER™ WHEEL 53118-2

Wheeling 18 Numbers in 5 games for a 3 of 4 Win

NUMBERS CORRECT***	MAXIMUM WINS				MINIMUM WINS			
	5x	4x	3x	2x	5x	4x	3x	2x
5 (w/o Jackpot)	0	1	1	3				
5	1	0	0	4	0	0	2	3
4	–	1	0	4	–	0	1	4
3	–	–	1	4	–	–	0	5
2	–	–	–	5	–	–	–	5

*** POWER NUMBER POSITIONS A* & B* MUST BE WINNERS.

Your 18 Numbers to Wheel

A*	B*	C	D	E	F	G	H	I
5	5	1	1	1	1	1	1	1

J	K	L	M	N	O	P	Q	R
1	1	1	0	1	1	1	1	1

(Continued Next Page)

POWER NUMBER™ WHEEL 53118-2 (Continued from previous page)
The 5 Games to Play

	A*	B*	C	K	R
1.					

	A*	B*	D	L	O
2.					

	A*	B*	E	H	Q
3.					

	A*	B*	F	J	P
4.					

	A*	B*	G	I	N
5.					

Copyright © 1983-1998 Gail Howard

POWER NUMBER™WHEEL 53121-2
Wheeling 21 Numbers in 6 games for a 3 of 4 Win

NUMBERS CORRECT***	MAXIMUM WINS				MINIMUM WINS			
	5x	4x	3x	2x	5x	4x	3x	2x
5 (w/o Jackpot)	0	1	1	4				
5	1	0	0	5	0	0	2	4
4	–	1	0	5	–	0	1	5
3	–	–	1	5	–	–	0	6
2	–	–	–	6	–	–	–	6

*** POWER NUMBER POSITIONS A* & B* MUST BE WINNERS.

Your 21 Numbers to Wheel

A*	B*	C	D	E	F	G	H	I	J	K
6	6	1	0	1	1	1	1	1	1	1

L	M	N	O	P	Q	R	S	T	U
1	1	1	1	1	1	1	1	1	1

The 6 Games to Play

	A*	B*	C	O	U
1.					

	A*	B*	E	L	T
2.					

	A*	B*	F	M	Q
3.					

	A*	B*	G	J	S
4.					

	A*	B*	H	K	R
5.					

	A*	B*	I	N	P
6.					

Copyright © 1983-1998 Gail Howard

POWER NUMBER™WHEEL 53124-2
Wheeling 24 Numbers in 7 games for a 3 of 4 Win

NUMBERS CORRECT***	MAXIMUM WINS				MINIMUM WINS			
	5x	4x	3x	2x	5x	4x	3x	2x
5 (w/o Jackpot)	0	1	1	5				
5	1	0	0	6	0	0	2	5
4	–	1	0	6	–	0	1	6
3	–	–	1	6	–	–	0	7
2	–	–	–	7	–	–	–	7

*** POWER NUMBER POSITIONS A* & B* MUST BE WINNERS.

Your 24 Numbers to Wheel

A*	B*	C	D	E	F	G	H	I	J	K	L
7	7	1	1	1	1	1	1	1	1	1	1

M	N	O	P	Q	R	S	T	U	V	W	X
1	0	1	1	1	1	1	1	1	1	1	1

The 7 Games to Play

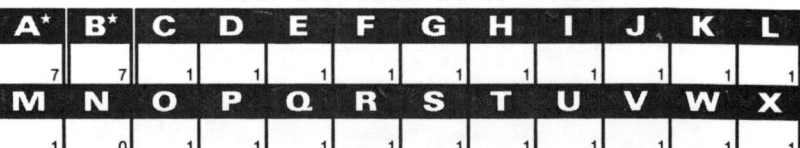

	A*	B*	C	P	W
1.					

	A*	B*	D	K	V
2.					

Copyright © 1983-1998 Gail Howard   (Continued Next Page)

POWER NUMBER™ WHEEL 53124-2 (Continued from previous page)

3.	A*	B*	E	J	X
4.	A*	B*	F	S	T
5.	A*	B*	G	L	U

6.	A*	B*	H	O	R
7.	A*	B*	I	M	Q

Copyright © 1983-1998 Gail Howard

POWER NUMBER™WHEEL 53127-2
Wheeling 27 Numbers in 8 games for a 3 of 4 Win

NUMBERS CORRECT***	MAXIMUM WINS				MINIMUM WINS			
	5x	4x	3x	2x	5x	4x	3x	2x
5 (w/o Jackpot)	0	1	1	6				
5	1	0	0	7	0	0	2	6
4	–	1	0	7	–	0	1	7
3	–	–	1	7	–	–	0	8
2	–	–	–	8	–	–	–	8

*** POWER NUMBER POSITIONS A* & B* MUST BE WINNERS.

Your 27 Numbers to Wheel

A*	B*	C	D	E	F	G	H	I
8	8	1	1	1	1	1	1	1

J	K	L	M	N	O	P	Q	R
1	1	0	1	1	1	1	1	1

S	T	U	V	W	X	Y	Z	AA
1	1	1	1	1	1	1	1	1

The 8 Games to Play

1.	A*	B*	C	X	Y
2.	A*	B*	D	T	Z
3.	A*	B*	E	P	W
4.	A*	B*	F	K	U

5.	A*	B*	G	O	S
6.	A*	B*	H	I	aa
7.	A*	B*	J	Q	R
8.	A*	B*	M	N	V

Copyright © 1983-1998 Gail Howard

POWER NUMBER™WHEEL 53130-2
Wheeling 30 Numbers in 9 games for a 3 of 4 Win

NUMBERS CORRECT***	MAXIMUM WINS				MINIMUM WINS			
	5x	4x	3x	2x	5x	4x	3x	2x
5 (w/o Jackpot)	0	1	1	7				
5	1	0	0	8	0	0	2	7
4	–	1	0	8	–	0	1	8
3	–	–	1	8	–	–	0	9
2	–	–	–	9	–	–	–	9

*** POWER NUMBER POSITIONS A* & B* MUST BE WINNERS.
(Continued Next Page)

POWER NUMBER™ WHEEL 53130-2 (Continued from previous page)
Your 30 Numbers to Wheel

A*	B*	C	D	E	F	G	H	I	J
9	9	1	1	1	1	1	1	1	1

K	L	M	N	O	P	Q	R	S	T
1	1	1	1	1	1	1	1	1	1

U	V	W	X	Y	Z	AA	BB	CC	DD
1	1	1	1	0	1	1	1	1	1

The 9 Games to Play

1.	A*	B*	C	R	cc
2.	A*	B*	D	Q	V
3.	A*	B*	E	P	T
4.	A*	B*	F	L	bb
5.	A*	B*	G	N	U

6.	A*	B*	H	S	Z
7.	A*	B*	I	M	aa
8.	A*	B*	J	W	X
9.	A*	B*	K	O	dd

POWER NUMBER™ WHEEL 53133-2
Wheeling 33 Numbers in 10 games for a 3 of 4 Win

NUMBERS CORRECT***	MAXIMUM WINS				MINIMUM WINS			
	5x	4x	3x	2x	5x	4x	3x	2x
5 (w/o Jackpot)	0	1	1	8				
5	1	0	0	9	0	0	2	8
4	–	1	0	9	–	0	1	9
3	–	–	1	9	–	–	0	10
2	–	–	–	10	–	–	–	10

*** POWER NUMBER POSITIONS A* & B* MUST BE WINNERS.

Your 33 Numbers to Wheel

A*	B*	C	D	E	F	G	H	I	J	K
10	10	1	1	1	1	1	1	1	1	1

L	M	N	O	P	Q	R	S	T	U	V
0	1	1	1	1	1	1	1	1	1	1

W	X	Y	Z	AA	BB	CC	DD	EE	FF	GG
1	1	1	1	1	1	1	1	1	1	1

The 10 Games to Play

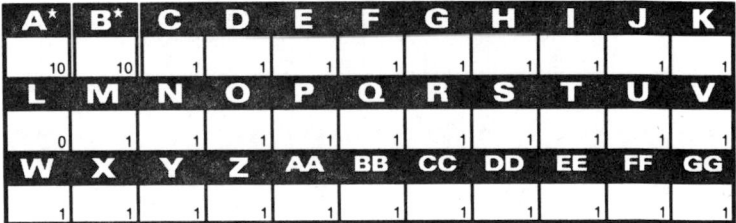

1.	A*	B*	C	Y	Z
2.	A*	B*	D	X	gg
3.	A*	B*	E	S	ff
4.	A*	B*	F	Q	aa
5.	A*	B*	G	H	ee

6.	A*	B*	I	O	dd
7.	A*	B*	J	R	W
8.	A*	B*	K	V	bb
9.	A*	B*	M	T	U
10.	A*	B*	N	P	cc

POWER NUMBER™WHEEL 53136-2
Wheeling 36 Numbers in 11 games for a 3 of 4 Win

NUMBERS CORRECT***	MAXIMUM WINS				MINIMUM WINS			
	5x	4x	3x	2x	5x	4x	3x	2x
5 (w/o Jackpot)	0	1	1	9	0	0	2	9
5	1	0	0	10	0	0	2	9
4	–	1	0	10	–	0	1	10
3	–	–	1	10	–	–	0	11
2	–	–	–	11	–	–	–	11

*** POWER NUMBER POSITIONS A* & B* MUST BE WINNERS.

Your 36 Numbers to Wheel

A*	B*	C	D	E	F	G	H	I	J	K	L
11	11	1	1	1	1	1	1	1	1	1	1

M	N	O	P	Q	R	S	T	U	V	W	X
1	1	1	1	1	1	1	1	1	0	1	1

Y	Z	AA	BB	CC	DD	EE	FF	GG	HH	II	JJ
1	1	1	1	1	1	1	1	1	1	1	1

The 11 Games to Play

1.	A*	B*	C	ee	ff
2.	A*	B*	D	P	gg
3.	A*	B*	E	X	Z
4.	A*	B*	F	Q	hh
5.	A*	B*	G	cc	dd
6.	A*	B*	H	N	jj
7.	A*	B*	I	R	aa
8.	A*	B*	J	T	Y
9.	A*	B*	K	O	ii
10.	A*	B*	L	S	bb
11.	A*	B*	M	U	W

Copyright © 1983-1998 Gail Howard

POWER NUMBER™WHEEL 53139-2
Wheeling 39 Numbers in 12 games for a 3 of 4 Win

NUMBERS CORRECT***	MAXIMUM WINS				MINIMUM WINS			
	5x	4x	3x	2x	5x	4x	3x	2x
5 (w/o Jackpot)	0	1	1	10				
5	1	0	0	11	0	0	2	10
4	–	1	0	11	–	0	1	11
3	–	–	1	11	–	–	0	12
2	–	–	–	12	–	–	–	12

*** POWER NUMBER POSITIONS A* & B* MUST BE WINNERS.

Your 39 Numbers to Wheel

A*	B*	C	D	E	F	G	H	I	J
12	12	1	1	1	1	1	1	1	1

K	L	M	N	O	P	Q	R	S	T
1	1	1	1	1	1	1	1	0	1

U	V	W	X	Y	Z	AA	BB	CC	DD
1	1	1	1	1	1	1	1	1	1

EE	FF	GG	HH	II	JJ	KK	LL	MM
1	1	1	1	1	1	1	1	1

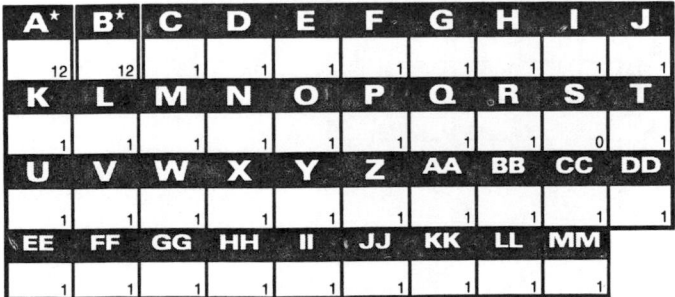

(Continued Next Page)

POWER NUMBER™ WHEEL 53139-2 (Continued from previous page)
The 12 Games to Play

1.	A*	B*	C	Y	ff
2.	A*	B*	D	O	mm
3.	A*	B*	E	Q	jj
4.	A*	B*	F	X	bb
5.	A*	B*	G	V	ii
6.	A*	B*	H	P	hh

7.	A*	B*	I	dd	ee
8.	A*	B*	J	T	ll
9.	A*	B*	K	U	z
10.	A*	B*	L	W	gg
11.	A*	B*	M	aa	cc
12.	A*	B*	N	R	kk

POWER NUMBER™WHEEL 53142-2
Wheeling 42 Numbers in 13 games for a 3 of 4 Win

NUMBERS CORRECT***	MAXIMUM WINS				MINIMUM WINS			
	5x	4x	3x	2x	5x	4x	3x	2x
5 (w/o Jackpot)	0	1	1	11				
5	1	0	0	12	0	0	2	11
4	–	1	0	12	–	0	1	12
3	–	–	1	12	–	–	0	13
2	–	–	–	13	–	–	–	13

*** POWER NUMBER POSITIONS A* & B* MUST BE WINNERS.

Your 42 Numbers to Wheel

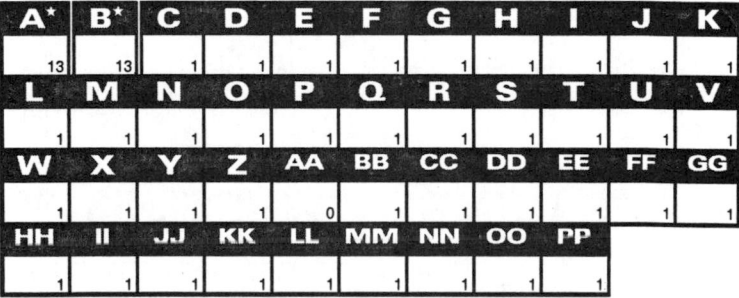

A*	B*	C	D	E	F	G	H	I	J	K
13	13	1	1	1	1	1	1	1	1	1

L	M	N	O	P	Q	R	S	T	U	V
1	1	1	1	1	1	1	1	1	1	1

W	X	Y	Z	AA	BB	CC	DD	EE	FF	GG
1	1	1	1	0	1	1	1	1	1	1

HH	II	JJ	KK	LL	MM	NN	OO	PP
1	1	1	1	1	1	1	1	1

The 13 Games to Play

1.	A*	B*	C	Y	mm
2.	A*	B*	D	R	oo
3.	A*	B*	E	dd	jj
4.	A*	B*	F	Q	kk
5.	A*	B*	G	S	ii
6.	A*	B*	H	X	ii
7.	A*	B*	I	W	ee

8.	A*	B*	J	U	gg
9.	A*	B*	K	P	hh
10.	A*	B*	L	V	pp
11.	A*	B*	M	bb	cc
12.	A*	B*	N	Z	ff
13.	A*	B*	O	T	nn

POWER NUMBER™WHEEL 53145-2
Wheeling 45 Numbers in 14 games for a 3 of 4 Win

NUMBERS CORRECT***	MAXIMUM WINS				MINIMUM WINS			
	5x	4x	3x	2x	5x	4x	3x	2x
5 (w/o Jackpot)	0	1	1	12				
5	1	0	0	13	0	0	2	12
4	–	1	0	13	–	0	1	13
3	–	–	1	13	–	–	0	14
2	–	–	–	14	–	–	–	14

*** POWER NUMBER POSITIONS A* & B* MUST BE WINNERS.

Your 45 Numbers to Wheel

A*	B*	C	D	E	F	G	H	I	J	K	L
14	14	1	1	1	1	1	1	1	1	1	1

M	N	O	P	Q	R	S	T	U	V	W	X
1	1	1	1	1	1	1	1	1	1	1	1

Y	Z	AA	BB	CC	DD	EE	FF	GG	HH	II	JJ
1	1	1	1	1	1	1	1	1	1	1	1

KK	LL	MM	NN	OO	PP	QQ	RR	SS
1	1	1	1	1	1	1	0	1

The 14 Games to Play

1.	A*	B*	C	bb	ii	8.	A*	B*	J	ee	kk
2.	A*	B*	D	Y	jj	9.	A*	B*	K	W	qq
3.	A*	B*	E	aa	oo	10.	A*	B*	L	U	hh
4.	A*	B*	F	V	ss	11.	A*	B*	M	Q	dd
5.	A*	B*	G	T	nn	12.	A*	B*	N	Z	ff
6.	A*	B*	H	S	ll	13.	A*	B*	O	X	pp
7.	A*	B*	I	cc	gg	14.	A*	B*	P	R	mm

Copyright © 1983-1998 Gail Howard

POWER NUMBER™WHEEL 53149-2
Wheeling 49 Numbers in 16 games for a 3 of 4 Win

NUMBERS CORRECT***	MAXIMUM WINS				MINIMUM WINS			
	5x	4x	3x	2x	5x	4x	3x	2x
5 (w/o Jackpot)	0	2	1	13				
5	1	1	0	14	0	0	2	14
4	–	2	0	14	–	0	1	15
3	–	–	2	14	–	–	0	16
2	–	–	–	16	–	–	–	16

*** POWER NUMBER POSITIONS A* & B* MUST BE WINNERS.
(Continued Next Page)

POWER NUMBER™ WHEEL 53149-2 (Continued from previous page)
Your 49 Numbers to Wheel

A*	B*	C	D	E	F	G	H	I	J
16	16	1	1	1	1	1	1	1	1

K	L	M	N	O	P	Q	R	S	T
1	1	1	1	1	1	1	1	1	1

U	V	W	X	Y	Z	AA	BB	CC	DD
1	1	1	1	1	1	0	1	2	2

EE	FF	GG	HH	II	JJ	KK	LL	MM	NN
1	1	1	1	1	1	1	1	1	1

OO	PP	QQ	RR	SS	TT	UU	VV	WW
1	1	1	1	1	1	1	1	1

The 16 Games to Play

#						#					
1.	A*	B*	C	mm	nn	9.	A*	B*	K	S	rr
2.	A*	B*	D	ff	qq	10.	A*	B*	L	cc	dd
3.	A*	B*	E	jj	pp	11.	A*	B*	M	ee	ll
4.	A*	B*	F	R	ss	12.	A*	B*	N	W	Z
5.	A*	B*	G	V	oo	13.	A*	B*	O	hh	kk
6.	A*	B*	H	Q	ii	14.	A*	B*	T	X	tt
7.	A*	B*	I	Y	vv	15.	A*	B*	U	bb	ww
8.	A*	B*	J	P	uu	16.	A*	B*	cc	dd	gg

POWER NUMBER™ WHEEL 55006-3
Wheeling 6 Numbers in 3 games for a 5 of 5 Win

NUMBERS CORRECT***	MAXIMUM WINS				MINIMUM WINS			
	5x	4x	3x	2x	5x	4x	3x	2x
5 (w/o Jackpot)	0	0	0	0				
5	1	2	0	0	1	2	0	0
4	–	2	1	0	–	2	1	0
3	–	–	3	3	–	–	3	3
2	–	–	–	3	–	–	–	3

*** POWER NUMBER POSITIONS A*, B* & C* MUST BE WINNERS.

Your 6 Numbers to Wheel

A*	B*	C*	D	E	F
3	3	3	2	2	2

The 3 Games to Play

#					
1.	A*	B*	C*	D	E
2.	A*	B*	C*	D	F
3.	A*	B*	C*	E	F

POWER NUMBER™WHEEL 55007-3

Wheeling 7 Numbers in 6 games for a 5 of 5 Win

NUMBERS CORRECT***	MAXIMUM WINS				MINIMUM WINS			
	5x	4x	3x	2x	5x	4x	3x	2x
5 (w/o Jackpot)	0	0	0	0				
5	1	4	1	0	1	4	1	0
4	-	3	3	0	-	3	3	0
3	-	-	6	6	-	-	6	6
2	-	-	-	6	-	-	-	6

*** POWER NUMBER POSITIONS A*, B* & C* MUST BE WINNERS.

Your 7 Numbers to Wheel

A*	B*	C*	D	E	F	G
6	6	6	3	3	3	3

The 6 Games to Play

	A*	B*	C*	D	E
1.	A*	B*	C*	D	E
2.	A*	B*	C*	D	F
3.	A*	B*	C*	D	G

	A*	B*	C*	E	F
4.	A*	B*	C*	E	F
5.	A*	B*	C*	E	G
6.	A*	B*	C*	F	G

Copyright © 1983-1998 Gail Howard

POWER NUMBER™WHEEL 55008-3

Wheeling 8 Numbers in 10 games for a 5 of 5 Win

NUMBERS CORRECT***	MAXIMUM WINS				MINIMUM WINS			
	5x	4x	3x	2x	5x	4x	3x	2x
5 (w/o Jackpot)	0	0	0	0				
5	1	6	3	0	1	6	3	0
4	-	4	6	0	-	4	6	0
3	-	-	10	10	-	-	10	10
2	-	-	-	10	-	-	-	10

*** POWER NUMBER POSITIONS A*, B* & C* MUST BE WINNERS.

Your 8 Numbers to Wheel

A*	B*	C*	D	E	F	G	H
10	10	10	4	4	4	4	4

The 10 Games to Play

	A*	B*	C*	D	E
1.	A*	B*	C*	D	E
2.	A*	B*	C*	D	F
3.	A*	B*	C*	D	G
4.	A*	B*	C*	D	H
5.	A*	B*	C*	E	F

	A*	B*	C*	E	G
6.	A*	B*	C*	E	G
7.	A*	B*	C*	E	H
8.	A*	B*	C*	F	G
9.	A*	B*	C*	F	H
10.	A*	B*	C*	G	H

Copyright © 1983-1998 Gail Howard

POWER NUMBER™WHEEL 55009-3
Wheeling 9 Numbers in 15 games for a 5 of 5 Win

NUMBERS CORRECT***	MAXIMUM WINS				MINIMUM WINS			
	5x	4x	3x	2x	5x	4x	3x	2x
5 (w/o Jackpot)	0	0	0	0				
5	1	8	6	0	1	8	6	0
4	–	5	10	0	–	5	10	0
3	–	–	15	15	–	–	15	15
2	–	–	–	15	–	–	–	15

*** POWER NUMBER POSITIONS A*, B* & C* MUST BE WINNERS.

Your 9 Numbers to Wheel

A*	B*	C*	D	E	F	G	H	I
15	15	15	5	5	5	5	5	5

The 15 Games to Play

	A*	B*	C*	D	E
1.	A*	B*	C*	D	E
2.	A*	B*	C*	D	F
3.	A*	B*	C*	D	G
4.	A*	B*	C*	D	H
5.	A*	B*	C*	D	I
6.	A*	B*	C*	E	F
7.	A*	B*	C*	E	G
8.	A*	B*	C*	E	H
9.	A*	B*	C*	E	I
10.	A*	B*	C*	F	G
11.	A*	B*	C*	F	H
12.	A*	B*	C*	F	I
13.	A*	B*	C*	G	H
14.	A*	B*	C*	G	I
15.	A*	B*	C*	H	I

Copyright © 1983-1998 Gail Howard

POWER NUMBER™WHEEL 55010-3
Wheeling 10 Numbers in 21 games for a 5 of 5 Win

NUMBERS CORRECT***	MAXIMUM WINS				MINIMUM WINS			
	5x	4x	3x	2x	5x	4x	3x	2x
5 (w/o Jackpot)	0	0	0	0				
5	1	10	10	0	1	10	10	0
4	–	6	15	0	–	6	15	0
3	–	–	21	21	–	–	21	21
2	–	–	–	21	–	–	–	21

*** POWER NUMBER POSITIONS A*, B* & C* MUST BE WINNERS.

Your 10 Numbers to Wheel

A*	B*	C*	D	E	F	G	H	I	J
21	21	21	6	6	6	6	6	6	6

The 21 Games to Play

	A*	B*	C*	D	E
1.	A*	B*	C*	D	E
2.	A*	B*	C*	D	F
3.	A*	B*	C*	D	G
4.	A*	B*	C*	D	H
5.	A*	B*	C*	D	I
6.	A*	B*	C*	D	J
7.	A*	B*	C*	E	F
8.	A*	B*	C*	E	G
9.	A*	B*	C*	E	H
10.	A*	B*	C*	E	I
11.	A*	B*	C*	E	J
12.	A*	B*	C*	F	G

Copyright © 1983-1998 Gail Howard   (Continued Next Page)

POWER NUMBER™ WHEEL 55010-3 (Continued from previous page)

13.	A*	B*	C*	F	H
14.	A*	B*	C*	F	I
15.	A*	B*	C*	F	J
16.	A*	B*	C*	G	H
17.	A*	B*	C*	G	I

18.	A*	B*	C*	G	J
19.	A*	B*	C*	H	I
20.	A*	B*	C*	H	J
21.	A*	B*	C*	I	J

Copyright © 1983-1998 Gail Howard

POWER NUMBER™WHEEL 55011-3
Wheeling 11 Numbers in 28 games for a 5 of 5 Win

NUMBERS CORRECT***	MAXIMUM WINS				MINIMUM WINS			
	5x	4x	3x	2x	5x	4x	3x	2x
6 (w/o Jackpot)	0	0	0	0				
5	1	12	15	0	1	12	15	0
4	–	7	21	0	–	7	21	0
3	–	–	28	28	–	–	28	28
2	–	–	–	28	–	–	–	28

*** POWER NUMBER POSITIONS A*, B* & C* MUST BE WINNERS.

Your 11 Numbers to Wheel

A*	B*	C*	D	E	F	G	H	I	J	K
28	28	28	7	7	7	7	7	7	7	7

The 28 Games to Play

1.	A*	B*	C*	D	E
2.	A*	B*	C*	D	F
3.	A*	B*	C*	D	G
4.	A*	B*	C*	D	H
5.	A*	B*	C*	D	I
6.	A*	B*	C*	D	J
7.	A*	B*	C*	D	K
8.	A*	B*	C*	E	F
9.	A*	B*	C*	E	G
10.	A*	B*	C*	E	H
11.	A*	B*	C*	E	I
12.	A*	B*	C*	E	J
13.	A*	B*	C*	E	K
14.	A*	B*	C*	F	G

15.	A*	B*	C*	F	H
16.	A*	B*	C*	F	I
17.	A*	B*	C*	F	J
18.	A*	B*	C*	F	K
19.	A*	B*	C*	G	H
20.	A*	B*	C*	G	I
21.	A*	B*	C*	G	J
22.	A*	B*	C*	G	K
23.	A*	B*	C*	H	I
24.	A*	B*	C*	H	J
25.	A*	B*	C*	H	K
26.	A*	B*	C*	I	J
27.	A*	B*	C*	I	K
28.	A*	B*	C*	J	K

Copyright © 1983-1998 Gail Howard

POWER NUMBER™ WHEEL 55012-3
Wheeling 12 Numbers in 36 games for a 5 of 5 Win

NUMBERS CORRECT***	MAXIMUM WINS				MINIMUM WINS			
	5x	4x	3x	2x	5x	4x	3x	2x
5 (w/o Jackpot)	0	0	0	0				
5	1	14	21	0	1	14	21	0
4	–	8	28	0	–	8	28	0
3	–	–	36	36	–	–	36	36
2	–	–	–	36	–	–	–	36

*** POWER NUMBER POSITIONS A*, B* & C* MUST BE WINNERS.

Your 12 Numbers to Wheel

A*	B*	C*	D	E	F	G	H	I	J	K	L
36	36	36	8	8	8	8	8	8	8	8	8

The 36 Games to Play

#							#					
1.	A*	B*	C*	D	E		19.	A*	B*	C*	F	J
2.	A*	B*	C*	D	F		20.	A*	B*	C*	F	K
3.	A*	B*	C*	D	G		21.	A*	B*	C*	F	L
4.	A*	B*	C*	D	H		22.	A*	B*	C*	G	H
5.	A*	B*	C*	D	I		23.	A*	B*	C*	G	I
6.	A*	B*	C*	D	J		24.	A*	B*	C*	G	J
7.	A*	B*	C*	D	K		25.	A*	B*	C*	G	K
8.	A*	B*	C*	D	L		26.	A*	B*	C*	G	L
9.	A*	B*	C*	E	F		27.	A*	B*	C*	H	I
10.	A*	B*	C*	E	G		28.	A*	B*	C*	H	J
11.	A*	B*	C*	E	H		29.	A*	B*	C*	H	K
12.	A*	B*	C*	E	I		30.	A*	B*	C*	H	L
13.	A*	B*	C*	E	J		31.	A*	B*	C*	I	J
14.	A*	B*	C*	E	K		32.	A*	B*	C*	I	K
15.	A*	B*	C*	E	L		33.	A*	B*	C*	I	L
16.	A*	B*	C*	F	G		34.	A*	B*	C*	J	K
17.	A*	B*	C*	F	H		35.	A*	B*	C*	J	L
18.	A*	B*	C*	F	I		36.	A*	B*	C*	K	L

POWER NUMBER™ WHEEL 55013-3
Wheeling 13 Numbers in 45 games for a 5 of 5 Win

NUMBERS CORRECT***	MAXIMUM WINS				MINIMUM WINS			
	5x	4x	3x	2x	5x	4x	3x	2x
5 (w/o Jackpot)	0	0	0	0				
5	1	16	28	0	1	16	28	0
4	–	9	36	0	–	9	36	0
3	–	–	45	45	–	–	45	45
2	–	–	–	45	–	–	–	45

*** POWER NUMBER POSITIONS A*, B* & C* MUST BE WINNERS.

Your 13 Numbers to Wheel

A*	B*	C*	D	E	F	G
45	45	45	9	9	9	9

H	I	J	K	L	M
9	9	9	9	9	9

The 45 Games to Play

#						#					
1.	A*	B*	C*	D	E	24.	A*	B*	C*	F	M
2.	A*	B*	C*	D	F	25.	A*	B*	C*	G	H
3.	A*	B*	C*	D	G	26.	A*	B*	C*	G	I
4.	A*	B*	C*	D	H	27.	A*	B*	C*	G	J
5.	A*	B*	C*	D	I	28.	A*	B*	C*	G	K
6.	A*	B*	C*	D	J	29.	A*	B*	C*	G	L
7.	A*	B*	C*	D	K	30.	A*	B*	C*	G	M
8.	A*	B*	C*	D	L	31.	A*	B*	C*	H	I
9.	A*	B*	C*	D	M	32.	A*	B*	C*	H	J
10.	A*	D*	C*	E	F	33.	A*	B*	C*	H	K
11.	A*	B*	C*	E	G	34.	A*	B*	C*	H	L
12.	A*	B*	C*	E	H	35.	A*	B*	C*	H	M
13.	A*	B*	C*	E	I	36.	A*	B*	C*	I	J
14.	A*	B*	C*	E	J	37.	A*	B*	C*	I	K
15.	A*	B*	C*	E	K	38.	A*	B*	C*	I	L
16.	A*	B*	C*	E	L	39.	A*	B*	C*	I	M
17.	A*	B*	C*	E	M	40.	A*	B*	C*	J	K
18.	A*	B*	C*	F	G	41.	A*	B*	C*	J	L
19.	A*	B*	C*	F	H	42.	A*	B*	C*	J	M
20.	A*	B*	C*	F	I	43.	A*	B*	C*	K	L
21.	A*	B*	C*	F	J	44.	A*	B*	C*	K	M
22.	A*	B*	C*	F	K	45.	A*	B*	C*	L	M
23.	A*	B*	C*	F	L						

POWER NUMBER™ WHEEL 55014-3
Wheeling 14 Numbers in 55 games for a 5 of 5 Win

NUMBERS CORRECT***	MAXIMUM WINS				MINIMUM WINS			
	5x	4x	3x	2x	5x	4x	3x	2x
5 (w/o Jackpot)	0	0	0	0				
5	1	18	36	0	1	18	36	0
4	-	10	45	0	-	10	45	0
3	-	-	55	55	-	-	55	55
2	-	-	-	55	-	-	-	55

*** POWER NUMBER POSITIONS A*, B* & C* MUST BE WINNERS.

Your 14 Numbers to Wheel

A*	B*	C*	D	E	F	G
55	55	55	10	10	10	10

H	I	J	K	L	M	N
10	10	10	10	10	10	10

The 55 Games to Play

#						#					
1.	A*	B*	C*	D	E	25.	A*	B*	C*	F	L
2.	A*	B*	C*	D	F	26.	A*	B*	C*	F	M
3.	A*	B*	C*	D	G	27.	A*	B*	C*	F	N
4.	A*	B*	C*	D	H	28.	A*	B*	C*	G	H
5.	A*	B*	C*	D	I	29.	A*	B*	C*	G	I
6.	A*	B*	C*	D	J	30.	A*	B*	C*	G	J
7.	A*	B*	C*	D	K	31.	A*	B*	C*	G	K
8.	A*	B*	C*	D	L	32.	A*	B*	C*	G	L
9.	A*	B*	C*	D	M	33.	A*	B*	C*	G	M
10.	A*	B*	C*	D	N	34.	A*	B*	C*	G	N
11.	A*	B*	C*	E	F	35.	A*	B*	C*	H	I
12.	A*	B*	C*	E	G	36.	A*	B*	C*	H	J
13.	A*	B*	C*	E	H	37.	A*	B*	C*	H	K
14.	A*	B*	C*	E	I	38.	A*	B*	C*	H	L
15.	A*	B*	C*	E	J	39.	A*	B*	C*	H	M
16.	A*	B*	C*	E	K	40.	A*	B*	C*	H	N
17.	A*	B*	C*	E	L	41.	A*	B*	C*	I	J
18.	A*	B*	C*	E	M	42.	A*	B*	C*	I	K
19.	A*	B*	C*	E	N	43.	A*	B*	C*	I	L
20.	A*	B*	C*	F	G	44.	A*	B*	C*	I	M
21.	A*	B*	C*	F	H	45.	A*	B*	C*	I	N
22.	A*	B*	C*	F	I	46.	A*	B*	C*	J	K
23.	A*	B*	C*	F	J	47.	A*	B*	C*	J	L
24.	A*	B*	C*	F	K	48.	A*	B*	C*	J	M

    (Continued Next Page)

POWER NUMBER™ WHEEL 55014-3 (Continued from previous page)

49.	A*	B*	C*	J	N
50.	A*	B*	C*	K	L
51.	A*	B*	C*	K	M
52.	A*	B*	C*	K	N

53.	A*	B*	C*	L	M
54.	A*	B*	C*	L	N
55.	A*	B*	C*	M	N

POWER NUMBER™ WHEEL 55015-3
Wheeling 15 Numbers in 66 games for a 5 of 5 Win

NUMBERS CORRECT***	MAXIMUM WINS				MINIMUM WINS			
	5x	4x	3x	2x	5x	4x	3x	2x
5 (w/o Jackpot)	0	0	0	0				
5	1	20	45	0	1	20	45	0
4	–	11	55	0	–	11	55	0
3	–	–	66	66	–	–	66	66
2	–	–	–	66	–	–	–	66

*** POWER NUMBER POSITIONS A*, B* & C* MUST BE WINNERS.

Your 15 Numbers to Wheel

A*	B*	C*	D	E	F	G	H
66	66	66	11	11	11	11	11

I	J	K	L	M	N	O
11	11	11	11	11	11	11

The 66 Games to Play

1.	A*	B*	C*	D	E
2.	A*	B*	C*	D	F
3.	A*	B*	C*	D	G
4.	A*	B*	C*	D	H
5.	A*	B*	C*	D	I
6.	A*	B*	C*	D	J
7.	A*	B*	C*	D	K
8.	A*	B*	C*	D	L
9.	A*	B*	C*	D	M
10.	A*	B*	C*	D	N
11.	A*	B*	C*	D	O
12.	A*	B*	C*	E	F
13.	A*	B*	C*	E	G
14.	A*	B*	C*	E	H
15.	A*	B*	C*	E	I
16.	A*	B*	C*	E	J
17.	A*	B*	C*	E	K
18.	A*	B*	C*	E	L

19.	A*	B*	C*	E	M
20.	A*	B*	C*	E	N
21.	A*	B*	C*	E	O
22.	A*	B*	C*	F	G
23.	A*	B*	C*	F	H
24.	A*	B*	C*	F	I
25.	A*	B*	C*	F	J
26.	A*	B*	C*	F	K
27.	A*	B*	C*	F	L
28.	A*	B*	C*	F	M
29.	A*	B*	C*	F	N
30.	A*	B*	C*	F	O
31.	A*	B*	C*	G	H
32.	A*	B*	C*	G	I
33.	A*	B*	C*	G	J
34.	A*	B*	C*	G	K
35.	A*	B*	C*	G	L
36.	A*	B*	C*	G	M

(Continued Next Page)

POWER NUMBER™ WHEEL 55015-3 (Continued from previous page)

#						#					
37.	A*	B*	C*	G	N	52.	A*	B*	C*	J	K
38.	A*	B*	C*	G	O	53.	A*	B*	C*	J	L
39.	A*	B*	C*	H	I	54.	A*	B*	C*	J	M
40.	A*	B*	C*	H	J	55.	A*	B*	C*	J	N
41.	A*	B*	C*	H	K	56.	A*	B*	C*	J	O
42.	A*	B*	C*	H	L	57.	A*	B*	C*	K	L
43.	A*	B*	C*	H	M	58.	A*	B*	C*	K	M
44.	A*	B*	C*	H	N	59.	A*	B*	C*	K	N
45.	A*	B*	C*	H	O	60.	A*	B*	C*	K	O
46.	A*	B*	C*	I	J	61.	A*	B*	C*	L	M
47.	A*	B*	C*	I	K	62.	A*	B*	C*	L	N
48.	A*	B*	C*	I	L	63.	A*	B*	C*	L	O
49.	A*	B*	C*	I	M	64.	A*	B*	C*	M	N
50.	A*	B*	C*	I	N	65.	A*	B*	C*	M	O
51.	A*	B*	C*	I	O	66.	A*	B*	C*	N	O

POWER NUMBER™ WHEEL 55016-3
Wheeling 16 Numbers in 78 games for a 5 of 5 Win

NUMBERS CORRECT***	MAXIMUM WINS				MINIMUM WINS			
	5x	4x	3x	2x	5x	4x	3x	2x
5 (w/o Jackpot)	0	0	0	0				
5	1	22	55	0	1	22	55	0
4	–	12	66	0	–	12	66	0
3	–	–	78	78	–	–	78	78
2	–	–	–	78	–	–	–	78

*** POWER NUMBER POSITIONS A*, B* & C* MUST BE WINNERS.

Your 16 Numbers to Wheel

A*	B*	C*	D	E	F	G	H
78	78	78	12	12	12	12	12

I	J	K	L	M	N	O	P
12	12	12	12	12	12	12	12

The 78 Games to Play

#						#					
1.	A*	B*	C*	D	E	8.	A*	B*	C*	D	L
2.	A*	B*	C*	D	F	9.	A*	B*	C*	D	M
3.	A*	B*	C*	D	G	10.	A*	B*	C*	D	N
4.	A*	B*	C*	D	H	11.	A*	B*	C*	D	O
5.	A*	B*	C*	D	I	12.	A*	B*	C*	D	P
6.	A*	B*	C*	D	J	13.	A*	B*	C*	E	F
7.	A*	B*	C*	D	K	14.	A*	B*	C*	E	G

     (Continued Next Page)

POWER NUMBER™ WHEEL 55016-3 (Continued from previous page)

#	A*	B*	C*	col	col	#	A*	B*	C*	col	col
15.	A*	B*	C*	E	H	47.	A*	B*	C*	H	M
16.	A*	B*	C*	E	I	48.	A*	B*	C*	H	N
17.	A*	B*	C*	E	J	49.	A*	B*	C*	H	O
18.	A*	B*	C*	E	K	50.	A*	B*	C*	H	P
19.	A*	B*	C*	E	L	51.	A*	B*	C*	I	J
20.	A*	B*	C*	E	M	52.	A*	B*	C*	I	K
21.	A*	B*	C*	E	N	53.	A*	B*	C*	I	L
22.	A*	B*	C*	E	O	54.	A*	B*	C*	I	M
23.	A*	B*	C*	E	P	55.	A*	B*	C*	I	N
24.	A*	B*	C*	F	G	56.	A*	B*	C*	I	O
25.	A*	B*	C*	F	H	57.	A*	B*	C*	I	P
26.	A*	B*	C*	F	I	58.	A*	B*	C*	J	K
27.	A*	B*	C*	F	J	59.	A*	B*	C*	J	L
28.	A*	B*	C*	F	K	60.	A*	B*	C*	J	M
29.	A*	B*	C*	F	L	61.	A*	B*	C*	J	N
30.	A*	B*	C*	F	M	62.	A*	B*	C*	J	O
31.	A*	B*	C*	F	N	63.	A*	B*	C*	J	P
32.	A*	B*	C*	F	O	64.	A*	B*	C*	K	L
33.	A*	B*	C*	F	P	65.	A*	B*	C*	K	M
34.	A*	B*	C*	G	H	66.	A*	B*	C*	K	N
35.	A*	B*	C*	G	I	67.	A*	B*	C*	K	O
36.	A*	B*	C*	G	J	68.	A*	B*	C*	K	P
37.	A*	B*	C*	G	K	69.	A*	B*	C*	L	M
38.	A*	B*	C*	G	L	70.	A*	B*	C*	L	N
39.	A*	B*	C*	G	M	71.	A*	B*	C*	L	O
40.	A*	B*	C*	G	N	72.	A*	B*	C*	L	P
41.	A*	B*	C*	G	O	73.	A*	B*	C*	M	N
42.	A*	B*	C*	G	P	74.	A*	B*	C*	M	O
43.	A*	B*	C*	H	I	75.	A*	B*	C*	M	P
44.	A*	B*	C*	H	J	76.	A*	B*	C*	N	O
45.	A*	B*	C*	H	K	77.	A*	B*	C*	N	P
46.	A*	B*	C*	H	L	78.	A*	B*	C*	O	P

POWER NUMBER™WHEEL 55017-3
Wheeling 17 Numbers in 91 games for a 5 of 5 Win

NUMBERS CORRECT***	MAXIMUM WINS				MINIMUM WINS			
	5x	4x	3x	2x	5x	4x	3x	2x
5 (w/o Jackpot)	0	0	0	0				
5	1	24	66	0	1	24	66	0
4	–	13	78	0	–	13	78	0
3	–	–	91	91	–	–	91	91
2	–	–	–	91	–	–	–	91

*** POWER NUMBER POSITIONS A*, B* & C* MUST BE WINNERS.

Your 17 Numbers to Wheel

A*	B*	C*	D	E	F	G	H	I
91	91	91	13	13	13	13	13	13

J	K	L	M	N	O	P	Q	
13	13	13	13	13	13	13	13	

The 91 Games to Play

#						#					
1.	A*	B*	C*	D	E	25.	A*	B*	C*	E	Q
2.	A*	B*	C*	D	F	26.	A*	B*	C*	F	G
3.	A*	B*	C*	D	G	27.	A*	B*	C*	F	H
4.	A*	B*	C*	D	H	28.	A*	B*	C*	F	I
5.	A*	B*	C*	D	I	29.	A*	B*	C*	F	J
6.	A*	B*	C*	D	J	30.	A*	B*	C*	F	K
7.	A*	B*	C*	D	K	31.	A*	B*	C*	F	L
8.	A*	B*	C*	D	L	32.	A*	B*	C*	F	M
9.	A*	B*	C*	D	M	33.	A*	B*	C*	F	N
10.	A*	B*	C*	D	N	34.	A*	B*	C*	F	O
11.	A*	B*	C*	D	O	35.	A*	B*	C*	F	P
12.	A*	B*	C*	D	P	36.	A*	B*	C*	F	Q
13.	A*	B*	C*	D	Q	37.	A*	B*	C*	G	H
14.	A*	B*	C*	E	F	38.	A*	B*	C*	G	I
15.	A*	B*	C*	E	G	39.	A*	B*	C*	G	J
16.	A*	B*	C*	E	H	40.	A*	B*	C*	G	K
17.	A*	B*	C*	E	I	41.	A*	B*	C*	G	L
18.	A*	B*	C*	E	J	42.	A*	B*	C*	G	M
19.	A*	B*	C*	E	K	43.	A*	B*	C*	G	N
20.	A*	B*	C*	E	L	44.	A*	B*	C*	G	O
21.	A*	B*	C*	E	M	45.	A*	B*	C*	G	P
22.	A*	B*	C*	E	N	46.	A*	B*	C*	G	Q
23.	A*	B*	C*	E	O	47.	A*	B*	C*	H	I
24.	A*	B*	C*	E	P	48.	A*	B*	C*	H	J

Copyright © 1983-1998 Gail Howard

(Continued Next Page)

POWER NUMBER™ WHEEL 55017-3 (Continued from previous page)

49.	A*	B*	C*	H	K
50.	A*	B*	C*	H	L
51.	A*	B*	C*	H	M
52.	A*	B*	C*	H	N
53.	A*	B*	C*	H	O
54.	A*	B*	C*	H	P
55.	A*	B*	C*	H	Q
56.	A*	B*	C*	I	J
57.	A*	B*	C*	I	K
58.	A*	B*	C*	I	L
59.	A*	B*	C*	I	M
60.	A*	B*	C*	I	N
61.	A*	B*	C*	I	O
62.	A*	B*	C*	I	P
63.	A*	B*	C*	I	Q
64.	A*	B*	C*	J	K
65.	A*	B*	C*	J	L
66.	A*	B*	C*	J	M
67.	A*	B*	C*	J	N
68.	A*	B*	C*	J	O
69.	A*	B*	C*	J	P
70.	A*	B*	C*	J	Q

71.	A*	B*	C*	K	L
72.	A*	B*	C*	K	M
73.	A*	B*	C*	K	N
74.	A*	B*	C*	K	O
75.	A*	B*	C*	K	P
76.	A*	B*	C*	K	Q
77.	A*	B*	C*	L	M
78.	A*	B*	C*	L	N
79.	A*	B*	C*	L	O
80.	A*	R*	C*	L	P
81.	A*	B*	C*	L	Q
82.	A*	B*	C*	M	N
83.	A*	B*	C*	M	O
84.	A*	B*	C*	M	P
85.	A*	B*	C*	M	Q
86.	A*	B*	C*	N	O
87.	A*	B*	C*	N	P
88.	A*	B*	C*	N	Q
89.	A*	B*	C*	O	P
90.	A*	B*	C*	O	Q
91.	A*	D*	O*	P	Q

POWER NUMBER™WHEEL 55018-3
Wheeling 18 Numbers in 105 games for a 5 of 5 Win

NUMBERS CORRECT***	MAXIMUM WINS				MINIMUM WINS			
	5x	4x	3x	2x	5x	4x	3x	2x
5 (w/o Jackpot)	0	0	0	0				
5	1	26	78	0	1	26	78	0
4	–	14	91	0	–	14	91	0
3	–	–	105	105	–	–	105	105
2	–	–	–	105	–	–	–	105

*** POWER NUMBER POSITIONS A*, B* & C* MUST BE WINNERS.

Your 18 Numbers to Wheel

A*	B*	C*	D	E	F	G	H	I
105	105	105	14	14	14	14	14	14

J	K	L	M	N	O	P	Q	R
14	14	14	14	14	14	14	14	14

(Continued Next Page)

POWER NUMBER™ WHEEL 55018-3 (Continued from previous page)
The 105 Games to Play

#	A*	B*	C*			#	A*	B*	C*		
1.	A*	B*	C*	D	E	36.	A*	B*	C*	F	O
2.	A*	B*	C*	D	F	37.	A*	B*	C*	F	P
3.	A*	B*	C*	D	G	38.	A*	B*	C*	F	Q
4.	A*	B*	C*	D	H	39.	A*	B*	C*	F	R
5.	A*	B*	C*	D	I	40.	A*	B*	C*	G	H
6.	A*	B*	C*	D	J	41.	A*	B*	C*	G	I
7.	A*	B*	C*	D	K	42.	A*	B*	C*	G	J
8.	A*	B*	C*	D	L	43.	A*	B*	C*	G	K
9.	A*	B*	C*	D	M	44.	A*	B*	C*	G	L
10.	A*	B*	C*	D	N	45.	A*	B*	C*	G	M
11.	A*	B*	C*	D	O	46.	A*	B*	C*	G	N
12.	A*	B*	C*	D	P	47.	A*	B*	C*	G	O
13.	A*	B*	C*	D	Q	48.	A*	B*	C*	G	P
14.	A*	B*	C*	D	R	49.	A*	B*	C*	G	Q
15.	A*	B*	C*	E	F	50.	A*	B*	C*	G	R
16.	A*	B*	C*	E	G	51.	A*	B*	C*	H	I
17.	A*	B*	C*	E	H	52.	A*	B*	C*	H	J
18.	A*	B*	C*	E	I	53.	A*	B*	C*	H	K
19.	A*	B*	C*	E	J	54.	A*	B*	C*	H	L
20.	A*	B*	C*	E	K	55.	A*	B*	C*	H	M
21.	A*	B*	C*	E	L	56.	A*	B*	C*	H	N
22.	A*	B*	C*	E	M	57.	A*	B*	C*	H	O
23.	A*	B*	C*	E	N	58.	A*	B*	C*	H	P
24.	A*	B*	C*	E	O	59.	A*	B*	C*	H	Q
25.	A*	B*	C*	E	P	60.	A*	B*	C*	H	R
26.	A*	B*	C*	E	Q	61.	A*	B*	C*	I	J
27.	A*	B*	C*	E	R	62.	A*	B*	C*	I	K
28.	A*	B*	C*	F	G	63.	A*	B*	C*	I	L
29.	A*	B*	C*	F	H	64.	A*	B*	C*	I	M
30.	A*	B*	C*	F	I	65.	A*	B*	C*	I	N
31.	A*	B*	C*	F	J	66.	A*	B*	C*	I	O
32.	A*	B*	C*	F	K	67.	A*	B*	C*	I	P
33.	A*	B*	C*	F	L	68.	A*	B*	C*	I	Q
34.	A*	B*	C*	F	M	69.	A*	B*	C*	I	R
35.	A*	B*	C*	F	N	70.	A*	B*	C*	J	K

(Continued Next Page)

POWER NUMBER™ WHEEL 55018-3 (Continued from previous page)

71.	A*	B*	C*	J	L	89.	A*	B*	C*	L	Q
72.	A*	B*	C*	J	M	90.	A*	B*	C*	L	R
73.	A*	B*	C*	J	N	91.	A*	B*	C*	M	N
74.	A*	B*	C*	J	O	92.	A*	B*	C*	M	O
75.	A*	B*	C*	J	P	93.	A*	B*	C*	M	P
76.	A*	B*	C*	J	Q	94.	A*	B*	C*	M	Q
77.	A*	B*	C*	J	R	95.	A*	B*	C*	M	R
78.	A*	B*	C*	K	L	96.	A*	B*	C*	N	O
79.	A*	B*	C*	K	M	97.	A*	B*	C*	N	P
80.	A*	B*	C*	K	N	98.	A*	B*	C*	N	Q
81.	A*	B*	C*	K	O	99.	A*	B*	C*	N	R
82.	A*	B*	C*	K	P	100.	A*	B*	C*	O	P
83.	A*	B*	C*	K	Q	101.	A*	B*	C*	O	Q
84.	A*	B*	C*	K	R	102.	A*	B*	C*	O	R
85.	A*	B*	C*	L	M	103.	A*	B*	C*	P	Q
86.	A*	B*	C*	L	N	104.	A*	B*	C*	P	R
87.	A*	B*	C*	L	O	105.	A*	B*	C*	Q	R
88.	A*	B*	C*	L	P						

Copyright © 1983-1998 Gail Howard

POWER NUMBER™WHEEL 55019-3
Wheeling 19 Numbers in 120 games for a 5 of 5 Win

NUMBERS CORRECT***	MAXIMUM WINS				MINIMUM WINS			
	5x	4x	3x	2x	5x	4x	3x	2x
5 (w/o Jackpot)	0	0	0	0				
5	1	28	91	0	1	28	91	0
4	–	15	105	0	–	15	105	0
3	–	–	120	120	–	–	120	120
2	–	–	–	120	–	–	–	120

*** POWER NUMBER POSITIONS A*, B* & C* MUST BE WINNERS.

Your 19 Numbers to Wheel

A*	B*	C*	D	E	F	G	H	I	J
120	120	120	15	15	15	15	15	15	15

K	L	M	N	O	P	Q	R	S
15	15	15	15	15	15	15	15	15

The 120 Games to Play

1.	A*	B*	C*	D	E	5.	A*	B*	C*	D	I
2.	A*	B*	C*	D	F	6.	A*	B*	C*	D	J
3.	A*	B*	C*	D	G	7.	A*	B*	C*	D	K
4.	A*	B*	C*	D	H	8.	A*	B*	C*	D	L

Copyright © 1983-1998 Gail Howard   (Continued Next Page)

POWER NUMBER™ WHEEL 55019-3 (Continued from previous page)

#						#					
9.	A*	B*	C*	D	M	44.	A*	B*	C*	G	I
10.	A*	B*	C*	D	N	45.	A*	B*	C*	G	J
11.	A*	B*	C*	D	O	46.	A*	B*	C*	G	K
12.	A*	B*	C*	D	P	47.	A*	B*	C*	G	L
13.	A*	B*	C*	D	Q	48.	A*	B*	C*	G	M
14.	A*	B*	C*	D	R	49.	A*	B*	C*	G	N
15.	A*	B*	C*	D	S	50.	A*	B*	C*	G	O
16.	A*	B*	C*	E	F	51.	A*	B*	C*	G	P
17.	A*	B*	C*	E	G	52.	A*	B*	C*	G	Q
18.	A*	B*	C*	E	H	53.	A*	B*	C*	G	R
19.	A*	B*	C*	E	I	54.	A*	B*	C*	G	S
20.	A*	B*	C*	E	J	55.	A*	B*	C*	H	I
21.	A*	B*	C*	E	K	56.	A*	B*	C*	H	J
22.	A*	B*	C*	E	L	57.	A*	B*	C*	H	K
23.	A*	B*	C*	E	M	58.	A*	B*	C*	H	L
24.	A*	B*	C*	E	N	59.	A*	B*	C*	H	M
25.	A*	B*	C*	E	O	60.	A*	B*	C*	H	N
26.	A*	B*	C*	E	P	61.	A*	B*	C*	H	O
27.	A*	B*	C*	E	Q	62.	A*	B*	C*	H	P
28.	A*	B*	C*	E	R	63.	A*	B*	C*	H	Q
29.	A*	B*	C*	E	S	64.	A*	B*	C*	H	R
30.	A*	B*	C*	F	G	65.	A*	B*	C*	H	S
31.	A*	B*	C*	F	H	66.	A*	B*	C*	I	J
32.	A*	B*	C*	F	I	67.	A*	B*	C*	I	K
33.	A*	B*	C*	F	J	68.	A*	B*	C*	I	L
34.	A*	B*	C*	F	K	69.	A*	B*	C*	I	M
35.	A*	B*	C*	F	L	70.	A*	B*	C*	I	N
36.	A*	B*	C*	F	M	71.	A*	B*	C*	I	O
37.	A*	B*	C*	F	N	72.	A*	B*	C*	I	P
38.	A*	B*	C*	F	O	73.	A*	B*	C*	I	Q
39.	A*	B*	C*	F	P	74.	A*	B*	C*	I	R
40.	A*	B*	C*	F	Q	75.	A*	B*	C*	I	S
41.	A*	B*	C*	F	R	76.	A*	B*	C*	J	K
42.	A*	B*	C*	F	S	77.	A*	B*	C*	J	L
43.	A*	B*	C*	G	H	78.	A*	B*	C*	J	M

     (Continued Next Page)

POWER NUMBER™ WHEEL 55019-3 (Continued from previous page)

#	1	2	3	4	5	#	1	2	3	4	5
79.	A*	B*	C*	J	N	100.	A*	B*	C*	M	N
80.	A*	B*	C*	J	O	101.	A*	B*	C*	M	O
81.	A*	B*	C*	J	P	102.	A*	B*	C*	M	P
82.	A*	B*	C*	J	Q	103.	A*	B*	C*	M	Q
83.	A*	B*	C*	J	R	104.	A*	B*	C*	M	R
84.	A*	B*	C*	J	S	105.	A*	B*	C*	M	S
85.	A*	B*	C*	K	L	106.	A*	B*	C*	N	O
86.	A*	B*	C*	K	M	107.	A*	B*	C*	N	P
87.	A*	B*	C*	K	N	108.	A*	B*	C*	N	Q
88.	A*	B*	C*	K	O	109.	A*	B*	C*	N	R
89.	A*	B*	C*	K	P	110.	A*	B*	C*	N	S
90.	A*	B*	C*	K	Q	111.	A*	B*	C*	O	P
91.	A*	B*	C*	K	R	112.	A*	B*	C*	O	Q
92.	A*	B*	C*	K	S	113.	A*	B*	C*	O	R
93.	A*	B*	C*	L	M	114.	A*	B*	C*	O	S
94.	A*	B*	C*	L	N	115.	A*	B*	C*	P	Q
95.	A*	B*	C*	L	O	116.	A*	B*	C*	P	R
96.	A*	B*	C*	L	P	117.	A*	B*	C*	P	S
97.	A*	B*	C*	L	Q	118.	A*	B*	C*	Q	R
98.	A*	B*	C*	L	R	119.	A*	B*	C*	Q	S
99.	A*	B*	C*	L	S	120.	A*	B*	C*	R	S

POWER NUMBER™WHEEL 55020-3
Wheeling 20 Numbers in 136 games for a 5 of 5 Win

NUMBERS CORRECT***	MAXIMUM WINS				MINIMUM WINS			
	5x	4x	3x	2x	5x	4x	3x	2x
5 (w/o Jackpot)	0	0	0	0				
5	1	30	105	0	1	30	105	0
4	-	16	120	0	-	16	120	0
3	-	-	136	136	-	-	136	136
2	-	-	-	136	-	-	-	136

*** POWER NUMBER POSITIONS A*, B* & C* MUST BE WINNERS.

Your 20 Numbers to Wheel

A*	B*	C*	D	E	F	G	H	I	J
136	136	136	16	16	16	16	16	16	16

K	L	M	N	O	P	Q	R	S	T
16	16	16	16	16	16	16	16	16	16

The 136 Games to Play

1.	A*	B*	C*	D	E		2.	A*	B*	C*	D	F

          (Continued Next Page)

POWER NUMBER™ WHEEL 55020-3 (Continued from previous page)

#						#					
3.	A*	B*	C*	D	G	38.	A*	B*	C*	F	M
4.	A*	B*	C*	D	H	39.	A*	B*	C*	F	N
5.	A*	B*	C*	D	I	40.	A*	B*	C*	F	O
6.	A*	B*	C*	D	J	41.	A*	B*	C*	F	P
7.	A*	B*	C*	D	K	42.	A*	B*	C*	F	Q
8.	A*	B*	C*	D	L	43.	A*	B*	C*	F	R
9.	A*	B*	C*	D	M	44.	A*	B*	C*	F	S
10.	A*	B*	C*	D	N	45.	A*	B*	C*	F	T
11.	A*	B*	C*	D	O	46.	A*	B*	C*	G	H
12.	A*	B*	C*	D	P	47.	A*	B*	C*	G	I
13.	A*	B*	C*	D	Q	48.	A*	B*	C*	G	J
14.	A*	B*	C*	D	R	49.	A*	B*	C*	G	K
15.	A*	B*	C*	D	S	50.	A*	B*	C*	G	L
16.	A*	B*	C*	D	T	51.	A*	B*	C*	G	M
17.	A*	B*	C*	E	F	52.	A*	B*	C*	G	N
18.	A*	B*	C*	E	G	53.	A*	B*	C*	G	O
19.	A*	B*	C*	E	H	54.	A*	B*	C*	G	P
20.	A*	B*	C*	E	I	55.	A*	B*	C*	G	Q
21.	A*	B*	C*	E	J	56.	A*	B*	C*	G	R
22.	A*	B*	C*	E	K	57.	A*	B*	C*	G	S
23.	A*	B*	C*	E	L	58.	A*	B*	C*	G	T
24.	A*	B*	C*	E	M	59.	A*	B*	C*	H	I
25.	A*	B*	C*	E	N	60.	A*	B*	C*	H	J
26.	A*	B*	C*	E	O	61.	A*	B*	C*	H	K
27.	A*	B*	C*	E	P	62.	A*	B*	C*	H	L
28.	A*	B*	C*	E	Q	63.	A*	B*	C*	H	M
29.	A*	B*	C*	E	R	64.	A*	B*	C*	H	N
30.	A*	B*	C*	E	S	65.	A*	B*	C*	H	O
31.	A*	B*	C*	E	T	66.	A*	B*	C*	H	P
32.	A*	B*	C*	F	G	67.	A*	B*	C*	H	Q
33.	A*	B*	C*	F	H	68.	A*	B*	C*	H	R
34.	A*	B*	C*	F	I	69.	A*	B*	C*	H	S
35.	A*	B*	C*	F	J	70.	A*	B*	C*	H	T
36.	A*	B*	C*	F	K	71.	A*	B*	C*	I	J
37.	A*	B*	C*	F	L	72.	A*	B*	C*	I	K

          (Continued Next Page)

POWER NUMBER™ WHEEL 55020-3 (Continued from previous page)

#						#					
73.	A*	B*	C*	I	L	105.	A*	B*	C*	L	Q
74.	A*	B*	C*	I	M	106.	A*	B*	C*	L	R
75.	A*	B*	C*	I	N	107.	A*	B*	C*	L	S
76.	A*	B*	C*	I	O	108.	A*	B*	C*	L	T
77.	A*	B*	C*	I	P	109.	A*	B*	C*	M	N
78.	A*	B*	C*	I	Q	110.	A*	B*	C*	M	O
79.	A*	B*	C*	I	R	111.	A*	B*	C*	M	P
80.	A*	B*	C*	I	S	112.	A*	B*	C*	M	Q
81.	A*	B*	C*	I	T	113.	A*	B*	C*	M	R
82.	A*	B*	C*	J	K	114.	A*	B*	C*	M	S
83.	A*	B*	C*	J	L	115.	A*	B*	C*	M	T
84.	A*	B*	C*	J	M	116.	A*	B*	C*	N	O
85.	A*	B*	C*	J	N	117.	A*	B*	C*	N	P
86.	A*	B*	C*	J	O	118.	A*	B*	C*	N	Q
87.	A*	B*	C*	J	P	119.	A*	B*	C*	N	R
88.	A*	B*	C*	J	Q	120.	A*	B*	C*	N	S
89.	A*	B*	C*	J	R	121.	A*	B*	C*	N	T
90.	A*	B*	C*	J	S	122.	A*	B*	C*	O	P
91.	A*	B*	C*	J	T	123.	A*	B*	C*	O	Q
92.	A*	B*	C*	K	L	124.	A*	B*	C*	O	R
93.	A*	B*	C*	K	M	125.	A*	B*	C*	O	S
94.	A*	B*	C*	K	N	126.	A*	B*	C*	O	T
95.	A*	B*	C*	K	O	127.	A*	B*	C*	P	Q
96.	A*	B*	C*	K	P	128.	A*	B*	C*	P	R
97.	A*	B*	C*	K	Q	129.	A*	B*	C*	P	S
98.	A*	B*	C*	K	R	130.	A*	B*	C*	P	T
99.	A*	B*	C*	K	S	131.	A*	B*	C*	Q	R
100.	A*	B*	C*	K	T	132.	A*	B*	C*	Q	S
101.	A*	B*	C*	L	M	133.	A*	B*	C*	Q	T
102.	A*	B*	C*	L	N	134.	A*	B*	C*	R	S
103.	A*	B*	C*	L	O	135.	A*	B*	C*	R	T
104.	A*	B*	C*	L	P	136.	A*	B*	C*	S	T

POWER NUMBER™WHEEL 55026-3
Wheeling 26 Numbers in 253 games for a 5 of 5 Win

NUMBERS CORRECT***	MAXIMUM WINS				MINIMUM WINS			
	5x	4x	3x	2x	5x	4x	3x	2x
5 (w/o Jackpot)	0	0	0	0				
5	1	42	210	0	1	42	210	0
4	–	22	231	0	–	22	231	0
3	–	–	253	253	–	–	253	253
2	–	–	–	253	–	–	–	253

*** POWER NUMBER POSITIONS A*, B* & C* MUST BE WINNERS.

Your 26 Numbers to Wheel

A*	B*	C*	D	E	F	G	H	I
253	253	253	22	22	22	22	22	22

J	K	L	M	N	O	P	Q	R
22	22	22	22	22	22	22	22	22

S	T	U	V	W	X	Y	Z
22	22	22	22	22	22	22	22

The 253 Games to Play

#	A*	B*	C*	D	E
1.	A*	B*	C*	D	E
2.	A*	B*	C*	D	F
3.	A*	B*	C*	D	G
4.	A*	B*	C*	D	H
5.	A*	B*	C*	D	I
6.	A*	B*	C*	D	J
7.	A*	B*	C*	D	K
8.	A*	B*	C*	D	L
9.	A*	B*	C*	D	M
10.	A*	B*	C*	D	N
11.	A*	B*	C*	D	O
12.	A*	B*	C*	D	P
13.	A*	B*	C*	D	Q
14.	A*	B*	C*	D	R
15.	A*	B*	C*	D	S
16.	A*	B*	C*	D	T
17.	A*	B*	C*	D	U
18.	A*	B*	C*	D	V
19.	A*	B*	C*	D	W
20.	A*	B*	C*	D	X
21.	A*	B*	C*	D	Y
22.	A*	B*	C*	D	Z

#	A*	B*	C*	E	F
23.	A*	B*	C*	E	F
24.	A*	B*	C*	E	G
25.	A*	B*	C*	E	H
26.	A*	B*	C*	E	I
27.	A*	B*	C*	E	J
28.	A*	B*	C*	E	K
29.	A*	B*	C*	E	L
30.	A*	B*	C*	E	M
31.	A*	B*	C*	E	N
32.	A*	B*	C*	E	O
33.	A*	B*	C*	E	P
34.	A*	B*	C*	E	Q
35.	A*	B*	C*	E	R
36.	A*	B*	C*	E	S
37.	A*	B*	C*	E	T
38.	A*	B*	C*	E	U
39.	A*	B*	C*	E	V
40.	A*	B*	C*	E	W
41.	A*	B*	C*	E	X
42.	A*	B*	C*	E	Y
43.	A*	B*	C*	E	Z
44.	A*	B*	C*	F	G

(Continued Next Page)

392

POWER NUMBER™ WHEEL 55026-3 (Continued from previous page)

#	A*	B*	C*			#	A*	B*	C*		
45.	A*	B*	C*	F	H	80.	A*	B*	C*	G	X
46.	A*	B*	C*	F	I	81.	A*	B*	C*	G	Y
47.	A*	B*	C*	F	J	82.	A*	B*	C*	G	Z
48.	A*	B*	C*	F	K	83.	A*	B*	C*	H	I
49.	A*	B*	C*	F	L	84.	A*	B*	C*	H	J
50.	A*	B*	C*	F	M	85.	A*	B*	C*	H	K
51.	A*	B*	C*	F	N	86.	A*	B*	C*	H	L
52.	A*	B*	C*	F	O	87.	A*	B*	C*	H	M
53.	A*	B*	C*	F	P	88.	A*	B*	C*	H	N
54.	A*	B*	C*	F	Q	89.	A*	B*	C*	H	O
55.	A*	B*	C*	F	R	90.	A*	B*	C*	H	P
56.	A*	B*	C*	F	S	91.	A*	B*	C*	H	Q
57.	A*	B*	C*	F	T	92.	A*	B*	C*	H	R
58.	A*	B*	C*	F	U	93.	A*	B*	C*	H	S
59.	A*	B*	C*	F	V	94.	A*	B*	C*	H	T
60.	A*	B*	C*	F	W	95.	A*	B*	C*	H	U
61.	A*	B*	C*	F	X	96.	A*	B*	C*	H	V
62.	A*	B*	C*	F	Y	97.	A*	B*	C*	H	W
63.	A*	B*	C*	F	Z	98.	A*	B*	C*	H	X
64.	A*	B*	C*	G	H	99.	A*	B*	C*	H	Y
65.	A*	B*	C*	G	I	100.	A*	B*	C*	H	Z
66.	A*	B*	C*	G	J	101.	A*	B*	C*	I	J
67.	A*	B*	C*	G	K	102.	A*	B*	C*	I	K
68.	A*	B*	C*	G	L	103.	A*	B*	C*	I	L
69.	A*	B*	C*	G	M	104.	A*	B*	C*	I	M
70.	A*	B*	C*	G	N	105.	A*	B*	C*	I	N
71.	A*	B*	C*	G	O	106.	A*	B*	C*	I	O
72.	A*	B*	C*	G	P	107.	A*	B*	C*	I	P
73.	A*	B*	C*	G	Q	108.	A*	B*	C*	I	Q
74.	A*	B*	C*	G	R	109.	A*	B*	C*	I	R
75.	A*	B*	C*	G	S	110.	A*	B*	C*	I	S
76.	A*	B*	C*	G	T	111.	A*	B*	C*	I	T
77.	A*	B*	C*	G	U	112.	A*	B*	C*	I	U
78.	A*	B*	C*	G	V	113.	A*	B*	C*	I	V
79.	A*	B*	C*	G	W	114.	A*	B*	C*	I	W

          (Continued Next Page)

POWER NUMBER™ WHEEL 55026-3 (Continued from previous page)

#						#					
115.	A*	B*	C*	I	X	150.	A*	B*	C*	L	N
116.	A*	B*	C*	I	Y	151.	A*	B*	C*	L	O
117.	A*	B*	C*	I	Z	152.	A*	B*	C*	L	P
118.	A*	B*	C*	J	K	153.	A*	B*	C*	L	Q
119.	A*	B*	C*	J	L	154.	A*	B*	C*	L	R
120.	A*	B*	C*	J	M	155.	A*	B*	C*	L	S
121.	A*	B*	C*	J	N	156.	A*	B*	C*	L	T
122.	A*	B*	C*	J	O	157.	A*	B*	C*	L	U
123.	A*	B*	C*	J	P	158.	A*	B*	C*	L	V
124.	A*	B*	C*	J	Q	159.	A*	B*	C*	L	W
125.	A*	B*	C*	J	R	160.	A*	B*	C*	L	X
126.	A*	B*	C*	J	S	161.	A*	B*	C*	L	Y
127.	A*	B*	C*	J	T	162.	A*	B*	C*	L	Z
128.	A*	B*	C*	J	U	163.	A*	B*	C*	M	N
129.	A*	B*	C*	J	V	164.	A*	B*	C*	M	O
130.	A*	B*	C*	J	W	165.	A*	B*	C*	M	P
131.	A*	B*	C*	J	X	166.	A*	B*	C*	M	Q
132.	A*	B*	C*	J	Y	167.	A*	B*	C*	M	R
133.	A*	B*	C*	J	Z	168.	A*	B*	C*	M	S
134.	A*	B*	C*	K	L	169.	A*	B*	C*	M	T
135.	A*	B*	C*	K	M	170.	A*	B*	C*	M	U
136.	A*	B*	C*	K	N	171.	A*	B*	C*	M	V
137.	A*	B*	C*	K	O	172.	A*	B*	C*	M	W
138.	A*	B*	C*	K	P	173.	A*	B*	C*	M	X
139.	A*	B*	C*	K	Q	174.	A*	B*	C*	M	Y
140.	A*	B*	C*	K	R	175.	A*	B*	C*	M	Z
141.	A*	B*	C*	K	S	176.	A*	B*	C*	N	O
142.	A*	B*	C*	K	T	177.	A*	B*	C*	N	P
143.	A*	B*	C*	K	U	178.	A*	B*	C*	N	Q
144.	A*	B*	C*	K	V	179.	A*	B*	C*	N	R
145.	A*	B*	C*	K	W	180.	A*	B*	C*	N	S
146.	A*	B*	C*	K	X	181.	A*	B*	C*	N	T
147.	A*	B*	C*	K	Y	182.	A*	B*	C*	N	U
148.	A*	B*	C*	K	Z	183.	A*	B*	C*	N	V
149.	A*	B*	C*	L	M	184.	A*	B*	C*	N	W

     (Continued Next Page)

POWER NUMBER™ WHEEL 55026-3 (Continued from previous page)

#	A*	B*	C*			#	A*	B*	C*		
185.	A*	B*	C*	N	X	220.	A*	B*	C*	R	U
186.	A*	B*	C*	N	Y	221.	A*	B*	C*	R	V
187.	A*	B*	C*	N	Z	222.	A*	B*	C*	R	W
188.	A*	B*	C*	O	P	223.	A*	B*	C*	R	X
189.	A*	B*	C*	O	Q	224.	A*	B*	C*	R	Y
190.	A*	B*	C*	O	R	225.	A*	B*	C*	R	Z
191.	A*	B*	C*	O	S	226.	A*	B*	C*	S	T
192.	A*	B*	C*	O	T	227.	A*	B*	C*	S	U
193.	A*	B*	C*	O	U	228.	A*	B*	C*	S	V
194.	A*	B*	C*	O	V	229.	A*	B*	C*	S	W
195.	A*	B*	C*	O	W	230.	A*	B*	C*	S	X
196.	A*	B*	C*	O	X	231.	A*	B*	C*	S	Y
197.	A*	B*	C*	O	Y	232.	A*	B*	C*	S	Z
198.	A*	B*	C*	O	Z	233.	A*	B*	C*	T	U
199.	A*	B*	C*	P	Q	234.	A*	B*	C*	T	V
200.	A*	B*	C*	P	R	235.	A*	B*	C*	T	W
201.	A*	B*	C*	P	S	236.	A*	B*	C*	T	X
202.	A*	B*	C*	P	T	237.	A*	B*	C*	T	Y
203.	A*	B*	C*	P	U	238.	A*	B*	C*	T	Z
204.	A*	B*	C*	P	V	239.	A*	B*	C*	U	V
205.	A*	B*	C*	P	W	240.	A*	B*	C*	U	W
206.	A*	B*	C*	P	X	241.	A*	B*	C*	U	X
207.	A*	B*	C*	P	Y	242.	A*	B*	C*	U	Y
208.	A*	B*	C*	P	Z	243.	A*	B*	C*	U	Z
209.	A*	B*	C*	Q	R	244.	A*	B*	C*	V	W
210.	A*	B*	C*	Q	S	245.	A*	B*	C*	V	X
211.	A*	B*	C*	Q	T	246.	A*	B*	C*	V	Y
212.	A*	B*	C*	Q	U	247.	A*	B*	C*	V	Z
213.	A*	B*	C*	Q	V	248.	A*	B*	C*	W	X
214.	A*	B*	C*	Q	W	249.	A*	B*	C*	W	Y
215.	A*	B*	C*	Q	X	250.	A*	B*	C*	W	Z
216.	A*	B*	C*	Q	Y	251.	A*	B*	C*	X	Y
217.	A*	B*	C*	Q	Z	252.	A*	B*	C*	X	Z
218.	A*	B*	C*	R	S	253.	A*	B*	C*	Y	Z
219.	A*	B*	C*	R	T						

POWER NUMBER™ WHEEL 55030-3
Wheeling 30 Numbers in 351 games for a 5 of 5 Win

NUMBERS CORRECT***	MAXIMUM WINS				MINIMUM WINS			
	5x	4x	3x	2x	5x	4x	3x	2x
5 (w/o Jackpot)	0	0	0	0				
5	1	50	300	0	1	50	300	0
4	–	26	325	0	–	26	325	0
3	–	–	351	351	–	–	351	351
2	–	–	–	351	–	–	–	351

*** POWER NUMBER POSITIONS A*, B* & C* MUST BE WINNERS.

Your 30 Numbers to Wheel

A*	B*	C*	D	E	F	G	H	I	J
351	351	351	26	26	26	26	26	26	26

K	L	M	N	O	P	Q	R	S	T
26	26	26	26	26	26	26	26	26	26

U	V	W	X	Y	Z	AA	BB	CC	DD
26	26	26	26	26	26	26	26	26	26

The 351 Games to Play

#						#					
1.	A*	B*	C*	D	E	23.	A*	B*	C*	D	aa
2.	A*	B*	C*	D	F	24.	A*	B*	C*	D	bb
3.	A*	B*	C*	D	G	25.	A*	B*	C*	D	cc
4.	A*	B*	C*	D	H	26.	A*	B*	C*	D	dd
5.	A*	B*	C*	D	I	27.	A*	B*	C*	E	F
6.	A*	B*	C*	D	J	28.	A*	B*	C*	E	G
7.	A*	B*	C*	D	K	29.	A*	B*	C*	E	H
8.	A*	B*	C*	D	L	30.	A*	B*	C*	E	I
9.	A*	B*	C*	D	M	31.	A*	B*	C*	E	J
10.	A*	B*	C*	D	N	32.	A*	B*	C*	E	K
11.	A*	B*	C*	D	O	33.	A*	B*	C*	E	L
12.	A*	B*	C*	D	P	34.	A*	B*	C*	E	M
13.	A*	B*	C*	D	Q	35.	A*	B*	C*	E	N
14.	A*	B*	C*	D	R	36.	A*	B*	C*	E	O
15.	A*	B*	C*	D	S	37.	A*	B*	C*	E	P
16.	A*	B*	C*	D	T	38.	A*	B*	C*	E	Q
17.	A*	B*	C*	D	U	39.	A*	B*	C*	E	R
18.	A*	B*	C*	D	V	40.	A*	B*	C*	E	S
19.	A*	B*	C*	D	W	41.	A*	B*	C*	E	T
20.	A*	B*	C*	D	X	42.	A*	B*	C*	E	U
21.	A*	B*	C*	D	Y	43.	A*	B*	C*	E	V
22.	A*	B*	C*	D	Z	44.	A*	B*	C*	E	W

Copyright © 1983-1998 Gail Howard   (Continued Next Page)

POWER NUMBER™ WHEEL 55030-3 (Continued from previous page)

#						#					
45.	A*	B*	C*	E	X	80.	A*	B*	C*	G	L
46.	A*	B*	C*	E	Y	81.	A*	B*	C*	G	M
47.	A*	B*	C*	E	Z	82.	A*	B*	C*	G	N
48.	A*	B*	C*	E	aa	83.	A*	B*	C*	G	O
49.	A*	B*	C*	E	bb	84.	A*	B*	C*	G	P
50.	A*	B*	C*	E	cc	85.	A*	B*	C*	G	Q
51.	A*	B*	C*	E	dd	86.	A*	B*	C*	G	R
52.	A*	B*	C*	F	G	87.	A*	B*	C*	G	S
53.	A*	B*	C*	F	H	88.	A*	B*	C*	G	T
54.	A*	B*	O*	F	I	89.	A*	R*	C*	G	U
55.	A*	B*	C*	F	J	90.	A*	B*	C*	G	V
56.	A*	B*	C*	F	K	91.	A*	B*	C*	G	W
57.	A*	B*	C*	F	L	92.	A*	B*	C*	G	X
58.	A*	B*	C*	F	M	93.	A*	B*	C*	G	Y
59.	A*	B*	C*	F	N	94.	A*	B*	C*	G	Z
60.	A*	B*	C*	F	O	95.	A*	B*	C*	G	aa
61.	A*	B*	C*	F	P	96.	A*	B*	C*	G	bb
62.	A*	B*	C*	F	Q	97.	A*	B*	C*	G	cc
63.	A*	B*	C*	F	R	98.	A*	B*	C*	G	dd
64.	A*	B*	C*	F	S	99.	A*	B*	C*	H	I
65.	A*	B*	C*	F	T	100.	A*	D*	C*	H	J
66.	A*	B*	C*	F	U	101.	A*	B*	C*	H	K
67.	A*	B*	C*	F	V	102.	A*	B*	C*	H	L
68.	A*	B*	C*	F	W	103.	A*	B*	C*	H	M
69.	A*	B*	C*	F	X	104.	A*	B*	C*	H	N
70.	A*	B*	C*	F	Y	105.	A*	B*	C*	H	O
71.	A*	B*	C*	F	Z	106.	A*	B*	C*	H	P
72.	A*	B*	C*	F	aa	107.	A*	B*	C*	H	Q
73.	A*	B*	C*	F	bb	108.	A*	B*	C*	H	R
74.	A*	B*	C*	F	cc	109.	A*	B*	C*	H	S
75.	A*	B*	C*	F	dd	110.	A*	B*	C*	H	T
76.	A*	B*	C*	G	H	111.	A*	B*	C*	H	U
77.	A*	B*	C*	G	I	112.	A*	B*	C*	H	V
78.	A*	B*	C*	G	J	113.	A*	B*	C*	H	W
79.	A*	B*	C*	G	K	114.	A*	B*	C*	H	X

(Continued Next Page)

POWER NUMBER™ WHEEL 55030-3 (Continued from previous page)

115.	A*	B*	C*	H	Y	150.	A*	B*	C*	J	S
116.	A*	B*	C*	H	Z	151.	A*	B*	C*	J	T
117.	A*	B*	C*	H	aa	152.	A*	B*	C*	J	U
118.	A*	B*	C*	H	bb	153.	A*	B*	C*	J	V
119.	A*	B*	C*	H	cc	154.	A*	B*	C*	J	W
120.	A*	B*	C*	H	dd	155.	A*	B*	C*	J	X
121.	A*	B*	C*	I	J	156.	A*	B*	C*	J	Y
122.	A*	B*	C*	I	K	157.	A*	B*	C*	J	Z
123.	A*	B*	C*	I	L	158.	A*	B*	C*	J	aa
124.	A*	B*	C*	I	M	159.	A*	B*	C*	J	bb
125.	A*	B*	C*	I	N	160.	A*	B*	C*	J	cc
126.	A*	B*	C*	I	O	161.	A*	B*	C*	J	dd
127.	A*	B*	C*	I	P	162.	A*	B*	C*	K	L
128.	A*	B*	C*	I	Q	163.	A*	B*	C*	K	M
129.	A*	B*	C*	I	R	164.	A*	B*	C*	K	N
130.	A*	B*	C*	I	S	165.	A*	B*	C*	K	O
131.	A*	B*	C*	I	T	166.	A*	B*	C*	K	P
132.	A*	B*	C*	I	U	167.	A*	B*	C*	K	Q
133.	A*	B*	C*	I	V	168.	A*	B*	C*	K	R
134.	A*	B*	C*	I	W	169.	A*	B*	C*	K	S
135.	A*	B*	C*	I	X	170.	A*	B*	C*	K	T
136.	A*	B*	C*	I	Y	171.	A*	B*	C*	K	U
137.	A*	B*	C*	I	Z	172.	A*	B*	C*	K	V
138.	A*	B*	C*	I	aa	173.	A*	B*	C*	K	W
139.	A*	B*	C*	I	bb	174.	A*	B*	C*	K	X
140.	A*	B*	C*	I	cc	175.	A*	B*	C*	K	Y
141.	A*	B*	C*	I	dd	176.	A*	B*	C*	K	Z
142.	A*	B*	C*	J	K	177.	A*	B*	C*	K	aa
143.	A*	B*	C*	J	L	178.	A*	B*	C*	K	bb
144.	A*	B*	C*	J	M	179.	A*	B*	C*	K	cc
145.	A*	B*	C*	J	N	180.	A*	B*	C*	K	dd
146.	A*	B*	C*	J	O	181.	A*	B*	C*	L	M
147.	A*	B*	C*	J	P	182.	A*	B*	C*	L	N
148.	A*	B*	C*	J	Q	183.	A*	B*	C*	L	O
149.	A*	B*	C*	J	R	184.	A*	B*	C*	L	P

Copyright © 1983-1998 Gail Howard   (Continued Next Page)

POWER NUMBER™ WHEEL 55030-3 (Continued from previous page)

#						#					
185.	A*	B*	C*	L	Q	220.	A*	B*	C*	N	S
186.	A*	B*	C*	L	R	221.	A*	B*	C*	N	T
187.	A*	B*	C*	L	S	222.	A*	B*	C*	N	U
188.	A*	B*	C*	L	T	223.	A*	B*	C*	N	V
189.	A*	B*	C*	L	U	224.	A*	B*	C*	N	W
190.	A*	B*	C*	L	V	225.	A*	B*	C*	N	X
191.	A*	B*	C*	L	W	226.	A*	B*	C*	N	Y
192.	A*	B*	C*	L	X	227.	A*	B*	C*	N	Z
193.	A*	B*	C*	L	Y	228.	A*	B*	C*	N	aa
194.	A*	B*	C*	L	Z	229.	A*	B*	C*	N	bb
195.	A*	B*	C*	L	aa	230.	A*	B*	C*	N	cc
196.	A*	B*	C*	L	bb	231.	A*	B*	C*	N	dd
197.	A*	B*	C*	L	cc	232.	A*	B*	C*	O	P
198.	A*	B*	C*	L	dd	233.	A*	B*	C*	O	Q
199.	A*	B*	C*	M	N	234.	A*	B*	C*	O	R
200.	A*	B*	C*	M	O	235.	A*	B*	C*	O	S
201.	A*	B*	C*	M	P	236.	A*	B*	C*	O	T
202.	A*	B*	C*	M	Q	237.	A*	B*	C*	O	U
203.	A*	B*	C*	M	R	238.	A*	B*	C*	O	V
204.	A*	B*	C*	M	S	239.	A*	B*	C*	O	W
205.	A*	B*	C*	M	T	240.	A*	B*	C*	O	X
206.	A*	B*	C*	M	U	241.	A*	B*	C*	O	Y
207.	A*	B*	C*	M	V	242.	A*	B*	C*	O	Z
208.	A*	B*	C*	M	W	243.	A*	B*	C*	O	aa
209.	A*	B*	C*	M	X	244.	A*	B*	C*	O	bb
210.	A*	B*	C*	M	Y	245.	A*	B*	C*	O	cc
211.	A*	B*	C*	M	Z	246.	A*	B*	C*	O	dd
212.	A*	B*	C*	M	aa	247.	A*	B*	C*	P	Q
213.	A*	B*	C*	M	bb	248.	A*	B*	C*	P	R
214.	A*	B*	C*	M	cc	249.	A*	B*	C*	P	S
215.	A*	B*	C*	M	dd	250.	A*	B*	C*	P	T
216.	A*	B*	C*	N	O	251.	A*	B*	C*	P	U
217.	A*	B*	C*	N	P	252.	A*	B*	C*	P	V
218.	A*	B*	C*	N	Q	253.	A*	B*	C*	P	W
219.	A*	B*	C*	N	R	254.	A*	B*	C*	P	X

          (Continued Next Page)

POWER NUMBER™ WHEEL 55030-3 (Continued from previous page)

	A*	B*	C*	P	Y		A*	B*	C*	S	X
255.	A*	B*	C*	P	Y	290.	A*	B*	C*	S	X
256.	A*	B*	C*	P	Z	291.	A*	B*	C*	S	Y
257.	A*	B*	C*	P	aa	292.	A*	B*	C*	S	Z
258.	A*	B*	C*	P	bb	293.	A*	B*	C*	S	aa
259.	A*	B*	C*	P	cc	294.	A*	B*	C*	S	bb
260.	A*	B*	C*	P	dd	295.	A*	B*	C*	S	cc
261.	A*	B*	C*	Q	R	296.	A*	B*	C*	S	dd
262.	A*	B*	C*	Q	S	297.	A*	B*	C*	T	U
263.	A*	B*	C*	Q	T	298.	A*	B*	C*	T	V
264.	A*	B*	C*	Q	U	299.	A*	B*	C*	T	W
265.	A*	B*	C*	Q	V	300.	A*	B*	C*	T	X
266.	A*	B*	C*	Q	W	301.	A*	B*	C*	T	Y
267.	A*	B*	C*	Q	X	302.	A*	B*	C*	T	Z
268.	A*	B*	C*	Q	Y	303.	A*	B*	C*	T	aa
269.	A*	B*	C*	Q	Z	304.	A*	B*	C*	T	bb
270.	A*	B*	C*	Q	aa	305.	A*	B*	C*	T	cc
271.	A*	B*	C*	Q	bb	306.	A*	B*	C*	T	dd
272.	A*	B*	C*	Q	cc	307.	A*	B*	C*	U	V
273.	A*	B*	C*	Q	dd	308.	A*	B*	C*	U	W
274.	A*	B*	C*	R	S	309.	A*	B*	C*	U	X
275.	A*	B*	C*	R	T	310.	A*	B*	C*	U	Y
276.	A*	B*	C*	R	U	311.	A*	B*	C*	U	Z
277.	A*	B*	C*	R	V	312.	A*	B*	C*	U	aa
278.	A*	B*	C*	R	W	313.	A*	B*	C*	U	bb
279.	A*	B*	C*	R	X	314.	A*	B*	C*	U	cc
280.	A*	B*	C*	R	Y	315.	A*	B*	C*	U	dd
281.	A*	B*	C*	R	Z	316.	A*	B*	C*	V	W
282.	A*	B*	C*	R	aa	317.	A*	B*	C*	V	X
283.	A*	B*	C*	R	bb	318.	A*	B*	C*	V	Y
284.	A*	B*	C*	R	cc	319.	A*	B*	C*	V	Z
285.	A*	B*	C*	R	dd	320.	A*	B*	C*	V	aa
286.	A*	B*	C*	S	T	321.	A*	B*	C*	V	bb
287.	A*	B*	C*	S	U	322.	A*	B*	C*	V	cc
288.	A*	B*	C*	S	V	323.	A*	B*	C*	V	dd
289.	A*	B*	C*	S	W	324.	A*	B*	C*	W	X

          (Continued Next Page)

POWER NUMBER™ WHEEL 55030-3 (Continued from previous page)

325.	A*	B*	C*	W	Y	339.	A*	B*	C*	Y	bb
326.	A*	B*	C*	W	Z	340.	A*	B*	C*	Y	cc
327.	A*	B*	C*	W	aa	341.	A*	B*	C*	Y	dd
328.	A*	B*	C*	W	bb	342.	A*	B*	C*	Z	aa
329.	A*	B*	C*	W	cc	343.	A*	B*	C*	Z	bb
330.	A*	B*	C*	W	dd	344.	A*	B*	C*	Z	cc
331.	A*	B*	C*	X	Y	345.	A*	B*	C*	Z	dd
332.	A*	B*	C*	X	Z	346.	A*	B*	C*	aa	bb
333.	A*	B*	C*	X	aa	347.	A*	B*	C*	aa	cc
334.	A*	B*	C*	X	bb	348.	A*	B*	C*	aa	dd
335.	A*	B*	C*	X	cc	349.	A*	B*	C*	bb	cc
336.	A*	B*	C*	X	dd	350.	A*	B*	C*	bb	dd
337.	A*	B*	C*	Y	Z	351.	A*	B*	C*	cc	dd
338.	A*	B*	C*	Y	aa						

Copyright © 1983-1998 Gail Howard

POWER NUMBER™WHEEL 55035-3
Wheeling 35 Numbers in 496 games for a 5 of 5 Win

NUMBERS CORRECT***	MAXIMUM WINS				MINIMUM WINS			
	5x	4x	3x	2x	5x	4x	3x	2x
5 (w/o Jackpot)	0	0	0	0				
5	1	60	435	0	1	60	435	0
4	-	31	465	0	-	31	465	0
3	-	-	496	496	-	-	496	496
2	-	-	-	496	-	-	-	496

*** POWER NUMBER POSITIONS A*, B* & C* MUST BE WINNERS.

Your 35 Numbers to Wheel

A*	B*	C*	D	E	F	G	H	I	J	K	L
496	496	496	31	31	31	31	31	31	31	31	31

M	N	O	P	Q	R	S	T	U	V	W	X
31	31	31	31	31	31	31	31	31	31	31	31

Y	Z	AA	BB	CC	DD	EE	FF	GG	HH	II
31	31	31	31	31	31	31	31	31	31	31

The 496 Games to Play

1.	A*	B*	C*	D	E	7.	A*	B*	C*	D	K
2.	A*	B*	C*	D	F	8.	A*	B*	C*	D	L
3.	A*	B*	C*	D	G	9.	A*	B*	C*	D	M
4.	A*	B*	C*	D	H	10.	A*	B*	C*	D	N
5.	A*	B*	C*	D	I	11.	A*	B*	C*	D	O
6.	A*	B*	C*	D	J	12.	A*	B*	C*	D	P

Copyright © 1983-1998 Gail Howard (Continued Next Page)

POWER NUMBER™ WHEEL 55035-3 (Continued from previous page)

#						#					
13.	A*	B*	C*	D	Q	48.	A*	B*	C*	E	V
14.	A*	B*	C*	D	R	49.	A*	B*	C*	E	W
15.	A*	B*	C*	D	S	50.	A*	B*	C*	E	X
16.	A*	B*	C*	D	T	51.	A*	B*	C*	E	Y
17.	A*	B*	C*	D	U	52.	A*	B*	C*	E	Z
18.	A*	B*	C*	D	V	53.	A*	B*	C*	E	aa
19.	A*	B*	C*	D	W	54.	A*	B*	C*	E	bb
20.	A*	B*	C*	D	X	55.	A*	B*	C*	E	cc
21.	A*	B*	C*	D	Y	56.	A*	B*	C*	E	dd
22.	A*	B*	C*	D	Z	57.	A*	B*	C*	E	ee
23.	A*	B*	C*	D	aa	58.	A*	B*	C*	E	ff
24.	A*	B*	C*	D	bb	59.	A*	B*	C*	E	gg
25.	A*	B*	C*	D	cc	60.	A*	B*	C*	E	hh
26.	A*	B*	C*	D	dd	61.	A*	B*	C*	E	ii
27.	A*	B*	C*	D	ee	62.	A*	B*	C*	F	G
28.	A*	B*	C*	D	ff	63.	A*	B*	C*	F	H
29.	A*	B*	C*	D	gg	64.	A*	B*	C*	F	I
30.	A*	B*	C*	D	hh	65.	A*	B*	C*	F	J
31.	A*	B*	C*	D	ii	66.	A*	B*	C*	F	K
32.	A*	B*	C*	E	F	67.	A*	B*	C*	F	L
33.	A*	B*	C*	E	G	68.	A*	B*	C*	F	M
34.	A*	B*	C*	E	H	69.	A*	B*	C*	F	N
35.	A*	B*	C*	E	I	70.	A*	B*	C*	F	O
36.	A*	B*	C*	E	J	71.	A*	B*	C*	F	P
37.	A*	B*	C*	E	K	72.	A*	B*	C*	F	Q
38.	A*	B*	C*	E	L	73.	A*	B*	C*	F	R
39.	A*	B*	C*	E	M	74.	A*	B*	C*	F	S
40.	A*	B*	C*	E	N	75.	A*	B*	C*	F	T
41.	A*	B*	C*	E	O	76.	A*	B*	C*	F	U
42.	A*	B*	C*	E	P	77.	A*	B*	C*	F	V
43.	A*	B*	C*	E	Q	78.	A*	B*	C*	F	W
44.	A*	B*	C*	E	R	79.	A*	B*	C*	F	X
45.	A*	B*	C*	E	S	80.	A*	B*	C*	F	Y
46.	A*	B*	C*	E	T	81.	A*	B*	C*	F	Z
47.	A*	B*	C*	E	U	82.	A*	B*	C*	F	aa

    (Continued Next Page)

POWER NUMBER™ WHEEL 55035-3 (Continued from previous page)

#						#					
83.	A*	B*	C*	F	bb	118.	A*	B*	C*	G	ii
84.	A*	B*	C*	F	cc	119.	A*	B*	C*	H	I
85.	A*	B*	C*	F	dd	120.	A*	B*	C*	H	J
86.	A*	B*	C*	F	ee	121.	A*	B*	C*	H	K
87.	A*	B*	C*	F	ff	122.	A*	B*	C*	H	L
88.	A*	B*	C*	F	gg	123.	A*	B*	C*	H	M
89.	A*	B*	C*	F	hh	124.	A*	B*	C*	H	N
90.	A*	B*	C*	F	ii	125.	A*	B*	C*	H	O
91.	A*	B*	C*	G	H	126.	A*	B*	C*	H	P
92.	A*	B*	C*	G	I	127.	A*	B*	C*	H	Q
93.	A*	B*	C*	G	J	128.	A*	B*	C*	H	R
94.	A*	B*	C*	G	K	129.	A*	B*	C*	H	S
95.	A*	B*	C*	G	L	130.	A*	B*	C*	H	T
96.	A*	B*	C*	G	M	131.	A*	B*	C*	H	U
97.	A*	B*	C*	G	N	132.	A*	B*	C*	H	V
98.	A*	B*	C*	G	O	133.	A*	B*	C*	H	W
99.	A*	B*	C*	G	P	134.	A*	B*	C*	H	X
100.	A*	B*	C*	G	Q	135.	A*	B*	C*	H	Y
101.	A*	B*	C*	G	R	136.	A*	B*	C*	H	Z
102.	A*	B*	C*	G	S	137.	A*	B*	C*	H	aa
103.	A*	B*	C*	G	T	138.	A*	B*	C*	H	bb
104.	A*	B*	C*	G	U	139.	A*	B*	C*	H	cc
105.	A*	B*	C*	G	V	140.	A*	B*	C*	H	dd
106.	A*	B*	C*	G	W	141.	A*	B*	C*	H	ee
107.	A*	B*	C*	G	X	142.	A*	B*	C*	H	ff
108.	A*	B*	C*	G	Y	143.	A*	B*	C*	H	gg
109.	A*	B*	C*	G	Z	144.	A*	B*	C*	H	hh
110.	A*	B*	C*	G	aa	145.	A*	B*	C*	H	ii
111.	A*	B*	C*	G	bb	146.	A*	B*	C*	I	J
112.	A*	B*	C*	G	cc	147.	A*	B*	C*	I	K
113.	A*	B*	C*	G	dd	148.	A*	B*	C*	I	L
114.	A*	B*	C*	G	ee	149.	A*	B*	C*	I	M
115.	A*	B*	C*	G	ff	150.	A*	B*	C*	I	N
116.	A*	B*	C*	G	gg	151.	A*	B*	C*	I	O
117.	A*	B*	C*	G	hh	152.	A*	B*	C*	I	P

     (Continued Next Page)

POWER NUMBER™ WHEEL 55035-3 (Continued from previous page)

#	A*	B*	C*			#	A*	B*	C*		
153.	A*	B*	C*	I	Q	188.	A*	B*	C*	J	aa
154.	A*	B*	C*	I	R	189.	A*	B*	C*	J	bb
155.	A*	B*	C*	I	S	190.	A*	B*	C*	J	cc
156.	A*	B*	C*	I	T	191.	A*	B*	C*	J	dd
157.	A*	B*	C*	I	U	192.	A*	B*	C*	J	ee
158.	A*	B*	C*	I	V	193.	A*	B*	C*	J	ff
159.	A*	B*	C*	I	W	194.	A*	B*	C*	J	gg
160.	A*	B*	C*	I	X	195.	A*	B*	C*	J	hh
161.	A*	B*	C*	I	Y	196.	A*	B*	C*	J	ii
162.	A*	B*	C*	I	Z	197.	A*	B*	C*	K	L
163.	A*	B*	C*	I	aa	198.	A*	B*	C*	K	M
164.	A*	B*	C*	I	bb	199.	A*	B*	C*	K	N
165.	A*	B*	C*	I	cc	200.	A*	B*	C*	K	O
166.	A*	B*	C*	I	dd	201.	A*	B*	C*	K	P
167.	A*	B*	C*	I	ee	202.	A*	B*	C*	K	Q
168.	A*	B*	C*	I	ff	203.	A*	B*	C*	K	R
169.	A*	B*	C*	I	gg	204.	A*	B*	C*	K	S
170.	A*	B*	C*	I	hh	205.	A*	B*	C*	K	T
171.	A*	B*	C*	I	ii	206.	A*	B*	C*	K	U
172.	A*	B*	C*	J	K	207.	A*	B*	C*	K	V
173.	A*	B*	C*	J	L	208.	A*	B*	C*	K	W
174.	A*	B*	C*	J	M	209.	A*	B*	C*	K	X
175.	A*	B*	C*	J	N	210.	A*	B*	C*	K	Y
176.	A*	B*	C*	J	O	211.	A*	B*	C*	K	Z
177.	A*	B*	C*	J	P	212.	A*	B*	C*	K	aa
178.	A*	B*	C*	J	Q	213.	A*	B*	C*	K	bb
179.	A*	B*	C*	J	R	214.	A*	B*	C*	K	cc
180.	A*	B*	C*	J	S	215.	A*	B*	C*	K	dd
181.	A*	B*	C*	J	T	216.	A*	B*	C*	K	ee
182.	A*	B*	C*	J	U	217.	A*	B*	C*	K	ff
183.	A*	B*	C*	J	V	218.	A*	B*	C*	K	gg
184.	A*	B*	C*	J	W	219.	A*	B*	C*	K	hh
185.	A*	B*	C*	J	X	220.	A*	B*	C*	K	ii
186.	A*	B*	C*	J	Y	221.	A*	B*	C*	L	M
187.	A*	B*	C*	J	Z	222.	A*	B*	C*	L	N

          (Continued Next Page)

POWER NUMBER™ WHEEL 55035-3 (Continued from previous page)

#	A*	B*	C*			#	A*	B*	C*		
223.	A*	B*	C*	L	O	258.	A*	B*	C*	M	bb
224.	A*	B*	C*	L	P	259.	A*	B*	C*	M	cc
225.	A*	B*	C*	L	Q	260.	A*	B*	C*	M	dd
226.	A*	B*	C*	L	R	261.	A*	B*	C*	M	ee
227.	A*	B*	C*	L	S	262.	A*	B*	C*	M	ff
228.	A*	B*	C*	L	T	263.	A*	B*	C*	M	gg
229.	A*	B*	C*	L	U	264.	A*	B*	C*	M	hh
230.	A*	B*	C*	L	V	265.	A*	B*	C*	M	ii
231.	A*	B*	C*	L	W	266.	A*	B*	C*	N	O
232.	A*	B*	C*	L	X	267.	A*	B*	C*	N	P
233.	A*	B*	C*	L	Y	268.	A*	B*	C*	N	Q
234.	A*	B*	C*	L	Z	269.	A*	B*	C*	N	R
235.	A*	B*	C*	L	aa	270.	A*	B*	C*	N	S
236.	A*	B*	C*	L	bb	271.	A*	B*	C*	N	T
237.	A*	B*	C*	L	cc	272.	A*	B*	C*	N	U
238.	A*	B*	C*	L	dd	273.	A*	B*	C*	N	V
239.	A*	B*	C*	L	ee	274.	A*	B*	C*	N	W
240.	A*	B*	C*	L	ff	275.	A*	B*	C*	N	X
241.	A*	B*	C*	L	gg	276.	A*	B*	C*	N	Y
242.	A*	B*	C*	L	hh	277.	A*	B*	C*	N	Z
243.	A*	B*	C*	L	ii	278.	A*	B*	C*	N	aa
244.	A*	B*	C*	M	N	279.	A*	B*	C*	N	bb
245.	A*	B*	C*	M	O	280.	A*	B*	C*	N	cc
246.	A*	B*	C*	M	P	281.	A*	B*	C*	N	dd
247.	A*	B*	C*	M	Q	282.	A*	B*	C*	N	ee
248.	A*	B*	C*	M	R	283.	A*	B*	C*	N	ff
249.	A*	B*	C*	M	S	284.	A*	B*	C*	N	gg
250.	A*	B*	C*	M	T	285.	A*	B*	C*	N	hh
251.	A*	B*	C*	M	U	286.	A*	B*	C*	N	ii
252.	A*	B*	C*	M	V	287.	A*	B*	C*	O	P
253.	A*	B*	C*	M	W	288.	A*	B*	C*	O	Q
254.	A*	B*	C*	M	X	289.	A*	B*	C*	O	R
255.	A*	B*	C*	M	Y	290.	A*	B*	C*	O	S
256.	A*	B*	C*	M	Z	291.	A*	B*	C*	O	T
257.	A*	B*	C*	M	aa	292.	A*	B*	C*	O	U

          (Continued Next Page)

POWER NUMBER™ WHEEL 55035-3 (Continued from previous page)

#						#					
293.	A*	B*	C*	O	V	328.	A*	B*	C*	Q	T
294.	A*	B*	C*	O	W	329.	A*	B*	C*	Q	U
295.	A*	B*	C*	O	X	330.	A*	B*	C*	Q	V
296.	A*	B*	C*	O	Y	331.	A*	B*	C*	Q	W
297.	A*	B*	C*	O	Z	332.	A*	B*	C*	Q	X
298.	A*	B*	C*	O	aa	333.	A*	B*	C*	Q	Y
299.	A*	B*	C*	O	bb	334.	A*	B*	C*	Q	Z
300.	A*	B*	C*	O	cc	335.	A*	B*	C*	Q	aa
301.	A*	B*	C*	O	dd	336.	A*	B*	C*	Q	bb
302.	A*	B*	C*	O	ee	337.	A*	B*	C*	Q	cc
303.	A*	B*	C*	O	ff	338.	A*	B*	C*	Q	dd
304.	A*	B*	C*	O	gg	339.	A*	B*	C*	Q	ee
305.	A*	B*	C*	O	hh	340.	A*	B*	C*	Q	ff
306.	A*	B*	C*	O	ii	341.	A*	B*	C*	Q	gg
307.	A*	B*	C*	P	Q	342.	A*	B*	C*	Q	hh
308.	A*	B*	C*	P	R	343.	A*	B*	C*	Q	ii
309.	A*	B*	C*	P	S	344.	A*	B*	C*	R	S
310.	A*	B*	C*	P	T	345.	A*	B*	C*	R	T
311.	A*	B*	C*	P	U	346.	A*	B*	C*	R	U
312.	A*	B*	C*	P	V	347.	A*	B*	C*	R	V
313.	A*	B*	C*	P	W	348.	A*	B*	C*	R	W
314.	A*	B*	C*	P	X	349.	A*	B*	C*	R	X
315.	A*	B*	C*	P	Y	350.	A*	B*	C*	R	Y
316.	A*	B*	C*	P	Z	351.	A*	B*	C*	R	Z
317.	A*	B*	C*	P	aa	352.	A*	B*	C*	R	aa
318.	A*	B*	C*	P	bb	353.	A*	B*	C*	R	bb
319.	A*	B*	C*	P	cc	354.	A*	B*	C*	R	cc
320.	A*	B*	C*	P	dd	355.	A*	B*	C*	R	dd
321.	A*	B*	C*	P	ee	356.	A*	B*	C*	R	ee
322.	A*	B*	C*	P	ff	357.	A*	B*	C*	R	ff
323.	A*	B*	C*	P	gg	358.	A*	B*	C*	R	gg
324.	A*	B*	C*	P	hh	359.	A*	B*	C*	R	hh
325.	A*	B*	C*	P	ii	360.	A*	B*	C*	R	ii
326.	A*	B*	C*	Q	R	361.	A*	B*	C*	S	T
327.	A*	B*	C*	Q	S	362.	A*	B*	C*	S	U

(Continued Next Page)

POWER NUMBER™ WHEEL 55035-3 (Continued from previous page)

#	A*	B*	C*			#	A*	B*	C*		
363.	A*	B*	C*	S	V	398.	A*	B*	C*	U	bb
364.	A*	B*	C*	S	W	399.	A*	B*	C*	U	cc
365.	A*	B*	C*	S	X	400.	A*	B*	C*	U	dd
366.	A*	B*	C*	S	Y	401.	A*	B*	C*	U	ee
367.	A*	B*	C*	S	Z	402.	A*	B*	C*	U	ff
368.	A*	B*	C*	S	aa	403.	A*	B*	C*	U	gg
369.	A*	B*	C*	S	bb	404.	A*	B*	C*	U	hh
370.	A*	B*	C*	S	cc	405.	A*	B*	C*	U	ii
371.	A*	B*	C*	S	dd	406.	A*	B*	C*	V	W
372.	A*	B*	C*	S	ee	407.	A*	B*	C*	V	X
373.	A*	B*	C*	S	ff	408.	A*	B*	C*	V	Y
374.	A*	B*	C*	S	gg	409.	A*	B*	C*	V	Z
375.	A*	B*	C*	S	hh	410.	A*	B*	C*	V	aa
376.	A*	B*	C*	S	ii	411.	A*	B*	C*	V	bb
377.	A*	B*	C*	T	U	412.	A*	B*	C*	V	cc
378.	A*	B*	C*	T	V	413.	A*	B*	C*	V	dd
379.	A*	B*	C*	T	W	414.	A*	B*	C*	V	ee
380.	A*	B*	C*	T	X	415.	A*	B*	C*	V	ff
381.	A*	B*	C*	T	Y	416.	A*	B*	C*	V	gg
382.	A*	B*	C*	T	Z	417.	A*	B*	C*	V	hh
383.	A*	B*	C*	T	aa	418.	A*	B*	C*	V	ii
384.	A*	B*	C*	T	bb	419.	A*	B*	C*	W	X
385.	A*	B*	C*	T	cc	420.	A*	B*	C*	W	Y
386.	A*	B*	C*	T	dd	421.	A*	B*	C*	W	Z
387.	A*	B*	C*	T	ee	422.	A*	B*	C*	W	aa
388.	A*	B*	C*	T	ff	423.	A*	B*	C*	W	bb
389.	A*	B*	C*	T	gg	424.	A*	B*	C*	W	cc
390.	A*	B*	C*	T	hh	425.	A*	B*	C*	W	dd
391.	A*	B*	C*	T	ii	426.	A*	B*	C*	W	ee
392.	A*	B*	C*	U	V	427.	A*	B*	C*	W	ff
393.	A*	B*	C*	U	W	428.	A*	B*	C*	W	gg
394.	A*	B*	C*	U	X	429.	A*	B*	C*	W	hh
395.	A*	B*	C*	U	Y	430.	A*	B*	C*	W	ii
396.	A*	B*	C*	U	Z	431.	A*	B*	C*	X	Y
397.	A*	B*	C*	U	aa	432.	A*	B*	C*	X	Z

          (Continued Next Page)

POWER NUMBER™ WHEEL 55035-3 (Continued from previous page)

No.						No.					
433.	A*	B*	C*	X	aa	465.	A*	B*	C*	aa	ff
434.	A*	B*	C*	X	bb	466.	A*	B*	C*	aa	gg
435.	A*	B*	C*	X	cc	467.	A*	B*	C*	aa	hh
436.	A*	B*	C*	X	dd	468.	A*	B*	C*	aa	ii
437.	A*	B*	C*	X	ee	469.	A*	B*	C*	bb	cc
438.	A*	B*	C*	X	ff	470.	A*	B*	C*	bb	dd
439.	A*	B*	C*	X	gg	471.	A*	B*	C*	bb	ee
440.	A*	B*	C*	X	hh	472.	A*	B*	C*	bb	ff
441.	A*	B*	C*	X	ii	473.	A*	B*	C*	bb	gg
442.	A*	B*	C*	Y	z	474.	A*	B*	C*	bb	hh
443.	A*	B*	C*	Y	aa	475.	A*	B*	C*	bb	ii
444.	A*	B*	C*	Y	bb	476.	A*	B*	C*	cc	dd
445.	A*	B*	C*	Y	cc	477.	A*	B*	C*	cc	ee
446.	A*	B*	C*	Y	dd	478.	A*	B*	C*	cc	ff
447.	A*	B*	C*	Y	ee	479.	A*	B*	C*	cc	gg
448.	A*	B*	C*	Y	ff	480.	A*	B*	C*	cc	hh
449.	A*	B*	C*	Y	gg	481.	A*	B*	C*	cc	ii
450.	A*	B*	C*	Y	hh	482.	A*	B*	C*	dd	ee
451.	A*	B*	C*	Y	ii	483.	A*	B*	C*	dd	ff
452.	A*	B*	C*	Z	aa	484.	A*	B*	C*	dd	gg
453.	A*	B*	C*	Z	bb	485.	A*	B*	C*	dd	hh
454.	A*	B*	C*	Z	cc	486.	A*	B*	C*	dd	ii
455.	A*	B*	C*	Z	dd	487.	A*	B*	C*	ee	ff
456.	A*	B*	C*	Z	ee	488.	A*	B*	C*	ee	gg
457.	A*	B*	C*	Z	ff	489.	A*	B*	C*	ee	hh
458.	A*	B*	C*	Z	gg	490.	A*	B*	C*	ee	ii
459.	A*	B*	C*	Z	hh	491.	A*	B*	C*	ff	gg
460.	A*	B*	C*	Z	ii	492.	A*	B*	C*	ff	hh
461.	A*	B*	C*	aa	bb	493.	A*	B*	C*	ff	ii
462.	A*	B*	C*	aa	cc	494.	A*	B*	C*	gg	hh
463.	A*	B*	C*	aa	dd	495.	A*	B*	C*	gg	ii
464.	A*	B*	C*	aa	ee	496.	A*	B*	C*	hh	ii

POWER NUMBER™ WHEEL 55039-3
Wheeling 39 Numbers in 630 games for a 5 of 5 Win

NUMBERS CORRECT***	MAXIMUM WINS				MINIMUM WINS			
	5x	4x	3x	2x	5x	4x	3x	2x
5 (w/o Jackpot)	0	0	0	0				
5	1	68	561	0	1	68	561	0
4	–	35	595	0	–	35	595	0
3	–	–	630	630	–	–	630	630
2	–	–	–	630	–	–	–	630

*** POWER NUMBER POSITIONS A*, B* & C* MUST BE WINNERS.

Your 39 Numbers to Wheel

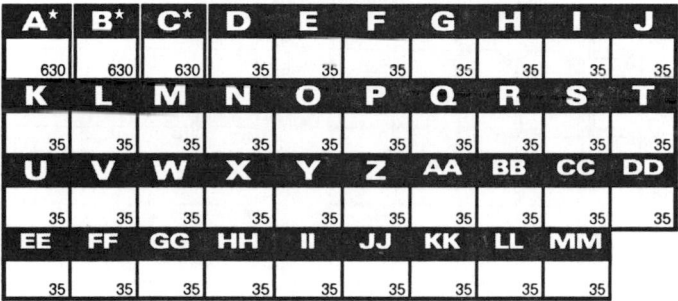

A*	B*	C*	D	E	F	G	H	I	J
630	630	630	35	35	35	35	35	35	35

K	L	M	N	O	P	Q	R	S	T
35	35	35	35	35	35	35	35	35	35

U	V	W	X	Y	Z	AA	BB	CC	DD
35	35	35	35	35	35	35	35	35	35

EE	FF	GG	HH	II	JJ	KK	LL	MM
35	35	35	35	35	35	35	35	35

The 630 Games to Play

#						#					
1.	A*	B*	C*	D	E	21.	A*	B*	C*	D	Y
2.	A*	B*	C*	D	F	22.	A*	B*	C*	D	Z
3.	A*	B*	C*	D	G	23.	A*	B*	C*	D	aa
4.	A*	B*	C*	D	H	24.	A*	B*	C*	D	bb
5.	A*	B*	C*	D	I	25.	A*	B*	C*	D	cc
6.	A*	B*	C*	D	J	26.	A*	B*	C*	D	dd
7.	A*	B*	C*	D	K	27.	A*	B*	C*	D	ee
8.	A*	B*	C*	D	L	28.	A*	B*	C*	D	ff
9.	A*	B*	C*	D	M	29.	A*	B*	C*	D	gg
10.	A*	B*	C*	D	N	30.	A*	B*	C*	D	hh
11.	A*	B*	C*	D	O	31.	A*	B*	C*	D	ii
12.	A*	B*	C*	D	P	32.	A*	B*	C*	D	jj
13.	A*	B*	C*	D	Q	33.	A*	B*	C*	D	kk
14.	A*	B*	C*	D	R	34.	A*	B*	C*	D	ll
15.	A*	B*	C*	D	S	35.	A*	B*	C*	D	mm
16.	A*	B*	C*	D	T	36.	A*	B*	C*	E	F
17.	A*	B*	C*	D	U	37.	A*	B*	C*	E	G
18.	A*	B*	C*	D	V	38.	A*	B*	C*	E	H
19.	A*	B*	C*	D	W	39.	A*	B*	C*	E	I
20.	A*	B*	C*	D	X	40.	A*	B*	C*	E	J

(Continued Next Page)

POWER NUMBER™ WHEEL 55039-3 (Continued from previous page)

#						#					
41.	A*	B*	C*	E	K	76.	A*	B*	C*	F	M
42.	A*	B*	C*	E	L	77.	A*	B*	C*	F	N
43.	A*	B*	C*	E	M	78.	A*	B*	C*	F	O
44.	A*	B*	C*	E	N	79.	A*	B*	C*	F	P
45.	A*	B*	C*	E	O	80.	A*	B*	C*	F	Q
46.	A*	B*	C*	E	P	81.	A*	B*	C*	F	R
47.	A*	B*	C*	E	Q	82.	A*	B*	C*	F	S
48.	A*	B*	C*	E	R	83.	A*	B*	C*	F	T
49.	A*	B*	C*	E	S	84.	A*	B*	C*	F	U
50.	A*	B*	C*	E	T	85.	A*	B*	C*	F	V
51.	A*	B*	C*	E	U	86.	A*	B*	C*	F	W
52.	A*	B*	C*	E	V	87.	A*	B*	C*	F	X
53.	A*	B*	C*	E	W	88.	A*	B*	C*	F	Y
54.	A*	B*	C*	E	X	89.	A*	B*	C*	F	Z
55.	A*	B*	C*	E	Y	90.	A*	B*	C*	F	aa
56.	A*	B*	C*	E	Z	91.	A*	B*	C*	F	bb
57.	A*	B*	C*	E	aa	92.	A*	B*	C*	F	cc
58.	A*	B*	C*	E	bb	93.	A*	B*	C*	F	dd
59.	A*	B*	C*	E	cc	94.	A*	B*	C*	F	ee
60.	A*	B*	C*	E	dd	95.	A*	B*	C*	F	ff
61.	A*	B*	C*	E	ee	96.	A*	B*	C*	F	gg
62.	A*	B*	C*	E	ff	97.	A*	B*	C*	F	hh
63.	A*	B*	C*	E	gg	98.	A*	B*	C*	F	ii
64.	A*	B*	C*	E	hh	99.	A*	B*	C*	F	jj
65.	A*	B*	C*	E	ii	100.	A*	B*	C*	F	kk
66.	A*	B*	C*	E	jj	101.	A*	B*	C*	F	ll
67.	A*	B*	C*	E	kk	102.	A*	B*	C*	F	mm
68.	A*	B*	C*	E	ll	103.	A*	B*	C*	G	H
69.	A*	B*	C*	E	mm	104.	A*	B*	C*	G	I
70.	A*	B*	C*	F	G	105.	A*	B*	C*	G	J
71.	A*	B*	C*	F	H	106.	A*	B*	C*	G	K
72.	A*	B*	C*	F	I	107.	A*	B*	C*	G	L
73.	A*	B*	C*	F	J	108.	A*	B*	C*	G	M
74.	A*	B*	C*	F	K	109.	A*	B*	C*	G	N
75.	A*	B*	C*	F	L	110.	A*	B*	C*	G	O

     (Continued Next Page)

POWER NUMBER™ WHEEL 55039-3 (Continued from previous page)

#						#					
111.	A*	B*	C*	G	P	146.	A*	B*	C*	H	T
112.	A*	B*	C*	G	Q	147.	A*	B*	C*	H	U
113.	A*	B*	C*	G	R	148.	A*	B*	C*	H	V
114.	A*	B*	C*	G	S	149.	A*	B*	C*	H	W
115.	A*	B*	C*	G	T	150.	A*	B*	C*	H	X
116.	A*	B*	C*	G	U	151.	A*	B*	C*	H	Y
117.	A*	B*	C*	G	V	152.	A*	B*	C*	H	Z
118.	A*	B*	C*	G	W	153.	A*	B*	C*	H	aa
119.	A*	B*	C*	G	X	154.	A*	B*	C*	H	bb
120.	A*	B*	C*	G	Y	155.	A*	B*	C*	H	cc
121.	A*	B*	C*	G	Z	156.	A*	B*	C*	H	dd
122.	A*	B*	C*	G	aa	157.	A*	B*	C*	H	ee
123.	A*	B*	C*	G	bb	158.	A*	B*	C*	H	ff
124.	A*	B*	C*	G	cc	159.	A*	B*	C*	H	gg
125.	A*	B*	C*	G	dd	160.	A*	B*	C*	H	hh
126.	A*	B*	C*	G	ee	161.	A*	B*	C*	H	ii
127.	A*	B*	C*	G	ff	162.	A*	B*	C*	H	jj
128.	A*	B*	C*	G	gg	163.	A*	B*	C*	H	kk
129.	A*	B*	C*	G	hh	164.	A*	B*	C*	H	ll
130.	A*	B*	C*	G	ii	165.	A*	B*	C*	H	mm
131.	A*	B*	C*	G	jj	166.	A*	B*	C*	I	J
132.	A*	B*	C*	G	kk	167.	A*	B*	C*	I	K
133.	A*	B*	C*	G	ll	168.	A*	B*	C*	I	L
134.	A*	B*	C*	G	mm	169.	A*	B*	C*	I	M
135.	A*	B*	C*	H	I	170.	A*	B*	C*	I	N
136.	A*	B*	C*	H	J	171.	A*	B*	C*	I	O
137.	A*	B*	C*	H	K	172.	A*	B*	C*	I	P
138.	A*	B*	C*	H	L	173.	A*	B*	C*	I	Q
139.	A*	B*	C*	H	M	174.	A*	B*	C*	I	R
140.	A*	B*	C*	H	N	175.	A*	B*	C*	I	S
141.	A*	B*	C*	H	O	176.	A*	B*	C*	I	T
142.	A*	B*	C*	H	P	177.	A*	B*	C*	I	U
143.	A*	B*	C*	H	Q	178.	A*	B*	C*	I	V
144.	A*	B*	C*	H	R	179.	A*	B*	C*	I	W
145.	A*	B*	C*	H	S	180.	A*	B*	C*	I	X

    (Continued Next Page)

POWER NUMBER™ WHEEL 55039-3 (Continued from previous page)

#	A*	B*	C*				#	A*	B*	C*		
181.	A*	B*	C*	I	Y		216.	A*	B*	C*	J	ee
182.	A*	B*	C*	I	Z		217.	A*	B*	C*	J	ff
183.	A*	B*	C*	I	aa		218.	A*	B*	C*	J	gg
184.	A*	B*	C*	I	bb		219.	A*	B*	C*	J	hh
185.	A*	B*	C*	I	cc		220.	A*	B*	C*	J	ii
186.	A*	B*	C*	I	dd		221.	A*	B*	C*	J	jj
187.	A*	B*	C*	I	ee		222.	A*	B*	C*	J	kk
188.	A*	B*	C*	I	ff		223.	A*	B*	C*	J	ll
189.	A*	B*	C*	I	gg		224.	A*	B*	C*	J	mm
190.	A*	B*	C*	I	hh		225.	A*	B*	C*	K	L
191.	A*	B*	C*	I	ii		226.	A*	B*	C*	K	M
192.	A*	B*	C*	I	jj		227.	A*	B*	C*	K	N
193.	A*	B*	C*	I	kk		228.	A*	B*	C*	K	O
194.	A*	B*	C*	I	ll		229.	A*	B*	C*	K	P
195.	A*	B*	C*	I	mm		230.	A*	B*	C*	K	Q
196.	A*	B*	C*	J	K		231.	A*	B*	C*	K	R
197.	A*	B*	C*	J	L		232.	A*	B*	C*	K	S
198.	A*	B*	C*	J	M		233.	A*	B*	C*	K	T
199.	A*	B*	C*	J	N		234.	A*	B*	C*	K	U
200.	A*	B*	C*	J	O		235.	A*	B*	C*	K	V
201.	A*	B*	C*	J	P		236.	A*	B*	C*	K	W
202.	A*	B*	C*	J	Q		237.	A*	B*	C*	K	X
203.	A*	B*	C*	J	R		238.	A*	B*	C*	K	Y
204.	A*	B*	C*	J	S		239.	A*	B*	C*	K	Z
205.	A*	B*	C*	J	T		240.	A*	B*	C*	K	aa
206.	A*	B*	C*	J	U		241.	A*	B*	C*	K	bb
207.	A*	B*	C*	J	V		242.	A*	B*	C*	K	cc
208.	A*	B*	C*	J	W		243.	A*	B*	C*	K	dd
209.	A*	B*	C*	J	X		244.	A*	B*	C*	K	ee
210.	A*	B*	C*	J	Y		245.	A*	B*	C*	K	ff
211.	A*	B*	C*	J	Z		246.	A*	B*	C*	K	gg
212.	A*	B*	C*	J	aa		247.	A*	B*	C*	K	hh
213.	A*	B*	C*	J	bb		248.	A*	B*	C*	K	ii
214.	A*	B*	C*	J	cc		249.	A*	B*	C*	K	jj
215.	A*	B*	C*	J	dd		250.	A*	B*	C*	K	kk

(Continued Next Page)

POWER NUMBER™ WHEEL 55039-3 (Continued from previous page)

#						#				
251.	A*	B*	C*	K	ll	286.	A*	B*	C*	M	T
252.	A*	B*	C*	K	mm	287.	A*	B*	C*	M	U
253.	A*	B*	C*	L	M	288.	A*	B*	C*	M	V
254.	A*	B*	C*	L	N	289.	A*	B*	C*	M	W
255.	A*	B*	C*	L	O	290.	A*	B*	C*	M	X
256.	A*	B*	C*	L	P	291.	A*	B*	C*	M	Y
257.	A*	B*	C*	L	Q	292.	A*	B*	C*	M	Z
258.	A*	B*	C*	L	R	293.	A*	B*	C*	M	aa
259.	A*	B*	C*	L	S	294.	A*	B*	C*	M	bb
260.	A*	B*	C*	L	T	295.	A*	B*	C*	M	cc
261.	A*	B*	C*	L	U	296.	A*	B*	C*	M	dd
262.	A*	B*	C*	L	V	297.	A*	B*	C*	M	ee
263.	A*	B*	C*	L	W	298.	A*	B*	C*	M	ff
264.	A*	B*	C*	L	X	299.	A*	B*	C*	M	gg
265.	A*	B*	C*	L	Y	300.	A*	B*	C*	M	hh
266.	A*	B*	C*	L	Z	301.	A*	B*	C*	M	ii
267.	A*	B*	C*	L	aa	302.	A*	B*	C*	M	jj
268.	A*	B*	C*	L	bb	303.	A*	B*	C*	M	kk
269.	A*	B*	C*	L	cc	304.	A*	B*	C*	M	ll
270.	A*	B*	C*	L	dd	305.	A*	B*	C*	M	mm
271.	A*	B*	C*	L	ee	306.	A*	B*	C*	N	O
272.	A*	B*	C*	L	ff	307.	A*	B*	C*	N	P
273.	A*	B*	C*	L	gg	308.	A*	B*	C*	N	Q
274.	A*	B*	C*	L	hh	309.	A*	B*	C*	N	R
275.	A*	B*	C*	L	ii	310.	A*	B*	C*	N	S
276.	A*	B*	C*	L	jj	311.	A*	B*	C*	N	T
277.	A*	B*	C*	L	kk	312.	A*	B*	C*	N	U
278.	A*	B*	C*	L	ll	313.	A*	B*	C*	N	V
279.	A*	B*	C*	L	mm	314.	A*	B*	C*	N	W
280.	A*	B*	C*	M	N	315.	A*	B*	C*	N	X
281.	A*	B*	C*	M	O	316.	A*	B*	C*	N	Y
282.	A*	B*	C*	M	P	317.	A*	B*	C*	N	Z
283.	A*	B*	C*	M	Q	318.	A*	B*	C*	N	aa
284.	A*	B*	C*	M	R	319.	A*	B*	C*	N	bb
285.	A*	B*	C*	M	S	320.	A*	B*	C*	N	cc

          (Continued Next Page)

413

POWER NUMBER™ WHEEL 55039-3 (Continued from previous page)

#						#					
321.	A*	B*	C*	N	dd	356.	A*	B*	C*	P	R
322.	A*	B*	C*	N	ee	357.	A*	B*	C*	P	S
323.	A*	B*	C*	N	ff	358.	A*	B*	C*	P	T
324.	A*	B*	C*	N	gg	359.	A*	B*	C*	P	U
325.	A*	B*	C*	N	hh	360.	A*	B*	C*	P	V
326.	A*	B*	C*	N	ii	361.	A*	B*	C*	P	W
327.	A*	B*	C*	N	jj	362.	A*	B*	C*	P	X
328.	A*	B*	C*	N	kk	363.	A*	B*	C*	P	Y
329.	A*	B*	C*	N	ll	364.	A*	B*	C*	P	Z
330.	A*	B*	C*	N	mm	365.	A*	B*	C*	P	aa
331.	A*	B*	C*	O	P	366.	A*	B*	C*	P	bb
332.	A*	B*	C*	O	Q	367.	A*	B*	C*	P	cc
333.	A*	B*	C*	O	R	368.	A*	B*	C*	P	dd
334.	A*	B*	C*	O	S	369.	A*	B*	C*	P	ee
335.	A*	B*	C*	O	T	370.	A*	B*	C*	P	ff
336.	A*	B*	C*	O	U	371.	A*	B*	C*	P	gg
337.	A*	B*	C*	O	V	372.	A*	B*	C*	P	hh
338.	A*	B*	C*	O	W	373.	A*	B*	C*	P	ii
339.	A*	B*	C*	O	X	374.	A*	B*	C*	P	jj
340.	A*	B*	C*	O	Y	375.	A*	B*	C*	P	kk
341.	A*	B*	C*	O	Z	376.	A*	B*	C*	P	ll
342.	A*	B*	C*	O	aa	377.	A*	B*	C*	P	mm
343.	A*	B*	C*	O	bb	378.	A*	B*	C*	Q	R
344.	A*	B*	C*	O	cc	379.	A*	B*	C*	Q	S
345.	A*	B*	C*	O	dd	380.	A*	B*	C*	Q	T
346.	A*	B*	C*	O	ee	381.	A*	B*	C*	Q	U
347.	A*	B*	C*	O	ff	382.	A*	B*	C*	Q	V
348.	A*	B*	C*	O	gg	383.	A*	B*	C*	Q	W
349.	A*	B*	C*	O	hh	384.	A*	B*	C*	Q	X
350.	A*	B*	C*	O	ii	385.	A*	B*	C*	Q	Y
351.	A*	B*	C*	O	jj	386.	A*	B*	C*	Q	Z
352.	A*	B*	C*	O	kk	387.	A*	B*	C*	Q	aa
353.	A*	B*	C*	O	ll	388.	A*	B*	C*	Q	bb
354.	A*	B*	C*	O	mm	389.	A*	B*	C*	Q	cc
355.	A*	B*	C*	P	Q	390.	A*	B*	C*	Q	dd

     (Continued Next Page)

POWER NUMBER™ WHEEL 55039-3 (Continued from previous page)

#						#					
391.	A*	B*	C*	Q	ee	426.	A*	B*	C*	S	Y
392.	A*	B*	C*	Q	ff	427.	A*	B*	C*	S	Z
393.	A*	B*	C*	Q	gg	428.	A*	B*	C*	S	aa
394.	A*	B*	C*	Q	hh	429.	A*	B*	C*	S	bb
395.	A*	B*	C*	Q	ii	430.	A*	B*	C*	S	cc
396.	A*	B*	C*	Q	jj	431.	A*	B*	C*	S	dd
397.	A*	B*	C*	Q	kk	432.	A*	B*	C*	S	ee
398.	A*	B*	C*	Q	ll	433.	A*	B*	C*	S	ff
399.	A*	B*	C*	Q	mm	434.	A*	B*	C*	S	gg
400.	A*	B*	C*	R	S	435.	A*	B*	C*	S	hh
401.	A*	B*	C*	R	T	436.	A*	B*	C*	S	ii
402.	A*	B*	C*	R	U	437.	A*	B*	C*	S	jj
403.	A*	B*	C*	R	V	438.	A*	B*	C*	S	kk
404.	A*	B*	C*	R	W	439.	A*	B*	C*	S	ll
405.	A*	B*	C*	R	X	440.	A*	B*	C*	S	mm
406.	A*	B*	C*	R	Y	441.	A*	B*	C*	T	U
407.	A*	B*	C*	R	Z	442.	A*	B*	C*	T	V
408.	A*	B*	C*	R	aa	443.	A*	B*	C*	T	W
409.	A*	B*	C*	R	bb	444.	A*	B*	C*	T	X
410.	A*	B*	C*	R	cc	445.	A*	B*	C*	T	Y
411.	A*	B*	C*	R	dd	446.	A*	B*	C*	T	Z
412.	A*	B*	C*	R	ee	447.	A*	B*	C*	T	aa
413.	A*	B*	C*	R	ff	448.	A*	B*	C*	T	bb
414.	A*	B*	C*	R	gg	449.	A*	B*	C*	T	cc
415.	A*	B*	C*	R	hh	450.	A*	B*	C*	T	dd
416.	A*	B*	C*	R	ii	451.	A*	B*	C*	T	ee
417.	A*	B*	C*	R	jj	452.	A*	B*	C*	T	ff
418.	A*	B*	C*	R	kk	453.	A*	B*	C*	T	gg
419.	A*	B*	C*	R	ll	454.	A*	B*	C*	T	hh
420.	A*	B*	C*	R	mm	455.	A*	B*	C*	T	ii
421.	A*	B*	C*	S	T	456.	A*	B*	C*	T	jj
422.	A*	B*	C*	S	U	457.	A*	B*	C*	T	kk
423.	A*	B*	C*	S	V	458.	A*	B*	C*	T	ll
424.	A*	B*	C*	S	W	459.	A*	B*	C*	T	mm
425.	A*	B*	C*	S	X	460.	A*	B*	C*	U	V

(Continued Next Page)

415

POWER NUMBER™ WHEEL 55039-3 (Continued from previous page)

#						#					
461.	A*	B*	C*	U	W	496.	A*	B*	C*	W	Y
462.	A*	B*	C*	U	X	497.	A*	B*	C*	W	Z
463.	A*	B*	C*	U	Y	498.	A*	B*	C*	W	aa
464.	A*	B*	C*	U	Z	499.	A*	B*	C*	W	bb
465.	A*	B*	C*	U	aa	500.	A*	B*	C*	W	cc
466.	A*	B*	C*	U	bb	501.	A*	B*	C*	W	dd
467.	A*	B*	C*	U	cc	502.	A*	B*	C*	W	ee
468.	A*	B*	C*	U	dd	503.	A*	B*	C*	W	ff
469.	A*	B*	C*	U	ee	504.	A*	B*	C*	W	gg
470.	A*	B*	C*	U	ff	505.	A*	B*	C*	W	hh
471.	A*	B*	C*	U	gg	506.	A*	B*	C*	W	ii
472.	A*	B*	C*	U	hh	507.	A*	B*	C*	W	jj
473.	A*	B*	C*	U	ii	508.	A*	B*	C*	W	kk
474.	A*	B*	C*	U	jj	509.	A*	B*	C*	W	ll
475.	A*	B*	C*	U	kk	510.	A*	B*	C*	W	mm
476.	A*	B*	C*	U	ll	511.	A*	B*	C*	X	Y
477.	A*	B*	C*	U	mm	512.	A*	B*	C*	X	Z
478.	A*	B*	C*	V	W	513.	A*	B*	C*	X	aa
479.	A*	B*	C*	V	X	514.	A*	B*	C*	X	bb
480.	A*	B*	C*	V	Y	515.	A*	B*	C*	X	cc
481.	A*	B*	C*	V	Z	516.	A*	B*	C*	X	dd
482.	A*	B*	C*	V	aa	517.	A*	B*	C*	X	ee
483.	A*	B*	C*	V	bb	518.	A*	B*	C*	X	ff
484.	A*	B*	C*	V	cc	519.	A*	B*	C*	X	gg
485.	A*	B*	C*	V	dd	520.	A*	B*	C*	X	hh
486.	A*	B*	C*	V	ee	521.	A*	B*	C*	X	ii
487.	A*	B*	C*	V	ff	522.	A*	B*	C*	X	jj
488.	A*	B*	C*	V	gg	523.	A*	B*	C*	X	kk
489.	A*	B*	C*	V	hh	524.	A*	B*	C*	X	ll
490.	A*	B*	C*	V	ii	525.	A*	B*	C*	X	mm
491.	A*	B*	C*	V	jj	526.	A*	B*	C*	Y	Z
492.	A*	B*	C*	V	kk	527.	A*	B*	C*	Y	aa
493.	A*	B*	C*	V	ll	528.	A*	B*	C*	Y	bb
494.	A*	B*	C*	V	mm	529.	A*	B*	C*	Y	cc
495.	A*	B*	C*	W	X	530.	A*	B*	C*	Y	dd

          (Continued Next Page)

POWER NUMBER™ WHEEL 55039-3 (Continued from previous page)

#	A*	B*	C*			#	A*	B*	C*		
531.	A*	B*	C*	Y	ee	566.	A*	B*	C*	bb	dd
532.	A*	B*	C*	Y	ff	567.	A*	B*	C*	bb	ee
533.	A*	B*	C*	Y	gg	568.	A*	B*	C*	bb	ff
534.	A*	B*	C*	Y	hh	569.	A*	B*	C*	bb	gg
535.	A*	B*	C*	Y	ii	570.	A*	B*	C*	bb	hh
536.	A*	B*	C*	Y	jj	571.	A*	B*	C*	bb	ii
537.	A*	B*	C*	Y	kk	572.	A*	B*	C*	bb	jj
538.	A*	B*	C*	Y	ll	573.	A*	B*	C*	bb	kk
539.	A*	B*	C*	Y	mm	574.	A*	B*	C*	bb	ll
540.	A*	B*	C*	Z	aa	575.	A*	B*	C*	bb	mm
541.	A*	B*	C*	Z	bb	576.	A*	B*	C*	cc	dd
542.	A*	B*	C*	Z	cc	577.	A*	B*	C*	cc	ee
543.	A*	B*	C*	Z	dd	578.	A*	B*	C*	cc	ff
544.	A*	B*	C*	Z	ee	579.	A*	B*	C*	cc	gg
545.	A*	B*	C*	Z	ff	580.	A*	B*	C*	cc	hh
546.	A*	B*	C*	Z	gg	581.	A*	B*	C*	cc	ii
547.	A*	B*	C*	Z	hh	582.	A*	B*	C*	cc	jj
548.	A*	B*	C*	Z	ii	583.	A*	B*	C*	cc	kk
549.	A*	B*	C*	Z	jj	584.	A*	B*	C*	cc	ll
550.	A*	B*	C*	Z	kk	585.	A*	B*	C*	cc	mm
551.	A*	B*	C*	Z	ll	586.	A*	B*	C*	dd	ee
552.	A*	B*	C*	Z	mm	587.	A*	B*	C*	dd	ff
553.	A*	B*	C*	aa	bb	588.	A*	B*	C*	dd	gg
554.	A*	B*	C*	aa	cc	589.	A*	B*	C*	dd	hh
555.	A*	B*	C*	aa	dd	590.	A*	B*	C*	dd	ii
556.	A*	B*	C*	aa	ee	591.	A*	B*	C*	dd	jj
557.	A*	B*	C*	aa	ff	592.	A*	B*	C*	dd	kk
558.	A*	B*	C*	aa	gg	593.	A*	B*	C*	dd	ll
559.	A*	B*	C*	aa	hh	594.	A*	B*	C*	dd	mm
560.	A*	B*	C*	aa	ii	595.	A*	B*	C*	ee	ff
561.	A*	B*	C*	aa	jj	596.	A*	B*	C*	ee	gg
562.	A*	B*	C*	aa	kk	597.	A*	B*	C*	ee	hh
563.	A*	B*	C*	aa	ll	598.	A*	B*	C*	ee	ii
564.	A*	B*	C*	aa	mm	599.	A*	B*	C*	ee	jj
565.	A*	B*	C*	bb	cc	600.	A*	B*	C*	ee	kk

          (Continued Next Page)

POWER NUMBER™ WHEEL 55039-3 (Continued from previous page)

	A*	B*	C*	ee	ll			A*	B*	C*	hh	ii
601.							616.					
602.	A*	B*	C*	ee	mm		617.	A*	B*	C*	hh	jj
603.	A*	B*	C*	ff	gg		618.	A*	B*	C*	hh	kk
604.	A*	B*	C*	ff	hh		619.	A*	B*	C*	hh	ll
605.	A*	B*	C*	ff	ii		620.	A*	B*	C*	hh	mm
606.	A*	B*	C*	ff	jj		621.	A*	B*	C*	ii	jj
607.	A*	B*	C*	ff	kk		622.	A*	B*	C*	ii	kk
608.	A*	B*	C*	ff	ll		623.	A*	B*	C*	ii	ll
609.	A*	B*	C*	ff	mm		624.	A*	B*	C*	ii	mm
610.	A*	B*	C*	gg	hh		625.	A*	B*	C*	jj	kk
611.	A*	B*	C*	gg	ii		626.	A*	B*	C*	jj	ll
612.	A*	B*	C*	gg	jj		627.	A*	B*	C*	jj	mm
613.	A*	B*	C*	gg	kk		628.	A*	B*	C*	kk	ll
614.	A*	B*	C*	gg	ll		629.	A*	B*	C*	kk	mm
615.	A*	B*	C*	gg	mm		630.	A*	B*	C*	ll	mm

POWER NUMBER™ WHEEL 54007-3
Wheeling 7 Numbers in 2 games for a 4 of 4 Win

NUMBERS CORRECT***	MAXIMUM WINS				MINIMUM WINS			
	5x	4x	3x	2x	5x	4x	3x	2x
5 (w/o Jackpot)	0	2	0	0				
5	1	0	1	0	0	2	0	0
4	–	1	1	0	–	1	1	0
3	–	–	2	2	–	–	2	2
2	–	–	–	2	–	–	–	2

*** POWER NUMBER POSITIONS A*, B* & C* MUST BE WINNERS.

Your 7 Numbers to Wheel

A*	B*	C*	D	E	F	G
2	2	2	1	1	1	1

The 2 Games to Play

1. | A* | B* | C* | D | G |

2. | A* | B* | C* | E | F |

POWER NUMBER™WHEEL 54009-3

Wheeling 9 Numbers in 3 games for a 4 of 4 Win

NUMBERS CORRECT***	MAXIMUM WINS				MINIMUM WINS			
	5x	4x	3x	2x	5x	4x	3x	2x
5 (w/o Jackpot)	0	2	1	0				
5	1	0	2	0	0	2	1	0
4	–	1	2	0	–	1	2	0
3	–	–	3	3	–	–	3	3
2	–	–	–	3	–	–	–	3

*** POWER NUMBER POSITIONS A*, B* & C* MUST BE WINNERS.

Your 9 Numbers to Wheel

A*	B*	C*	D	E	F	G	H	I
3	3	3	1	1	1	1	1	1

The 3 Games to Play

1. | A* | B* | C* | D | I |

2. | A* | B* | C* | E | H |

3. | A* | B* | C* | F | G |

Copyright © 1983-1998 Gail Howard

POWER NUMBER™WHEEL 54011-3

Wheeling 11 Numbers in 4 games for a 4 of 4 Win

NUMBERS CORRECT***	MAXIMUM WINS				MINIMUM WINS			
	5x	4x	3x	2x	5x	4x	3x	2x
5 (w/o Jackpot)	0	2	2	0				
5	1	0	3	0	0	2	2	0
4	–	1	3	0	–	1	3	0
3	–	–	4	4	–	–	4	4
2	–	–	–	4	–	–	–	4

*** POWER NUMBER POSITIONS A*, B* & C* MUST BE WINNERS.

Your 11 Numbers to Wheel

A*	B*	C*	D	E	F	G	H	I	J	K
4	4	4	1	1	1	1	1	1	1	1

The 4 Games to Play

1. | A* | B* | C* | D | J |

2. | A* | B* | C* | E | K |

3. | A* | B* | C* | F | H |

4. | A* | B* | C* | G | I |

Copyright © 1983-1998 Gail Howard

POWER NUMBER™WHEEL 54013-3

Wheeling 13 Numbers in 5 games for a 4 of 4 Win

NUMBERS CORRECT***	MAXIMUM WINS				MINIMUM WINS			
	5x	4x	3x	2x	5x	4x	3x	2x
5 (w/o Jackpot)	0	2	3	0				
5	1	0	4	0	0	2	3	0
4	–	1	4	0	–	1	4	0
3	–	–	5	5	–	–	5	5
2	–	–	–	5	–	–	–	5

*** POWER NUMBER POSITIONS A*, B* & C* MUST BE WINNERS.

(Continued Next Page)

POWER NUMBER™ WHEEL 54013-3 (Continued from previous page)
Your 13 Numbers to Wheel

A*	B*	C*	D	E	F	G
5	5	5	1	1	1	1

H	I	J	K	L	M
1	1	1	1	1	1

The 5 Games to Play

1. | A* | B* | C* | D | L |

2. | A* | B* | C* | E | K |

3. | A* | B* | C* | F | M |

4. | A* | B* | C* | G | I |

5. | A* | B* | C* | H | J |

Copyright © 1983-1998 Gail Howard

POWER NUMBER™ WHEEL 54015-3
Wheeling 15 Numbers in 6 games for a 4 of 4 Win

NUMBERS CORRECT***	MAXIMUM WINS				MINIMUM WINS			
	5x	4x	3x	2x	5x	4x	3x	2x
5 (w/o Jackpot)	0	2	4	0				
5	1	0	5	0	0	2	4	0
4	-	1	5	0	-	1	5	0
3	-	-	6	6	-	-	6	6
2	-	-	-	6	-	-	-	6

*** POWER NUMBER POSITIONS A*, B* & C* MUST BE WINNERS.

Your 15 Numbers to Wheel

A*	B*	C*	D	E	F	G	H
6	6	6	1	1	1	1	1

I	J	K	L	M	N	O
1	1	1	1	1	1	1

The 6 Games to Play

1. | A* | B* | C* | D | N |

2. | A* | B* | C* | E | M |

3. | A* | B* | C* | F | O |

4. | A* | B* | C* | G | K |

5. | A* | B* | C* | H | L |

6. | A* | B* | C* | I | J |

Copyright © 1983-1998 Gail Howard

POWER NUMBER™ WHEEL 54017-3
Wheeling 17 Numbers in 7 games for a 4 of 4 Win

NUMBERS CORRECT***	MAXIMUM WINS				MINIMUM WINS			
	5x	4x	3x	2x	5x	4x	3x	2x
5 (w/o Jackpot)	0	2	5	0				
5	1	0	6	0	0	2	5	0
4	-	1	6	0	-	1	6	0
3	-	-	7	7	-	-	7	7
2	-	-	-	7	-	-	-	7

*** POWER NUMBER POSITIONS A*, B* & C* MUST BE WINNERS.

(Continued Next Page)

420

POWER NUMBER™ WHEEL 54017-3 (Continued from previous page)
Your 17 Numbers to Wheel

A*	B*	C*	D	E	F	G	H	I
7	7	7	1	1	1	1	1	1

J	K	L	M	N	O	P	Q
1	1	1	1	1	1	1	1

The 7 Games to Play

1.	A*	B*	C*	D	P
2.	A*	B*	C*	E	O
3.	A*	B*	C*	F	N
4.	A*	B*	C*	G	Q

5.	A*	B*	C*	H	M
6.	A*	B*	C*	I	L
7.	A*	B*	C*	J	K

Copyright © 1983-1998 Gail Howard

POWER NUMBER™WHEEL 54019-3
Wheeling 19 Numbers in 8 games for a 4 of 4 Win

NUMBERS CORRECT***	MAXIMUM WINS				MINIMUM WINS			
	5x	4x	3x	2x	5x	4x	3x	2x
5 (w/o Jackpot)	0	2	6	0				
5	1	0	7	0	0	2	6	0
4	–	1	7	0	–	1	7	0
3	–	–	8	8	–	–	8	8
2	–	–	–	8	–	–	–	8

*** POWER NUMBER POSITIONS A*, B* & C* MUST BE WINNERS.

Your 19 Numbers to Wheel

A*	B*	C*	D	E	F	G	H	I	J
8	8	8	1	1	1	1	1	1	1

K	L	M	N	O	P	Q	R	S
1	1	1	1	1	1	1	1	1

The 8 Games to Play

1.	A*	B*	C*	D	R
2.	A*	B*	C*	E	O
3.	A*	B*	C*	F	S
4.	A*	B*	C*	G	P

5.	A*	B*	C*	H	M
6.	A*	B*	C*	I	Q
7.	A*	B*	C*	J	N
8.	A*	B*	C*	K	L

Copyright © 1983-1998 Gail Howard

POWER NUMBER™WHEEL 54021-3
Wheeling 21 Numbers in 9 games for a 4 of 4 Win

NUMBERS CORRECT***	MAXIMUM WINS				MINIMUM WINS			
	5x	4x	3x	2x	5x	4x	3x	2x
5 (w/o Jackpot)	0	2	7	0				
5	1	0	8	0	0	2	7	0
4	–	1	8	0	–	1	8	0
3	–	–	9	9	–	–	9	9
2	–	–	–	9	–	–	–	9

*** POWER NUMBER POSITIONS A*, B* & C* MUST BE WINNERS.

(Continued Next Page)

POWER NUMBER™ WHEEL 54021-3 (Continued from previous page)
Your 21 Numbers to Wheel

A*	B*	C*	D	E	F	G	H	I	J	K
9	9	9	1	1	1	1	1	1	1	1

L	M	N	O	P	Q	R	S	T	U
1	1	1	1	1	1	1	1	1	1

The 9 Games to Play

1. A* B* C* D S
2. A* B* C* E T
3. A* B* C* F Q
4. A* B* C* G U
5. A* B* C* H M
6. A* B* C* I N
7. A* B* C* J R
8. A* B* C* K P
9. A* B* C* L O

POWER NUMBER™ WHEEL 54023-3
Wheeling 23 Numbers in 10 games for a 4 of 4 Win

NUMBERS CORRECT***	MAXIMUM WINS 5x	4x	3x	2x	MINIMUM WINS 5x	4x	3x	2x
5 (w/o Jackpot)	0	2	8	0				
5	1	0	9	0	0	2	8	0
4	–	1	9	0	–	1	9	0
3	–	–	10	10	–	–	10	10
2	–	–	–	10	–	–	–	10

*** POWER NUMBER POSITIONS A*, B* & C* MUST BE WINNERS.

Your 23 Numbers to Wheel

A*	B*	C*	D	E	F	G	H	I	J	K	L
10	10	10	1	1	1	1	1	1	1	1	1

M	N	O	P	Q	R	S	T	U	V	W
1	1	1	1	1	1	1	1	1	1	1

The 10 Games to Play

1. A* B* C* D R
2. A* B* C* E U
3. A* B* C* F V
4. A* B* C* G N
5. A* B* C* H Q
6. A* B* C* I T
7. A* B* C* J W
8. A* B* C* K L
9. A* B* C* M S
10. A* B* C* O P

422

POWER NUMBER™ WHEEL 54025-3
Wheeling 25 Numbers in 11 games for a 4 of 4 Win

NUMBERS CORRECT***	MAXIMUM WINS				MINIMUM WINS			
	5x	4x	3x	2x	5x	4x	3x	2x
5 (w/o Jackpot)	0	2	9	0				
5	1	0	10	0	0	2	9	0
4	–	1	10	0	–	1	10	0
3	–	–	11	11	–	–	11	11
2	–	–	–	11	–	–	–	11

*** POWER NUMBER POSITIONS A*, B* & C* MUST BE WINNERS.

Your 25 Numbers to Wheel

A*	B*	C*	D	E	F	G	H	I
11	11	11	1	1	1	1	1	1

J	K	L	M	N	O	P	Q	R
1	1	1	1	1	1	1	1	1

S	T	U	V	W	X	Y
1	1	1	1	1	1	1

The 11 Games to Play

1. A* B* C* D V
2. A* B* C* E R
3. A* B* C* F X
4. A* B* C* G Y
5. A* B* C* H T
6. A* B* C* I S
7. A* B* C* J U
8. A* B* C* K W
9. A* B* C* L Q
10. A* B* C* M O
11. A* B* C* N P

Copyright © 1983-1998 Gail Howard

POWER NUMBER™ WHEEL 54029-3
Wheeling 29 Numbers in 13 games for a 4 of 4 Win

NUMBERS CORRECT***	MAXIMUM WINS				MINIMUM WINS			
	5x	4x	3x	2x	5x	4x	3x	2x
5 (w/o Jackpot)	0	2	11	0				
5	1	0	12	0	0	2	11	0
4	–	1	12	0	–	1	12	0
3	–	–	13	13	–	–	13	13
2	–	–	–	13	–	–	–	13

*** POWER NUMBER POSITIONS A*, B* & C* MUST BE WINNERS.

Your 29 Numbers to Wheel

A*	B*	C*	D	E	F	G	H	I	J
13	13	13	1	1	1	1	1	1	1

K	L	M	N	O	P	Q	R	S	T
1	1	1	1	1	1	1	1	1	1

U	V	W	X	Y	Z	AA	BB	CC
1	1	1	1	1	1	1	1	1

The 13 Games to Play

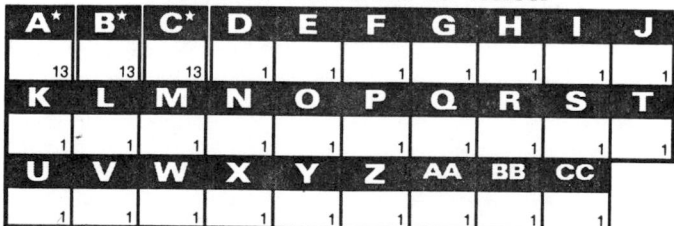

1. A* B* C* D Y
2. A* B* C* E V

POWER NUMBER™ WHEEL 54029-3 (Continued from previous page)

3.	A*	B*	C*	F	aa	9.	A*	B*	C*	L	S
4.	A*	B*	C*	G	U	10.	A*	B*	C*	M	T
5.	A*	B*	C*	H	Z	11.	A*	B*	C*	O	W
6.	A*	B*	C*	I	bb	12.	A*	B*	C*	P	cc
7.	A*	B*	C*	J	R	13.	A*	B*	C*	Q	X
8.	A*	B*	C*	K	N						

POWER NUMBER™ WHEEL 54031-3
Wheeling 31 Numbers in 14 games for a 4 of 4 Win

NUMBERS CORRECT***	MAXIMUM WINS				MINIMUM WINS			
	5x	4x	3x	2x	5x	4x	3x	2x
5 (w/o Jackpot)	0	2	12	0				
5	1	0	13	0	0	2	12	0
4	–	1	13	0	–	1	13	0
3	–	–	14	14	–	–	14	14
2	–	–	–	14	–	–	–	14

*** POWER NUMBER POSITIONS A*, B* & C* MUST BE WINNERS.

Your 31 Numbers to Wheel

The 14 Games to Play

1.	A*	B*	C*	D	X	8.	A*	B*	C*	K	ee
2.	A*	B*	C*	E	Y	9.	A*	B*	C*	L	Z
3.	A*	B*	C*	F	U	10.	A*	B*	C*	M	W
4.	A*	B*	C*	G	bb	11.	A*	B*	C*	N	aa
5.	A*	B*	C*	H	V	12.	A*	B*	C*	O	S
6.	A*	B*	C*	I	R	13.	A*	B*	C*	P	dd
7.	A*	B*	C*	J	T	14.	A*	B*	C*	Q	cc

POWER NUMBER™WHEEL 54034-3
Wheeling 34 Numbers in 16 games for a 4 of 4 Win

NUMBERS CORRECT***	MAXIMUM WINS				MINIMUM WINS			
	5x	4x	3x	2x	5x	4x	3x	2x
5 (w/o Jackpot)	0	3	13	0				
5	1	1	14	0	0	2	14	0
4	–	2	14	0	–	1	15	0
3	–	–	16	16	–	–	16	16
2	–	–	–	16	–	–	–	16

*** POWER NUMBER POSITIONS A*, B* & C* MUST BE WINNERS.

Your 34 Numbers to Wheel

A*	B*	C*	D	E	F	G	H	I	J	K	L
16	16	16	1	1	1	1	1	2	1	1	1

M	N	O	P	Q	R	S	T	U	V	W	X
1	1	1	1	1	1	1	1	1	1	1	1

Y	Z	AA	BB	CC	DD	EE	FF	GG	HH
1	1	1	1	1	1	1	1	1	1

The 16 Games to Play

1.	A*	B*	C*	D	dd
2.	A*	B*	C*	E	gg
3.	A*	B*	C*	F	Z
4.	A*	B*	C*	G	ff
5.	A*	B*	C*	H	Q
6.	A*	B*	C*	I	aa
7.	A*	B*	C*	I	hh
8.	A*	B*	C*	J	L

9.	A*	B*	C*	K	W
10.	A*	B*	C*	M	Y
11.	A*	B*	C*	N	S
12.	A*	B*	C*	O	ee
13.	A*	B*	C*	P	R
14.	A*	B*	C*	T	cc
15.	A*	B*	C*	U	bb
10.	A*	B*	C*	V	X

POWER NUMBER™WHEEL 54035-3
Wheeling 35 Numbers in 16 games for a 4 of 4 Win

NUMBERS CORRECT***	MAXIMUM WINS				MINIMUM WINS			
	5x	4x	3x	2x	5x	4x	3x	2x
5 (w/o Jackpot)	0	2	14	0				
5	1	0	15	0	0	2	14	0
4	–	1	15	0	–	1	15	0
3	–	–	16	16	–	–	16	16
2	–	–	–	16	–	–	–	16

*** POWER NUMBER POSITIONS A*, B* & C* MUST BE WINNERS.

Your 35 Numbers to Wheel

A*	B*	C*	D	E	F	G	H	I	J	K	L
16	16	16	1	1	1	1	1	1	1	1	1

M	N	O	P	Q	R	S	T	U	V	W	X
1	1	1	1	1	1	1	1	1	1	1	1

Y	Z	AA	BB	CC	DD	EE	FF	GG	HH	II
1	1	1	1	1	1	1	1	1	1	1

(Continued Next Page)

POWER NUMBER™ WHEEL 54035-3 (Continued from previous page)
The 16 Games to Play

1.	A*	B*	C*	D	bb
2.	A*	B*	C*	E	U
3.	A*	B*	C*	F	hh
4.	A*	B*	C*	G	Y
5.	A*	B*	C*	H	O
6.	A*	B*	C*	I	Q
7.	A*	B*	C*	J	M
8.	A*	B*	C*	K	dd

9.	A*	B*	C*	L	gg
10.	A*	B*	C*	N	ii
11.	A*	B*	C*	P	X
12.	A*	B*	C*	R	cc
13.	A*	B*	C*	S	V
14.	A*	B*	C*	T	ff
15.	A*	B*	C*	W	ee
16.	A*	B*	C*	Z	aa

POWER NUMBER™WHEEL 54038-3
Wheeling 38 Numbers in 18 games for a 4 of 4 Win

NUMBERS CORRECT***	MAXIMUM WINS				MINIMUM WINS			
	5x	4x	3x	2x	5x	4x	3x	2x
5 (w/o Jackpot)	0	3	15	0				
5	1	1	16	0	0	2	16	0
4	-	2	16	0	-	1	17	0
3	-	-	18	18	-	-	18	18
2	-	-	-	18	-	-	-	18

*** POWER NUMBER POSITIONS A*, B* & C* MUST BE WINNERS.

Your 38 Numbers to Wheel

A*	B*	C*	D	E	F	G	H	I	J
18	18	18	1	1	1	1	2	1	1

K	L	M	N	O	P	Q	R	S	T
1	1	1	1	1	1	1	1	1	1

U	V	W	X	Y	Z	AA	BB	CC	DD
1	1	1	1	1	1	1	1	1	1

EE	FF	GG	HH	II	JJ	KK	LL
1	1	1	1	1	1	1	1

The 18 Games to Play

1.	A*	B*	C*	D	hh
2.	A*	B*	C*	E	ff
3.	A*	B*	C*	F	jj
4.	A*	B*	C*	G	X
5.	A*	B*	C*	H	kk
6.	A*	B*	C*	H	ll
7.	A*	B*	C*	I	T
8.	A*	B*	C*	J	ii
9.	A*	B*	C*	K	Y

10.	A*	B*	C*	L	S
11.	A*	B*	C*	M	R
12.	A*	B*	C*	N	dd
13.	A*	B*	C*	O	ee
14.	A*	B*	C*	P	bb
15.	A*	B*	C*	Q	cc
16.	A*	B*	C*	U	aa
17.	A*	B*	C*	V	Z
18.	A*	B*	C*	W	gg

POWER NUMBER™WHEEL 54039-3
Wheeling 39 Numbers in 18 games for a 4 of 4 Win

NUMBERS CORRECT***	MAXIMUM WINS				MINIMUM WINS			
	5x	4x	3x	2x	5x	4x	3x	2x
5 (w/o Jackpot)	0	2	16	0				
5	1	0	17	0	0	2	16	0
4	–	1	17	0	–	1	17	0
3	–	–	18	18	–	–	18	18
2	–	–	–	18	–	–	–	18

*** POWER NUMBER POSITIONS A*, B* & C* MUST BE WINNERS.

Your 39 Numbers to Wheel

A*	B*	C*	D	E	F	G	H	I	J
18	18	18	1	1	1	1	1	1	1

K	L	M	N	O	P	Q	R	S	T
1	1	1	1	1	1	1	1	1	1

U	V	W	X	Y	Z	AA	BB	CC	DD
1	1	1	1	1	1	1	1	1	1

EE	FF	GG	HH	II	JJ	KK	LL	MM
1	1	1	1	1	1	1	1	1

The 18 Games to Play

1.	A*	B*	C*	D	hh
2.	A*	B*	C*	E	mm
3.	A*	B*	C*	F	kk
4.	A*	B*	C*	G	z
5.	A*	B*	C*	H	dd
6.	A*	B*	C*	I	T
7.	A*	B*	C*	J	V
8.	A*	B*	C*	K	bb
9.	A*	B*	C*	L	X
10.	A*	B*	C*	M	N
11.	A*	B*	C*	O	jj
12.	A*	B*	C*	P	W
13.	A*	B*	C*	Q	gg
14.	A*	B*	C*	R	S
15.	A*	B*	C*	U	ll
16.	A*	B*	C*	Y	ee
17.	A*	B*	C*	aa	ii
18.	A*	B*	C*	cc	ff

POWER NUMBER™WHEEL 54049-3
Wheeling 49 Numbers in 23 games for a 4 of 4 Win

NUMBERS CORRECT***	MAXIMUM WINS				MINIMUM WINS			
	5x	4x	3x	2x	5x	4x	3x	2x
5 (w/o Jackpot)	0	2	21	0				
5	1	0	22	0	0	2	21	0
4	–	1	22	0	–	1	22	0
3	–	–	23	23	–	–	23	23
2	–	–	–	23	–	–	–	23

*** POWER NUMBER POSITIONS A*, B* & C* MUST BE WINNERS.
(Continued Next Page)

POWER NUMBER™ WHEEL 54049-3 (Continued from previous page)
Your 49 Numbers to Wheel

A*	B*	C*	D	E	F	G	H	I	J
23	23	23	1	1	1	1	1	1	1

K	L	M	N	O	P	Q	R	S	T
1	1	1	1	1	1	1	1	1	1

U	V	W	X	Y	Z	AA	BB	CC	DD
1	1	1	1	1	1	1	1	1	1

EE	FF	GG	HH	II	JJ	KK	LL	MM	NN
1	1	1	1	1	1	1	1	1	1

OO	PP	QQ	RR	SS	TT	UU	VV	WW
1	1	1	1	1	1	1	1	1

The 23 Games to Play

1. | A* | B* | C* | D | ii |
2. | A* | B* | C* | E | mm |
3. | A* | B* | C* | F | ee |
4. | A* | B* | C* | G | ww |
5. | A* | B* | C* | H | bb |
6. | A* | B* | C* | I | ss |
7. | A* | B* | C* | J | qq |
8. | A* | B* | C* | K | oo |
9. | A* | B* | C* | L | tt |
10. | A* | B* | C* | M | rr |
11. | A* | B* | C* | N | z |
12. | A* | B* | C* | O | vv |
13. | A* | B* | C* | P | gg |
14. | A* | B* | C* | Q | pp |
15. | A* | B* | C* | R | dd |
16. | A* | B* | C* | S | ll |
17. | A* | B* | C* | T | X |
18. | A* | B* | C* | U | V |
19. | A* | B* | C* | W | ff |
20. | A* | B* | C* | Y | nn |
21. | A* | B* | C* | aa | hh |
22. | A* | B* | C* | cc | uu |
23. | A* | B* | C* | jj | kk |

428

INSTANT WHEEL FINDER™

Index of Pick 5 Wheels Available in Lotto Wheel Five to Win

	No Power						One Power						Two Power					Three		
	5/5	4/4	4/5	3/3	3/4	3/5	5/5	4/4	4/5	3/3	3/4	3/5	5/5	4/4	4/5	3/3	3/4	5/5	4/4	
06	6	5	–	4	–	–	5	4	–	–	–	–	4	3	–	–	–	3	–	06
07	21	9	3	5	–	–	15	6	3	3	–	–	10	4	2	–	–	6	2	07
08	56	20	5	8	3	–	35	12	4	5	–	–	20	6	2	–	–	10	–	08
09	126	30	9	12	5	–	70	14	6	6	2	–	35	7	4	–	–	15	3	09
10	252	51	14	17	7	2	126	25	10	8	–	2	56	11	5	–	–	21	–	10
11	462	66	26	20	10	5	210	30	14	9	4	3	84	12	7	3	–	28	4	11
12	–	113	37	30	12	6	–	47	20	11	6	3	120	17	8	4	3	36	–	12
13	–	166	58	34	18	9	–	57	28	12	6	3	–	21	10	4	4	45	5	13
14	–	245	76	46	23	10	–	81	37	13	8	5	–	24	12	4	4	55	–	14
15	–	311	118	57	28	13	–	100	49	18	9	5	–	28	13	–	4	66	6	15
16	–	–	159	67	37	16	–	130	61	20	11	7	–	33	14	5	–	78	–	16
17	–	–	217	68	46	20	–	140	77	20	12	8	–	35	18	–	–	91	7	17
18	–	–	285	94	56	24	–	183	95	26	14	9	–	43	21	6	5	105	–	18
19	–	–	–	117	66	28	–	–	116	28	15	9	–	47	23	–	–	120	8	19
20	–	–	–	146	76	32	–	274	138	32	17	11	–	54	24	6	–	136	–	20
21	–	–	–	173	84	37	–	–	164	36	18	12	–	–	–	–	6	–	9	21
22	–	–	–	205	98	40	–	–	188	39	20	14	–	67	31	7	–	–	–	22
23	–	–	–	–	–	50	–	–	–	44	21	16	–	–	–	–	–	–	10	23
24	–	–	–	–	132	54	–	–	–	47	22	17	–	81	38	8	7	–	–	24
25	–	–	–	–	–	64	–	–	–	51	24	19	–	–	–	–	–	–	11	25
26	–	–	–	331	174	68	–	–	337	56	25	21	–	96	48	8	–	253	–	26
27	–	–	–	–	–	–	–	–	–	–	–	–	–	–	–	–	8	–	–	27
28	–	–	–	–	–	88	–	–	–	–	31	–	–	–	–	9	–	–	–	28
29	–	–	–	–	–	–	–	–	–	–	–	–	–	–	–	–	–	–	13	29
30	–	–	–	–	–	102	–	–	–	76	36	26	–	131	63	10	9	351	–	30
31	–	–	–	–	–	–	–	–	–	–	–	–	–	–	–	–	–	–	14	31
32	–	–	–	–	–	–	–	–	–	–	40	–	–	–	–	–	–	–	–	32
33	–	–	–	–	–	–	–	–	–	–	–	32	–	–	78	–	10	–	–	33
34	–	–	–	–	–	–	–	–	–	–	–	–	–	–	–	11	–	–	16	34
35	–	–	–	–	470	162	–	–	–	106	50	37	–	185	89	11	–	496	16	35
36	–	–	–	–	–	–	–	–	–	–	–	–	–	–	–	–	11	–	–	36
37	–	–	–	–	–	–	–	–	–	–	–	–	–	–	–	–	–	–	–	37
38	–	–	–	–	–	–	–	–	–	–	–	–	–	–	–	12	–	–	18	38
39	–	–	–	–	–	263	–	–	–	130	64	47	–	230	112	13	12	630	18	39
40	·	·	·	·	·	·	·	·	·	·	·	·	–	–	–	–	–	–	–	40
41	·	·	·	·	·	·	·	·	·	·	·	·	–	–	–	–	–	–	–	41
42	·	·	·	·	·	·	·	·	·	·	·	·	–	–	–	14	13	–	–	42
43	·	·	·	·	·	·	·	·	·	·	·	·	–	–	–	–	–	–	–	43
44	·	·	·	·	·	·	·	·	·	·	·	·	–	–	–	–	–	–	–	44
45	·	·	·	·	·	·	·	·	·	·	·	·	–	–	–	–	14	–	–	45
46	·	·	·	·	·	·	·	·	·	·	·	·	–	–	–	–	–	–	–	46
47	·	·	·	·	·	·	·	·	·	·	·	·	–	–	–	–	–	–	–	47
48	·	·	·	·	·	·	·	·	·	·	·	·	–	–	–	–	–	–	–	48
49	·	·	·	·	·	·	·	·	·	·	·	·	–	–	–	–	16	–	23	49

BUDGET WHEEL FINDER™ — By GAMES to Play

GAMES	##-P	WIN	PAGE	GAMES	##-P	WIN	PAGE	GAMES	##-P	WIN	PAGE
2	10-0	3 of 5	177	6	12-1	3 of 4	278	12	38-2	3 of 3	363
2	10-1	3 of 5	293	6	9-1	3 of 3	257	12	21-1	3 of 5	299
2	9-1	3 of 4	277	6	9-1	4 of 5	231	12	17-1	3 of 4	281
2	8-2	4 of 5	339	6	8-2	4 of 4	314	12	14-2	4 of 5	341
2	7-2	4 of 5	338	6	7-1	4 of 4	210	12	13-1	3 of 3	259
2	7-3	4 of 4	418	6	7-3	5 of 5	374	12	12-0	3 of 4	153
3	13-1	3 of 5	294	6	6-0	5 of 5	73	12	11-2	4 of 4	316
3	12-1	3 of 5	294	7	24-2	3 of 4	368	12	9-0	3 of 3	125
3	12-2	3 of 4	365	7	22-2	3 of 3	359	12	8-1	4 of 4	210
3	11-1	3 of 5	293	7	17-3	4 of 4	420	13	42-2	3 of 4	372
3	11-2	3 of 3	356	7	16-1	3 of 5	296	13	39-2	3 of 3	364
3	9-3	4 of 4	418	7	11-2	4 of 5	340	13	29-3	4 of 4	423
3	8-0	3 of 4	151	7	10-0	3 of 4	152	13	15-0	3 of 5	179
3	7-0	4 of 5	105	7	9-2	4 of 4	315	13	15-2	4 of 5	342
3	7-1	3 of 3	257	8	27-2	3 of 4	369	13	14-1	3 of 3	260
3	7-1	4 of 5	230	8	26-2	3 of 3	360	14	45-2	3 of 4	372
3	6-2	4 of 4	314	8	24-2	3 of 3	360	14	42-2	3 of 3	365
3	6-3	5 of 5	374	8	19-3	4 of 4	421	14	31-3	4 of 4	424
4	15-2	3 of 4	367	8	17-1	3 of 5	296	14	22-1	3 of 5	299
4	14-2	3 of 4	366	8	14-1	3 of 4	279	14	18-1	3 of 4	281
4	14-2	3 of 3	357	8	12-2	4 of 5	340	14	16-2	4 of 5	343
4	13-2	3 of 3	357	8	10-1	3 of 3	258	14	11-1	4 of 5	232
4	13-2	3 of 4	366	8	8-0	3 of 3	125	14	10-0	4 of 5	107
4	12-2	3 of 3	356	9	30-2	3 of 4	369	14	9-1	4 of 4	211
4	11-1	3 of 4	278	9	28-2	3 of 3	361	15	19-1	3 of 4	282
4	11-3	4 of 4	419	9	21-3	4 of 4	421	15	9-3	5 of 5	375
4	9-2	4 of 5	339	9	19-1	3 of 5	297	15	7-1	5 of 5	201
4	8-1	4 of 5	231	9	18-1	3 of 5	297	16	49-2	3 of 4	373
4	7-2	4 of 4	314	9	15-1	3 of 4	279	16	35-3	4 of 4	425
4	6-0	3 of 3	124	9	13-0	3 of 5	178	16	34-3	4 of 4	424
4	6-1	4 of 4	210	9	11-1	3 of 3	258	16	23-1	3 of 5	300
4	6-2	5 of 5	307	9	9-0	4 of 5	106	16	16-0	3 of 5	180
5	18-2	3 of 4	367	9	7-0	4 of 4	88	17	24-1	3 of 5	300
5	16-2	3 of 3	358	10	33-2	3 of 4	370	17	20-1	3 of 4	282
5	15-1	3 of 5	295	10	30-2	3 of 3	361	17	12-2	4 of 4	316
5	14-1	3 of 5	295	10	23-3	4 of 4	422	17	10-0	3 of 3	126
5	13-3	4 of 4	419	10	14-0	3 of 5	179	18	39-3	4 of 4	426
5	11-0	3 of 5	177	10	13-2	4 of 5	341	18	38-3	4 of 4	426
5	10-2	4 of 5	340	10	11-0	3 of 4	152	18	21-1	3 of 4	283
5	9-0	3 of 4	152	10	10-1	4 of 5	232	18	17-2	4 of 5	343
5	8-0	4 of 5	106	10	8-3	5 of 5	375	18	15-1	3 of 3	261
5	8-1	3 of 3	257	10	7-2	5 of 5	307	18	13-0	3 of 4	153
5	7-0	3 of 3	124	11	36-2	3 of 4	370	19	25-1	3 of 5	301
5	6-0	4 of 4	87	11	35-2	3 of 3	363	20	22-1	3 of 4	284
5	6-1	5 of 5	201	11	34-2	3 of 3	362	20	17-0	3 of 5	181
6	21-2	3 of 4	368	11	25-3	4 of 4	422	20	17-1	3 of 4	262
6	20-2	3 of 3	359	11	20-1	3 of 5	298	20	16-1	3 of 3	261
6	18-2	3 of 3	358	11	16-1	3 of 4	280	20	12-1	4 of 5	233
6	15-3	4 of 4	420	11	12-1	3 of 3	259	20	11-0	3 of 3	126
6	13-1	3 of 4	278	11	10-2	4 of 5	315	20	8-0	4 of 4	88
6	12-0	3 of 5	178	12	39-2	3 of 4	371	20	8-2	5 of 5	307

(Continued Next Page)

BUDGET WHEEL FINDER™ — By GAMES to Play (Continued)

GAMES	##-P	WIN	PAGE	GAMES	##-P	WIN	PAGE	GAMES	##-P	WIN	PAGE
21	26-1	3 of 5	302	44	23-1	3 of 3	267	96	26-2	4 of 4	327
21	23-1	3 of 4	284	45	13-3	5 of 5	378	98	22-0	3 of 4	163
21	18-2	4 of 5	344	46	17-0	3 of 4	156	100	15-1	4 of 4	217
21	13-2	4 of 4	317	46	14-0	3 of 3	129	102	30-0	3 of 5	192
21	10-3	5 of 5	376	47	39-1	3 of 5	305	105	18-3	5 of 5	385
21	7-0	5 of 5	73	47	24-1	3 of 3	268	106	35-1	3 of 3	273
22	24-1	3 of 4	285	47	19-2	4 of 4	322	112	39-2	4 of 5	354
23	49-3	4 of 4	427	47	12-1	4 of 4	213	113	12-0	4 of 4	92
23	19-2	4 of 5	345	48	26-2	4 of 5	348	116	19-1	4 of 5	241
23	14-0	3 of 4	154	49	15-1	4 of 5	235	117	19-0	3 of 3	135
24	25-1	3 of 4	286	50	35-1	3 of 4	290	118	15-0	4 of 5	111
24	20-2	4 of 5	345	50	23-0	3 of 5	185	120	19-3	5 of 5	387
24	18-0	3 of 5	181	51	25-1	3 of 3	269	120	12-2	5 of 5	312
24	14-2	4 of 4	318	51	10-0	4 of 4	90	126	10-1	5 of 5	204
25	26-1	3 of 4	287	54	24-0	3 of 5	186	126	9-0	5 of 5	75
25	10-1	4 of 4	211	54	20-2	4 of 4	323	130	39-1	3 of 3	275
26	30-1	3 of 5	303	55	14-3	5 of 5	379	130	16-1	4 of 4	218
26	18-1	3 of 3	263	56	26-1	3 of 3	270	131	30-2	4 of 4	329
26	11-0	4 of 5	107	56	18-0	3 of 4	157	132	24-0	3 of 4	165
28	19-0	3 of 5	182	56	10-2	5 of 5	309	136	20-3	5 of 5	389
28	19-1	3 of 3	263	56	8-0	5 of 5	73	138	20-1	4 of 5	243
28	15-0	3 of 4	155	57	15-0	3 of 3	130	140	17-1	4 of 4	221
28	15-2	4 of 4	318	57	13-1	4 of 4	214	146	20-0	3 of 3	137
28	13-1	4 of 5	233	58	13-0	4 of 5	109	159	16-0	4 of 5	113
28	11-3	5 of 5	377	61	16-1	4 of 5	236	162	35-0	3 of 5	194
30	12-0	3 of 3	127	63	30-2	4 of 5	349	164	21-1	4 of 5	245
30	11-1	4 of 4	212	64	39-1	3 of 4	292	166	13-0	4 of 4	94
30	9-0	4 of 4	89	64	25-0	3 of 5	188	173	21-0	3 of 3	140
31	28-1	3 of 4	287	66	19-0	3 of 4	159	174	26-0	3 of 4	167
31	22-2	4 of 5	346	66	15-3	5 of 5	381	183	18-1	4 of 4	223
32	33-1	3 of 4	303	66	11-0	4 of 4	91	185	35-2	4 of 4	331
32	20-0	3 of 5	183	67	22-2	4 of 4	324	188	22-1	4 of 5	248
32	20-1	3 of 3	264	67	16-0	3 of 3	131	205	22-0	3 of 3	143
33	16-2	4 of 4	319	68	26-0	3 of 5	189	210	11-1	5 of 5	206
34	13-0	3 of 3	128	68	17-0	3 of 3	132	217	17-0	4 of 5	116
35	17-2	4 of 4	320	70	9-1	5 of 5	203	230	39-2	4 of 4	335
35	9-2	5 of 5	308	76	30-1	3 of 3	271	245	14-0	4 of 4	97
35	8-1	5 of 5	202	76	20-0	3 of 4	160	252	10-0	5 of 5	77
36	30-1	3 of 4	288	76	14-0	4 of 5	110	253	26-3	5 of 5	391
36	21-1	3 of 3	265	77	17-1	4 of 5	238	263	39-0	3 of 5	197
36	12-3	5 of 5	377	78	33-2	4 of 5	351	274	20-1	4 of 4	226
37	35-1	3 of 5	304	78	16-3	5 of 5	382	285	18-0	4 of 5	120
37	21-0	3 of 5	184	81	24-2	4 of 4	326	311	15-0	4 of 4	101
37	16-0	3 of 4	156	81	14-1	4 of 4	215	331	26-0	3 of 3	146
37	14-1	4 of 5	234	84	21-0	3 of 4	161	337	26-1	4 of 5	251
37	12-0	4 of 5	108	84	11-2	5 of 5	310	351	30-3	5 of 5	395
38	24-2	4 of 5	347	88	28-0	3 of 5	190	462	11-0	5 of 5	81
39	22-1	3 of 3	266	89	35-2	4 of 5	352	470	35-0	3 of 4	170
40	32-1	3 of 4	289	91	17-3	5 of 5	383	496	35-3	5 of 5	401
40	22-0	3 of 5	184	94	18-0	3 of 3	134	630	39-3	5 of 5	408
43	18-2	4 of 4	321	95	18-1	4 of 5	239				

BUDGET WHEEL FINDER™ — By NUMBERS to Play

##-P	GAMES	WIN	PAGE
6-2	3	4 of 4	314
6-3	3	5 of 5	374
6-0	4	3 of 3	124
6-1	4	4 of 4	210
6-2	4	5 of 5	307
6-0	5	4 of 4	87
6-1	5	5 of 5	201
6-0	6	5 of 5	73
7-2	2	4 of 5	338
7-3	2	4 of 4	418
7-0	3	4 of 5	105
7-1	3	3 of 3	257
7-1	3	4 of 5	230
7-2	4	4 of 4	314
7-0	5	3 of 3	124
7-1	6	4 of 4	210
7-3	6	5 of 5	374
7-0	9	4 of 4	88
7-2	10	5 of 5	307
7-1	15	5 of 5	201
7-0	21	5 of 5	73
8-2	2	4 of 5	339
8-0	3	3 of 4	151
8-1	4	4 of 5	231
8-0	5	4 of 5	106
8-1	5	3 of 3	257
8-2	6	4 of 4	314
8-0	8	3 of 3	125
8-3	10	5 of 5	375
8-1	12	4 of 4	210
8-0	20	4 of 4	88
8-2	20	5 of 5	307
8-1	35	5 of 5	202
8-0	56	5 of 5	73
9-1	2	3 of 4	277
9-3	3	4 of 4	418
9-2	4	4 of 5	339
9-0	5	3 of 4	152
9-1	6	4 of 5	231
9-1	6	3 of 3	257
9-2	7	4 of 4	315
9-0	9	4 of 5	106
9-0	12	3 of 3	125
9-1	14	4 of 4	211
9-3	15	5 of 5	375
9-0	30	4 of 4	89
9-2	35	5 of 5	308
9-1	70	5 of 5	203
9-0	126	5 of 5	75
10-0	2	3 of 5	177
10-1	2	3 of 5	293

##-P	GAMES	WIN	PAGE
10-2	5	4 of 5	340
10-0	7	3 of 4	152
10-1	8	3 of 3	258
10-1	10	4 of 5	232
10-2	11	4 of 4	315
10-0	14	4 of 5	107
10-0	17	3 of 3	126
10-3	21	5 of 5	376
10-1	25	4 of 4	211
10-0	51	4 of 4	90
10-2	56	5 of 5	309
10-1	126	5 of 5	204
10-0	252	5 of 5	77
11-1	3	3 of 5	293
11-2	3	3 of 3	356
11-1	4	3 of 4	278
11-3	4	4 of 4	419
11-0	5	3 of 5	177
11-2	7	4 of 5	340
11-1	9	3 of 3	258
11-0	10	3 of 4	152
11-2	12	4 of 4	316
11-1	14	4 of 5	232
11-0	20	3 of 3	126
11-0	26	4 of 5	107
11-3	28	5 of 5	377
11-1	30	4 of 4	212
11-0	66	4 of 4	91
11-2	84	5 of 5	310
11-1	210	5 of 5	206
11-0	462	5 of 5	81
12-1	3	3 of 5	294
12-2	3	3 of 4	365
12-2	4	3 of 3	356
12-0	6	3 of 5	178
12-1	6	3 of 4	278
12-2	8	4 of 5	340
12-1	11	3 of 3	259
12-0	12	3 of 4	153
12-2	17	4 of 4	316
12-1	20	4 of 5	233
12-0	30	3 of 3	127
12-3	36	5 of 5	377
12-0	37	4 of 5	108
12-1	47	4 of 4	213
12-0	113	4 of 4	92
12-2	120	5 of 5	312
13-1	3	3 of 5	294
13-2	4	3 of 4	366
13-2	4	3 of 3	357
13-3	5	4 of 4	419

##-P	GAMES	WIN	PAGE
13-1	6	3 of 4	278
13-0	9	3 of 5	178
13-2	10	4 of 5	341
13-1	12	3 of 3	259
13-0	18	3 of 4	153
13-2	21	4 of 4	317
13-1	28	4 of 5	233
13-0	34	3 of 3	128
13-3	45	5 of 5	378
13-1	57	4 of 4	214
13-0	58	4 of 5	109
13-0	166	4 of 4	94
14-2	4	3 of 4	366
14-2	4	3 of 3	357
14-1	5	3 of 5	295
14-1	8	3 of 4	279
14-0	10	3 of 5	179
14-2	12	4 of 5	341
14-1	13	3 of 3	260
14-0	23	3 of 4	154
14-2	24	4 of 4	318
14-1	37	4 of 5	234
14-0	46	3 of 3	129
14-3	55	5 of 5	379
14-0	76	4 of 5	110
14-1	81	4 of 4	215
14-0	245	4 of 4	97
15-2	4	3 of 4	367
15-1	5	3 of 5	295
15-3	6	4 of 4	420
15-1	9	3 of 4	279
15-0	13	3 of 5	179
15-2	13	4 of 5	342
15-1	18	3 of 3	261
15-0	28	3 of 4	155
15-2	28	4 of 4	318
15-1	49	4 of 5	235
15-0	57	3 of 3	130
15-3	66	5 of 5	381
15-1	100	4 of 4	217
15-0	118	4 of 5	111
15-0	311	4 of 4	101
16-2	5	3 of 3	358
16-1	7	3 of 5	296
16-1	11	3 of 4	280
16-2	14	4 of 5	343
16-0	16	3 of 5	180
16-1	20	3 of 3	261
16-2	33	4 of 4	319
16-0	37	3 of 4	156
16-1	61	4 of 5	236

(Continued Next Page)

BUDGET WHEEL FINDER™ — By NUMBERS to Play (Continued)

##-P	GAMES	WIN	PAGE
16-0	67	3 of 3	131
16-3	78	5 of 5	382
16-1	130	4 of 4	218
16-0	159	4 of 5	113
17-3	7	4 of 4	420
17-1	8	3 of 5	296
17-1	12	3 of 4	281
17-2	18	4 of 5	343
17-0	20	3 of 5	181
17-1	20	3 of 3	262
17-2	35	4 of 4	320
17-0	46	3 of 4	156
17-0	68	3 of 3	132
17-1	77	4 of 5	238
17-3	91	5 of 5	383
17-1	140	4 of 4	221
17-0	217	4 of 5	116
18-2	5	3 of 4	367
18-2	6	3 of 3	358
18-1	9	3 of 5	297
18-1	14	3 of 4	281
18-2	21	4 of 5	344
18-0	24	3 of 5	181
18-1	26	3 of 3	263
18-2	43	4 of 4	321
18-0	56	3 of 4	157
18-0	94	3 of 3	134
18-1	95	4 of 5	239
18-3	105	5 of 5	385
18-1	183	4 of 4	223
18-0	285	4 of 5	120
19-3	8	4 of 4	421
19-1	9	3 of 5	297
19-1	15	3 of 4	282
19-2	23	4 of 5	345
19-0	28	3 of 5	182
19-1	28	3 of 3	263
19-2	47	4 of 4	322
19-0	66	3 of 4	159
19-1	116	4 of 5	241
19-0	117	3 of 3	135
19-3	120	5 of 5	387
20-2	6	3 of 3	359
20-1	11	3 of 5	298
20-1	17	3 of 4	282
20-2	24	4 of 5	345
20-0	32	3 of 5	183
20-1	32	3 of 3	264
20-2	54	4 of 4	323
20-0	76	3 of 4	160
20-3	136	5 of 5	389

##-P	GAMES	WIN	PAGE
20-1	138	4 of 5	243
20-0	146	3 of 3	137
20-1	274	4 of 4	226
21-2	6	3 of 4	368
21-3	9	4 of 4	421
21-1	12	3 of 5	299
21-1	18	3 of 4	283
21-1	36	3 of 3	265
21-0	37	3 of 5	184
21-0	84	3 of 4	161
21-1	164	4 of 5	245
21-0	173	3 of 3	140
22-2	7	3 of 3	359
22-1	14	3 of 5	299
22-1	20	3 of 4	284
22-2	31	4 of 5	346
22-1	39	3 of 3	266
22-0	40	3 of 5	184
22-2	67	4 of 4	324
22-0	98	3 of 4	163
22-1	188	4 of 5	248
22-0	205	3 of 3	143
23-3	10	4 of 4	422
23-1	16	3 of 5	300
23-1	21	3 of 4	284
23-1	44	3 of 3	267
23-0	50	3 of 5	185
24-2	7	3 of 4	368
24-2	8	3 of 3	360
24-1	17	3 of 5	300
24-1	22	3 of 4	285
24-2	38	4 of 5	347
24-1	47	3 of 3	268
24-0	54	3 of 5	186
24-2	81	4 of 4	326
24-0	132	3 of 4	165
25-3	11	4 of 4	422
25-1	19	3 of 5	301
25-1	24	3 of 4	286
25-1	51	3 of 3	269
25-0	64	3 of 5	188
26-2	8	3 of 3	360
26-1	21	3 of 5	302
26-1	25	3 of 4	287
26-2	48	4 of 5	348
26-1	56	3 of 3	270
26-0	68	3 of 5	189
26-2	96	4 of 4	327
26-0	174	3 of 4	167
26-3	253	5 of 5	391
26-0	331	3 of 3	146

##-P	GAMES	WIN	PAGE
26-1	337	4 of 5	251
27-2	8	3 of 4	369
28-2	9	3 of 3	361
28-1	31	3 of 4	287
28-0	88	3 of 5	190
29-3	13	4 of 4	423
30-2	9	3 of 4	369
30-2	10	3 of 3	361
30-1	26	3 of 5	303
30-1	36	3 of 4	288
30-2	63	4 of 5	349
30-1	76	3 of 3	271
30-0	102	3 of 5	192
30-2	131	4 of 4	329
30-3	351	5 of 5	395
31-3	14	4 of 4	424
32-1	40	3 of 4	289
33-2	10	3 of 4	370
33-1	32	3 of 5	303
33-2	78	4 of 5	351
34-2	11	3 of 3	362
34-3	16	4 of 4	424
35-2	11	3 of 3	363
35-3	16	4 of 4	425
35-1	37	3 of 5	304
35-1	50	3 of 4	290
35-2	89	4 of 5	352
35-1	106	3 of 3	273
35-0	162	3 of 5	194
35-2	185	4 of 4	331
35-0	470	3 of 5	170
35-3	496	5 of 5	401
36-2	11	3 of 4	370
38-2	12	3 of 3	363
38-3	18	4 of 4	426
39-2	12	3 of 4	371
39-2	13	3 of 3	364
39-3	18	4 of 4	426
39-1	47	3 of 5	305
39-1	64	3 of 4	292
39-2	112	4 of 5	354
39-1	130	3 of 3	275
39-2	230	4 of 4	335
39-0	263	3 of 5	197
39-3	630	5 of 5	408
42-2	13	3 of 4	372
42-2	14	3 of 3	365
45-2	14	3 of 4	372
49-2	16	3 of 4	373
49-3	23	4 of 4	427

Pick-5 Jackpot Winners
Thank Gail Howard's Systems ...

❖ "I have been using Lotto Wheel Five to Win and I have had countless third and forth place wins and some second place wins, and then the day came on 4/11/97 I had all five numbers in New York's Take 5 and won $35,634.50 plus four tickets with 3#s that paid $27 each for a total of $35,742.50. Thank you for your systems and all the interesting reading."   — **Pete Bulwidas**

❖ "I was using Wheel Five for only about six weeks when I was rewarded by winning the Cash-5 Jackpot for $100,000 dollars. I also had 20 prizes of $20 each for a total of $100,400 dollars using your Power Wheel #3810[54016-1]. Thank you, Gail. I never would have won without the help of your Wheel Five and Advantage Plus programs. I will be forever grateful to you. Thank you, again, Gail."   — **Donald Marcil**

❖ "We decided to invest in your book. This is when our luck changed! After eight tries with System #3009[53014] we chose four of the five numbers correctly in our wheel–and we received $500.00 for four correct numbers on one ticket. After eight more tries, on April 12, 1994, we had all five numbers drawn in our wheel. I saw we had hit several $5.00 winners. Then, I couldn't believe my eyes when I saw the ticket with all five numbers correct on one ticket. A $50,000.00 winner!!!!! We felt you must know of our good fortune right away. Gail, thanks again for your help and encouraging book."   — **Tom and Annette W.**

❖ "Just a few words about your Smart Luck lottery programs: Super! Magnificent! Excellent! Fantastic! Best! Extraordinary! Incredible! Wonderful! Fabulous! Terrific! Outstanding! Great! Outta Sight! Simply Marvelous!!! On May 22nd, I moved to Florida and started playing the Florida Fantasy Five game. On June 16th I hit the first prize of $16,286.73 using your Wheel Five Plus system #541. I've also hit several 3 & 4 number prizes during this three week period! Will someone pinch me please! Thank you 16,000 times over!"   — **Daniel P. Salustro**

❖ "My pool hit the Illinois Little Lotto. After splitting the grand prize with one other person, we ended up with $103,475.00 before taxes, plus $174.00 cash from 22 three number prizes. I pick my numbers from several different charts in your Advantage Plus program and I used Wheel 54019-2 from your computer program, Smart Luck Wheel Five Plus(tm). When we won, I had five people in the pool besides myself. You made five people very happy."

— **Mark Kern**

❖ "The second (2nd) time I used your system I hit the Indiana Lucky 5 Jackpot for $50,000.00 using system #3009[53014], wheeling 17 numbers. I also won six (6) three-number winners, two of which appear on my winning Jackpot ticket. Needless to say, I think you are awesome and the greatest! Gail, I tell everyone that I bought your system and gladly encourage them to do the same if they wish to be a winner when they play the lottery."

— **Willie Hoover**

❖ "Your system is awesome! Using your system I won $34,708.00 in the Illinois CASH-5 lottery. It took less than 30 days after I put your system into use. I made the front page of my neighbor-hood paper. It was a great feeling and I owe it all to you."

— **Thomas J. McGill**

❖ "As a direct result of using your system I am $50,000.00 richer today, as I won the Match 5 jackpot in the Maryland lottery. I used the Advantage Plus Smart Picks to pick the numbers, then used the Balanced Wheel System #3014[53122] to wheel the numbers. Works great and I'm looking forward to more big money jackpots thanks to your great software. Keep up the good work, Gail, so everyone who has or orders your Advantage Plus and wheel systems will get their fair share of the big money." — **Richard T. Whisman**

❖ "Thanks to your 5-number Lotto System #3014[53122] wheeling 22 numbers for a 3 of 4 win, I won a TAKE-5 Lotto jackpot on 4-17-92. I won $61,661.50. God Bless You. Please don't publish our names. Thank you." — **P. & Y. S.**

❖ "I used Gail Howard's wheeling system #3009[53117] and I hit the jackpot ($51,762.50) plus 11 second prizes on August 8, 1995 on the Take-5 game. Thanks, Gail."   — Santiago Alvarez

❖ "I thought I would drop you a line to let you know that after using your book for three months, using System #3005[53113] on the Illinois Little Lotto my wife and I hit the 1st Prize on Sept. 9. Our total prize winnings were $234,941.50. Along with the 1st prize we also hit 4 numbers and 3 numbers twice."   — Richard Shepardson

❖ "I want to tell you that it was a great joy using your system #3010[53118] and winning over $36,000. My wife and I are happy that we are a part or your winning team. Thank you for your systems. Without them I couldn't have hit the Take-5 jackpot."
    — Vinny Licata

❖ "It is my pleasure to write to you telling you that I have been fortunate in winning a Powerball Jackpot of $100,000.00 using your 20-number Wheeling System. I have appreciated your help and above all a word of gratitude that words cannot express. I am eternally grateful to a new wonderful friend." —Alberta M. Worth

❖ "On December 17th, we became a CASH-5 jackpot winner in the Colorado lottery. Our total winning was $23,317.00. We used your system 3103[55008] of the book entitled 'Lotto Wheel Five to Win.' Just as your system stated, we won 1 five number prize, 15 four number prizes, 30 three number prizes and we also had 17 two number prizes.

I have used your systems for approximately 9 years for the regular game and have won several second prizes (5 out of 6), plus more third prizes than I can count. We never play lotto without using your systems."   — Mary L. Green

❖ "On Jan. 26,1990 we hit our first jackpot for $395,832 using one of your systems. Then on April 1, 1993, we won first prize again. I have you to thank for being a jackpot winner again for the SECOND time."   — Fred Gscheidle

❖ "We are so excited about winning first prize in Florida with your 5-number Lotto System 3014[53122] for a total winning of

$244,114.50 that we had to share the good news with you. We won on the first try."   — **Nancy & Ralph Crapse**

❖ "I am excited to tell you that I recently won my first jackpot on Sept. 2, 1994, a mere 11 drawings after my 18th birthday. The prize paid $25,000 plus $334 in other small prizes. I knew your system would not fail me because my father used it and managed to cash in three prizes of over $1,000."   — **Chad Casson**

❖ "I am pleased to let you know that I jackpotted on our Californian Fantasy Five. To choose my numbers, I used Charts B, 6 and 7 in your Advantage Plus. Together with the 10-number wheel 54110, I was able to land the five numbers for a jackpot valued at $27,297.00. I can't say enough about your programs except that they are right on time. Especially the Smart Picks which make it so easy to make number selections. I play all the time. Most of the time I win. But without your program, I would not play."   — **Bettie & Robert Carter**

❖ "Thanks for the Smart Luck Computer Wheel. On Nov. 27, 1995 I won the Virginia Cash-5 using your system. My winning ticket paid me $25,000 plus $1.25 for a three-number win on the same ticket. Thanks so much for your information and help."
               — **Douglas R. Roper, Sr.**

❖ "I am writing to inform you of a recent win by our group, 'The Magnificent Seven' in the New Jersey Cash 5 lottery. Your computer programs are superior to anything on the market and make all other programs totally inadequate. On January 31, 1995, our group held one of the two winning tickets for a NJ Cash 5 prize worth $99,350. What a great feeling it was! All the group members were simply ecstatic and grateful for this top win."
               — **Gerald Galanowsky**

❖ "Gail Howard's lottery wheels brought me home winners 2 times. On May 16 1990, I won $245,350.97 by playing 10 games in Gail's system #3003[53111] in (Florida's) Fantasy 5. In December 1992, I won 5 out of 6 in Lotto. I had one 5 of 6 for $4,300 plus several 4of 6 and 3 of 6, giving me a total of $7,600. My advice — Don't count on dumb luck alone."
               — **Patricia McDevitt**

A FEW NEWSPAPER QUOTES

NEW YORK DAILY NEWS:

"Wheeling systems like Howard's have the most respectability among critics since they concede that the wheels offer a systematic way of reducing the odds..."

THE WASHINGTON TIMES:

"Gail Howard is the nation's leading lottery handicapper. Leavelle Carter...and Sherry Jaynes...both won big jackpots by using Miss Howard's system. Mr. Carter bet $13 and won $606,023 in the D.C. Lotto game; Mrs. Jaynes hit a $13.8 million jack-pot in the New York state lottery...On Aug. 2, an Indiana couple hit the Canadian lottery for $516,000. Two days later, 16 co-workers at a Miller Brewing plant in Clay, NY, split more than $1.4 million. All used Miss Howard's system."

NY NEWSDAY (UPI):

"Sharon Jaynes used a booklet by Gail Howard to become the sole winner of the $13.8 million."

BUTTERFIELD EXPRESS:

"Mitchell Drummond believes there is a system of picking the numbers and he recently proved it by winning $454,434 in the Nov. 21 Lotto 6-49 drawing. 'I use the Gail Howard system...I saw her on television while I was working the night shift in January and it seemed logical,' Drummond said. 'So I've been using her system since then and knew it would be only a matter of time.'"

DAILY NEWS

"Jim Shivley won $9.48 million in the California State Lottery last August, using a 'wheeling' system devised by Gail Howard. The system, says Shivley, helped him reduce his odds. Willy Richey is another winner who swears by Howard's system. 'I don't play unless I use the system,' says Richey, who last year won $1.2 million in the Michigan lottery."

ABOUT GAIL HOWARD

Gail Howard is universally recognized as the creator of the most highly acclaimed and successful lottery systems used in the world today. Gail's are the ONLY lottery systems that have been credited with winning **dozens of first prize** lottery jackpots.

To date, **59** documented first prize Lotto jackpot winners have won a combined total of **$97.4 million dollars** with her systems. Documentation consists of more than 150 pages of letters from her jackpot winners, copies of their jackpot winning tickets, checks and/or congratulatory letters from the lottery, lottery press releases, newspaper articles, etc.

Gail was America's original lottery expert — the pioneer of scientific lottery strategy. Since she created her lottery systems in 1982, Gail has turned thousands of lottery losers into winners, and she has made dozens of people rich. Her ability to turn people into millionaires has made lottery history!

Her remarkable track record in helping people win big money in Lotto has led to appearances on hundreds of radio and TV shows, including *The Today Show* and *Good Morning America*.

She has also been featured or quoted in articles in many major magazines and newspapers, including *Newsweek, U.S. News & World Report, Insight Magazine, Playboy, Family Circle, The Wall Street Journal, Los Angeles Times, New York Daily News, Chicago Tribune, Toronto Star, The New York Times*.

Earlier in her fascinating career, she had spent 12 years traveling throughout the world (in 130 countries), as an import-export specialist. For nine years after that, she was a highly successful stock broker and commodity futures trader. Gail has used her Wall Street skills, and her fascination with games of chance, to focus on creating winning lottery systems — with amazing results!

In 1986, she won national recognition for her accuracy in predicting two weeks in advance the closing prices of seven different commodity futures contracts. In 1987, she placed 11th in the world in the prestigious Commodity Perspectives Chartist of the Year contest for her accurate predictions. Commodity Perspective is a Knight Ridder Business Information Service.

In her capacity as lottery expert, Gail Howard:

- Has written articles for many national magazines, including *Family Circle*.
- Was Lottery Editor of *Gambling Times* magazine from November 1984 through April 1987.
- Wrote and published *Lottery Advantage*® a 32-page monthly publication, with editions in New York/New Jersey and Canada, from May 1985 through January 1990.
- Wrote *Lottery Bu$ter*, an eight-page monthly newsletter, from June 1986 through January 1988. (The paid circulation grew to 500,000 during the time she was writing it.)
- Has written a weekly column for 15 years for *New York Lottery News*.
- Gail Howard's Special Report: *State Lotteries: How to Get In It and How to Win It* (first edition published in 1985), was sold through full page display ads in major magazines and newspapers, and also on 30-minute TV infomercials. More than two million copies of her Special Report were sold by mail.
- Her books are sold all over the world, including foreign language editions translated into Spanish, French, German, and Norwegian.

Books by Gail Howard include:

Special Report: *State Lotteries: How to Get In It and How to Win It*

Gail Howard's *Winning Lottery Strategies*

Gail Howard's *Encyclopedia of Winning Lottery Numbers*

Lotto How to Wheel a Fortune

Lotto Wheel Five to Win

Lottery Winning Systems

Lottery Master Guide

Gail Howard's Smart Luck® ORDER FORM
Lottery Books and Printed Charts

- ❏ LOTTO HOW TO WHEEL A FORTUNE .... $19.50 + $4.50 S/H
- ❏ LOTTO WHEEL FIVE TO WIN .... $19.95 + $4.50 S/H
- ❏ LOTTERY MASTER GUIDE .... $24.50 + $4.50 S/H
- ❏ LOTTERY ADVANTAGE® Charts .... $15.00 + $4.00 S/H

Printed for your Game Choice: State: _____ Nr.Field _____

$$$ SAVE $$$ GET DISCOUNTS for Buying Two or More

- ❏ TWO sets of LOTTERY ADVANTAGE® Charts $34.00
  State: _____ Nr.Field _____   State: _____ Nr.Field _____

- ❏ THREE sets of LOTTERY ADVANTAGE® Charts $49.00
  State: _____ Nr.Field _____   State: _____ Nr.Field _____
  State: _____ Nr.Field _____

Books and Charts are mailed separately and require separate postage.

Lottery Software for Your Computer

- ❏ ADVANTAGE PLUS™ .... $79.95 + S/H
- ❏ INTERNATIONAL ADVANTAGE PLUS™ .... $79.95 + S/H
- ❏ U.S.A. KENO ADVANTAGE PLUS™ .... $79.95 + S/H
- ❏ COMPUTER WHEEL™ .... $39.50 + S/H
- ❏ WHEEL FIVE™ .... $37.50 + S/H
- ❏ FULL WHEEL GENERATOR™ .... $34.50 + S/H
- ❏ KENO WHEEL™ ... (NO DISCOUNT) .... $59.95 + S/H

$$$ SAVE $$$ GET DISCOUNTS for Buying Two or More

- ❏ ADVANTAGE PLUS™ & ANY ONE WHEEL™ .... $99.95 + S/H
- ❏ ADVANTAGE PLUS™ & TWO Wheel programs .... $129.95 + S/H
- ❏ ADVANTAGE PLUS™ & ALL THREE Wheel programs . $154.95 + S/H

THE ABOVE ORDERS DO NOT INCLUDE SHIPPING. PLEASE ADD:
- ❏ $3 within U.S.A.   ❏ $5 to Canada   ❏ $10 to all other countries.

We Ship 3 ½" Disks UNLESS You CHECK ❏ 5 ¼"

$ _____ **TOTAL $ ENCLOSED** (ONLY U.S.$ accepted.)

Make Checks or money orders payable to: **SMART LUCK PUBLISHERS**
VISA/ MASTERCARD Orders Call: **1-800-692-4245**

Or Call: 1-702-365-1818 or visit us at: **www.smartluck.com**

VISA

SMART LUCK Publishers
Dept. B-5, P.O. Box 81770
Las Vegas, Nevada 89180-1770

Name:	
Address:	
City:	State: Zip:
Phone: ( )	
❏ VISA ❏ MC Card #:	Exp Date:
Signature:	

Fold here and tape or staple.

‾‾‾‾‾‾‾‾‾‾‾‾‾‾‾‾‾‾‾
‾‾‾‾‾‾‾‾‾‾‾‾‾‾‾‾‾‾‾
‾‾‾‾‾‾‾‾‾‾‾‾‾‾‾‾‾‾‾

SMART LUCK Publishers
Dept. B-5, P.O. Box 81770
Las Vegas, Nevada 89180-1770

DELUXE Lottery Software ORDER FORM

- ❏ ADVANTAGE PLUS™ .... $79.95+S/H
- ❏ INTERNATIONAL ADVANTAGE PLUS™ .... $79.95+S/H
- ❏ WHEEL SIX PLUS™ .... $59.95+S/H
- ❏ WHEEL FIVE PLUS™ .... $57.95+S/H
- ❏ FULL WHEEL GENERATOR™ .... $34.50+S/H

$$$ SAVE $$$$ DISCOUNTS For Buying Two or More
Buy Advantage Plus™ OR International Advantage Plus™ with:

- ❏ with Wheel Six Plus (Save $20 from $139.90) .... $119.95+S/H
- ❏ with Wheel Five Plus (Save $18 from $137.90) .... $119.95+S/H
- ❏ with Full Wheel Generator (Save $15 from $114.45) .... $99.95+S/H
- ❏ with Wheel Five Plus & Wheel Six plus .... $167.95+S/H
  (Save $30 from $197.85)
- ❏ with Wheel Six Plus & Full Wheel Generator .... $147.50+S/H
  (Save $27 from $174.40)
- ❏ with Wheel Five Plus & Full Wheel Generator .... $145.50+S/H
  (Save $27 from $172.40)
- ❏ with Wheel Six Plus & Wheel Five Plus & .... $192.95+S/H
  Full Wheel Generator (Save $40 from $232.35)

A WHEEL BARGAIN!

- ❏ Buy ONLY Wheel Six Plus & Wheel Five Plus .... $99.95+S/H
  (Save $18 from $117.90)
- ❏ Buy ONLY Wheel Six Plus & Wheel Five Plus & ...... $129.50+S/H
  Full Wheel Generator (Save $23 from $152.40)

THE ABOVE ORDERS DO NOT INCLUDE SHIPPING. PLEASE ADD:
❏ $3 within U.S.A.   ❏ $5 to Canada   ❏ $10 to all other countries.

We Ship 3 ½" Disks UNLESS You CHECK ❏ 5 ¼"

$ _____ **TOTAL $ ENCLOSED** (ONLY U.S.$ accepted.)

Make Checks or money orders payable to: **SMART LUCK PUBLISHERS**
VISA/ MASTERCARD Orders Call: **1-800-692-4245**

Or Call: 1-702-365-1818 or visit us at: **www.smartluck.com**

SMART LUCK Publishers
Dept. B-5, P.O. Box 81770
Las Vegas, Nevada 89180-1770

Name:		
Address:		
City:	State:	Zip:
Phone: ( )		
☐ VISA ☐ MC Card #:		Exp Date:
Signature:		

SMART LUCK Publishers
Dept. B-5, P.O. Box 81770
Las Vegas, Nevada 89180-1770

Fold here and tape or staple.

SMART LUCK Publishers
Dept. B-5, P.O. Box 81770
Las Vegas, Nevada 89180-1770